Get the eBook FREE!
(PDF, ePub, Kindle, and liveBook all included)

We believe that once you buy a book from us, you should be able to read it in any format we have available. To get electronic versions of this book at no additional cost to you, purchase and then register this book at the Manning website.

Go to https://www.manning.com/freebook and follow the instructions to complete your pBook registration.

That's it!
Thanks from Manning!

Java Persistence with Spring Data and Hibernate

CĂTĂLIN TUDOSE

A revised and extended new edition of *Java Persistence with Hibernate*

CHRISTIAN BAUER, GAVIN KING, AND GARY GREGORY

FOREWORDS BY DMITRY ALEKSANDROV
AND MOHAMED TAMAN

MANNING
SHELTER ISLAND

For online information and ordering of this and other Manning books, please visit www.manning.com. The publisher offers discounts on this book when ordered in quantity. For more information, please contact

Special Sales Department
Manning Publications Co.
20 Baldwin Road
PO Box 761
Shelter Island, NY 11964
Email: orders@manning.com

Manning Publications Co.
20 Baldwin Road
PO Box 761
Shelter Island, NY 11964

Development editors:	Katie Sposato Johnson and Christina Taylor
Technical development editor:	Víctor Durán
Review editor:	Adriana Sabo
Production editor:	Kathleen Rossland
Copy editor:	Andy Carroll
Proofreader:	Keri Hales
Technical proofreader:	Jean-François Morin
Typesetter:	Gordan Salinovic
Cover designer:	Marija Tudor

ISBN 9781617299186
Printed in the United States of America

This book is dedicated to all those people who made it possible: family, friends, colleagues, professors, students, readers of previous books, and participants and watchers of my courses.

brief contents

contents

forewords

When Cătălin asked me to write this foreword, I realized that for 17 years of my career, I've mostly been dealing with the problems that are discussed and solved in this book. Historically, we've come to a state where most data is persisted in relational DBMSs. The task may sound quite simple; save data in a database, read it, modify it if needed, and finally delete it. Many (even senior) developers don't realize how much computer science there is in those several operations. Talking to a relational database from an OOP language like Java is like speaking to a person from another world who lives by completely different rules.

In the early years of my career, I spent most of my time just mapping "ResultSets" to Java objects without any sophisticated logic. It wasn't hard, but it was really time-consuming. I was only dreaming, thinking that our architects wouldn't suddenly change the object structure so that I'd have to rewrite everything from scratch. And I wasn't the only one!

To save manual work and automate these translation tasks, frameworks like Hibernate, and later Spring Data, were created. They really do a lot of work for you. You just need to add them as a dependency, add some annotations to your code, and the magic will happen! This works perfectly on small projects, but in real life, projects are way bigger with a lot of corner cases!

Hibernate and Spring Data have quite a long history with tremendous effort invested to make this magic work. In this book, you'll find definitive descriptions of the functionality of each framework, their corner cases, suggested optimizations, and best practices.

The flow of this book is designed so that you first understand the fundamental theory of relational databases and the main problems of object/relational mapping (ORM). Then, you'll see how this is solved with Hibernate, and how the functionality is extended in Spring Data for the Spring Framework universe. Finally, you'll get acquainted with the usage of ORM for NoSQL solutions.

And I can say that these technologies are everywhere! Like literally everywhere! Should you open your bank account, buy an airline ticket, send a request to your government, or write a comment on a blog post, behind the curtains, with high probability, Hibernate and/or Spring Data are handling the persistence in those applications! These technologies are important, and this book provides information about their various applications.

Knowing your tools is essential for doing your job right. In this book, you will find everything you need to work effectively with Hibernate and Spring Data, backed by theory in computer science. It is absolutely a must-read for all Java developers, especially those working in enterprise technology.

—DMITRY ALEKSANDROV
SOFTWARE DEVELOPER AT ORACLE, JAVA CHAMPION,
CO-LEAD OF BULGARIAN JAVA USER GROUP, AUTHOR OF *HELIDON IN ACTION*

Data persistence is a crucial part of any application, and databases are indisputably at the core of the modern enterprise. While programming languages like Java provide an object-oriented view of business entities, the data underlying these entities are usually relational in nature. It is this challenge—bridging relational data and Java objects—that Hibernate and Spring Data take on through object/relational mapping (ORM).

As Cătălin demonstrates in this book, the effective use of ORM technology in all but the simplest of enterprise environments requires understanding and configuring the mediation between relational data and objects. This demands that the developer be knowledgeable about the application and its data requirements, as well as the SQL query language, relational storage structures, and the potential for optimization.

This book provides a comprehensive overview of Java persistence using the industry-leading tools Spring Data and Hibernate. It covers how to use their type-mapping capabilities and facilities for modeling associations and inheritance; how to retrieve objects efficiently by querying JPA with Querydsl; how to process and manage transactions with Spring Data and Hibernate; how to create fetch plans, strategies, and profiles; how to filter data; how to configure Hibernate for use in both managed and unmanaged environments; and how to use their commands. In addition, you will learn about building Spring Data REST projects, using Java persistence with non-relational databases, and testing Java persistence applications. Throughout the book, the author provides insights into the underlying problems of ORM and the design choices behind Hibernate. These insights will give the reader a deep understanding of the effective use of ORM as an enterprise technology.

Java Persistence with Spring Data and Hibernate is the definitive guide to persistence with these popular tools. You will benefit from detailed coverage of Spring Data JPA, Spring Data JDBC, Spring Data REST, JPA, and Hibernate, comparing and contrasting the alternatives to be able to choose what is best for your code in enterprise computing today.

For two reasons, it is an honor to recommend this book. Firstly, I share with its author the hope that it will assist you in the production of increasingly performant, secure, testable software with a quality upon which others may rely with confidence. Secondly, I know the author personally, and he is outstanding on both personal and technical levels. He has long experience in the software development industry, and his professional activity, including videos, books, and articles, is oriented to benefit the worldwide developer community.

—Mohamed Tamam
Chief Solutions Architect, Nortal
Java Champion, Oracle ACE, JCP Member

preface

I am fortunate to have been in the IT industry for more than 25 years. I started programming in C++ and Delphi in my student years and the first years of my career. I made the step from my mathematics background as a teenager to computer science and continuously tried to keep both sides in my mind.

In 2000, my attention turned for the first time to the Java programming language. It was very new then, but many people were predicting a great future for it. I was part of a development team for online games, and the particular technology we worked with was applets, which was extremely fashionable during those years. Behind the application, the program needed to access a database, and our team spent some time developing the logic to access and interact with the database. Things such as ORM weren't used yet, but we were able to develop our own library to interact with the database, shaping the incipient ideas of ORM.

After 2004, I spent more than 90% of my time working with Java. It was the dawn of a new era for me, and things like code refactoring, unit testing, and object/relational mapping were becoming normal in our professional lives.

Currently, there are a lot of Java programs that access databases and rely on higher-level techniques and frameworks, such as JPA, Hibernate, and Spring Data. The old days of working with JDBC are hardly remembered. One of my activities as Java and Web Technologies Expert and Java Chapter Lead at Luxoft is to conduct courses on Java persistence topics and to coach my colleagues regarding the topic.

I wrote my first book for Manning Publications in 2020, *JUnit in Action*, and I have been fortunate to continue working with them. The previous versions of this book focused on Hibernate, whereas today Spring and Spring Data play a more and more important role in Java programs. Of course, we also dedicated a chapter to testing Java persistence applications.

Object/relational mapping and Java persistence have come a long way since their early days and since I began working with them. These concepts need careful consideration and planning, as particular applications and technologies require particular knowledge and approaches. This book effectively provides that information, with many examples. You'll also find concise and easy-to-follow procedures to solving a series of tasks. I hope that the methods outlined here will help you decide what to do when you face new situations in your work.

acknowledgments

First, I would like to thank my professors and colleagues for all their support over the years and to the many participants in my face-to-face and online courses—they stimulated me to achieve top quality work and to always look for improvements.

I would like to thank Luxoft, where I have been active for almost 20 years and where I currently work as Java and Web Technologies Expert and Java Chapter Lead.

Many thanks to Christian Bauer, Gavin King, and Gary Gregory, the co-authors of *Java Persistence with Hibernate*, which provided a strong foundation for this book. I hope to meet all of you in person someday.

Best thoughts for my colleagues from Luxoft, Vladimir Sonkin and Oleksii Kvitsynskyi, with whom I investigate new technologies and develop Java courses and the Java Chapter. It is a rare opportunity to work so effectively with both a Russian and a Ukrainian engineer at this time in history.

I would also like to thank the staff at Manning: acquisition editor Mike Stephens, development editors Katie Sposato Johnson and Christina Taylor, technical proofreader Jean-François Morin, copy editor Andy Carroll, as well as the behind-the-scenes production crew. The Manning team helped me to create a high-level book, and I look forward to more opportunities of this kind.

I am happy that two prominent experts, Dmitry Aleksandrov and Mohamed Taman, appreciated the book and wrote forewords for it—it's always a great pleasure to analyze technical matters together.

To all the reviewers: Amrah Umudlu, Andres Sacco, Bernhard Schuhmann, Bhagvan Kommadi, Damián Mazzini, Daniel Carl, Abayomi Otebolaku, Fernando

Bernardino, Greg Gendron, Hilde Van Gysel, Jan van Nimwegen, Javid Asgarov, Kim Gabrielsen, Kim Kjærsulf, Marcus Geselle, Matt Deimel, Mladen Knezic, Najeeb Arif, Nathan B. Crocker, Özay Duman, Piotr Gliźniewicz, Rajinder Yadav, Richard Meinsen, Sergiy Pylypets, Steve Prior, Yago Rubio, Yogesh Shetty, and Zorodzayi Mukuy—your suggestions helped make this a better book.

about this book

Java Persistence with Spring Data and Hibernate explores persistence with the most popular available tools. You'll benefit from detailed coverage of Spring Data JPA, Spring Data JDBC, Spring Data REST, JPA, and Hibernate, comparing and contrasting the alternatives so you can pick what's best for your code.

We'll begin with a hands-on introduction to object/relational mapping (ORM) and then dive into mapping strategies for linking up objects and your database. You'll learn about the different approaches to transactions in Hibernate and Spring Data, and even how to deliver Java persistence with non-relational databases. Finally, we'll explore testing strategies for persistent applications to keep your code clean and bug free.

Who should read this book

This book is for application developers who are already proficient in writing Java Core code and are interested in learning how to develop applications to interact easily and effectively with databases. You should be familiar with object-oriented programming and have at least a working knowledge of Java. You will also need a working knowledge of Maven and be able to build a Maven project and open a Java program in IntelliJ IDEA, edit it, and launch it in execution. Some of the chapters require basic knowledge about technologies like Spring or REST.

How this book is organized: A road map

This book has 20 chapters in 6 parts. Part 1 will help you get started with ORM.

- Chapter 1 introduces the object/relational paradigm mismatch and several strategies for dealing with it, foremost object/relational mapping (ORM).

- Chapter 2 guides you step by step through a tutorial with Jakarta Persistence API, Hibernate, and Spring Data—you'll implement and test a "Hello World" example.
- Chapter 3 teaches you how to design and implement complex business domain models in Java, and which mapping metadata options you have available.
- Chapter 4 will provide a first view of Spring Data JPA, introducing how you can work with it and use its capabilities.

Part 2 is about ORM, from classes and properties to tables and columns.

- Chapter 5 starts with regular class and property mappings and explains how you can map fine-grained Java domain models.
- Chapter 6 demonstrates how to map basic properties and embeddable components, and how to control mapping between Java and SQL types.
- Chapter 7 demonstrates how to map inheritance hierarchies of entities to the database using four basic inheritance-mapping strategies.
- Chapter 8 is about mapping collections and entity associations.
- Chapter 9 dives deeper into advanced entity association mappings like mapping one-to-one entity associations, one-to-many mapping options, and many-to-many and ternary entity relationships.
- Chapter 10 deals with managing data, examining the lifecycle and states of objects and effectively working with the Jakarta Persistence API.

Part 3 is about loading and storing data with Hibernate and Java Persistence. It introduces the programming interfaces, how to write transactional applications, and how Hibernate can load data from the database most efficiently.

- Chapter 11 defines database and system transaction essentials and explains how to control concurrent access with Hibernate, JPA, and Spring.
- Chapter 12 examines lazy and eager loading, fetch plans, strategies, and profiles, and wraps up with a discussion of optimizing SQL execution.
- Chapter 13 covers cascading state transitions, listening to and intercepting events, auditing and versioning with Hibernate Envers, and filtering data dynamically.

Part 4 connects Java persistence with the most widely used Java framework nowadays: Spring.

- Chapter 14 teaches you the most important strategies for creating a JPA or Hibernate application and integrating it with Spring.
- Chapter 15 introduces and analyzes the possibilities for developing persistence applications using another part of the large Spring Data framework: Spring Data JDBC.
- Chapter 16 examines Spring Data REST, which you can use to build applications in the representational state transfer (REST) architectural style.

Part 5 connects Java applications to frequently used NoSQL databases: MongoDB and Neo4j.

- Chapter 17 teaches you the most important features of the Spring Data MongoDB framework and compares them with the already discussed Spring Data JPA and Spring Data JDBC.
- Chapter 18 introduces the Hibernate OGM framework and demonstrates how to use JPA code to connect to different NoSQL databases (MongoDB and Neo4j).

Part 6 teaches you how to write queries and how to test Java persistence applications.

- Chapter 19 discusses working with Querydsl, one of the alternatives for querying a database using Java programs.
- Chapter 20 examines how to test Java persistence applications, introducing the testing pyramid and analyzing persistence testing in its context.

About the code

This book contains (mostly) large blocks of code, rather than short snippets. Therefore, all the code listings are annotated and explained.

You can get the full source code for all these examples by downloading it from GitHub at https://github.com/ctudose/java-persistence-spring-data-hibernate. You can also get executable snippets of code from the liveBook (online) version of this book at https://livebook.manning.com/book/java-persistence-with-spring-data-and-hibernate. The complete code for the examples in the book is available for download from the Manning website at https://www.manning.com/books/java-persistence-with-spring-data-and-hibernate.

liveBook discussion forum

Purchase of *Java Persistence with Spring Data and Hibernate* includes free access to liveBook, Manning's online reading platform. Using liveBook's exclusive discussion features, you can attach comments to the book globally or to specific sections or paragraphs. It's a snap to make notes for yourself, ask and answer technical questions, and receive help from the author and other users. To access the forum, go to https://livebook.manning.com/book/java-persistence-with-spring-data-and-hibernate/discussion. You can also learn more about Manning's forums and the rules of conduct at https://livebook.manning.com/discussion.

Manning's commitment to our readers is to provide a venue where a meaningful dialogue between individual readers and between readers and the author can take place. It is not a commitment to any specific amount of participation on the part of the author, whose contribution to the forum remains voluntary (and unpaid). We suggest you try asking the author some challenging questions lest his interest stray! The forum and the archives of previous discussions will be accessible from the publisher's website as long as the book is in print.

about the author

CĂTĂLIN TUDOSE was born in Piteşti, Argeş, Romania and graduated with a degree in computer science in 1997 in Bucharest. He also holds a PhD in this field. He has more than 20 years of experience in the Java area and is currently acting as a Java and web technologies expert at Luxoft Romania. He has taught more than 2,000 hours of courses and applications as a teaching assistant and professor at the Faculty of Automation and Computers in Bucharest. Cătălin has also taught more than 3,000 hours of Java inside the company, including the Corporate Junior Program, which has prepared about 50 new Java programmers in Poland. He has taught online courses at UMUC (University of Maryland University College): Computer Graphics with Java (CMSC 405), Intermediate Programming in Java (CMIS 242), and Advanced Programming in Java (CMIS 440). Cătălin has developed six courses for Pluralsight on topics related to JUnit 5, Spring, and Hibernate: "TDD with JUnit 5," "Java BDD Fundamentals," "Implementing a Test Pyramid Strategy in Java," "Spring Framework: Aspect Oriented Programming with Spring AOP," "Migrating from the JUnit 4 to the JUnit 5 Testing Platform," and "Java Persistence with Hibernate 5 Fundamentals." Besides the IT field and mathematics, Cătălin is interested in world culture and in soccer. He is a lifelong supporter of FC Argeş Piteşti.

authors of *Java Persistence with Hibernate, Second Edition*

CHRISTIAN BAUER is a member of the Hibernate developer team; he works as a trainer and consultant.

GAVIN KING is the creator of Hibernate and is a Distinguished Engineer at Red Hat. He helped design JPA and EJB 3, and was the spec lead and author of the CDI specification. He recently worked on Hibernate 6 and Hibernate Reactive, and advised on the design of Quarkus. Gavin has presented at hundreds of conferences and Java user groups around the world.

GARY GREGORY is a principal software engineer at Rocket Software, working on application servers and legacy integration. He is a co-author of Manning's *JUnit in Action* and *Spring Batch in Action* and is a member of the Project Management Committees for the Apache Software Foundation projects: Commons, HttpComponents, Logging Services, and Xalan.

about the cover illustration

The figure on the cover of *Java Persistence with Spring Data and Hibernate* is "Homme Maltois," or "Man from Malta," taken from a collection by Jacques Grasset de Saint-Sauveur, published in 1788. Each illustration is finely drawn and colored by hand.

In those days, it was easy to identify where people lived and what their trade or station in life was just by their dress. Manning celebrates the inventiveness and initiative of the computer business with book covers based on the rich diversity of regional culture centuries ago, brought back to life by pictures from collections such as this one.

Part 1

Getting started with ORM

In part 1 we'll show you why object persistence is such a complex topic and what solutions you can apply in practice. Chapter 1 introduces the object/relational paradigm mismatch and several strategies for dealing with it, foremost object/relational mapping (ORM). In chapter 2, we'll guide you step by step through a tutorial with Jakarta Persistence API (JPA), Hibernate, and Spring Data—you'll implement and test a "Hello World" example. Thus prepared, in chapter 3 you'll be ready to learn how to design and implement complex business domain models in Java, and which mapping metadata options you have available. Then chapter 4 will examine working with Spring Data JPA and its features.

After reading this part of the book, you'll understand why you need ORM and how JPA, Hibernate, and Spring Data work in practice. You'll have written your first small project, and you'll be ready to take on more complex problems. You'll also understand how real-world business entities can be implemented as Java domain models and in what format you prefer to work with ORM metadata.

Understanding object/relational persistence

This chapter covers

- Persisting with SQL databases in Java applications
- Analyzing the object/relational paradigm mismatch
- Introducing ORM, JPA, Hibernate, and Spring Data

This book is about JPA, Hibernate, and Spring Data; our focus is on using Hibernate as a provider of the Jakarta Persistence API (formerly Java Persistence API) and Spring Data as a Spring-based programming model for data access. We'll cover basic and advanced features and describe some ways to develop new applications using the Java Persistence API. Often these recommendations aren't specific to Hibernate or Spring Data. Sometimes they're our own ideas about the *best* ways to do things when working with persistent data, explained in the context of Hibernate and Spring Data.

The choice of approach to managing persistent data may be a key design decision in many software projects. Persistence has always been a hot topic of debate in the Java community. Is persistence a problem that has already been solved by SQL and extensions such as stored procedures, or is it a more pervasive problem that must be addressed by special Java frameworks? Should we hand-code even the most primitive CRUD (create, read, update, delete) operations in SQL and JDBC, or should this work be handed to an intermediary layer? How can we achieve portability if every database management system has its own SQL dialect? Should we abandon SQL completely and adopt a different database technology, such as object database systems or NoSQL systems? The debate may never end, but a solution called *object/relational mapping* (ORM) now has wide acceptance. This is due in large part to Hibernate, an open source ORM service implementation, and Spring Data, an umbrella project from the Spring family whose purpose is to unify and facilitate access to different kinds of persistence stores, including relational database systems and NoSQL databases.

Before we can get started with Hibernate and Spring Data, however, you need to understand the core problems of object persistence and ORM. This chapter explains why you need tools like Hibernate and Spring Data and specifications such as the *Jakarta Persistence API* (JPA).

First we'll define persistent data management in the context of software applications and discuss the relationships between SQL, JDBC, and Java, the underlying technologies and standards that Hibernate and Spring Data build on. We'll then discuss the so-called *object/relational paradigm mismatch* and the generic problems we encounter in object-oriented software development with SQL databases. These problems make it clear that we need tools and patterns to minimize the time we have to spend on persistence-related code in our applications.

The best way to learn Hibernate and Spring Data isn't necessarily linear. We understand that you may want to try Hibernate or Spring Data right away. If this is how you'd like to proceed, skip to the next chapter and set up a project with the "Hello World" example. We recommend that you return here at some point as you go through this book; that way, you'll be prepared and have the background concepts you need for the rest of the material.

1.1 What is persistence?

Most applications require persistent data. Persistence is one of the fundamental concepts in application development. If an information system didn't preserve data when it was powered off, the system would be of little practical use. *Object persistence* means individual objects can outlive the application process; they can be saved to a data store and be re-created at a later point in time. When we talk about persistence in Java, we're generally talking about mapping and storing object instances in a database using SQL.

We'll start by taking a brief look at persistence and how it's used in Java. Armed with this information, we'll continue our discussion of persistence and look at how it's implemented in object-oriented applications.

1.1.1 Relational databases

You, like most other software engineers, have probably worked with SQL and relational databases; many of us handle such systems every day. Relational database management systems have SQL-based application programming interfaces, so we call today's relational database products SQL *database management systems* (DBMS) or, when we're talking about particular systems, SQL *databases*.

Relational technology is a well-known technology, and this alone is sufficient reason for many organizations to choose it. Relational databases are also an incredibly flexible and robust approach to data management. Due to the well-researched theoretical foundation of the relational data model, relational databases can guarantee and protect the integrity of stored data, along with having other desirable characteristics. You may be familiar with E.F. Codd's five-decade-old introduction of the relational model, "A Relational Model of Data for Large Shared Data Banks" (Codd, 1970). A more recent compendium worth reading, with a focus on SQL, is C.J. Date's *SQL and Relational Theory* (Date, 2015).

Relational DBMSs aren't specific to Java, nor is an SQL database specific to a particular application. This important principle is known as *data independence*. In other words, *data usually lives longer than an application does*. Relational technology provides a way of sharing data among different applications, or among different parts of the same overall system (a data entry application and a reporting application, for example). Relational technology is a common denominator of many disparate systems and technology platforms. Hence, the relational data model is often the foundation for the enterprise-wide representation of business entities.

Before we go into more detail about the practical aspects of SQL databases, we need to mention an important concern: although marketed as relational, a database system providing only an SQL data language interface isn't really relational, and in many ways it isn't even close to the original concept. Naturally, this has led to confusion. SQL practitioners blame the relational data model for shortcomings in the SQL language, and relational data management experts blame the SQL standard for being a weak implementation of the relational model and ideals. We'll highlight some significant aspects of this problem throughout this book, but generally we'll focus on the practical aspects. If you're interested in more background material, we highly recommend *Fundamentals of Database Systems* by Ramez Elmasri and Shamkant B. Navathe (Elmasri, 2016) for the theory and concepts of relational database systems.

1.1.2 Understanding SQL

To use JPA, Hibernate, and Spring Data effectively, you must start with a solid understanding of the relational model and SQL. You'll need to understand the relational model and the information model and topics such as normalization to guarantee the integrity of your data, and you'll need to use your knowledge of SQL to tune the performance of your application—these are all prerequisites for reading this book. Hibernate and Spring Data simplify many repetitive coding tasks, but your knowledge of persistence technology must extend beyond the frameworks themselves if you want to take advantage of the full power of modern SQL databases. To dig deeper, consult the sources in the references list at the end of this book.

You've probably used SQL for many years and are familiar with the basic operations and statements written in this language. Still, we know from our own experience that SQL is sometimes hard to remember, and some terms vary in usage.

You should be comfortable with them, so let's briefly review some of the SQL terms we'll use in this book. SQL is used as a *data definition language* (DDL), with syntax for *creating*, *altering*, and *dropping* artifacts such as tables and constraints in the catalog of the DBMS. When this *schema* is ready, you can use SQL as a *data manipulation language* (DML) to perform operations on data, including *insertions, updates*, and *deletions*. You can retrieve data by executing *data query language* (DQL) statements with *restrictions, projections*, and *Cartesian products*. For efficient reporting, you can use SQL to *join, aggregate*, and *group* data as necessary. You can even nest SQL statements inside each other—a technique that uses *subselects*. When your business requirements change, you'll have to modify the database schema again with DDL statements after data has been stored; this is known as *schema evolution*. You may also use SQL as a *data control language* (DCL) to *grant and revoke* access to the database or parts of it.

If you're an SQL veteran and you want to know more about optimization and how SQL is executed, get a copy of the excellent book *SQL Tuning* by Dan Tow (Tow, 2003). For a look at the practical side of SQL through the lens of how not to use SQL, *SQL Antipatterns: Avoiding the Pitfalls of Database Programming*, by Bill Karwin (Karwin, 2010) is a good resource.

Although the SQL database is one part of ORM, the other part, of course, consists of the data in your Java application that needs to be persisted to and loaded from the database.

1.1.3   *Using SQL in Java*

When you work with an SQL database in a Java application, you issue SQL statements to the database via the Java Database Connectivity (JDBC) API. Whether the SQL was written by hand and embedded in the Java code or generated on the fly by Java code, you use the JDBC API to bind arguments when preparing query parameters, executing a query, scrolling through query results, retrieving values from a result set, and so on. These are low-level data access tasks; as application engineers, we're more interested in the business problem that requires this data access. What we'd really like to write is code that saves and retrieves instances of our classes, relieving us of this low-level labor.

Because these data access tasks are often so tedious, we have to ask: are the relational data model and (especially) SQL the right choices for persistence in object-oriented applications? We can answer this question unequivocally: yes! There are many reasons why SQL databases dominate the computing industry—relational database management systems are the only proven generic data management technology, and they're almost always a *requirement* in Java projects.

Note that we aren't claiming that relational technology is *always* the best solution. Many data management requirements warrant a completely different approach. For example, internet-scale distributed systems (web search engines, content distribution networks, peer-to-peer sharing, instant messaging) have to deal with exceptional transaction volumes. Many of these systems don't require that after a data update completes, all processes see the same updated data (strong transactional consistency). Users might be happy with weak consistency; after an update, there might be a window of inconsistency before all processes see the updated data. In contrast, some scientific applications work with enormous but very specialized datasets. Such systems and their unique challenges typically require equally unique and often custom-made persistence solutions. Generic data management tools such as ACID-compliant transactional SQL databases, JDBC, Hibernate, and Spring Data would play only a minor role for these types of systems.

Relational systems at internet scale

To understand why relational systems, and the data-integrity guarantees associated with them, are difficult to scale, we recommend that you first familiarize yourself with the *CAP theorem*. According to this rule, a distributed system cannot be *consistent*, *available*, and *tolerant against partition failures* all at the same time.

A system may guarantee that all nodes will see the same data at the same time and that data read and write requests are always answered. But when a part of the system fails due to a host, network, or data center problem, you must either give up strong consistency or 100% availability. In practice, this means you need a strategy that detects partition failures and restores either consistency or availability to a certain degree (for example, by making some part of the system temporarily unavailable so data synchronization can occur in the background). Often, the data, the user, or the operation will determine whether strong consistency is necessary.

In this book, we'll consider the problems of data storage and sharing in the context of an object-oriented application that uses a *domain model*. Instead of directly working with the rows and columns of a `java.sql.ResultSet`, the business logic of the application will interact with the application-specific object-oriented domain model. If the SQL database schema of an online auction system has `ITEM` and `BID` tables, for example, the Java application defines corresponding `Item` and `Bid` classes. Instead of reading and writing the value of a particular row and column with the `ResultSet` API, the application loads and stores instances of `Item` and `Bid` classes.

At runtime, the application therefore operates with instances of these classes. Each instance of a `Bid` has a reference to an auction `Item`, and each `Item` may have a collection of references to `Bid` instances. The business logic isn't executed in the database (as an SQL stored procedure); it's implemented in Java and executed in the application tier. This allows the business logic to use sophisticated object-oriented concepts such as inheritance and polymorphism. For example, we could use well-known design patterns such as *strategy, mediator,* and *composite* (see *Design Patterns: Elements of Reusable Object-Oriented Software* [Gamma, 1994]), all of which depend on polymorphic method calls.

Now a warning: not all Java applications are designed this way, nor should they be. Simple applications may be much better off without a domain model. Use the JDBC ResultSet if that's all you need. Call existing stored procedures, and read their SQL result sets, too. Many applications need to execute procedures that modify large sets of data, close to the data. You might also implement some reporting functionality with plain SQL queries and render the results directly onscreen. SQL and the JDBC API are perfectly serviceable for dealing with tabular data representations, and the JDBC RowSet makes CRUD operations even easier. Working with such a representation of persistent data is straightforward and well understood.

But for applications with nontrivial business logic, the domain model approach helps to improve code reuse and maintainability significantly. In practice, *both* strategies are common and needed.

For several decades, developers have spoken of a *paradigm mismatch*. The *paradigms* referred to are object modeling and relational modeling, or, more practically, object-oriented programming and SQL. This mismatch explains why every enterprise project expends so much effort on persistence-related concerns. With this conception, you can begin to see the problems—some well understood and some less well understood—that must be solved in an application that combines an object-oriented domain model and a persistent relational model. Let's take a closer look at this so-called paradigm mismatch.

1.2   *The paradigm mismatch*

The object/relational paradigm mismatch can be broken into several parts, which we'll examine one at a time. Let's start our exploration with a simple example that is problem-free. As we build on it, you'll see the mismatch begin to appear.

Suppose you have to design and implement an online e-commerce application. In this application, you need a class to represent information about a user of the system, and you need another class to represent information about the user's billing details, as shown in figure 1.1.

Figure 1.1   A simple UML diagram of the User and BillingDetails entities

In this diagram, you can see that a User has many BillingDetails. This is a composition, indicated by the full diamond. A composition is the type of association where an object (BillingDetails in our case) cannot conceptually exist without the container (User in our case). You can navigate the relationship between the classes in both directions; this means you can iterate through collections or call methods to get to the "other" side of the relationship. The classes representing these entities may be extremely simple:

```
Path: Ch01/e-commerce/src/com/manning/javapersistence/ch01/User.java

public class User {
    private String username;
    private String address;
```

```
        private Set<BillingDetails> billingDetails = new HashSet<>();

        // Constructor, accessor methods (getters/setters), business methods
}
```

Path: Ch01/e-commerce/src/com/manning/javapersistence/ch01
➡ /BillingDetails.java

```
public class BillingDetails {
    private String account;
    private String bankname;
    private User user;

    // Constructor, accessor methods (getters/setters), business methods
}
```

Note that we're only interested in the state of the entities' persistence, so we've omitted the implementation of constructors, accessor methods, and business methods.

It's easy to come up with an SQL schema design for this case (the syntax of the following queries is applicable to MySQL):

```
CREATE TABLE USERS (
    USERNAME VARCHAR(15) NOT NULL PRIMARY KEY,
    ADDRESS VARCHAR(255) NOT NULL
);

CREATE TABLE BILLINGDETAILS (
    ACCOUNT VARCHAR(15) NOT NULL PRIMARY KEY,
    BANKNAME VARCHAR(255) NOT NULL,
    USERNAME VARCHAR(15) NOT NULL,
    FOREIGN KEY (USERNAME) REFERENCES USERS(USERNAME)
);
```

The foreign key–constrained column USERNAME in BILLINGDETAILS represents the relationship between the two entities. For this simple domain model, the object/relational mismatch is barely in evidence; it's straightforward to write JDBC code to insert, update, and delete information about users and billing details.

Now let's see what happens when we consider something a little more realistic. The paradigm mismatch will be visible when we add more entities and entity relationships to the application.

1.2.1 *The problem of granularity*

The most obvious problem with the current implementation is that we've designed an address as a simple String value. In most systems, it's necessary to store street, city, state, country, and ZIP code information separately. Of course, you could add these properties directly to the User class, but because other classes in the system will likely also carry address information, it makes more sense to create an Address class to reuse it. Figure 1.2 shows the updated model.

The relationship between `User` and `Address` is an aggregation, indicated by the empty diamond. Should we also add an `ADDRESS` table? Not necessarily; it's common to keep address information in the `USERS` table, in individual columns. This design is likely to perform better because a table join isn't needed if you want to retrieve the user and address in a single query. The nicest solution may be to create

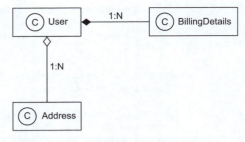

Figure 1.2   The `User` has an `Address`.

a new SQL data type to represent addresses and to add a single column of that new type in the `USERS` table, instead of adding several new columns.

This choice of adding either several columns or a single column of a new SQL data type is a problem of *granularity*. Broadly speaking, granularity refers to the relative size of the types you're working with.

Let's return to the example. Adding a new data type to the database catalog to store `Address` Java instances in a single column sounds like the best approach:

```
CREATE TABLE USERS (
    USERNAME VARCHAR(15) NOT NULL PRIMARY KEY,
    ADDRESS ADDRESS NOT NULL
);
```

A new `Address` type (class) in Java and a new `ADDRESS` SQL data type should guarantee interoperability. But you'll find various problems if you check on the support for user-defined data types (UDTs) in today's SQL database management systems.

UDT support is one of several so-called *object/relational extensions* to traditional SQL. This term alone is confusing, because it means the database management system has (or is supposed to support) a sophisticated data type system. Unfortunately, UDT support is a somewhat obscure feature of most SQL DBMSs, and it certainly isn't portable between different products. Furthermore, the SQL standard supports user-defined data types, but poorly.

This limitation isn't the fault of the relational data model. You can consider the failure to standardize such an important piece of functionality to be a result of the object/relational database wars between vendors in the mid-1990s. Today most engineers accept that SQL products have limited type systems—no questions asked. Even with a sophisticated UDT system in your SQL DBMS, you would still likely duplicate the type declarations, writing the new type in Java and again in SQL. Attempts to find a better solution for the Java space, such as SQLJ, unfortunately have not had much success. DBMS products rarely support deploying and executing Java classes directly on the database, and if support is available, it's typically limited to very basic functionality in everyday usage.

For these and whatever other reasons, the use of UDTs or Java types in an SQL database isn't common practice at this time, and it's unlikely that you'll encounter a legacy schema that makes extensive use of UDTs. We therefore can't and won't store instances of our new `Address` class in a single new column that has the same data type as the Java layer.

The pragmatic solution for this problem has several columns of built-in vendor-defined SQL types (such as Boolean, numeric, and string data types). You'd usually define the `USERS` table as follows:

```
CREATE TABLE USERS (
    USERNAME VARCHAR(15) NOT NULL PRIMARY KEY,
    ADDRESS_STREET VARCHAR(255) NOT NULL,
    ADDRESS_ZIPCODE VARCHAR(5) NOT NULL,
    ADDRESS_CITY VARCHAR(255) NOT NULL
);
```

Classes in the Java domain model come in a range of levels of granularity: from coarse-grained entity classes like `User` to finer-grained classes like `Address`, down to simple `SwissZipCode` extending `AbstractNumericZipCode` (or whatever your desired level of abstraction is). In contrast, just two levels of type granularity are visible in the SQL database: relation types created by you, like `USERS` and `BILLINGDETAILS`, and built-in data types such as `VARCHAR`, `BIGINT`, and `TIMESTAMP`.

Many simple persistence mechanisms fail to recognize this mismatch and so end up forcing the less flexible representation of SQL products on the object-oriented model, effectively flattening it. It turns out that the granularity problem isn't especially difficult to solve, even if it's visible in so many existing systems. We'll look at the solution to this problem in section 5.1.1.

A much more difficult and interesting problem arises when we consider domain models that rely on *inheritance*, a feature of object-oriented design you may use to bill the users of your e-commerce application in new and interesting ways.

1.2.2 *The problem of inheritance*

In Java, you implement type inheritance using superclasses and subclasses. To illustrate why this can present a mismatch problem, let's modify our e-commerce application so that we now can accept not only bank account billing, but also credit cards. The most natural way to reflect this change in the model is to use inheritance for the `BillingDetails` superclass, along with multiple concrete subclasses: `CreditCard`, `BankAccount`. Each of these subclasses defines slightly different data (and completely different functionality that acts on that data). The UML class diagram in figure 1.3 illustrates this model.

What changes must we make to support this updated Java class structure? Can we create a `CREDITCARD` table that *extends* `BILLINGDETAILS`? SQL database products don't generally implement table inheritance (or even data type inheritance), and if they do implement it, they don't follow a standard syntax.

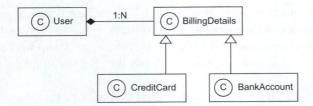

Figure 1.3   Using inheritance for different billing strategies

We haven't finished with inheritance. As soon as we introduce inheritance into the model, we have the possibility of *polymorphism*. The User class has a *polymorphic association* with the BillingDetails superclass. At runtime, a User instance may reference an instance of any of the subclasses of BillingDetails. Similarly, we want to be able to write *polymorphic queries* that refer to the BillingDetails class and have the query return instances of its subclasses.

SQL databases lack an obvious way (or at least a standardized way) to represent a polymorphic association. A foreign key constraint refers to exactly one target table; it isn't straightforward to define a foreign key that refers to multiple tables.

The result of this mismatch of subtypes is that the inheritance structure in a model must be persisted in an SQL database that doesn't offer an inheritance mechanism. In chapter 7 we'll discuss how ORM solutions such as Hibernate solve the problem of persisting a class hierarchy to an SQL database table or tables, and how polymorphic behavior can be implemented. Fortunately, this problem is now well understood in the community, and most solutions support approximately the same functionality.

The next aspect of the object/relational mismatch problem is the issue of *object identity*.

1.2.3   *The problem of identity*

You probably noticed that the example defined USERNAME as the primary key of the USERS table. Was that a good choice? How do you handle identical objects in Java?

Although the problem of identity may not be obvious at first, you'll encounter it often in your growing and expanding e-commerce system, such as when you need to check whether two instances are identical. There are three ways to tackle this problem: two in the Java world and one in the SQL database. As expected, they work together only with some help.

Java defines two different notions of *sameness*:

- Instance identity (roughly equivalent to a memory location, checked with a == b)
- Instance equality, as determined by the implementation of the equals() method (also called *equality by value*)

On the other hand, the identity of a database row is expressed as a comparison of primary key values. As you'll see in section 9.1.2, neither equals() nor == is always equivalent to a comparison of primary key values. It's common for several non-identical instances in Java to simultaneously represent the same row of a database, such as in concurrently running application threads. Furthermore, some subtle difficulties are involved in implementing `equals()` correctly for a persistent class and in understanding when this might be necessary.

Let's use an example to discuss another problem related to database identity. In the table definition for USERS, USERNAME is the primary key. Unfortunately, this decision makes it difficult to change a user's name; you need to update not only the row in USERS but also the foreign key values in (many) rows of BILLINGDETAILS. To solve this problem, later in this book we'll recommend that you use *surrogate keys* whenever you can't find a good natural key. We'll also discuss what makes a good primary key. A surrogate key column is a primary key column with no meaning to the application user—in other words, a key that isn't presented to the application user. Its only purpose is to identify data inside the application.

For example, you may change your table definitions to look like this:

```
CREATE TABLE USERS (
    ID BIGINT NOT NULL PRIMARY KEY,
    USERNAME VARCHAR(15) NOT NULL UNIQUE,
    . . .
);
CREATE TABLE BILLINGDETAILS (
    ID BIGINT NOT NULL PRIMARY KEY,
    ACCOUNT VARCHAR(15) NOT NULL,
    BANKNAME VARCHAR(255) NOT NULL,
    USER_ID BIGINT NOT NULL,
    FOREIGN KEY (USER_ID) REFERENCES USERS(ID)
);
```

The ID columns contain system-generated values. These columns were introduced purely for the benefit of the data model, so how (if at all) should they be represented in the Java domain model? We'll discuss this question in section 5.2, and we'll find a solution with ORM.

In the context of persistence, identity is closely related to how the system handles caching and transactions. Different persistence solutions have chosen different strategies, and this has been an area of confusion. We'll cover all these interesting topics—and look at how they're related—in section 9.1.

So far, the skeleton e-commerce application we've designed has exposed the paradigm mismatch problems with mapping granularity, subtypes, and identity. We need to discuss further the important concept of *associations*: how the relationships between entities are mapped and handled. Is the foreign key constraint in the database all you need?

1.2.4 *The problem of associations*

In the domain model, associations represent the relationships between entities. The User, Address, and BillingDetails classes are all associated; but unlike Address, BillingDetails stands on its own. BillingDetails instances are stored in their own table. Association mapping and the management of entity associations are central concepts in any object persistence solution.

Object-oriented languages represent associations using *object references*, but in the relational world, a *foreign key–constrained column* represents an association with copies of key values. The constraint is a rule that guarantees the integrity of the association. There are substantial differences between the two mechanisms.

Object references are inherently directional; the association is from one instance to the other. They're pointers. If an association between instances should be navigable in both directions, you must define the association *twice*, once in each of the associated classes. The UML class diagram in figure 1.4 illustrates this model with a one-to-many association.

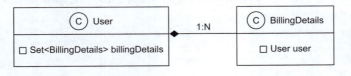

Figure 1.4 One-to-many association between `User` and `BillingDetails`

You've already seen this in the domain model classes:

```
Path: Ch01/e-commerce/src/com/manning/javapersistence/ch01/User.java

public class User {
    private Set<BillingDetails> billingDetails = new HashSet<>();
}
```

```
Path: Ch01/e-commerce/src/com/manning/javapersistence/ch01
➥ /BillingDetails.java

public class BillingDetails {
    private User user;
}
```

Navigation in a particular direction has no meaning for a relational data model because you can create data associations with *join* and *projection* operators. The challenge is to map a completely open data model that is independent of the application that works with the data to an application-dependent navigational model—a constrained view of the associations needed by this particular application.

Java associations can have *many-to-many* multiplicity. The UML class diagram in figure 1.5 illustrates this model.

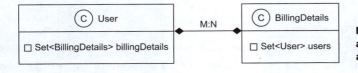

Figure 1.5 Many-to-many association between `User` and `BillingDetails`

The classes could look like this:

```
Path: Ch01/e-commerce/src/com/manning/javapersistence/ch01/User.java

public class User {
    private Set<BillingDetails> billingDetails = new HashSet<>();
}

Path: Ch01/e-commerce/src/com/manning/javapersistence/ch01
➥ /BillingDetails.java

public class BillingDetails {
    private Set<User> users = new HashSet<>();
}
```

However, the foreign key declaration on the BILLINGDETAILS table is a *many-to-one* association: each bank account is linked to a particular user, but each user may have multiple linked bank accounts.

If you wish to represent a *many-to-many* association in an SQL database, you must introduce a new table, usually called a *link table*. In most cases, this table doesn't appear anywhere in the domain model. For this example, if you consider the relationship between the user and the billing information to be many-to-many, you would define the link table as follows:

```
CREATE TABLE USER_BILLINGDETAILS (
    USER_ID BIGINT,
    BILLINGDETAILS_ID BIGINT,
    PRIMARY KEY (USER_ID, BILLINGDETAILS_ID),
    FOREIGN KEY (USER_ID) REFERENCES USERS(ID),
    FOREIGN KEY (BILLINGDETAILS_ID) REFERENCES BILLINGDETAILS(ID)
);
```

You no longer need the USER_ID foreign key column and constraint on the BILLING-DETAILS table; this additional table now manages the links between the two entities. We'll discuss association and collection mappings in detail in chapter 8.

So far, the problems we've considered are mainly *structural*: you can see them by considering a purely static view of the system. Perhaps the most difficult problem in object persistence is a *dynamic* problem: how data is accessed at runtime.

1.2.5 *The problem of data navigation*

There is a fundamental difference between how you access data in Java code and within a relational database. In Java, when you access a user's billing information, you call someUser.getBillingDetails().iterator().next() or something similar. Or, starting from Java 8, you may call someUser.getBillingDetails().stream() .filter(someCondition).map(someMapping).forEach(billingDetails-> {doSomething (billingDetails)}). This is the most natural way to access object-oriented data, and it's often described as *walking the object network*. You navigate from one instance to another, even iterating collections, following prepared pointers between classes. Unfortunately, this isn't an efficient way to retrieve data from an SQL database.

The single most important thing you can do to improve the performance of data access code is to *minimize the number of requests to the database.* The most obvious way to do this is to minimize the number of SQL queries. (Of course, other, more sophisticated, ways—such as extensive caching—follow as a second step.)

Therefore, efficient access to relational data with SQL usually requires joins between the tables of interest. The number of tables included in the join when retrieving data determines the depth of the object network you can navigate in memory. For example, if you need to retrieve a User and aren't interested in the user's billing information, you can write this simple query:

```
SELECT * FROM USERS WHERE ID = 123
```

On the other hand, if you need to retrieve a User and then subsequently visit each of the associated BillingDetails instances (let's say, to list the user's bank accounts), you would write a different query:

```
SELECT * FROM USERS, BILLINGDETAILS
WHERE USERS.ID = 123 AND
BILLINGDETAILS.ID = USERS.ID
```

As you can see, to use joins efficiently you need to know what portion of the object network you plan to access *before* you start navigating the object network! Careful, though: if you retrieve too much data (probably more than you might need), you're wasting memory in the application tier. You may also overwhelm the SQL database with huge Cartesian product result sets. Imagine retrieving not only users and bank accounts in one query, but also all orders paid from each bank account, the products in each order, and so on.

Any object persistence solution permits you to fetch the data of associated instances only when the association is first accessed in the Java code. This is known as *lazy loading*: retrieving data only on demand. This piecemeal style of data access is fundamentally inefficient in the context of an SQL database, because it requires executing one statement for each node or collection of the object network that is accessed. This is the dreaded *n+1 selects* problem. In our example, you will need one *select* to retrieve a User and then *n selects* for each of the *n* associated BillingDetails instances.

This mismatch in the way you access data in Java code and within a relational database is perhaps the single most common source of performance problems in Java information systems. Avoiding the Cartesian product and *n*+1 selects problems is still a problem for many Java programmers. Hibernate provides sophisticated features for efficiently and transparently fetching networks of objects from the database to the application accessing them. We'll discuss these features in chapter 12.

We now have quite a list of object/relational mismatch problems: the problem of granularity, the problem of inheritance, the problem of identity, the problem of associations, and the problem of data navigation. It can be costly (in time and effort) to find solutions, as you may know from experience. It will take us a large part of this book to provide detailed answers to these questions and to demonstrate ORM as a viable solution. Let's get started with an overview of ORM, the Java Persistence standard (JPA), and the Hibernate and Spring Data projects.

1.3   ORM, JPA, Hibernate, and Spring Data

In a nutshell, object/relational mapping (ORM) is the automated (and transparent) persistence of objects in a Java application to the tables in an RDBMS (relational database management system), using metadata that describes the mapping between the classes of the application and the schema of the SQL database. In essence, ORM works by transforming (reversibly) data from one representation to another. A program using ORM will provide the meta-information about how to map the objects from the memory to the database, and the effective transformation will be fulfilled by ORM.

Some people may consider one advantage of ORM to be that it shields developers from messy SQL. This view holds that object-oriented developers shouldn't be expected to go deep into SQL or relational databases. On the contrary, Java developers must have a sufficient level of familiarity with—and appreciation of—relational modeling and SQL to work with Hibernate and Spring Data. ORM is an advanced technique used by developers who have already done it the hard way.

JPA (Jakarta Persistence API, formerly Java Persistence API) is a specification defining an API that manages the persistence of objects and object/relational mappings. Hibernate is the most popular implementation of this specification. So, JPA will specify what must be done to persist objects, while Hibernate will determine how to do it. Spring Data Commons, as part of the Spring Data family, provides the core Spring framework concepts that support all Spring Data modules. Spring Data JPA, another project from the Spring Data family, is an additional layer on top of JPA implementations (such as Hibernate). Not only can Spring Data JPA use all the capabilities of JPA, but it adds its own capabilities, such as generating database queries from method names. We'll go into many details in this book, but if you would like an overall view right now, you can quickly jump ahead to figure 4.1.

To use Hibernate effectively, you must be able to view and interpret the SQL statements it issues and understand their performance implications. To take advantage of the benefits of Spring Data, you must be able to anticipate how the boilerplate code and the generated queries are created.

The JPA specification defines the following:

- A facility for specifying mapping metadata—how persistent classes and their properties relate to the database schema. JPA relies heavily on Java annotations in domain model classes, but you can also write mappings in XML files.
- APIs for performing basic CRUD operations on instances of persistent classes, most prominently `javax.persistence.EntityManager` for storing and loading data.

- A language and APIs for specifying queries that refer to classes and properties of classes. This language is the Jakarta Persistence Query Language (JPQL) and it looks similar to SQL. The standardized API allows for the programmatic creation of *criteria queries* without string manipulation.
- How the persistence engine interacts with transactional instances to perform dirty checking, association fetching, and other optimization functions. The JPA specification covers some basic caching strategies.

Hibernate implements JPA and supports all the standardized mappings, queries, and programming interfaces. Let's look at some of the benefits of Hibernate:

- *Productivity*—Hibernate eliminates much of the repetitive work (more than you'd expect) and lets you concentrate on the business problem. No matter which application-development strategy you prefer—top-down (starting with a domain model) or bottom-up (starting with an existing database schema)—Hibernate, used together with the appropriate tools, will significantly reduce development time.
- *Maintainability*—Automated ORM with Hibernate reduces lines of code, making the system more understandable and easier to refactor. Hibernate provides a buffer between the domain model and the SQL schema, isolating each model from minor changes to the other.
- *Performance*—Although hand-coded persistence might be faster in the same sense that assembly code can be faster than Java code, automated solutions like Hibernate allow the use of many optimizations *at all times*. One example is the efficient and easily tunable caching in the application tier. This means developers can spend more energy hand-optimizing the few remaining real bottlenecks instead of prematurely optimizing everything.
- *Vendor independence*—Hibernate can help mitigate some of the risks associated with vendor lock-in. Even if you plan never to change your DBMS product, ORM tools that support several different DBMSs enable a certain level of portability. Also, DBMS independence helps in development scenarios where engineers use a lightweight local database but deploy for testing and production on a different system.

Spring Data makes the implementation of the persistence layer even more efficient. Spring Data JPA, one of the projects of the family, sits on top of the JPA layer. Spring Data JDBC, another project of the family, sits on top of JDBC. Let's look at some of the benefits of Spring Data:

- *Shared infrastructure*—Spring Data Commons, part of the umbrella Spring Data project, provides a metadata model for persisting Java classes and technology-neutral repository interfaces. It provides its capabilities to the other Spring Data projects.

- *Removes DAO implementations*—JPA implementations use the *data access object* (DAO) pattern. This pattern starts with the idea of an abstract interface to a database and maps application calls to the persistence layer while hiding the details of the database. Spring Data JPA makes it possible to fully remove DAO implementations, so the code will be shorter.
- *Automatic class creation*—Using Spring Data JPA, a DAO interface needs to extend the JPA-specific `Repository` interface—`JpaRepository`. Spring Data JPA will automatically create an implementation for this interface—the programmer will not have to take care of this.
- *Default implementations for methods*—Spring Data JPA will generate default implementations for each method defined by its repository interfaces. Basic CRUD operations do not need to be implemented any longer. This reduces the boilerplate code, speeds up development, and removes the possibility of introducing bugs.
- *Generated queries*—You may define a method on your repository interface following a naming pattern. There's no need to write your queries by hand; Spring Data JPA will parse the method name and create a query for it.
- *Close to the database if needed*—Spring Data JDBC can communicate directly with the database and avoid the "magic" of Spring Data JPA. It allows you to interact with the database through JDBC, but it removes the boilerplate code by using the Spring framework facilities.

This chapter has focused on understanding object/relational persistence and the problems generated by the object/relational paradigm mismatch. Chapter 2 will look at some of the persistence alternatives for a Java application: JPA, Hibernate Native, and Spring Data JPA.

Summary

- With object persistence, individual objects can outlive their application process, be saved to a data store, and be re-created later. The object/relational mismatch comes into play when the data store is an SQL-based relational database management system. For example, a network of objects can't be saved to a database table; it must be disassembled and persisted to columns of portable SQL data types. A good solution to this problem is object/relational mapping (ORM).
- ORM isn't a silver bullet for all persistence tasks; its job is to relieve the developer of about 95% of object persistence work, such as writing complex SQL statements with many table joins and copying values from JDBC result sets to objects or graphs of objects.
- A full-featured ORM middleware solution may provide database portability, certain optimization techniques like caching, and other viable functions that aren't easy to hand-code in a limited time with SQL and JDBC. An ORM solution

implies, in the Java world, the JPA specification and a JPA implementation—Hibernate being the most popular nowadays.

- Spring Data may come on top of the JPA implementations, and it simplifies, even more, the data persistence process. It is an umbrella project that adheres to the Spring framework principles and comes with an even simpler approach, including removing the DAO pattern, automatic code generation, and automatic query generation.

Starting a project

2

This chapter covers

- Introducing the Hibernate and Spring Data projects
- Developing a "Hello World" with Jakarta Persistence API, Hibernate, and Spring Data
- Examining the configuration and integration options

In this chapter, we'll start with the Jakarta Persistence API (JPA), Hibernate, and Spring Data and work through a step-by-step example. We'll look at the persistence APIs and see the benefits of using either standardized JPA, native Hibernate, or Spring Data.

We'll begin with a tour through JPA, Hibernate, and Spring Data, looking at a straightforward "Hello World" application. JPA (Jakarta Persistence API, formerly Java Persistence API) is the specification defining an API that manages the persistence of objects and object/relational mappings—it specifies what must be done to persist objects. Hibernate, the most popular implementation of this specification, will make the persistence happen. Spring Data makes the implementation of the persistence layer even more efficient; it's an umbrella project that adheres to the Spring framework principles and offers an even simpler approach.

2.1   *Introducing Hibernate*

Object/relational mapping (ORM) is a programming technique for making the connection between the incompatible worlds of object-oriented systems and relational databases. Hibernate is an ambitious project that aims to provide a complete solution to the problem of managing persistent data in Java. Today, Hibernate is not only an ORM service but also a collection of data management tools extending well beyond ORM.

The Hibernate project suite includes the following:

- *Hibernate ORM*—Hibernate ORM consists of a core, a base service for persistence with SQL databases, and a native proprietary API. Hibernate ORM is the foundation for several of the other projects in the suite, and it's the oldest Hibernate project. You can use Hibernate ORM on its own, independent of any framework or any particular runtime environment with all JDKs. As long as a data source is accessible, you can configure it for Hibernate, and it works.
- *Hibernate EntityManager*—This is Hibernate's implementation of the standard Jakarta Persistence API. It's an optional module you can stack on top of Hibernate ORM. Hibernate's native features are a superset of the JPA persistence features in every respect.
- *Hibernate Validator*—Hibernate provides the reference implementation of the Bean Validation (JSR 303) specification. Independent of other Hibernate projects, it provides declarative validation for domain model (or any other) classes.
- *Hibernate Envers*—Envers is dedicated to audit logging and keeping multiple versions of data in the SQL database. This helps add data history and audit trails to the application, similar to any version control systems you might already be familiar with, such as Subversion or Git.
- *Hibernate Search*—Hibernate Search keeps an index of the domain model data up to date in an Apache Lucene database. It lets you query this database with a powerful and naturally integrated API. Many projects use Hibernate Search in addition to Hibernate ORM, adding full-text search capabilities. If you have a free text search form in your application's user interface, and you want happy users, work with Hibernate Search. Hibernate Search isn't covered in this book, but you can get a good start with *Hibernate Search in Action* by Emmanuel Bernard (Bernard, 2008).
- *Hibernate OGM*—This Hibernate project is an object/grid mapper. It provides JPA support for NoSQL solutions, reusing the Hibernate core engine but persisting mapped entities into key/value-, document-, or graph-oriented data stores.
- *Hibernate Reactive*—Hibernate Reactive is a reactive API for Hibernate ORM, interacting with a database in a non-blocking manner. It supports non-blocking database drivers. Hibernate Reactive isn't covered in this book.

The Hibernate source code is freely downloadable from https://github.com/hibernate.

2.2 Introducing Spring Data

Spring Data is a family of projects belonging to the Spring framework whose purpose is to simplify access to both relational and NoSQL databases:

- *Spring Data Commons*—Spring Data Commons, part of the umbrella Spring Data project, provides a metadata model for persisting Java classes and technology-neutral repository interfaces.

- *Spring Data JPA*—Spring Data JPA deals with the implementation of JPA-based repositories. It provides improved support for JPA-based data access layers by reducing the boilerplate code and creating implementations for the repository interfaces.

- *Spring Data JDBC*—Spring Data JDBC deals with the implementation of JDBC-based repositories. It provides improved support for JDBC-based data access layers. It does not offer a series of JPA capabilities, such as caching or lazy loading, resulting in a simpler and limited ORM.

- *Spring Data REST*—Spring Data REST deals with exporting Spring Data repositories as RESTful resources.

- *Spring Data MongoDB*—Spring Data MongoDB deals with access to the MongoDB document database. It relies on the repository-style data access layer and the POJO programming model.

- *Spring Data Redis*—Spring Data Redis deals with access to the Redis key/value database. It relies on freeing the developer from managing the infrastructure and providing high- and low-level abstractions for access to the data store. Spring Data Redis isn't covered in this book.

The Spring Data source code (together with other Spring projects) is freely downloadable from https://github.com/spring-projects.

Let's get started with our first JPA, Hibernate, and Spring Data project.

2.3 "Hello World" with JPA

In this section we'll write our first JPA application, which will store a message in the database and then retrieve it. The machine we are running our code on has MySQL Release 8.0 installed. To install MySQL Release 8.0, follow the instructions in the official documentation: https://dev.mysql.com/doc/refman/8.0/en/installing.html.

In order to execute the examples in the source code, you'll need first to run the Ch02.sql script, as shown in figure 2.1. Open MySQL Workbench, go to File > Open SQL Script, and choose the SQL file and run it. The examples use a MySQL server with the default credentials: the username *root* and no password.

In the "Hello World" application, we want to store messages in the database and load them from the database. Hibernate applications define persistent classes that are mapped to database tables. We define these classes based on our analysis of the business domain; hence, they're a model of the domain. This example will consist of one class and its mapping. We'll write the examples as executable tests, with assertions that

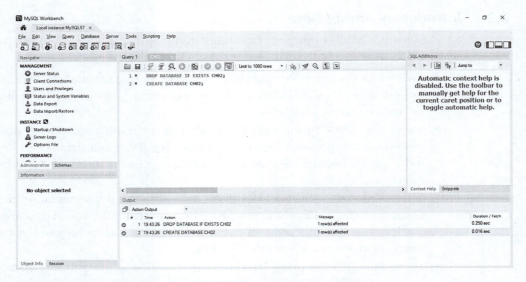

Figure 2.1   Creating the MySQL database by running the Ch02.sql script

verify the correct outcome of each operation. We've tested all the examples in this book, so we can be sure they work properly.

Let's start by installing and configuring JPA, Hibernate, and the other needed dependencies. We'll use Apache Maven as the project build tool for all the examples in this book. For basic Maven concepts and details on how to set up Maven, see appendix A.

We'll declare the dependencies shown in the following listing.

> **Listing 2.1   The Maven dependencies on Hibernate, JUnit Jupiter, and MySQL**

Path: Ch02/helloworld/pom.xml

```xml
<dependency>
    <groupId>org.hibernate</groupId>
    <artifactId>hibernate-entitymanager</artifactId>
    <version>5.6.9.Final</version>
</dependency>
<dependency>
    <groupId>org.junit.jupiter</groupId>
    <artifactId>junit-jupiter-engine</artifactId>
    <version>5.8.2</version>
    <scope>test</scope>
</dependency>
<dependency>
    <groupId>mysql</groupId>
    <artifactId>mysql-connector-java</artifactId>
    <version>8.0.29</version>
</dependency>
```

The `hibernate-entitymanager` module includes transitive dependencies on other modules we'll need, such as `hibernate-core` and the JPA interface stubs. We also need the `junit-jupiter-engine` dependency to run the tests with the help of JUnit 5, and the `mysql-connector-java` dependency, which is the official JDBC driver for MySQL.

Our starting point in JPA is the *persistence unit*. A persistence unit is a pairing of our domain model class mappings with a database connection, plus some other configuration settings. Every application has at least one persistence unit; some applications have several if they're talking to several (logical or physical) databases. Hence, our first step is setting up a persistence unit in our application's configuration.

2.3.1 Configuring a persistence unit

The standard configuration file for persistence units is located on the classpath in META-INF/persistence.xml. Create the following configuration file for the "Hello World" application.

Listing 2.2 The persistence.xml configuration file

```
Path: Ch02/helloworld/src/main/resources/META-INF/persistence.xml

<persistence xmlns="http://java.sun.com/xml/ns/persistence"
            xmlns:xsi="http://www.w3.org/2001/XMLSchema-instance"
            xsi:schemaLocation="http://java.sun.com/xml/ns/persistence
            ➥ http://java.sun.com/xml/ns/persistence/persistence_2_0.xsd"
            version="2.0">                          A                                    B

    <persistence-unit name="ch02">   ←
        <provider>org.hibernate.jpa.HibernatePersistenceProvider</provider> ←
        <properties>
            <property name="javax.persistence.jdbc.driver"
                    value="com.mysql.cj.jdbc.Driver"/>          C
            <property name="javax.persistence.jdbc.url"                            D
     E       value="jdbc:mysql://localhost:3306/CH02?serverTimezone=UTC "/>
       └→    <property name="javax.persistence.jdbc.user" value="root"/>
       ┌→    <property name="javax.persistence.jdbc.password" value=""/>
     F
            <property name="hibernate.dialect"
                    value="org.hibernate.dialect.MySQL8Dialect"/>    G

       ┌→    <property name="hibernate.show_sql" value="true"/>           I
     H       <property name="hibernate.format_sql" value="true"/>   ←

            <property name="hibernate.hbm2ddl.auto" value="create"/>   ←
        </properties>                                                         J
    </persistence-unit>

</persistence>
```

A The persistence.xml file configures at least one persistence unit; each unit must have a unique name.

B As JPA is only a specification, we need to indicate the vendor-specific Persistence-Provider implementation of the API. The persistence we define will be backed by a Hibernate provider.

C Indicate the JDBC properties—the driver.

D The URL of the database.

E The username.

F There is no password for access. The machine we are running the programs on has MySQL 8 installed, and the access credentials are the ones from persistence.xml. You should modify the credentials to correspond to the ones on your machine.

G The Hibernate dialect is MySQL8, as the database to interact with is MySQL Release 8.0.

H While executing, show the SQL code.

I Hibernate will format the SQL nicely and generate comments in the SQL string so we know why Hibernate executed the SQL statement.

J Every time the program is executed, the database will be created from scratch. This is ideal for automated testing, when we want to work with a clean database for every test run.

Let's see what a simple persistent class looks like, how the mapping is created, and some of the things we can do with instances of the persistent class in JPA.

2.3.2 *Writing a persistent class*

The objective of this example is to store messages in a database and retrieve them for display. The application has a simple persistent class, `Message`.

Listing 2.3 The Message class

Path: Ch02/helloworld/src/main/java/com/manning/javapersistence/ch02
➡ /Message.java

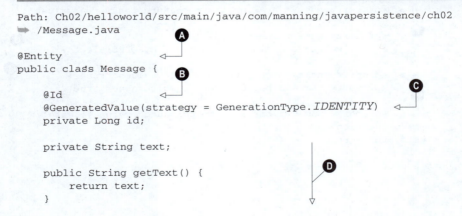

```
@Entity
public class Message {

    @Id
    @GeneratedValue(strategy = GenerationType.IDENTITY)
    private Long id;

    private String text;

    public String getText() {
        return text;
    }
}
```

```
public void setText(String text) {
    this.text = text;
}
```
D

```
}
```

A Every persistent entity class must have at least the `@Entity` annotation. Hibernate maps this class to a table called `MESSAGE`.

B Every persistent entity class must have an identifier attribute annotated with `@Id`. Hibernate maps this attribute to a column named `id`.

C Someone must generate identifier values; this annotation enables automatic generation of ids.

D We usually implement regular attributes of a persistent class with private fields and public getter/setter method pairs. Hibernate maps this attribute to a column called `text`.

The identifier attribute of a persistent class allows the application to access the database identity—the primary key value—of a persistent instance. If two instances of `Message` have the same identifier value, they represent the same row in the database. This example uses `Long` for the type of identifier attribute, but this isn't a requirement. Hibernate allows you to use virtually anything for the identifier type, as you'll see later in the book.

You may have noticed that the `text` attribute of the `Message` class has JavaBeans-style property accessor methods. The class also has a (default) constructor with no parameters. The persistent classes we'll show in the examples will usually look something like this. Note that we don't need to implement any particular interface or extend any special superclass.

Instances of the `Message` class can be managed (made persistent) by Hibernate, but they don't have to be. Because the `Message` object doesn't implement any persistence-specific classes or interfaces, we can use it just like any other Java class:

```
Message msg = new Message();
msg.setText("Hello!");
System.out.println(msg.getText());
```

It may look like we're trying to be cute here; in fact, we're demonstrating an important feature that distinguishes Hibernate from some other persistence solutions. We can use the persistent class in any execution context—*no special container is needed.*

We don't have to use annotations to map a persistent class. Later we'll show other mapping options, such as the JPA orm.xml mapping file and the native hbm.xml mapping files, and we'll look at when they're a better solution than source annotations, which are the most frequently used approach nowadays.

The `Message` class is now ready. We can store instances in our database and write queries to load them again into application memory.

2.3.3 *Storing and loading messages*

What you really came here to see is JPA with Hibernate, so let's save a new `Message` to the database.

> **Listing 2.4   The `HelloWorldJPATest` class**

```
Path: Ch02/helloworld/src/test/java/com/manning/javapersistence/ch02
➥ /HelloWorldJPATest.java

public class HelloWorldJPATest {

    @Test
    public void storeLoadMessage() {

        EntityManagerFactory emf =                                          A
                Persistence.createEntityManagerFactory("ch02");

    B  try {
           EntityManager em = emf.createEntityManager();              C
           em.getTransaction().begin();                          ←

           Message message = new Message();              D
           message.setText("Hello World!");
    E
           em.persist(message);
                                                    F
           em.getTransaction().commit();          ←
           //INSERT into MESSAGE (ID, TEXT) values (1, 'Hello World!')
    G
           em.getTransaction().begin();


           List<Message> messages =
               em.createQuery("select m from Message m", Message.class)   H
                 .getResultList();
           //SELECT * from MESSAGE

           messages.get(messages.size() - 1).              I
                   setText("Hello World from JPA!");
    J
           em.getTransaction().commit();
           //UPDATE MESSAGE set TEXT = 'Hello World from JPA!'
           ➥ where ID = 1

           assertAll(                                          K
                   () -> assertEquals(1, messages.size()),
                   () -> assertEquals("Hello World from JPA!",     L
                           messages.get(0).getText())
           );

           em.close();          ←
                             M
        } finally {
```

```
            emf.close();        ⊲─┐
        }                         │
    }                            (N)

}
```

(A) First we need an `EntityManagerFactory` to talk to the database. This API represents the persistence unit, and most applications have one `EntityManager-Factory` for one configured persistence unit. Once it starts, the application should create the `EntityManagerFactory`; the factory is thread-safe, and all code in the application that accesses the database should share it.

(B) Begin a new session with the database by creating an `EntityManager`. This is the context for all persistence operations.

(C) Get access to the standard transaction API, and begin a transaction on this thread of execution.

(D) Create a new instance of the mapped domain model class `Message`, and set its `text` property.

(E) Enlist the transient instance with the persistence context; we make it persistent. Hibernate now knows that we wish to store that data, but it doesn't necessarily call the database immediately.

(F) Commit the transaction. Hibernate automatically checks the persistence context and executes the necessary SQL `INSERT` statement. To help you understand how Hibernate works, we show the automatically generated and executed SQL statements in source code comments when they occur. Hibernate inserts a row in the `MESSAGE` table, with an automatically generated value for the `ID` primary key column, and the `TEXT` value.

(G) Every interaction with the database should occur within transaction boundaries, even if we're only reading data, so we start a new transaction. Any potential failure appearing from now on will not affect the previously committed transaction.

(H) Execute a query to retrieve all instances of `Message` from the database.

(I) We can change the value of a property. Hibernate detects this automatically because the loaded `Message` is still attached to the persistence context it was loaded in.

(J) On commit, Hibernate checks the persistence context for dirty state, and it executes the SQL `UPDATE` automatically to synchronize in-memory objects with the database state.

(K) Check the size of the list of messages retrieved from the database.

(L) Check that the message we persisted is in the database. We use the JUnit 5 `assert-All` method, which always checks all the assertions that are passed to it, even if some of them fail. The two assertions that we verify are conceptually related.

(M) We created an `EntityManager`, so we must close it.

(N) We created an `EntityManagerFactory`, so we must close it.

The query language you've seen in this example isn't SQL, it's the Jakarta Persistence Query Language (JPQL). Although there is syntactically no difference in this trivial example, the `Message` in the query string doesn't refer to the database table name but to the persistent class name. For this reason, the `Message` class name in the query is case-sensitive. If we map the class to a different table, the query will still work.

Also, notice how Hibernate detects the modification to the text property of the message and automatically updates the database. This is the automatic dirty-checking feature of JPA in action. It saves us the effort of explicitly asking the persistence manager to update the database when we modify the state of an instance inside a transaction.

Figure 2.2 shows the result of checking for the existence of the record we inserted and updated on the database side. As you'll recall, we created a database named CH02 by running the Ch02.sql script from the chapter's source code.

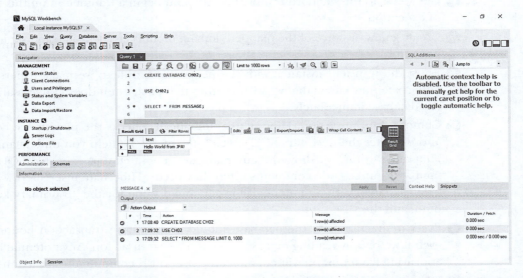

Figure 2.2   The result of checking for the existence of the inserted and updated record on the database side

You've just completed your first JPA and Hibernate application. Let's now take a quick look at the native Hibernate bootstrap and configuration API.

2.4   *Native Hibernate configuration*

Although basic (and extensive) configuration is standardized in JPA, we can't access all the configuration features of Hibernate with properties in persistence.xml. Note that most applications, even quite sophisticated ones, don't need such special configuration options and hence don't have to access the bootstrap API we'll show in this section. If you aren't sure, you can skip this section and come back to it later when you need to extend Hibernate type adapters, add custom SQL functions, and so on.

When using native Hibernate we'll use the Hibernate dependencies and API directly, rather than the JPA dependencies and classes. JPA is a specification, and it can use different implementations (Hibernate is one example, but EclipseLink is another alternative) through the same API. Hibernate, as an implementation, provides its own dependencies and classes. While using JPA provides more flexibility, you'll see throughout the book that accessing the Hibernate implementation directly allows you to use features that are not covered by the JPA standard (we'll point this out where it's relevant).

The native equivalent of the standard JPA `EntityManagerFactory` is the `org.hibernate.SessionFactory`. We have usually one per application, and it involves the same pairing of class mappings with database connection configuration.

To configure the native Hibernate, we can use a hibernate.properties Java properties file or a hibernate.cfg.xml XML file. We'll choose the second option, and the configuration will contain database and session-related options. This XML file is generally placed in the src/main/resource or src/test/resource folder. As we need the information for the Hibernate configuration in our tests, we'll choose the second location.

Listing 2.5   The hibernate.cfg.xml configuration file

Path: Ch02/helloworld/src/test/resources/hibernate.cfg.xml

```xml
<?xml version='1.0' encoding='utf-8'?>
<!DOCTYPE hibernate-configuration PUBLIC
"-//Hibernate/Hibernate Configuration DTD//EN"
    "http://www.hibernate.org/dtd/hibernate-configuration-3.0.dtd">    A
<hibernate-configuration>                                               B
    <session-factory>
        <property name="hibernate.connection.driver_class">
            com.mysql.cj.jdbc.Driver                                    C
        </property>
        <property name="hibernate.connection.url">
            jdbc:mysql://localhost:3306/CH02?serverTimezone=UTC         D
        </property>                                                     E
        <property name="hibernate.connection.username">root</property>
        <property name="hibernate.connection.password"></property>     F
        <property name="hibernate.connection.pool_size">50</property>  G
        <property name="show_sql">true</property>                      H
        <property name="hibernate.hbm2ddl.auto">create</property>      I
    </session-factory>
</hibernate-configuration>
```

A We use the tags to indicate that we are configuring Hibernate.

B More exactly, we are configuring the `SessionFactory` object. `SessionFactory` is an interface, and we need one `SessionFactory` to interact with one database.

C Indicate the JDBC properties—the driver.

D The URL of the database.

E The username.

F No password is required to access it. The machine we are running the programs on has MySQL 8 installed and the access credentials are the ones from hibernate .cfg.xml. You should modify the credentials to correspond to the ones on your machine.

G Limit the number of connections waiting in the Hibernate database connection pool to 50.

H While executing, the SQL code is shown.

I Every time the program is executed, the database will be created from scratch. This is ideal for automated testing, when we want to work with a clean database for every test run.

Let's save a Message to the database using native Hibernate.

Listing 2.6   The HelloWorldHibernateTest class

Path: Ch02/helloworld/src/test/java/com/manning/javapersistence/ch02
➡ /HelloWorldHibernateTest.java

```java
public class HelloWorldHibernateTest {

    private static SessionFactory createSessionFactory() {
        Configuration configuration = new Configuration();          // A
        configuration.configure().addAnnotatedClass(Message.class); // B
        ServiceRegistry serviceRegistry = new
                StandardServiceRegistryBuilder().
                applySettings(configuration.getProperties()).build();  // C
        return configuration.buildSessionFactory(serviceRegistry);     // D
    }

    @Test
    public void storeLoadMessage() {

        try (SessionFactory sessionFactory = createSessionFactory();  // E
             Session session = sessionFactory.openSession()) {        // F

            session.beginTransaction();                               // G

            Message message = new Message();
            message.setText("Hello World from Hibernate!");           // H

            session.persist(message);                                 // I

            session.getTransaction().commit();                        // J
            // INSERT into MESSAGE (ID, TEXT)
            // values (1, 'Hello World from Hibernate!')
            session.beginTransaction();                               // K

            CriteriaQuery<Message> criteriaQuery =
                    session.getCriteriaBuilder().createQuery(Message.class);  // L
            criteriaQuery.from(Message.class);                        // M
```

```
          List<Message> messages =
              session.createQuery(criteriaQuery).getResultList();      N
          // SELECT * from MESSAGE                                 O

          session.getTransaction().commit();            ⟵

          assertAll(
                  () -> assertEquals(1, messages.size()),            P
                  () -> assertEquals("Hello World from Hibernate!",
                              messages.get(0).getText())             Q
          );

      }
    }
  }
```

A To create a `SessionFactory`, we first need to create a configuration.

B We need to call the `configure` method on it and to add `Message` to it as an annotated class. The execution of the `configure` method will load the content of the default hibernate.cfg.xml file.

C The builder pattern helps us create the immutable service registry and configure it by applying settings with chained method calls. A `ServiceRegistry` hosts and manages services that need access to the `SessionFactory`. Services are classes that provide pluggable implementations of different types of functionality to Hibernate.

D Build a `SessionFactory` using the configuration and the service registry we have previously created.

E The `SessionFactory` created with the `createSessionFactory` method we previously defined is passed as an argument to a `try` with resources, as `SessionFactory` implements the `AutoCloseable` interface.

F Similarly, we begin a new session with the database by creating a `Session`, which also implements the `AutoCloseable` interface. This is our context for all persistence operations.

G Get access to the standard transaction API and begin a transaction on this thread of execution.

H Create a new instance of the mapped domain model class `Message`, and set its `text` property.

I Enlist the transient instance with the persistence context; we make it persistent. Hibernate now knows that we wish to store that data, but it doesn't necessarily call the database immediately. The native Hibernate API is pretty similar to the standard JPA, and most methods have the same name.

J Synchronize the session with the database, and close the current session on commit of the transaction automatically.

K Begin another transaction. Every interaction with the database should occur within transaction boundaries, even if we're only reading data.

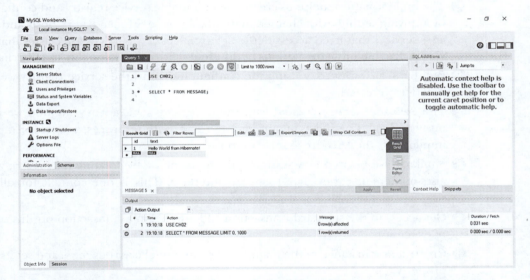

L Create an instance of `CriteriaQuery` by calling the `CriteriaBuilder` `create-Query()` method. A `CriteriaBuilder` is used to construct criteria queries, compound selections, expressions, predicates, and orderings. A `CriteriaQuery` defines functionality that is specific to top-level queries. `CriteriaBuilder` and `Criteria-Query` belong to the Criteria API, which allows us to build a query programmatically.

M Create and add a query root corresponding to the given `Message` entity.

N Call the `getResultList()` method of the query object to get the results. The query that is created and executed will be `SELECT * FROM MESSAGE`.

O Commit the transaction.

P Check the size of the list of messages retrieved from the database.

Q Check that the message we persisted is in the database. We use the JUnit 5 `assert-All` method, which always checks all the assertions that are passed to it, even if some of them fail. The two assertions that we verify are conceptually related.

Figure 2.3 shows the result of checking for the existence of the record we inserted on the database side by using native Hibernate.

Figure 2.3   The result of checking for the existence of the inserted record on the database side

Most of the examples in this book won't use the `SessionFactory` or `Session` API. From time to time, when a particular feature is only available in Hibernate, we'll show you how to `unwrap()` the native interface.

2.5   *Switching between JPA and Hibernate*

Suppose you're working with JPA and need to access the Hibernate API. Or, vice versa, you're working with native Hibernate and you need to create an `EntityManagerFactory` from the Hibernate configuration. To obtain a `SessionFactory` from an `Entity-ManagerFactory`, you'll have to unwrap the first one from the second one.

Listing 2.7   Obtaining a `SessionFactory` from an `EntityManagerFactory`

Path: Ch02/helloworld/src/test/java/com/manning/javapersistence/ch02
➥ /HelloWorldJPAToHibernateTest.java

```
private static SessionFactory getSessionFactory
                (EntityManagerFactory entityManagerFactory) {
    return entityManagerFactory.unwrap(SessionFactory.class);
}
```

Starting with JPA version 2.0, you can get access to the APIs of the underlying implementations. The `EntityManagerFactory` (and also the `EntityManager`) declares an unwrap method that will return objects belonging to the classes of the JPA implementation. When using the Hibernate implementation, you can get the corresponding `SessionFactory` or `Session` objects and start using them as demonstrated in listing 2.6. When a particular feature is only available in Hibernate, you can switch to it using the unwrap method.

You may be interested in the reverse operation: creating an `EntityManager-Factory` from an initial Hibernate configuration.

Listing 2.8   Obtaining an `EntityManagerFactory` from a Hibernate configuration

Path: Ch02/helloworld/src/test/java/com/manning/javapersistence/ch02
➥ /HelloWorldHibernateToJPATest.java

```
private static EntityManagerFactory createEntityManagerFactory() {     Ⓑ
    Configuration configuration = new Configuration();
    configuration.configure().addAnnotatedClass(Message.class);

    Map<String, String> properties = new HashMap<>();
    Enumeration<?> propertyNames =                                     Ⓓ
                configuration.getProperties().propertyNames();
    while (propertyNames.hasMoreElements()) {
        String element = (String) propertyNames.nextElement();        Ⓔ
        properties.put(element,
            configuration.getProperties().getProperty(element));
    }

    return Persistence.createEntityManagerFactory("ch02", properties);
}
```

Ⓐ Create a new Hibernate configuration.

Ⓑ Call the `configure` method, which adds the content of the default hibernate .cfg.xml file to the configuration, and then explicitly add `Message` as an annotated class.

C Create a new hash map to be filled in with the existing properties.

D Get all the property names from the Hibernate configuration.

E Add the property names one by one to the previously created map.

F Return a new `EntityManagerFactory`, providing to it the ch02.ex01 persistence unit name and the previously created map of properties.

2.6   *"Hello World" with Spring Data JPA*

Let's now write our first Spring Data JPA application, which will store a message in the database and then retrieve it.

We'll first add the Spring dependencies to the Apache Maven configuration.

Listing 2.9   The Maven dependencies on Spring

Path: `Ch02/helloworld/pom.xml`

```xml
<dependency>
    <groupId>org.springframework.data</groupId>          A
    <artifactId>spring-data-jpa</artifactId>
    <version>2.7.0</version>
</dependency>
<dependency>
    <groupId>org.springframework</groupId>
    <artifactId>spring-test</artifactId>                 B
    <version>5.3.20</version>
</dependency>
```

A The `spring-data-jpa` module provides repository support for JPA and includes transitive dependencies on other modules we'll need, such as `spring-core` and `spring-context`.

B We also need the `spring-test` dependency to run the tests.

The standard configuration file for Spring Data JPA is a Java class that creates and sets up the beans needed by Spring Data. The configuration can be done using either an XML file or Java code, and we've chosen the second alternative. Create the following configuration file for the "Hello World" application.

Listing 2.10   The `SpringDataConfiguration` class

Path: `Ch02/helloworld/src/test/java/com/manning/javapersistence/ch02`   A
➥ `/configuration/SpringDataConfiguration.java`

```java
@EnableJpaRepositories("com.manning.javapersistence.ch02.repositories")   ◁─── A
public class SpringDataConfiguration {
    @Bean
    public DataSource dataSource() {                                          B
        DriverManagerDataSource dataSource = new DriverManagerDataSource();
        dataSource.setDriverClassName("com.mysql.cj.jdbc.Driver");          C
        dataSource.setUrl(
            "jdbc:mysql://localhost:3306/CH02?serverTimezone=UTC");         D
```

```
      ⊳    dataSource.setUsername("root");
  E        dataSource.setPassword("");           ◀──F
           return dataSource;      ◀──
      }                           B

      @Bean
      public JpaTransactionManager
              transactionManager(EntityManagerFactory emf) {      G
          return new JpaTransactionManager(emf);
      }

      @Bean
      public JpaVendorAdapter jpaVendorAdapter() {
          HibernateJpaVendorAdapter jpaVendorAdapter = new      H
                  HibernateJpaVendorAdapter();
  I       jpaVendorAdapter.setDatabase(Database.MYSQL);
      ⊳   jpaVendorAdapter.setShowSql(true);          ◀──J
          return jpaVendorAdapter;      ◀──
      }                              H

      @Bean
      public LocalContainerEntityManagerFactoryBean entityManagerFactory() {      K
          LocalContainerEntityManagerFactoryBean
  L         localContainerEntityManagerFactoryBean =
      ⊳           new LocalContainerEntityManagerFactoryBean();
          localContainerEntityManagerFactoryBean.setDataSource(dataSource());
          Properties properties = new Properties();
          properties.put("hibernate.hbm2ddl.auto", "create");      M
          localContainerEntityManagerFactoryBean.
                  setJpaProperties(properties);
          localContainerEntityManagerFactoryBean.              N
                  setJpaVendorAdapter(jpaVendorAdapter());
  K       localContainerEntityManagerFactoryBean.                  O
      ⊳           setPackagesToScan("com.manning.javapersistence.ch02");
          return localContainerEntityManagerFactoryBean;
      }
  }
```

Ⓐ The @EnableJpaRepositories annotation enables scanning of the package received as an argument for Spring Data repositories.

Ⓑ Create a data source bean.

Ⓒ Specify the JDBC properties—the driver.

Ⓓ The URL of the database.

Ⓔ The username.

Ⓕ No password is required for access. The machine we are running the programs on has MySQL 8 installed, and the access credentials are the ones from this configuration. You should modify the credentials to correspond to the ones on your machine.

G Create a transaction manager bean based on an entity manager factory. Every interaction with the database should occur within transaction boundaries, and Spring Data needs a transaction manager bean.

H Create the JPA vendor adapter bean needed by JPA to interact with Hibernate.

I Configure this vendor adapter to access a MySQL database.

J Show the SQL code while it is executed.

K Create a `LocalContainerEntityManagerFactoryBean`. This is a factory bean that produces an `EntityManagerFactory` following the JPA standard container bootstrap contract.

L Set the data source.

M Set the database to be created from scratch every time the program is executed.

N Set the vendor adapter.

O Set the packages to scan for entity classes. As the `Message` entity is located in `com.manning.javapersistence.ch02`, we set this package to be scanned.

Spring Data JPA provides support for JPA-based data access layers by reducing the boilerplate code and creating implementations for the repository interfaces. We only need to define our own repository interface to extend one of the Spring Data interfaces.

Listing 2.11   The `MessageRepository` interface

Path: Ch02/helloworld/src/main/java/com/manning/javapersistence/ch02
➡ /repositories/MessageRepository.java

```
public interface MessageRepository extends CrudRepository<Message, Long> {

}
```

The `MessageRepository` interface extends `CrudRepository` `<Message, Long>`. This means that it is a repository of Message entities with a `Long` identifier. Remember, the `Message` class has an id field annotated as `@Id` of type `Long`. We can directly call methods such as `save`, `findAll`, or `findById`, which are inherited from `CrudRepository`, and we can use them without any other additional information to execute the usual operations against a database. Spring Data JPA will create a proxy class implementing the `MessageRepository` interface and implement its methods (figure 2.4).

Let's save a `Message` to the database using Spring Data JPA.

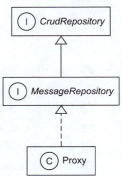

Figure 2.4   The Spring Data JPA `Proxy` class implements the `MessageRepository` interface.

Listing 2.12 The `HelloWorldSpringDataJPATest` class

Path: Ch02/helloworld/src/test/java/com/manning/javapersistence/ch02
➡ /HelloWorldSpringDataJPATest.java

Ⓐ

```
@ExtendWith(SpringExtension.class)                                        Ⓑ
@ContextConfiguration(classes = {SpringDataConfiguration.class})      ◁─┘
public class HelloWorldSpringDataJPATest {

    @Autowired                                                    Ⓒ
    private MessageRepository messageRepository;

    @Test
    public void storeLoadMessage() {
        Message message = new Message();
        message.setText("Hello World from Spring Data JPA!");    Ⓓ
 Ⓔ
        messageRepository.save(message);

        List<Message> messages =                                 Ⓕ
        ➡ (List<Message>)messageRepository.findAll();        ◁─┘

        assertAll(
                () -> assertEquals(1, messages.size()),          Ⓖ
                () -> assertEquals("Hello World from Spring Data JPA!",  Ⓗ
                                   messages.get(0).getText())
        );

    }
}
```

Ⓐ Extend the test using `SpringExtension`. This extension is used to integrate the Spring test context with the JUnit 5 Jupiter test.

Ⓑ The Spring test context is configured using the beans defined in the previously presented `SpringDataConfiguration` class.

Ⓒ A `MessageRepository` bean is injected by Spring through autowiring. This is possible as the `com.manning.javapersistence.ch02.repositories` package where `MessageRepository` is located was used as the argument of the `@EnableJpaRepositories` annotation in listing 2.8. If we call `messageRepository.getClass()`, we'll see that it returns something like `com.sun.proxy.$Proxy41`—a proxy generated by Spring Data, as explained in figure 2.4.

Ⓓ Create a new instance of the mapped domain model class `Message`, and set its `text` property.

Ⓔ Persist the `message` object. The `save` method is inherited from the `CrudRepository` interface, and its body will be generated by Spring Data JPA when the proxy class is created. It will simply save a `Message` entity to the database.

Ⓕ Retrieve the messages from the repository. The `findAll` method is inherited from the `CrudRepository` interface, and its body will be generated by Spring Data JPA when the proxy class is created. It will simply return all entities belonging to the `Message` class.

G Check the size of the list of messages retrieved from the database and that the message we persisted is in the database.

H Use the JUnit 5 `assertAll` method, which checks all the assertions that are passed to it, even if some of them fail. The two assertions that we verify are conceptually related.

You'll notice that the Spring Data JPA test is considerably shorter than the ones using JPA or native Hibernate. This is because the boilerplate code has been removed—there's no more explicit object creation or explicit control of the transactions. The repository object is injected, and it provides the generated methods of the proxy class. The burden is now heavier on the configuration side, but this should be done only once per application.

Figure 2.5 shows the result of checking that the record we inserted with Spring Data JPA exists in the database.

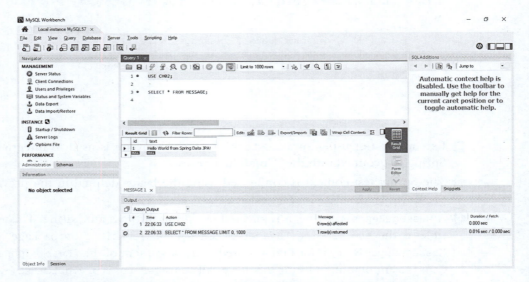

Figure 2.5   The result of checking that the inserted record exists in the database

2.7   *Comparing the approaches of persisting entities*

We have implemented a simple application that interacts with a database and uses, alternatively, JPA, native Hibernate, and Spring Data JPA. Our purpose was to analyze each approach and see how the configuration and code varies. Table 2.1 summarizes the characteristics of these approaches.

Table 2.1   Comparison of working with JPA, native Hibernate, and Spring Data JPA

Framework	Characteristics
JPA	<ul><li>Uses the general JPA API and requires a persistence provider.</li><li>We can switch between persistence providers from the configuration.</li><li>Requires explicit management of the `EntityManagerFactory`, `EntityManager`, and transactions.</li><li>The configuration and the amount of code to be written is similar to the native Hibernate native approach.</li><li>We can switch to the JPA approach by constructing an `EntityManagerFactory` from a native Hibernate configuration.</li></ul>
Native Hibernate	<ul><li>Uses the native Hibernate API. You are locked into using this chosen framework.</li><li>Builds its configuration starting with the default Hibernate configuration files (hibernate.cfg.xml or hibernate.properties).</li><li>Requires explicit management of the `SessionFactory`, `Session`, and transactions.</li><li>The configuration and the amount of code to be written are similar to the JPA approach.</li><li>We can switch to the native Hibernate native approach by unwrapping a `SessionFactory` from an `EntityManagerFactory` or a `Session` from an `EntityManager`.</li></ul>
Spring Data JPA	<ul><li>Needs additional Spring Data dependencies in the project.</li><li>The configuration will also take care of the creation of beans needed for the project, including the transaction manager.</li><li>The repository interface only needs to be declared, and Spring Data will create an implementation for it as a proxy class with generated methods that interact with the database.</li><li>The necessary repository is injected and not explicitly created by the programmer.</li><li>This approach requires the least amount of code to be written, as the configuration takes care of most of the burden.</li></ul>

For more information on the performance of each approach, see the article "Object-Relational Mapping Using JPA, Hibernate and Spring Data JPA," by Cătălin Tudose and Carmen Odubăşteanu (Tudose, 2021).

To analyze the running times, we executed a batch of insert, update, select, and delete operations using the three approaches, progressively increasing the number of records from 1,000 to 50,000. Tests were made on Windows 10 Enterprise, running on a four-core Intel i7-5500U processor at 2.40 GHz with 8 GB of RAM.

The insert execution times of Hibernate and JPA are very close (see table 2.2 and figure 2.6). The execution time for Spring Data JPA increases much faster with the increase of the number of records.

Table 2.2   Insert execution times by framework (times in ms)

Number of records	Hibernate	JPA	Spring Data JPA
1,000	1,138	1,127	2,288
5,000	3,187	3,307	8,410
10,000	5,145	5,341	14,565
20,000	8,591	8,488	26,313

Table 2.2   Insert execution times by framework (times in ms) *(continued)*

Number of records	Hibernate	JPA	Spring Data JPA
30,000	11,146	11,859	37,579
40,000	13,011	13,300	48,913
50,000	16,512	16,463	59,629

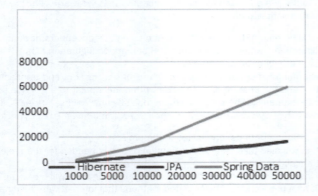

Figure 2.6   Insert execution times by framework (times in ms)

The update execution times of Hibernate and JPA are also very close (see table 2.3 and figure 2.7). Again, the execution time for Spring Data JPA increases much faster with the increase of the number of records.

Table 2.3   Update execution times by framework (times in ms)

Number of records	Hibernate	JPA	Spring Data JPA
1,000	706	759	2,683
5,000	2,081	2,256	10,211
10,000	3,596	3,958	17,594
20,000	6,669	6,776	33,090
30,000	9,352	9,696	46,341
40,000	12,720	13,614	61,599
50,000	16,276	16,355	75,071

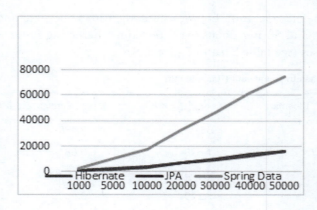

Figure 2.7   Update execution times by framework (times in ms)

The situation is similar for the select operations, with practically no difference between Hibernate and JPA, and a steep curve for Spring Data as the number of records increases (see table 2.4 and figure 2.8).

Table 2.4   Select execution times by framework (times in ms)

Number of records	Hibernate	JPA	Spring Data JPA
1,000	1,138	1,127	2,288
5,000	3,187	3,307	8,410
10,000	5,145	5,341	14,565
20,000	8,591	8,488	26,313
30,000	11,146	11,859	37,579
40,000	13,011	13,300	48,913
50,000	16,512	16,463	59,629

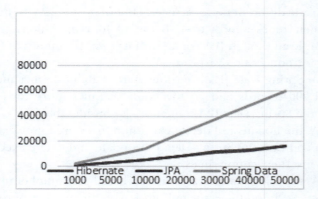

Figure 2.8   Select execution times by framework (times in ms)

It's no surprise that the delete operation behaves similarly, with Hibernate and JPA being close to each other, and Spring Data's execution time increasing faster as the number of records increases (see table 2.5 and figure 2.9).

Table 2.5 Delete execution times by framework (times in ms)

Number of records	Hibernate	JPA	Spring Data JPA
1,000	584	551	2,430
5,000	1,537	1,628	9,685
10,000	2,992	2,763	17,930
20,000	5,344	5,129	32,906
30,000	7,478	7,852	47,400
40,000	10,061	10,493	62,422
50,000	12,857	12,768	79,799

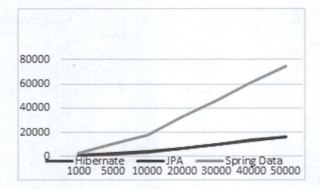

Figure 2.9 Delete execution times by framework (times in ms)

The three approaches provide different performances. Hibernate and JPA go head to head—the graphics of their times almost overlap for all four operations (insert, update, select, and delete). Even though JPA comes with its own API on top of Hibernate, this additional layer introduces no overhead.

The execution times of Spring Data JPA insertions start at about 2 times those of Hibernate and JPA for 1,000 records and go to about 3.5 times more for 50,000 records. The overhead of the Spring Data JPA framework is considerable.

For Hibernate and JPA, the update and delete execution times are lower than the insert execution times. In contrast, the Spring Data JPA update and delete execution times are longer than the insert execution times.

For Hibernate and JPA, the select times grow very slowly with the number of rows. The Spring Data JPA select execution times strongly grow with the number of rows.

Using Spring Data JPA is mainly justified in particular situations: if the project already uses the Spring framework and needs to rely on its existing paradigm (such as inversion of control or automatically managed transactions), or if there is a strong need to decrease the amount of code and thus shorten the development time (nowadays it is cheaper to acquire more computing power than to acquire more developers).

This chapter has focused on alternatives for working with databases from a Java application—JPA, native Hibernate, and Spring Data JPA—and we looked at introductory examples for each of them. Chapter 3 will introduce a more complex example and will deal in more depth with domain models and metadata.

Summary

- A Java persistence project can be implemented using three alternatives: JPA, native Hibernate, and Spring Data JPA.
- You can create, map, and annotate a persistent class.
- Using JPA, you can implement the configuration and bootstrapping of a persistence unit, and you can create the `EntityManagerFactory` entry point.
- You can call the `EntityManager` to interact with the database, storing and loading an instance of the persistent domain model class.
- Native Hibernate provides bootstrapping and configuration options, as well as the equivalent basic Hibernate APIs: `SessionFactory` and `Session`.
- You can switch between the JPA approach and Hibernate approach by unwrapping a `SessionFactory` from an `EntityManagerFactory` or obtaining an `EntityManagerFactory` from a Hibernate configuration.
- You can implement the configuration of a Spring Data JPA application by creating the repository interface, and then use it to store and load an instance of the persistent domain model class.
- Comparing and contrasting these three approaches (JPA, native Hibernate, and Spring Data JPA) demonstrates the advantages and shortcomings of each of them, in terms of portability, needed dependencies, amount of code, and execution speed.

Domain models
and metadata

3

This chapter covers

- Introducing the CaveatEmptor example application
- Implementing the domain model
- Examining object/relational mapping metadata options

The "Hello World" example in the previous chapter introduced you to Hibernate, Spring Data, and JPA, but it isn't useful for understanding the requirements of real-world applications with complex data models. For the rest of the book, we'll use a much more sophisticated example application—CaveatEmptor, an online auction system—to demonstrate JPA, Hibernate, and later Spring Data. (*Caveat emptor* means "Let the buyer beware.")

We'll start our discussion of the CaveatEmptor application by introducing its layered application architecture. Then you'll learn how to identify the business entities of a problem domain. You'll create a conceptual model of these entities and their attributes, called a *domain model*, and you'll implement it in Java by creating

46

> **Major new features in JPA 2**
>
> A JPA persistence provider now integrates automatically with a Bean Validation provider. When data is stored, the provider automatically validates constraints on persistent classes.
>
> The `Metamodel` API has also been added. You can obtain the names, properties, and mapping metadata of the classes in a persistence unit.

persistent classes. We'll spend some time exploring exactly what these Java classes should look like and where they fit within a typical layered application architecture. We'll also look at the persistence capabilities of the classes and at how this influences the application's design and implementation. We'll add Bean Validation, which will help you to automatically verify the integrity of the domain model data—both the persistent information and the business logic.

We'll then explore some mapping metadata options—the ways you tell Hibernate how the persistent classes and their properties relate to database tables and columns. This can be as simple as adding annotations directly in the Java source code of the classes or writing XML documents that you eventually deploy along with the compiled Java classes that Hibernate accesses at runtime.

After reading this chapter, you'll know how to design the persistent parts of your domain model in complex real-world projects and what mapping metadata option you'll primarily prefer to use. Let's start with the example application.

3.1   The example CaveatEmptor application

The CaveatEmptor example is an online auction application that demonstrates ORM techniques, JPA, Hibernate, and Spring Data functionality. We won't pay much attention to the user interface in this book (it could be web-based or a rich client); we'll concentrate instead on the data access code.

To understand the design challenges involved in ORM, let's pretend the Caveat-Emptor application doesn't yet exist and that we're building it from scratch. Let's start by looking at the architecture.

3.1.1   A layered architecture

With any nontrivial application, it usually makes sense to organize classes by concern. Persistence is one concern; others include presentation, workflow, and business logic. A typical object-oriented architecture includes layers of code that represent these concerns.

> **Cross-cutting concerns**
>
> There are also so-called *cross-cutting concerns*, which may be implemented generically, such as by framework code. Typical cross-cutting concerns include logging, authorization, and transaction demarcation.

A layered architecture defines interfaces between the code that implements the various concerns, allowing changes to be made to the way one concern is implemented without significant disruption to code in the other layers. Layering determines the kinds of inter-layer dependencies that occur. The rules are as follows:

- Layers communicate from top to bottom. A layer is dependent only on the interface of the layer directly below it.
- Each layer is unaware of any other layers except for the layer just below it and eventually of the layer above if it receives explicit requests from it.

Different systems group concerns differently, so they define different layers. The typical, proven, high-level application architecture uses three layers: one each for presentation, business logic, and persistence, as shown in figure 3.1.

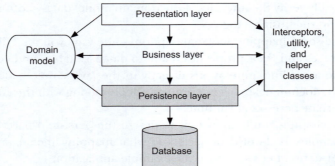

Figure 3.1   A persistence layer is the basis of a layered architecture.

- *Presentation layer*—The user interface logic is topmost. Code responsible for the presentation and control of page and screen navigation is in the presentation layer. The user interface code may directly access business entities of the shared domain model and render them on the screen, along with controls to execute actions. In some architectures, business entity instances might not be directly accessible by user interface code, such as when the presentation layer isn't running on the same machine as the rest of the system. In such cases, the presentation layer may require its own special data-transfer model, representing only a transmittable subset of the domain model. A good example of the presentation layer is working with a browser to interact with an application.
- *Business layer*—The business layer is generally responsible for implementing any business rules or system requirements that are part of the problem domain. This layer usually includes some kind of controlling component—code that knows when to invoke which business rule. In some systems, this layer has its own internal representation of the business domain entities. Alternatively, it may rely on a domain model implementation that's shared with the other layers of the application. A good example of the business layer is the code responsible for executing the business logic.

- *Persistence layer*—The persistence layer is a group of classes and components responsible for storing data to, and retrieving it from, one or more data stores. This layer needs a model of the business domain entities for which you'd like to keep a persistent state. The persistence layer is where the bulk of JPA, Hibernate, and Spring Data use takes place.

- *Database*—The database is usually external. It's the actual persistent representation of the system state. If an SQL database is used, the database includes a schema and possibly stored procedures for the execution of business logic close to the data. The database is the place where data is persisted for the long term.

- *Helper and utility classes*—Every application has a set of infrastructural helper or utility classes that are used in every layer of the application. These may include general-purpose classes or cross-cutting concern classes (for logging, security, and caching). These shared infrastructural elements don't form a layer because they don't obey the rules for inter-layer dependency in a layered architecture.

Now that we have a high-level architecture, we can focus on the business problem.

3.1.2   *Analyzing the business domain*

At this stage, you, with the help of domain experts, should analyze the business problems your software system needs to solve, identifying the relevant main entities and their interactions. The main goal behind the analysis and design of a domain model is to capture the essence of the business information for the application's purpose.

Entities are usually notions understood by users of the system: payment, customer, order, item, bid, and so forth. Some entities may be abstractions of less concrete things the user thinks about, such as a pricing algorithm, but even these are usually understandable to the user. You can find all these entities in the conceptual view of the business, sometimes called an *information model*.

From this business model, engineers and architects of object-oriented software create an object-oriented model, still at the conceptual level (no Java code). This model may be as simple as a mental image that exists only in the mind of the developer, or it may be as elaborate as a UML class diagram. Figure 3.2 shows a simple model expressed in UML.

Figure 3.2 . A class diagram of a typical online auction model

This model contains entities that you're bound to find in any typical e-commerce system: category, item, and user. This domain model represents all the entities and their relationships (and perhaps their attributes). This kind of object-oriented model of entities from the problem domain, encompassing only those entities that are of interest to the user, is called a *domain model*. It's an abstract view of the real world.

Instead of using an object-oriented model, engineers and architects may start the application design with a data model. This can be expressed with an entity-relationship diagram, and it will contain the CATEGORY, ITEM, and USER entities, together with the relationships between them. We usually say that, concerning persistence, there is little difference between the two types of models; they're merely different starting points. In the end, which modeling language you use is secondary; we're most interested in the structure of and relationships between the business entities. We care about the rules that have to be applied to guarantee the integrity of the data (for example, the multiplicity of relationships included in the model) and the code procedures used to manipulate the data (usually not included in the model).

In the next section we'll complete our analysis of the CaveatEmptor problem domain. The resulting domain model will be the central theme of this book.

3.1.3   *The CaveatEmptor domain model*

The CaveatEmptor site will allow users to auction many different kinds of items, from electronic equipment to airline tickets. Auctions proceed according to the English auction strategy: users continue to place bids on an item until the bid period for that item expires, and the highest bidder wins.

In any store, goods are categorized by type and grouped with similar goods into sections and onto shelves. The auction catalog requires some kind of hierarchy of item categories so that a buyer can browse the categories or arbitrarily search by category and item attributes. Lists of items will appear in the category browser and search result screens. Selecting an item from a list will take the buyer to an item-detail view where an item may have images attached to it.

An auction consists of a sequence of bids, and one is the winning bid. User details will include name, address, and billing information.

The result of this analysis, the high-level overview of the domain model, is shown in figure 3.3. Let's briefly discuss some interesting features of this model:

- Each item can be auctioned only once, so you don't need to make Item distinct from any auction entities. Instead, you have a single auction item entity named Item. Thus, Bid is associated directly with Item. You model the Address information of a User as a separate class—a User may have three addresses for home, billing, and shipping. You allow the user to have many BillingDetails. Subclasses of an abstract class represent the various billing strategies (allowing for future extension).

- The application may nest a Category inside another Category, and so on. A recursive association, from the Category entity to itself, expresses this relationship. Note that a single Category may have multiple child categories but at most one parent. Each Item belongs to at least one Category.

- This representation isn't the *complete* domain model; it's only the classes for which you need persistence capabilities. You'll want to store and load instances of Category, Item, User, and so on. We have simplified this high-level overview a little; we'll make modifications to these classes when needed for more complex examples.

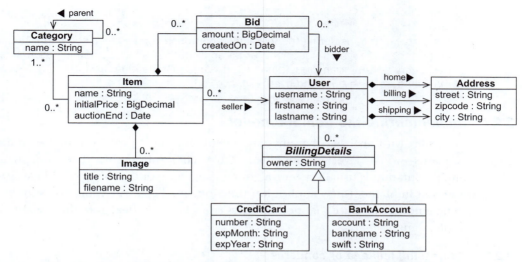

Figure 3.3   Persistent classes of the CaveatEmptor domain model and their relationships

- The entities in a domain model should encapsulate state and behavior. For example, the User entity should define the name and address of a customer *and* the logic required to calculate the shipping costs for items (to this particular customer).

- There might be other classes in the domain model that only have transient runtime instances. Consider a WinningBidStrategy class encapsulating the fact that the highest bidder wins an auction. This might be called by the business layer (controller) code when checking the state of an auction. At some point you might have to figure out how the tax should be calculated for sold items or how the system should approve a new user account. We don't consider such business rules or domain model behavior to be unimportant; rather, those concerns are mostly orthogonal to the problem of persistence.

Now that you have a (rudimentary) application design with a domain model, the next step is to implement it in Java.

ORM without a domain model

Object persistence with full ORM is most suitable for applications based on a rich domain model. If your application doesn't implement complex business rules or complex interactions between entities, or if you have few entities, you may not need a domain model. Many simple and some not-so-simple problems are perfectly suited to table-oriented solutions, where the application is designed around the database data model instead of around an object-oriented domain model and the logic is often executed in the database (with stored procedures).

> **(continued)**
> It's also worth considering the learning curve: once you're proficient with Hibernate and Spring Data, you'll use them for all applications—even something as a simple SQL query generator and result mapper. If you're just learning ORM, a trivial use case may not justify the time and overhead involved.

3.2   *Implementing the domain model*

Let's start with an issue that any implementation must deal with: the separation of concerns—which layer is concerned with what responsibility. The domain model implementation is usually a central, organizing component; it's reused heavily whenever you implement new application functionality. For this reason, you should go to some lengths to ensure that non-business concerns don't leak into the domain model implementation.

3.2.1   *Addressing leakage of concerns*

When concerns such as persistence, transaction management, or authorization start to appear in the domain model classes, this is an example of leakage of concerns. The domain model implementation is important code that shouldn't depend on orthogonal APIs. For example, code in the domain model shouldn't call the database directly or through an intermediate abstraction. This will allow you to reuse the domain model classes virtually anywhere.

The architecture of the application includes the following layers:

- The presentation layer can access instances and attributes of domain model entities when rendering views. The user may use the front end (such as a browser) to interact with the application. This concern should be separate from the concerns of the other layers.
- The controller components in the business layer can access the state of domain model entities and call methods of these entities. This is where the business calculations and logic are executed. This concern should be separate from the concerns of the other layers.
- The persistence layer can load instances of domain model entities from and store them to the database, preserving their state. This is where the information is persisted for a long time. This concern should also be separate from the concerns of the other layers.

Preventing the leakage of concerns makes it easy to unit test the domain model without the need for a particular runtime environment or container or for mocking any service dependencies. You can write unit tests that verify the correct behavior of your domain model classes without any special test harness. (Here we're talking about unit tests such as "calculate the shipping cost and tax," not performance and integration tests such as "load from the database" and "store in the database.")

The Jakarta EE standard solves the problem of leaky concerns with metadata such as annotations within your code or external XML descriptors. This approach allows the runtime container to implement some predefined cross-cutting concerns—security, concurrency, persistence, transactions, and remoteness—in a generic way by intercepting calls to application components.

JPA defines the *entity class* as the primary programming artifact. This programming model enables transparent persistence, and a JPA provider such as Hibernate also offers automated persistence. Hibernate isn't a Jakarta EE runtime environment, and it's not an application server. It's an implementation of the ORM technique.

3.2.2   *Transparent and automated persistence*

We use the term *transparent* to refer to a complete separation of concerns between the persistent classes of the domain model and the persistence layer. The persistent classes are unaware of—and have no dependency on—the persistence mechanism. From inside the persistent classes, there is no reference to the outside persistence mechanism. We use the term *automatic* to refer to a persistence solution (your annotated domain, the layer, and the mechanism) that relieves you of handling low-level mechanical details, such as writing most SQL statements and working with the JDBC API. As a real-world use case, let's analyze how transparent and automated persistence is reflected at the level of the `Item` class.

The `Item` class of the CaveatEmptor domain model shouldn't have any runtime dependency on any Jakarta Persistence or Hibernate API. Furthermore, JPA doesn't require that any special superclasses or interfaces be inherited or implemented by persistent classes. Nor are any special classes used to implement attributes and associations. You can reuse persistent classes outside the context of persistence, such as in unit tests or in the presentation layer. You can create instances in any runtime environment with the regular Java `new` operator, preserving testability and reusability.

In a system with transparent persistence, instances of entities aren't aware of the underlying data store; they need not even be aware that they're being persisted or retrieved. JPA externalizes persistence concerns to a generic persistence manager API. Hence, most of your code, and certainly your complex business logic, doesn't have to concern itself with the current state of a domain model entity instance in a single thread of execution. We regard transparency as a requirement because it makes an application easier to build and maintain. Transparent persistence should be one of the primary goals of any ORM solution.

Clearly, no automated persistence solution is completely transparent: every automated persistence layer, including JPA and Hibernate, imposes some requirements on the persistent classes. For example, JPA requires that collection-valued attributes be typed to an interface such as `java.util.Set` or `java.util.List` and not to an actual implementation such as `java.util.HashSet` (this is good practice anyway). Similarly, a JPA entity class has to have a special attribute, called the *database identifier* (which is also less of a restriction but is usually convenient).

You now know that the persistence mechanism should have minimal effect on how you implement a domain model and that transparent and automated persistence is required. Our preferred programming model for achieving this is POJO.

> **NOTE**   POJO is the acronym for *Plain Old Java Objects*. Martin Fowler, Rebecca Parsons, and Josh Mackenzie coined this term in 2000.

At the beginning of the 2000s, many developers started talking about POJO, a back-to-basics approach that essentially revives JavaBeans, a component model for UI development, and reapplies it to the other layers of a system. Several revisions of the EJB and JPA specifications brought us new lightweight entities, and it would be appropriate to call them *persistence-capable JavaBeans*. Java engineers often use all these terms as synonyms for the same basic design approach.

You shouldn't be too concerned about which terms we use in this book; our ultimate goal is to apply the persistence aspect as transparently as possible to Java classes. Almost any Java class can be persistence-capable if you follow some simple practices. Let's see what this looks like in code.

> **NOTE**   To be able to execute the examples from the chapter's source code, you'll need first to run the Ch03.sql script. The examples use a MySQL server with the default credentials: a username of *root* and no password.

3.2.3   *Writing persistence-capable classes*

Supporting fine-grained and rich domain models is a major Hibernate objective. This is one reason we work with POJOs. In general, using fine-grained objects means having more classes than tables.

A persistence-capable plain old Java class declares attributes, which represent state, and business methods, which define behavior. Some attributes represent associations to other persistence-capable classes.

The following listing shows a POJO implementation of the User entity of the domain model (example 1 in the domainmodel folder in the source code). Let's walk through this code.

Listing 3.1   POJO implementation of the User class

```
Path: Ch03/domainmodel/src/main/java/com/manning/javapersistence/ch03/ex01
    /User.java

public class User {

    private String username;

    public String getUsername() {
        return username;
    }

    public void setUsername(String username) {
```

```
        this.username = username;
    }

}
```

The class can be abstract and, if needed, extend a non-persistent class or implement an interface. It must be a top-level class, not be nested within another class. The persistence-capable class and any of its methods *shouldn't* be final (this is a requirement of the JPA specification). Hibernate is not so strict, and it will allow you to declare final classes as entities or as entities with final methods that access persistent fields. However, this is not a good practice, as this will prevent Hibernate from using the proxy pattern for performance improvement. In general, you should follow the JPA requirements if you would like your application to remain portable between different JPA providers.

Hibernate and JPA require a constructor with no arguments for every persistent class. Alternatively, if you do not write a constructor at all, Hibernate will use the default Java constructor. Hibernate calls classes using the Java Reflection API on such no-argument constructors to create instances. The constructor need not be public, but it has to be at least package-visible for Hibernate to use runtime-generated proxies for performance optimization.

The properties of the POJO implement the attributes of the business entities, such as the username of User. You'll usually implement properties as private or protected member fields, together with public or protected property accessor methods: for each field you'll need a method for retrieving its value and another for setting its value. These methods are known as the *getter* and *setter*, respectively. The example POJO in listing 3.1 declares getter and setter methods for the username property.

The JavaBean specification defines the guidelines for naming accessor methods; this allows generic tools like Hibernate to easily discover and manipulate property values. A getter method name begins with get, followed by the name of the property (with the first letter in uppercase). A setter method name begins with set and similarly is followed by the name of the property. You may begin getter method names for Boolean properties with is instead of get.

Hibernate doesn't require accessor methods. You can choose how the state of an instance of your persistent classes should be persisted. Hibernate will either directly access fields or call accessor methods. Your class design isn't disturbed much by these considerations. You can make some accessor methods non-public or completely remove them and then configure Hibernate to rely on field access for these properties.

Making property fields and accessor methods private, protected, or package visible

Typically you will not allow direct access to the internal state of your class, so you won't make attribute fields public. If you make fields or methods private, you're effectively declaring that nobody should ever access them; only you are allowed to do that (or a service like Hibernate). This is a definitive statement.

(continued)
There are often good reasons for someone to access your "private" internals—usually to fix one of your bugs—and you only make people angry if they have to fall back to reflection access in an emergency. Instead, you might assume or know that the engineer who comes after you has access to your code and knows what they're doing.

Although trivial accessor methods are common, one of the reasons we like to use JavaBeans-style accessor methods is that they provide encapsulation: you can change the hidden internal implementation of an attribute without making any changes to the public interface. If you configure Hibernate to access attributes through methods, you abstract the internal data structure of the class—the instance variables—from the design of the database.

For example, if your database stores the name of a user as a single NAME column, but your User class has firstname and lastname fields, you can add the following persistent name property to the class (this is example 2 from the domainmodel folder source code).

Listing 3.2   POJO implementation of the `User` class with logic in accessor methods

Path: Ch03/domainmodel/src/main/java/com/manning/javapersistence/ch03/ex02
➥ /User.java

```
public class User {

    private String firstname;
    private String lastname;

    public String getName() {
        return firstname + ' ' + lastname;
    }

    public void setName(String name) {
        StringTokenizer tokenizer = new StringTokenizer(name);
        firstname = tokenizer.nextToken();
        lastname = tokenizer.nextToken();
    }

}
```

Later you'll see that a custom type converter in the persistence service is a better way to handle many of these kinds of situations. It helps to have several options.

Another issue to consider is *dirty checking*. Hibernate automatically detects state changes so that it can synchronize the updated state with the database. It's usually safe to return a different instance from the getter method than the instance passed by Hibernate to the setter. Hibernate compares them by value—not by object identity—

to determine whether the attribute's persistent state needs to be updated. For example, the following getter method doesn't result in unnecessary SQL UPDATEs:

```
public String getFirstname() {
    return new String(firstname);
}
```

There is an important point to note about *dirty checking* when persisting collections. If you have an Item entity with a Set<Bid> field that's accessed through the setBids setter, this code will result in an unnecessary SQL UPDATE:

```
item.setBids(bids);
em.persist(item);
item.setBids(bids);
```

This happens because Hibernate has its own collection implementations: PersistentSet, PersistentList, or PersistentMap. Providing setters for an entire collection is not good practice anyway.

How does Hibernate handle exceptions when your accessor methods throw them? If Hibernate uses accessor methods when loading and storing instances, and a RuntimeException (unchecked) is thrown, the current transaction is rolled back, and the exception is yours to handle in the code that called the Jakarta Persistence (or native Hibernate) API. If you throw a checked application exception, Hibernate wraps the exception into a RuntimeException.

Next we'll focus on the relationships between entities and the associations between persistent classes.

3.2.4 *Implementing POJO associations*

Let's now look at how you can associate and create different kinds of relationships between objects: one-to-many, many-to-one, and bidirectional relationships. We'll look at the scaffolding code needed to create these associations, how you can simplify relationship management, and how you can enforce the integrity of these relationships.

You can create properties to express associations between classes, and you will (typically) call accessor methods to navigate from instance to instance at runtime. Let's consider the associations defined by the Item and Bid persistent classes, as shown in figure 3.4.

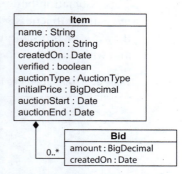

Figure 3.4 Associations between the Item and Bid classes

We left the association-related attributes, Item#bids and Bid#item, out of figure 3.4. These properties and the methods that manipulate their values are called *scaffolding code*. This is what the scaffolding code for the Bid class looks like:

Path: Ch03/domainmodel/src/main/java/com/manning/javapersistence/ch03/ex03
➡ /Bid.java

```java
public class Bid {

    private Item item;

    public Item getItem() {
        return item;
    }

    public void setItem(Item item) {
        this.item = item;
    }

}
```

The item property allows navigation from a Bid to the related Item. This is an association with *many-to-one* multiplicity; users can make many bids for each item.

Here is the Item class's scaffolding code:

Path: Ch03/domainmodel/src/main/java/com/manning/javapersistence/ch03/ex03
➡ /Item.java

```java
public class Item {
    private Set<Bid> bids = new HashSet<>();

    public Set<Bid> getBids() {
        return Collections.unmodifiableSet(bids);
    }
}
```

This association between the two classes allows for *bidirectional* navigation: the *many-to-one* is from this perspective a *one-to-many* multiplicity. One item can have many bids—they are of the same type but were generated during the auction by different users and with different amounts, as shown in table 3.1.

Table 3.1   One Item has many Bids generated during the auction

Item	Bid	User	Amount
1	1	John	100
1	2	Mike	120
1	3	John	140

The scaffolding code for the bids property uses a collection interface type, java.util.Set. JPA requires interfaces for collection-typed properties, where you must use java.util.Set, java.util.List, or java.util.Collection rather than HashSet, for example. It's good practice to program to collection interfaces anyway, rather than concrete implementations, so this restriction shouldn't bother you.

You can choose a `Set` and initialize the field to a new `HashSet`, because the application disallows duplicate bids. This is good practice, because you'll avoid any `NullPointer-Exceptions` when someone is accessing the property of a new `Item`, which will have an empty set of bids. The JPA provider is also required to set a non-empty value on any mapped collection-valued property, such as when an `Item` without bids is loaded from the database. (It doesn't have to use a `HashSet`; the implementation is up to the provider. Hibernate has its own collection implementations with additional capabilities, such as dirty checking.)

Shouldn't bids on an item be stored in a list?

The first reaction is often to preserve the order of elements as they're entered by users, because this may also be the order in which you will show them later. Certainly, in an auction application, there has to be a defined order in which the user sees bids for an item, such as the highest bid first or the newest bid last. You might even work with a `java.util.List` in your user interface code to sort and display bids for an item.

That doesn't mean this display order should be durable, however. The data integrity isn't affected by the order in which bids are displayed. You'll need to store the amount of each bid, so you can always find the highest bid, and you'll need to store a timestamp for when each bid is created, so you can always find the newest bid. When in doubt, keep your system flexible, and sort the data when it's retrieved from the data store (in a query) or shown to the user (in Java code), not when it's stored.

Accessor methods for associations need to be declared `public` only if they're part of the external interface of the persistent class used by the application logic to create a link between two instances. We'll now focus on this issue, because managing the link between an `Item` and a `Bid` is much more complicated in Java code than it is in an SQL database, with declarative foreign key constraints. In our experience, engineers are often unaware of this complication, which arises from a network object model with bidirectional references (pointers). Let's walk through the issue step by step.

The basic procedure for linking a `Bid` with an `Item` looks like this:

```
anItem.getBids().add(aBid);
aBid.setItem(anItem);
```

Whenever you create this bidirectional link, two actions are required:

- You must add the `Bid` to the `bids` collection of the `Item` (shown in figure 3.5).
- The `item` property of the `Bid` must be set (shown in figure 3.6).

JPA doesn't manage persistent associations. If you want to manipulate an association, you must write the same code you would write without Hibernate. If an association is bidirectional, you must consider both sides of the relationship. If you ever have

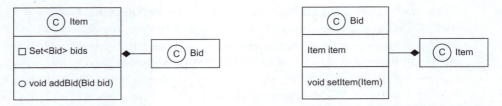

Figure 3.5   Step 1 of linking a Bid with an Item: adding a Bid to the set of Bids from the Item

Figure 3.6   Step 2 of linking a Bid with an Item: setting the Item on the Bid side

problems understanding the behavior of associations in JPA, just ask yourself, "What would I do without Hibernate?" Hibernate doesn't change the regular Java semantics.

We recommend that you add convenience methods to group these operations, allowing reuse and helping ensure correctness, and in the end guaranteeing data integrity (a Bid *is required* to have a reference to an Item). The next listing shows such a convenience method in the Item class (this is example 3 from the domainmodel folder source code).

Listing 3.3   A convenience method simplifies relationship management

Path: Ch03/domainmodel/src/main/java/com/manning/javapersistence/ch03/ex03
➥ /Item.java

```
public void addBid(Bid bid) {
    if (bid == null)
        throw new NullPointerException("Can't add null Bid");
    if (bid.getItem() != null)
        throw new IllegalStateException(
                "Bid is already assigned to an Item");
    bids.add(bid);
    bid.setItem(this);
}
```

The addBid() method not only reduces the lines of code when dealing with Item and Bid instances but also enforces the cardinality of the association. You avoid errors that arise from leaving out one of the two required actions. You should always provide this kind of grouping of operations for associations, if possible. If you compare this with the relational model of foreign keys in an SQL database, you can easily see how a network and a pointer model complicate a simple operation: instead of a declarative constraint, you need procedural code to guarantee data integrity.

Because you want addBid() to be the only externally visible mutator method for the bids of an item (possibly in addition to a removeBid() method), consider making the Bid#setItem() method package-visible.

The Item#getBids() getter method should not return a modifiable collection, so that clients can't use the collection to make changes that aren't reflected on the other side. Bids added directly to the collection may belong to an item, but they wouldn't have a reference to that item, which would create an inconsistent state, according to the database constraints. To prevent this problem, you can wrap the internal collection before returning it from the getter method with `Collections.unmodifiableCollection(c)` and `Collections.unmodifiableSet(s)`. The client will then get an exception if it tries to modify the collection You can therefore force every modification to go through the relationship management method, guaranteeing integrity. It is always good practice to return an unmodifiable collection from your classes so that the client does not have direct access to it.

An alternative strategy is to use immutable instances. For example, you could enforce integrity by requiring an `Item` argument in the constructor of `Bid`, as shown in the following listing (example 4 from the `domainmodel` folder source code).

Listing 3.4 Enforcing the integrity of relationships with a constructor

Path: Ch03/domainmodel/src/main/java/com/manning/javapersistence/ch03/ex04
➡ /Bid.java

```java
public class Bid {

    private Item item;

    public Bid(Item item) {
        this.item = item;
        item.bids.add(this); // Bidirectional
    }

    public Item getItem() {
        return item;
    }
}
```

In this constructor, the `item` field is set; no further modification of the field value should occur. The collection on the other side is also updated for a bidirectional relationship, while the `bids` field from the `Item` class is now package-private. There is no `Bid#setItem()` method.

There are several problems with this approach, however. First, Hibernate can't call this constructor. You need to add a no-argument constructor for Hibernate, and it needs to be at least package-visible. Furthermore, because there is no `setItem()` method, Hibernate would have to be configured to access the `item` field directly. This means the field can't be `final`, so the class isn't guaranteed to be immutable.

It's up to you how many convenience methods and layers you want to wrap around the persistent association properties or fields, but we recommend being consistent and applying the same strategy to all your domain model classes. For the sake of readability, we won't always show our convenience methods, special constructors, and other such scaffolding in future code samples; you should add them according to your own taste and requirements.

You now have seen domain model classes and how to represent their attributes and the relationships between them. Next we'll increase the level of abstraction: we'll add metadata to the domain model implementation and declare aspects such as validation and persistence rules.

3.3   *Domain model metadata*

Metadata is data about data, so domain model metadata is information about your domain model. For example, when you use the Java Reflection API to discover the names of classes in your domain model or the names of their attributes, you're accessing domain model metadata.

ORM tools also require metadata to specify the mapping between classes and tables, properties and columns, associations and foreign keys, Java types and SQL types, and so on. This object/relational mapping metadata governs the transformation between the different type systems and relationship representations in object-oriented and SQL systems. JPA has a metadata API that you can call to obtain details about the persistence aspects of your domain model, such as the names of persistent entities and attributes. It's your job as an engineer to create and maintain this information.

JPA standardizes two metadata options: annotations in Java code and externalized XML descriptor files. Hibernate has some extensions for native functionality, also available as annotations or XML descriptors. We usually prefer annotations as the primary source of mapping metadata. After reading this section, you'll have the information to make an informed decision for your own project.

We'll also discuss *Bean Validation* (JSR 303) in this section, and how it provides declarative validation for your domain model (or any other) classes. The reference implementation of this specification is the *Hibernate Validator* project. Most engineers today prefer Java annotations as the primary mechanism for declaring metadata.

3.3.1   *Annotation-based metadata*

The big advantage of annotations is that they put metadata, such as `@Entity`, next to the information it describes, instead of separating it in a different file. Here's an example:

```
import javax.persistence.Entity;
@Entity
public class Item {
}
```

You can find the standard JPA mapping annotations in the `javax.persistence` package. This example declares the `Item` class as a persistent entity using the `@javax.persistence.Entity` annotation. All of its attributes are now automatically made persistent with a default strategy. That means you can load and store instances of `Item`, and all the properties of the class are part of the managed state.

Annotations are type-safe, and the JPA metadata is included in the compiled class files. The annotations are still accessible at runtime, and Hibernate reads the classes and metadata with Java reflection when the application starts. The IDE can also easily validate and highlight annotations—they're regular Java types, after all. When you refactor your code, you rename, delete, and move classes and properties. Most development tools and editors can't refactor XML elements and attribute values, but annotations are part of the Java language and are included in all refactoring operations.

> ### Is my class now dependent on JPA?
> You need JPA libraries on your classpath when you compile the source of your domain model class. JPA isn't required on the classpath when you create an instance of the class, such as in a client application that doesn't execute any JPA code. Only when you access the annotations through reflection at runtime (as Hibernate does internally when it reads your metadata) will you need the packages on the classpath.

When the standardized Jakarta Persistence annotations are insufficient, a JPA provider may offer additional annotations.

USING VENDOR EXTENSIONS

Even if you map most of your application's model with JPA-compatible annotations from the `javax.persistence` package, you may have to use vendor extensions at some point. For example, some performance-tuning options you'd expect to be available in high-quality persistence software are only available as Hibernate-specific annotations. This is how JPA providers compete, so you can't avoid annotations from other packages—there's a reason why you chose to use Hibernate.

The following snippet shows the `Item` entity source code again with a Hibernate-only mapping option:

```
import javax.persistence.Entity;
@Entity
@org.hibernate.annotations.Cache(
    usage = org.hibernate.annotations.CacheConcurrencyStrategy.READ_WRITE
)
public class Item {
}
```

We prefer to prefix Hibernate annotations with the full `org.hibernate.annotations` package name. Consider this good practice, because it enables you to easily see which metadata for this class is from the JPA specification and which is vendor-specific. You can also easily search your source code for `org.hibernate.annotations` and get a complete overview of all nonstandard annotations in your application in a single search result.

If you switch your Jakarta Persistence provider, you'll only have to replace the vendor-specific extensions, and you can expect a similar feature set to be available from most mature JPA implementations. Of course, we hope you'll never have to do this, and it doesn't often happen in practice—just be prepared.

Annotations on classes only cover metadata that applies to that particular class. You'll often also need metadata at a higher level for an entire package or even the whole application.

GLOBAL ANNOTATION METADATA

The @Entity annotation maps a particular class. JPA and Hibernate also have annotations for global metadata. For example, a @NamedQuery has a global scope; you don't apply it to a particular class. Where should you place this annotation?

Although it's possible to place such global annotations in the source file of a class (at the top of any class), we prefer to keep global metadata in a separate file. Package-level annotations are a good choice; they're in a file called package-info.java in a particular package directory. You will be able to look for them in a single place instead of browsing through several files. The following listing shows an example of global named query declarations (example 5 from the domainmodel folder source code).

Listing 3.5   Global metadata in a package-info.java file

```
Path: Ch03/domainmodel/src/main/java/com/manning/javapersistence/ch03/ex05
  /package-info.java

@org.hibernate.annotations.NamedQueries({
    @org.hibernate.annotations.NamedQuery(
        name = "findItemsOrderByName",
        query = "select i from Item i order by i.name asc"
    )
    ,
    @org.hibernate.annotations.NamedQuery(
        name = "findItemBuyNowPriceGreaterThan",
        query = "select i from Item i where i.buyNowPrice > :price",
        timeout = 60, // Seconds!
        comment = "Custom SQL comment"
    )
})

package com.manning.javapersistence.ch03.ex05;
```

Unless you've used package-level annotations before, the syntax of this file with the package and import declarations at the bottom is probably new to you.

Annotations will be our primary tool for ORM metadata throughout this book, and there is much to learn about this subject. Before we look at the alternative mapping style using XML files, let's use some simple annotations to improve our domain model classes with validation rules.

3.3.2 Applying constraints to Java objects

Most applications contain a multitude of data integrity checks. When you violate one of the simplest data-integrity constraints, you may get a NullPointerException because a value isn't available. You may similarly get this exception when a string-valued property shouldn't be empty (an empty string isn't null), when a string has to match a particular regular expression pattern, or when a number or date value must be within a certain range.

These business rules affect every layer of an application: The user interface code has to display detailed and localized error messages. The business and persistence layers must check input values received from the client before passing them to the data store. The SQL database must be the final validator, guaranteeing the integrity of durable data.

The idea behind Bean Validation is that declaring rules such as "This property can't be null" or "This number has to be in the given range" is much easier and less error-prone than repeatedly writing if-then-else procedures. Furthermore, declaring these rules on the central component of your application, the domain model implementation, enables integrity checks in every layer of the system. The rules are then available to the presentation and persistence layers. And if you consider how data-integrity constraints affect not only your Java application code but also your SQL database schema—which is a collection of integrity rules—you might think of Bean Validation constraints as additional ORM metadata.

Look at the following extended Item domain model class from the validation folder source code.

> **Listing 3.6 Applying validation constraints on Item entity fields**

```
Path: Ch03/validation/src/main/java/com/manning/javapersistence/ch03
➥ /validation/Item.java

import javax.validation.constraints.Future;
import javax.validation.constraints.NotNull;
import javax.validation.constraints.Size;
import java.util.Date;

public class Item {
    @NotNull
    @Size(
            min = 2,
            max = 255,
            message = "Name is required, maximum 255 characters."
    )
    private String name;

    @Future
    private Date auctionEnd;
}
```

We add two attributes when an auction concludes: the `name` of an item and the `auctionEnd` date. Both are typical candidates for additional constraints. First, we want to guarantee that the name is always present and human-readable (one-character item names don't make much sense) but not too long—your SQL database will be most efficient with variable-length strings up to 255 characters, and your user interface will also have some constraints on visible label space. Second, the ending time of an auction should obviously be in the future. If we don't provide an error message for a constraint, a default message will be used. Messages can be keys to external property files for internationalization.

The validation engine will access the fields directly if you annotate the fields. If you prefer to use calls through accessor methods, annotate the getter method with validation constraints, not the setter (annotations on setters are not supported). Then the constraints will be part of the class's API and will be included in its Javadoc, making the domain model implementation easier to understand. Note that constraints being part of the class's API is independent of access by the JPA provider; for example, Hibernate Validator may call accessor methods, whereas Hibernate ORM may call fields directly.

Bean Validation isn't limited to built-in annotations; you can create your own constraints and annotations. With a custom constraint, you can even use class-level annotations and validate several attribute values at the same time on an instance of a class. The following test code shows how you could manually check the integrity of an `Item` instance.

> **Listing 3.7   Testing an `Item` instance for constraint violations**

```
Path: Ch03/validation/src/test/java/com/manning/javapersistence/ch03
 ➦ /validation/ModelValidation.java

ValidatorFactory factory = Validation.buildDefaultValidatorFactory();
Validator validator = factory.getValidator();

Item item = new Item();
item.setName("Some Item");
item.setAuctionEnd(new Date());

Set<ConstraintViolation<Item>> violations = validator.validate(item);

ConstraintViolation<Item> violation = violations.iterator().next();
String failedPropertyName =
        violation.getPropertyPath().iterator().next().getName();

// Validation error, auction end date was not in the future!
assertAll(() -> assertEquals(1, violations.size()),
        () -> assertEquals("auctionEnd", failedPropertyName),
        () -> {
            if (Locale.getDefault().getLanguage().equals("en"))
                assertEquals(violation.getMessage(),
                        "must be a future date");
        });
```

We're not going to explain this code in detail but offer it for you to explore. You'll rarely write this kind of validation code; usually this validation is automatically handled by your user interface and persistence framework. It's therefore important to look for Bean Validation integration when selecting a UI framework.

Hibernate, as required from any JPA provider, also automatically integrates with Hibernate Validator if the libraries are available on the classpath, and it offers the following features:

- You don't have to manually validate instances before passing them to Hibernate for storage.
- Hibernate recognizes constraints on persistent domain model classes and triggers validation before database insert or update operations. When validation fails, Hibernate throws a `ConstraintViolationException` containing the failure details to the code calling persistence-management operations.
- The Hibernate toolset for automatic SQL schema generation understands many constraints and generates SQL DDL-equivalent constraints for you. For example, a `@NotNull` annotation translates into an SQL `NOT NULL` constraint, and a `@Size(n)` rule defines the number of characters in a `VARCHAR(n)`-typed column.

You can control this behavior of Hibernate with the `<validation-mode>` element in your persistence.xml configuration file. The default mode is `AUTO`, so Hibernate will only validate if it finds a Bean Validation provider (such as Hibernate Validator) on the classpath of the running application. With the `CALLBACK` mode, validation will always occur, and you'll get a deployment error if you forget to bundle a Bean Validation provider. The `NONE` mode disables automatic validation by the JPA provider.

You'll see Bean Validation annotations again later in this book; you'll also find them in the example code bundles. We could write much more about Hibernate Validator, but we'd only repeat what is already available in the project's excellent reference guide (http://mng.bz/ne65). Take a look and find out more about features such as validation groups and the metadata API for the discovery of constraints.

3.3.3 Externalizing metadata with XML files

You can replace or override every annotation in JPA with an XML descriptor element. In other words, you don't have to use annotations if you don't want to, or if keeping mapping metadata separate from source code is advantageous to your system design for whatever reason. Keeping the mapping metadata separate has the benefit of not cluttering the JPA annotations with Java code and of making your Java classes more reusable, though you lose the type-safety. This approach is less in use nowadays, but we'll analyze it anyway, as you may still encounter it or choose this approach for your own projects.

XML METADATA WITH JPA

The following listing shows a JPA XML descriptor for a particular persistence unit (the
metadataxmljpa folder source code).

Listing 3.8   JPA XML descriptor containing the mapping metadata of a persistence unit

Path: Ch03/metadataxmljpa/src/test/resources/META-INF/orm.xml

```
<entity-mappings
        version="2.2"
        xmlns="http://xmlns.jcp.org/xml/ns/persistence/orm"
        xmlns:xsi="http://www.w3.org/2001/XMLSchema-instance"
        xsi:schemaLocation="http://xmlns.jcp.org/xml/ns/persistence/orm
            http://xmlns.jcp.org/xml/ns/persistence/orm_2_2.xsd">

    <persistence-unit-metadata>                                        B
            <xml-mapping-metadata-complete/>
            <persistence-unit-defaults>
                <delimited-identifiers/>
            </persistence-unit-defaults>                    C
    </persistence-unit-metadata>
    <entity class="com.manning.javapersistence.ch03.metadataxmljpa.Item"
                    access="FIELD">                                         E
        <attributes>
            <id name="id">
                <generated-value strategy="AUTO"/>
            </id>                                           F
            <basic name="name"/>
            <basic name="auctionEnd">
                <temporal>TIMESTAMP</temporal>
            </basic>
        </attributes>
    </entity>
</entity-mappings>
```

Ⓐ Declare the global metadata.

Ⓑ Ignore all mapping annotations. If we include the `<xml-mapping-metadata-complete>` element, the JPA provider ignores all annotations on the domain model classes in this persistence unit and relies only on the mappings as defined in the XML descriptors.

Ⓒ The default settings escape all SQL columns, tables, and other names.

Ⓓ Escaping is useful if the SQL names are actually keywords (a "USER" table, for example).

Ⓔ Declare the `Item` class as an entity with field access.

Ⓕ Its attributes are the `id`, which is autogenerated, the `name`, and the `auctionEnd`, which is a temporal field.

The JPA provider automatically picks up this descriptor if you place it in a META-INF/
orm.xml file on the classpath of the persistence unit. If you prefer to use a different

filename or several files, you'll have to change the configuration of the persistence unit in your META-INF/persistence.xml file:

```
<persistence-unit name="persistenceUnitName">
    . . .
    <mapping-file>file1.xml</mapping-file>
    <mapping-file>file2.xml</mapping-file>
    . . .
</persistence-unit>
```

If you don't want to ignore the annotation metadata but override it instead, don't mark the XML descriptors as "complete," and name the class and property you want to override:

```
<entity class="com.manning.javapersistence.ch03.metadataxmljpa.Item">
    <attributes>
        <basic name="name">
            <column name="ITEM_NAME"/>
        </basic>
    </attributes>
</entity>
```

Here we map the name property to the ITEM_NAME column; by default, the property would map to the NAME column. Hibernate will now ignore any existing annotations from the javax.persistence.annotation and org.hibernate.annotations packages on the name property of the Item class. But Hibernate won't ignore Bean Validation annotations and still applies them for automatic validation and schema generation! All other annotations on the Item class are also recognized. Note that we don't specify an access strategy in this mapping, so field access or accessor methods are used, depending on the position of the @Id annotation in Item. (We'll get back to this detail in the next chapter.)

We won't talk much about JPA XML descriptors in this book. The syntax of these documents is the same as the JPA annotation syntax, so you shouldn't have any problems writing them. We'll focus on the important aspect: the mapping strategies.

3.3.4   Accessing metadata at runtime

The JPA specification provides programming interfaces for accessing the metamodel (information about the model) of persistent classes. There are two flavors of the API. One is more dynamic in nature and similar to basic Java reflection. The second option is a static metamodel. For both options, access is read-only; you can't modify the metadata at runtime.

THE DYNAMIC METAMODEL API IN JAKARTA PERSISTENCE

Sometimes you'll want to get programmatic access to the persistent attributes of an entity, such as when you want to write custom validation or generic UI code. You'd like to know dynamically what persistent classes and attributes your domain model has.

The code in the following listing shows how you can read metadata with Jakarta Persistence interfaces (from the `metamodel` folder source code).

```
Path: Ch03/metamodel/src/test/java/com/manning/javapersistence/ch03
➥ /metamodel/MetamodelTest.java

Metamodel metamodel = emf.getMetamodel();
Set<ManagedType<?>> managedTypes = metamodel.getManagedTypes();
ManagedType<?> itemType = managedTypes.iterator().next();

assertAll(() -> assertEquals(1, managedTypes.size()),
        () -> assertEquals(
                Type.PersistenceType.ENTITY,
                itemType.getPersistenceType())));
```

You can get the `Metamodel` object from either the `EntityManagerFactory`, of which you'll typically have only one instance per data source in an application, or, if it's more convenient, by calling `EntityManager#getMetamodel()`. The set of managed types contains information about all persistent entities and embedded classes (which we'll discuss in the next chapter). In this example, there's only one managed type: the `Item` entity. This is how you can dig deeper and find out more about each attribute.

```
Path: Ch03/metamodel/src/test/java/com/manning/javapersistence/ch03
➥ /metamodel/MetamodelTest.java

SingularAttribute<?, ?> idAttribute =                                    Ⓐ
        itemType.getSingularAttribute("id");       ←
Ⓑ
    assertFalse(idAttribute.isOptional());

SingularAttribute<?, ?> nameAttribute =                                  Ⓒ
        itemType.getSingularAttribute("name");     ←

assertAll(() -> assertEquals(String.class, nameAttribute.getJavaType()),
        () -> assertEquals(                                              Ⓓ
                Attribute.PersistentAttributeType.BASIC,
                nameAttribute.getPersistentAttributeType()
        ));

SingularAttribute<?, ?> auctionEndAttribute =                           Ⓔ
        itemType.getSingularAttribute("auctionEnd");   ←
assertAll(() -> assertEquals(Date.class,
                        auctionEndAttribute.getJavaType()),             Ⓕ
        () -> assertFalse(auctionEndAttribute.isCollection()),
        () -> assertFalse(auctionEndAttribute.isAssociation())
);
```

Ⓐ The attributes of the entity are accessed with a string: the `id`.

Ⓑ Check that the `id` attribute is not optional. This means that it cannot be NULL, since it is the primary key.

Ⓒ The `name`.

Ⓓ Check that the `name` attribute has the `String` Java type and the basic persistent attribute type.

Ⓔ The `auctionEnd` date. This obviously isn't type-safe, and if you change the names of the attributes, this code will be broken and obsolete. The strings aren't automatically included in the refactoring operations of your IDE.

Ⓕ Check that the `auctionEnd` attribute has the `Date` Java type and that it is not a collection or an association.

JPA also offers a static type-safe metamodel.

USING A STATIC METAMODEL

In Java (at least up to version 17), you can't access the fields or accessor methods of a bean in a type-safe fashion—only by their names, using strings. This is particularly inconvenient with JPA criteria querying, which is a type-safe alternative to string-based query languages. Here's an example:

```
Path: Ch03/metamodel/src/test/java/com/manning/javapersistence/ch03
    /metamodel/MetamodelTest.java

CriteriaBuilder cb = em.getCriteriaBuilder();
CriteriaQuery<Item> query = cb.createQuery(Item.class);    ← Ⓐ
Root<Item> fromItem = query.from(Item.class);
query.select(fromItem);
List<Item> items = em.createQuery(query).getResultList();

assertEquals(2, items.size());
```

Ⓐ The query is the equivalent of `select i from Item i`. This query returns all items in the database, and there are two in this case. If you want to restrict this result and only return items with a particular name, you will have to use a `like` expression, comparing the `name` attribute of each item with the pattern set in a parameter.

The following code introduces a filter on the read operation:

```
Path: Ch03/metamodel/src/test/java/com/manning/javapersistence/ch03
    /metamodel/MetamodelTest.java

Path<String> namePath = fromItem.get("name");
query.where(cb.like(namePath, cb.parameter(String.class, "pattern")));
List<Item> items = em.createQuery(query).
                setParameter("pattern", "%Item 1%").    ← Ⓐ
                getResultList();
assertAll(() -> assertEquals(1, items.size()),
        () -> assertEquals("Item 1", items.iterator().next().getName()));
```

Ⓐ The query is the equivalent of `select i from Item i where i.name like :pattern`. Notice that the `namePath` lookup requires the `name` string. This is where the type-safety of the criteria query breaks down. You can rename the `Item` entity class with your IDE's refactoring tools, and the query will still work. But as soon as you touch the `Item#name` property, manual adjustments are necessary. Luckily, you'll catch this when the test fails.

A much better approach that's safe for refactoring and that detects mismatches at compile time and not runtime is the type-safe static metamodel:

Path: Ch03/metamodel/src/test/java/com/manning/javapersistence/ch03
➡ /metamodel/MetamodelTest.java

```
query.where(
    cb.like(
        fromItem.get(Item_.name),
        cb.parameter(String.class, "pattern")
    )
);
```

The special class here is `Item_`; note the underscore. This class is a metadata class, and it lists all the attributes of the `Item` entity class:

Path: Ch03/metamodel/target/classes/com/manning/javapersistence/ch03
➡ /metamodel/Item_.class

```
@Generated(value = "org.hibernate.jpamodelgen.JPAMetaModelEntityProcessor")
@StaticMetamodel(Item.class)
public abstract class Item_ {

    public static volatile SingularAttribute<Item, Date> auctionEnd;
    public static volatile SingularAttribute<Item, String> name;
    public static volatile SingularAttribute<Item, Long> id;

    public static final String AUCTION_END = "auctionEnd";
    public static final String NAME = "name";
    public static final String ID = "id";

}
```

This class will be automatically generated. The Hibernate JPA 2 Metamodel Generator (a subproject of the Hibernate suite) takes care of this. Its only purpose is to generate static metamodel classes from your managed persistent classes. You need to add this Maven dependency to your pom.xml file:

Path: Ch03/metamodel/pom.xml

```
<dependency>
    <groupId>org.hibernate</groupId>
    <artifactId>hibernate-jpamodelgen</artifactId>
    <version>5.6.9.Final</version>
</dependency>
```

It will run automatically whenever you build your project and will generate the appropriate `Item_` metadata class. You will find the generated classes in the target\generated-sources folder.

This chapter discussed the construction of the domain model and the dynamic and static metamodel. Although you've seen some mapping constructs in the previous sections, we haven't introduced any more sophisticated class and property mappings so far. You should now decide which mapping metadata strategy you'd like to use in your project—we recommend the more commonly used annotations, instead of the already less used XML. Then you can read more about class and property mappings in part 2 of this book, starting with chapter 5.

Summary

- We analyzed different abstract notions like the information model and data model, and then jumped into JPA/Hibernate so that we could work with databases from Java programs.
- You can implement persistent classes free of any cross-cutting concerns like logging, authorization, and transaction demarcation.
- The persistent classes only depend on JPA at compile time.
- Persistence-related concerns should not leak into the domain model implementation.
- Transparent persistence is important if you want to execute and test the business objects independently.
- The POJO concept and the JPA entity programming model have several things in common, arising from the old JavaBean specification: they implement properties as private or protected member fields, while property accessor methods are generally public or protected.
- We can access the metadata using either the dynamic metamodel or the static metamodel.

Working with Spring Data JPA

This chapter covers

- Introducing Spring Data and its modules
- Examining the main concepts of Spring Data JPA
- Investigating the query builder mechanisms
- Examining projections, and modifying and deleting queries
- Examining Query by Example

Spring Data is an umbrella project containing many projects specific to various databases. These projects are developed in partnership with the companies creating the database technologies themselves. Spring Data's goal is to provide an abstraction for data access while retaining the underlying specifics of the various data stores.

We'll discuss the following general features provided by Spring Data:

- Integration with Spring via JavaConfig and XML configuration
- Repository and custom object-mapping abstractions
- Integration with custom repository code

- Dynamic query creation based on repository method names
- Integration with other Spring projects, such as Spring Boot

We enumerated the main Spring Data modules in chapter 2. We'll focus on Spring Data JPA here, which is largely used as an alternative for accessing databases from Java programs. It provides a layer of abstraction on top of a JPA provider (such as Hibernate), in the spirit of the Spring framework, taking control of the configuration and transactions management. We'll use it to interact with the databases in many of our examples in the following chapters, so this chapter will analyze its capabilities in depth. We will still define and manage our entities using JPA and Hibernate, but we'll provide Spring Data JPA as an alternative for interacting with them.

4.1 Introducing Spring Data JPA

Spring Data JPA provides support for interacting with JPA repositories. As you can see in figure 4.1, it is built on top of the functionality offered by the Spring Data Commons project and the JPA provider (Hibernate in our case). To review the main Spring Data modules, refer to chapter 2.

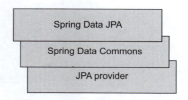

Figure 4.1 Spring Data JPA is built on top of Spring Data Commons and the JPA provider.

Throughout the book, we'll generally interact with databases using both Hibernate JPA and Spring Data as alternatives. This chapter, along with the background provided in chapters 1–3, will help you start using the most important capabilities of Spring Data JPA. We'll examine further Spring Data JPA features when they are needed, and we'll look at other Spring Data projects in their dedicated chapters.

As you saw in section 2.6 when we created the "Hello World" application, Spring Data JPA can do several things to facilitate interaction with a database:

- Configure the data source bean
- Configure the entity manager factory bean
- Configure the transaction manager bean
- Manage transactions through annotations

4.2 Starting a new Spring Data JPA project

We'll use the CaveatEmptor example application that we introduced in chapter 3 to demonstrate and analyze the capabilities of Spring Data JPA. We'll use Spring Data JPA as a persistence framework to manage and persist the CaveatEmptor users, with Hibernate JPA as the underlying JPA provider. Spring Data JPA can execute CRUD operations and queries against a database, and it can be backed by different JPA implementations. It provides another layer of abstraction to interact with the databases.

> **NOTE** To be able to execute the examples from the source code, you'll first need to run the Ch04.sql script. The source code is in the `springdatajpa` folder.

We'll create a Spring Boot application to use Spring Data JPA. To do this, we'll use the Spring Initializr website at https://start.spring.io/ to create a new Spring Boot project (see figure 4.2) with the following characteristics:

- Group: com.manning.javapersistence
- Artifact: springdatajpa
- Description: Spring Data with Spring Boot

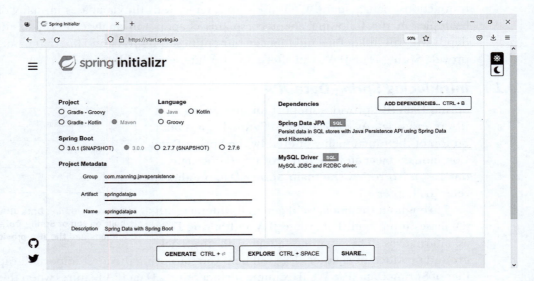

Figure 4.2   Creating a new Spring Boot project using Spring Data JPA and MySQL

We'll also add the following dependencies:

- Spring Data JPA (this will add `spring-boot-starter-data-jpa` in the Maven pom.xml file)
- MySQL Driver (this will add `mysql-connector-java` in the Maven pom.xml file)

After you click the Generate button (shown in figure 4.2), the Spring Initializr website will provide an archive to be downloaded. This archive contains a Spring Boot project that uses Spring Data JPA and MySQL. Figure 4.3 shows this project opened in the IntelliJ IDEA IDE.

The skeleton of the project contains four files:

- `SpringDataJpaApplication` includes a skeleton `main` method.
- `SpringDataJpaApplicationTests` includes a skeleton test method.
- `application.properties` is empty at the beginning.
- `pom.xml` includes the management information needed by Maven.

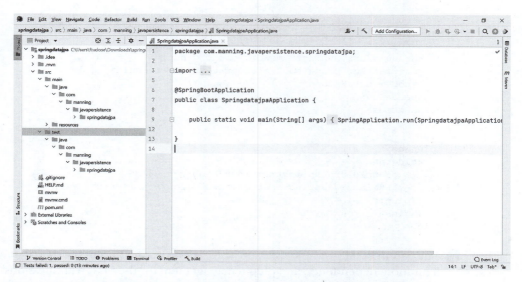

Figure 4.3 Opening the Spring Boot project that uses Spring Data JPA and MySQL

As the first three files in the preceding list are standard ones, we'll take a closer look now at the pom.xml file generated by Spring Initializr.

Listing 4.1   The pom.xml Maven file

Path: Ch04/springdatajpa/pom.xml

```
<parent>
    <groupId>org.springframework.boot</groupId>
    <artifactId>spring-boot-starter-parent</artifactId>
    <version>2.7.0</version>
    <relativePath/> <!-- lookup parent from repository -->
</parent>
<groupId>com.manning.javapersistence</groupId>
<artifactId>springdatajpa</artifactId>
<version>0.0.1-SNAPSHOT</version>
<name>springdatajpa</name>
<description>Spring Data with Spring Boot</description>
<properties>
    <java.version>17</java.version>
</properties>
<dependencies>
    <dependency>
        <groupId>org.springframework.boot</groupId>
        <artifactId>spring-boot-starter-data-jpa</artifactId>
    </dependency>

    <dependency>
        <groupId>mysql</groupId>
        <artifactId>mysql-connector-java</artifactId>
```

A

B

C

D

```
            <scope>runtime</scope>
        </dependency>
        <dependency>
            <groupId>org.springframework.boot</groupId>
            <artifactId>spring-boot-starter-test</artifactId>
            <scope>test</scope>
        </dependency>
    </dependencies>

<build>
    <plugins>
        <plugin>
            <groupId>org.springframework.boot</groupId>
            <artifactId>spring-boot-maven-plugin</artifactId>
        </plugin>
    </plugins>
</build>
```

A The parent POM is `spring-boot-starter-parent`. This parent provides default configuration, dependency, and plugin management for the Maven applications. It also inherits dependency management from its parent, `spring-boot-dependencies`.

B Indicates the `groupId`, `artifactId`, `version`, `name`, and `description` of the project, plus the Java version.

C `spring-boot-starter-data-jpa` is the starter dependency used by Spring Boot to connect to a relational database through Spring Data JPA with Hibernate. It uses Hibernate as a transitive dependency.

D `mysql-connector-java` is the JDBC driver for MySQL. It is a runtime dependency, indicating that it is not needed in the classpath for compiling, but only at runtime.

E `spring-boot-starter-test` is the Spring Boot starter dependency for testing. This dependency is needed only for the test compilation and execution phases.

F `spring-boot-maven-plugin` is a utility plugin for building and running a Spring Boot project.

4.3 *First steps for configuring a Spring Data JPA project*

We'll now write the class that will describe a `User` entity. The CaveatEmptor application has to keep track of the users interacting with it, so it is natural to start with the implementation of this class.

Listing 4.2   The `User` entity

Path: Ch04/springdatajpa/src/main/java/com/manning/javapersistence
➥ /springdatajpa/model/User.java

```
@Entity
@Table(name = "USERS")
public class User {
```

```
    @Id
    @GeneratedValue        B
    private Long id;

    private String username;                        C

    private LocalDate registrationDate;

    public User() {

    }

    public User(String username) {
        this.username = username;
    }                                                          D

    public User(String username, LocalDate registrationDate) {
        this.username = username;
        this.registrationDate = registrationDate;
    }

    public Long getId() {         E
        return id;
    }

    public String getUsername() {
        return username;
    }

    public void setUsername(String username) {
        this.username = username;
    }                                                          F

    public LocalDate getRegistrationDate() {
        return registrationDate;
    }

    public void setRegistrationDate(LocalDate registrationDate) {
        this.registrationDate = registrationDate;
    }

    @Override
    public String toString() {
        return "User{" +
                "id=" + id +                                   G
                ", username='" + username + '\'' +
                ", registrationDate=" + registrationDate +
                '}';
    }
}
```

Ⓐ Create the User entity and annotate it with the @Entity and @Table annotations. We specify USERS as the name of the corresponding table, because the default USER name is reserved in most database systems.

B Specify the `id` field as the primary key and include a getter for it. The `@Generated-Value` annotation enables the automatic generation of `ids`. We'll look at this more in chapter 5.

C Declare the `username` and `registrationDate` fields, together with getters and setters.

D Declare three constructors, including a no-arguments one. Recall that JPA requires a constructor with no arguments for every persistent class. JPA uses the Java Reflection API on such a no-argument constructor to create instances.

E Create the `toString` method to nicely display the instances of the `User` class.

We'll also create the `UserRepository` interface.

Listing 4.3   The `UserRepository` interface

Path: Ch04/springdatajpa/src/main/java/com/manning/javapersistence
➥ /springdatajpa/repositories/UserRepository.java

```
public interface UserRepository extends CrudRepository<User, Long> {
}
```

The `UserRepository` interface extends `CrudRepository<User, Long>`. This means that it is a repository of `User` entities, which have a `Long` identifier. Remember, the `User` class has an `id` field of type `Long` annotated as `@Id`. We can directly call methods such as `save`, `findAll`, and `findById`, inherited from `CrudRepository`, and we can use them without any additional information to execute the usual operations against the database. Spring Data JPA will create a proxy class implementing the `UserRepository` interface and implement its methods.

It is worth mentioning that `CrudRepository` is a generic technology-agnostic persistence interface that we can use not only for JPA/relational databases but also for NoSQL databases. For example, we can easily change the database from MySQL to MongoDB without touching the implementation by changing the dependency from the original `spring-boot-starter-data-jpa` to `spring-boot-starter-data-mongodb`.

The next step will be to fill in the Spring Boot application.properties file. Spring Boot will automatically find and load the application.properties file from the classpath; the src/main/resources folder is added by Maven to the classpath.

Listing 4.4   The application.properties file

Path: Ch04/springdatajpa/src/main/resources/application.properties

```
spring.datasource.url=jdbc:mysql://localhost:3306/CH04_SPRINGDATAJPA    Ⓐ
                     ?serverTimezone=UTC
spring.datasource.username=root                              Ⓑ
spring.datasource.password=
spring.jpa.properties.hibernate.dialect=org.hibernate.dialect.MySQL8Dialect    Ⓓ
spring.jpa.show-sql=true
spring.jpa.hibernate.ddl-auto=create    ←Ⓔ
```
Ⓒ

Ⓐ The application.properties file will indicate the URL of the database.

Ⓑ The username, and no password for access.

Ⓒ The Hibernate dialect is MySQL8, as the database we'll interact with is MySQL Release 8.0.

Ⓓ While executing, the SQL code is shown.

Ⓔ Every time the program is executed, the database will be created from scratch.

We'll now write code that saves two users to the database and then tries to find them.

Listing 4.5   Persisting and finding `User` entities

```
Path: Ch04/springdatajpa/src/main/java/com/manning/javapersistence
    /springdatajpa/SpringDataJpaApplication.java
```

```java
@SpringBootApplication                          ◄── Ⓐ
public class SpringDataJpaApplication {

    public static void main(String[] args) {                        Ⓑ
        SpringApplication.run(SpringDataJpaApplication.class, args);   ◄──┘
    }

    @Bean                                                             Ⓒ
    public ApplicationRunner configure(UserRepository userRepository) {
        return env ->
        {
            User user1 = new User("beth", LocalDate.of(2020,
                Month.AUGUST, 3));
            User user2 = new User("mike",                              Ⓓ
                            LocalDate.of(2020, Month.JANUARY, 18));

            userRepository.save(user1);    Ⓔ
            userRepository.save(user2);
                                                                      Ⓕ
            userRepository.findAll().forEach(System.out::println);   ◄──┘
        };
    }

}
```

Ⓐ The `@SpringBootApplication` annotation, added by Spring Boot to the class containing the `main` method, will enable the Spring Boot autoconfiguration mechanism and the scan on the package where the application is located, and it will allow the registration of extra beans in the context.

Ⓑ `SpringApplication.run` will load the standalone Spring application from the `main` method. It will create an appropriate `ApplicationContext` instance and load beans.

Ⓒ Spring Boot will run the `@Bean` annotated method, returning an `Application-Runner` just before `SpringApplication.run()` finishes.

D Create two users.

E Save them to the database.

F Retrieve them and display the information about them.

When we run this application, we'll get the following output (determined by the way the `toString()` method of the `User` class works):

```
User{id=1, username='beth', registrationDate=2020-08-03}
User{id=2, username='mike', registrationDate=2020-01-18}
```

4.4   *Defining query methods with Spring Data JPA*

We'll extend the `User` class by adding the fields `email`, `level`, and `active`. A user may have different levels, which will allow them to execute particular actions (such as bidding above some amount). A user may be active or may be retired (previously active in the CaveatEmptor auction system, but not anymore). This is important information that the CaveatEmptor application needs to keep about its users.

> **NOTE**   The source code we'll discuss in the rest of this chapter can be found in the `springdatajpa2` folder.

Listing 4.6   The modified `User` class

Path: Ch04/springdatajpa2/src/main/java/com/manning/javapersistence
➥ /springdatajpa/model/User.java

```java
@Entity
@Table(name = "USERS")
public class User {

    @Id
    @GeneratedValue
    private Long id;

    private String username;

    private LocalDate registrationDate;

    private String email;

    private int level;

    private boolean active;

    public User() {

    }

    public User(String username) {
        this.username = username;
    }
```

```java
    public User(String username, LocalDate registrationDate) {
        this.username = username;
        this.registrationDate = registrationDate;
    }

    //getters and setters
}
```

We'll now start to add new methods to the `UserRepository` interface and use them inside newly created tests. We'll change the `UserRepository` interface to extend `Jpa-Repository` instead of `CrudRepository`. `JpaRepository` extends `PagingAndSorting-Repository`, which, in turn, extends `CrudRepository`.

CrudRepository provides basic CRUD functionality, whereas `PagingAndSorting-Repository` offers convenient methods that sort and paginate the records (which we'll address later in the chapter). `JpaRepository` offers JPA-related methods, such as flushing the persistence context and deleting records in a batch. Additionally, `JpaRepository` overwrites a few methods from `CrudRepository`, such as `findAll`, `findAllById`, and `saveAll` to return `List` instead of `Iterable`.

We'll also add a series of query methods to the `UserRepository` interface, as shown in the following listing

Listing 4.7 The `UserRepository` interface with new methods

Path: Ch04/springdatajpa2/src/main/java/com/manning/javapersistence
➡ /springdatajpa/repositories/UserRepository.java

```java
public interface UserRepository extends JpaRepository<User, Long> {

    User findByUsername(String username);
    List<User> findAllByOrderByUsernameAsc();
    List<User> findByRegistrationDateBetween(LocalDate start,
    ➥ LocalDate end);
    List<User> findByUsernameAndEmail(String username, String email);
    List<User> findByUsernameOrEmail(String username, String email);
    List<User> findByUsernameIgnoreCase(String username);
    List<User> findByLevelOrderByUsernameDesc(int level);
    List<User> findByLevelGreaterThanEqual(int level);
    List<User> findByUsernameContaining(String text);
    List<User> findByUsernameLike(String text);
    List<User> findByUsernameStartingWith(String start);
    List<User> findByUsernameEndingWith(String end);
    List<User> findByActive(boolean active);
    List<User> findByRegistrationDateIn(Collection<LocalDate> dates);
    List<User> findByRegistrationDateNotIn(Collection<LocalDate> dates);

}
```

The purpose of these query methods is to retrieve information from the database. Spring Data JPA provides a query builder mechanism that will create behavior for the repository methods based on their names. Later we'll look at modifying queries, which modify the data they find; for now, we'll focus on queries whose purpose is to find information. This query mechanism removes prefixes and suffixes such as `find...By`, `get...By`, `query...By`, `read...By`, and `count...By` from the name of the method and parses the remainder of it.

You can declare methods containing expressions as `Distinct` to set a distinct clause; declare operators as `LessThan`, `GreaterThan`, `Between`, or `Like`; or declare compound conditions with `And` or `Or`. You can apply static ordering with the `OrderBy` clause in the name of the query method, referencing a property and providing a sorting direction (`Asc` or `Desc`). You can use `IgnoreCase` for properties that support such a clause. For deleting rows, you'd have to replace `find` with `delete` in the names of the methods. Also, Spring Data JPA will look at the return type of the method. If you want to find a `User` and return it in an `Optional` container, the method return type will be `Optional<User>`. A full list of possible return types, together with detailed explanations, can be found in appendix D of the Spring Data JPA reference documentation (http://mng.bz/o51y).

The names of the methods need to follow the rules. If the method naming is wrong (for example, the entity property does not match in the query method), you will get an error when the application context is loaded. Table 4.1 describes the essential keywords that Spring Data JPA supports and how each method name is transposed in JPQL. For a more comprehensive list, see appendix B at the end of this book.

Table 4.1   Essential Spring Data JPA keywords and the generated JPQL

Keyword	Example	Generated JPQL

Is, Equals	`findByUsername`
	`findByUsernameIs`
	`findByUsernameEquals`
		`. . .where`
		`e.username = ?1`

And	`findByUsernameAndRegistrationDate`	`. . .where`
		`e.username = ?1 and`
		`e.registrationdate = ?2`

Or	`findByUsernameOrRegistrationDate`	`. . . where`
		`e.username = ?1 or`
		`e.registrationdate = ?2`

LessThan	`findByRegistrationDateLessThan`	`. . . where` `e.registrationdate < ?1`
LessThanEqual	`findByRegistrationDateLessThanEqual`	`. . . where` `e.registrationdate <= ?1`
GreaterThan	`findByRegistrationDateGreaterThan`	`. . . where` `e.registrationdate > ?1`
GreaterThanEqual	`findByRegistrationDateGreaterThanEqual`	`. . . where` `e.registrationdate >= ?1`

Table 4.1   Essential Spring Data JPA keywords and the generated JPQL *(continued)*

Keyword	Example	Generated JPQL
Between	findByRegistrationDateBetween	. . . where e.registrationdate between ?1 and ?2
OrderBy	findByRegistrationDateOrderByUsernameDesc	. . . where e.registrationdate = ?1 order by e.username desc
Like	findByUsernameLike	. . . where e.username like ?1
NotLike	findByUsernameNotLike	. . . where e.username not like ?1
Before	findByRegistrationDateBefore	. . . where e.registrationdate < ?1
After	findByRegistrationDateAfter	. . . where e.registrationdate > ?1
Null, IsNull	findByRegistrationDate(Is)Null	. . . where e.registrationdate is null
NotNull, IsNotNull	findByRegistrationDate(Is)NotNull	. . . where e.registrationdate is not null
Not	findByUsernameNot	. . . where e.username <> ?1

As a base class for future tests, we'll write a `SpringDataJpaApplicationTests` abstract class.

Listing 4.8   The `SpringDataJpaApplicationTests` abstract class

```
Path: Ch04/springdatajpa2/src/test/java/com/manning/javapersistence
   /springdatajpa/SpringDataJpaApplicationTests.java

@SpringBootTest
@TestInstance(TestInstance.Lifecycle.PER_CLASS)
abstract class SpringDataJpaApplicationTests {
    @Autowired
    UserRepository userRepository;

    @BeforeAll
    void beforeAll() {
        userRepository.saveAll(generateUsers());
    }

    private static List<User> generateUsers() {
        List<User> users = new ArrayList<>();
```

```
        User john = new User("john", LocalDate.of(2020, Month.APRIL, 13));
        john.setEmail("john@somedomain.com");
        john.setLevel(1);
        john.setActive(true);

        //create and set a total of 10 users

        users.add(john);
        //add a total of 10 users to the list

        return users;
    }

    @AfterAll
    void afterAll() {                              E
        userRepository.deleteAll();
    }

}
```

Ⓐ The @SpringBootTest annotation, added by Spring Boot to the initially created class, tells Spring Boot to search the main configuration class (the @SpringBoot-Application annotated class, for instance) and create the ApplicationContext to be used in the tests. Recall that the @SpringBootApplication annotation added by Spring Boot to the class containing the main method will enable the Spring Boot autoconfiguration mechanism, enable the scan on the package where the application is located, and allow the registration of extra beans in the context.

Ⓑ Using the @TestInstance(TestInstance.Lifecycle.PER_CLASS) annotation, we ask JUnit 5 to create a single instance of the test class and reuse it for all test methods. This will allow us to make the @BeforeAll and @AfterAll annotated methods non-static and to directly use the autowired UserRepository instance field inside them.

Ⓒ Autowire a UserRepository instance. This autowiring is possible due to the @SpringBootApplication annotation, which enables the scan on the package where the application is located and registers the beans in the context.

Ⓓ The @BeforeAll annotated method will be executed once before executing all tests from a class that extends SpringDataJpaApplicationTests. This method will not be static (see Ⓑ above).

Ⓔ The @AfterAll annotated method will be executed once, after executing all tests from a class that extends SpringDataJpaApplicationTests. This method will not be static (see Ⓑ above).

The next tests will extend this class and use the already populated database. To test the methods that now belong to UserRepository, we'll create the FindUsersUsing-QueriesTest class and follow the same recipe for writing tests: call the repository method and verify its results.

Listing 4.9   The `FindUsersUsingQueriesTest` class

Path: Ch04/springdatajpa2/src/test/java/com/manning/javapersistence
➥ /springdatajpa/FindUsersUsingQueriesTest.java

```java
public class FindUsersUsingQueriesTest extends
    SpringDataJpaApplicationTests {

    @Test
    void testFindAll() {
        List<User> users = userRepository.findAll();
        assertEquals(10, users.size());
    }

    @Test
    void testFindUser() {
        User beth = userRepository.findByUsername("beth");
        assertEquals("beth", beth.getUsername());
    }

    @Test
    void testFindAllByOrderByUsernameAsc() {
        List<User> users = userRepository.findAllByOrderByUsernameAsc();
        assertAll(() -> assertEquals(10, users.size()),
                () -> assertEquals("beth", users.get(0).getUsername()),
                () -> assertEquals("stephanie",
                        users.get(users.size() - 1).getUsername()));
    }

    @Test
    void testFindByRegistrationDateBetween() {
        List<User> users = userRepository.findByRegistrationDateBetween(
                LocalDate.of(2020, Month.JULY, 1),
                LocalDate.of(2020, Month.DECEMBER, 31));
        assertEquals(4, users.size());
    }

    //more tests
}
```

4.5 Limiting query results, sorting, and paging

The `first` and `top` keywords (used equivalently) can limit the results of query methods. The `top` and `first` keywords may be followed by an optional numeric value to indicate the maximum result size to be returned. If this numeric value is missing, the result size will be 1.

`Pageable` is an interface for pagination information, but in practice we use the `PageRequest` class that implements it. This one can specify the page number, the page size, and the sorting criterion.

We'll add the methods shown in listing 4.10 to the `UserRepository` interface.

Listing 4.10   Limiting query results, sorting, and paging

Path: Ch04/springdatajpa2/src/main/java/com/manning/javapersistence
➡ /springdatajpa/repositories/UserRepository.java

```
User findFirstByOrderByUsernameAsc();
User findTopByOrderByRegistrationDateDesc();
Page<User> findAll(Pageable pageable);
List<User> findFirst2ByLevel(int level, Sort sort);
List<User> findByLevel(int level, Sort sort);
List<User> findByActive(boolean active, Pageable pageable);
```

Next we'll write the following tests to verify how these newly added methods work.

Listing 4.11   Testing limiting query results, sorting, and paging

Path: Ch04/springdatajpa2/src/test/java/com/manning/javapersistence
➡ /springdatajpa/FindUsersSortingAndPagingTest.java

```
public class FindUsersSortingAndPagingTest extends
            SpringDataJpaApplicationTests {

    @Test
    void testOrder() {

        User user1 = userRepository.findFirstByOrderByUsernameAsc();      Ⓐ
        User user2 = userRepository.findTopByOrderByRegistrationDateDesc();
        Page<User> userPage = userRepository.findAll(PageRequest.of(1, 3));
        List<User> users = userRepository.findFirst2ByLevel(2,            Ⓒ
                                        Sort.by("registrationDate"));

        assertAll(
                () -> assertEquals("beth", user1.getUsername()),
                () -> assertEquals("julius", user2.getUsername()),
                () -> assertEquals(2, users.size()),
                () -> assertEquals(3, userPage.getSize()),
                () -> assertEquals("beth", users.get(0).getUsername()),
                () -> assertEquals("marion", users.get(1).getUsername())
        );

    }

    @Test
    void testFindByLevel() {                                              Ⓓ
        Sort.TypedSort<User> user = Sort.sort(User.class);

        List<User> users = userRepository.findByLevel(3,                  Ⓔ
                user.by(User::getRegistrationDate).descending());
        assertAll(
                () -> assertEquals(2, users.size()),
                () -> assertEquals("james", users.get(0).getUsername())
        );

    }
```

Ⓑ

```
    @Test
    void testFindByActive() {
        List<User> users = userRepository.findByActive(true,
                PageRequest.of(1, 4, Sort.by("registrationDate")));
        assertAll(
                () -> assertEquals(4, users.size()),
                () -> assertEquals("burk", users.get(0).getUsername())
        );

    }
}
```

Ⓐ The first test will find the first user by ascending order of the username and the second user by descending order of the registration date.

Ⓑ Find all users, split them into pages, and return page number 1 of size 3 (the page numbering starts with 0).

Ⓒ Find the first two users with level 2, ordered by registration date.

Ⓓ The second test will define a sorting criterion on the User class. Sort.TypedSort extends Sort and can use method handles to define the properties to sort by.

Ⓔ Find users of level 3 and sort by registration date, descending.

Ⓕ The third test will find the active users sorted by registration date, split them into pages, and return page number 1 of size 4 (the page numbering starts with 0).

4.6   Streaming results

Query methods returning more than one result can use standard Java interfaces such as Iterable, List, Set. Additionally, Spring Data supports Streamable, which can be used as an alternative to Iterable or any collection type. You can concatenate Streamables and directly filter and map over the elements.

We'll add the following methods to the UserRepository interface.

Listing 4.12   Adding methods that return Streamable in the UserRepository interface

```
Path: Ch04/springdatajpa2/src/main/java/com/manning/javapersistence
➡ /springdatajpa/repositories/UserRepository.java

Streamable<User> findByEmailContaining(String text);
Streamable<User> findByLevel(int level);
```

We'll write the following tests to verify that these newly added methods work.

Listing 4.13   Testing methods that return Streamable

```
Path: Ch04/springdatajpa2/src/test/java/com/manning/javapersistence
➡ /springdatajpa/QueryResultsTest.java

@Test
```

```
void testStreamable() {
    try(Stream<User> result =
            userRepository.findByEmailContaining("someother")    Ⓐ
            .and(userRepository.findByLevel(2))     Ⓑ
            .stream().distinct())   {      Ⓒ
        assertEquals(6, result.count());    Ⓓ
    }
}
```

Ⓐ The test will call the findByEmailContaining method, searching for emails containing "someother."

Ⓑ The test will concatenate the resulting Streamable with the Streamable providing the users of level 2.

Ⓒ It will transform this into a stream and will keep the distinct users. The stream is given as a resource of the try block, so it will automatically be closed. An alternative is to explicitly call the close() method. Otherwise, the stream would keep the underlying connection to the database.

Ⓓ Check that the resulting stream contains six users.

4.7   *The @Query annotation*

With the @Query annotation, you can create a method and then write a custom query on it. When you use the @Query annotation, the method name does not need to follow any naming convention. The custom query can be parameterized, identifying the parameters by position or by name, and binding these names in the query with the @Param annotation. The @Query annotation can generate native queries with the nativeQuery flag set to true. You should be aware, however, that native queries can affect the portability of the application. To sort the results, you can use a Sort object. The properties you order by must resolve to a query property or a query alias.

Spring Data JPA supports Spring Expression Language (SpEL) expressions in queries defined using the @Query annotation, and Spring Data JPA supports the entityName variable. In a query such as select e from #{#entityName} e, entityName is resolved based on the @Entity annotation. In our case, in UserRepository extends JpaRepository<User, Long>, entityName will resolve to User.

We'll add the following methods to the UserRepository interface.

Listing 4.14   Limiting query results, sorting, and paging

Path: Ch04/springdatajpa2/src/main/java/com/manning/javapersistence
➥ /springdatajpa/repositories/UserRepository.java

```
@Query("select count(u) from User u where u.active = ?1")     Ⓐ
int findNumberOfUsersByActivity(boolean active);

@Query("select u from User u where u.level = :level
➥ and u.active = :active")
List<User> findByLevelAndActive(@Param("level") int level,     Ⓑ
                                @Param("active") boolean active);
```

```
@Query(value = "SELECT COUNT(*) FROM USERS WHERE ACTIVE = ?1",
               nativeQuery = true)
int findNumberOfUsersByActivityNative(boolean active);
```
C

```
@Query("select u.username, LENGTH(u.email) as email_length from
       #{#entityName} u where u.username like %?1%")
List<Object[]> findByAsArrayAndSort(String text, Sort sort);
```
D

A The `findNumberOfUsersByActivity` method will return the number of active users.

B The `findByLevelAndActive` method will return the users with the `level` and `active` status given as named parameters. The `@Param` annotation will match the `:level` parameter of the query with the `level` argument of the method and the `:active` parameter of the query with the `active` argument of the method. This is especially useful when you change the order of the parameters from the signature of the method and the query is not updated.

C The `findNumberOfUsersByActivityNative` method will return the number of users with a given `active` status. Setting the `nativeQuery` flag to `true` indicates that, unlike the previous queries, which are written with JPQL, this query is written using a native SQL that's specific to the database.

D The `findByAsArrayAndSort` method will return a list of arrays, with each array containing the `username` and the length of the `email`, after filtering based on the `username`. The second `Sort` parameter will allow you to order the result of the query based on different criteria.

We'll write the tests for these query methods, which are pretty straightforward. We'll discuss only the test written for the fourth query method, which allows a few variations of the sorting criterion.

Listing 4.15 Testing the query methods

Path: Ch04/springdatajpa2/src/test/java/com/manning/javapersistence
➡ /springdatajpa/QueryResultsTest.java

```
public class QueryResultsTest extends SpringDataJpaApplicationTests {

    // testing the first 3 query methods

    @Test
    void testFindByAsArrayAndSort() {
        List<Object[]> usersList1 =
            userRepository.findByAsArrayAndSort("ar", Sort.by("username"));     A
        List<Object[]> usersList2 =
            userRepository.findByAsArrayAndSort("ar",
                Sort.by("email_length").descending());                          B
        List<Object[]> usersList3 = userRepository.findByAsArrayAndSort(
            "ar", JpaSort.unsafe("LENGTH(u.email)"));                           C
```

```
        assertAll(
                () -> assertEquals(2, usersList1.size()),
                () -> assertEquals("darren", usersList1.get(0)[0]),
                () -> assertEquals(21, usersList1.get(0)[1]),
                () -> assertEquals(2, usersList2.size()),
                () -> assertEquals("marion", usersList2.get(0)[0]),
                () -> assertEquals(26, usersList2.get(0)[1]),
                () -> assertEquals(2, usersList3.size()),
                () -> assertEquals("darren", usersList3.get(0)[0]),
                () -> assertEquals(21, usersList3.get(0)[1])
        );
    }
}
```

Ⓐ The `findByAsArrayAndSort` method will return the users whose `username` is like `%ar%`, and it will order them by `username`.

Ⓑ The `findByAsArrayAndSort` method will return the users whose `username` is like `%ar%`, and it will order them by `email_length`, descending. Note that the `email_length` alias needed to be specified inside the query to be used for ordering.

Ⓒ The `findByAsArrayAndSort` method will return the users whose `username` is like `%ar%`, and it will order them by `LENGTH(u.email)`. `JpaSort` is a class that extends `Sort`, and it can use something other than property references and aliases for sorting. The `unsafe` property handling means that the provided String is not necessarily a property or an alias but can be an arbitrary expression inside the query.

If the method naming is wrong for any of the previous methods that follow the Spring Data JPA naming conventions (for example, the entity property does not match in the query method), you will get an error when the application context is loaded. If you are using the `@Query` annotation and the query you wrote is wrong, you will get an error at runtime when executing that method. Thus, the `@Query` annotated methods are more flexible, but they also provide less safety.

4.8 *Projections*

Not all attributes of an entity are always needed, so we may sometimes access only some of them. For example, the frontend may reduce I/O and display only the information that will be of interest to the end user. Consequently, instead of returning instances of the root entity managed by the repository, you may want to create projections based on certain attributes of those entities. Spring Data JPA can shape return types to selectively return attributes of entities.

An interface-based projection requires the creation of an interface that declares getter methods for the properties to be included in the projection. Such an interface can also compute specific values using the `@Value` annotation and SpEL expressions. By executing queries at runtime, the execution engine creates proxy instances of the interface for each returned element and forwards the calls to the exposed methods to the target object.

We'll create a `Projection` class and add `UserSummary` as a nested interface. We'll group the projections, as they are logically connected.

Listing 4.16   Interface-based projection

Path: Ch04/springdatajpa2/src/main/java/com/manning/javapersistence
➡ /springdatajpa/model/Projection.java

```
public class Projection {

    public interface UserSummary {        Ⓐ

        String getUsername();            ⟵┐

        @Value("#{target.username} #{target.email}")   Ⓑ
        String getInfo();

    }
}
```

Ⓐ The `getUsername` method will return the `username` field.

Ⓑ The `getInfo` method is annotated with the `@Value` annotation and will return the concatenation of the `username` field, a space, and the `email` field.

How should we approach projections in practice? If we include only methods such as Ⓐ in listing 4.16, we'll create a closed projection—this is an interface whose getters all correspond to properties of the target entity. When you're working with a closed projection, the query execution can be optimized by Spring Data JPA because all the properties needed by the projection proxy are known from the beginning.

If we include methods such as Ⓑ, we create an open projection, which is more flexible. However, Spring Data JPA will not be able to optimize the query execution, because the SpEL expression is evaluated at runtime and may include any properties or combination of properties of the entity root.

In general, you should use projections when you need to provide limited information and not expose the full entity. For performance reasons, you should prefer closed projections whenever you know from the beginning which information you want to return. If you have a query that returns the full object, and you have a similar query that only returns a projection, you can use alternate naming conventions, such as naming one method `find...By` and the other method `get...By`.

A class-based projection requires the creation of a data transfer object (DTO) class that declares the properties to be included in the projection and the getter methods. Using a class-based projection is similar to using interface-based projections. However, Spring Data JPA doesn't need to create proxy classes for managing projections. Spring Data JPA will instantiate the class that declares the projection, and the properties to be included are determined by the parameter names of the constructor of the class.

The following listing adds `UsernameOnly` as a nested class of the `Projection` class.

Listing 4.17   Class-based projection

Path: Ch04/springdatajpa2/src/main/java/com/manning/javapersistence
➥ /springdatajpa/model/Projection.java

```java
public class Projection {

    // . . .

    public static class UsernameOnly {
        private String username;

        public UsernameOnly(String username) {
            this.username = username;
        }

        public String getUsername() {
            return username;
        }

    }

}
```

Ⓐ The `UsernameOnly` class
Ⓑ The username field
Ⓒ The declared constructor
Ⓓ The username field exposed through a getter

The methods that we'll add to the `UserRepository` interface will look like these:

Path: Ch04/springdatajpa2/src/main/java/com/manning/javapersistence
➥ /springdatajpa/repositories/UserRepository.java

```java
List<Projection.UserSummary> findByRegistrationDateAfter(LocalDate date);
List<Projection.UsernameOnly> findByEmail(String username);
```

These repository methods use the same naming conventions we applied in the previous examples in this section, and they know their return types from compile time as collections of projection types. However, we can generify the return types of repository methods, which will make them dynamic. We'll add a new method to the `UserRepository` interface:

Path: Ch04/springdatajpa2/src/main/java/com/manning/javapersistence
➥ /springdatajpa/repositories/UserRepository.java

```java
<T> List<T> findByEmail(String username, Class<T> type);
```

We'll write the tests for these query methods using projections.

Listing 4.18   Testing query methods using projections

Path: Ch04/springdatajpa2/src/test/java/com/manning/javapersistence
➡ /springdatajpa/ProjectionTest.java

```java
public class ProjectionTest extends SpringDataJpaApplicationTests {

    @Test
    void testProjectionUsername() {

        List<Projection.UsernameOnly> users =
            userRepository.findByEmail("john@somedomain.com");        Ⓐ

        assertAll(
                () -> assertEquals(1, users.size()),
                () -> assertEquals("john", users.get(0).getUsername())   Ⓑ
        );
    }

    @Test
    void testProjectionUserSummary() {
        List<Projection.UserSummary> users =
            userRepository.findByRegistrationDateAfter(        Ⓒ
                LocalDate.of(2021, Month.FEBRUARY, 1));

        assertAll(
                () -> assertEquals(1, users.size()),
                () -> assertEquals("julius", users.get(0).getUsername()),   Ⓓ
                () -> assertEquals("julius julius@someotherdomain.com",
                                    users.get(0).getInfo())
        );
    }

    @Test
    void testDynamicProjection() {
        List<Projection.UsernameOnly> usernames =
                userRepository.findByEmail("mike@somedomain.com",        Ⓔ
                Projection.UsernameOnly.class);
        List<User> users =
        ➡ userRepository.findByEmail("mike@somedomain.com",        Ⓕ
                User.class);

        assertAll(
                () -> assertEquals(1, usernames.size()),
                () -> assertEquals("mike", usernames.get(0).getUsername()),   Ⓖ
                () -> assertEquals(1, users.size()),
                () -> assertEquals("mike", users.get(0).getUsername())
        );
    }
}
```

Ⓐ The `findByEmail` method will return a list of `Projection.UsernameOnly` instances.

Ⓑ Verify the assertions.

Ⓒ The `findByRegistrationDateAfter` method will return a list of `Projection.UserSummary` instances.

Ⓓ Verify the assertions.

Ⓔ This `findByEmail` method provides a dynamic projection. It will return a list of `Projection.UsernameOnly` instances.

Ⓕ This `findByEmail` method may also return a list of `User` instances, depending on the class that it is generified by.

Ⓖ Verify the assertions.

4.9 *Modifying queries*

You can define modifying methods with the `@Modifying` annotation. For example, `INSERT`, `UPDATE`, and `DELETE` queries, or DDL statements, modify the content of the database. The `@Query` annotation will have the modifying query as an argument, and it may need binding parameters. Such a method must also be annotated with `@Transactional` or be run from a programmatically managed transaction. Modifying queries have the advantage of clearly emphasizing which column they address, and they may include conditions, so they can make the code clearer, compared to persisting or deleting the whole object. Also, changing a limited number of columns in the database will execute more quickly.

Spring Data JPA can also generate delete queries based on method names. The mechanism works much like the examples in table 4.1, but replacing the `find` keyword with `delete`.

We'll add the following methods to the `UserRepository` interface.

Listing 4.19   Adding modifying methods to the `UserRepository` interface

Path: Ch04/springdatajpa2/src/main/java/com/manning/javapersistence
➡ /springdatajpa/repositories/UserRepository.java

```
@Modifying
@Transactional
@Query("update User u set u.level = ?2 where u.level = ?1")     Ⓐ
int updateLevel(int oldLevel, int newLevel);


@Transactional                    Ⓑ
int deleteByLevel(int level);


@Transactional
@Modifying
@Query("delete from User u where u.level = ?1")                 Ⓒ
int deleteBulkByLevel(int level);
```

Ⓐ The updateLevel method will change level for users with the oldLevel parameter and set it to newLevel, as the argument of the @Query annotation indicates. The method is also annotated with @Modifying and @Transactional.

Ⓑ The deleteByLevel method will generate a query based on the method name; it will remove all users with the level given as a parameter. The method is annotated with @Transactional. @Modifying isn't necessary in this case, since the query is generated by the framework.

Ⓒ The deleteBulkByLevel method will remove all users with the level given as a parameter, as the argument of the @Query annotation indicates. The method is also annotated with @Modifying and @Transactional.

What is the difference between the deleteByLevel and deleteBulkByLevel methods? The first one runs a query, and it will then remove the returned instances one by one. If there are callback methods that control the lifecycle of each instance (for example, a method to be run when a user is removed), they will be executed. The second method will remove the users in bulk, executing a single JPQL query. No User instance (not even the ones that are already loaded in memory) will execute lifecycle callback methods.

We can now write tests for the modifying methods.

Listing 4.20 Testing modifying methods

```
Path: Ch04/springdatajpa2/src/test/java/com/manning/javapersistence
  /springdatajpa/ModifyQueryTest.java

@Test
void testModifyLevel() {
    int updated = userRepository.updateLevel(5, 4);
    List<User> users = userRepository.findByLevel(4, Sort.by("username"));

    assertAll(
            () -> assertEquals(1, updated),
            () -> assertEquals(3, users.size()),
            () -> assertEquals("katie", users.get(1).getUsername())
    );
}
```

We'll also write tests for the deleting methods.

Listing 4.21 Testing deleting methods

```
Path: Ch04/springdatajpa2/src/test/java/com/manning/javapersistence
  /springdatajpa/DeleteQueryTest.java

@Test
void testDeleteByLevel() {
    int deleted = userRepository.deleteByLevel(2);
    List<User> users = userRepository.findByLevel(2, Sort.by("username"));
```

```
        assertEquals(0, users.size());
}

@Test
void testDeleteBulkByLevel() {
    int deleted = userRepository.deleteBulkByLevel(2);
    List<User> users = userRepository.findByLevel(2, Sort.by("username"));
    assertEquals(0, users.size());
}
```

4.10   *Query by Example*

Query by Example (QBE) is a querying technique that does not require you to write classical queries to include entities and properties. It allows dynamic query creation and consists of three pieces: a probe, an `ExampleMatcher`, and an `Example`.

The probe is a domain object with already-set properties. The `ExampleMatcher` provides the rules for matching particular properties. An `Example` puts the probe and the `ExampleMatcher` together and generates the query. Multiple `Examples` may reuse a single `ExampleMatcher`.

These are the most appropriate use cases for QBE:

- When you are decoupling the code from the underlying data store API.
- When there are frequent changes to the internal structure of the domain objects, and they aren't propagated to the existing queries.
- When you are building a set of static or dynamic constraints to query the repository.

QBE has a couple of limitations:

- It only supports starting/ending/containing regex matching for String properties, and exact matching for other types.
- It does not support nested or grouped property constraints, such as username = ?0 or (username = ?1 and email = ?2).

We won't add any more methods to the `UserRepository` interface. We'll only write tests to build the probe, the `ExampleMatchers`, and the `Examples`.

> **Listing 4.22   Query By Example tests**

Path: Ch04/springdatajpa2/src/test/java/com/manning/javapersistence
➥ /springdatajpa/QueryByExampleTest.java

```
public class QueryByExampleTest extends SpringDataJpaApplicationTests {

    @Test
    void testEmailWithQueryByExample() {
        User user = new User();
        user.setEmail("@someotherdomain.com");
```
Ⓐ

```
        ExampleMatcher matcher = ExampleMatcher.matching()
                .withIgnorePaths("level", "active")
                .withMatcher("email", match -> match.endsWith());

        Example<User> example = Example.of(user, matcher);

        List<User> users = userRepository.findAll(example);

        assertEquals(4, users.size());
    }

    @Test
    void testUsernameWithQueryByExample() {
        User user = new User();
        user.setUsername("J");

        ExampleMatcher matcher = ExampleMatcher.matching()
                .withIgnorePaths("level", "active")
                .withStringMatcher(ExampleMatcher.StringMatcher.STARTING)
                .withIgnoreCase();

        Example<User> example = Example.of(user, matcher);

        List<User> users = userRepository.findAll(example);

        assertEquals(3, users.size());
    }
}
```

A Initialize a `User` instance and set up an `email` for it. This will represent the probe.

B Create the `ExampleMatcher` with the help of the builder pattern. Any `null` reference property will be ignored by the matcher. However, we need to explicitly ignore the `level` and `active` properties, which are primitives. If they were not ignored, they would be included in the matcher with their default values (0 for `level` and `false` for `active`) and would change the generated query. We'll configure the matcher condition so that the `email` property will end with a given string.

C Create an `Example` that puts the probe and `ExampleMatcher` together and generates the query. The query will search for users that have an `email` property ending with the string defining the `email` of the probe.

D Execute the query to find all users matching the probe.

E Verify that there are four users of this kind.

F Initialize a `User` instance and set up a `name` for it. This will represent the second probe.

G Create the `ExampleMatcher` with the help of the builder pattern. Any `null` reference property will be ignored by the matcher. Again, we need to explicitly ignore the `level` and `active` properties, which are primitives. We configure the matcher condition so that the match will be made on starting strings for the configured properties (the `username` property from the probe, in our case).

H Create an `Example` that puts the probe and the `ExampleMatcher` together and generates the query. The query will search for users having a `username` property that starts with the string defining the `username` of the probe.

I Execute the query to find all users matching the probe.

J Verify that there are six users of this kind.

To emphasize the importance of ignoring the default primitive properties, we'll compare the generated queries with and without the calls to the `withIgnorePaths` `("level", "active")` methods. For the first test, this is the query generated with the call to the `withIgnorePaths("level", "active")` method:

```
select user0_.id as id1_0_, user0_.active as active2_0_, user0_.email as
➥ email3_0_, user0_.level as level4_0_, user0_.registration_date as
➥ registra5_0_, user0_.username as username6_0_ from users user0_ where
➥ user0_.email like ? escape ?
```

This is the query generated without the call to the `withIgnorePaths("level", "active")` method:

```
select user0_.id as id1_0_, user0_.active as active2_0_, user0_.email as
➥ email3_0_, user0_.level as level4_0_, user0_.registration_date as
➥ registra5_0_, user0_.username as username6_0_ from users user0_ where
➥ user0_.active=? and (user0_.email like ? escape ?) and user0_.level=0
```

For the second test, this is the query generated with the call to the `withIgnore-Paths("level", "active")` method:

```
select user0_.id as id1_0_, user0_.active as active2_0_, user0_.email as
➥ email3_0_, user0_.level as level4_0_, user0_.registration_date as
➥ registra5_0_, user0_.username as username6_0_ from users user0_ where
➥ lower(user0_.username) like ? escape ?
```

This is the query generated without the call to the `withIgnorePaths("level", "active")` method:

```
select user0_.id as id1_0_, user0_.active as active2_0_, user0_.email as
➥ email3_0_, user0_.level as level4_0_, user0_.registration_date as
➥ registra5_0_, user0_.username as username6_0_ from users user0_ where
➥ user0_.active=? and user0_.level=0 and (lower(user0_.username) like ?
➥ escape ?)
```

Note the conditions added on primitive properties when the `withIgnore-Paths("level", "active")` method was removed:

```
user0_.active=? and user0_.level=0
```

This will change the query result.

Summary

- You can create and configure a Spring Data JPA project using Spring Boot.
- You can define and use a series of query methods to access repositories by using the Spring Data JPA query builder mechanisms.
- Spring Data JPA provides capabilities for limiting query results, sorting, paging, and streaming the results.
- You can use the `@Query` annotation to define both non-native and native custom queries.
- You can implement projections to shape the return types and selectively return attributes of entities, and you can create and use modifying queries to update and delete entities.
- The Query by Example (QBE) querying technique allows for dynamic query creation and consists of three pieces: a probe, an `ExampleMatcher`, and an `Example`.

Part 2

Mapping strategies

This part of the book is all about ORM, from classes and properties to tables and columns. The knowledge you will gain here is essential, whether you work with Hibernate or Spring Data JPA as your persistence framework. Chapter 5 starts with regular class and property mappings and explains how you can map fine-grained Java domain models. Next, in chapter 6, you'll see how to map basic properties and embeddable components, and how to control mapping between Java and SQL types. In chapter 7, you'll map inheritance hierarchies of entities to the database using four basic inheritance-mapping strategies; you'll also map polymorphic associations. Chapter 8 is all about mapping collections and entity associations: you'll map persistent collections, collections of basic and embeddable types, and simple many-to-one and one-to-many entity associations. Chapter 9 dives deeper with advanced entity association mappings like mapping one-to-one entity associations, one-to-many mapping options, and many-to-many and ternary entity relationships.

After reading this part of the book, you'll be ready to create even the most complex mappings quickly and with the right strategy. You'll understand how the problem of inheritance mapping can be solved and how to map collections and associations.

5
Mapping persistent classes

This chapter covers
- Understanding entities and value types
- Mapping entity classes with identity
- Controlling entity-level mapping options

This chapter presents some fundamental mapping options and explains how to map entity classes to SQL tables. This is essential knowledge for structuring classes in an application, no matter whether you work with Hibernate, Spring Data JPA, or some other persistence framework that implement the JPA specification. We'll demonstrate and analyze how you can handle database identity and primary keys, and how you can use various other metadata settings to customize how Hibernate or Spring Data JPA using Hibernate as a persistence provider will load and store instances of your domain model classes.

Spring Data JPA, as a data access abstraction, sits on top of a JPA provider (such as Hibernate) and will significantly reduce the boilerplate code required to interact with the database. That is why, once the mapping of persistent classes is made, it can be used both from Hibernate and from Spring Data JPA. Our examples will demonstrate this, and all our mapping examples will use JPA annotations.

Before we look at mapping, though, we'll define the essential distinction between entities and value types and explain how you should approach the object/relational mapping of your domain model. The role of the engineer is to make the connection between the *application domain*, which is the environment of the problem that the system needs to address, and the *solution domain*, which is the software and the technologies that will build this system. In figure 5.1, the application domain is represented by the application domain model (the real entities), while the solution domain is represented by the system model (the objects from the software application).

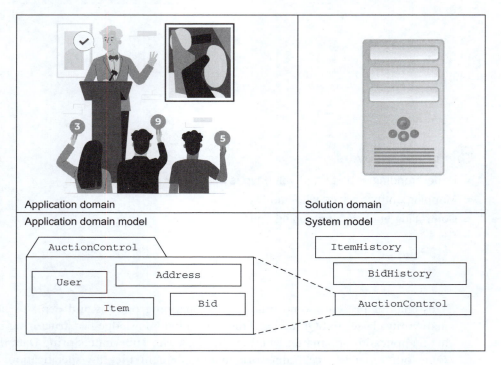

Figure 5.1   The different domains and models to be connected

5.1   *Understanding entities and value types*

When you look at your domain model, you'll notice a difference between classes: some of the types seem more important, representing first-class business objects (the term *object* is used here in its natural sense). Some examples are the `Item`, `Category`, and `User` classes: these are entities in the real world that you're trying to represent (refer to figure 3.3 for a view of the example domain model). Other types present in your domain model, such as `Address`, seem less important. In this section, we'll look at what it means to use fine-grained domain models and make the distinction between entities and value types.

5.1.1   *Fine-grained domain models*

A major objective of Hibernate and Spring Data JPA using Hibernate as a persistence provider is providing support for fine-grained and rich domain models. It's one reason we work with POJOs (Plain Old Java Objects)—regular Java objects not bound to any framework. In crude terms, *fine-grained* means having more classes than tables.

For example, a user may have a home address in your domain model. In the database, you may have a single USERS table with the columns HOME_STREET, HOME_CITY, and HOME_ZIPCODE. (Remember the problem of SQL types we discussed in section 1.2.1?) In the domain model, you could use the same approach, representing the address as three string-valued properties of the User class. But it's much better to model this using an Address class, where User has a homeAddress property. This domain model achieves improved cohesion and greater code reuse, and it's more understandable than SQL with inflexible type systems.

JPA emphasizes the usefulness of fine-grained classes for implementing type safety and behavior. For example, many people model an email address as a string-valued property of User. However, a more sophisticated approach is to define an EmailAddress class, which adds higher-level semantics and behavior. It may provide a prepareMail() method (but it shouldn't have a sendMail() method, because you don't want your domain model classes to depend on the mail subsystem).

This granularity problem leads us to a distinction of central importance in ORM. In Java, all classes are of equal standing—all instances have their own identity and lifecycle. When you introduce persistence, some instances may not have their own identity and lifecycle but instead depend on others. Let's walk through an example.

5.1.2   *Defining application concepts*

Suppose two people live in the same house, and they both register user accounts in CaveatEmptor. Let's call them John and Jane. An instance of User represents each account. Because you want to load, save, and delete these User instances independently, User is an entity class and not a value type. Finding entity classes is easy.

The User class has a homeAddress property; it's an association with the Address class. Do both User instances have a runtime reference to the same Address instance, or does each User instance have a reference to its own Address? Does it matter that John and Jane live in the same house?

In figure 5.2, you can see how two User instances share a single Address instance representing their home address (this is a UML object diagram, not a class diagram). If Address is supposed to support shared runtime references, it's an entity type. The Address instance has its own life. You can't delete it when John removes his User account—Jane might still have a reference to the Address.

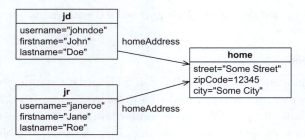

Figure 5.2   Two User instances have a reference to a single Address.

Now let's look at the alternative model, where each User has a reference to its own homeAddress instance, as shown in figure 5.3. In this case, you can make an instance of Address dependent on an instance of User: you make it a value type. When John removes his User account, you can safely delete his Address instance. Nobody else will hold a reference to it.

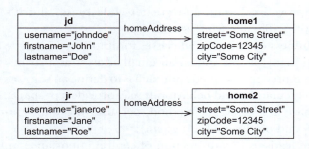

Figure 5.3   Two User instances each have their own dependent Address.

Hence, we can make the following essential distinction:

- *Entity type*—You can retrieve an instance of an *entity type* using its persistent identity; for example, a User, Item, or Category instance. A reference to an entity instance (a pointer in the JVM) is persisted as a reference in the database (a foreign key–constrained value). An entity instance has its own lifecycle; it can exist independently of any other entity. You map selected classes of your domain model as entity types.
- *Value type*—An instance of a *value type* has no persistent identifier property; it belongs to an entity instance, and its lifespan is bound to the owning entity instance. A value-type instance doesn't support shared references. You can map your own domain model classes as value types; for example, Address and MonetaryAmount.

If you read the JPA specification, you'll find the same concepts, but value types are called *basic property types* or *embeddable classes* in JPA. We'll come back to this in the next chapter.

Identifying entities and value types in your domain model isn't an ad hoc task but follows a certain procedure.

5.1.3   *Distinguishing entities and value types*

You may find it helpful to add stereotype information to your UML class diagrams so you can immediately recognize entities and value types (stereotypes are a UML extensibility mechanism). This practice will also force you to think about this distinction for all your classes, which is the first step toward an optimal mapping and well-performing persistence layer. Figure 5.4 shows an example, with the stereotype information in the double angle brackets.

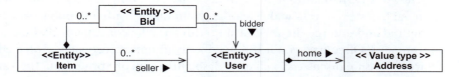

Figure 5.4   Diagramming stereotypes for entities and value types

The `Item` and `User` classes are obvious entities. They each have their own identity, their instances have references from many other instances (shared references), and they have independent lifespans.

Marking `Address` as a value type is also easy: a single `User` instance references a particular `Address` instance. You know this because the association has been created as a composition, with the `User` instance being fully responsible for the lifecycle of the referenced `Address` instance. Therefore, `Address` instances can't be referenced by anyone else and don't need their own identity.

The `Bid` class could be a problem. In object-oriented modeling, this is marked as a composition (the association between `Item` and `Bid` with the full diamond). Composition is a type of association where an object can only exist as part of a container. If the container is destroyed, then the included object is also destroyed. Thus, an `Item` is the owner of its `Bid` instances and holds a collection of references. The `Bid` instances cannot exist without the `Item`. At first, this seems reasonable, because bids in an auction system are useless when the item they were made for disappears.

But what if a future extension of the domain model requires a `User#bids` collection containing all bids made by a particular `User`? Right now, the association between `Bid` and `User` is unidirectional; a `Bid` has a `bidder` reference. What if this was bidirectional?

In that case, you would have to deal with possible shared references to `Bid` instances, so the `Bid` class would need to be an entity. It has a dependent lifecycle, but it must have its own identity to support (future) shared references.

You'll often find this kind of mixed behavior, but your first reaction should be to make everything a value-typed class and promote it to an entity only when absolutely necessary. `Bid` is a value type because its identity is defined by `Item` and `User`. This does not necessarily mean that it won't live in its own table. Try to simplify your associations; persistent collections, for example, frequently add complexity without offering any advantages. Instead of mapping the `Item#bids` and `User#bids` collections, you can write queries to obtain all the bids for an Item and those made by a particular User. The associations in the UML diagram will point from the Bid *to* the Item and User, unidirectionally, and not the other way. The stereotype on the Bid class would then be <<Value type>>. We'll come back to this point in chapter 8.

Next, you can take your domain model diagram and implement POJOs for all entities and value types. You'll have to take care of three things:

- *Shared references*—Avoid shared references to value type instances when you write your POJO classes. For example, make sure only one User can reference an Address. You can make Address immutable with no public setUser() method and enforce the relationship with a public constructor that has a User argument. Of course, you'll still need a no-argument, probably protected constructor, as we discussed in chapter 3, so Hibernate or Spring Data JPA can also create an instance.
- *Lifecycle dependencies*—If a User is deleted, its Address dependency will have to be deleted as well. Persistence metadata will include cascading rules for all such dependencies, so Hibernate, Spring Data JPA, or the database can take care of removing the obsolete Address. You must design your application procedures and user interface to respect and expect such dependencies—write your domain model POJOs accordingly.
- *Identity*—Entity classes need an identifier property in almost all cases. Value type classes (and, of course, JDK classes such as String and Integer) don't have an identifier property because instances are identified through the owning entity.

We'll come back to references, associations, and lifecycle rules when we discuss more advanced mappings in later chapters. Object identity and identifier properties are our next topic.

5.2   *Mapping entities with identity*

Mapping entities with identity requires you to understand Java identity and equality. Once you know that, we can walk through an entity class example and its mapping, discuss terms like *database identity*, and look at how JPA manages identity. After that, we'll be able to dig in deeper and select a primary key, configure key generators, and finally go through identifier generator strategies.

5.2.1   *Understanding Java identity and equality*

Java developers understand the difference between Java object identity and equality. Object identity (==) is a notion defined by the Java virtual machine. Two references are identical if they point to the same memory location.

Object equality, on the other hand, is a notion defined by a class's equals() method, sometimes also referred to as *equivalence*. Equivalence means two different (non-identical) instances have the same value—the same state. If you have a stack of freshly printed books of the same kind, and you have to choose one of them, it means you will have to choose one from several non-identical but equivalent objects.

Two different instances of `String` are equal if they represent the same sequence of characters, even though each has its own location in the memory space of the virtual machine. (If you're a Java guru, we acknowledge that `String` is a special case. Assume we used a different class to make the same point.)

Persistence complicates this picture. With object/relational persistence, a persistent instance is an in-memory representation of a particular row (or rows) of a database table (or tables). Along with Java identity and equality, we define *database identity*. You now have three methods for distinguishing references:

- *Object identify*—Objects are identical if they occupy the same memory location in the JVM. This can be checked with the a == b operator. This concept is known as *object identity*.
- *Object equality*—Objects are equal if they have the same state, as defined by the `a.equals(Object b)` method. Classes that don't explicitly override this method inherit the implementation defined by `java.lang.Object`, which compares object identity with ==. This concept is known as *object equality*. As you'll probably recall, the properties of object equality are reflexivity, symmetry, and transitivity. One thing they imply is that if a == b, then both `a.equals(b)` and `b.equals(a)` should be true.
- *Database identity*—Objects stored in a relational database are identical if they share the same table and primary key value. This concept, mapped into the Java space, is known as *database identity*.

We now need to look at how database identity relates to object identity and how we can express database identity in the mapping metadata. As an example, you'll map an entity of a domain model.

5.2.2 A first entity class and mapping

The `@Entity` annotation isn't enough to map a persistent class. You'll also need an `@Id` annotation, as shown in the following listing (see the `generator` folder for the source code).

> **NOTE** To execute the examples from the source code, you'll first need to run the Ch05.sql script.

Listing 5.1 Mapped `Item` entity class with an identifier property

```
Path: Ch05/generator/src/main/java/com/manning/javapersistence/ch05/model
➡ /Item.java

@Entity
public class Item {
    @Id
    @GeneratedValue(generator = "ID_GENERATOR")
```

```
    private Long id;
    public Long getId() {
        return id;
    }
}
```

This is the most basic entity class, marked as "persistence capable" with the `@Entity` annotation and with an `@Id` mapping for the database identifier property. The class maps by default to a table named `ITEM` in the database schema.

Every entity class has to have an `@Id` property; it's how JPA exposes database identity to the application. We haven't shown the identifier property in our diagrams, but we assume that each entity class has one. In our examples, we always name the identifier property `id`. This is a good practice for your own projects; use the same identifier property name for all your domain model entity classes. If you specify nothing else, this property maps to a primary key column named `ID` in the table in your database schema.

Hibernate and Spring Data JPA will use the field to access the identifier property value when loading and storing items, not getter or setter methods. Because `@Id` is on a field, Hibernate or Spring Data JPA will enable every field of the class as a persistent property by default. The rule in JPA is this: if `@Id` is on a field, the JPA provider will access fields of the class directly and consider all fields to be part of the persistent state by default. In our experience, field access is often a better choice than using an accessor, because it gives you more freedom for accessor method design.

Should you have a public getter method for the identifier property? Applications often use database identifiers as convenient handles for particular instances, even outside the persistence layer. For example, it's common for web applications to display the results of a search to the user as a list of summaries. When the user selects a particular element, the application may need to retrieve the selected item, and it's common to use a lookup by identifier for this purpose—you've probably already used identifiers this way, even in applications that rely on JDBC.

Should you have a setter method? Primary key values never change, so you shouldn't allow the identifier property value to be modified. Hibernate and Spring Data JPA using Hibernate as a provider won't update a primary key column, and you shouldn't expose a public identifier setter method on an entity.

The Java type of the identifier property, `java.lang.Long` in the previous example, depends on the primary key column type in the `ITEM` table and how key values are produced. This brings us to the `@GeneratedValue` annotation, and to primary keys in general.

5.2.3   *Selecting a primary key*

The database identifier of an entity is mapped to a table's primary key, so let's first get some background on primary keys without worrying about mappings. Take a step back and think about how you identify entities.

A *candidate key* is a column or set of columns that you could use to identify a particular row in a table. To become the primary key, a candidate key must satisfy the following requirements:

- The value of any candidate key column is never null. You can't identify something with data that is unknown, and there are no nulls in the relational model. Some SQL products allow you to define (composite) primary keys with nullable columns, so you must be careful.
- The value of the candidate key column (or columns) is a unique value for any row.
- The value of the candidate key column (or columns) never changes; it's immutable.

> **Must primary keys be immutable?**
> The relational model requires that a candidate key must be unique and irreducible (no subset of the key attributes has the uniqueness property). Beyond that, picking a candidate key as *the* primary key is a matter of taste. But Hibernate and Spring Data JPA expect a candidate key to be immutable when it's used as the primary key. Hibernate and Spring Data JPA with Hibernate as a provider don't support updating primary key values with an API; if you try to work around this requirement, you'll run into problems with Hibernate's caching and dirty-checking engine. If your database schema relies on updatable primary keys (and maybe uses ON UPDATE CASCADE foreign key constraints), you must change the schema before it will work with Hibernate or Spring Data JPA using Hibernate as provider.

If a table has only one identifying attribute, it becomes, by definition, the primary key. But several columns or combinations of columns may satisfy these properties for a particular table; you can choose between candidate keys to decide on the best primary key for the table. You should declare candidate keys that are not chosen as the primary key as unique keys in the database if their values are indeed unique (but maybe not immutable).

Many legacy SQL data models use natural primary keys. A *natural key* is a key with business meaning: an attribute or combination of attributes that is unique by virtue of its business semantics. Examples of natural keys are the US Social Security Number and Australian Tax File Number. Distinguishing natural keys is simple: if a candidate key attribute has meaning outside the database context, it's a natural key, regardless of whether it's automatically generated. Think about the application's users: if they refer to a key attribute when talking about and working with the application, it's a natural key: "Can you send me the pictures of item #A23-abc?"

Experience has shown that natural primary keys usually cause problems in the end. A good primary key must be unique, immutable, and never null. Few entity attributes satisfy these requirements, and some that do can't be efficiently indexed by SQL databases (although this is an implementation detail and shouldn't be the deciding factor for or against a particular key). You should also make certain that a candidate key definition never changes throughout the lifetime of the database. Changing the value (or even the definition) of a primary key and all foreign keys that refer to it is a frustrating task. Expect your database schema to survive decades, even if your application won't.

Furthermore, you can often only find natural candidate keys by combining several columns in a *composite* natural key. These composite keys, although certainly appropriate for some schema artifacts (like a link table in a many-to-many relationship), potentially make maintenance, ad hoc queries, and schema evolution much more difficult.

For these reasons, we strongly recommend that you add synthetic identifiers, also called *surrogate keys*. Surrogate keys have no business meaning—they have unique values generated by the database or application. Application users ideally won't see or refer to these key values; they're part of the system's internals. Introducing a surrogate key column is also appropriate in the common situation where there are no candidate keys. In other words, almost every table in your schema should have a dedicated surrogate primary key column with only this purpose.

There are several well-known approaches to generating surrogate key values. The aforementioned @GeneratedValue annotation is how you configure this.

5.2.4   *Configuring key generators*

The @Id annotation is required to mark the identifier property of an entity class. Without the @GeneratedValue next to it, the JPA provider assumes that you'll take care of creating and assigning an identifier value before you save an instance. We call this an *application-assigned* identifier. Assigning an entity identifier manually is necessary when you're dealing with a legacy database or natural primary keys.

Usually you'll want the system to generate a primary key value when you save an entity instance, so you can write the @GeneratedValue annotation next to @Id. JPA standardizes several value-generation strategies with the javax.persistence.GenerationType enum, which you select with @GeneratedValue(strategy = ...):

- GenerationType.AUTO—Hibernate (or Spring Data JPA using Hibernate as a persistence provider) picks an appropriate strategy, asking the SQL dialect of your configured database what is best. This is equivalent to @GeneratedValue() without any settings.
- GenerationType.SEQUENCE—Hibernate (or Spring Data JPA using Hibernate as a persistence provider) expects (and creates, if you use the tools) a sequence named HIBERNATE_SEQUENCE in your database. The sequence will be called separately before every INSERT, producing sequential numeric values.
- GenerationType.IDENTITY—Hibernate (or Spring Data JPA using Hibernate as a persistence provider) expects (and creates in table DDL) a special auto-incremented primary key column that automatically generates a numeric value on INSERT in the database.

- `GenerationType.TABLE`—Hibernate (or Spring Data JPA using Hibernate as a persistence provider) will use an extra table in your database schema that holds the next numeric primary key value, with one row for each entity class. This table will be read and updated before `INSERT`s. The default table name is `HIBERNATE_SEQUENCES` with the columns `SEQUENCE_NAME` and `NEXT_VALUE`.

Although `AUTO` seems convenient, you'll sometimes need more control over how IDs are created, so you usually should instead explicitly configure a primary key generation strategy. Most applications work with database sequences, but you may want to customize the name and other settings of the database sequence. Therefore, instead of picking one of the JPA strategies, you can map the identifier with `@GeneratedValue (generator = "ID_GENERATOR")`, as shown in listing 5.1. This is a *named* identifier generator; you are now free to set up the `ID_GENERATOR` configuration independently of your entity classes.

JPA has two built-in annotations you can use to configure named generators: `@javax .persistence.SequenceGenerator` and `@javax.persistence.TableGenerator`. With these annotations, you can create a named generator with your own sequence and table names. As usual with JPA annotations, you can unfortunately only use them at the top of a (maybe otherwise empty) class and not in a package-info.java file.

For this reason, and because the JPA annotations don't give you access to the full Hibernate feature set, we prefer the native `@org.hibernate.annotations.Generic-Generator` annotation as an alternative. It supports all Hibernate identifier generator strategies and their configuration details. Unlike the rather limited JPA annotations, you can use the Hibernate annotation in a package-info.java file, typically in the same package as your domain model classes. The following listing shows a recommended configuration, which can also be found in the `generator` folder.

Listing 5.2 Hibernate identifier generator configured as package-level metadata

Path: Ch05/generator/src/main/java/com/manning/javapersistence/ch05
➥ /package-info.java

```
@org.hibernate.annotations.GenericGenerator(
  name = "ID_GENERATOR",
  strategy = "enhanced-sequence",          ←Ⓐ
  parameters = {
    @org.hibernate.annotations.Parameter(
      name = "sequence_name",              ←Ⓑ
      value = "JPWHSD_SEQUENCE"
    ),
    @org.hibernate.annotations.Parameter(
      name = "initial_value",              ←Ⓒ
      value = "1000"
    )
})
```

A The enhanced-sequence strategy produces sequential numeric values. If your SQL dialect supports sequences, Hibernate (or Spring Data JPA using Hibernate as a persistence provider) will use an actual database sequence. If your DBMS doesn't support native sequences, Hibernate (or Spring Data JPA using Hibernate as a persistence provider) will manage and use an extra "sequence table," simulating the behavior of a sequence. This gives you real portability: the generator can always be called before performing an SQL INSERT, unlike, for example, auto-increment identity columns, which produce a value on INSERT that has to be returned to the application afterward.

B You can configure the sequence_name. Hibernate (or Spring Data JPA using Hibernate as a persistence provider) will either use an existing sequence or create one when you generate the SQL schema automatically. If your DBMS doesn't support sequences, this will be the special "sequence table" name.

C You can start with an initial_value that gives you room for test data. For example, when your integration test runs, Hibernate (or Spring Data JPA using Hibernate as a persistence provider) will make any new data insertions from test code with identifier values greater than 1,000. Any test data you want to import before the test can use numbers 1 to 999, and you can refer to the stable identifier values in your tests: "Load item with id 123 and run some tests on it." This is applied when Hibernate (or Spring Data JPA using Hibernate as a persistence provider) generates the SQL schema and sequence; it's a DDL option.

You can share the same database sequence among all your domain model classes. There is no harm in specifying @GeneratedValue(generator = "ID_GENERATOR") in all your entity classes. It doesn't matter if primary key values aren't contiguous for a particular entity, as long as they're unique within one table.

Finally, you can use java.lang.Long as the type of the identifier property in the entity class, which maps perfectly to a numeric database sequence generator. You could also use a long primitive. The main difference is what someItem.getId() returns on a new item that hasn't been stored in the database: either null or 0. If you want to test whether an item is new, a null check is probably easier for someone else reading your code to understand. You shouldn't use another integral type, such as int or short, for identifiers. Although they will work for a while (perhaps even years), as your database size grows, you may be limited by their range. An Integer would work for almost two months if you generated a new identifier each millisecond with no gaps, and a Long would last for about 300 million years.

Although it is recommended for most applications, the enhanced-sequence strategy, as shown in listing 5.2, is just one of the strategies built into Hibernate. The key generator's configuration is unaware of the framework that uses it, and the programmer will never manage the value of the primary key. This is done at the level of the frameworks. The code will look like listings 5.3 and 5.4.

Listing 5.3   Persisting an `Item` with a generated primary key from Hibernate JPA

Path: Ch05/generator/src/test/java/com/manning/javapersistence/ch05
➥ /HelloWorldJPATest.java

```
em.getTransaction().begin();

Item item = new Item();
item.setName("Some Item");
item.setAuctionEnd(Helper.tomorrow());
em.persist(item);

em.getTransaction().commit();
```

Listing 5.4   Persisting an `Item` with a generated primary key from Spring Data JPA

Path: Ch05/generator/src/test/java/com/manning/javapersistence/ch05
➥ /HelloWorldSpringDataJPATest.java

```
Item item = new Item();
item.setName("Some Item");
item.setAuctionEnd(Helper.tomorrow());
itemRepository.save(item);
```

After running any of the Hibernate JPA or Spring Data JPA programs, a new `ITEM` will be inserted in the database with the `id` 1000, the first one specified by the generator (figure 5.5). The value to be generated for the next insertion is kept inside `JPWHSD_SEQUENCE` (figure 5.6).

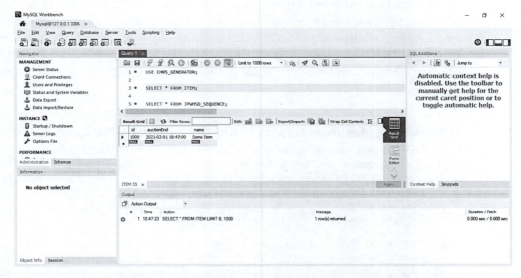

Figure 5.5   The content of the `ITEM` table after inserting a row with a generated primary key

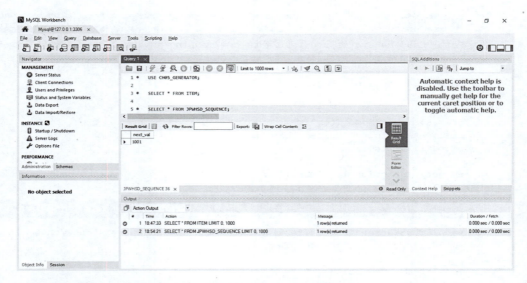

Figure 5.6   The next generated value kept by `JPWHSD_SEQUENCE`

5.2.5   *Identifier generator strategies*

Hibernate and Spring Data JPA using Hibernate as a provider offer several identifier generator strategies, and we'll list and discuss them in this section. We won't address the deprecated generator strategies.

If you don't want to read the whole list now, enable `GenerationType.AUTO` and check what Hibernate defaults to for your database dialect. It's most likely `sequence` or `identity`—good choices, but maybe not the most efficient or portable choices. If you require consistent, portable behavior and identifier values that are available before `INSERT`s, use `enhanced-sequence`, as shown in the previous section. This is a portable, flexible, and modern strategy that also offers various optimizers for large datasets.

Generating identifiers before or after `INSERT`: what's the difference?

An ORM service tries to optimize SQL `INSERT`s, such as by batching several at the JDBC level. Hence, SQL execution occurs as late as possible during a unit of work, and not when you call `entityManager.persist(someItem)`. This merely queues the insertion for later execution and, if possible, assigns the identifier value. However, if you now call `someItem.getId()`, you might get `null` back if the engine wasn't able to generate an identifier before the `INSERT`.

In general, we prefer *pre-insert* generation strategies that produce identifier values independently before `INSERT`. A common choice is to use a shared and concurrently accessible database sequence. Auto-incremented columns, column default values, and trigger-generated keys are available only after the `INSERT`.

Before we discuss the full list of identifier generator strategies, the recommendations for these strategies are as follows:

- In general, prefer pre-insert generation strategies that produce identifier values independently before `INSERT`.
- Use `enhanced-sequence`, which uses a native database sequence when that's supported and otherwise falls back to using an extra database table with a single column and row, emulating a sequence.

The following list outlines Hibernate's identifier generator strategies with their options and our usage recommendations. We also discuss the relationship between each standard JPA strategy and its native Hibernate equivalent. Hibernate has been growing organically, so there are now two sets of mappings between standard and native strategies; we refer to them as *old* and *new* in the list. You can switch this mapping with the `hibernate.id.new_generator_mappings` setting in your persistence.xml file. The default is `true`, which means the new mapping is used. Software doesn't age quite as well as wine.

- `native`—This option automatically selects a strategy, such as `sequence` or `identity`, depending on the configured SQL dialect. You have to look at the Javadoc (or even the source) of the SQL dialect you configured in persistence.xml to determine which strategy will be selected. This is equivalent to JPA `GenerationType.AUTO` with the old mapping.
- `sequence`—This strategy uses a native database sequence named `HIBERNATE_SEQUENCE`. The sequence is called before each `INSERT` of a new row. You can customize the sequence name and provide additional DDL settings; see the Javadoc for the `org.hibernate.id.SequenceGenerator` class.
- `enhanced-sequence`—This strategy uses a native database sequence when it's supported; otherwise it falls back to using an extra database table with a single column and row, emulating a sequence (the default table name is `HIBERNATE_SEQUENCE`). Using this strategy always calls the database "sequence" before an `INSERT`, providing the same behavior independently of whether the DBMS supports real sequences. This strategy also supports an `org.hibernate.id.enhanced.Optimizer` to avoid hitting the database before each `INSERT`, and it defaults to no optimization and fetching a new value for each `INSERT`. This is equivalent to JPA `GenerationType.SEQUENCE` and `GenerationType.AUTO` with the new mapping enabled, and it's probably your best option of the built-in strategies. For all the parameters, see the Javadoc for the `org.hibernate.id.enhanced.SequenceStyleGenerator` class.
- `enhanced-table`—This strategy uses an extra table named `HIBERNATE_SEQUENCES`, with one row by default representing the sequence and storing the next value. This value is selected and updated when an identifier value has to be generated. You can configure this generator to use multiple rows instead: one for each generator (see the Javadoc for `org.hibernate.id.enhanced.TableGenerator`). This is equivalent to JPA `GenerationType.TABLE` with the

new mapping enabled. It replaces the outdated but similar `org.hibernate` `.id.MultipleHiLoPerTableGenerator`, which was the old mapping for JPA `GenerationType.TABLE`.

- `identity`—This strategy supports `IDENTITY` and auto-increment columns in DB2, MySQL, MS SQL Server, and Sybase. The identifier value for the primary key column will be generated on the `INSERT` of a row. It has no options. Unfortunately, due to a quirk in Hibernate's code, you *cannot* configure this strategy in `@GenericGenerator`. The DDL generation will not include the identity or auto-increment option for the primary key column. The only way to use it is with JPA `GenerationType.IDENTITY` and the old or new mapping, making it the default for `GenerationType.IDENTITY`.

- `increment`—At Hibernate startup, this strategy reads the maximum (numeric) primary key column value of each entity's table and increments the value by one each time a new row is inserted. This is especially efficient if a non-clustered Hibernate application has exclusive access to the database, but don't use it in any other scenario.

- `select`—With this strategy, Hibernate won't generate a key value or include the primary key column in an `INSERT` statement. Hibernate expects the DBMS to assign a value to the column on insertion (the default value in the schema or the value given by a trigger). Hibernate then retrieves the primary key column with a `SELECT` query after insertion. The required parameter is `key`, naming the database identifier property (such as `id`) for the `SELECT`. This strategy isn't very efficient and should only be used with old JDBC drivers that can't return generated keys directly.

- `uuid2`—This strategy produces a unique 128-bit UUID in the application layer. This is useful when you need globally unique identifiers across databases (such as if you merge data from several distinct production databases in batch runs every night into an archive). The UUID can be encoded either as a `java.lang.String`, a `byte[16]`, or a `java.util.UUID` property in your entity class. This replaces the legacy `uuid` and `uuid.hex` strategies. You configure it with an `org.hibernate` `.id.UUIDGenerationStrategy`; see the Javadoc for the `org.hibernate.id.UUID-Generator` class for more details.

- `guid`—This strategy uses a globally unique identifier produced by the database, with an SQL function available on Oracle, Ingres, MS SQL Server, and MySQL. Hibernate calls the database function before an `INSERT`. The value maps to a `java.lang.String` identifier property. If you need full control over identifier generation, configure the strategy of `@GenericGenerator` with the fully qualified name of a class that implements the `org.hibernate.id.IdentityGenerator` interface.

If you haven't already, go ahead and add identifier properties to the entity classes of your domain model. Make sure you do not expose the identifier outside the business logic, such as through an API—this identifier has no business logic meaning and it is related only to the persistence.

After you complete the basic mapping of each entity and its identifier property, you can continue to map the value-typed properties of the entities. We'll talk about value-type mappings in the next chapter. First, though, read on for some special options that can simplify and enhance your class mappings.

5.3 Entity-mapping options

You've now mapped a persistent class with `@Entity`, using defaults for all the other settings, such as the mapped SQL table name. We'll now explore some class-level options and how you can control them:

- Naming defaults and strategies
- Dynamic SQL generation
- Entity mutability

These are options. If you prefer, you can skip this section for now, and come back later when you have to deal with specific problems.

5.3.1 Controlling names

Let's talk about the naming of entity classes and tables. If you only specify `@Entity` on a persistence-capable class, the default mapped table name will be the same as the class name. For example, the Java entity class `Item` maps to the `ITEM` table. A Java entity class named `BidItem` will map to the `BID_ITEM` table (here, the camel case will be converted into snake case). You can override the table name with the JPA `@Table` annotation, as shown next. (See the `mapping` folder for the source code.)

> **NOTE** We write SQL artifact names in UPPERCASE to make them easier to distinguish—SQL is actually case insensitive.

> **Listing 5.5 Overriding the mapped table name with the `@Table` annotation**

```
Path: Ch05/mapping/src/main/java/com/manning/javapersistence/ch05/model
➥ /User.java

@Entity

@Table(name = "USERS")

public class User {
    //  . . .
}
```

The `User` entity would map to the `USER` table, but this is a reserved keyword in most SQL DBMSs, so you can't have a table with that name. Instead we have mapped it to `USERS`. The `@javax.persistence.Table` annotation also has `catalog` and `schema` options if your database layout requires these as naming prefixes.

If you really have to, quoting allows you to use reserved SQL names and even work with case-sensitive names.

QUOTING SQL IDENTIFIERS

From time to time, especially in legacy databases, you'll encounter identifiers with strange characters or whitespace, or you'll wish to force case sensitivity. Or, as in the previous example, the automatic mapping of a class or property would require a table or column name that is a reserved keyword. Hibernate and Spring Data JPA using Hibernate as a provider know the reserved keywords of your DBMS through the configured database dialect, and they can automatically put quotes around such strings when generating SQL. You can enable this automatic quoting with `hibernate` `.auto_quote_keyword=true` in your persistence unit configuration. If you're using an older version of Hibernate, or you find that the dialect's information is incomplete, you must still apply quotes on names manually in your mappings if there is a conflict with a keyword.

If you quote a table or column name in your mapping with backticks, Hibernate always quotes this identifier in the generated SQL. This still works in the latest versions of Hibernate, but JPA 2.0 standardized this functionality as *delimited identifiers* with double quotes.

This is the Hibernate-only quoting with backticks, modifying the previous example:

```
@Table(name = "`USER`")
```

To be JPA-compliant, you also have to escape the quotes in the string:

```
@Table(name = "\"USER\"")
```

Either way works fine with Hibernate and Spring Data JPA using Hibernate as a provider. It knows the native quote character for your dialect and now generates SQL accordingly: `[USER]` for MS SQL Server, `'USER'` for MySQL, `"USER"` for H2, and so on.

If you have to quote *all* SQL identifiers, create an orm.xml file and add the setting `<delimited-identifiers/>` to its `<persistence-unit-defaults>` section, as you saw earlier in listing 3.8. Hibernate then enforces quoted identifiers everywhere.

You should consider renaming tables or columns with reserved keyword names whenever possible. Ad hoc SQL queries are difficult to write in an SQL console if you have to quote and escape everything properly by hand. Also, you should avoid using quoted identifiers for databases that are also accessed by other means than Hibernate, JPA, or Spring Data (such as for reporting). Having to use delimiters for all identifiers in a (complex) report query is really painful.

Next, let's see how Hibernate and Spring Data JPA with Hibernate as a provider can help when you encounter organizations with strict conventions for database table and column names.

IMPLEMENTING NAMING CONVENTIONS

Hibernate provides a feature that allows you to enforce naming standards automatically. Suppose that all table names in CaveatEmptor should follow the pattern

CE_<table name>. One solution is to manually specify the @Table annotation on all entity classes, but this approach is time-consuming and easily forgotten. Instead, you can implement Hibernate's PhysicalNamingStrategy interface or override an existing implementation, as in the following listing.

> **Listing 5.6 Overriding default naming conventions with `PhysicalNamingStrategy`**

Path: Ch05/mapping/src/main/java/com/manning/javapersistence/ch05
➡ /CENamingStrategy.java

```
public class CENamingStrategy extends PhysicalNamingStrategyStandardImpl {

    @Override

    public Identifier toPhysicalTableName(Identifier name,

                                        JdbcEnvironment context) {

        return new Identifier("CE_" + name.getText(), name.isQuoted());

    }

}
```

The overridden toPhysicalTableName() method prepends CE_ to all generated table names in your schema. Look at the Javadoc of the PhysicalNamingStrategy interface; it offers methods for custom naming of columns, sequences, and other artifacts.

You have to enable the naming strategy implementation. With Hibernate JPA, this is done in persistence.xml:

Path: Ch05/mapping/src/main/resources/META-INF/persistence.xml

```
<persistence-unit name="ch05.mapping">
    ...
    <properties>
        ...
        <property name="hibernate.physical_naming_strategy"
                value="com.manning.javapersistence.ch05.CENamingStrategy"/>
    </properties>
</persistence-unit>
```

With Spring Data JPA using Hibernate as a persistence provider, this is done from the LocalContainerEntityManagerFactoryBean configuration:

Path: Ch05/mapping/src/test/java/com/manning/javapersistence/ch05
➡ /configuration/SpringDataConfiguration.java

```
properties.put("hibernate.physical_naming_strategy",
            CENamingStrategy.class.getName());
```

Let's now take a quick look at another related problem, the naming of entities for queries.

NAMING ENTITIES FOR QUERYING

By default, all entity names are automatically imported into the namespace of the query engine. In other words, you can use short class names without a package prefix in JPA query strings, which is convenient:

```
Path: Ch05/generator/src/test/java/com/manning/javapersistence/ch05
➥ /HelloWorldJPATest.java

List<Item> items = em.createQuery("select i from Item i",
➥ Item.class).getResultList();
```

This only works when you have one `Item` class in your persistence unit. If you add another `Item` class in a different package, you should rename one of them for JPA if you want to continue using the short form in queries:

```
package my.other.model;
@javax.persistence.Entity(name = "AuctionItem")
public class Item {
    // . . .

}
```

The short query form is now `select i from AuctionItem i` for the `Item` class in the `my.other.model` package. Thus you resolve the naming conflict with another `Item` class in another package. Of course, you can always use fully qualified long names with the package prefix.

This completes our tour of the naming options. Next we'll discuss how Hibernate and Spring Data JPA using Hibernate generate the SQL that contains these names.

5.3.2   *Dynamic SQL generation*

By default, Hibernate and Spring Data JPA using Hibernate as a provider create SQL statements for each persistent class when the persistence unit is created on startup. These statements are simple create, read, update, and delete (CRUD) operations for reading a single row, deleting a row, and so on. It's cheaper to create and cache them instead of generating SQL strings every time such a simple query has to be executed at runtime. Besides, prepared statement caching at the JDBC level is much more efficient if there are fewer statements.

How can Hibernate create an UPDATE statement on startup? After all, the columns to be updated aren't known at this time. The answer is that the generated SQL statement updates all columns, and if the value of a particular column isn't modified, the statement sets it to its old value.

In some situations, such as a legacy table with hundreds of columns, where the SQL statements will be large for even the simplest operations (such as when only one column needs updating), you should disable this startup SQL generation and switch to dynamic statements generated at runtime. An extremely large number of entities can also influence startup time because Hibernate has to generate all the SQL statements for CRUD up front. Memory consumption for this query statement cache will also be high if a dozen statements must be cached for thousands of entities. This can be a concern in virtual environments with memory limitations or on low-power devices.

To disable the generation of INSERT and UPDATE SQL statements on startup, you need to use native Hibernate annotations:

```
@Entity
@org.hibernate.annotations.DynamicInsert
@org.hibernate.annotations.DynamicUpdate
public class Item {
    //  . . .
}
```

By enabling dynamic insertion and updates, you tell Hibernate to produce the SQL strings when needed, not up front. The UPDATE will only contain columns with updated values, and the INSERT will only contain non-nullable columns.

5.3.3   *Making an entity immutable*

Instances of a particular class may be immutable. For example, in CaveatEmptor, a Bid made for an item is immutable. Hence, Hibernate or Spring Data JPA using Hibernate as a provider never needs to execute UPDATE statements on the BID table. Hibernate can also make a few other optimizations, such as avoiding dirty checking if you map an immutable class, as shown in the next example. Here the Bid class is immutable, and instances are never modified:

```
@Entity
@org.hibernate.annotations.Immutable
public class Bid {
    //  . . .
}
```

A POJO is immutable if no public setter methods for any properties of the class are exposed—all values are set in the constructor. Hibernate or Spring Data JPA using Hibernate as a provider should access the fields directly when loading and storing instances. We talked about this earlier in this chapter: if the @Id annotation is on a field, Hibernate will access the fields directly, and you are free to design your getter and setter methods. Also, remember that not all frameworks work with POJOs without setter methods.

When you can't create a view in your database schema, you can map an immutable entity class to an SQL SELECT query.

5.3.4   *Mapping an entity to a subselect*

Sometimes your DBA won't allow you to change the database schema. Even adding a new view might not be possible. Let's say you want to create a view that contains the identifier of an auction `Item` and the number of bids made for that item (see the `sub-select` folder for the source code). Using a Hibernate annotation, you can create an application-level view, a read-only entity class mapped to an SQL `SELECT`:

Path: Ch05/subselect/src/main/java/com/manning/javapersistence/ch05/model
➡ /ItemBidSummary.java

```
@Entity
@org.hibernate.annotations.Immutable
@org.hibernate.annotations.Subselect(
    value = "select i.ID as ITEMID, i.NAME as NAME, " +
            "count(b.ID) as NUMBEROFBIDS " +
            "from ITEM i left outer join BID b on i.ID = b.ITEM_ID " +
               "group by i.ID, i.NAME"
)
@org.hibernate.annotations.Synchronize({"ITEM", "BID"})
public class ItemBidSummary {
    @Id
    private Long itemId;
    private String name;
    private long numberOfBids;
    public ItemBidSummary() {
    }
    // Getter methods . . .
    // . . .
}
```

You should list all the table names referenced in your `SELECT` in the `@org.hibernate`
`.annotations.Synchronize` annotation. The framework will then know it has to flush modifications of `Item` and `Bid` instances before it executes a query against `ItemBid-Summary`. If there are in-memory modifications that haven't yet been persisted to the database but that may affect the query, Hibernate (or Spring Data JPA using Hibernate as a provider) detects this and flushes the changes before executing the query. Otherwise the result may be a stale state. As there is no `@Table` annotation on the `ItemBid-Summary` class, the framework doesn't know when it must auto-flush before executing a query. The `@org.hibernate.annotations.Synchronize` annotation indicates that the framework needs to flush the `ITEM` and `BID` tables before executing the query.

Using the read-only `ItemBidSummary` entity class from Hibernate JPA will look like this:

Path: Ch05/subselect/src/test/java/com/manning/javapersistence/ch05
➡ /ItemBidSummaryTest.java

```
TypedQuery<ItemBidSummary> query =
    em.createQuery("select ibs from ItemBidSummary ibs where
➡ ibs.itemId = :id",
                    ItemBidSummary.class);
ItemBidSummary itemBidSummary =
                    query.setParameter("id", 1000L).getSingleResult();
```

To use the read-only `ItemBidSummary` entity class from Spring Data JPA, you'll first need to introduce a new Spring Data repository:

```
Path: Ch05/mapping/src/main/java/com/manning/javapersistence/ch05
➥ /repositories/ItemBidSummaryRepository.java

public interface ItemBidSummaryRepository extends
                CrudRepository<ItemBidSummary, Long> {
}
```

The repository will be effectively used like this:

```
Path: Ch05/subselect/src/test/java/com/manning/javapersistence/ch05
➥ /ItemBidSummarySpringDataTest.java

Optional<ItemBidSummary> itemBidSummary =
                itemBidSummaryRepository.findById(1000L);
```

Summary

- Entities are coarser-grained classes of a system. Their instances have independent lifecycles and their own identities, and many other instances can reference them.
- Value types are dependent on a particular entity class. A value type instance is bound to its owning entity instance, and only one entity instance can reference it—it has no individual identity.
- Java identity, object equality, and database identity are different concepts: the first two apply in the object-oriented world and the last one in the relational database world.
- A good primary key is never null, is unique, and never changes.
- Generators for primary keys can be configured using different strategies.
- You can use entities, mapping options, and naming strategies both from Hibernate JPA and from Spring Data JPA.

Mapping value types

This chapter covers

- Mapping basic properties
- Mapping embeddable components
- Controlling mapping between Java and SQL types

After spending the previous chapter almost exclusively on entities and their class- and identity-mapping options, we'll now focus on value types in their various forms. Value types are frequently encountered in classes under development. We'll separate value types into two categories: basic value-typed classes that come with the JDK, such as String, Date, primitives, and their wrappers; and developer-defined value-type classes, such as Address and MonetaryAmount in CaveatEmptor.

In this chapter, we'll first map persistent properties with JDK types and discuss the basic mapping annotations. We'll look at how you can work with various aspects of properties: overriding defaults, customizing access, and generated values. We'll also see how SQL is used with derived properties and transformed column values. We'll work with basic properties, temporal properties, and mapping enumerations.

We'll then examine custom value-type classes and map them as embeddable components. We'll look at how classes relate to the database schema and we'll make the classes embeddable while allowing for overriding embedded attributes.

We'll complete our look at embeddable components by mapping nested components. Finally, we'll analyze how you can customize the loading and storing of property values at a lower level with flexible JPA converters, which are standardized extension points of every JPA provider.

> **Major new features in JPA 2**
> JPA 2.2 supports the Java 8 Date and Time API. There is no longer any need to use additional mapping annotations, such as `@Temporal`, that formerly were needed to annotate fields of type `java.util.Date`.

6.1 *Mapping basic properties*

Mapping is at the heart of the ORM technique. It makes the connection between the object-oriented world and the relational world. When we map a persistent class, whether it's an entity or an embeddable type (more about these in section 6.2), all of its properties are considered persistent by default.

These are the default JPA rules for properties of persistent classes:

- If the property is a primitive or a primitive wrapper, or of type `String`, `BigInteger`, `BigDecimal`, `java.time.LocalDateTime`, `java.time.LocalDate`, `java.time.LocalDate`, `java.util.Date`, `java.util.Calendar`, `java.sql.Date`, `java.sql.Time`, `java.sql.Timestamp`, `byte[]`, `Byte[]`, `char[]`, or `Character[]`, it's automatically persistent. Hibernate or Spring Data JPA using Hibernate loads and stores the value of the property in a column with an appropriate SQL type and the same name as the property.

- Otherwise, if we annotate the class of the property as `@Embeddable`, or we map the property itself as `@Embedded`, the property is mapped as an embedded component of the owning class. We'll analyze the embedding of components later in this chapter, when we look at the `Address` and `MonetaryAmount` embeddable classes of CaveatEmptor.

- Otherwise, if the type of the property is `java.io.Serializable`, its value is stored in its serialized form. This may raise compatibility problems (we might have stored the information using one class format and would like to retrieve it later using another class format) and performance problems (the serialization/deserialization operations are costly). We should always map Java classes instead of storing a series of bytes in the database. Maintaining a database with this binary information when the application may be gone in a few years will mean that the classes that the serialized version maps to are no longer available.

- Otherwise, an exception will be thrown on startup, complaining that the type of the property isn't understood.

This *configuration by exception* approach means we don't have to annotate a property to make it persistent; we only have to configure the mapping in exceptional cases.

Several annotations are available in JPA to customize and control basic property mappings.

6.1.1   *Overriding basic property defaults*

We might not want all the properties of an entity class to be persistent. So which information ought to be persisted and which not? For example, although it makes sense to have a persistent `Item#initialPrice` property, an `Item#totalPriceIncludingTax` property shouldn't be persisted in the database if we only compute and use its value at runtime. To exclude a property, mark the field or the getter method of the property with the annotation `@javax.persistence.Transient` or use the Java `transient` keyword. The `transient` keyword excludes fields both for Java serialization and for persistence, as it is also recognized by JPA providers. The `@javax.persistence.Transient` annotation will only exclude the field from being persisted.

To decide whether a property should be persistent or not, ask yourself these questions: Is this a basic attribute that shapes the instance? Do we need it from the very beginning, or will we calculate it based on some other properties? Does it make sense to rebuild the information after some time, or will the information no longer be significant? Is it sensitive information that we would rather avoid persisting so it can't later be revealed (such as a password in clear)? Is it information that does not have significance in some other environment (such as a local IP address that is meaningless in another network)?

We'll come back to the placement of the annotation on fields or getter methods in a moment. First, let's assume, as we have before, that Hibernate or Spring Data JPA using Hibernate will access fields directly because `@Id` has been placed on these fields. Therefore, all other JPA and Hibernate mapping annotations are also on fields.

> **NOTE**   To execute the examples from the source code, you'll first need to run the Ch06.sql script. The source code can be found in the `mapping-value-types` folder.

In our CaveatEmptor application, our goal is to not only take care of the persistence logic from the program, but also to build flexible and easy-to-change code. If we do not want to rely on property mapping defaults, we can apply the `@Basic` annotation to a particular property, such as the `initialPrice` of an `Item`:

```
@Basic(optional = false)
BigDecimal initialPrice;
```

This annotation doesn't provide many alternatives. It only has two parameters: `optional` and `fetch`. We'll talk the `fetch` option when we explore optimization strategies in section 12.1. The option shown here, `optional`, marks the property as not optional at the Java object level.

By default, all persistent properties are nullable and optional, which would mean an `Item` could have an unknown `initialPrice`. Mapping the `initialPrice` property as non-optional makes sense if you want a NOT NULL constraint on the INITIALPRICE column in the SQL schema. The generated SQL schema will automatically include a NOT NULL constraint for non-optional properties.

Now if the application attempts to store an Item without setting a value on the initialPrice field, an exception will be thrown before an SQL statement is sent to the database. A value is required for initialPrice in order to perform an INSERT or UPDATE. If we do not mark the initialPrice property as optional and try to save a NULL, the database will reject the SQL statement, and a constraint-violation exception will be thrown.

Instead of @Basic, we can use the @Column annotation to declare nullability:

```
@Column(nullable = false)
BigDecimal initialPrice;
```

We've now demonstrated three ways to declare whether a property value is required: with the @Basic annotation, with the @Column annotation, and earlier with the Bean Validation @NotNull annotation (in section 3.3.2). All have the same effect on the JPA provider: a null check is performed when saving, and a NOT NULL constraint is generated in the database schema. We recommend using the Bean Validation @NotNull annotation so that you can manually validate an Item instance and have your user interface code in the presentation layer execute validation checks automatically. There isn't much difference in the end result, but not hitting the database with a statement that fails is cleaner.

The @Column annotation can also override the mapping of the property name to the database column:

```
@Column(name = "START_PRICE", nullable = false)
BigDecimal initialPrice;
```

The @Column annotation has a few other parameters, most of which control SQL-level details such as catalog and schema names. They're rarely needed, and we only demonstrate them in this book when necessary.

Property annotations aren't always on fields, and we may not want the JPA provider to access fields directly. Let's look at customizing property access.

6.1.2 Customizing property access

The persistence engine accesses the properties of a class either directly through fields or indirectly through getter and setter methods. We will try now to answer the question, "how should we access each persistent property?" An annotated entity inherits the default from the position of the mandatory @Id annotation. For example, if we declare @Id on a field, rather than using a getter method, all other mapping annotations for that entity are expected to be fields. Annotations are not supported on the setter methods.

The default access strategy isn't only applicable to a single entity class. Any @Embedded class inherits the default or explicitly declared access strategy of its owning root entity class. We'll cover embedded components later in this chapter. Furthermore, any @MappedSuperclass properties are accessed with the default or explicitly declared access strategy of the mapped entity class. Inheritance is the topic of chapter 7.

The JPA specification offers the @Access annotation for overriding the default behavior, using the parameters AccessType.FIELD (access through fields) and AccessType.PROPERTY (access through getters). When you set @Access on the class or entity level, all properties of the class will be accessed according to the selected strategy. Any other mapping annotations, including the @Id, can be set on either fields or getter methods.

We can also use the @Access annotation to override the access strategy of individual properties, as in the following example. Note that the position of other mapping annotations, like @Column, doesn't change—only how instances are accessed at runtime.

> **Listing 6.1   Overriding access strategy for the name property**

Path: Ch06/mapping-value-types/src/main/java/com/manning/javapersistence
➡ /ch06/model/Item.java

```
@Entity
public class Item {

    @Id
    @GeneratedValue(generator = "ID_GENERATOR")          Ⓐ
    private Long id;

    @Access(AccessType.PROPERTY)
    @Column(name = "ITEM_NAME")               Ⓑ
    private String name;

    public String getName() {
        return name;
    }                                                                  Ⓒ

    public void setName(String name) {
        this.name =
                !name.startsWith("AUCTION: ") ? "AUCTION: " + name : name;
    }

}
```

Ⓐ The Item entity defaults to field access. The @Id is on the field.

Ⓑ The @Access(AccessType.PROPERTY) setting on the name field switches this particular property to be accessed at runtime by the JPA provider through getter/setter.

Ⓒ Hibernate or Spring Data JPA using Hibernate calls getName() and setName() when loading and storing items.

Now turn it around: if the default (or explicit) access type of the entity were through property getter and setter methods, @Access(AccessType.FIELD) on a getter method would tell Hibernate or Spring Data JPA using Hibernate to access the field directly. All other mapping information would still have to be on the getter method, not the field.

Some properties don't map to a column. In particular, a derived property (like a calculated field) takes its value from an SQL expression.

6.1.3   Using derived properties

We have now come to derived properties—properties resulting from some other properties. The value of a derived property is calculated at runtime by evaluating an SQL expression declared with the @org.hibernate.annotations.Formula annotation, as shown in the next listing.

Listing 6.2   Two read-only derived properties

Path: Ch06/mapping-value-types/src/main/java/com/manning/javapersistence
➥ /ch06/model/Item.java

```
@Formula(
        "CONCAT(SUBSTR(DESCRIPTION, 1, 12), '...')"
)
private String shortDescription;

@Formula(
        "(SELECT AVG(B.AMOUNT) FROM BID B WHERE B.ITEM_ID = ID)"
)
private BigDecimal averageBidAmount;
```

The SQL formulas are evaluated every time the Item entity is retrieved from the database and not at any other time, so the result can become outdated if other properties are modified. The properties never appear in an SQL INSERT or UPDATE, only in SELECTs. Evaluation occurs in the database; the SQL formula is embedded in the SELECT clause when loading the instance.

The SQL formulas may refer to columns of the database table, they can call specific database SQL functions, and they can even include SQL subselects. In the previous example, the SUBSTR() and CONCAT() functions are called.

The SQL expression is passed to the underlying database as-is. Relying on vendor-specific operators or keywords may bind the mapping metadata to a particular database product. For example, the CONCAT() function in the preceding listing is specific to MySQL, so you should be aware that portability may be affected. Notice that unqualified column names refer to columns of the table of the class to which the derived property belongs.

Hibernate also supports a variation of formulas called *column transformers*, which allow you to write a custom SQL expression for reading *and* writing a property value. Let's investigate this capability.

6.1.4   *Transforming column values*

Let's now deal with information that has different representations in the object-oriented system and the relational system. Suppose a database has a column called IMPERIALWEIGHT, storing the weight of an Item in pounds. The application, however, has the property Item#metricWeight in kilograms, so we would have to convert the value of the database column when reading a row from *and* writing it to the ITEM table. We can implement this with a Hibernate extension: the @org.hibernate .annotations.ColumnTransformer annotation.

> **Listing 6.3   Transforming column values with SQL expressions**

Path: Ch06/mapping-value-types/src/main/java/com/manning/javapersistence
➡ /ch06/model/Item.java

```
@Column(name = "IMPERIALWEIGHT")
@ColumnTransformer(
    read = "IMPERIALWEIGHT / 2.20462",
    write = "? * 2.20462"
)
private double metricWeight;
```

When reading a row from the ITEM table, Hibernate or Spring Data JPA using Hibernate embeds the expression IMPERIALWEIGHT / 2.20462, so the calculation occurs in the database, and the metric value is returned in the result to the application layer. For writing to the column, Hibernate or Spring Data JPA using Hibernate sets the metric value on the mandatory, single placeholder (the question mark), and the SQL expression calculates the actual value to be inserted or updated.

Hibernate also applies column converters in query restrictions. For example, the query in the following listing retrieves all items with a weight of 2 kilograms.

> **Listing 6.4   Applying column converters in query restrictions**

Path: Ch06/mapping-value-types/src/test/java/com/manning/javapersistence
➡ /ch06/MappingValuesJPATest.java

```
List<Item> result =
    em.createQuery("SELECT i FROM Item i WHERE i.metricWeight = :w")
        .setParameter("w", 2.0)
        .getResultList();
```

The actual SQL executed for this query contains the following restriction in the WHERE clause:

```
// ...
where
    i.IMPERIALWEIGHT / 2.20462=?
```

Note that the database will probably not be able to rely on an index for this restriction; a full table scan would be performed because the weights for *all* ITEM rows have to be calculated to evaluate the restriction.

Another special kind of property relies on database-generated values.

6.1.5 Generated and default property values

The database sometimes generates a property value, and this usually happens when we insert a row for the first time. Examples of database-generated values are creation timestamps, a default price for an item, or a trigger that runs for every modification.

Typically, Hibernate (or Spring Data JPA using Hibernate) applications need to refresh instances that contain properties for which the database generates values after saving. This means the application would have to make another round trip to the database to read the value after inserting or updating a row. Marking properties as generated, however, lets the application delegate this responsibility to Hibernate or Spring Data JPA using Hibernate. Essentially, whenever an SQL INSERT or UPDATE is issued for an entity that has declared generated properties, the SQL does a SELECT immediately afterward to retrieve the generated values.

We use the @org.hibernate.annotations.Generated annotation to mark generated properties. For temporal properties, we use the @CreationTimestamp and @UpdateTimestamp annotations. The @CreationTimestamp annotation is used to mark the createdOn property. This tells Hibernate or Spring Data using Hibernate to generate the property value automatically. In this case, the value is set to the current date before the entity instance is inserted into the database. The other similar built-in annotation is @UpdateTimestamp, which generates the property value automatically when an entity instance is updated.

Listing 6.5   Database-generated property values

Path: Ch06/mapping-value-types/src/main/java/com/manning/javapersistence
➡ /ch06/model/Item.java

```
@CreationTimestamp
private LocalDate createdOn;

@UpdateTimestamp
private LocalDateTime lastModified;

@Column(insertable = false)
@ColumnDefault("1.00")
@Generated(
    org.hibernate.annotations.GenerationTime.INSERT
)
private BigDecimal initialPrice;
```

Available settings for the GenerationTime enum are ALWAYS and INSERT. With GenerationTime.ALWAYS, Hibernate or Spring Data JPA using Hibernate refreshes the entity instance after every SQL UPDATE or INSERT. With GenerationTime.INSERT, the refreshing only occurs after an SQL INSERT to retrieve the default value provided by the database. We can also map the initialPrice property as not insertable. The @ColumnDefault annotation sets the default value of the column when Hibernate or Spring Data JPA using Hibernate exports and generates the SQL schema DDL.

Timestamps are frequently automatically generated either by the database, as in the previous example, or by the application. As long as we are using JPA 2.2 and the Java 8 LocalDate, LocalDateTime, and LocalTime classes, we don't need to use the @Temporal annotation. The enumerated Java 8 classes from the java.time package include the temporal precision by themselves: the date, the date and the time, or only the time. Let's take a look at the uses of the @Temporal annotation that you may still encounter.

6.1.6   The @Temporal annotation

The JPA specification allows you to annotate temporal properties with @Temporal to declare the accuracy of the SQL data type of the mapped column. The Java temporal types before Java 8 are java.util.Date, java.util.Calendar, java.sql.Date, java .sql.Time, and java.sql.Timestamp. The following listing provides an example of using the @Temporal annotation.

> **Listing 6.6   Property of a temporal type that must be annotated with `@Temporal`**

```
@CreationTimestamp
@Temporal(TemporalType.DATE)
private Date createdOn;

@UpdateTimestamp
@Temporal(TemporalType.TIMESTAMP)
private Date lastModified;
```

Available TemporalType options are DATE, TIME, and TIMESTAMP, establishing which part of the temporal value should be stored in the database. The default is Temporal-Type.TIMESTAMP when no @Temporal annotation is present.

Another special property type is represented by the enumerations.

6.1.7   Mapping enumerations

An *enumeration type* is a common Java idiom where a class has a constant (small) number of immutable instances. In CaveatEmptor, for example, we can apply this to auctions having a limited number of types:

```
Path: Ch06/mapping-value-types/src/main/java/com/manning/javapersistence
    /ch06/model/AuctionType.java

public enum AuctionType {
    HIGHEST_BID,
    LOWEST_BID,
    FIXED_PRICE
}
```

We can now set the appropriate `auctionType` on each `Item`:

Path: Ch06/mapping-value-types/src/main/java/com/manning/javapersistence
➥ /ch06/model/Item.java

```
@NotNull
@Enumerated(EnumType.STRING)
private AuctionType auctionType = AuctionType.HIGHEST_BID;
```

Without the `@Enumerated` annotation, Hibernate or Spring Data JPA using Hibernate
would store the `ORDINAL` position of the value. That is, it would store 1 for `HIGHEST_BID`,
2 for `LOWEST_BID`, and 3 for `FIXED_PRICE`. This is a brittle default; if you make changes
to the `AuctionType` enum and add a new instance, existing values may no longer map
to the same position and break the application. The `EnumType.STRING` option is, therefore, a better choice; Hibernate or Spring Data JPA using Hibernate can store the label
of the enum value as is.

This completes our tour of basic properties and their mapping options. So far we
have looked at the properties of JDK-supplied types such as `String`, `Date`, and `Big-
Decimal`. The domain model also has custom value-typed classes—those with a compo-
sition association in the UML diagram.

6.2   Mapping embeddable components

The mapped classes of our domain model
have all been entity classes so far, each with
its own lifecycle and identity. The `User`
class, however, has a special kind of association with the `Address` class, as shown in
figure 6.1.

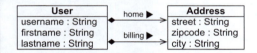

**Figure 6.1   Composition of `User` and
`Address`**

In object-modeling terms, this association is a kind of *aggregation*—a *part-of* relationship. An aggregation is a form of association, but it has some additional semantics
concerning the lifecycle of objects. In this case, we have an even stronger form, *composition*, where the lifecycle of the part is fully dependent on the lifecycle of the whole.
An `Address` object cannot exist in the absence of the
`User` object, so a composed class in UML, such as
`Address`, is often a candidate value type for the
object/relational mapping.

6.2.1   The database schema

We can map such a composition relationship with
`Address` as a value type (with the same semantics as
`String` or `BigDecimal`) and with `User` as an entity.
The targeted SQL schema is shown in figure 6.2.

There is only one mapped table, `USERS`, for the
`User` entity. This table embeds all the details of the

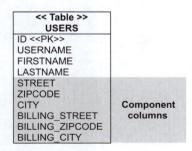

**Figure 6.2   The columns of the
components are embedded in the
entity table.**

components, where a single row holds a particular `User` and their `homeAddress` and `billingAddress`. If another entity has a reference to an `Address`—such as `Shipment#deliveryAddress`—the `SHIPMENT` table will also have all the columns needed to store an `Address`.

This schema reflects value type semantics: a particular `Address` can't be shared; it doesn't have its own identity. Its primary key is the mapped database identifier of the owning entity. An embedded component has a dependent lifecycle: when the owning entity instance is saved, the component instance is saved. When the owning entity instance is deleted, the component instance is deleted. No special SQL needs to be executed for this; all the data is in a single row.

Having "more classes than tables" is how fine-grained domain models are supported. Let's write the classes and mappings for this structure.

6.2.2 *Making classes embeddable*

Java has no concept of composition—a class or property can't be marked as a component. The only difference between a component and an entity is the database identifier: a component class has no individual identity, so the component class requires no identifier property or identifier mapping. It's a simple POJO, as in the following listing.

> **Listing 6.7 `Address` class: An embeddable component**

```
Path: Ch06/mapping-value-types/src/main/java/com/manning/javapersistence
⟹ /ch06/model/Address.java       Ⓐ

@Embeddable                              ⟵
public class Address {
    @NotNull                             ⟵
    @Column(nullable = false)
    private String street;           Ⓑ
                                                              Ⓓ
    @NotNull
    @Column(nullable = false, length = 5)    ⟵
    private String zipcode;

    @NotNull
    @Column(nullable = false)        Ⓔ
    private String city;
Ⓕ
⟶   public Address() {
    }
                                                                  Ⓖ
    public Address(String street, String zipcode, String city) {    ⟵
        this.street = street;
        this.zipcode = zipcode;
        this.city = city;
    }
    //getters and setters
}
```

Ⓐ Instead of @Entity, this component POJO is marked with @Embeddable. It has no identifier property.

Ⓑ The @NotNull annotation is ignored by the DDL generation.

Ⓒ @Column(nullable=false) is used for DDL generation.

Ⓓ The length argument of the @Column annotation will override the default generation of a column as VARCHAR(255).

Ⓔ The type of the city column will by default be VARCHAR(255).

Ⓕ Hibernate or Spring Data JPA using Hibernate call this no-argument constructor to create an instance and then populate the fields directly.

Ⓖ We can have additional (public) constructors for convenience.

In the preceding listing the properties of the embeddable class are all persistent by default, just like the properties of a persistent entity class. The property mappings can be configured with the same annotations, such as @Column or @Basic. The properties of the Address class map to the columns STREET, ZIPCODE, and CITY, and they are constrained with NOT NULL. That's the entire mapping.

> **Problem: Hibernate Validator doesn't generate NOT NULL constraints**
>
> At the time of writing, an open flaw remains with Hibernate Validator: Hibernate won't map @NotNull constraints on embeddable component properties to NOT NULL constraints when generating the database schema. Hibernate will only use @NotNull on the components' properties at runtime for Bean Validation. We have to map the property with @Column(nullable = false) to generate the constraint in the schema. The Hibernate bug database is tracking this problem as HVAL-3 (see http://mng.bz/IROR).

There's nothing special about the User entity.

Listing 6.8 User class containing a reference to an Address

Path: Ch06/mapping-value-types/src/main/java/com/manning/javapersistence
➡ /ch06/model/User.java

```
@Entity
@Table(name = "USERS")
public class User {
    @Id
    @GeneratedValue(generator = Constants.ID_GENERATOR)
    private Long id;
                                        Ⓐ
    private Address homeAddress;    ←⅃

    // ...
}
```

Ⓐ The Address is @Embeddable so no annotation is needed here.

In the preceding listing, Hibernate or Spring Data using Hibernate detects that the `Address` class is annotated with `@Embeddable`; the `STREET`, `ZIPCODE`, and `CITY` columns are mapped on the `USERS` table, the owning entity's table.

When we talked about property access earlier in this chapter, we mentioned that embeddable components inherit their access strategy from their owning entity. This means Hibernate or Spring Data using Hibernate will access the properties of the `Address` class with the same strategy as for `User` properties. This inheritance also affects the placement of mapping annotations in embeddable component classes. The rules are as follows:

- If the owning `@Entity` of an embedded component is mapped with field access, either implicitly with `@Id` on a field or explicitly with `@Access(AccessType.FIELD)` on the class, all mapping annotations of the embedded component class are expected on fields of the component class. Annotations are expected on the fields of the `Address` class, and the fields are directly read and written at runtime. Getter and setter methods on `Address` are optional.

- If the owning `@Entity` of an embedded component is mapped with property access, either implicitly with `@Id` on a getter method or explicitly with `@Access(AccessType.PROPERTY)` on the class, all mapping annotations of the embedded component class are expected on getter methods of the component class. Values are read and written by calling getter and setter methods on the embeddable component class.

- If the embedded property of the owning entity class—`User#homeAddress` in listing 6.8—is marked with `@Access(AccessType.FIELD)`, annotations are expected on the fields of the `Address` class, and fields are accessed at runtime.

- If the embedded property of the owning entity class—`User#homeAddress` in listing 6.8—is marked with `@Access(AccessType.PROPERTY)`, annotations are expected on getter methods of the `Address` class, and access is made using getter and setter methods at runtime.

- If `@Access` annotates the embeddable class itself, the selected strategy will be used for reading mapping annotations on the embeddable class and runtime access.

Let's now compare field-based and property-based access. Why should you use one or the other?

- *Field-based access*—When you use field-based access, you can omit getter methods for the fields that should not be exposed. Also, fields are declared on a single line, while accessor methods are spread out on multiple lines, so field-based access will make the code more readable.

- *Property-based access*—Accessor methods may execute additional logic. If this is what you want to happen when persisting an object, you can use property-based access. If the persistence would like to avoid these additional actions, you can use field-based access.

There's one more thing to remember: there's no elegant way to represent a null reference to an `Address`. Consider what would happen if the columns STREET, ZIPCODE, and CITY were nullable. If you load a `User` without any address information, what should be returned by `someUser.getHomeAddress()`? A null would be returned in this case. Hibernate or Spring Data using Hibernate also stores a null embedded property as NULL values in all mapped columns of the component. Consequently, if you store a `User` with an "empty" `Address` (an `Address` instance exists, but all its properties are null), no `Address` instance will be returned when loading the `User`. This can be counterintuitive; you probably shouldn't have nullable columns anyway, and avoid ternary logic, as you will most probably want your user to have a real address.

We should override the `equals()` and `hashCode()` methods of `Address` to compare instances by value. However, this isn't critically important as long as we don't have to compare instances, such as by putting them in a `HashSet`. We'll discuss this problem in the context of collections in section 8.2.1.

In a realistic scenario, a user would probably have separate addresses for different purposes. Figure 6.1 showed an additional composition relationship between `User` and `Address`: the `billingAddress`.

6.2.3 Overriding embedded attributes

The `billingAddress` is another embedded component property of the `User` class that we'll need to use, so another `Address` has to be stored in the USERS table. This creates a mapping conflict: so far, we only have STREET, ZIPCODE, and CITY columns in the schema to store one `Address`.

We'll need additional columns to store another `Address` for each USERS row. When we map the `billingAddress`, we can override the column names.

Listing 6.9 Overriding the column names

Path: Ch06/mapping-value-types/src/main/java/com/manning/javapersistence
➡ /ch06/model/User.java

```java
@Entity
@Table(name = "USERS")
public class User {                                    A
    @Embedded
    @AttributeOverride(name = "street",
        column = @Column(name = "BILLING_STREET"))
    @AttributeOverride(name = "zipcode",                        B
        column = @Column(name = "BILLING_ZIPCODE", length = 5))
    @AttributeOverride(name = "city",
        column = @Column(name = "BILLING_CITY"))
    private Address billingAddress;

    public Address getBillingAddress() {
        return billingAddress;
    }
```

```
    public void setBillingAddress(Address billingAddress) {
        this.billingAddress = billingAddress;
    }
    // ...
}
```

Ⓐ The `billingAddress` field is marked as embedded. The `@Embedded` annotation actually isn't necessary. You can mark either the component class or the property in the owning entity class (using both doesn't hurt but it offers no advantage). The `@Embedded` annotation is useful if you want to map a third-party component class without a source and no annotations but using the right getter and setter methods (like regular JavaBeans).

Ⓑ The repeatable `@AttributeOverride` annotation selectively overrides property mappings of the embedded class. In this example we override all three properties and provide different column names. Now we can store two `Address` instances in the `USERS` table, with each instance in a different set of columns (look back at the schema again in figure 6.2).

Each `@AttributeOverride` annotation for a component property is "complete"; any JPA or Hibernate annotation on the overridden property is ignored. This means the `@Column` annotations on the `Address` class are ignored, so all `BILLING_*` columns are `NULL`able! (Bean Validation still recognizes the `@NotNull` annotation on the component property, though; only the persistence annotations are overridden.)

We'll create two Spring Data JPA repository interfaces to interact with the database. The `UserRepository` interface only extends `CrudRepository`, and it will inherit all the methods from this interface. It is generified by `User` and `Long`, as it manages `User` entities having `Long` IDs.

Listing 6.10   The `UserRepository` interface

Path: Ch06/mapping-value-types/src/main/java/com/manning/javapersistence
➥ /ch06/repositories/UserRepository.java

```java
public interface UserRepository extends CrudRepository<User, Long> {
}
```

The `ItemRepository` interface extends `CrudRepository`, and it will inherit all the methods from this interface. Additionally, it declares the `findByMetricWeight` method, following the Spring Data JPA naming conventions. It is generified by `Item` and `Long`, as it manages `Item` entities having `Long` IDs.

Listing 6.11   The `ItemRepository` interface

Path: Ch06/mapping-value-types/src/main/java/com/manning/javapersistence
➥ /ch06/repositories/ItemRepository.java

```
public interface ItemRepository extends CrudRepository<Item, Long> {
    Iterable<Item> findByMetricWeight(double weight);
}
```

We'll test the functionality of the code we wrote using the Spring Data JPA framework, as demonstrated in the following listing. The source code for the book also contains testing code alternatives that use JPA and Hibernate.

Listing 6.12   Testing the functionality of the persistence code

Path: Ch06/mapping-value-types/src/test/java/com/manning/javapersistence
➥ /ch06/MappingValuesSpringDataJPATest.java Ⓐ

```
@ExtendWith(SpringExtension.class)                              ← Ⓐ
@ContextConfiguration(classes = {SpringDataConfiguration.class})   ←  Ⓑ
public class MappingValuesSpringDataJPATest {

    @Autowired                                                  Ⓒ
    private UserRepository userRepository;

    @Autowired                                                  Ⓓ
    private ItemRepository itemRepository;

    @Test
    void storeLoadEntities() {

        User user = new User();
        user.setUsername("username");
        user.setHomeAddress(new Address("Flowers Street",        Ⓔ
                                        "12345", "Boston"));
Ⓕ
    └─▷ userRepository.save(user);

        Item item = new Item();
        item.setName("Some Item");
        item.setMetricWeight(2);                                Ⓖ
Ⓗ      item.setDescription("descriptiondescription");
    └─▷ itemRepository.save(item);
                                                                Ⓘ
        List<User> users = (List<User>) userRepository.findAll(); ←
        List<Item> items = (List<Item>)                          Ⓙ
                           itemRepository.findByMetricWeight(2.0);

                                          Ⓚ
        assertAll(                                              Ⓛ
            () -> assertEquals(1, users.size()),          ←
            () -> assertEquals("username", users.get(0).getUsername()), ←
     Ⓜ     () -> assertEquals("Flowers Street",
                        users.get(0).getHomeAddress().getStreet()),
            () -> assertEquals("12345",                          Ⓝ
                        users.get(0).getHomeAddress().getZipcode()),
     Ⓞ     () -> assertEquals("Boston",
                        users.get(0).getHomeAddress().getCity()),
            () -> assertEquals(1, items.size()),          ←
     Ⓠ ─▷  () -> assertEquals("AUCTION: Some Item",
                                                                Ⓟ
```

```
                                 items.get(0).getName()),
           () -> assertEquals("descriptiondescription",
                                 items.get(0).getDescription()),
           () -> assertEquals(AuctionType.HIGHEST_BID,
                                 items.get(0).getAuctionType()),
           () -> assertEquals("descriptiond...",
                                 items.get(0).getShortDescription()),
           () -> assertEquals(2.0, items.get(0).getMetricWeight()),
           () -> assertEquals(LocalDate.now(),
                                 items.get(0).getCreatedOn()),
           () ->
                 assertTrue(ChronoUnit.SECONDS.between(
                          LocalDateTime.now(),
                          items.get(0).getLastModified()) < 1),
           () -> assertEquals(new BigDecimal("1.00"),
                                 items.get(0).getInitialPrice())
       );

   }
}
```

A We extend the test using `SpringExtension`. This extension is used to integrate the Spring test context with the JUnit 5 Jupiter test.

B The Spring test context is configured using the beans defined in the `SpringData-Configuration` class.

C A `UserRepository` bean is injected by Spring through autowiring.

D An `ItemRepository` bean is injected by Spring through autowiring. This is possible as the `com.manning.javapersistence.ch06.repositories` package where `UserRepository` and `ItemRepository` are located was used as the argument of the `@EnableJpaRepositories` annotation on the `SpringDataConfiguration` class. You can look back at chapter 2 for a refresher on what the `SpringDataConfiguration` class looks like.

E Create and set a user.

F Save it to the repository.

G Create and set an item.

H Save it to the repository.

I Get the list of all users.

J Get the list of items having the metric 2.0.

K Check the size of the list of users.

L Check the name.

M Check the street address.

N Check the ZIP code.

O Check the city of the first user in the list.

P Check the size of the list of items.

Q Check the name of the first item.

R Check its description.

S Check the auction type.

T Check the short description.

U Check its metric weight.

V Check the creation date.

W Check the last modification date and time.

X Check the initial price of the first item in the list. The last modification date and time is checked against the current date and time, to ensure it is within 1 second (allowing for the retrieval delay).

The domain model in the preceding listing can further improve reusability and be made more fine-grained by nesting embedded components.

6.2.4 *Mapping nested embedded components*

Let's consider the `Address` class and how it encapsulates address details; instead of a having a simple `city` string, we can move this detail into a new `City` embeddable class. The revised domain model diagram is shown in figure 6.3. The SQL schema targeted for the mapping still has only one `USERS` table, as shown in figure 6.4. The source code that follows in listings 6.13 and 6.14 can be found in the mapping-value-types2 folder.

Figure 6.3   Nested composition of `Address` and `City`

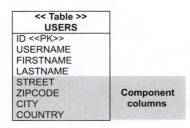

Figure 6.4   Embedded columns hold `Address` and `City` details.

An embeddable class can have an embedded property, and `Address` has a `city` property.

Listing 6.13   The `Address` class with a `city` property

Path: Ch06/mapping-value-types2/src/main/java/com/manning/javapersistence
➥ /ch06/model/Address.java

```
@Embeddable
public class Address {
```

```
    @NotNull
    @Column(nullable = false)
    private String street;

    @NotNull
    @AttributeOverride(
        name = "name",
        column = @Column(name = "CITY", nullable = false)
    )
    private City city;
    // ...
}
```

We'll create the embeddable `City` class with only basic properties.

Listing 6.14   The embeddable `City` class

Path: Ch06/mapping-value-types2/src/main/java/com/manning/javapersistence
➥ /ch06/model/City.java

```
@Embeddable
public class City {
    @NotNull
    @Column(nullable = false, length = 5)
    private String zipcode;

    @NotNull
    @Column(nullable = false)
    private String name;

    @NotNull
    @Column(nullable = false)
    private String country;
    // ...
}
```

We could continue this kind of nesting by creating a `Country` class, for example. All embedded properties, no matter how deep they are in the composition, are mapped to columns of the owning entity's table, which here is the USERS table.

The `name` property of the `City` class is mapped to the CITY column. This can be achieved with either an `@AttributeOverride` in `Address` (as demonstrated) or an override in the root entity class, `User`. Nested properties can be referenced with dot notation; for example, on `User#address`, `@AttributeOverride(name = "city.name")` references the `Address#city#name` attribute.

We'll come back to embedded components in section 8.2, where we'll look at mapping collections of components and using references from a component to an entity.

At the beginning of this chapter, we analyzed basic properties and how Hibernate or Spring Data JPA using Hibernate can map a JDK type such as `java.lang.String` to an appropriate SQL type. Let's find out more about this type system and how values are converted at a lower level.

6.3 Mapping Java and SQL types with converters

Until now, we've assumed that Hibernate or Spring Data JPA using Hibernate will select the right SQL type when we map a `java.lang.String` property. But what is the correct mapping between the Java and SQL types, and how can we control it? We'll shape a correspondence between these types as we delve into the specifics.

6.3.1 Built-in types

Any JPA provider has to support a minimum set of Java-to-SQL type conversions. Hibernate and Spring Data JPA using Hibernate support all of these mappings, as well as some additional adapters that aren't standard but are useful in practice. First let's look at the Java primitives and their SQL equivalents.

PRIMITIVE AND NUMERIC TYPES

The built-in types shown in table 6.1 map Java primitives and their wrappers to appropriate SQL standard types. We've also included some other numeric types. The names in the Name column are Hibernate-specific; we'll use them later when customizing type mappings.

Table 6.1 Java primitive types that map to SQL standard types

Name	Java type	ANSI SQL type
integer	int, java.lang.Integer	INTEGER
long	long, java.lang.Long	BIGINT
short	short, java.lang.Short	SMALLINT
float	float, java.lang.Float	FLOAT
double	double, java.lang.Double	DOUBLE
byte	byte, java.lang.Byte	TINYINT
boolean	boolean, java.lang.Boolean	BOOLEAN
big_decimal	java.math.BigDecimal	NUMERIC
big_integer	java.math.BigInteger	NUMERIC

You probably noticed that your DBMS product doesn't support some of the SQL types listed. These SQL type names are ANSI-standard type names. Most DBMS vendors ignore this part of the SQL standard, usually because their legacy type systems preceded the standard. However, JDBC provides a partial abstraction of vendor-specific data types, allowing Hibernate to work with ANSI-standard types when executing DML statements such as `INSERT` and `UPDATE`. For product-specific schema generation, Hibernate translates from the ANSI-standard type to an appropriate vendor-specific type using the configured SQL dialect. This means we usually don't have to worry about SQL data types if we let Hibernate create the schema for us.

If we have an existing schema or we need to know the native data type for our DBMS, we can look at the source of our configured SQL dialect. For example, the `H2Dialect` that ships with Hibernate contains this mapping from the ANSI `NUMERIC` type to the vendor-specific `DECIMAL` type: `registerColumnType(Types.NUMERIC, "decimal($p,$s)")`.

The `NUMERIC` SQL type supports decimal precision and scale settings. The default precision and scale setting for a `BigDecimal` property, for example, is `NUMERIC(19, 2)`. To override this for schema generation, apply the `@Column` annotation on the property and set its `precision` and `scale` parameters.

Next are the types that map to strings in the database.

CHARACTER TYPES

Table 6.2 shows types that map character and string value representations.

Table 6.2 Adapters for character and string values

Name	Java type	ANSI SQL type
string	`java.lang.String`	VARCHAR
character	`char[]`, `Character[]`, `java.lang.String`	CHAR
yes_no	`boolean`, `java.lang.Boolean`	CHAR(1), 'Y' or 'N'
true_false	`boolean`, `java.lang.Boolean`	CHAR(1), 'T' or 'F'
class	`java.lang.Class`	VARCHAR
locale	`java.util.Locale`	VARCHAR
timezone	`java.util.TimeZone`	VARCHAR
currency	`java.util.Currency`	VARCHAR

The Hibernate type system picks an SQL data type depending on the declared length of a string value: if the `String` property is annotated with `@Column(length = ...)` or `@Length` in Bean Validation, Hibernate selects the right SQL data type for the given string size. This selection also depends on the configured SQL dialect. For example, for MySQL, a length of up to 65,535 produces a regular `VARCHAR(length)` column when the schema is generated by Hibernate. For a length of up to 16,777,215, a MySQL-specific `MEDIUMTEXT` data type is produced, and even greater lengths use a `LONGTEXT`. The default length of Hibernate for all `java.lang.String` properties is 255, so without any further mapping, a `String` property maps to a `VARCHAR(255)` column. You can customize this type selection by extending the class of your SQL dialect; read the dialect documentation and source code to find out the details for your DBMS product.

A database usually enables the internationalization of text with a sensible (UTF-8) default character set for the entire database or at least whole tables. This is a DBMS-specific setting. If you need more fine-grained control and want to switch to the nationalized variants of character data types (e.g., NVARCHAR, NCHAR, or NCLOB), annotate the property mapping with @org.hibernate.annotations.Nationalized.

Also built in are some special converters for legacy databases or DBMSs with limited type systems, such as Oracle. The Oracle DBMS doesn't even have a truth-valued data type; the only data type required by the relational model. Many existing Oracle schemas, therefore, represent Boolean values with Y/N or T/F characters. Or—and this is the default in Hibernate's Oracle dialect—a column of type NUMBER(1,0) is expected and generated. Again, refer to the SQL dialect of the DBMS if you want to know all mappings from ANSI data type to vendor-specific type.

Next are the types that map to dates and times in the database.

DATE AND TIME TYPES

Table 6.3 lists types associated with dates, times, and timestamps.

Table 6.3   Date and time types

Name	Java type	ANSI SQL type
date	java.util.Date, java.sql.Date	DATE
time	java.util.Date, java.sql.Time	TIME
timestamp	java.util.Date, java.sql.Timestamp	TIMESTAMP
calendar	java.util.Calendar	TIMESTAMP
calendar_date	java.util.Calendar	DATE
duration	java.time.Duration	BIGINT
instant	java.time.Instant	TIMESTAMP
localdatetime	java.time.LocalDateTime	TIMESTAMP
localdate	java.time.LocalDate	DATE
localtime	java.time.LocalTime	TIME
offsetdatetime	java.time.OffsetDateTime	TIMESTAMP
offsettime	java.time.OffsetTime	TIME
zoneddatetime	java.time.ZonedDateTime	TIMESTAMP

In the domain model, we can represent date and time data as either java.util.Date, java.util.Calendar, or the subclasses of java.util.Date defined in the java.sql package, or the Java 8 classes from the java.time package. The best decision at this time is to use the Java 8 API in the java.time package. These classes may represent a date, a time, a date with a time, or they may even include the offset to the UTC zone (OffsetDateTime and OffsetTime). JPA 2.2 officially supports the Java 8 date and time classes.

Hibernate's behavior for java.util.Date properties might be a surprise at first: when storing a java.util.Date, Hibernate won't return a java.util.Date after loading. It will return a java.sql.Date, a java.sql.Time, or a java.sql.Timestamp, depending on whether the property is mapped with TemporalType.DATE, TemporalType.TIME, or TemporalType.TIMESTAMP.

Hibernate has to use the JDBC subclass when loading data from the database because the database types have higher accuracy than java.util.Date. A java.util.Date has millisecond accuracy, but a java.sql.Timestamp includes nanosecond information that may be present in the database. Hibernate won't cut off this information to fit the value into java.util.Date, which may lead to problems when trying to compare java.util.Date values with the equals() method; it's not symmetric with the java.sql.Timestamp subclass's equals() method.

The solution in such a case is simple and not even specific to Hibernate: don't call aDate.equals(bDate). You should always compare dates and times by comparing Unix time milliseconds (assuming you don't care about the nanoseconds): aDate.getTime() > bDate.getTime(), for example, is true if aDate is a later time than bDate. But be careful: collections such as HashSet call the equals() method as well. Don't mix java.util.Date and java.sql.Date|Time|Timestamp values in such a collection.

You won't have this kind of problem with a Calendar property. When storing a Calendar value, Hibernate will always return a Calendar value, created with Calendar.getInstance()—the actual type depends on locale and time zone.

Alternatively, you can write your own *converter*, as shown in section 6.3.2, and transform any instance of a java.sql temporal type from Hibernate into a plain java.util.Date instance. A custom converter is also a good starting point if, for example, a Calendar instance should have a non-default time zone after the value is loaded from the database.

All these concerns will go away if you choose to represent date and time data using the Java 8 classes LocalDate, LocalTime, LocalDateTime, as previously demonstrated in section 6.1.5. As you may still encounter a lot of code that uses the old classes, you should be aware of the problems that these can raise.

Next are types that map to binary data and large values in the database.

BINARY AND LARGE VALUE TYPES

Table 6.4 lists types for handling binary data and large values. Note that only binary is supported as the type of an identifier property.

If a property in the persistent Java class is of type byte[], Hibernate maps it to a VARBINARY column. The real SQL data type will depend on the dialect; for example, in PostgreSQL, the data type is BYTEA, and in Oracle DBMS it's RAW. In some dialects, the length set with @Column also affects the selected native type; for example, LONG RAW is used for a length of 2,000 and greater in Oracle. In MySQL, the default SQL data type will be TINYBLOB. Depending on the length set with @Column, it may be BLOB, MEDIUMBLOB, or LONGBLOB.

Table 6.4 Binary and large value types

Name	Java type	ANSI SQL type
binary	byte[], java.lang.Byte[]	VARBINARY
text	java.lang.String	CLOB
clob	java.sql.Clob	CLOB
blob	java.sql.Blob	BLOB
serializable	java.io.Serializable	VARBINARY

A `java.lang.String` property is mapped to an SQL VARCHAR column and the same is true for `char[]` and `Character[]`. As we've discussed, some dialects register different native types depending on the declared length.

Hibernate initializes the property value right away when the entity instance that holds the property variable is loaded. This is inconvenient when you have to deal with potentially large values, so you'll usually want to override this default mapping. The JPA specification has a convenient shortcut annotation for this purpose, `@Lob`:

```
@Entity
public class Item {
    @Lob
    private byte[] image;
    @Lob
    private String description;
}
```

This maps the `byte[]` to an SQL BLOB data type and the `String` to a CLOB. Unfortunately, you still won't get lazy loading with this design. Hibernate or Spring Data JPA using Hibernate would have to intercept field access and, for example, load the bytes of the image when you call `someItem.getImage()`. This approach requires bytecode instrumentation of the classes after compilation, for the injection of extra code. We'll discuss lazy loading through bytecode instrumentation and interception in section 12.1.2.

Alternatively, you can switch the type of property in the Java class. JDBC supports large objects (LOBs) directly. If the Java property is `java.sql.Clob` or `java.sql.Blob`, you'll get lazy loading without bytecode instrumentation:

```
@Entity
public class Item {
    @Lob
    private java.sql.Blob imageBlob;
    @Lob
    private java.sql.Clob description;
}
```

> **What does BLOB/CLOB mean?**
>
> Jim Starkey, who came up with the idea of LOBs, says that the marketing department created the terms BLOB and CLOB. BLOB is interpreted as Binary Large Object: binary data (usually a multimedia object—image, video, or audio) stored as a single entity. CLOB means Character Large Object—character data stored in a separate location that the table only references.

These JDBC classes include behavior for loading values on demand. When the owning entity instance is loaded, the property value is a placeholder, and the real value isn't immediately materialized. Once you access the property, within the same transaction, the value is materialized or even streamed directly (to the client) without consuming temporary memory:

```
Item item = em.find(Item.class, ITEM_ID);
InputStream imageDataStream = item.getImageBlob().getBinaryStream();
ByteArrayOutputStream outStream = new ByteArrayOutputStream();
StreamUtils.copy(imageDataStream, outStream);
byte[] imageBytes = outStream.toByteArray();
```

Ⓐ Stream the bytes directly.

Ⓑ Or materialize them into memory.

Ⓒ `org.springframework.util.StreamUtils` is a class providing utility methods for dealing with streams.

The downside is that the domain model is then bound to JDBC; in unit tests you can't access LOB properties without a database connection.

To create and set a `Blob` or `Clob` value, Hibernate offers some convenience methods. This example reads `byteLength` bytes from an `InputStream` directly into the database, without consuming temporary memory:

```
Session session = em.unwrap(Session.class);
Blob blob = session.getLobHelper()
        .createBlob(imageInputStream, byteLength);
someItem.setImageBlob(blob);
em.persist(someItem);
```

Ⓐ We need the native Hibernate API, so we have to unwrap the `Session` from the `EntityManager`.

Ⓑ Then we need to know the number of bytes we want to read from the stream.

Finally, Hibernate provides fallback serialization for any property type that is `java.io.Serializable`. This mapping converts the value of the property to a byte stream stored in a `VARBINARY` column. Serialization and deserialization occur when the owning entity instance is stored and loaded. Naturally, you should use this strategy with extreme caution because data lives longer than applications. One day, nobody will know what those bytes in the database mean. Serialization is sometimes useful for temporary data, such as user preferences, login session data, and so on.

Hibernate will pick the right type of adapter depending on the Java type of the property. If you don't like the default mapping, read on to override it.

SELECTING A TYPE ADAPTER

You have seen many adapters and their Hibernate names in the previous sections. Use the name when overriding Hibernate's default type selection and explicitly select a particular adapter:

```
@Entity
public class Item {
    @org.hibernate.annotations.Type(type = "yes_no")
    private boolean verified = false;
}
```

Instead of BIT, this boolean now maps to a CHAR column with values Y or N.

You can also override an adapter globally in the Hibernate boot configuration with a custom user type, which we'll demonstrate how to write in the next section:

```
metaBuilder.applyBasicType(new MyUserType(), new String[]{"date"});
```

This setting will override the built-in date type adapter and delegate value conversion for java.util.Date properties to the custom implementation.

We consider this extensible type system to be one of Hibernate's core features and an important aspect that makes it so flexible. Next we'll explore the type system and JPA custom converters in more detail.

6.3.2 Creating custom JPA converters

A new requirement for the online auction system is using multiple currencies, and rolling out this kind of change can be complex. We have to modify the database schema, we may have to migrate existing data from the old to the new schema, and we have to update all applications that access the database. In this section, we'll demonstrate how JPA converters and the extensible Hibernate type system can assist in this process, providing an additional, flexible buffer between the application and the database.

To support multiple currencies, we'll introduce a new class in the CaveatEmptor domain model: MonetaryAmount, shown in the following listing.

Listing 6.15 Immutable `MonetaryAmount` value-type class

Path: Ch06/mapping-value-types2/src/main/java/com/manning/javapersistence
➡ /ch06/model/MonetaryAmount.java   **Ⓐ**

```
public class MonetaryAmount implements Serializable {   ⬅
    private final BigDecimal value;                      Ⓑ
    private final Currency currency;
```

```
    public MonetaryAmount(BigDecimal value, Currency currency) {    ◄──┐
        this.value = value;                                              │  B
        this.currency = currency;                                        │
    }                                          B
                                               │
    public BigDecimal getValue() {    ◄────────┘
        return value;
    }                                          B
                                               │
    public Currency getCurrency() {    ◄───────┘
        return currency;
    }

    @Override                                          C
                                                       │
    public boolean equals(Object o) {    ◄─────────────┘
      if (this == o) return true;
      if (o == null || getClass() != o.getClass()) return false;
      MonetaryAmount that = (MonetaryAmount) o;
      return Objects.equals(value, that.value) &&
            Objects.equals(currency, that.currency);
    }
                                                       C
                                                       │
    public int hashCode() {                       ◄────┘
        return Objects.hash(value, currency);
    }                                          D
                                               │
    public String toString() {         ◄───────┘
        return value + " " + currency;
    }                                                  E
                                                       │
    public static MonetaryAmount fromString(String s) {    ◄───┘
        String[] split = s.split(" ");
        return new MonetaryAmount(
            new BigDecimal(split[0]),
            Currency.getInstance(split[1])
        );
    }

}
```

A This value-typed class should be `java.io.Serializable`: When Hibernate stores entity instance data in the shared second-level cache, it *disassembles* the entity's state. If an entity has a `MonetaryAmount` property, the serialized representation of the property value is stored in the second-level cache region. When entity data is retrieved from the cache region, the property value is deserialized and reassembled.

B The class defines the value and currency fields, a constructor using both of them, and getters on these fields.

C The class implements the `equals()` and `hashCode()` methods and compares monetary amounts "by value."

D The class implements the `toString()` method.

E The class implements a static method to create an instance from a `String`.

CONVERTING BASIC PROPERTY VALUES

As is often the case, the database folks can't implement multiple currencies right away. All they can provide quickly is a column data type change in the database schema.

We'll add the buyNowPrice field to the Item class.

Path: Ch06/mapping-value-types/src/main/java/com/manning/javapersistence
➥ /ch06/model/Item.java

```
@NotNull
@Convert(converter = MonetaryAmountConverter.class)
@Column(name = "PRICE", length = 63)
private MonetaryAmount buyNowPrice;
```

We'll store the BUYNOWPRICE in the ITEM table in a VARCHAR column and we'll append the currency code of the monetary amount to its string value. We will store, for example, the value 11.23 USD or 99 EUR.

We'll convert an instance of MonetaryAmount to such a String representation when storing data. When loading data, we'll convert the String back into a Monetary-Amount. The simplest solution for this is to implement a standardized extension point in JPA, javax.persistence.AttributeConverter, in the MonetaryAmoutConverter class used in the @Convert annotation in the preceding snippet. It's shown in the next listing.

Listing 6.16 Converting between strings and MonetaryValue

Path: Ch06/mapping-value-types2/src/main/java/com/manning/javapersistence
➥ /ch06/converter/MonetaryAmountConverter.java

```
@Converter
public class MonetaryAmountConverter                                   Ⓐ
    implements AttributeConverter<MonetaryAmount, String> {

    @Override
    public String convertToDatabaseColumn(MonetaryAmount monetaryAmount) {    Ⓑ
        return monetaryAmount.toString();
    }

    @Override
    public MonetaryAmount convertToEntityAttribute(String s) {         Ⓒ
        return MonetaryAmount.fromString(s);
    }
}
```

Ⓐ A converter has to implement the AttributeConverter interface; the two arguments are the type of the Java property and the type in the database schema. The Java type is MonetaryAmount, and the database type is String, which maps, as usual, to an SQL VARCHAR. We must annotate the class with @Converter.

B The `convertToDatabaseColumn` method will convert from the `MonetaryAmount` entity type to the string database column.

C The `convertToEntityAttribute` method will convert from the string database column to the `MonetaryAmount` entity type.

To test the functionality of the persistence code, we'll use the Spring Data JPA framework, as demonstrated in the following listing. The source code for this book also contains the testing code alternatives that use JPA and Hibernate.

Listing 6.17 | **Testing the functionality of the persistence code**

Path: Ch06/mapping-value-types2/src/test/java/com/manning/javapersistence
➥ /ch06/MappingValuesSpringDataJPATest.java

```
@ExtendWith(SpringExtension.class)                                          A
@ContextConfiguration(classes = {SpringDataConfiguration.class})            B
public class MappingValuesSpringDataJPATest {

    @Autowired                                                              C
    private UserRepository userRepository;

    @Autowired                                                              D
    private ItemRepository itemRepository;

    @Test
    void storeLoadEntities() {

        City city = new City();
        city.setName("Boston");                                             E
        city.setZipcode("12345");
        city.setCountry("USA");
        User user = new User();                                             F
        user.setUsername("username");
        user.setHomeAddress(new Address("Flowers Street", city));
        userRepository.save(user);                                          G

        Item item = new Item();
        item.setName("Some Item");
        item.setMetricWeight(2);                                            H
        item.setBuyNowPrice(new MonetaryAmount(
            BigDecimal.valueOf(1.1), Currency.getInstance("USD")));
I       item.setDescription("descriptiondescription");
        itemRepository.save(item);                                          J

        List<User> users = (List<User>) userRepository.findAll();
        List<Item> items = (List<Item>)                                     K
                            itemRepository.findByMetricWeight(2.0);

        assertAll(                                                          L
                () -> assertEquals(1, users.size()),
                () -> assertEquals("username", users.get(0).getUsername()), M
N               () -> assertEquals("Flowers Street",
                        users.get(0).getHomeAddress().getStreet()),
```

```
        () -> assertEquals("Boston",
            users.get(0).getHomeAddress().getCity().getName()),                O
        () -> assertEquals("12345",
P           users.get(0).getHomeAddress().getCity().getZipcode()),
        () -> assertEquals("USA",                                              Q
            users.get(0).getHomeAddress().getCity().getCountry()),
        () -> assertEquals(1, items.size()),
R       () -> assertEquals("AUCTION: Some Item",               S
                items.get(0).getName()),
        () -> assertEquals("1.1 USD",                                   T
                items.get(0).getBuyNowPrice().toString()),
U       () -> assertEquals("descriptiondescription",
                items.get(0).getDescription()),
        () -> assertEquals(AuctionType.HIGHEST_BID,     V
                items.get(0).getAuctionType()),
W       () -> assertEquals("descriptiond...",                              X
                items.get(0).getShortDescription()),
        () -> assertEquals(2.0, items.get(0).getMetricWeight()),
Y       () -> assertEquals(LocalDate.now(),
                items.get(0).getCreatedOn()),
        () ->
            assertTrue(ChronoUnit.SECONDS.between(
                    LocalDateTime.now(),
                    items.get(0).getLastModified()) < 1),
        () -> assertEquals(new BigDecimal("1.00"),
                items.get(0).getInitialPrice())
                                                          Z
    );
                                                        AA

    }
}
```

A Extend the test using `SpringExtension`. This extension is used to integrate the Spring test context with the JUnit 5 Jupiter test.

B The Spring test context is configured using the beans defined in the `SpringData-Configuration` class.

C A `UserRepository` bean is injected by Spring through autowiring.

D An `ItemRepository` bean is injected by Spring through autowiring. This is possible as the `com.manning.javapersistence.ch06.repositories` package where `UserRepository` and `ItemRepository` are located was used as the argument of the `@EnableJpaRepositories` annotation on the `SpringDataConfiguration` class. To recall what the `SpringDataConfiguration` class looks like, refer to chapter 2.

E Create and set a city.

F Create and set a user.

G Save it to the repository.

H Create and set an item.

I Save it to the repository.

J Get the list of all users.

K Get the list of items having the metric 2.0.

L Check the size of the list of users.

M Check the name of the first user in the list.

N Check the street address of the first user in the list.

O Check the city of the first user in the list.

P Check the ZIP code of the first user in the list.

Q Check the country of the first user in the list.

R Check the size of the list of items.

S Check the name of the first item.

T Check its current buying price.

U Check its description.

V Check the auction type.

W Check its short description.

X Check its metric weight.

Y Check the creation date.

Z Check the last modification date and time and the initial price of the first item in the list. The last modification date and time is checked against the current date and time to be within 1 second (allowing for the retrieval delay).

AA Check the initial price of the first item.

Later, when the DBA upgrades the database schema and offers separate columns for the monetary amount and currency, we'll only have to change the application in a few places. We'll drop the `MonetaryAmountConverter` from the project and make `MonetaryAmount` an `@Embeddable`; it will then map automatically to two database columns. It's easy to selectively enable and disable converters, too, if some tables in the schema haven't been upgraded.

The converter we just wrote is for `MonetaryAmount`, a new class in the domain model. Converters aren't limited to custom classes—we can even override Hibernate's built-in type adapters. For example, we could create a custom converter for some or even all `java.util.Date` properties in the domain model.

We can apply converters to properties of entity classes, like `Item#buyNowPrice` in listing 6.17. We can also apply them to properties of embeddable classes.

CONVERTING PROPERTIES OF COMPONENTS

We've been making a case for fine-grained domain models in this chapter. Earlier we isolated the address information of the `User` and mapped the embeddable `Address` class. We'll continue the process and introduce inheritance with an abstract `Zipcode` class, as shown in figure 6.5. The source code that follows can be found in the mapping-value-types3 folder.

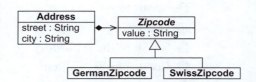

Figure 6.5   The abstract `Zipcode` class has two concrete subclasses.

The `Zipcode` class is trivial, but we have to implement equality by value:

Path: Ch06/mapping-value-types3/src/main/java/com/manning/javapersistence
➥ /ch06/model/Zipcode.java

```java
public abstract class Zipcode {
    private String value;

    public Zipcode(String value) {
        this.value = value;
    }

    public String getValue() {
        return value;
    }

    @Override
    public boolean equals(Object o) {
        if (this == o) return true;
        if (o == null || getClass() != o.getClass()) return false;
        Zipcode zipcode = (Zipcode) o;
        return Objects.equals(value, zipcode.value);
    }

    @Override
    public int hashCode() {
        return Objects.hash(value);
    }
}
```

We can now encapsulate domain subclasses, the difference between German and Swiss postal codes, and any processing:

Path: Ch06/mapping-value-types3/src/main/java/com/manning/javapersistence
➥ /ch06/model/GermanZipcode.java

```java
public class GermanZipcode extends Zipcode {
    public GermanZipcode(String value) {
        super(value);
    }
}
```

We haven't implemented any special processing in the subclass. We'll start with the most obvious difference: German ZIP codes are five numbers long, Swiss are four. A custom converter will take care of this.

Listing 6.18   The `ZipcodeConverter` class

Path: Ch06/mapping-value-types3/src/main/java/com/manning/javapersistence
➥ /ch06/converter/ZipcodeConverter.java

```java
@Converter
```

```
public class ZipcodeConverter
    implements AttributeConverter<Zipcode, String> {

    @Override
    public String convertToDatabaseColumn(Zipcode attribute) {        A
        return attribute.getValue();
    }

    @Override
    public Zipcode convertToEntityAttribute(String s) {               B
        if (s.length() == 5)
            return new GermanZipcode(s);
        else if (s.length() == 4)                                     D
            return new SwissZipcode(s);
        throw new IllegalArgumentException(
            "Unsupported zipcode in database: " + s                   E
        );
    }
}
```

Ⓐ Hibernate calls the `convertToDatabaseColumn()` method of this converter when storing a property value; we return a `String` representation. The column in the schema is VARCHAR. When loading a value, we examine its length and create either a `GermanZipcode` or `SwissZipcode` instance. This is a custom type discrimination routine; we can pick the Java type of the given value.

Ⓑ Hibernate calls the `convertToEntityAttribute` method of this converter when loading a property from the database.

Ⓒ If the length of the string is 5, a new `GermanZipcode` is created.

Ⓓ If the length of the string is 4, a new `SwissZipcode` is created.

Ⓔ Otherwise, an exception is thrown—the ZIP code in the database is not supported.

Now we'll apply this converter on some `Zipcode` properties, such as the embedded homeAddress of a User:

Path: Ch06/mapping-value-types3/src/main/java/com/manning/javapersistence
➥ /ch06/model/User.java

```
@Entity
@Table(name = "USERS")
public class User {
    @Convert(
        converter = ZipcodeConverter.class,
        attributeName = "city.zipcode"
    )
    private Address homeAddress;
    // ...
}
```

The `attributeName` declares the `zipcode` attribute of the embeddable `Address` class. This setting supports a dot syntax for the attribute path; if `zipcode` isn't a property of the `Address` class but is a property of a nested embeddable `City` class, it is referenced with `city.zipcode`, its nested path.

In JPA 2.2, we can apply several `@Convert` annotations on a single embedded property to convert several attributes of the `Address`. Up to JPA 2.1, we had to group them within a single `@Converts` annotation. We can also apply converters to values of collections, and maps if their values or keys are of basic or embeddable types. For example, we can add the `@Convert` annotation on a persistent `Set<Zipcode>`. We'll demonstrate how to map persistent collections later, with `@ElementCollection`, in chapter 8.

For persistent maps, the `attributeName` option of the `@Convert` annotation has some special syntax:

- On a persistent `Map<Address, String>`, we can apply a converter for the zipcode property of each map key with the attribute name `key.zipcode`.
- On a persistent `Map<String, Address>`, we can apply a converter for the zipcode property of each map value with the attribute name `value.zipcode`.
- On a persistent `Map<Zipcode, String>`, we can apply a converter for the key of each map entry with the attribute name `key`.
- On a persistent `Map<String, Zipcode>`, we can apply a converter for the value of each map entry by not setting any `attributeName`.

As before, the attribute name can be a dot-separated path if the embeddable classes are nested; we can write `key.city.zipcode` to reference the `zipcode` property of the `City` class in a composition with the `Address` class.

Some limitations of the JPA converters are as follows:

- We can't apply them to identifier or version properties of an entity.
- We shouldn't apply a converter on a property mapped with `@Enumerated` or `@Temporal` because these annotations already declare what kind of conversion has to occur. If we want to apply a custom converter for enums or date/time properties, we shouldn't annotate them with `@Enumerated` or `@Temporal`.

We'll have to change the testing code we wrote a little. We'll replace this line,

```
city.setZipcode("12345");
```

with this one:

```
city.setZipcode(new GermanZipcode("12345"));
```

We'll also replace this line,

```
() -> assertEquals("12345",
        users.get(0).getHomeAddress().getCity().getZipcode())
```

with this one:

```
() -> assertEquals("12345",
    users.get(0).getHomeAddress().getCity().getZipcode().getValue())
```

The source code for the book contains these tests using Spring Data JPA, Hibernate, and JPA.

Let's get back to multiple currency support in CaveatEmptor. The database administrators have changed the schema again, and we now have to update the application.

6.3.3 *Extending Hibernate with UserTypes*

Finally, new columns have been added to the database schema to support multiple currencies. The ITEM table now has a BUYNOWPRICE_AMOUNT and a separate column for the currency of the amount, BUYNOWPRICE_CURRENCY. There are also INITIALPRICE_AMOUNT and INITIALPRICE_CURRENCY columns. We have to map these columns to the MonetaryAmount properties of the Item class, buyNowPrice, and initialPrice.

Ideally, we don't want to change the domain model; the properties already use the MonetaryAmount class. Unfortunately, the standardized JPA converters don't support the transformation of values from or to multiple columns. Another limitation of JPA converters is integration with the query engine. We can't write the following query: select i from Item i where i.buyNowPrice.amount > 100. Thanks to the converter from the previous section, Hibernate knows how to convert a MonetaryAmount to and from a string. However, it doesn't know that MonetaryAmount has an amount attribute, so it can't parse such a query.

A simple solution would be to map MonetaryAmount as @Embeddable, as you saw earlier in this chapter for the Address class (listing 6.13). Each property of MonetaryAmount—amount and currency—maps to its respective database column.

The database admins, however, added a twist to their requirements: because other old applications also access the database, we'll have to convert each amount to a target currency before storing it in the database. For example, Item#buyNowPrice should be stored in US dollars, and Item#initialPrice should be stored in Euros. (If this example seems far-fetched, we can assure you that you'll see worse in the real world. The evolution of a shared database schema can be costly but is, of course, necessary, because data always lives longer than applications.) Hibernate offers a native converter API: an extension point that allows much more detailed and low-level customization access.

THE EXTENSION POINTS

Hibernate's extension interfaces for its type system can be found in the org.hibernate.usertype package. The following interfaces are available:

- UserType—You can transform values by interacting with the plain JDBC: PreparedStatement (when storing data) and ResultSet (when loading data). By implementing this interface, you can also control how Hibernate caches and dirty-checks values.
- CompositeUserType—You can tell Hibernate that the MonetaryAmount component has two properties: amount and currency. You can then reference these properties in queries with dot notation, such as select avg(i.buyNowPrice .amount) from Item i.

- ParameterizedType—This provides settings to the adapter in mappings. We could implement this interface for the MonetaryAmount conversion because, in some mappings we'll want to convert the amount to US dollars and in other mappings to Euros. We'll only have to write a single adapter and we can then customize its behavior when mapping a property.

- DynamicParameterizedType—This more powerful settings API gives access to dynamic information in the adapter, such as the mapped column and table names. We might as well use this instead of ParameterizedType; there is no additional cost or complexity.

- EnhancedUserType—This is an optional interface for adapters of identifier properties and discriminators. Unlike JPA converters, a UserType in Hibernate can be an adapter for any kind of entity property. Because MonetaryAmount won't be the type of an identifier property or discriminator, we won't need it.

- UserVersionType—This is an optional interface for adapters of version properties.

- UserCollectionType—This rarely-needed interface is used to implement custom collections. We'll have to implement it to persist a non-JDK collection (such as the Google Guava collections: Multiset, Multimap, BiMap, Table, etc.) and preserve additional semantics.

The custom type adapter for MonetaryAmount will implement several of these interfaces. The source code that follows can be found in the mapping-value-types4 folder.

IMPLEMENTING THE USERTYPE

MonetaryAmountUserType is a large class, as you can see in the following listing.

Listing 6.19 The MonetaryAmountUserType class

Path: Ch06/mapping-value-types4/src/main/java/com/manning/javapersistence
➥ /ch06/converter/MonetaryAmountUserType.java

```java
public class MonetaryAmountUserType
        implements CompositeUserType, DynamicParameterizedType {    A

    private Currency convertTo;    B

    public void setParameterValues(Properties parameters) {    C
        String convertToParameter = parameters.getProperty("convertTo");    D
        this.convertTo = Currency.getInstance(
                convertToParameter != null ? convertToParameter : "USD"    E
        );
    }

    public Class returnedClass() {
        return MonetaryAmount.class;    F
    }
```

```java
public boolean isMutable() {                              G
    return false;
}

public Object deepCopy(Object value) {              H
    return value;
}

public Serializable disassemble(Object value,
                        SharedSessionContractImplementor session){    I
    return value.toString();
}

public Object assemble(Serializable cached,
            SharedSessionContractImplementor session, Object owner) {    J
    return MonetaryAmount.fromString((String) cached);
}

public Object replace(Object original, Object target,
            SharedSessionContractImplementor session, Object owner) {    K
    return original;
}

public boolean equals(Object x, Object y) {
    return x == y || !(x == null || y == null) && x.equals(y);
}
                                                          L
public int hashCode(Object x) {
    return x.hashCode();
}

public Object nullSafeGet(ResultSet resultSet,
                        String[] names,                   M
                        SharedSessionContractImplementor session,
                        Object owner) throws SQLException {
    BigDecimal amount = resultSet.getBigDecimal(names[0]);
    if (resultSet.wasNull())                              N
        return null;
    Currency currency =
            Currency.getInstance(resultSet.getString(names[1]));
    return new MonetaryAmount(amount, currency);    <--
}                                                         O

public void nullSafeSet(PreparedStatement statement,      P
        Object value, int index,
        SharedSessionContractImplementor session) throws SQLException {
    if (value == null) {
        statement.setNull(
                index,
                StandardBasicTypes.BIG_DECIMAL.sqlType());    Q
        statement.setNull(
                index + 1,
                StandardBasicTypes.CURRENCY.sqlType());
    } else {
```

```
            MonetaryAmount amount = (MonetaryAmount) value;
            MonetaryAmount dbAmount = convert(amount, convertTo);
            statement.setBigDecimal(index, dbAmount.getValue());
            statement.setString(index + 1, convertTo.getCurrencyCode());
        }
    }

    public MonetaryAmount convert(MonetaryAmount amount,
                                  Currency toCurrency) {
        return new MonetaryAmount(
                amount.getValue().multiply(new BigDecimal(2)),
                toCurrency
        );
    }

    public String[] getPropertyNames() {
        return new String[]{"value", "currency"};
    }

    public Type[] getPropertyTypes() {
        return new Type[]{
                StandardBasicTypes.BIG_DECIMAL,
                StandardBasicTypes.CURRENCY
        };
    }

    public Object getPropertyValue(Object component,
                                   int property) {
        MonetaryAmount monetaryAmount = (MonetaryAmount) component;
        if (property == 0)
            return monetaryAmount.getValue();
        else
            return monetaryAmount.getCurrency();
    }

    public void setPropertyValue(Object component,
                                 int property,
                                 Object value) {
        throw new UnsupportedOperationException(
                "MonetaryAmount is immutable"
        );
    }
}
```

Ⓐ The interfaces we implement are `CompositeUserType` and `DynamicParameterizedType`.

Ⓑ The target currency.

Ⓒ The `setParameterValues` method is inherited from the `DynamicParameterizedType` interface.

Ⓓ Use the `convertTo` parameter to determine the target currency when saving a value into the database.

Ⓔ If the parameter hasn't been set, default to US dollars.

F The `returnedClass` method adapts the given class, in this case, `MonetaryAmount`. This method and the ones to follow are inherited from the `CompositeUserType` interface.

G Hibernate can enable some optimizations if it knows that `MonetaryAmount` is immutable.

H If Hibernate has to make a copy of the value, it calls this `deepCopy` method. For simple immutable classes like `MonetaryAmount`, we can return the given instance.

I Hibernate calls the `disassemble` method when it stores a value in the global shared second-level cache. We need to return a `Serializable` representation. For `MonetaryAmount`, a `String` representation is an easy solution. Or, because `Monetary-Amount` is `Serializable`, we could return it directly.

J Hibernate calls the `assemble` method when it reads the serialized representation from the global shared second-level cache. We create a `MonetaryAmount` instance from the `String` representation. Or, if we stored a serialized `MonetaryAmount`, we could return it directly.

K The `replace` method is called during `EntityManager#merge()` operations. We need to return a copy of the original. Or, if the value type is immutable, like `Monetary-Amount`, we can return the original.

L Hibernate uses value equality to determine whether the value was changed and the database needs to be updated. We rely on the equality and hash code routines we have already written on the `MonetaryAmount` class.

M The `nullSafeGet` method is called to read the `ResultSet` when a `MonetaryAmount` value has to be retrieved from the database.

N Take the `amount` and `currency` values as given in the query result.

O Create a new instance of `MonetaryAmount`.

P The `nullSafeSet` method is called when a `MonetaryAmount` value has to be stored in the database.

Q If `MonetaryAmount` was null, we call `setNull()` to prepare the statement.

R Otherwise, we convert the value to the target currency.

S We then set the `amount` and `currency` on the provided `PreparedStatement()`.

T We can implement whatever currency conversion routine we need.

U For the sake of this example, we double the value so we can easily test whether the conversion was successful. We'd have to replace this code with a real currency converter in a real application. This `convert` method is not a method of the Hibernate `UserType` API.

V The remaining methods inherited from `CompositeUserType` provide the details of the `MonetaryAmount` properties, so Hibernate can integrate the class with the query engine. The `getPropertyNames` method will return a `String` array with two elements, `value` and `currency`—the names of the properties of the `Monetary-Amount` class.

W The getPropertyTypes method will return a Type array with two elements, BIG_DECIMAL and CURRENCY—the types of the properties of the MonetaryAmount class.

X The getPropertyValue method will return either the value field or the currency field of the MonetaryAmount object, depending on the property index.

Y The setPropertyValue method will not allow any field of the MonetaryAmount object to be set, as this one is immutable.

The MonetaryAmountUserType class is now complete, and we can already use it in mappings with its fully qualified class name in @org.hibernate.annotations.Type, as demonstrated in the "Selecting a type adapter" section (in section 6.3.1). This annotation also supports parameters, so we can set the convertTo argument to the target currency.

However, we recommend creating *type definitions*, bundling the adapter with some parameters.

USING TYPE DEFINITIONS

We need an adapter that converts to US dollars, and another that converts to Euros. If we declare these parameters once as a *type definition*, we won't have to repeat them in property mappings. A good location for type definitions is package metadata, in a package-info.java file:

Path: Ch06/mapping-value-types4/src/main/java/com/manning/javapersistence
➡ /ch06/converter/package-info.java

```
@org.hibernate.annotations.TypeDefs({
    @org.hibernate.annotations.TypeDef(
        name = "monetary_amount_usd",
        typeClass = MonetaryAmountUserType.class,
        parameters = {@Parameter(name = "convertTo", value = "USD")}
    ),
    @org.hibernate.annotations.TypeDef(
        name = "monetary_amount_eur",
        typeClass = MonetaryAmountUserType.class,
        parameters = {@Parameter(name = "convertTo", value = "EUR")}
    )
})
package com.manning.javapersistence.ch06.converter;
import org.hibernate.annotations.Parameter;
```

We are now ready to use the adapters in mappings, using the names monetary_amount_usd and monetary_amount_eur.

We can map the buyNowPrice and initialPrice of Item:

Path: Ch06/mapping-value-types4/src/main/java/com/manning/javapersistence
➡ /ch06/model/Item.java

```
@Entity
public class Item {
    @NotNull
    @org.hibernate.annotations.Type(
```

```
            type = "monetary_amount_usd"
    )
    @org.hibernate.annotations.Columns(columns = {
        @Column(name = "BUYNOWPRICE_AMOUNT"),
        @Column(name = "BUYNOWPRICE_CURRENCY", length = 3)
    })
    private MonetaryAmount buyNowPrice;

    @NotNull
    @org.hibernate.annotations.Type(
            type = "monetary_amount_eur"
    )
    @org.hibernate.annotations.Columns(columns = {
        @Column(name = "INITIALPRICE_AMOUNT"),
        @Column(name = "INITIALPRICE_CURRENCY", length = 3)
    })
    private MonetaryAmount initialPrice;
    // ...
}
```

If `UserType` transforms values for only a single column, we don't need an `@Column` annotation. `MonetaryAmountUserType`, however, accesses two columns, so we need to explicitly declare two columns in the property mapping. Because JPA doesn't support multiple `@Column` annotations on a single property, we'll have to group them with the proprietary `@org.hibernate.annotations.Columns` annotation. Note that the order of the annotations is now important! Recheck the code for `MonetaryAmountUserType`; many operations rely on indexed access of arrays. The order when accessing `PreparedStatement` or `ResultSet` is the same as that for the declared columns in the mapping. Also, note that the number of columns isn't relevant for the choice of `UserType` versus `CompositeUserType`—only the desire to expose value type properties for queries.

We'll have to change the testing code we wrote. We'll add this line to set the `Item`:

```
item.setBuyNowPrice(new MonetaryAmount(BigDecimal.valueOf(1.1),
                    Currency.getInstance("USD")));
```

We'll replace this line,

```
() -> assertEquals("1.1 USD",
                items.get(0).getBuyNowPrice().toString())
```

with this one:

```
() -> assertEquals("2.20 USD",
                items.get(0).getBuyNowPrice().toString())
```

We'll also replace this line,

```
() -> assertEquals(new BigDecimal("1.00"),
                items.get(0).getInitialPrice())
```

with this one:

```
() -> assertEquals("2.00 EUR",
                   items.get(0).getInitialPrice().toString())
```

This is because the `convert` method from the `MonetaryAmountUserType` class doubles the value of the amount (shown in listing 6.19 at **U**). The source code for this book contains the tests using Spring Data JPA, Hibernate, and JPA.

With `MonetaryAmountUserType`, we've extended the buffer between the Java domain model and the SQL database schema. Both representations are now more robust with respect to changes, and we can handle even rather eccentric requirements without modifying the essence of the domain model classes.

Summary

- You can map the basic and embedded properties of an entity class.
- You can override basic mappings, change the name of a mapped column, use derived, default, temporal, and enumeration properties, and test them.
- You can implement embeddable component classes and create fine-grained domain models.
- You can map the properties of several Java classes in a composition, such as `Address` and `City`, to one entity table.
- Any JPA provider supports a minimum set of Java-to-SQL type conversions, as well as some additional adapters.
- You can write a custom type converter, as we did for the `MonetaryAmount` class, with the standard JPA extension interfaces. You can also write a low-level adapter, as we did with the native Hibernate `UserType` API.

Mapping inheritance

We deliberately haven't talked much about inheritance mapping so far. Mapping makes the connection between the object-oriented world and the relational world, but inheritance is specific to object-oriented systems. Consequently, mapping a hierarchy of classes to tables can be a complex problem, and we'll demonstrate various strategies in this chapter.

A basic strategy for mapping classes to database tables might be "one table for every persistent entity class." This approach sounds simple enough and indeed works well until we encounter inheritance.

Inheritance is such a visible structural mismatch between the object-oriented and relational worlds because the object-oriented model provides both *is a* and *has a* relationships. SQL-based models provide only *has a* relationships; SQL database management systems don't support type inheritance, and even when it's available, it's usually proprietary or incomplete.

There are four different strategies for representing an inheritance hierarchy:

- Use one table per concrete class and default runtime polymorphic behavior.
- Use one table per concrete class, but discard polymorphism and inheritance relationships completely from the SQL schema. Use SQL `UNION` queries for runtime polymorphic behavior.
- Use one table per class hierarchy: enable polymorphism by denormalizing the SQL schema and rely on row-based discrimination to determine supertypes and subtypes.
- Use one table per subclass: represent *is a* (inheritance) relationships as *has a* (foreign key) relationships, and use SQL `JOIN` operations.

This chapter takes a top-down approach, assuming that we're starting with a domain model and trying to derive a new SQL schema. The mapping strategies described here are just as relevant if you're working from the bottom up, starting with existing database tables. We'll examine some tricks along the way to help you deal with imperfect table layouts.

7.1 Table per concrete class with implicit polymorphism

We are working on the CaveatEmptor application, implementing persistence for a hierarchy of classes. We could stick with the simplest approach suggested: use exactly one table for each concrete class. We can map all the properties of a class, including inherited properties, to columns of a table, as shown in figure 7.1.

NOTE To be able to execute the examples from this chapter's source code, you will first need to run the Ch07.sql script.

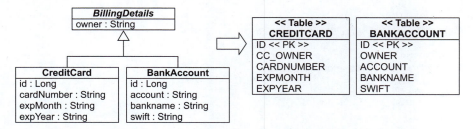

Figure 7.1 Mapping all concrete classes to an independent table

Relying on this implicit polymorphism, we'll map concrete classes with `@Entity`, as usual. By default, properties of the superclass are ignored and not persistent! We'll have to annotate the superclass with `@MappedSuperclass` to enable the embedding of its properties in the concrete subclass tables; see listing 7.1, which can be found in the mapping-inheritance-mappedsuperclass folder.

Path: Ch07/mapping-inheritance-mappedsuperclass/src/main/java/com/manning
➥ /javapersistence/ch07/model/BillingDetails.java

```java
@MappedSuperclass
public abstract class BillingDetails {
    @Id
    @GeneratedValue(generator = "ID_GENERATOR")
    private Long id;

    @NotNull
    private String owner;
    // . . .
}
```

Now we'll map the concrete subclasses.

Listing 7.2   Mapping `CreditCard` (concrete subclass)

Path: Ch07/mapping-inheritance-mappedsuperclass/src/main/java/com/manning
➥ /javapersistence/ch07/model/CreditCard.java

```java
@Entity
@AttributeOverride(
        name = "owner",
        column = @Column(name = "CC_OWNER", nullable = false))
public class CreditCard extends BillingDetails {

    @NotNull
    private String cardNumber;

    @NotNull
    private String expMonth;

    @NotNull
    private String expYear;

    // . . .
}
```

We can override column mappings from the superclass in a subclass with the
@AttributeOverride annotation. Starting with JPA 2.2, we can use several @Attribute-
Override annotations on the same class; up to JPA 2.1, we had to group the @Attribute-
Override annotations within an @AttributeOverrides annotation. The previous
example renames the OWNER column to CC_OWNER in the CREDITCARD table.

The following listing shows the mapping of the BankAccount subclass.

Listing 7.3   Mapping `BankAccount` (concrete subclass)

Path: Ch07/mapping-inheritance-mappedsuperclass/src/main/java/com/manning
➡ /javapersistence/ch07/model/BankAccount.java

```
@Entity
   public class BankAccount extends BillingDetails {

       @NotNull
       private String account;

       @NotNull
       private String bankname;

       @NotNull
       private String swift;
// ...
}
```

We can declare the identifier property in the superclass, with a shared column name and generator strategy for all subclasses (as in listing 7.3), or we can repeat it inside each concrete class.

To work with these classes, we'll create three Spring Data JPA repository interfaces.

Listing 7.4   The `BillingDetailsRepository` interface

Path: Ch07/mapping-inheritance-mappedsuperclass/src/main/java/com/manning
➡ /javapersistence/ch07/repositories/BillingDetailsRepository.java

```
@NoRepositoryBean
public interface BillingDetailsRepository<T extends BillingDetails, ID>
                extends JpaRepository<T, ID> {
    List<T> findByOwner(String owner);
}
```

In the preceding listing, the `BillingDetailsRepository` interface is annotated with `@NoRepositoryBean`. This prevents its instantiation as a Spring Data JPA repository instance. This is necessary because, following the schema from figure 7.1, there will be no `BILLINGDETAILS` table. However, the `BillingDetailsRepository` interface intends to be extended by the repository interfaces to deal with the `CreditCard` and `BankAccount` subclasses. That is why `BillingDetailsRepository` is generified by a `T` that extends `BillingDetails`. Additionally, it contains the `findByOwner` method. The `owner` field from `BillingDetails` will be included in both the `CREDITCARD` and `BANK-ACCOUNT` tables.

We'll now create two more Spring Data repository interfaces.

Listing 7.5   The `BankAccountRepository` interface

```
Path: Ch07/mapping-inheritance-mappedsuperclass/src/main/java/com/manning
➥ /javapersistence/ch07/repositories/BankAccountRepository.java

public interface BankAccountRepository
        extends BillingDetailsRepository<BankAccount, Long> {
    List<BankAccount> findBySwift(String swift);
}
```

The `BankAccountRepository` interface extends `BillingDetailsRepository`, generi-fied by `BankAccount` (as it deals with `BankAccount` instances) and by `Long` (as the ID of the class is of this type). It adds the `findBySwift` method, whose name follows the Spring Data JPA conventions (see chapter 4).

Listing 7.6   The `CreditCardRepository` interface

```
Path: Ch07/mapping-inheritance-mappedsuperclass/src/main/java/com/manning
➥ /javapersistence/ch07/repositories/CreditCardRepository.java

public interface CreditCardRepository
        extends BillingDetailsRepository<CreditCard, Long> {
    List<CreditCard> findByExpYear(String expYear);
}
```

The `CreditCardRepository` interface extends `BillingDetailsRepository`, generi-fied by `CreditCard` (as it deals with `CreditCard` instances) and by `Long` (as the ID of the class is of this type). It adds the `findByExpYear` method, whose name follows the Spring Data JPA conventions (see chapter 4).

We'll create the following test to check the functionality of the persistence code.

Listing 7.7   Testing the functionality of the persistence code

```
Path: Ch07/mapping-inheritance-mappedsuperclass/src/test/java/com/manning
➥ /javapersistence/ch07/MappingInheritanceSpringDataJPATest.java
```

A

```
@ExtendWith(SpringExtension.class)                                      ⓑ
@ContextConfiguration(classes = {SpringDataConfiguration.class})    ◁──┘
public class MappingInheritanceSpringDataJPATest {

    @Autowired                                                      ⓒ
    private CreditCardRepository crediCardRepository;

    @Autowired                                                      ⓓ
    private BankAccountRepository bankAccountRepository;

    @Test
    void storeLoadEntities() {

        CreditCard creditCard = new CreditCard(                     ⓔ
                "John Smith", "123456789", "10", "2030");
        creditCardRepository.save(creditCard);
```

```
        BankAccount bankAccount = new BankAccount(
                "Mike Johnson", "12345", "Delta Bank", "BANKXY12");
        bankAccountRepository.save(bankAccount);
```
Ⓕ

```
        List<CreditCard> creditCards =
            creditCardRepository.findByOwner("John Smith");
```
Ⓖ
```
        List<BankAccount> bankAccounts =
            bankAccountRepository.findByOwner("Mike Johnson");
```
Ⓗ
Ⓘ
```
        List<CreditCard> creditCards2 =
            creditCardRepository.findByExpYear("2030");
        List<BankAccount> bankAccounts2 =
            bankAccountRepository.findBySwift("BANKXY12");
```
Ⓙ

Ⓚ
```
assertAll(
        () -> assertEquals(1, creditCards.size()),
```
Ⓛ
```
        () -> assertEquals("123456789",
```
Ⓜ
```
            creditCards.get(0).getCardNumber()),
        () -> assertEquals(1, bankAccounts.size()),
```
Ⓝ
```
        () -> assertEquals("12345",
```
Ⓞ
```
            bankAccounts.get(0).getAccount()),
        () -> assertEquals(1, creditCards2.size()),
```
Ⓟ
```
        () -> assertEquals("John Smith",
```
Ⓠ
```
            creditCards2.get(0).getOwner()),
        () -> assertEquals(1, bankAccounts2.size()),
```
Ⓡ
```
        () -> assertEquals("Mike Johnson",
            bankAccounts2.get(0).getOwner())
);
```
```
    }
}
```

Ⓐ Extend the test using `SpringExtension`. This extension is used to integrate the Spring test context with the JUnit 5 Jupiter test.

Ⓑ The Spring test context is configured using the beans defined in the `SpringData-Configuration` class.

Ⓒ A `CreditCardRepository` bean is injected by Spring through autowiring.

Ⓓ A `BankAccountRepository` bean is injected by Spring through autowiring. This is possible as the `com.manning.javapersistence.ch07.repositories` package where `CreditCardRepository` and `BankAccountRepository` are located was used as the argument of the `@EnableJpaRepositories` annotation on the `SpringData-Configuration` class. To recall what the `SpringDataConfiguration` class looks like, refer to chapter 2.

Ⓔ Create a credit card and save it to the repository.

Ⓕ Create a bank account and save it to the repository.

Ⓖ Get the list of all credit cards having John Smith as owner.

Ⓗ Get the list of all bank accounts having Mike Johnson as owner.

Ⓘ Get the credit cards expiring in 2030.

(J) Get the bank accounts with SWIFT BANKXY12.

(K) Check the size of the list of credit cards.

(L) Get the number of the first credit card in the list.

(M) Check the size of the list of bank accounts.

(N) Check the number of the first bank account in the list.

(O) Check the size of the list of credit cards expiring in 2030.

(P) Check the owner of the first credit card in this list.

(Q) Check the size of the list of bank accounts with SWIFT BANKXY12.

(R) Check the owner of the first bank account in this list.

The source code for this chapter also demonstrates how to test these classes using JPA and Hibernate.

The main problem with implicit inheritance mapping is that it doesn't support polymorphic associations very well. In the database, we usually represent associations as foreign key relationships. In the schema from figure 7.1, if the subclasses are all mapped to different tables, a polymorphic association to their superclass (the abstract `BillingDetails`) can't be represented as a simple foreign key relationship. We can't have another entity mapped with a foreign key "referencing BILLINGDETAILS"—there is no such table. This would be problematic in the domain model because `Billing-Details` is associated with `User`; both the `CREDITCARD` and `BANKACCOUNT` tables would need a foreign key reference to the `USERS` table. None of these problems can be easily resolved, so we should consider an alternative mapping strategy.

Polymorphic queries that return instances of all classes that match the interface of the queried class are also problematic. Hibernate must execute a query against the superclass as several SQL `SELECT`s—one for each concrete subclass. The JPA query `select bd from BillingDetails bd` requires two SQL statements:

```
select
    ID, OWNER, ACCOUNT, BANKNAME, SWIFT
from
    BANKACCOUNT
select
    ID, CC_OWNER, CARDNUMBER, EXPMONTH, EXPYEAR
from
    CREDITCARD
```

Hibernate or Spring Data JPA using Hibernate uses a separate SQL query for each concrete subclass. On the other hand, queries against the concrete classes are trivial and perform well—Hibernate uses only one of the statements.

A further conceptual problem with this mapping strategy is that several different columns of different tables share exactly the same semantics. This makes schema evolution more complex. For example, renaming or changing the type of a superclass property results in changes to multiple columns in multiple tables. Many of the standard refactoring operations offered by your IDE would require manual adjustments, because the automatic procedures usually don't count for things like `@Attribute-Override` or `@AttributeOverrides`. It is much more difficult to implement database integrity constraints that apply to all subclasses.

We recommend this approach only for the top level of your class hierarchy, where polymorphism isn't usually required and when modification of the superclass in the future is unlikely. This may work for particular domain models that you face in your real-life applications, but it isn't a good fit for the CaveatEmptor domain model, where queries and other entities refer to `BillingDetails`. We'll look for other alternatives.

With the help of the SQL UNION operation, we can eliminate most of the concerns with polymorphic queries and associations.

7.2 Table per concrete class with unions

Let's consider a union subclass mapping with `BillingDetails` as an abstract class (or interface), as in the previous section. In this situation, there are again two tables and superclass columns that are duplicated in both: `CREDITCARD` and `BANKACCOUNT`. What's new here is an inheritance strategy known as `TABLE_PER_CLASS`, declared on the superclass, as shown in the following listing. The source code can be found in the `mapping-inheritance-tableperclass` folder.

> **NOTE** The JPA standard specifies that `TABLE_PER_CLASS` is optional, so not all JPA implementations support it.

Listing 7.8 Mapping `BillingDetails` with `TABLE_PER_CLASS`

Path: Ch07/mapping-inheritance-tableperclass/src/main/java/com/manning
➥ /javapersistence/ch07/model/BillingDetails.java

```
@Entity
@Inheritance(strategy = InheritanceType.TABLE_PER_CLASS)
public abstract class BillingDetails {
    @Id
    @GeneratedValue(generator = "ID_GENERATOR")
    private Long id;
    @NotNull
    private String owner;
    // . . .
}
```

The database identifier and its mapping have to be present in the superclass to share it in all subclasses and their tables. This is no longer optional, as it was for the previous mapping strategy. The `CREDITCARD` and `BANKACCOUNT` tables both have an `ID` primary key column. All concrete class mappings inherit persistent properties from the superclass (or interface). An `@Entity` annotation on each subclass is all that is required.

Listing 7.9   Mapping `CreditCard`

Path: Ch07/mapping-inheritance-tableperclass/src/main/java/com/manning
➥ /javapersistence/ch07/model/CreditCard.java

```
@Entity
@AttributeOverride(
        name = "owner",
        column = @Column(name = "CC_OWNER", nullable = false))
public class CreditCard extends BillingDetails {
    @NotNull
    private String cardNumber;
    @NotNull
    private String expMonth;
    @NotNull
    private String expYear;
    // . . .
}
```

Listing 7.10   Mapping `BankAccount`

Path: Ch07/mapping-inheritance-tableperclass/src/main/java/com/manning
➥ /javapersistence/ch07/model/BankAccount.java

```
@Entity
public class BankAccount extends BillingDetails {
    @NotNull
    private String account;
    @NotNull
    private String bankName;
    @NotNull
    private String swift;
    // . . .
}
```

We'll have to change the `BillingDetailsRepository` interface and remove the `@NoRepositoryBean` annotation. This change, together with the fact that the `BillingDetails` class is now annotated as `@Entity`, will allow this repository to interact with the database. This is what the `BillingDetailsRepository` interface looks like now.

Listing 7.11   The `BillingDetailsRepository` interface

Path: Ch07/mapping-inheritance-tableperclass/src/main/java/com/manning
➥ /javapersistence/ch07/model/BillingDetailsRepository.java

```
public interface BillingDetailsRepository<T extends BillingDetails, ID>
                extends JpaRepository<T, ID> {
    List<T> findByOwner(String owner);
}
```

Keep in mind that the SQL schema still isn't aware of the inheritance; the tables look exactly alike, as shown in figure 7.1.

If `BillingDetails` were concrete, we'd need an additional table to hold instances. Keep in mind that there is still no relationship between the database tables, except for the fact that they have some (many) similar columns.

The advantages of this mapping strategy are clearer if we examine polymorphic queries.

We can use the Spring Data JPA `BillingDetailsRepository` interface to query the database, like this:

```
billingDetailsRepository.findAll();
```

Or from JPA or Hibernate, we can execute the following query:

```
select bd from BillingDetails bd
```

Both approaches will generate the following SQL statement:

```
select
    ID, OWNER, EXPMONTH, EXPYEAR, CARDNUMBER,
    ACCOUNT, BANKNAME, SWIFT, CLAZZ_
 from
    ( select
        ID, OWNER, EXPMONTH, EXPYEAR, CARDNUMBER,
        null as ACCOUNT,
        null as BANKNAME,
        null as SWIFT,
        1 as CLAZZ_
    from
        CREDITCARD
    union all
    select
        id, OWNER,
        null as EXPMONTH,
        null as EXPYEAR,
        null as CARDNUMBER,
        ACCOUNT, BANKNAME, SWIFT,
        2 as CLAZZ_
    from
        BANKACCOUNT
    ) as BILLINGDETAILS
```

This `SELECT` uses a `FROM`-clause subquery to retrieve all instances of `BillingDetails` from all concrete class tables. The tables are combined with a `UNION` operator, and a literal (in this case, 1 and 2) is inserted into the intermediate result; Hibernate reads this to instantiate the correct class given the data from a particular row. A union requires that the queries that are combined project over the same columns, so you have to pad and fill nonexistent columns with `NULL`. You may wonder whether this query will really perform better than two separate statements. Here you can let the database optimizer find the best execution plan to combine rows from several tables instead of merging two result sets in memory as Hibernate's polymorphic loader engine would do.

An important advantage is the ability to handle polymorphic associations; for example, an association mapping from `User` to `BillingDetails` will now be possible. Hibernate can use a `UNION` query to simulate a single table as the target of the association mapping.

So far, the inheritance-mapping strategies we've examined don't require extra consideration of the SQL schema. This situation changes with the next strategy.

7.3 Table per class hierarchy

We could map an entire class hierarchy to a single table. This table includes columns for all properties of all classes in the hierarchy. The value of an extra type discriminator column or formula identifies the concrete subclass represented by a particular row. Figure 7.2 shows this approach. The source code that follows can be found in the mapping-inheritance-singletable folder.

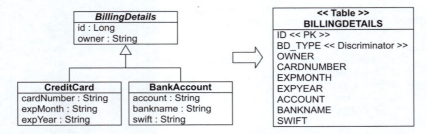

Figure 7.2   Mapping an entire class hierarchy to a single table

This mapping strategy is a winner in terms of both performance and simplicity. It's the best-performing way to represent polymorphism—both polymorphic and non-polymorphic queries perform well, and it's even easy to write queries by hand. Ad hoc reporting is possible without complex joins or unions. Schema evolution is straightforward.

There is one major problem: data integrity. We must declare columns for properties declared by subclasses to be nullable. If the subclasses each define several non-nullable properties, the loss of `NOT NULL` constraints may be a serious problem from the point of view of data correctness. Imagine that an expiration date for credit cards is required, but the database schema can't enforce this rule because all columns of the table can be `NULL`. A simple application programming error can lead to invalid data.

Another important concern is normalization. We've created functional dependencies between non-key columns, violating the third normal form. As always, denormalization for performance reasons can be misleading because it sacrifices long-term stability, maintainability, and the integrity of data for immediate gains that may also be achieved by proper optimization of the SQL execution plans (in other words, ask the DBA).

We'll use the SINGLE_TABLE inheritance strategy to create a table-per-class hierarchy mapping, as shown in the following listing.

Listing 7.12 Mapping `BillingDetails` with SINGLE_TABLE

Path: Ch07/mapping-inheritance-singletable/src/main/java/com/manning
➥ /javapersistence/ch07/model/BillingDetails.java

```java
@Entity
@Inheritance(strategy = InheritanceType.SINGLE_TABLE)
@DiscriminatorColumn(name = "BD_TYPE")
public abstract class BillingDetails {

    @Id
    @GeneratedValue(generator = "ID_GENERATOR")
    private Long id;

    @NotNull
    @Column(nullable = false)
    private String owner;

    //  . . .
}
```

The root class of the inheritance hierarchy, BillingDetails, is mapped to the BILLINGDETAILS table automatically. Shared properties of the superclass can be NOT NULL in the schema; every subclass instance must have a value. An implementation quirk of Hibernate requires that we declare nullability with @Column because Hibernate ignores Bean Validation's @NotNull when it generates the database schema.

We have to add a special discriminator column to distinguish what each row represents. This isn't a property of the entity; it's used internally by Hibernate. The column name is BD_TYPE, and the values are strings—in this case, "CC" or "BA". Hibernate or Spring Data JPA using Hibernate automatically sets and retrieves the discriminator values.

If we don't specify a discriminator column in the superclass, its name defaults to DTYPE, and the values are strings. All concrete classes in the inheritance hierarchy can have a discriminator value, such as CreditCard.

Listing 7.13 Mapping `CreditCard` using the SINGLE_TABLE inheritance strategy

Path: Ch07/mapping-inheritance-singletable/src/main/java/com/manning
➥ /javapersistence/ch07/model/CreditCard.java

```java
@Entity
@DiscriminatorValue("CC")
public class CreditCard extends BillingDetails {
    @NotNull
    private String cardNumber;
    @NotNull
```

```
    private String expMonth;
    @NotNull
    private String expYear;
    //  . . .
}
```

Without an explicit discriminator value, Hibernate defaults to the fully qualified class name if we use Hibernate XML files and to the simple entity name if we use annotations or JPA XML files. Note that JPA doesn't specify a default for non-string discriminator types; each persistence provider can have different defaults. Therefore, we should always specify discriminator values for the concrete classes.

We'll annotate every subclass with `@Entity`, and then map properties of a subclass to columns in the `BILLINGDETAILS` table. Remember that `NOT NULL` constraints aren't allowed in the schema because a `BankAccount` instance won't have an `expMonth` property, and the `EXPMONTH` column must be `NULL` for that row. Hibernate and Spring Data JPA using Hibernate ignore the `@NotNull` for schema DDL generation, but they observe it at runtime before inserting a row. This helps us avoid programming errors; we don't want to accidentally save credit card data without its expiration date. (Other, less well-behaved applications can, of course, still store incorrect data in this database.)

We can use the Spring Data JPA `BillingDetailsRepository` interface to query the database, like this:

```
billingDetailsRepository.findAll();
```

Or, from JPA or Hibernate, we can execute the following query:

```
select bd from BillingDetails bd
```

Both approaches will generate the following SQL statement:

```
select
    ID, OWNER, EXPMONTH, EXPYEAR, CARDNUMBER,
    ACCOUNT, BANKNAME, SWIFT, BD_TYPE
from
    BILLINGDETAILS
```

To query the `CreditCard` subclass, we also have alternatives.

We can use the Spring Data JPA `CreditCardRepository` interface to query the database, like this:

```
creditCardRepository.findAll();
```

Or, from JPA or Hibernate, we can execute the following query:

```
select cc from CreditCard cc
```

Hibernate adds a restriction on the discriminator column:

```
select
    ID, OWNER, EXPMONTH, EXPYEAR, CARDNUMBER
from
    BILLINGDETAILS
where
    BD_TYPE='CC'
```

Sometimes, especially in legacy schemas, we don't have the freedom to include an extra discriminator column in the entity tables. In this case, we can apply an expression to calculate a discriminator value for each row. Formulas for discrimination aren't part of the JPA specification, but Hibernate has an extension annotation, `@DiscriminatorFormula`.

Listing 7.14   Mapping `BillingDetails` with a `@DiscriminatorFormula`

Path: Ch07/mapping-inheritance-singletableformula/src/main/java/com/manning
➡ /javapersistence/ch07/model/BillingDetails.java

```
@Entity
@Inheritance(strategy = InheritanceType.SINGLE_TABLE)
@org.hibernate.annotations.DiscriminatorFormula(
        "case when CARDNUMBER is not null then 'CC' else 'BA' end"
)
public abstract class BillingDetails {
    //  . . .
}
```

There is no discriminator column in the schema, so this mapping relies on an SQL `CASE`/`WHEN` expression to determine whether a particular row represents a credit card or a bank account (many developers have never used this kind of SQL expression; check the ANSI standard if you aren't familiar with it). The result of the expression is a literal, `CC` or `BA`, declared on the subclass mappings.

The disadvantages of the table-per-class hierarchy strategy may be too serious for your design—denormalized schemas can become a major burden in the long term, and your DBA may not like it at all. The next inheritance-mapping strategy doesn't expose you to this problem.

7.4   Table per subclass with joins

The fourth option is to represent inheritance relationships as SQL foreign key associations. Every class or subclass that declares persistent properties—including abstract classes and even interfaces—has its own table. The source code that follows can be found in the mapping-inheritance-joined folder.

Unlike the table-per-concrete-class strategy we mapped first, the table of a concrete `@Entity` here contains columns only for each non-inherited property declared by the subclass itself, along with a primary key that is also a foreign key of the superclass table. This is easier than it sounds; have a look at figure 7.3.

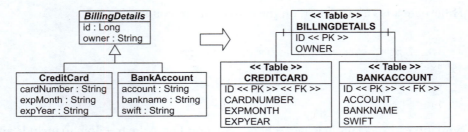

Figure 7.3   Mapping all classes of the hierarchy to their own tables

If we make an instance of the `CreditCard` subclass persistent, Hibernate inserts two rows: The values of properties declared by the `BillingDetails` superclass are stored in a new row of the `BILLINGDETAILS` table. Only the values of properties declared by the subclass are stored in a new row of the `CREDITCARD` table. The primary key shared by the two rows links them together. Later, the subclass instance can be retrieved from the database by joining the subclass table with the superclass table.

The primary advantage of this strategy is that it normalizes the SQL schema. Schema evolution and integrity-constraint definition are straightforward. A foreign key referencing the table of a particular subclass may represent a polymorphic association to that particular subclass. We'll use the `JOINED` inheritance strategy to create a table-per-subclass hierarchy mapping.

Listing 7.15   Mapping `BillingDetails` with `JOINED`

Path: Ch07/mapping-inheritance-joined/src/main/java/com/manning
➥ /javapersistence/ch07/model/BillingDetails.java

```
@Entity
@Inheritance(strategy = InheritanceType.JOINED)
public abstract class BillingDetails {
    @Id
    @GeneratedValue(generator = "ID_GENERATOR")
    private Long id;
    @NotNull
    private String owner;

    // . . .
}
```

The root class `BillingDetails` is mapped to the table `BILLINGDETAILS`. Note that no discriminator is required with this strategy.

In subclasses, we don't need to specify the join column if the primary key column of the subclass table has (or is supposed to have) the same name as the primary key column of the superclass table. In the following listing, `BankAccount` will be a subclass of `BillingDetails`.

Listing 7.16   Mapping `BankAccount` (concrete class)

Path: Ch07/mapping-inheritance-joined/src/main/java/com/manning
➡ /javapersistence/ch07/model/BankAccount.java

```
@Entity
public class BankAccount extends BillingDetails {

    @NotNull
    private String account;

    @NotNull
    private String bankname;

    @NotNull
    private String swift;

    //  . . .
}
```

This entity has no identifier property; it automatically inherits the ID property and column from the superclass, and Hibernate knows how to join the tables if we want to retrieve instances of BankAccount.

Of course, we could specify the column name explicitly, using the @PrimaryKey-JoinColumn annotation, as shown in the following listing.

Listing 7.17   Mapping `CreditCard`

Path: Ch07/mapping-inheritance-joined/src/main/java/com/manning
➡ /javapersistence/ch07/model/CreditCard.java

```
@Entity
@PrimaryKeyJoinColumn(name = "CREDITCARD_ID")
public class CreditCard extends BillingDetails {
    @NotNull
    private String cardNumber;
    @NotNull
    private String expMonth;
    @NotNull
    private String expYear;
    //  . . .
}
```

The primary key columns of the BANKACCOUNT and CREDITCARD tables each also have a foreign key constraint referencing the primary key of the BILLINGDETAILS table.

We can use the Spring Data JPA BillingDetailsRepository interface to query the database, like this:

```
billingDetailsRepository.findAll();
```

Or, from JPA or Hibernate, we can execute the following query:

```
select bd from BillingDetails bd
```

Hibernate relies on an SQL outer join and will generate the following:

```
select
    BD.ID, BD.OWNER,
    CC.EXPMONTH, CC.EXPYEAR, CC.CARDNUMBER,
    BA.ACCOUNT, BA.BANKNAME, BA.SWIFT,
    case
        when CC.CREDITCARD_ID is not null then 1
        when BA.ID is not null then 2
        when BD.ID is not null then 0
    end
from
    BILLINGDETAILS BD
    left outer join CREDITCARD CC on BD.ID=CC.CREDITCARD_ID
    left outer join BANKACCOUNT BA on BD.ID=BA.ID
```

The SQL `CASE . . . WHEN` clause detects the existence (or absence) of rows in the subclass tables `CREDITCARD` and `BANKACCOUNT`, so Hibernate or Spring Data using Hibernate can determine the concrete subclass for a particular row of the `BILLING-DETAILS` table.

For a narrow subclass query like this,

```
creditCardRepository.findAll();
```

or this,

```
select cc from CreditCard cc,
```

Hibernate uses an inner join:

```
select
    CREDITCARD_ID, OWNER, EXPMONTH, EXPYEAR, CARDNUMBER
from
    CREDITCARD
    inner join BILLINGDETAILS on CREDITCARD_ID=ID
```

As you can see, this mapping strategy is more difficult to implement by hand—even ad hoc reporting is more complex. This is an important consideration if you plan to mix Spring Data JPA or Hibernate code with handwritten SQL. A usual approach and a portable solution may be working with JPQL (Jakarta Persistence Query Language) and annotating methods with JPQL queries.

Furthermore, even though this mapping strategy is deceptively simple, our experience is that performance can be unacceptable for complex class hierarchies. Queries always require a join across many tables or many sequential reads.

Inheritance with joins and a discriminator

Hibernate doesn't need a special discriminator database column to implement the `InheritanceType.JOINED` strategy, and the JPA specification doesn't contain any requirements either. The `CASE . . . WHEN` clause in the SQL `SELECT` statement is a smart way to distinguish the entity type of each retrieved row.

Some JPA examples you might find elsewhere, however, use `Inheritance-Type.JOINED` *and* a `@DiscriminatorColumn` mapping. Apparently some other JPA providers don't use `CASE . . . WHEN` clauses and rely only on a discriminator value, even for the `InheritanceType.JOINED` strategy. Hibernate doesn't need the discriminator but uses a declared `@DiscriminatorColumn`, even with a `JOINED` mapping strategy. If you prefer to ignore the discriminator mapping with `JOINED` (it was ignored in older Hibernate versions), enable the configuration property `hibernate.discriminator.ignore_explicit_for_joined`.

Before we look at when you should choose which strategy, let's consider mixing inheritance-mapping strategies in a single class hierarchy.

7.5 *Mixing inheritance strategies*

We can map an entire inheritance hierarchy with the `TABLE_PER_CLASS`, `SINGLE_TABLE`, or `JOINED` strategy. We can't mix them—for example, switching from a table-per-class hierarchy with a discriminator to a normalized table-per-subclass strategy. Once we've decided on an inheritance strategy, we have to stick with it.

Except, this isn't completely true. By using some tricks, we can switch the mapping strategy for a particular subclass. For example, we can map a class hierarchy to a single table, but, for a particular subclass, switch to a separate table with a foreign key–mapping strategy, just as with table-per-subclass. Look at the schema in figure 7.4. The source code that follows can be found in the mapping-inheritance-mixed folder.

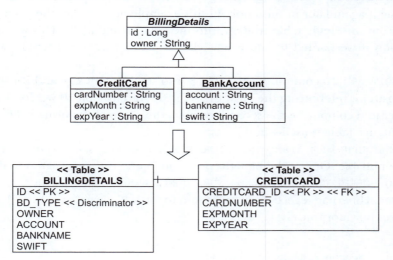

Figure 7.4 Breaking out a subclass to its own secondary table

We'll map the superclass `BillingDetails` with `InheritanceType.SINGLE_TABLE`, as we did before. Then we'll map the `CreditCard` subclass we want to break out of the single table to a secondary table.

Listing 7.18　Mapping `CreditCard`

Path: Ch07/mapping-inheritance-mixed/src/main/java/com/manning
➥ /javapersistence/ch07/model/CreditCard.java

```java
@Entity
@DiscriminatorValue("CC")
@SecondaryTable(
        name = "CREDITCARD",
        pkJoinColumns = @PrimaryKeyJoinColumn(name = "CREDITCARD_ID")
)
public class CreditCard extends BillingDetails {
    @NotNull
    @Column(table = "CREDITCARD", nullable = false)
    private String cardNumber;

    @Column(table = "CREDITCARD", nullable = false)
    private String expMonth;

    @Column(table = "CREDITCARD", nullable = false)
    private String expYear;
    // . . .
}
```

The `@SecondaryTable` and `@Column` annotations group some properties and tell Hibernate to get them from a secondary table. We map all the properties that we moved into the secondary table with the name of that secondary table. This is done with the `table` parameter of `@Column`, which we haven't shown before. This mapping has many uses, and you'll see it again later in this book. In this example, it separates the `CreditCard` properties from the single table strategy into the `CREDITCARD` table. This would be a viable solution if we wanted to add a new class to extend `BillingDetails`; `Paypal` for example.

The `CREDITCARD_ID` column of this table is also the primary key, and it has a foreign key constraint referencing the `ID` of the single hierarchy table. If we don't specify a primary key join column for the secondary table, the name of the primary key of the single inheritance table is used—in this case, `ID`.

Remember that `InheritanceType.SINGLE_TABLE` enforces all columns of subclasses to be nullable. One of the benefits of this mapping is that we can now declare columns of the `CREDITCARD` table as `NOT NULL`, guaranteeing data integrity.

At runtime, Hibernate executes an outer join to fetch `BillingDetails` and all subclass instances polymorphically:

```sql
select
    ID, OWNER, ACCOUNT, BANKNAME, SWIFT,
    EXPMONTH, EXPYEAR, CARDNUMBER,
    BD_TYPE
from
    BILLINGDETAILS
    left outer join CREDITCARD on ID=CREDITCARD_ID
```

We can also use this trick for other subclasses in the class hierarchy. For an exception-ally wide class hierarchy, the outer join can become a problem. Some database systems (Oracle, for example) limit the number of tables in an outer join operation. For a wide hierarchy, you may want to switch to a different fetching strategy that executes an immediate second SQL select instead of an outer join.

7.6   Inheritance of embeddable classes

An embeddable class is a component of its owning entity, so the normal entity inheri-tance rules presented in this chapter don't apply. As a Hibernate extension, we can map an embeddable class that inherits some persistent properties from a superclass (or interface). Let's consider two new attributes of an auction item: dimensions and weight.

An item's dimensions are its width, height, and depth, expressed in a given unit and its symbol: for example, inches (") or centimeters (cm). An item's weight also car-ries a unit of measurement: for example, pounds (lbs) or kilograms (kg). To capture the common attributes (name and symbol) of measurement, we'll define a superclass for `Dimensions` and `Weight` called `Measurement`. The source code that follows can be found in the mapping-inheritance-embeddable folder.

> **Listing 7.19   Mapping the `Measurement` abstract embeddable superclass**

```
Path: Ch07/mapping-inheritance-embeddable/src/main/java/com/manning
➥ /javapersistence/ch07/model/Measurement.java

@MappedSuperclass
public abstract class Measurement {
    @NotNull
    private String name;
    @NotNull
    private String symbol;
    //  . . .
}
```

We've used the `@MappedSuperclass` annotation on the superclass of the embeddable class we're mapping, just like we would for an entity. Subclasses will inherit the proper-ties of this class as persistent properties.

We'll define the `Dimensions` and `Weight` subclasses as `@Embeddable`. For `Dimen-sions`, we'll override all the superclass attributes and add a column-name prefix.

> **Listing 7.20   Mapping the `Dimensions` class**

```
Path: Ch07/mapping-inheritance-embeddable/src/main/java/com/manning
➥ /javapersistence/ch07/model/Dimensions.java

@Embeddable
@AttributeOverride(name = "name",
        column = @Column(name = "DIMENSIONS_NAME"))
@AttributeOverride(name = "symbol",
```

```
        column = @Column(name = "DIMENSIONS_SYMBOL"))
public class Dimensions extends Measurement {
    @NotNull
    private BigDecimal depth;
    @NotNull
    private BigDecimal height;
    @NotNull
    private BigDecimal width;
    //  . . .
}
```

Without this override, an `Item` embedding both `Dimensions` and `Weight` would map to a table with conflicting column names.

Next is the `Weight` class; its mapping also overrides the column names with a prefix (for uniformity, we avoid the conflict with the previous override).

Listing 7.21   Mapping the `Weight` class

Path: Ch07/mapping-inheritance-embeddable/src/main/java/com/manning
➡ /javapersistence/ch07/model/Weight.java

```
@Embeddable
@AttributeOverride(name = "name",
        column = @Column(name = "WEIGHT_NAME"))
@AttributeOverride(name = "symbol",
        column = @Column(name = "WEIGHT_SYMBOL"))
public class Weight extends Measurement {
    @NotNull
    @Column(name = "WEIGHT")
    private BigDecimal value;
    //  . . .
}
```

The owning entity `Item` defines two regular persistent embedded properties.

Listing 7.22   Mapping the `Item` class

Path: Ch07/mapping-inheritance-embeddable/src/main/java/com/manning
➡ /javapersistence/ch07/model/Item.java

```
@Entity
public class Item {
    private Dimensions dimensions;
    private Weight weight;
    //  . . .
}
```

Figure 7.5 illustrates this mapping.

Alternatively, we could override the conflicting `Measurement` column names of the embedded properties in the `Item` class, as was demonstrated in section 6.2. However,

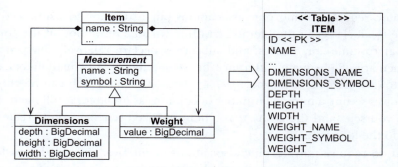

Figure 7.5   Mapping concrete embeddable classes with their inherited properties

we prefer to override them once in the `@Embeddable` classes, so consumers of these classes don't have to resolve the conflict.

A pitfall to watch out for is embedding a property of an abstract superclass type (like `Measurement`) in an entity (like `Item`). This can never work; the JPA provider doesn't know how to store and load `Measurement` instances polymorphically. It doesn't have the information necessary to decide whether the values in the database are `Dimensions` or `Weight` instances because there is no discriminator. This means although we *can* have an `@Embeddable` class inherit some persistent properties from a `@MappedSuperclass`, the reference *to* an instance isn't polymorphic—it always names a concrete class.

Compare this with the alternative inheritance strategy for embeddable classes examined in the section "Converting properties of components" (within section 6.3.2), which supported polymorphism but required some custom type-discrimination code.

Next we'll provide some tips on how to choose an appropriate combination of mapping strategies for an application's class hierarchies.

7.7   *Choosing a strategy*

Which inheritance-mapping strategy you choose will depend on how superclasses are used in the entity hierarchy. You'll have to consider how frequently you query for instances of the superclasses and whether you have associations targeting the superclasses. Another important aspect is the attributes of super- and subtypes: whether subtypes have many additional attributes or only different behavior than their supertypes. Here are some rules of thumb:

- If you don't require polymorphic associations or queries, lean toward table-per-concrete class—in other words, if you never or rarely `select bd from Billing-Details bd`, and you have no class that has an association to `BillingDetails`. An explicit `UNION`-based mapping with `InheritanceType.TABLE_PER_CLASS` should be preferred because (optimized) polymorphic queries and associations will be possible later.

- If you do require polymorphic associations (an association to a superclass, and hence to all classes in the hierarchy with a dynamic resolution of the concrete class at runtime) or queries, and subclasses declare relatively few properties (particularly if the main difference between subclasses is in their behavior), lean toward InheritanceType.SINGLE_TABLE. This approach can be chosen if it involves setting a minimal number of columns as nullable. You'll need to convince yourself (and the DBA) that a denormalized schema won't create problems in the long run.

- If you do require polymorphic associations or queries, and subclasses declare many (non-optional) properties (subclasses differ mainly by the data they hold), lean toward InheritanceType.JOINED. Alternatively, depending on the width and depth of the inheritance hierarchy and the possible cost of joins versus unions, use InheritanceType.TABLE_PER_CLASS. This decision might require the evaluation of SQL execution plans with real data.

By default, choose InheritanceType.SINGLE_TABLE only for simple problems. For complex cases, or when a data modeler insists on the importance of NOT NULL constraints and normalization overrules you, you should consider the Inheritance-Type .JOINED strategy. At that point, you should ask yourself whether it may not be better to remodel inheritance as delegation in the class model. Complex inheritance is often best avoided for all sorts of reasons unrelated to persistence or ORM. Hibernate acts as a buffer between the domain and relational models, but that doesn't mean you can ignore persistence concerns completely when designing the classes.

When you start thinking about mixing inheritance strategies, you must remember that implicit polymorphism in Hibernate is smart enough to handle exotic cases. Also, you must consider that you can't put inheritance annotations on interfaces; this isn't standardized in JPA.

For example, suppose you needed to add an interface in the CaveatEmptor application: ElectronicPaymentOption. This is a business interface that doesn't have a persistence aspect except that a persistent class such as CreditCard will likely implement this interface. No matter how we map the BillingDetails hierarchy, Hibernate can answer the query select o from ElectronicPaymentOption o correctly. This even works if other classes, which aren't part of the BillingDetails hierarchy, are mapped as persistent and implement this interface. Hibernate always knows what tables to query, which instances to construct, and how to return a polymorphic result.

We can apply all mapping strategies to abstract classes. Hibernate won't try to instantiate an abstract class, even if we query or load it.

We mentioned the relationship between User and BillingDetails several times, and we looked at how it influences the selection of an inheritance-mapping strategy. In the following and last section of this chapter, we'll explore this more advanced topic in detail: polymorphic associations. If you don't have such a relationship in your model right now, you may want to come back to this topic later, when you encounter the issue in your application.

7.8 Polymorphic associations

Polymorphism is a defining feature of object-oriented languages like Java. Support for polymorphic associations and polymorphic queries is a fundamental feature of an ORM solution like Hibernate. Surprisingly, we've managed to get this far without needing to talk much about polymorphism. Refreshingly, there isn't much to say on the topic—polymorphism is so easy to use in Hibernate that we don't need to expend a lot of effort explaining it.

To provide an overview, we'll first consider a *many-to-one* association to a class that may have subclasses and then a *one-to-many* relationship. For both examples, the classes of the domain model are the same; see figure 7.6.

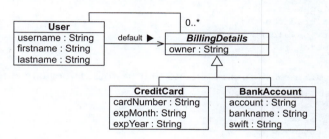

Figure 7.6   A user has either a credit card or a bank account as the default billing details.

7.8.1 Polymorphic many-to-one associations

First, consider the `defaultBilling` property of `User`. It references one particular `BillingDetails` instance, which at runtime can be any concrete instance of that class. The source code that follows can be found in the mapping-inheritance-manytoone folder.

We'll map this unidirectional association to the abstract class `BillingDetails` as follows:

Path: Ch07/mapping-inheritance-manytoone/src/main/java/com/manning
➥ /javapersistence/ch07/model/User.java

```
@Entity
@Table(name = "USERS")
public class User {
    @ManyToOne
    private BillingDetails defaultBilling;
    //  . . .
}
```

The `USERS` table now has the join/foreign-key column `DEFAULTBILLING_ID` representing this relationship. It's a nullable column because a `User` might not have a default billing method assigned. Because `BillingDetails` is abstract, the association must refer to an instance of one of its subclasses—`CreditCard` or `BankAccount`—at runtime.

We don't have to do anything special to enable polymorphic associations in Hibernate. If the target class of an association is mapped with @Entity and @Inheritance, the association is naturally polymorphic.

The following Spring Data JPA code demonstrates the creation of an association to an instance of the CreditCard subclass:

Path: Ch07/mapping-inheritance-manytoone/src/test/java/com/manning
➡ /javapersistence/ch07/MappingInheritanceSpringDataJPATest.java

```
CreditCard creditCard = new CreditCard(
    "John Smith", "123456789", "10", "2030"
);
User john = new User("John Smith");
john.setDefaultBilling(creditCard);
    creditCardRepository.save(creditCard);
    userRepository.save(john);
```

Now, when we navigate the association in a second unit of work, Hibernate automatically retrieves the CreditCard instance:

```
List<User> users = userRepository.findAll();
users.get(0).getDefaultBilling().pay(123);
```

The second line here will invoke the pay method from the concrete subclass of BillingDetails.

We can handle *one-to-one* associations the same way. What about plural associations, like the collection of billingDetails for each User? Let's look at that next.

7.8.2 *Polymorphic collections*

A User may have references to many BillingDetails, not only a single default (one of the many is the default, but let's ignore that for now). We can map this with a bidirectional *one-to-many* association. The source code that follows can be found in the mapping-inheritance-onetomany folder.

Path: Ch07/mapping-inheritance-onetomany/src/main/java/com/manning
➡ /javapersistence/ch07/model/User.java

```
@Entity
@Table(name = "USERS")
public class User {
    @OneToMany(mappedBy = "user")
    private Set<BillingDetails> billingDetails = new HashSet<>();
    //  . . .
}
```

Next, here's the owning side of the relationship (declared with mappedBy in the previous mapping). By the *owning side*, we mean that side of the relationship that owns the foreign key in the database, which is BillingDetails in this example.

```
Path: Ch07/mapping-inheritance-onetomany/src/main/java/com/manning
➡ /javapersistence/ch07/model/BillingDetails.java

@Entity
@Inheritance(strategy = InheritanceType.TABLE_PER_CLASS)
public abstract class BillingDetails {
    @ManyToOne
    private User user;
    //  . . .
}
```

So far, there is nothing special about this association mapping. The `BillingDetails` class hierarchy can be mapped with `TABLE_PER_CLASS`, `SINGLE_TABLE`, or a `JOINED` inheritance type. Hibernate is smart enough to use the right SQL queries, with either `JOIN` or `UNION` operators, when loading the collection elements.

There is one limitation, however: the `BillingDetails` class can't be a `@Mapped-Superclass`, as discussed in section 7.1. It has to be mapped with `@Entity` and `@Inheritance`.

Summary

- Table-per-concrete-class with implicit polymorphism is the simplest strategy for mapping inheritance hierarchies of entities, and it doesn't support polymorphic associations very well.
- Different columns from different tables share exactly the same semantics, making schema evolution more complex.
- This table-per-concrete-class approach is recommended for the top level of the class hierarchy only, where polymorphism isn't usually required and when modification of the superclass in the future is unlikely.
- The table-per-concrete-class-with-unions strategy is optional, and JPA implementations may not support it, but it does handle polymorphic associations.
- The table-per-class-hierarchy strategy is a winner in terms of both performance and simplicity. Ad hoc reporting is possible without complex joins or unions, and schema evolution is straightforward.
- The one major problem with the single-table strategy is data integrity, because we must declare some columns as nullable. Another concern is normalization: this strategy creates functional dependencies between non-key columns, violating the third normal form.
- The table-per-subclass-with-joins strategy has as its primary advantage the fact that it normalizes the SQL schema, making schema evolution and integrity constraint definition straightforward. The disadvantages are that it's more difficult to implement by hand, and performance can be unacceptable for complex class hierarchies.

Mapping collections and entity associations

The first thing many developers try to do when they begin using Hibernate or Spring Data JPA is to map a *parent/child relationship*. This is usually the first time they encounter collections. It's also the first time they have to think about the differences between entities and value types or get lost in the complexity of ORM.

Managing the associations between classes and the relationships between tables is at the heart of ORM. Most of the difficult problems involved in implementing an ORM solution relate to collections and entity association management. We'll start this chapter with some basic collection-mapping concepts and simple examples. After that, you'll be prepared for the first collection in an entity association—we'll come back to more complicated entity association mappings in the next chapter. To get the full picture, we recommend you read both this chapter and the next.

> **Major new features in JPA 2**
>
> Support was added for collections and maps of basic and embeddable types.
>
> Support was added for persistent lists where the index of each element is stored in an additional database column.
>
> One-to-many associations now have an orphan removal option.

8.1   Sets, bags, lists, and maps of value types

Java has a rich collection API, from which we can choose the interface and implementation that best fits the domain model design. We'll use the Java Collections framework for our implementation in this chapter, and we'll walk through the most common collection mappings, repeating the same `Image` and `Item` example with minor variations.

We'll start by looking at the database schema and creating and mapping a collection property in general. The database goes first, as it is generally designed first and our programs must work with it. Then we'll proceed to selecting a specific collection interface and mapping various collection types: a set, an identifier bag, a list, a map, and finally sorted and ordered collections.

8.1.1   The database schema

We'll extend CaveatEmptor to support attaching images to auction items. An item with an associated image is more interesting for the potential buyer. We'll ignore the Java code for now and consider only the database schema. The source code that follows can be found in the mapping-collections folder.

> **NOTE**   To execute the examples from the source code, you will first need to run the Ch08.sql script.

For the auction item and images example, assume that the image is stored somewhere on the filesystem and that we store just the filename in the database. When an image is deleted from the database, a separate process must delete the file from the disk.

We need an `IMAGE` table in the database to hold the images, or maybe just the filenames of images. This table will also have a foreign key column, say `ITEM_ID`, referencing the `ITEM` table. Look at the schema shown in figure 8.1.

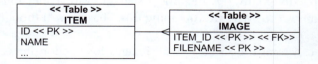

Figure 8.1   The `IMAGE` table holds image filenames, each referencing an `ITEM_ID`.

That's all there is to the schema—no collections or composition.

8.1.2 *Creating and mapping a collection property*

How would we map this IMAGE table with what we know so far? We'd probably map it as an @Entity class named Image. Later in this chapter we'll map a foreign key column with a @ManyToOne property to make the association between entities. We'd also need a composite primary key mapping for the entity class, as we'll first demonstrate in section 10.2.2. What we need to know for now is that a composite primary key is a combination of more than one column to uniquely identify a row in a table. Individual columns may not be unique, but their combination must be unique.

There are no mapped collections of images; they aren't necessary. When we need an item's images, we can write and execute a query in the JPA query language:

```
select img from Image img where img.item = :itemParameter
```

Persistent collections are *always* optional.

A collection we could create is Item#images, referencing all images for a particular item. We could create and map this collection property to do the following:

- Execute the SQL query SELECT * from IMAGE where ITEM_ID = ? automatically when we call someItem.getImages(). As long as the domain model instances are in a *managed* state (more on that later), we can read from the database on demand while navigating the associations between the classes. We don't have to manually write and execute a query to load data. On the other hand, when we start iterating the collection, the collection query is always "all images for this item," never "only images that match criteria XYZ."
- Avoid saving each Image with entityManager.persist() or imageRepository .save(). If we have a mapped collection, adding the Image to the collection with someItem.getImages().add() will make it persistent automatically when the Item is saved. This cascading persistence is convenient because we can save instances without calling the repository or the EntityManager.
- Have a dependent lifecycle of Images. When an Item is deleted, Hibernate deletes all attached Images with an extra SQL DELETE. We don't have to worry about the lifecycle of images and cleaning up orphans (assuming the database foreign key constraint doesn't ON DELETE CASCADE). The JPA provider handles the composition lifecycle.

It's important to realize that although these benefits sound great, the price we'll pay is additional mapping complexity. Many JPA beginners struggle with collection mappings, and frequently the answer to "Why are you doing this?" has been "I thought this collection was required."

If we analyze how we can treat the scenario with images for auction items, we'll find that we'll benefit from a collection mapping. The images have a dependent lifecycle; when an item is deleted, all the attached images should be deleted. When an item is stored, all attached images should be stored. And when an item is displayed, we'll often also display all images, so someItem.getImages() is convenient in UI code—this is rather an eager loading of the information. We don't have to call the persistence service again to get the images; they're just *there*.

Now we'll move on to choosing the collection interface and implementation that best fits the domain model design. Let's walk through the most common collection mappings, repeating the same `Image` and `Item` example with minor variations.

8.1.3   *Selecting a collection interface*

This is the idiom for a collection property in the Java domain model:

```
<<Interface>> images = new <<Implementation>>();
// Getter and setter methods
//   . . .
```

Use an interface to declare the type of the property, not an implementation. Pick a matching implementation, and initialize the collection right away; doing so avoids uninitialized collections. We don't recommend initializing collections late in constructors or setter methods.

Using generics, here's a typical `Set`:

```
Set<Image> images = new HashSet<Image>();
```

> **Raw collections without generics**
>
> If we don't specify the type of collection elements with generics, or the key/value types of a map, we need to tell Hibernate the type (or types). For example, instead of a `Set<String>`, we can map a raw `Set` with `@ElementCollection(targetClass=String.class)`. This also applies to type parameters of a `Map`. Specify the key type of a `Map` with `@MapKeyClass`.
>
> All the examples in this book use generic collections and maps, and so should you.

Out of the box, Hibernate supports the most important JDK collection interfaces and preserves the semantics of JDK collections, maps, and arrays in a persistent fashion. Each JDK interface has a matching implementation supported by Hibernate, and it's important that we use the right combination. Hibernate wraps the already initialized collection on the declaration of the field or sometimes replaces it if it's not the right one. It does that to enable, among other things, lazy loading and dirty checking of collection elements.

Without extending Hibernate, we can choose from the following collections:

- A `java.util.Set` property, initialized with a `java.util.HashSet`. The order of elements isn't preserved, and duplicate elements aren't allowed. All JPA providers support this type.
- A `java.util.SortedSet` property, initialized with a `java.util.TreeSet`. This collection supports a stable order of elements: sorting occurs in memory after

Hibernate loads the data. This is a Hibernate-only extension; other JPA providers may ignore the "sorted" aspect of the set.

- A `java.util.List` property, initialized with a `java.util.ArrayList`. Hibernate preserves the position of each element with an additional index column in the database table. All JPA providers support this type.
- A `java.util.Collection` property, initialized with a `java.util.ArrayList`. This collection has *bag* semantics; duplicates are possible, but the order of elements isn't preserved. All JPA providers support this type.
- A `java.util.Map` property, initialized with a `java.util.HashMap`. The key and value pairs of a map can be preserved in the database. All JPA providers support this type.
- A `java.util.SortedMap` property, initialized with a `java.util.TreeMap`. It supports a stable order of elements: sorting occurs in memory after Hibernate loads the data. This is a Hibernate-only extension; other JPA providers may ignore the "sorted" aspect of the map.
- Hibernate supports persistent arrays, but JPA doesn't. They're rarely used, and we won't show them in this book. Hibernate can't wrap array properties, so many benefits of collections, such as on-demand lazy loading, won't work. Only use persistent arrays in your domain model if you're sure you won't need lazy loading. (You can load arrays on demand, but this requires interception with bytecode enhancement, as explained in section 12.1.3.)

If we want to map collection interfaces and implementations that are not directly supported by Hibernate, we need to tell Hibernate about the semantics of the custom collections. The extension point in Hibernate is the `PersistentCollection` interface in the `org.hibernate.collection.spi` package, where we usually extend one of the existing `PersistentSet`, `PersistentBag`, and `PersistentList` classes. Custom persistent collections aren't easy to write, and we don't recommend doing this if you aren't an experienced Hibernate user.

Transactional filesystems

If we only keep the filenames of images in the SQL database, we have to store the binary data of each picture—the files—somewhere. We could store the image data in the SQL database in BLOB columns (see "Binary and large value types" in section 6.3.1).

If we decide not to store the images in the database, but as regular files, we should be aware that the standard Java filesystem APIs, `java.io.File` and `java.nio.file.Files`, aren't transactional. Filesystem operations aren't enlisted in a Java Transaction API (JTA) system transaction; a transaction might successfully complete with Hibernate writing the filename into the SQL database, but the storing or deleting of the file in the filesystem might fail. We won't be able to roll back these operations as one atomic unit, and we won't get proper isolation of operations.

You could use a separate system transaction manager such as Bitronix. File operations are then enlisted, committed, and rolled back together with Hibernate's SQL operations in the same transaction.

Let's map a collection of image filenames for an `Item`.

8.1.4 Mapping a set

The simplest implementation of mapping a set is a `Set` of `String` image filenames. Add a collection property to the `Item` class, as demonstrated in the following listing.

> **Listing 8.1 Images mapped as a simple set of strings**

Path: Ch08/mapping-collections/src/main/java/com/manning/javapersistence
➡ /ch08/setofstrings/Item.java

```
@Entity
public class Item {
    // . . .

    @ElementCollection                              A
    @CollectionTable(                               B
            name = "IMAGE",
            joinColumns = @JoinColumn(name = "ITEM_ID"))   C
    @Column(name = "FILENAME")                      D
    private Set<String> images = new HashSet<>();    E
```

A Declare the `images` field as an `@ElementCollection`. We refer here to image paths on the system, but for brevity we'll use the names of the fields and columns, such as `image` or `images`.

B The collection table will be named `IMAGE`. Otherwise it would default to `ITEM_IMAGES`.

C The join column between the `ITEM` and the `IMAGE` tables will be `ITEM_ID` (the default name, in fact).

D The name of the column that will contain the string information from the `images` collection will be `FILENAME`. Otherwise it would default to `IMAGES`.

E Initialize the `images` collection as a `HashSet`.

The `@ElementCollection` JPA annotation in the preceding listing is required for a collection of value-typed elements. Without the `@CollectionTable` and `@Column` annotations, Hibernate would use default schema names. Look at the schema in figure 8.2: the primary key columns are underlined.

The `IMAGE` table has a composite primary key of both the `ITEM_ID` and `FILENAME` columns. That means we can't have duplicate rows: each image file can only be attached once to one item. Also, the order of images isn't stored. This fits the domain

ITEM	
ID	NAME
1	Foo

IMAGE	
ITEM_ID	FILENAME
1	landscape.jpg
1	foreground.jpg
1	background.jpg
1	portrait.jpg

Figure 8.2   Table structure and example data for a set of strings

model and `Set` collection. The image is stored somewhere on the filesystem, and we keep just the filename in the database.

To interact with the `Item` entities, we'll create the following Spring Data JPA repository.

Listing 8.2   The `ItemRepository` interface

Path: Ch08/mapping-collections/src/main/java/com/manning/javapersistence
➡ /ch08/repositories/setofstrings/ItemRepository.java

```
public interface ItemRepository extends JpaRepository<Item, Long> {

    @Query("select i from Item i inner join fetch i.images where i.id = :id")   Ⓐ
    Item findItemWithImages(@Param("id") Long id);

    @Query(value = "SELECT FILENAME FROM IMAGE WHERE ITEM_ID = ?1",             Ⓑ
            nativeQuery = true)
    Set<String> findImagesNative(Long id);
}
```

Ⓐ Declare a `findItemWithImages` method that will get the `Item` by id, including the images collection. To fetch this collection eagerly, we'll use the `inner join fetch` capability of Jakarta Persistence Query Language (JPQL).

Ⓑ Declare the `findImagesNative` method, which is annotated as a native query and will get the set of strings representing the `images` of a given id.

We'll also create the following test.

Listing 8.3   The `MappingCollectionsSpringDataJPATest` class

Path: Ch08/mapping-collections/src/test/java/com/manning/javapersistence
➡ /ch08//setofstrings/MappingCollectionsSpringDataJPATest.java

```
@ExtendWith(SpringExtension.class)
@ContextConfiguration(classes = {SpringDataConfiguration.class})
public class MappingCollectionsSpringDataJPATest {

    @Autowired
    private ItemRepository itemRepository;

    @Test
```

```
void storeLoadEntities() {                         A

    Item item = new Item("Foo");

    item.addImage("background.jpg");
    item.addImage("foreground.jpg");               B
    item.addImage("landscape.jpg");
    item.addImage("portrait.jpg");

    itemRepository.save(item);          C                              D

    Item item2 = itemRepository.findItemWithImages(item.getId());
E
    List<Item> items2 = itemRepository.findAll();
    Set<String> images = itemRepository.findImagesNative(item.getId());
                                                                       F
    assertAll(
        () -> assertEquals(4, item2.getImages().size()),
        () -> assertEquals(1, items2.size()),                 G
        () -> assertEquals(4, images.size())
    );

}
}
```

A Create an `Item`.

B Add 4 image paths to it.

C Save it to the database.

D Access the repository to get the item together with the `images` collection. As we specified in the JPQL query with which the `findItemWithImages` method is annotated, the collection will also be fetched from the database.

E Get all `Items` from the database.

F Get the set of strings representing the images, using the `findImagesNative` method.

G Check the sizes of the different collections we have obtained.

It doesn't seem likely that we'd allow the user to attach the same image more than once to the same item, but let's suppose we did. What kind of mapping would be appropriate in that case?

8.1.5   Mapping an identifier bag

A *bag* is an unordered collection that allows duplicate elements, like the `java.util` `.Collection` interface. Curiously, the Java Collections framework doesn't include a bag implementation. We can initialize the property with an `ArrayList`, and Hibernate ignores the index of elements when storing and loading elements.

Listing 8.4 Bag of strings, allowing duplicate elements

Path: Ch08/mapping-collections/src/main/java/com/manning/javapersistence
➥ /ch08/bagofstrings/Item.java

```
@Entity
public class Item {
    // . . .

    @ElementCollection
    @CollectionTable(name = "IMAGE")
    @Column(name = "FILENAME")
    @GenericGenerator(name = "sequence_gen", strategy = "sequence")
    @org.hibernate.annotations.CollectionId(
            columns = @Column(name = "IMAGE_ID"),
            type = @org.hibernate.annotations.Type(type = "long"),
            generator = "sequence_gen")
    private Collection<String> images = new ArrayList<>();
```

Ⓐ Declare a `@GenericGenerator` with the name `"sequence_gen"` and the `"sequence"` strategy to take care of the surrogate keys in the `IMAGE` table.

Ⓑ The `IMAGE` collection table needs a different primary key to allow duplicate `FILE-NAME` values for each `ITEM_ID`.

Ⓒ Introduce a surrogate primary key column named `IMAGE_ID`. You may retrieve all images at the same time or store them all at the same time, but a database table still needs a primary key.

Ⓓ Use a Hibernate-only annotation.

Ⓔ Configure how the primary key is generated.

Ⓕ There is no bag implementation in JDK. We initialize the collection as `ArrayList`.

Usually you'll want the system to generate a primary key value when you save an entity instance. If you need to refresh your memory about key generators, refer to section 5.2.4. The modified schema is shown in figure 8.3. The Spring Data JPA repository and the test will be just like in the previous example.

ITEM

ID	NAME
1	Foo

IMAGE

IMAGE_ID	ITEM_ID	FILENAME
1	1	landscape.jpg
2	1	foreground.jpg
3	1	background.jpg
4	1	portrait.jpg

Figure 8.3 Surrogate primary key column for a bag of strings

Here's an interesting question: if all you see is this schema, can you tell how the tables are mapped in Java? The `ITEM` and `IMAGE` tables look the same: each has a surrogate primary key column and some other normalized columns. Each table could be mapped with an `@Entity` class. However, we could decide to use a JPA feature and map a collection to `IMAGE`, even with a composition lifecycle. This is, effectively, a design decision that some predefined query and manipulation rules are all we need for this table instead of the more generic `@Entity` mapping. When you make such a decision, be sure you know the reasons why and the consequences.

The next mapping technique preserves the order of images within a list.

8.1.6   Mapping a list

If you haven't used ORM software before, a persistent list seems to be a very powerful concept; imagine how much work storing and loading a `java.util.List <String>` is with plain JDBC and SQL. If we add an element to the middle of the list, the list shifts all subsequent elements to the right or rearranges pointers, depending on the list implementation. If we remove an element from the middle of the list, something else happens, and so on. If the ORM software can do all of this automatically for database records, a persistent list starts to look more appealing than it actually is.

As we noted in section 3.2.4, the first reaction is often to preserve the order of data elements as users enter them because you'll often have to show them later in the same order. But if another criterion can be used for sorting the data, like an entry time-stamp, you should sort the data when querying rather than store the display order. What if the display order you need to use changes? The order in which data is displayed is usually not an integral part of the data but an orthogonal concern, so think twice before mapping a persistent `List`; Hibernate isn't as smart as you might think, as you'll see in the next example.

Let's change the `Item` entity and its collection property.

Listing 8.5   Persistent list, preserving the order of elements in the database

Path: Ch08/mapping-collections/src/main/java/com/manning/javapersistence
➡ /ch08/listofstrings/Item.java

```
@Entity
public class Item {
    // . . .

    @ElementCollection
    @CollectionTable(name = "IMAGE")
    @OrderColumn // Enables persistent order, Defaults to IMAGES_ORDER
    @Column(name = "FILENAME")
    private List<String> images = new ArrayList<>();
```

There is a new annotation in this example: `@OrderColumn`. This column stores an index in the persistent list, starting at zero. The column name will default to `IMAGES_ORDER`. Note that Hibernate stores the index to be contiguous in the database and expects it to be that way. If there are gaps, Hibernate will add `null` elements when loading and constructing the `List`. Look at the schema in figure 8.4.

ITEM	
ID	NAME
1	Foo
2	Bar

IMAGE		
ITEM_ID	IMAGES_ORDER	FILENAME
1	0	landscape.jpg
1	1	foreground.jpg
1	2	background.jpg
1	3	background.jpg
2	0	portrait.jpg
2	1	foreground.jpg

Figure 8.4 The collection table preserves the position of each list element.

The primary key of the IMAGE table is a composite of ITEM_ID and IMAGES_ORDER. This allows duplicate FILENAME values, which is consistent with the semantics of a List. Remember, the image is stored somewhere on the filesystem, and we keep just the filename in the database. The Spring Data JPA repository and the test will be just like the previous example.

We said earlier that Hibernate isn't as smart as you might think. Consider making modifications to the list: say the list has three images, A, B, and C, in that order. What happens if you remove A from the list? Hibernate executes one SQL DELETE for that row. Then it executes two UPDATEs, for B and C, shifting their positions to the left to close the gap in the index. For each element to the right of the deleted element, Hibernate executes an UPDATE. If we wrote SQL for this by hand, we could do it with one UPDATE. The same is true for insertions in the middle of the list—Hibernate shifts all existing elements to the right one by one. At least Hibernate is smart enough to execute a single DELETE when we clear() the list.

Now suppose the images for an item have user-supplied names in addition to the filename. One way to model this in Java is with a map, using key/value pairs.

8.1.7 Mapping a map

To accommodate user-supplied names for the image files, we'll change the Java class to use a Map property.

Listing 8.6 Persistent map storing its key and value pairs

Path: Ch08/mapping-collections/src/main/java/com/manning/javapersistence
➥ /ch08/mapofstrings/Item.java

```
@Entity
public class Item {
    // . . .

    @ElementCollection                              Ⓐ
    @CollectionTable(name = "IMAGE")
Ⓑ  @MapKeyColumn(name = "FILENAME")    ⟵
    └▷ @Column(name = "IMAGENAME")
    private Map<String, String> images = new HashMap<>();
```

A Each map entry is a key/value pair. Here the key is mapped with `@MapKeyColumn` to `FILENAME`.

B The value is the `IMAGENAME` column. This means the user can only use a file once because a `Map` doesn't allow duplicate keys.

As you can see from the schema in figure 8.5, the primary key of the collection table is a composite of `ITEM_ID` and `FILENAME`. The example uses a `String` as the key for the map, but Hibernate supports any basic type, such as `BigDecimal` or `Integer`. If the key is a Java enum, we must use `@MapKeyEnumerated`. With any temporal types such as `java.util.Date`, use `@MapKeyTemporal`.

ITEM

ID	NAME
1	Foo
2	Bar

IMAGE

ITEM_ID	FILENAME	IMAGENAME
1	landscape.jpg	Landscape
1	foreground.jpg	Foreground
1	background.jpg	Background
1	portrait.jpg	Portrait
2	landscape.jpg	Landscape
2	foreground.jpg	Foreground

Figure 8.5 Tables for a map, using strings as indexes and elements

The map in the previous example was unordered. If the list of files is long, and we would like to quickly look for something at a glance, how can we always sort map entries by filename?

8.1.8 Sorted and ordered collections

We can *sort* a collection in memory by using a Java comparator. We can *order* a collection when it's loaded from the database by using an SQL query with an `ORDER BY` clause.

Let's make the map of images a sorted map. We need to change the Java property and the mapping.

Listing 8.7 Sorting map entries in memory using a comparator

Path: Ch08/mapping-collections/src/main/java/com/manning/javapersistence
➡ /ch08/sortedmapofstrings/Item.java

```
@Entity
public class Item {
    // . . .

    @ElementCollection
    @CollectionTable(name = "IMAGE")
    @MapKeyColumn(name = "FILENAME")
    @Column(name = "IMAGENAME")
    @org.hibernate.annotations.SortComparator(ReverseStringComparator.class)
    private SortedMap<String, String> images = new TreeMap<>();
```

Sorted collections are a Hibernate feature; hence the annotation `org.hibernate` `.annotations.SortComparator` with an implementation of `java.util.Comparator` `<String>`—the one shown here sorts strings in reverse order. The database schema doesn't change, which is also the case for all the following examples. Look at figures 8.1–8.5 in the previous sections if you need a reminder.

We'll add the following two lines to the test, which will check that the keys are now in reverse order:

```
() -> assertEquals("Portrait", item2.getImages().firstKey()),
() -> assertEquals("Background", item2.getImages().lastKey())
```

We'll map a `java.util.SortedSet` as demonstrated next. You can find it in the sortedsetofstrings example in the mapping-collections folder.

Listing 8.8   Sorting set elements in memory with `String#compareTo()`

Path: Ch08/mapping-collections/src/main/java/com/manning/javapersistence
➥ /ch08/sortedsetofstrings/Item.java

```
@Entity
public class Item {
    //...

    @ElementCollection
    @CollectionTable(name = "IMAGE")
    @Column(name = "FILENAME")
    @org.hibernate.annotations.SortNatural
    private SortedSet<String> images = new TreeSet< >();
```

Here natural sorting is used, falling back on the `String#compareTo()` method.

Unfortunately, we can't sort a bag; there is no `TreeBag`. The indexes of list elements predefine their order. Alternatively, instead of switching to `Sorted*` interfaces, we may want to retrieve the elements of a collection in the right order from the database, rather than sorting in memory. Instead of a `java.util.SortedSet`, we'll use a `java.util.LinkedHashSet` in the following listing.

Listing 8.9   `LinkedHashSet` offers insertion order for iteration

Path: Ch08/mapping-collections/src/main/java/com/manning/javapersistence
➥ /ch08/setofstringsorderby/Item.java

```
@Entity
public class Item {
    //...

    @ElementCollection
    @CollectionTable(name = "IMAGE")
    @Column(name = "FILENAME")
```

```
// @javax.persistence.OrderBy // One possible order: "FILENAME asc"
@org.hibernate.annotations.OrderBy(clause = "FILENAME desc")
private Set<String> images = new LinkedHashSet<>();
```

The `LinkedHashSet` class has a stable iteration order over its elements, and Hibernate will fill it in the right order when loading a collection. To do this, Hibernate applies an `ORDER BY` clause to the SQL statement that loads the collection. We must declare this SQL clause with the proprietary `@org.hibernate.annotations.OrderBy` annotation. We could call an SQL function, like `@OrderBy("substring(FILENAME, 0, 3) desc")`, which would sort by the first three letters of the filename, but be careful to check that the DBMS supports the SQL function you're calling. Furthermore, you can use the SQL:2003 syntax `ORDER BY . . . NULLS FIRST|LAST`, and Hibernate will automatically transform it into the dialect supported by your DBMS.

If the expression is just a column name with `ASC` or `DESC`, a `@javax .persistence.OrderBy` annotation works fine as well. If you need a more elaborate clause (such as the `substring()` example in the previous paragraph), an `@org .hibernate.annotations.OrderBy` annotation is required.

Hibernate's `@OrderBy` vs. JPA's `@OrderBy`

You can apply the annotation `@org.hibernate.annotations.OrderBy` to any collection; its parameter is a plain SQL fragment that Hibernate attaches to the SQL statement loading the collection.

Java Persistence has a similar annotation, `@javax.persistence.OrderBy`. Its only parameter is not SQL but `someProperty DESC|ASC`. A `String` or `Integer` element value has no properties, so when we apply JPA's `@OrderBy` annotation on a collection of a basic type, as in listing 8.9 with `Set<String>`, "the ordering will be by value of the basic objects," according to the specification. This means we can't change the ordering value (just the direction, `asc` or `desc`). We'll use the JPA annotation in section 8.2.2 when the element value class has persistent properties and isn't of basic/scalar type.

The next example from `bagofstringsorderby` demonstrates the same ordering at load time with a bag mapping. You can find it in the mapping-collections folder.

Listing 8.10   `ArrayList` provides a stable iteration order

Path: Ch08/mapping-collections/src/main/java/com/manning/javapersistence
➡ /ch08/bagofstringsorderby/Item.java

```
@Entity
public class Item {
    //...

    @ElementCollection
    @CollectionTable(name = "IMAGE")
```

```
@Column(name = "FILENAME")
@GenericGenerator(name = "sequence_gen", strategy = "sequence")
@org.hibernate.annotations.CollectionId(
        columns = @Column(name = "IMAGE_ID"),
        type = @org.hibernate.annotations.Type(type = "long"),
        generator = "sequence_gen")
@org.hibernate.annotations.OrderBy(clause = "FILENAME desc")
private Collection<String> images = new ArrayList<>();
```

Finally, we can load ordered key/value pairs with a `LinkedHashMap`.

Listing 8.11   `LinkedHashMap` keeps key/value pairs in order

Path: Ch08/mapping-collections/src/main/java/com/manning/javapersistence
➥ /ch08/mapofstringsorderby/Item.java

```
@Entity
public class Item {
    //...

    @ElementCollection
    @CollectionTable(name = "IMAGE")
    @MapKeyColumn(name = "FILENAME")
    @Column(name = "IMAGENAME")
    @org.hibernate.annotations.OrderBy(clause = "FILENAME desc")
    private Map<String, String> images = new LinkedHashMap<>();
```

Keep in mind that the elements of ordered collections are only in the desired order when they're loaded. As soon as we add or remove elements, the iteration order of the collections might be different than "by filename"; they behave like regular linked sets, maps, or lists. We demonstrated the technical approach, but we need to be aware of its shortcomings and to conclude that these make it a somewhat unreliable solution.

In a real system, it's likely that we'll need to store more than just the image name and filename. We'll probably need to create an `Image` class for extra information (such as title, width, and height). This is the perfect use case for a collection of components.

8.2   *Collections of components*

We mapped an embeddable component earlier: the `address` of a `User`. The example we're working with in this chapter is different because an `Item` has many references to an `Image`, as shown in figure 8.6. The association in the UML diagram is a composition (the black diamond); hence, the referenced `Images` are bound to the lifecycle of the owning `Item`.

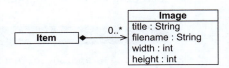

Figure 8.6   Collection of `Image` components in `Item`

The code in the following listing demonstrates the new `Image` embeddable class, capturing all the properties of an image that interest us.

> **Listing 8.12 Encapsulating all properties of an image**

Path: Ch08/mapping-collections/src/main/java/com/manning/javapersistence
➡ /ch08/setofembeddables/Image.java

```
@Embeddable
public class Image {
    @Column(nullable = false)
    private String filename;
    private int width;
    private int height;
    //...
}
```

First, note that all the properties are non-optional, NOT NULL. The size properties are non-nullable because their values are primitives. Second, we have to consider equality, and how the database and Java tier compare two images.

8.2.1 Equality of component instances

Let's say we want to keep several `Image` instances in a `HashSet`. We know that sets don't allow duplicate elements, but how do sets detect duplicates? The `HashSet` calls the `equals()` method on each `Image` we put in the `Set`. (It also calls the `hashCode()` method to get a hash, obviously.)

How many images are in the following collection?

```
someItem.addImage(new Image("background.jpg", 640, 480));
someItem.addImage(new Image("foreground.jpg", 800, 600));
someItem.addImage(new Image("landscape.jpg", 1024, 768));
someItem.addImage(new Image("landscape.jpg", 1024, 768));
assertEquals(3, someItem.getImages().size());
```

Did you expect four images instead of three? You're right: the regular Java equality check relies on identity. The `java.lang.Object#equals()` method compares instances with a==b. Using this procedure, we'd have four instances of `Image` in the collection. Clearly, three is the "correct" answer for this use case.

For the `Image` class, we don't rely on Java identity—we override the `equals()` and `hashCode()` methods.

> **Listing 8.13 Implementing custom equality with `equals()` and `hashCode()`**

Path: Ch08/mapping-collections/src/main/java/com/manning/javapersistence
➡ /ch08/setofembeddables/Image.java

```
@Embeddable
public class Image {
    //...
@Override                                    ⓐ
public boolean equals(Object o) {      ⟵─┘
    if (this == o) return true;
```

```
    if (o == null || getClass() != o.getClass()) return false;
    Image image = (Image) o;
    return width == image.width &&
           height == image.height &&
           filename.equals(image.filename) &&
           item.equals(image.item);
}

@Override                                    B
public int hashCode() {              ◄─┐
    return Objects.hash(filename, width, height, item);
}
    //...
}
```

Ⓐ This custom equality check in `equals()` compares all values of one `Image` to the values of another `Image`. If all values are the same, the images must be the same.

Ⓑ The `hashCode()` method has to fulfill the contract requiring that if two instances are equal, they must have the same hash code.

Why didn't we override equality in section 6.2, when we mapped the `Address` of a `User`? Well, the truth is, we probably should have done that. Our only excuse is that we won't have any problems with the regular identity equality unless we put embeddable components into a `Set` or use them as keys in a `Map` that uses `equals()` and `hashCode()` for storing and comparison (this means it is not a `TreeMap`, which compares items with one another to sort and locate them). We should also redefine equality based on values, not identity. It's best if we override these methods on every `@Embeddable` class; all value types should be compared "by value."

Now consider the database primary key: Hibernate will generate a schema that includes all non-nullable columns of the `IMAGE` collection table in a composite primary key. The columns have to be non-nullable because we can't identify what we don't know. This reflects the equality implementation in the Java class. We'll look at the schema in the next section, with more details about the primary key.

> **NOTE** There is a minor problem with Hibernate's schema generator: if we annotate an embeddable's property with `@NotNull` instead of `@Column (nullable=false)`, Hibernate won't generate a `NOT NULL` constraint for the collection table's column. A Bean Validation check of an instance works as expected, but the database schema is missing the integrity rule. Use `@Column(nullable=false)` if the embeddable class is mapped in a collection and the property should be part of the primary key.

The component class is now ready, and we can use it in collection mappings.

8.2.2 *Set of components*

We can map a `Set` of components as shown next. Keep in mind that a `Set` is a type of collection that allows only unique items.

Listing 8.14   A Set of embeddable components with an override

Path: Ch08/mapping-collections/src/main/java/com/manning/javapersistence,
↪ /ch08/setofembeddables/Item.java

```
@Entity
public class Item {
    //...

    @ElementCollection           ◄──┐   Ⓐ
    @CollectionTable(name = "IMAGE") ◄──┐   Ⓑ
    @AttributeOverride(
            name = "filename",
            column = @Column(name = "FNAME", nullable = false)
    )
    private Set<Image> images = new HashSet<>();
```

Ⓐ As before, the `@ElementCollection` annotation is required. Hibernate automatically knows that the target of the collection is an `@Embeddable` type from the declaration of a generic collection.

Ⓑ The `@CollectionTable` annotation overrides the default name for the collection table, which would have been `ITEM_IMAGES`.

The `Image` mapping defines the columns of the collection table. Just as for a single embedded value, we can use `@AttributeOverride` to customize the mapping without modifying the target embeddable class.

Look at the database schema in figure 8.7. We're mapping a set, so the primary key of the collection table is a composite of the foreign key column `ITEM_ID` and all "embedded" non-nullable columns: `FNAME`, `WIDTH`, and `HEIGHT`.

ITEM

ID	NAME
1	Foo
2	Bar

IMAGE

ITEM_ID	FNAME	WIDTH	HEIGHT
1	landscape.jpg	640	480
1	foreground.jpg	800	600
1	background.jpg	1024	768
1	portrait.jpg	480	640
2	landscape.jpg	640	480
2	foreground.jpg	800	600

Figure 8.7   Example data tables for a collection of components

The `ITEM_ID` value wasn't included in the overridden `equals()` and `hashCode()` methods of `Image`, as discussed in the previous section. Therefore, if we mix images of different items in one set, we'll run into equality problems in the Java tier. In the database table, we obviously can distinguish the images of different items because the item's identifier is included in primary key equality checks.

If we want to include the `Item` in the equality routine of the `Image`, to be symmetric with the database primary key, we'll need an `Image#item` property. This is a simple back-pointer provided by Hibernate when `Image` instances are loaded:

Path: Ch08/mapping-collections/src/main/java/com/manning/javapersistence
➥ /ch08/setofembeddables/Image.java

```java
@Embeddable
public class Image {
    //...
    @org.hibernate.annotations.Parent
    private Item item;
    //...
}
```

We can now include the parent `Item` value in the `equals()` and `hashCode()` implementations.

In the next code snippet, we'll match the `FILENAME` field to the `FNAME` column using the `@AttributeOverride` annotation:

Path: Ch08/mapping-collections/src/main/java/com/manning/javapersistence
➥ /ch08/setofembeddables/Item.java

```java
@AttributeOverride(
        name = "filename",
        column = @Column(name = "FNAME", nullable = false)
)
```

We'll similarly have to change the native query in the `ItemRepository` interface:

Path: Ch08/mapping-collections/src/main/java/com/manning/javapersistence
➥ /ch08/repositories/setofembeddables/ItemRepository.java

```java
@Query(value = "SELECT FNAME FROM IMAGE WHERE ITEM_ID = ?1",
        nativeQuery = true)
Set<String> findImagesNative(Long id);
```

If we need load-time ordering of elements and a stable iteration order with a `Linked-HashSet`, we can use the JPA `@OrderBy` annotation:

Path: Ch08/mapping-collections/src/main/java/com/manning/javapersistence
➥ /ch08/setofembeddablesorderby/Item.java

```java
@Entity
public class Item {
    //...
    @ElementCollection
    @CollectionTable(name = "IMAGE")
    @OrderBy("filename DESC, width DESC")
    private Set<Image> images = new LinkedHashSet<>();
```

The arguments of the @OrderBy annotation are properties of the Image class, followed by either ASC for ascending or DESC for descending order. The default is ascending. This example sorts descending by image filename and then descending by the width of each image. Note that this is different from the proprietary @org.hibernate.annotations .OrderBy annotation, which takes a plain SQL clause, as discussed in section 8.1.8.

Declaring all properties of Image as @NotNull may not be something we want. If any of the properties are optional, we'll need a different primary key for the collection table.

8.2.3   *Bag of components*

We used the @org.hibernate.annotations.CollectionId annotation before adding a surrogate key column to the collection table. The collection type, however, was not a Set but a general Collection, a bag. This is consistent with our updated schema: if we have a surrogate primary key column, duplicate element values are allowed. Let's walk through this with the bagofembeddables example.

First, the Image class can now have nullable properties, as we'll have a surrogate key:

Path: Ch08/mapping-collections/src/main/java/com/manning/javapersistence
➥ /ch08/bagofembeddables/Image.java

```
@Embeddable
public class Image {
    @Column(nullable = true)
    private String title;
    @Column(nullable = false)
    private String filename;
    private int width;
    private int height;
    //  . . .
}
```

Remember to account for the optional title of the Image in the overridden equals() and hashCode() methods when comparing instances by value. For example, the comparison of the title fields will be done in the equals method like this:

```
Objects.equals(title, image.title)
```

Next, take a look at the mapping of the bag collection in Item. As before, in section 8.1.5, we declare an additional surrogate primary key column, IMAGE_ID, with the proprietary @org.hibernate.annotations.CollectionId annotation:

Path: Ch08/mapping-collections/src/main/java/com/manning/javapersistence
➥ /ch08/bagofembeddables/Item.java

```
@Entity
public class Item {
    //...
```

```
@ElementCollection
@CollectionTable(name = "IMAGE")
    @GenericGenerator(name = "sequence_gen", strategy = "sequence")
@org.hibernate.annotations.CollectionId(
        columns = @Column(name = "IMAGE_ID"),
        type = @org.hibernate.annotations.Type(type = "long"),
        generator = "sequence_gen")
private Collection<Image> images = new ArrayList<>();
// . . .
}
```

Figure 8.8 shows the database schema. The `title` of the `Image` with identifier 2 is null.

ITEM

ID	NAME
1	Foo
2	Bar

IMAGE

IMAGE_ID	ITEM_ID	TITLE	FILENAME	WIDTH	HEIGHT
1	1	Landscape	landscape.jpg	640	480
2	1		foreground.jpg	800	600
3	1	Background	background.jpg	1024	768
4	1	Portrait	portrait.jpg	480	640
5	2	Landscape	landscape.jpg	640	480
6	2	Foreground	foreground.jpg	800	600

Figure 8.8 Collection of components table with a surrogate primary key column

Next, we'll analyze another way to change the primary key of the collection table with a `Map`.

8.2.4 *Map of component values*

A map keeps the information as pairs of keys and values. If the `Images` are stored in a `Map`, the filename can be the map key:

Path: Ch08/mapping-collections/src/main/java/com/manning/javapersistence
➥ /ch08/mapofstringsembeddables/Item.java

```
@Entity
public class Item {
    //...

    @ElementCollection                           A
    @CollectionTable(name = "IMAGE")
    @MapKeyColumn(name = "TITLE")          ←┘
    private Map<String, Image> images = new HashMap<>();
    //  . . .
}
```

A The key column of the map is set to `TITLE`. Otherwise, it will default to `IMAGES_KEY`.

The test will set the TITLE column by executing instructions of this kind:

```
item.putImage("Background", new Image("background.jpg", 640, 480));
```

The primary key of the collection table, as shown in figure 8.9, is now the foreign key column ITEM_ID and the key column of the map, TITLE.

ITEM

ID	NAME
1	Foo
2	Bar

IMAGE

ITEM_ID	TITLE	FILENAME	WIDTH	HEIGHT
1	Landscape	landscape.jpg	640	480
1	Foreground	foreground.jpg	800	600
1	Background	background.jpg	1024	768
1	Portrait	portrait.jpg	480	640
2	Landscape	landscape.jpg	640	480
2	Foreground	foreground.jpg	800	600

Figure 8.9   Database tables for a map of components

The embeddable Image class maps all other columns, which may be nullable:

Path: Ch08/mapping-collections/src/main/java/com/manning/javapersistence
➡ /ch08/mapofstringsembeddables/Image.java

```
@Embeddable                              Ⓐ
public class Image {
    @Column(nullable = true)          ←─┘
    private String filename;
    private int width;
    private int height;
    //  . . .
}
```

Ⓐ The filename field can now be null; it is not part of the primary key.

Here the values in the map are instances of an embeddable component class and the keys of the map a basic string. Next we'll use embeddable types for both key and value.

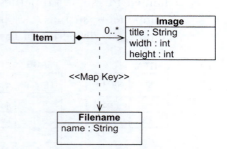

8.2.5   Components as map keys

Our final example is mapping a Map, with both keys and values of embeddable type, as you can see in figure 8.10.

Instead of a string representation, we can represent a filename with a custom type.

Figure 8.10   The Item has a Map keyed by Filename.

Listing 8.15	Representing a filename with a custom type

Path: Ch08/mapping-collections/src/main/java/com/manning/javapersistence
➥ /ch08/mapofembeddables/Filename.java

```
@Embeddable
public class Filename {                              Ⓐ
    @Column(nullable = false)
    private String name;
    //  . . .
}
```

Ⓐ The `name` field must not be null, as it is part of the primary key. If we want to use this class for the keys of a map, the mapped database columns can't be nullable because they're all part of a composite primary key. We also have to override the `equals()` and `hashCode()` methods because the keys of a map are a set, and each `Filename` must be unique within a given key set.

We don't need any special annotations to map the collection:

Path: Ch08/mapping-collections/src/main/java/com/manning/javapersistence
➥ /ch08/mapofsembeddables/Item.java

```
@Entity
public class Item {
    @ElementCollection
    @CollectionTable(name = "IMAGE")
    private Map<Filename, Image> images = new HashMap<>();
    //  . . .
}
```

In fact, we can't apply `@MapKeyColumn` and `@AttributeOverrides`; they have no effect when the map's key is an `@Embeddable` class.

The composite primary key of the IMAGE table includes the ITEM_ID and NAME columns, as you can see in figure 8.11. A composite embeddable class like `Image` isn't limited to simple properties of basic types. You've already seen how to nest other components, such as `City` in `Address`. We could extract and encapsulate the width and height properties of `Image` in a new `Dimensions` class.

ITEM

ID	NAME
1	Foo
2	Bar

IMAGE

ITEM_ID	NAME	TITLE	WIDTH	HEIGHT
1	landscape.jpg	Landscape	640	480
1	foreground.jpg	Foreground	800	600
1	background.jpg	Background	1024	768
1	portrait.jpg	Portrait	480	640
2	landscape.jpg	Landscape	640	480
2	foreground.jpg	Foreground	800	600

Figure 8.11 Database tables for a Map of Images keyed on Filenames

An embeddable class can also have its own collections.

8.2.6   *Collection in an embeddable component*

Suppose that for each `Address`, we want to store a list of contacts. This is a simple `Set<String>` in the embeddable class:

Path: Ch08/mapping-collections/src/main/java/com/manning/javapersistence
➥ /ch08/embeddablesetofstrings/Address.java

```
@Embeddable
public class Address {
    @NotNull
    @Column(nullable = false)
    private String street;
    @NotNull
    @Column(nullable = false, length = 5)
    private String zipcode;
    @NotNull
    @Column(nullable = false)
    private String city;

    @ElementCollection
    @CollectionTable(
            name = "CONTACT",
            joinColumns = @JoinColumn(name = "USER_ID"))
    @Column(name = "NAME", nullable = false)
    private Set<String> contacts = new HashSet<>();
    //  . . .
}
```

Ⓐ The `@ElementCollection` is the only required annotation; the table and column names have default values. The table name would default to `USER_CONTACTS`.

Ⓑ The join column would be `USER_ID` by default.

Ⓒ The column name would default to `CONTACTS`.

Look at the schema in figure 8.12: the `USER_ID` column has a foreign key constraint referencing the owning entity's table, `USERS`. The primary key of the collection table is a composite of the `USER_ID` and `NAME` columns, preventing duplicate elements, so a `Set` is appropriate.

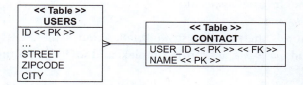

Figure 8.12   `USER_ID` has a foreign key constraint referencing `USERS`.

Instead of a `Set`, we could map a list, bag, or map of basic types. Hibernate also supports collections of embeddable types, so instead of a simple contact string, we could write an embeddable `Contact` class and have `Address` hold a collection of `Contacts`.

Although Hibernate gives a lot of flexibility with component mappings and fine-grained models, be aware that code is read more often than it's written. Think about the next developer who will have to maintain this in a few years.

Switching focus, let's turn our attention to entity associations: in particular, simple *many-to-one* and *one-to-many* associations.

8.3 *Mapping entity associations*

At the beginning of this chapter, we promised to talk about parent/child relationships. So far, we've looked at the mapping of an entity, Item. Let's say this is the parent, and it has a collection of children: the collection of Image instances. The term *parent/child* implies some kind of lifecycle dependency, so a collection of strings or embeddable components is appropriate. The children are fully dependent on the parent; they will always be saved, updated, and removed with the parent, never alone.

We've already mapped a parent/child relationship! The parent was an entity, and the many children were of value type. When an Item is removed, its collection of Image instances will also be removed. (The actual images may be removed in a transactional way, meaning we'll either delete the rows from the database together with the files from the disk, or nothing at all. This is, however, a separate problem that we won't deal with here.)

We now want to map relationships of a different kind: associations between two entity classes. Their instances won't have dependent lifecycles—one instance can be saved, updated, and removed without affecting another. Naturally, *sometimes* there will be dependencies, even between entity instances, but we'll need more fine-grained control over how the relationship between the two classes affects instance state, unlike with completely dependent (embedded) types. Are we still talking about a parent/child relationship here? It turns out that the *parent/child* term is vague, and everyone has their own definition. We'll try not to use that term from now on, and we'll instead rely on more precise, or at least well-defined, vocabulary.

The relationship we'll explore in the following sections will remain the same: a relationship between the Item and Bid entity classes, as shown in figure 8.13. The association from Bid to Item is a *many-to-one* association. Later we'll make this association bidirectional, so the inverse association from Item to Bid will be *one-to-many*.

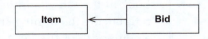

Figure 8.13 Relationship between Item and Bid

The *many-to-one* association is the simplest, so we'll talk about it first. The other associations, *many-to-many* and *one-to-one*, are more complex, and we'll discuss them in the next chapter.

Let's start with the *many-to-one* association that we need to implement in the Caveat-Emptor application, and let's see what alternatives we have. The source code that follows can be found in the mapping-associations folder.

8.3.1   The simplest possible association

We call the mapping of the `Bid#item` property a *unidirectional many-to-one association*. Before we analyze this mapping, look at the database schema in figure 8.14 and the code in listing 8.16.

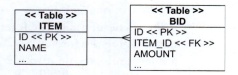

Figure 8.14   **A *many-to-one* relationship in the SQL schema**

Listing 8.16   Bid has a single reference to an `Item`

Path: Ch08/mapping-associations/src/main/java/com/manning/javapersistence
➡ /ch08/onetomany/bidirectional/Bid.java

```
@Entity
public class Bid {                                    A
    @ManyToOne(fetch = FetchType.LAZY)        ◄─┐
    @JoinColumn(name = "ITEM_ID", nullable = false)
    private Item item;
    // . . .
}
```

Ⓐ The `@ManyToOne` annotation marks a property as an entity association, and it's required. Its fetch parameter defaults to `EAGER`, which means the associated Item is loaded whenever the `Bid` is loaded. We usually prefer lazy loading as a default strategy, and we'll talk more about it later in section 12.1.1.

A *many-to-one* entity association maps naturally to a foreign key column: `ITEM_ID` in the BID table. In JPA, this is called the *join column*. We don't need anything but the `@ManyToOne` annotation on the property. The default name for the join column is `ITEM_ID`: Hibernate automatically uses a combination of the target entity name and its identifier property, separated with an underscore.

We can override the foreign key column with the `@JoinColumn` annotation, but we used it here for a different reason: to make the foreign key column `NOT NULL` when Hibernate generates the SQL schema. A bid always has to have a reference to an item; it can't survive on its own. (Note that this already indicates some kind of lifecycle dependency we have to keep in mind.) Alternatively, we could mark this association as non-optional with either `@ManyToOne(optional = false)` or, as usual, with Bean Validation's `@NotNull`.

That was easy. It's critically important to realize that we can write a complete and complex application without using anything else.

We don't need to map the other side of this relationship; we can ignore the *one-to-many* association from `Item` to `Bid`. There is only a foreign key column in the database schema, and we've already mapped it. We are serious about this: when you see a foreign key column and two entity classes involved, you should probably map it with `@ManyToOne` and nothing else.

We can now get the `Item` of each `Bid` by calling `someBid.getItem()`. The JPA provider will dereference the foreign key and load the `Item` for us, and it will also take care of managing the foreign key values. How can we get all of an item's bids? We can write a query and execute it with `EntityManager` or `JpaRepository` in whatever query language Hibernate supports. For example, in JPQL, we'd use `select b from Bid b where b.item = :itemParameter`. One of the reasons we use Hibernate or Spring Data JPA is, of course, that in most cases we don't want to write and execute that query ourselves.

8.3.2 *Making it bidirectional*

At the beginning of this chapter, in section 8.1.2, we had a list of reasons why a mapping of the `Item#images` collection was a good idea. Let's do the same for the `Item#bids` collection. This collection will implement the *one-to-many* association between `Item` and `Bid` entity classes. If we create and map this collection property, we'll get the following:

- Hibernate executes the SQL query `SELECT * from BID where ITEM_ID = ?` automatically when we call `someItem.getBids()` and start iterating through the collection elements.

- We can *cascade* state changes from an `Item` to all referenced `Bids` in the collection. We can select what lifecycle events should be transitive; for example, we could declare that all referenced `Bid` instances should be saved when an `Item` is saved, so we don't have to call `EntityManager#persist()` or `ItemRepository#save()` repeatedly for all bids.

Well, that isn't a very long list. The primary benefit of one-to-many mappings is navigational access to data. It's one of the core promises of ORM, enabling us to access data by calling only methods of our Java domain model. The ORM engine is supposed to take care of loading the required data in a smart way while we work with a high-level interface of our own design: `someItem.getBids().iterator().next().getAmount()`, and so on.

The fact that you can optionally cascade some state changes to related instances is a nice bonus. Consider, though, that some dependencies indicate value types at the Java level, and they do not indicate entities. Ask yourself if any table in the schema will have a `BID_ID` foreign key column. If not, map the `Bid` class as `@Embeddable`, not `@Entity`, using the same tables as before but with a different mapping with fixed rules for transitive state changes. If any other table has a foreign key reference on any `BID` row, we'll need a shared `Bid` entity; it can't be mapped embedded with an `Item`.

So should we map the `Item#bids` collection at all? We'll get navigational data access, but the price we'll pay is additional Java code and significantly more complexity. This is frequently a difficult decision; the choice of mapping the collection should rarely be taken. How often will we call `someItem.getBids()` in the application and then access or display all bids in a predefined order? If we only want to display a subset of the bids, or if we need to retrieve them in a different order every time, we'd need to write and execute queries manually anyway. The one-to-many mapping and its collection would only be maintenance baggage. In our experience, this is a frequent source of problems and bugs, especially for ORM beginners.

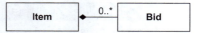

Figure 8.15 Bidirectional association between `Item` and `Bid`

In CaveatEmptor's case, the answer is yes, we'll frequently call `someItem.getBids()` and then show a list to the user who wants to participate in an auction. Figure 8.15 shows the updated UML diagram with the bidirectional association that we need to implement.

The mapping of the collection and the one-to-many side is as follows.

Listing 8.17 `Item` has a collection of `Bid` references

Path: Ch08/mapping-associations/src/main/java/com/manning/javapersistence
➥ /ch08/onetomany/bidirectional/Item.java

```
@Entity
public class Item {
    //...

                                       Ⓐ
    @OneToMany(mappedBy = "item",          Ⓑ
               fetch = FetchType.LAZY)
    private Set<Bid> bids = new HashSet<>();
    //  . . .
}
```

Ⓐ The `@OneToMany` annotation is required to make the association bidirectional. In this case, we also have to set the `mappedBy` parameter.

Ⓑ The argument is the name of the property on the "other side." The fetching will be `LAZY` by default.

Look again at the other side—the many-to-one mapping in listing 8.16. The property name in the `Bid` class is `item`. The bid side is responsible for the foreign key column, `ITEM_ID`, which we mapped with `@ManyToOne`. Here, `mappedBy` tells Hibernate to "load this collection using the foreign key column already mapped by the given property"—in this case, `Bid#item`. The `mappedBy` parameter is always required when the one-to-many is bidirectional and we've already mapped the foreign key column. We'll talk about that again in the next chapter.

The default for the `fetch` parameter of a collection mapping is always `FetchType`
`.LAZY`, so we won't need this option in the future. It's a good default setting; the opposite would be the rarely needed `EAGER`. We don't want all the `bids` eagerly loaded every time we load an `Item`. They should be loaded when accessed, on demand.

We can now create the following two Spring Data JPA repositories.

Listing 8.18   The `ItemRepository` interface

Path: Ch08/mapping-associations/src/test/java/com/manning/javapersistence
➡ /ch08/repositories/onetomany/bidirectional/ItemRepository.java

```
public interface ItemRepository extends JpaRepository<Item, Long> {
}
```

Listing 8.19   The `BidRepository` interface

Path: Ch08/mapping-associations/src/test/java/com/manning/javapersistence
➡ /ch08/repositories/onetomany/bidirectional/BidRepository.java

```
public interface BidRepository extends JpaRepository<Bid, Long> {
Set<Bid> findByItem(Item item);
}
```

These are regular Spring Data JPA repositories, with the `BidRepository` adding a method to get the bids by `Item`.

The second reason for mapping the `Item#bids` collection is the ability to cascade state changes, so let's look at that.

8.3.3   *Cascading state*

If an entity state change can be cascaded across an association to another entity, we need fewer lines of code to manage relationships. But this may have a serious performance consequence.

The following code creates a new `Item` and a new `Bid` and then links them:

```
Item someItem = new Item("Some Item");
Bid someBid = new Bid(new BigDecimal("123.00"), someItem);
someItem.addBid(someBid);
```

We have to consider both sides of this relationship: the `Bid` constructor accepts an item that's used to populate `Bid#item`. To maintain the integrity of the instances in memory, we need to add the bid to `Item#bids`. Now the link is complete from the perspective of the Java code; all the references are set. If you aren't sure why you need this code, please refer to section 3.2.4.

Let's save the item and its bids in the database, first without and then with transitive persistence.

ENABLING TRANSITIVE PERSISTENCE

With the current mapping of `@ManyToOne` and `@OneToMany`, we need to write the following code to save a new `Item` and several `Bid` instances.

Listing 8.20   Managing independent entity instances separately

Path: Ch08/mapping-associations/src/test/java/com/manning/javapersistence
➡ /ch08/onetomany/bidirectional/MappingAssociationsSpringDataJPATest.java

```
Item item = new Item("Foo");
```

```
Bid bid = new Bid(BigDecimal.valueOf(100), item);
Bid bid2 = new Bid(BigDecimal.valueOf(200), item);

itemRepository.save(item);
item.addBid(bid);
item.addBid(bid2);
bidRepository.save(bid);
bidRepository.save(bid2);
```

When we create several bids, calling `EntityManager#persist()` or `BidRepository` `#save()` on each seems redundant. New instances are transient and have to be made persistent. The relationship between `Bid` and `Item` doesn't influence their lifecycles. If `Bid` were to be a value type, the state of a `Bid` would automatically be the same as the owning `Item`. In this case, however, `Bid` has its own completely independent state.

We said earlier that fine-grained control is sometimes necessary to express the dependencies between associated entity classes; this is such a case. The mechanism for this in JPA is the `cascade` option. For example, to save all bids when the item is saved, map the collection as demonstrated next.

Listing 8.21   Cascading persistent state from `Item` to all `bids`

Path: Ch08/mapping-associations/src/main/java/com/manning/javapersistence
➡ /ch08/onetomany/cascadepersist/Item.java

```
@Entity
public class Item {
    //...

    @OneToMany(mappedBy = "item", cascade = CascadeType.PERSIST)
    private Set<Bid> bids = new HashSet<>();
    //  . . .
}
```

Cascading options here intend to be transitive, so we use `CascadeType.PERSIST` for the `ItemRepository#save()` or `EntityManager#persist()` operation. We can now simplify the code that links items and bids and then saves them.

Listing 8.22   All referenced `bids` are automatically made persistent

Path: Ch08/mapping-associations/src/test/java/com/manning/javapersistence
➡ /ch08/onetomany/cascadepersist/MappingAssociationsSpringDataJPATest.java

```
Item item = new Item("Foo");

Bid bid = new Bid(BigDecimal.valueOf(100), item);
Bid bid2 = new Bid(BigDecimal.valueOf(200), item);
item.addBid(bid);
item.addBid(bid2);
                              Ⓐ
itemRepository.save(item);   ⬅
```

A We save the bids automatically, but later. At commit time, Spring Data JPA using Hibernate examines the managed/persistent `Item` instance and looks into the bids collection. It then calls `save()` internally on each of the referenced `Bid` instances, saving them as well. The value stored in the column `BID#ITEM_ID` is taken from each `Bid` by inspecting the `Bid#item` property. The foreign key column is `mappedBy` with `@ManyToOne` on that property.

The `@ManyToOne` annotation also has the `cascade` option. We won't use this often. For example, we can't really say, "when the bid is saved, also save the item." The item has to exist beforehand; otherwise the bid won't be valid in the database. Think about another possible `@ManyToOne` relationship: the `Item#seller` property. The `User` has to exist before they can sell an `Item`.

Transitive persistence is a simple concept, frequently useful with `@OneToMany` or `@ManyToMany` mappings. On the other hand, we have to apply transitive deletion carefully.

CASCADING DELETION

It seems reasonable that the deletion of an item implies the deletion of all the bids for the item, because they're not relevant alone. This is what the *composition* (the filled-out diamond) in the UML diagram means. With the current cascading options, we'll have to write the following code to delete an item:

```
Path: Ch08/mapping-associations/src/test/java/com/manning/javapersistence
➡ /ch08/onetomany/cascadepersist/MappingAssociationsSpringDataJPATest.java

Item retrievedItem = itemRepository.findById(item.getId()).get();

for (Bid someBid : bidRepository.findByItem(retrievedItem)) {
    bidRepository.delete(someBid);           ◄─┐
}                                              A
itemRepository.delete(retrievedItem);    B
```

A First we remove the bids.

B Then we remove the Item owner.

JPA offers a cascading option to help with this. The persistence engine can remove an associated entity instance automatically.

Listing 8.23   Cascading removal from `Item` to all bids

```
Path: Ch08/mapping-associations/src/main/java/com/manning/javapersistence
➡ /ch08/onetomany/cascaderemove/Item.java

@Entity
public class Item {
    // ...
```

```
@OneToMany(mappedBy = "item",
           cascade = {CascadeType.PERSIST, CascadeType.REMOVE})
private Set<Bid> bids = new HashSet<>();
// . . .
}
```

Just as before with `PERSIST`, the `delete()` operations on this association will be cascaded. If we call `ItemRepository#delete()` or `EntityManager#remove()` on an `Item`, Hibernate loads the `bids` collection elements and internally calls `remove()` on each instance:

Path: Ch08/mapping-associations/src/test/java/com/manning/javapersistence
➡ /ch08/onetomany/cascaderemove/MappingAssociationsSpringDataJPATest.java

```
itemRepository.delete(item);
```

One line of code will be enough to also delete bids one by one.

This deletion process is inefficient, however: Hibernate or Spring Data JPA must always load the collection and delete each `Bid` individually. A single SQL statement would have the same effect on the database: `delete from BID where ITEM_ID = ?`.

Nobody in the database has a foreign key reference on the `BID` table. Hibernate doesn't know this, however, and it can't search the whole database for any row that might have a linked `BID_ID` (that is, a `BID_ID` that is actually an `Item` foreign key).

If `Item#bids` was instead a collection of embeddable components, `someItem.getBids().clear()` would execute a single SQL `DELETE`. With a collection of value types, Hibernate assumes that nobody can possibly hold a reference to the bids, and removing only the reference from the collection makes it orphan removable data.

ENABLING ORPHAN REMOVAL

JPA offers a flag that enables the same behavior for `@OneToMany` (and only `@OneTo-Many`) entity associations.

> **Listing 8.24   Enabling orphan removal on a `@OneToMany` collection**

Path: Ch08/mapping-associations/src/main/java/com/manning/javapersistence
➡ /ch08/onetomany/orphanremoval/Item.java

```
@Entity
public class Item {
    //...

    @OneToMany(mappedBy = "item",
               cascade = CascadeType.PERSIST, orphanRemoval = true)
    private Set<Bid> bids = new HashSet<>();
    // . . .
}
```

The `orphanRemoval=true` argument tells Hibernate that we want to permanently remove a `Bid` when it's removed from the collection.

We'll change the `ItemRepository` interface as in the following listing.

Listing 8.25   The modified `ItemRepository` interface

Path: Ch08/mapping-associations/src/test/java/com/manning/javapersistence
➥ /ch08/repositories/onetomany/orphanremoval/ItemRepository.java

```java
public interface ItemRepository extends JpaRepository<Item, Long> {

    @Query("select i from Item i inner join fetch i.bids where i.id = :id")    A
    Item findItemWithBids(@Param("id") Long id);

}
```

A The new `findItemWithBids` method will get the Item by `id`, including the bids collection. To fetch this collection, we'll use the inner join fetch capability of JPQL.

Here is an example of deleting a single `Bid`:

Path: Ch08/mapping-associations/src/test/java/com/manning/javapersistence
➥ /ch08/onetomany/orphanremoval/MappingAssociationsSpringDataJPATest.java

```java
Item item1 = itemRepository.findItemWithBids(item.getId());
Bid firstBid = item1.getBids().iterator().next();
item1.removeBid(firstBid);

itemRepository.save(item1);
```

Hibernate or Spring Data JPA using Hibernate will monitor the collection, and on transaction commit will notice that we removed an element from the collection. Hibernate now considers the `Bid` to be orphaned. We have guaranteed that nobody else had a reference to it; the only reference was the one we just removed from the collection. Thus, Hibernate or Spring Data JPA using Hibernate will automatically execute an SQL `DELETE` to remove the `Bid` instance in the database.

We still won't get the `clear()` one-shot `DELETE`, as with a collection of components. Hibernate respects the regular entity-state transitions, and the bids are all loaded and removed individually.

Orphan removal is a questionable process. It's fine in this example, where there is no other table in the database with a foreign key reference on `BID`. There are no consequences to deleting a row from the `BID` table; the only in-memory references to bids are in `Item#bids`.

As long as all of this is true, there is no problem with enabling orphan removal. It's a convenient option when the presentation layer can remove an element from a collection to delete something. We only need to work with domain model instances, and we don't need to call a service to perform this operation.

But consider what happens when we create a `User#bids` collection mapping—another `@OneToMany`—as shown in figure 8.16. This is a good time to test your knowledge of Hibernate: what will the tables and schema look like after this change? (Answer: the BID table has a BIDDER_ID foreign key column, referencing USERS.)

Figure 8.16 Bidirectional associations between Item, Bid, and User

The test shown in the following listing won't pass.

Listing 8.26 No clean up in-memory references after database removal

Path: Ch08/mapping-associations/src/test/java/com/manning/javapersistence
➥ /ch08/onetomany/orphanremoval/MappingAssociationsSpringDataJPATest.java

```
User user = userRepository.findUserWithBids(john.getId());
assertAll(
    () -> assertEquals(1, items.size()),
    () -> assertEquals(2, bids.size()),
    () -> assertEquals(2, user.getBids().size())
);
Item item1 = itemRepository.findItemWithBids(item.getId());
Bid firstBid = item1.getBids().iterator().next();
item1.removeBid(firstBid);
itemRepository.save(item1);
//FAILURE
//assertEquals(1, user.getBids().size());
assertEquals(2, user.getBids().size());
List<Item> items2 = itemRepository.findAll();
List<Bid> bids2 = bidRepository.findAll();

assertAll(
    () -> assertEquals(1, items2.size()),
    () -> assertEquals(1, bids2.size()),
    () -> assertEquals(2, user.getBids().size())
    //FAILURE
    //() -> assertEquals(1, user.getBids().size())
);
```

Hibernate or Spring Data JPA thinks the removed Bid is orphaned and deletable; it will be deleted automatically in the database, but we still hold a reference to it in the other collection, User#bids. The database state is fine when this transaction commits; the deleted row of the BID table contained both foreign keys, ITEM_ID and BIDDER_ID. But we now have an inconsistency in memory, because saying, "Remove the entity instance when the reference is removed from the collection" naturally conflicts with shared references.

Instead of orphan removal, or even CascadeType.REMOVE, always consider a simpler mapping. Here, Item#bids would be fine as a collection of components, mapped with @ElementCollection. The Bid would be @Embeddable and have a @ManyToOne bidder property, referencing a User. (Embeddable components can own unidirectional associations to entities.)

This would provide the lifecycle we're looking for: a full dependency on the owning entity. We'll have to avoid shared references; the UML diagram in figure 8.16 makes the association from Bid to User unidirectional. Drop the User#bids collection—we don't need this @OneToMany. If we need all the bids made by a user, we can write a query: select b from Bid b where b.bidder = :userParameter. (In the next chapter, we'll complete this mapping with a @ManyToOne in an embeddable component.)

ENABLING ON DELETE CASCADE ON THE FOREIGN KEY

All the removal operations we've shown so far are inefficient. Bids have to be loaded into memory, and many SQL DELETEs are necessary. SQL databases support a more efficient foreign key feature: the ON DELETE option. In DDL, it looks like this: foreign key (ITEM_ID) references ITEM on delete cascade for the BID table.

This option tells the database to maintain the referential integrity of composites transparently for all applications accessing the database. Whenever we delete a row in the ITEM table, the database will automatically delete any row in the BID table with the same ITEM_ID key value. We only need one DELETE statement to remove all dependent data recursively, and nothing has to be loaded into application (server) memory.

You should check whether your schema already has this option enabled on foreign keys. If you want this option added to the Hibernate-generated schema, use the Hibernate @OnDelete annotation.

You should also check whether this option works with your DBMS and if Hibernate or Spring Data JPA using Hibernate generates a foreign key with the ON DELETE CASCADE option. This does not work with MySQL, so we chose to demonstrate this particular example on the H2 database. You will find it this way in the source code (Maven dependency in pom.xml and Spring Data JPA configuration).

Listing 8.27   Generating foreign key ON DELETE CASCADE in the schema

Path: Ch08/mapping-associations/src/main/java/com/manning/javapersistence
➥ /ch08/onetomany/ondeletecascade/Item.java

```
@Entity
public class Item {
    //...

    @OneToMany(mappedBy = "item", cascade = CascadeType.PERSIST)
    @org.hibernate.annotations.OnDelete(
        action = org.hibernate.annotations.OnDeleteAction.CASCADE
    )
    private Set<Bid> bids = new HashSet<>();
    //  . . .
}
```

Ⓐ

A One of the Hibernate's quirks is visible here: the `@OnDelete` annotation affects only the schema generation by Hibernate. Settings that affect schema generation are usually on the "other" `mappedBy` side, where the foreign key/join column is mapped. The `@OnDelete` annotation is usually next to the `@ManyToOne` in `Bid`. When the association is mapped bidirectionally, however, Hibernate will only recognize it on the `@OneToMany` side.

Enabling foreign key cascade deletion in the database doesn't influence Hibernate's runtime behavior. We can still run into the same problem as shown in listing 8.26. Data in memory may no longer accurately reflect the state in the database. If all related rows in the `BID` table are automatically removed when a row in the `ITEM` table is deleted, the application code is responsible for cleaning up references and catching up with the database state. If we aren't careful, we may even end up saving something that we or someone else previously deleted.

The `Bid` instances don't go through the regular lifecycle, and callbacks such as `@PreRemove` have no effect. Additionally, Hibernate doesn't automatically clear the optional second-level global cache, which potentially contains stale data. Fundamentally, the kinds of problems encountered with database-level foreign key cascading are the same as when another application besides ours is accessing the same database, or any other database trigger makes changes. Hibernate can be a very effective utility in such a scenario, but there are other moving parts to consider.

If you work on a new schema, the easiest approach is to not enable database-level cascading and to map a composition relationship in your domain model as embedded/embeddable, not as an entity association. Hibernate or Spring Data JPA using Hibernate can then execute efficient SQL `DELETE` operations to remove the entire composite. We made this recommendation in the previous section: if you can avoid shared references, map the `Bid` as an `@ElementCollection` in `Item`, not as a standalone entity with `@ManyToOne` and `@OneToMany` associations. Alternatively, of course, you might not map any collections at all and use only the simplest mapping: a foreign key column with `@ManyToOne`, unidirectional between `@Entity` classes.

Summary

- Using simple collection mappings, such as a `Set<String>`, you can work through a rich set of interfaces and implementations.
- You can use sorted collections as well as Hibernate's options for letting the database return the collection elements in the desired order.
- You can use complex collections of user-defined embeddable types and sets, bags, and maps of components.
- You can use components as both keys and values in maps.
- You can use a collection in an embeddable component.
- Mapping the first foreign key column to an entity many-to-one association makes it bidirectional as a one-to-many. You can implement cascading options.

Advanced entity
association mappings

This chapter covers

- Applying mapping through one-to-one entity associations
- Using one-to-many mapping options
- Creating many-to-many and ternary entity relationships
- Working with entity associations with maps

In the previous chapter, we demonstrated a unidirectional *many-to-one* association, made it bidirectional, and finally enabled transitive state changes with cascading options. One reason we are discussing more advanced entity mappings in a separate chapter is that we consider quite a few of them rare or at least optional. It's possible to only use component mappings and many-to-one (occasionally *one-to-one*) entity associations. You can write a sophisticated application without ever mapping a collection! We've demonstrated the particular benefits to be gained from collection mappings in the previous chapter, and the rules for when a collection mapping is appropriate also apply to all the examples in this chapter. Always make sure you actually need a collection before attempting a complex collection mapping.

We'll start with mappings that don't involve collections: one-to-one entity associations.

Major new features in JPA 2

Many-to-one and *one-to-one* associations may now be mapped with an intermediate join/link table.

Embeddable component classes may have unidirectional associations to entities, even many-valued with collections.

9.1 One-to-one associations

We argued in section 6.2 that the relationships between `User` and `Address` (the user has a `billingAddress`, `homeAddress`, and `shippingAddress`) are best represented with an `@Embeddable` component mapping. This is usually the simplest way to represent one-to-one relationships because the lifecycle is typically dependent in such a case. It's either aggregation or composition in UML.

What about using a dedicated `ADDRESS` table and mapping both `User` and `Address` as entities? One benefit of this model is that shared references are possible—another entity class (let's say `Shipment`) can also have a reference to a particular `Address` instance. If a `User` also has a reference to this instance as their `shippingAddress`, the `Address` instance has to support shared references and needs its own identity.

In this case, `User` and `Address` classes have a true one-to-one association. Look at the revised class diagram in figure 9.1.

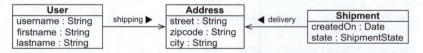

Figure 9.1 `Address` as an entity with two associations, supporting shared references

We are working on the CaveatEmptor application, and we need to map the entities from figure 9.1. There are several possible mappings for one-to-one associations. The first strategy we'll consider is a shared primary key value.

> **NOTE** To be able to execute the examples from the source code, you'll first need to run the Ch09.sql script.

9.1.1 Sharing a primary key

Rows in two tables related by a primary key association share the same primary key values. If each user has exactly one shipping address, then the approach would be that the `User` has the same primary key value as the (shipping) `Address`. The main difficulty with this approach is ensuring that associated instances are assigned the same primary key value when the instances are saved.

Before we look at this problem, let's create the basic mapping. The `Address` class is now a standalone entity; it's no longer a component. The source code that follows can be found in the onetoone-sharedprimarykey folder.

Listing 9.1   Address class as a standalone entity

Path: onetoone-sharedprimarykey/src/main/java/com/manning/javapersistence
➥ /ch09/onetoone/sharedprimarykey/Address.java

```
@Entity
public class Address {
    @Id
    @GeneratedValue(generator = Constants.ID_GENERATOR)
    private Long id;
    @NotNull
    private String street;
    @NotNull
    private String zipcode;
    @NotNull
    private String city;
    //  . . .
}
```

The `User` class is also an entity with the `shippingAddress` association property. We'll introduce two new annotations here: `@OneToOne` and `@PrimaryKeyJoinColumn`.

`@OneToOne` does what you'd expect: it's required to mark an entity-valued property as a one-to-one association. We'll require that a `User` has an `Address` with the `optional=false` clause. We'll force the cascading of changes from `User` to `Address` with the `cascade = CascadeType.ALL` clause. The `@PrimaryKeyJoinColumn` annotation selects the shared primary key strategy we'd like to map.

Listing 9.2   User entity and shippingAddress association

Path: onetoone-sharedprimarykey/src/main/java/com/manning/javapersistence
➥ /ch09/onetoone/sharedprimarykey/User.java

```
@Entity
@Table(name = "USERS")
public class User {          A
    @Id
    private Long id;

        private String username;

B
    @OneToOne(                      C
        fetch = FetchType.LAZY,
D       optional = false,              E
            cascade = CascadeType.ALL
```

```
    )
    @PrimaryKeyJoinColumn                          ←  F
    private Address shippingAddress;

    public User() {
    }
                                                                        G
    public User(Long id, String username) {        ←
        this.id = id;
        this.username = username;
    }
    //  . . .
}
```

A For the User, we don't declare an identifier generator. As mentioned in section 5.2.4, this is one of the rare cases where we'll use an *application-assigned* identifier value.

B The relationship between User and Address is one-to-one.

C As usual, we should prefer the lazy-loading strategy, so we override the default FetchType.EAGER with LAZY.

D The optional=false switch specifies that a User must have a shippingAddress.

E The Hibernate-generated database schema reflects this with a foreign key constraint. Any change here must be cascaded to Address. The primary key of the USERS table also has a foreign key constraint referencing the primary key of the ADDRESS table. See the tables in figure 9.2.

F Using @PrimaryKeyJoinColumn makes this a unidirectional shared primary key one-to-one association mapping, from User to Address.

G The constructor design weakly enforces this: the public API of the class requires an identifier value to create an instance.

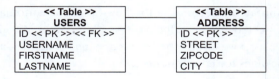

<< Table >> USERS		<< Table >> ADDRESS
ID << PK >> << FK >>		ID << PK >>
USERNAME		STREET
FIRSTNAME		ZIPCODE
LASTNAME		CITY

Figure 9.2 The USERS table has a foreign key constraint on its primary key.

For some of the examples in this chapter, we'll need to make a few changes to our usual configuration for the tests, as the execution will need to be transactional. The SpringDataConfiguration class will require more annotations:

Path: onetoone-sharedprimarykey/src/test/java/com/manning/javapersistence
➥ /ch09/configuration/onetoone/sharedprimarykey
➥ /SpringDataConfiguration.java

B
```
@Configuration                         ←  A
@EnableTransactionManagement                                              C
@ComponentScan(basePackages = "com.manning.javapersistence.ch09.*")  ←
```

```
@EnableJpaRepositories("com.manning.javapersistence.ch09.repositories.
                        onetoone.sharedprimarykey")
public class SpringDataConfiguration {
// . . .
}
```
Ⓓ

Ⓐ `@Configuration` specifies that this class declares one or more bean definitions to be used by the Spring container.

Ⓑ `@EnableTransactionManagement` enables the transaction management capabilities of Spring through annotations.

Ⓒ We'll need to execute a few operations in a transactional way to test the code from this chapter. `@ComponentScan` requires Spring to scan the package provided as an argument, and its subpackages, for components.

Ⓓ `@EnableJpaRepositories` scans the indicated package to find Spring Data repositories.

We'll isolate the operations against the database in a dedicated `TestService` class:

Path: onetoone-sharedprimarykey/src/test/java/com/manning/javapersistence
➡ /ch09/onetoone/sharedprimarykey/TestService.java

```
@Service
public class TestService {            Ⓐ
    @Autowired
    private UserRepository userRepository;
                                                      Ⓑ
    @Autowired
    private AddressRepository addressRepository;

    @Transactional            Ⓒ
    public void storeLoadEntities() {
// . . .
```

Ⓐ The `TestService` class is annotated as `@Service` to allow Spring to automatically create a bean, later to be injected in the effective test. Remember that in the `SpringDataConfiguration` class, we scan the `com.manning.javapersistence` `.ch09` package and its subpackages for components.

Ⓑ Inject two repository beans.

Ⓒ Define the `storeLoadEntities` method, annotating it with `@Transactional`. The operations we'll need to execute against the database need to be transactional, and we'll let Spring control this.

The testing class will differ from the previously presented ones, as it will delegate to the `TestService` class. This will allow us to keep the transactional operations isolated in their own methods and to call those methods from the test.

Path: onetoone-sharedprimarykey/src/test/java/com/manning/javapersistence
➡ /ch09/onetoone/sharedprimarykey/AdvancedMappingSpringDataJPATest.java

```
@ExtendWith(SpringExtension.class)
@ContextConfiguration(classes = {SpringDataConfiguration.class})
public class AdvancedMappingSpringDataJPATest {

    @Autowired
    private TestService testService;

    @Test
    void testStoreLoadEntities() {

        testService.storeLoadEntities();

    }
}
```

The JPA specification doesn't include a standardized method for dealing with the problem of shared primary key generation. This means we're responsible for setting the identifier value of a `User` instance correctly before we save it to the identifier value of the linked `Address` instance:

Path: onetoone-sharedprimarykey/src/test/java/com/manning/javapersistence
➥ /ch09/onetoone/sharedprimarykey/TestService.java

```
Address address =
        new Address("Flowers Street", "01246", "Boston");
addressRepository.save(address);

User john = new User(address.getId(),"John Smith");
john.setShippingAddress(address);

userRepository.save(john);
```

A Persist the `Address`.

B Take its generated identifier value and set it on `User`.

C Save it.

There are three problems with the mapping and code:

- We have to remember that the `Address` must be saved first and then get its identifier value. This is only possible if the `Address` entity has an identifier generator that produces values on `save()` before the `INSERT`, as we discussed in section 5.2.5. Otherwise, `someAddress.getId()` returns `null`, and we can't manually set the identifier value of the `User`.

- Lazy loading with proxies only works if the association is non-optional. This is often a surprise for developers new to JPA. The default for `@OneToOne` is `FetchType.EAGER`: when Hibernate or Spring Data JPA using Hibernate loads a `User`, it loads the `shippingAddress` right away. Conceptually, lazy loading with proxies only makes sense if Hibernate knows that there is a linked `shipping-Address`. If the property were nullable, Hibernate would have to check in the database whether the property value is `NULL` by querying the `ADDRESS` table. If we have to check the database, we might as well load the value right away, because there would be no benefit in using a proxy.

- The one-to-one association is unidirectional; sometimes we need bidirectional navigation.

The first problem has no other solution. In the preceding example we are doing exactly this: saving the `Address`, getting its primary key, and manually setting it as the identifier value of the `User`. This is one of the reasons we should always prefer identifier generators capable of producing values before any SQL `INSERT`.

A `@OneToOne(optional=true)` association doesn't support lazy loading with proxies. This is consistent with the JPA specification. `FetchType.LAZY` is a hint for the persistence provider, not a requirement. We could get lazy loading of nullable `@OneToOne` with bytecode instrumentation, as you'll see in section 12.1.3.

As for the last problem, if we make the association bidirectional (where the `Address` references the `User` and the `User` references the `Address`), we can also use a special Hibernate-only identifier generator to help with assigning key values.

9.1.2   *The foreign primary key generator*

A bidirectional mapping always requires a `mappedBy` side. We'll pick the `User` side—this is a matter of taste and perhaps other, secondary requirements. (The source code that follows can be found in the onetoone-foreigngenerator folder.)

Path: onetoone-foreigngenerator/src/main/java/com/manning/javapersistence
➥ /ch09/onetoone/foreigngenerator/User.java

```
@Entity
@Table(name = "USERS")
public class User {
    @Id
    @GeneratedValue(generator = Constants.ID_GENERATOR)
    private Long id;

    private String username;

    @OneToOne(
        mappedBy = "user",
        cascade = CascadeType.PERSIST
    )
    private Address shippingAddress;
    // . . .
}
```

We have added the `mappedBy` option, telling Hibernate or Spring Data JPA using Hibernate that the lower-level details are now mapped by "the property on the other side," named user. As a convenience, we enable `CascadeType.PERSIST`; transitive persistence will make it easier to save the instances in the right order. When we make the `User` persistent, Hibernate makes the `shippingAddress` persistent and generates the identifier for the primary key automatically.

Next, let's look at the "other side": the Address. We'll use the @GenericGenerator
on the identifier property to define a special-purpose primary key value generator
with the Hibernate-only foreign strategy. We didn't mention this generator in the
overview in section 5.2.5 because the shared primary key one-to-one association is its
only use case. When persisting an instance of Address, this special generator grabs the
value of the user property and takes the identifier value of the referenced entity
instance, the User.

Listing 9.3   Address has the special foreign key generator

Path: onetoone-foreigngenerator/src/main/java/com/manning/javapersistence
➡ /ch09/onetoone/foreigngenerator/Address.java

```
@Entity
public class Address {
    @Id
    @GeneratedValue(generator = "addressKeyGenerator")        Ⓐ
    @org.hibernate.annotations.GenericGenerator(
        name = "addressKeyGenerator",
        strategy = "foreign",
        parameters =
            @org.hibernate.annotations.Parameter(
                name = "property", value = "user"
            )
    )
    private Long id;

    // . . .

                                                              Ⓑ
    @OneToOne(optional = false)
    @PrimaryKeyJoinColumn                           Ⓒ
    private User user;

    public Address() {
    }
                                                    Ⓓ
    public Address(User user) {
        this.user = user;
    }

    public Address(User user, String street,        Ⓓ
                   String zipcode, String city) {
        this.user = user;
        this.street = street;
        this.zipcode = zipcode;
        this.city = city;
    }
    // . . .
}
```

A With the `@GenericGenerator` annotation, when we persist an instance of `Address`, this special generator grabs the value of the `user` property and takes the identifier value of the referenced entity instance, the `User`.

B The `@OneToOne` mapping is set to `optional=false`, so an `Address` must have a reference to a `User`.

C The `user` property is marked as a shared primary key entity association with the `@PrimaryKeyJoinColumn` annotation.

D The public constructors of `Address` now require a `User` instance. The foreign key constraint reflecting `optional=false` is now on the primary key column of the `ADDRESS` table, as you can see in the schema in figure 9.3.

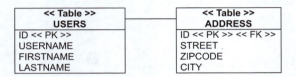

<< Table >> USERS
ID << PK >>
USERNAME
FIRSTNAME
LASTNAME

<< Table >> ADDRESS
ID << PK >> << FK >>
STREET
ZIPCODE
CITY

Figure 9.3   The `ADDRESS` table has a foreign key constraint on its primary key.

Thanks to this new code, we no longer have to call `address.getId()` or `user.getId()` in our unit of work. Storing data is simplified:

Path: onetoone-foreigngenerator/src/test/java/com/manning/javapersistence
➡ /ch09/onetoone/foreigngenerator/AdvancedMappingJPATest.java

```
User john = new User("John Smith");
Address address =
    new Address(                                          A
        john,
        "Flowers Street", "01246", "Boston"
    );
john.setShippingAddress(address);            A
userRepository.save(john);
```

B (arrow pointing to `userRepository.save(john);`)

A We must link both sides of a bidirectional entity association. Note that with this mapping, we won't get lazy loading of `User#shippingAddress` (it's optional/nullable), but we can load `Address#user` on demand with proxies (it's non-optional).

B When we persist the user, we'll get the transitive persistence of `shippingAddress`.

Shared primary key one-to-one associations are relatively rare. Instead, we'll often map a "to-one" association with a foreign key column and a unique constraint.

9.1.3   *Using a foreign key join column*

Instead of sharing a primary key, two rows can have a relationship based on a simple additional foreign key column. One table has a foreign key column that references the primary key of the associated table. (The source and target of this foreign key constraint can even be the same table: we call this a *self-referencing relationship*.) The source code that follows can be found in the onetoone-foreignkey folder.

Let's change the mapping for `User#shippingAddress`. Instead of having a shared primary key, we'll now add a `SHIPPINGADDRESS_ID` column in the `USERS` table. This column has a `UNIQUE` constraint, so no two users can reference the same shipping address. Look at the schema in figure 9.4.

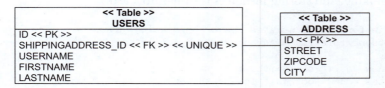

Figure 9.4   **A one-to-one join column association between the USERS and ADDRESS tables**

The `Address` is a regular entity class, like the first one we demonstrated in this chapter, in listing 9.1. The `User` entity class has the `shippingAddress` property, implementing this unidirectional association.

We should enable lazy loading for this `User–Address` association. Unlike with shared primary keys, we don't have a problem with lazy loading here: when a row of the `USERS` table has been loaded, it contains the value of the `SHIPPINGADDRESS_ID` column. Hibernate or Spring Data using Hibernate, therefore, knows whether an `ADDRESS` row is present, and a proxy can be used to load the `Address` instance on demand.

Path: onetoone-foreignkey/src/main/java/com/manning/javapersistence
➥ /ch09/onetoone/foreignkey/User.java

```
@Entity
@Table(name = "USERS")
public class User {
    @Id
    @GeneratedValue(generator = Constants.ID_GENERATOR)
    private Long id;

    @OneToOne(
        fetch = FetchType.LAZY,                    Ⓐ
        optional = false,
        cascade = CascadeType.PERSIST             Ⓑ
    )
    @JoinColumn(unique = true)
    private Address shippingAddress;
    //  . . .
}
```

Ⓐ We don't need any special identifier generators or primary key assignments; we'll make sure the `shippingAddress` is not null.

Ⓑ Instead of `@PrimaryKeyJoinColumn`, we apply the regular `@JoinColumn`, which will default to `SHIPPINGADDRESS_ID`. If you're more familiar with SQL than JPA, it helps to think "foreign key column" every time you see `@JoinColumn` in a mapping.

In the mapping, we set `optional=false`, so the user must have a shipping address. This won't affect the loading behavior but it is a logical consequence of the unique=true setting on the @JoinColumn. This setting adds a unique constraint to the generated SQL schema. If the values of the SHIPPINGADDRESS_ID column must be unique for all users, only one user could possibly have "no shipping address." Hence, nullable unique columns typically aren't meaningful.

Creating, linking, and storing instances is straightforward:

Path: onetoone-foreignkey/src/test/java/com/manning/javapersistence
➡ /ch09/onetoone/foreignkey/AdvancedMappingSpringDataJPATest.java

```
User john = new User("John Smith");
Address address = new Address("Flowers Street", "01246", "Boston");
john.setShippingAddress(address);
userRepository.save(john);          ← B
```

A Create the link between the user and the address.

B When we save john, we'll transitively save the address.

We've now completed two basic one-to-one association mappings: the first with a shared primary key, and the second with a foreign key reference and a unique column constraint. The last option we want to discuss is a bit more exotic: mapping a one-to-one association with the help of an additional table.

9.1.4   *Using a join table*

You've probably noticed that nullable columns can be problematic. Sometimes a better solution for optional values is to use an intermediate table, which contains a row if a link is present and doesn't if it's not.

Let's consider the Shipment entity in CaveatEmptor and discuss its purpose. Sellers and buyers interact in CaveatEmptor by starting and bidding on auctions. Shipping goods seems outside the scope of the application; the seller and the buyer agree on a method of shipment and payment after the auction ends. They can do this offline, outside of CaveatEmptor.

On the other hand, we could offer an escrow service in CaveatEmptor. Sellers would use this service to create a trackable shipment once the auction ends. The buyer would pay the price of the auction item to a trustee (us), and we'd inform the seller that the money is available. Once the shipment arrives and the buyer accepts it, we'd transfer the money to the seller.

If you've ever participated in an online auction of significant value, you've probably used such an escrow service. But we want more in CaveatEmptor: not only will we provide trust services for completed auctions, but we also allow users to create trackable and trusted shipments for any deals they make outside an auction, outside CaveatEmptor. This scenario calls for a Shipment entity with an optional one-to-one association to Item. The class diagram for this domain model is shown in figure 9.5.

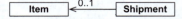

Figure 9.5   Shipment has an optional link with an auction Item.

NOTE We briefly considered abandoning the CaveatEmptor example for this section because we couldn't find a natural scenario that requires optional one-to-one associations. If this escrow example seems contrived, consider the equivalent problem of assigning employees to workstations. This is also an optional one-to-one relationship.

In the database schema, we'll add an intermediate link table called ITEM_SHIPMENT. A row in this table represents a Shipment made in the context of an auction. Figure 9.6 shows the tables.

Figure 9.6 The intermediate table links items and shipments.

Note how the schema enforces uniqueness and the one-to-one relationship: the primary key of ITEM_SHIPMENT is the SHIPMENT_ID column, and the ITEM_ID column is unique. An item can therefore be in only one shipment. Of course, that also means a shipment can contain only one item.

We'll map this model with a @OneToOne annotation in the Shipment entity class. The source code that follows can be found in the onetoone-jointable folder.

Path: onetoone-jointable/src/main/java/com/manning/javapersistence
➥ /ch09/onetoone/jointable/Shipment.java

```java
@Entity
public class Shipment {
    // . . .
    @OneToOne(fetch = FetchType.LAZY)      ⬅ Ⓐ
    @JoinTable(                             Ⓑ
        name = "ITEM_SHIPMENT",
        joinColumns =
            @JoinColumn(name = "SHIPMENT_ID"),    ⬅ Ⓒ
        inverseJoinColumns =                      Ⓓ
            @JoinColumn(name = "ITEM_ID",
                        nullable = false,
                        unique = true)      ⬅ Ⓔ
    )
    private Item auction;

    // . . .
}
```

Ⓐ Lazy loading has been enabled, with a twist: when Hibernate or Spring Data JPA using Hibernate loads a Shipment, it queries both the SHIPMENT and the ITEM_SHIPMENT join table. Hibernate has to know if a link to an Item is present before it can use a proxy. It does that in one outer join SQL query, so we won't see any extra SQL statements. If there is a row in ITEM_SHIPMENT, Hibernate uses an Item placeholder.

B The @JoinTable annotation is new; we always have to specify the name of the inter-mediate table. This mapping effectively hides the join table; there is no correspond-ing Java class. The annotation defines the column names of the ITEM_SHIPMENT table.

C The join column is SHIPMENT_ID (it would default to ID).

D The inverse join column is ITEM_ID (it would default to AUCTION_ID).

E Hibernate generates the UNIQUE constraint on the ITEM_ID column in the schema. Hibernate also generates the appropriate foreign key constraints on the columns of the join table.

Here we store a Shipment without Items and another linked to a single Item:

```
Path: onetoone-jointable/src/test/java/com/manning/javapersistence
➥ /ch09/onetoone/jointable/AdvancedMappingSpringDataJPATest.java
```

```
Shipment shipment = new Shipment();
shipmentRepository.save(shipment);
Item item = new Item("Foo");
itemRepository.save(item);
Shipment auctionShipment = new Shipment(item);
shipmentRepository.save(auctionShipment);
```

This completes our discussion of one-to-one association mappings. To summarize, you should use a shared primary key association if one of the two entities is always stored before the other and can act as the primary key source. Use a foreign key association in all other cases, or a hidden intermediate join table when the one-to-one association is optional.

We'll now focus on plural, or *many-valued*, entity associations, beginning with some advanced options for one-to-many.

9.2 *One-to-many associations*

A *plural entity association* is, by definition, a collection of entity references. We mapped one of these, a one-to-many association, in section 8.3.2. One-to-many associations are the most important kind of entity association involving a collection. We'll go so far as to discourage the use of more complex association styles when a simple bidirectional many-to-one or one-to-many will do the job.

Also, remember that you don't have to map any collection of entities if you don't want to; you can always write an explicit query instead of direct access through itera-tion. If you decide to map collections of entity references, you have a few options, and we'll analyze some more complex situations now.

9.2.1 *Considering one-to-many bags*

So far, we have only seen a @OneToMany on a Set, but it's possible to use a bag mapping for a bidirectional one-to-many association. Why would we do this?

Bags have the most efficient performance characteristics of all the collections we can use for a bidirectional one-to-many entity association. By default, collections in Hibernate are loaded when they're accessed for the first time in the application. Because a bag doesn't have to maintain the index of its elements (like a list) or check for duplicate elements (like a set), we can add new elements to the bag without triggering the loading. This is an important feature if we're going to map a possibly large collection of entity references.

On the other hand, we can't eager-fetch two collections of bag type simultaneously, as the generated SELECT queries are unrelated and need to be kept separately. This might happen if bids and images of an Item were one-to-many bags, for example. This is no big loss, because fetching two collections simultaneously always results in a Cartesian product; we want to avoid this kind of operation, whether the collections are bags, sets, or lists. We'll come back to fetching strategies in chapter 12. In general, we'd say that a bag is the best inverse collection for a one-to-many association if it is mapped as a @OneToMany(mappedBy = "...").

To map our bidirectional one-to-many association as a bag, we have to replace the type of the bids collection in the Item entity with a Collection and an ArrayList implementation. The mapping for the association between Item and Bid remains essentially unchanged. (The source code that follows can be found in the onetomany-bag folder.)

Path: onetomany-bag/src/main/java/com/manning/javapersistence/ch09
➥ /onetomany/bag/Item.java

```
@Entity
public class Item {
    / . . .
    @OneToMany(mappedBy = "item")
    private Collection<Bid> bids = new ArrayList<>();
    // . . .
}
```

The Bid side with its @ManyToOne (which is the "mapped by" side) and even the tables are the same as in section 8.3.1.

A bag also allows duplicate elements, which a set does not:

Path: onetomany-bag/src/test/java/com/manning/javapersistence/ch09
➥ /onetomany/bag/AdvancedMappingSpringDataJPATest.java

```
    Item item = new Item("Foo");
    itemRepository.save(item);
Bid someBid = new Bid(new BigDecimal("123.00"), item);
item.addBid(someBid);
item.addBid(someBid);
bidRepository.save(someBid);
assertEquals(2, someItem.getBids().size());
```

It turns out that isn't relevant in this case because *duplicate* means we've added a particular reference to the same `Bid` instance several times We wouldn't do this in our application code. Even if we added the same reference several times to this collection, though, Hibernate or Spring Data JPA using Hibernate would ignore it—there is no persistent effect. The side relevant for updates of the database is the `@ManyToOne`, and the relationship is already "mapped by" that side. When we load the `Item`, the collection doesn't contain the duplicate:

Path: onetomany-bag/src/test/java/com/manning/javapersistence/ch09/
➥ onetomany/bag/AdvancedMappingSpringDataJPATest.java

```
Item item2 = itemRepository.findItemWithBids(item.getId());
assertEquals(1, item2.getBids().size());
```

As mentioned previously, the advantage of bags is that the collection doesn't have to be initialized when we add a new element:

Path: onetomany-bag/src/test/java/com/manning/javapersistence/ch09/
➥ onetomany/bag/AdvancedMappingSpringDataJPATest.java

```
Bid bid = new Bid(new BigDecimal("456.00"), item);
item.addBid(bid);
bidRepository.save(bid);
```

A This code example triggers one SQL `SELECT` to load the Item. Hibernate still initializes and returns an `Item` proxy with a `SELECT` as soon as we call `item.addBid()`. But as long as we don't iterate the `Collection`, no more queries are necessary, and an `INSERT` for the new `Bid` will be made without loading all the bids. If the collection is a `Set` or a `List`, Hibernate loads all the elements when we add another element.

We'll now change the collection to a persistent `List`.

9.2.2 Unidirectional and bidirectional list mappings

If we need a real list to hold the position of the elements in a collection, we have to store that position in an additional column. For a one-to-many mapping, this also means we should change the `Item#bids` property to `List` and initialize the variable with an `ArrayList`. This will be a unidirectional mapping: there will be no other "mapped by" side. The `Bid` will not have a `@ManyToOne` property. For persistent list indexes, we'll use the annotation `@OrderColumn`. (The source code that follows can be found in the onetomany-list folder.)

Path: onetomany-list/src/main/java/com/manning/javapersistence/ch09/
➥ onetomany/list/Item.java

```
@Entity
public class Item {
    @OneToMany
    @JoinColumn(
```

```
        name = "ITEM_ID",
        nullable = false
    )
    @OrderColumn(
        name = "BID_POSITION",
        nullable = false
    )
    private List<Bid> bids = new ArrayList<>();
    //  . . .
}
```

A As mentioned, this is a unidirectional mapping: there is no other "mapped by" side. The Bid doesn't have a @ManyToOne property. The @OrderColumn annotation will set the name of the index column to be BID_POSITION. Otherwise, it would default to BIDS_ORDER.

B As usual, we should make the column NOT NULL.

The database view of the BID table, with the join and order columns, is shown in figure 9.7.

BID

ID	ITEM_ID	BID_POSITION	AMOUNT
1	1	0	99.00
2	1	1	100.00
3	1	2	101.00
4	2	0	4.99

Figure 9.7 The BID table contains the ITEM_ID (join column) and BID_POSITION (order column).

The stored index of each collection starts at zero and is contiguous (there are no gaps). Hibernate or Spring Data JPA using Hibernate will execute potentially many SQL statements when we add, remove, and shift elements of the List. We talked about this performance issue in section 8.1.6.

Let's make this mapping bidirectional, with a @ManyToOne property on the Bid entity:

Path: onetomany-list/src/main/java/com/manning/javapersistence/ch09/
➥ onetomany/list/Bid.java

```
@Entity
public class Bid {
    // . . .

    @ManyToOne
    @JoinColumn(
        name = "ITEM_ID",
        updatable = false, insertable = false
    )
    @NotNull
```

```
        private Item item;
        //  . . .
    }
```

Ⓐ The `Item#bids` collection is no longer read-only because Hibernate now has to store the index of each element. If the `Bid#item` side was the owner of the relationship, Hibernate would ignore the collection when storing data and not write the element indexes. We have to map the `@JoinColumn` twice and then disable writing on the `@ManyToOne` side with `updatable=false` and `insertable=false`. Hibernate now considers the collection side when storing data, including the index of each element. The `@ManyToOne` is effectively read-only, as it would be if it had a `mappedBy` attribute.

You probably expected different code—maybe `@ManyToOne(mappedBy="bids")` and no additional `@JoinColumn` annotation. But `@ManyToOne` doesn't have a `mappedBy` attribute: it's always the "owning" side of the relationship. We'd have to make the other side, `@OneToMany`, the `mappedBy` side.

Finally, the Hibernate schema generator always relies on the `@JoinColumn` of the `@ManyToOne` side. Hence, if we want the correct schema produced, we should add the `@NotNull` on this side or declare `@JoinColumn(nullable=false)`. The generator ignores the `@OneToMany` side and its join column if there is a `@ManyToOne`.

In a real application, we wouldn't map this association with a `List`. Preserving the order of elements in the database seems like a common use case, but it isn't actually very useful: sometimes we'll want to show a list with the highest or newest bid first, or only show bids made by a certain user, or show bids made within a certain time range. None of these operations requires a persistent list index. As mentioned in section 3.2.4, it's best to avoid storing a display order in the database, as the display order may change frequently; keep it flexible with queries instead of using hardcoded mappings. Furthermore, maintaining the index when the application removes, adds, or shifts elements in a list can be expensive and may trigger many SQL statements. Map the foreign key join column with `@ManyToOne`, and drop the collection.

Next we'll work on one more scenario with a one-to-many relationship: an association mapped to an intermediate join table.

9.2.3 *Optional one-to-many with a join table*

A useful addition to the `Item` class is a `buyer` property. We can then call `someItem.getBuyer()` to access the `User` who made the winning bid. If it's made bidirectional, this association will also help us render a screen that shows all the auctions a particular user has won: we could call `someUser.get-BoughtItems()` instead of writing a query.

From the point of view of the `User` class, the association is one-to-many. Figure 9.8 shows the classes and their relationship.

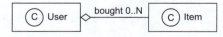

Figure 9.8   The `User–Item` "bought" relationship

Why is this association different from the one between `Item` and `Bid`? The multiplicity `0..*` in UML indicates that the reference is optional. This doesn't influence the Java domain model much, but it has consequences for the underlying tables. We expect a `BUYER_ID` foreign key column in the `ITEM` table, but now the column has to be nullable because a user may not have bought a particular `Item` (as long as the auction is still running).

We could accept that the foreign key column can be `NULL` and apply additional constraints: "Allowed to be `NULL` only if the auction end time hasn't been reached or if no bid has been made." However, we always try to avoid nullable columns in a relational database schema. Unknown information degrades the quality of the data we store. Tuples represent propositions that are true, and we can't assert something we don't know. Moreover, in practice, many developers and DBAs don't create the right constraints and rely on often buggy application code to provide data integrity.

An optional entity association, be it one-to-one or one-to-many, is best represented in an SQL database with a join table. Figure 9.9 shows an example schema.

Figure 9.9 An intermediate table links users and items.

We added a join table earlier in this chapter for a one-to-one association. To guarantee the multiplicity of one-to-one, we applied a unique constraint on a foreign key column of the join table. In the current case, we have a one-to-many multiplicity, so only the `ITEM_ID` primary key column has to be unique: only one `User` can buy any given `Item` once. The `BUYER_ID` column isn't unique because a `User` can buy many `Items`. (The source code that follows can be found in the `onetomany-jointable` folder.)

The mapping of the `User#boughtItems` collection is simple:

Path: onetomany-jointable/src/main/java/com/manning/javapersistence/ch09/
➥ onetomany/jointable/User.java

```
@Entity
@Table(name = "USERS")
public class User {
    // . . .
    @OneToMany(mappedBy = "buyer")
    private Set<Item> boughtItems = new HashSet<>();
    // . . .
}
```

This is the usual read-only side of a bidirectional association, with the actual mapping to the schema on the "mapped by" side, the `Item#buyer`. It will be a clean, optional one-to-many/many-to-one relationship.

Path: onetomany-jointable/src/main/java/com/manning/javapersistence/ch09/
➥ onetomany/jointable/Item.java

```java
@Entity
public class Item {
    // . . .
    @ManyToOne(fetch = FetchType.LAZY)
    @JoinTable(
        name = "ITEM_BUYER",
        joinColumns =
            @JoinColumn(name = "ITEM_ID"),
        inverseJoinColumns =
            @JoinColumn(nullable = false)
    )
    private User buyer;
    // . . .
}
```

A If an `Item` hasn't been bought, there is no corresponding row in the `ITEM_BUYER` join table. The relationship will thus be optional. The join column is named `ITEM_ID` (it would default to `ID`).

B The inverse join column will default to `BUYER_ID`, and it is not nullable.

We don't have any problematic nullable columns in our schema. Still, we should write a procedural constraint and a trigger that runs on `INSERT` for the `ITEM_BUYER` table: "Only allow insertion of a buyer if the auction end time for the given item has been reached and the user made the winning bid."

The next example is our last with one-to-many associations. So far, you've seen one-to-many associations from an entity to another entity. An embeddable component class may also have a one-to-many association to an entity, and this is what we'll deal with now.

9.2.4 *One-to-many association in an embeddable class*

Consider again the embeddable component mapping we've been repeating for a few chapters: the `Address` of a `User`. We'll now extend this example by adding a one-to-many association from `Address` to `Shipment`: a collection called `deliveries`. Figure 9.10 shows the UML class diagram for this model.

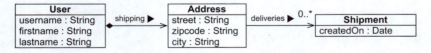

Figure 9.10   The one-to-many relationship from `Address` to `Shipment`

The `Address` is an `@Embeddable` class, not an entity. It can own a unidirectional association to an entity; here, it's a one-to-many multiplicity to `Shipment`. We'll look at an embeddable class having a many-to-one association with an entity in the next section. (The source code that follows can be found in the onetomany-embeddable folder.)

The `Address` class has a `Set<Shipment>` representing this association:

Path: onetomany-embeddable/src/main/java/com/manning/javapersistence/ch09/
➥ onetomany/embeddable/Address.java

```java
@Embeddable
public class Address {
    @NotNull
    @Column(nullable = false)
    private String street;
    @NotNull
    @Column(nullable = false, length = 5)
    private String zipcode;
    @NotNull
    @Column(nullable = false)
    private String city;
    @OneToMany
    @JoinColumn(                                          A
        name = "DELIVERY_ADDRESS_USER_ID",  ◁
        nullable = false
    )
    private Set<Shipment> deliveries = new HashSet<>();
    //  . . .
}
```

A The first mapping strategy for this association is with a `@JoinColumn` named `DELIVERY_ADDRESS_USER_ID` (it would default to `DELIVERIES_ID`).

This foreign key-constrained column is in the `SHIPMENT` table, as you can see in figure 9.11.

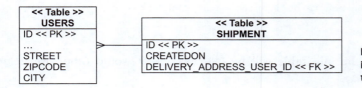

Figure 9.11 A primary key in the USERS table links the USERS and SHIPMENT tables.

Embeddable components don't have their own identifier, so the value in the foreign key column is the value of a `User`'s identifier, which embeds the `Address`. Here we also declare the join column `nullable = false`, so a `Shipment` must have an associated delivery address. Of course, bidirectional navigation isn't possible: the `Shipment` can't have a reference to the `Address` because embedded components can't have shared references.

If the association is optional and we don't want a nullable column, we can map the association to an intermediate join/link table, as shown in figure 9.12.

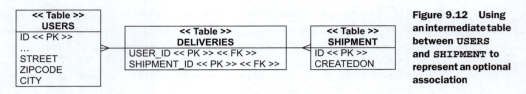

Figure 9.12   Using an intermediate table between USERS and SHIPMENT to represent an optional association

The mapping of the collection in `Address` now uses a `@JoinTable` instead of a `@JoinColumn`. (The source code that follows can be found in the onetomany-embeddable-jointable folder.)

Path: onetomany-embeddable-jointable/src/main/java/com/manning
➥ /javapersistence/ch09/onetomany/embeddablejointable/Address.java

```
@Embeddable
public class Address {
    @NotNull
    @Column(nullable = false)
    private String street;
    @NotNull
    @Column(nullable = false, length = 5)
    private String zipcode;
    @NotNull
    @Column(nullable = false)
    private String city;

    @OneToMany
    @JoinTable(                              Ⓐ
        name = "DELIVERIES",      ←┐
        joinColumns =                   Ⓑ
        @JoinColumn(name = "USER_ID"),   ←┐
        inverseJoinColumns =
        @JoinColumn(name = "SHIPMENT_ID")    ← Ⓒ
    )
    private Set<Shipment> deliveries = new HashSet<>();
    //  . . .
}
```

Ⓐ The name of the join table will be `DELIVERIES` (it would otherwise default to `USERS_SHIPMENT`).

Ⓑ The name of the join column will be `USER_ID` (it would otherwise default to `USERS_ID`).

Ⓒ The name of the inverse join column will be `SHIPMENT_ID` (it would otherwise default to `SHIPMENTS_ID`).

Note that if we declare neither `@JoinTable` nor `@JoinColumn`, the `@OneToMany` in an embeddable class defaults to a join table strategy.

From within the owning entity class, we can override property mappings of an embedded class with `@AttributeOverride`, as demonstrated in section 6.2.3. If we want to override the join table or column mapping of an entity association in an embeddable class, we can use `@AssociationOverride` in the owning entity class instead. We can't, however, switch the mapping strategy; the mapping in the embeddable component class decides whether a join table or join column is used.

A join table mapping is, of course, also applicable in true *many-to-many* mappings.

9.3   *Many-to-many and ternary associations*

The association between `Category` and `Item` is a *many-to-many* association, as you can see in figure 9.13. In a real system, we may not have a many-to-many association—our experience is that there is almost always other information that must be attached to each link between associated instances. Some examples are the timestamp when an `Item` was added to a `Category`, and the `User` responsible for creating the link. We'll expand the example later in this section to cover such cases, but we'll start with a regular and simpler many-to-many association.

Figure 9.13   A many-to-many association between `Category` and `Item`

9.3.1   *Unidirectional and bidirectional many-to-many associations*

A join table in the database represents a regular many-to-many association, which some developers also call a *link table* or *association table*. Figure 9.14 shows a many-to-many relationship with a link table.

The `CATEGORY_ITEM` link table has two columns, both with foreign key constraints referencing the `CATEGORY` and `ITEM` tables, respectively. Its primary key is a composite key of both columns. We can only link a particular `Category` and `Item` once, but we can link the same item to several categories. The source code that follows can be found in the `manytomany-bidirectional` folder.

In JPA, we map many-to-many associations with `@ManyToMany` on a collection:

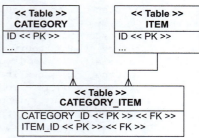

Figure 9.14   `CategorizedItem` is the link between `Category` and `Item`.

Path: manytomany-bidirectional/src/main/java/com/manning
➥ /javapersistence/ch09/manytomany/bidirectional/Category.java

```
@Entity
public class Category {
    // . . .
    @ManyToMany(cascade = CascadeType.PERSIST)
    @JoinTable(
        name = "CATEGORY_ITEM",
        joinColumns = @JoinColumn(name = "CATEGORY_ID"),
        inverseJoinColumns = @JoinColumn(name = "ITEM_ID")
    )
    private Set<Item> items = new HashSet<>();
    // . . .
}
```

As usual, we can enable `CascadeType.PERSIST` to make it easier to save data. When we reference a new `Item` from the collection, Hibernate or Spring Data JPA using Hibernate makes it persistent. Let's make this association bidirectional (we don't have to if we don't need to):

Path: manytomany-bidirectional/src/main/java/com/manning
➥ /javapersistence/ch09/manytomany/bidirectional/Item.java

```
@Entity
public class Item {
    // . . .
    @ManyToMany(mappedBy = "items")
    private Set<Category> categories = new HashSet<>();
    //  . . .
}
```

As in any bidirectional mapping, one side is "mapped by" the other side. The `Item#categories` collection is effectively read-only; Hibernate will analyze the content of the `Category#items` side when storing data.

Next we'll create two categories and two items and link them with many-to-many multiplicity:

Path: manytomany-bidirectional/src/test/java/com/manning
➥ /javapersistence/ch09/manytomany/bidirectional/TestService.java

```
Category someCategory = new Category("Some Category");
Category otherCategory = new Category("Other Category");
Item someItem = new Item("Some Item");
Item otherItem = new Item("Other Item");
someCategory.addItem(someItem);
someItem.addCategory(someCategory);
someCategory.addItem(otherItem);
otherItem.addCategory(someCategory);
otherCategory.addItem(someItem);
someItem.addCategory(otherCategory);
categoryRepository.save(someCategory);
categoryRepository.save(otherCategory);
```

Because we enabled transitive persistence, saving the categories makes the entire network of instances persistent. On the other hand, the cascading options ALL, REMOVE, and orphan deletion (discussed in section 8.3.3) aren't meaningful for many-to-many associations. This is a good point for testing whether we understand entities and value types. Try to come up with reasonable answers as to why these cascading types don't make sense for a many-to-many association. Hint: Think about what may happen if deleting a record will automatically delete a related record.

Could we use a `List` instead of a `Set`, or even a bag? The `Set` matches the database schema perfectly because there can be no duplicate links between `Category` and `Item`. A bag implies duplicate elements, so we would need a different primary key for the join table. Hibernate's proprietary `@CollectionId` annotation can provide this, as demonstrated in section 8.1.5. However, one of the alternative many-to-many strategies we'll discuss in a moment is a better choice if we need to support duplicate links.

We can map indexed collections such as a `List` with the regular `@ManyToMany`, but only on one side. Remember that in a bidirectional relationship, one side has to be "mapped by" the other side, meaning its value is ignored when Hibernate synchronizes with the database. If both sides are lists, we can only make the index of one side persistent.

A regular `@ManyToMany` mapping hides the link table; there is no corresponding Java class, only some collection properties. So whenever someone says, "My link table has more columns with information about the link" (and, in our experience, someone always says this sooner rather than later), we need to map this information to a Java class.

9.3.2   *Many-to-many with an intermediate entity*

We can always represent a many-to-many association as two many-to-one associations to an intervening class, and this is what we'll do next. We won't hide the link table; we'll represent it with a Java class. This model is usually more easily extensible, so we tend not to use regular many-to-many associations in applications. It's a lot of work to change the code later when more columns are inevitably added to a link table, so before mapping a `@ManyToMany` as shown in the previous section, consider the alternative shown in figure 9.15.

Figure 9.15 `CategorizedItem` will be the link between `Category` and `Item`.

Imagine that we need to record some information each time we add an `Item` to a `Category`. The `CategorizedItem` entity captures the timestamp and the user who created the link. This domain model requires additional columns on the join table, as you can see figure 9.16

The `CategorizedItem` entity maps to the link table, as you'll see in listing 9.4. (The source code that follows can be found in the manytomany-linkentity folder.) This will involve a large chunk of code with some new annotations. First, it will be an immutable entity class

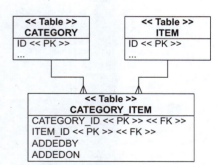

Figure 9.16   Additional columns on the join table in a many-to-many relationship

(annotated with `@org.hibernate.annotations.Immutable`), so we'll never update properties after creation. Hibernate can make some optimizations, such as avoiding dirty checking during flushing of the persistence context, if we declare the class immutable.

The entity class will have a composite key, which we'll encapsulate in a static nested embeddable component class for convenience. The identifier property and its composite key columns will be mapped to the entity's table through the `@EmbeddedId` annotation.

Listing 9.4   Mapping a many-to-many relationship with `CategorizedItem`

Path: manytomany-linkentity/src/main/java/com/manning/javapersistence
➡ /ch09/manytomany/linkentity/CategorizedItem.java

```java
@Entity
@Table(name = "CATEGORY_ITEM")                            (A)
@org.hibernate.annotations.Immutable    ←
public class CategorizedItem {                                (B)
    @Embeddable
    public static class Id implements Serializable {   ←
        @Column(name = "CATEGORY_ID")
        private Long categoryId;
        @Column(name = "ITEM_ID")
        private Long itemId;

        public Id() {
        }

        public Id(Long categoryId, Long itemId) {
            this.categoryId = categoryId;
            this.itemId = itemId;
        }
        //implementing equals and hashCode
(C) }
    @EmbeddedId
    private Id id = new Id();
    @Column(updatable = false)      (D)
    @NotNull
    private String addedBy;    ←
    @Column(updatable = false)
    @NotNull                                   (E)
    @CreationTimestamp
    private LocalDateTime addedOn;    ←
    @ManyToOne
    @JoinColumn(
        name = "CATEGORY_ID",
(F)     insertable = false, updatable = false)
    private Category category;
    @ManyToOne
    @JoinColumn(
        name = "ITEM_ID",
(G)     insertable = false, updatable = false)
    private Item item;
    public CategorizedItem(                (H)
        String addedByUsername,    ←
        Category category,
        Item item) {                           (I)
        this.addedBy = addedByUsername;    ←
        this.category = category;
        this.item = item;                          (J)
        this.id.categoryId = category.getId();    ←
        this.id.itemId = item.getId();
(I)     category.addCategorizedItem(this);
        item.addCategorizedItem(this);
```

```
    }
    //  . . .
}
```

Ⓐ The class is immutable, as annotated with `@org.hibernate.annotations` `.Immutable`.

Ⓑ An entity class needs an identifier property. The primary key of the link table is the composite of `CATEGORY_ID` and `ITEM_ID`. We can externalize this `Id` class into its own file, of course.

Ⓒ The new `@EmbeddedId` annotation maps the identifier property and its composite key columns to the entity's table.

Ⓓ The basic property mapping the `addedBy` username to a column of the join table.

Ⓔ The basic property mapping the `addedOn` timestamp to a column of the join table. This is the "additional information about the link" that interests us.

Ⓕ The `@ManyToOne` property `category` is already mapped in the identifier.

Ⓖ The `@ManyToOne` property `item` is already mapped in the identifier. The trick here is to make them read-only, with the `updatable=false`, `insertable=false` settings. This means Hibernate or Spring Data JPA using Hibernate writes the values of these columns by taking the identifier value of `CategorizedItem`. At the same time, we can read and browse the associated instances through `categorizedItem` `.getItem()` and `getCategory()`. (If we map the same column twice without making one mapping read-only, Hibernate or Spring Data JPA using Hibernate will complain on startup about a duplicate column mapping.)

Ⓗ We can also see that constructing a `CategorizedItem` involves setting the values of the identifier. The application always assigns composite key values; Hibernate doesn't generate them.

Ⓘ The constructor sets the `addedBy` field value and guarantees referential integrity by managing collections on both sides of the association.

Ⓙ The constructor sets the `categoryId` field value. We'll map these collections next to enable bidirectional navigation. This is a unidirectional mapping and enough to support the many-to-many relationship between `Category` and `Item`. To create a link, we instantiate and persist a `CategorizedItem`. If we want to break a link, we remove the `CategorizedItem`. The constructor of `CategorizedItem` requires that we provide already persistent `Category` and `Item` instances.

If bidirectional navigation is required, we can map a `@OneToMany` collection in `Category` and/or `Item`. Here it is in `Category`:

Path: manytomany-linkentity/src/main/java/com/manning/javapersistence
➡ /ch09/manytomany/linkentity/Category.java

```
@Entity
public class Category {
    //  . . .
```

```
@OneToMany(mappedBy = "category")
private Set<CategorizedItem> categorizedItems = new HashSet<>();
//  . . .
}
```

Here it is in `Item`:

Path: manytomany-linkentity/src/main/java/com/manning
➡ /javapersistence/ch09/manytomany/linkentity/Item.java

```
@Entity
public class Item {
    //  . . .
    @OneToMany(mappedBy = "item")
    private Set<CategorizedItem> categorizedItems = new HashSet<>();
    //  . . .
}
```

Both sides are "mapped by" the annotations in `CategorizedItem`, so Hibernate already knows what to do when we iterate through the collection returned by either `getCategorizedItems()` method.

This is how we create and store links:
Path: manytomany-linkentity/src/test/java/com/manning/javapersistence
➡ /ch09/manytomany/linkentity/TestService.java

```
Category someCategory = new Category("Some Category");
Category otherCategory = new Category("Other Category");
categoryRepository.save(someCategory);
categoryRepository.save(otherCategory);
Item someItem = new Item("Some Item");
Item otherItem = new Item("Other Item");
itemRepository.save(someItem);
itemRepository.save(otherItem);
CategorizedItem linkOne = new CategorizedItem(
    "John Smith", someCategory, someItem
);
CategorizedItem linkTwo = new CategorizedItem(
    "John Smith", someCategory, otherItem
);
CategorizedItem linkThree = new CategorizedItem(
    "John Smith", otherCategory, someItem
);
categorizedItemRepository.save(linkOne);
categorizedItemRepository.save(linkTwo);
categorizedItemRepository.save(linkThree);
```

The primary advantage of this strategy is the possibility of bidirectional navigation: we can get all items in a category by calling `someCategory.getCategorizedItems()`, and we can also navigate from the opposite direction with `someItem` `.getCategorizedItems()`. A disadvantage is the more complex code needed to manage the `CategorizedItem` entity instances to create and remove links, which we have to save and delete independently. We also need some infrastructure in the `CategorizedItem` class, such as the composite identifier. One small improvement would be to enable `CascadeType.PERSIST` on some of the associations, reducing the number of calls to `save()`.

In this example, we stored the user who created the link between `Category` and `Item` as a simple name string. If the join table instead had a foreign key column called `USER_ID`, we'd have a ternary relationship. The `CategorizedItem` would have a `@ManyToOne` for `Category`, `Item`, and `User`.

In the following section, we'll demonstrate another many-to-many strategy. To make it a bit more interesting, we'll make it a ternary association.

9.3.3 *Ternary associations with components*

In the previous section, we represented a many-to-many relationship with an entity class mapped to a link table. A potentially simpler alternative is mapping to an embeddable component class. The source code that follows can be found in the manytomany-ternary folder.

Path: manytomany-ternary/src/main/java/com/manning/javapersistence
➥ /ch09/manytomany/ternary/CategorizedItem.java

```java
@Embeddable
public class CategorizedItem {
    @ManyToOne
    @JoinColumn(
        name = "ITEM_ID",
        nullable = false, updatable = false
    )
    private Item item;
    @ManyToOne
    @JoinColumn(
        name = "USER_ID",
        updatable = false
    )                            A
    @NotNull
    private User addedBy;
A
    @Column(updatable = false)
    @NotNull
    private LocalDateTime addedOn = LocalDateTime.now();
    public CategorizedItem() {
    }
    public CategorizedItem(User addedBy,
                           Item item) {
        this.addedBy = addedBy;
        this.item = item;
    }
    //  . . .
}
```

A The `@NotNull` annotations do not generate an SQL constraint, so the annotated fields will not be part of the primary key.

The new mappings here are `@ManyToOne` associations in an `@Embeddable` and the additional foreign key join column `USER_ID`, making this a ternary relationship. Look at the database schema in figure 9.17.

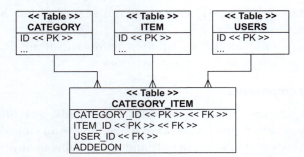

Figure 9.17   A link table with three foreign key columns

The owner of the embeddable component collection is the `Category` entity:

Path: manytomany-ternary/src/main/java/com/manning/javapersistence
➥ /ch09/manytomany/ternary/Category.java

```
@Entity
public class Category {
    // . . .
    @ElementCollection
    @CollectionTable(
        name = "CATEGORY_ITEM",
        joinColumns = @JoinColumn(name = "CATEGORY_ID")
    )
    private Set<CategorizedItem> categorizedItems = new HashSet<>();
    // . . .
}
```

Unfortunately, this mapping isn't perfect: when we map an `@ElementCollection` of embeddable type, all properties of the target type that are `nullable=false` become part of the (composite) primary key. We want all columns in `CATEGORY_ITEM` to be NOT NULL. Only the `CATEGORY_ID` and `ITEM_ID` columns should be part of the primary key, though. The trick is to use the Bean Validation `@NotNull` annotation on properties that shouldn't be part of the primary key. In that case (because it's an embeddable class), Hibernate ignores the Bean Validation annotation for primary key realization and SQL schema generation. The downside is that the generated schema won't have the appropriate NOT NULL constraints on the `USER_ID` and `ADDEDON` columns, which we should fix manually.

The advantage of this strategy is the implicit lifecycle of the link components. To create an association between a `Category` and an `Item`, add a new `CategorizedItem` instance to the collection. To break the link, remove the element from the collection. No extra cascading settings are required, and the Java code is simplified (albeit spread over more lines):

Path: manytomany-ternary/src/test/java/com/manning/javapersistence
➡ /ch09/manytomany/ternary/TestService.java

```java
Category someCategory = new Category("Some Category");
Category otherCategory = new Category("Other Category");
categoryRepository.save(someCategory);
categoryRepository.save(otherCategory);
Item someItem = new Item("Some Item");
Item otherItem = new Item("Other Item");
itemRepository.save(someItem);
itemRepository.save(otherItem);
User someUser = new User("John Smith");
userRepository.save(someUser);
CategorizedItem linkOne = new CategorizedItem(
    someUser, someItem
);
someCategory.addCategorizedItem(linkOne);
CategorizedItem linkTwo = new CategorizedItem(
    someUser, otherItem
);
someCategory.addCategorizedItem(linkTwo);
CategorizedItem linkThree = new CategorizedItem(
    someUser, someItem
);
otherCategory.addCategorizedItem(linkThree);
```

There is no way to enable bidirectional navigation: an embeddable component, such as `CategorizedItem`, by definition can't have shared references. We can't navigate from `Item` to `CategorizedItem`, and there is no mapping of this link in `Item`. Instead, we can write a query to retrieve the categories, given an `Item`:

Path: manytomany-ternary/src/test/java/com/manning/javapersistence
➡ /ch09/manytomany/ternary/TestService.java

```java
List<Category> categoriesOfItem =
    categoryRepository.findCategoryWithCategorizedItems(item1);
assertEquals(2, categoriesOfItem.size());
```

The `findCategoryWithCategorizedItems` method is annotated with the `@Query` annotation:

Path: manytomany-ternary/src/main/java/com/manning/javapersistence
➡ /ch09/repositories/manytomany/ternary/CategoryRepository.java

```java
@Query("select c from Category c join c.categorizedItems ci where
        ci.item = :itemParameter")
List<Category> findCategoryWithCategorizedItems(
        @Param("itemParameter") Item itemParameter);
```

We've now completed our first ternary association mapping. In the previous chapters, we saw ORM examples with maps; the keys and values of those maps were always of basic or embeddable type. In the following section, we'll use more complex key/value pair types and their mappings.

9.4   *Entity associations with maps*

Map keys and values can be references to other entities, providing another strategy for mapping many-to-many and ternary relationships. First, let's assume that only the value of each map entry is a reference to another entity.

9.4.1   *One-to-many with a property key*

If the value of each map entry is a reference to another entity, we have a one-to-many entity relationship. The key of the map is of a basic type, such as a Long value. (The source code that follows can be found in the maps-mapkey folder.)

An example of this structure would be an Item entity with a map of Bid instances, where each map entry is a pair consisting of Bid identifier and reference to a Bid instance. When we iterate through someItem.getBids(), we iterate through map entries that look like (1, <reference to Bid with PK 1>), (2, <reference to Bid with PK 2>), and so on:

Path: maps-mapkey/src/test/java/com/manning/javapersistence
➡ /ch09/maps/mapkey/TestService.java

```
    Item item = itemRepository.findById(someItem.getId()).get();
assertEquals(2, item.getBids().size());
for (Map.Entry<Long, Bid> entry : item.getBids().entrySet()) {
    assertEquals(entry.getKey(), entry.getValue().getId());
}
```

The underlying tables for this mapping are nothing special; we have ITEM and BID tables, with an ITEM_ID foreign key column in the BID table. This is the same schema as demonstrated in figure 8.14 for a one-to-many/many-to-one mapping with a regular collection instead of a Map. Our motivation here is a slightly different representation of the data in the application.

In the Item class, we'll include a Map property named bids:

Path: maps-mapkey/src/main/java/com/manning/javapersistence
➡ /ch09/maps/mapkey/Item.java

```
@Entity
public class Item {
    // . . .
    @MapKey(name = "id")
    @OneToMany(mappedBy = "item")
    private Map<Long, Bid> bids = new HashMap<>();
    // . . .
}
```

New here is the `@MapKey` annotation. It maps a property of the target entity: in this case, the `Bid` entity, as the key of the map. The default if we omit the `name` attribute is the identifier property of the target entity, so the `name` option here is redundant. Because the keys of a map form a set, we should expect values to be unique for a particular map. This is the case for `Bid` primary keys but likely not for any other property of `Bid`. It's up to us to ensure that the selected property has unique values—Hibernate or Spring Data JPA using Hibernate won't check.

The primary and rare use case for this mapping technique is to iterate map entries with some property of the entry entity value as the entry key, maybe because it's convenient for how we'd like to render the data. A more common situation is a map in the middle of a ternary association.

9.4.2   *Key/value ternary relationship*

You may be a little bored by now with all the mapping experiments that we've executed, but we promise this is the last time we'll show another way of mapping the association between Category and Item. Previously, in section 9.3.3, we used an embeddable `CategorizedItem` component to represent the link. Here we'll show a representation of the relationship with a `Map` instead

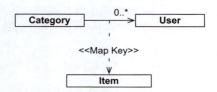

Figure 9.18   A `Map` with entity associations as key/value pairs

of an additional Java class. The key of each map entry is an `Item`, and the related value is the `User` who added the `Item` to the `Category`, as shown in figure 9.18.

The link/join table in the schema, as you can see in figure 9.19, has three columns: `CATEGORY_ID`, `ITEM_ID`, and `USER_ID`. The `Map` is owned by the `Category` entity. The source code that follows can be found in the maps-ternary folder.

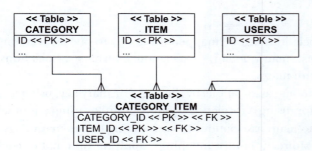

Figure 9.19   The link table represents the `Map` key/value pairs.

The following code models the relationship between Category and Item using a map.

Path: maps-ternary/src/main/java/com/manning/javapersistence
➡ /ch09/maps/ternary/Category.java

```
@Entity
public class Category {
```

```
// . . .
@ManyToMany(cascade = CascadeType.PERSIST)
@MapKeyJoinColumn(name = "ITEM_ID")                    A
@JoinTable(
    name = "CATEGORY_ITEM",
    joinColumns = @JoinColumn(name = "CATEGORY_ID"),
    inverseJoinColumns = @JoinColumn(name = "USER_ID")
)
private Map<Item, User> itemAddedBy = new HashMap<>();
// . . .
}
```

A The `@MapKeyJoinColumn` is optional; Hibernate or Spring Data JPA using Hibernate will default to the column name `ITEMADDEDBY_KEY` for the join/foreign key column referencing the `ITEM` table.

To create a link between all three entities, all instances must already be in persistent state and then put into the map:

Path: maps-ternary/src/test/java/com/manning/javapersistence
➥ /ch09/maps/ternary/TestService.java

```
someCategory.putItemAddedBy(someItem, someUser);
someCategory.putItemAddedBy(otherItem, someUser);
otherCategory.putItemAddedBy(someItem, someUser);
```

To remove the link, remove the entry from the map. This manages a complex relationship, hiding a database link table with three columns. But remember that, in practice, link tables often grow additional columns, and changing all the Java application code later is expensive if you depend on a `Map` API. Earlier, we had an `ADDEDON` column with a timestamp when the link was created, but we had to drop it for this mapping.

Summary

- Complex entity associations can be mapped using one-to-one associations, one-to-many associations, many-to-many associations, ternary associations, and entity associations with maps.
- You can create one-to-one associations by sharing a primary key, using a foreign primary key generator, using a foreign key join column, or using a join table.
- You can create one-to-many associations by considering one-to-many bags, using unidirectional and bidirectional list mappings, applying optional one-to-many with a join table, or creating one-to-many associations in an embeddable class.
- You can create unidirectional and bidirectional many-to-many associations and many-to-many associations with an intermediate entity.
- You can build ternary associations with components and entity associations with maps.

- You can often best represent many-to-many entity associations as two many-to-one associations from an intermediate entity class or with a collection of components.
- Before attempting a complex collection mapping, always make sure you actually need a collection. Ask yourself whether you frequently iterate through its elements.
- The Java structures used in this chapter may sometimes make data access easier, but typically they complicate data storage, updates, and deletion.

Part 3

Transactional data processing

In part 3, you'll load and store data with Hibernate and Java Persistence. You'll be introduced to the programming interfaces, to writing transactional applications, and to how Hibernate can load data from the database most efficiently.

Starting with chapter 10, you'll learn the most important strategies for interacting with entity instances in a JPA application. You'll see the lifecycle of entity instances: how they become persistent, detached, and removed. This chapter is where you'll get to know the most important interface in JPA: the `EntityManager`. Next, chapter 11 defines database and system transaction essentials and how to control concurrent access with Hibernate, JPA, and Spring. You'll also see non-transactional data access. In chapter 12, we'll go through lazy and eager loading, fetch plans, strategies, and profiles, and wrap up with optimizing SQL execution. Finally, chapter 13 covers cascading state transitions, listening to and intercepting events, auditing and versioning with Hibernate Envers, and filtering data dynamically.

After reading this part of the book, you'll know how to work with Hibernate and Java Persistence programming interfaces and how to load, modify, and store objects efficiently. You'll understand how transactions work and why conversational processing can open up new approaches for application design. You'll be ready to optimize any object-modification scenarios and apply the best fetching and caching strategy to increase performance and scalability.

Managing data

10

This chapter covers

- Examining the lifecycle and states of objects
- Working with the EntityManager interface
- Working with detached state

You now understand how ORM solves the static aspects of the object/relational mismatch. With what you know so far, you can create a mapping between Java classes and an SQL schema, solving the structural mismatch problem. As you'll recall, the paradigm mismatch covers the problems of granularity, inheritance, identity, association, and data navigation. For a deeper review, take a look back at section 1.2.

Beyond that, though, an efficient application solution requires something more: you must investigate strategies for runtime data management. These strategies are crucial to the performance and correct behavior of the applications.

In this chapter, we'll analyze the lifecycle of entity instances—how an instance becomes persistent, and how it stops being considered persistent—and the method calls and management operations that trigger these transitions. The JPA `Entity-Manager` is the primary interface for accessing data.

Before we look at JPA, let's start with entity instances, their lifecycle, and the events that trigger a change of state. Although some of this material may be formal, a solid understanding of the persistence lifecycle is essential.

Major new features in JPA 2

We can get a vendor-specific variation of the persistence manager API with `Entity-Manager#unwrap()`, such as the `org.hibernate.Session` API. Use the already demonstrated `EntityManagerFactory#unwrap()` method to obtain an instance of `org.hibernate.SessionFactory` (see section 2.5).

The new `detach()` operation provides fine-grained management of the persistence context, evicting individual entity instances.

From an existing `EntityManager`, we can obtain the `EntityManagerFactory` used to create the persistence context with `getEntityManagerFactory()`.

The new static `PersistenceUtil` and `PersistenceUnitUtil` helper methods determine whether an entity instance (or one of its properties) was fully loaded or is an uninitialized reference (a Hibernate proxy or an unloaded collection wrapper).

10.1 *The persistence lifecycle*

Because JPA is a transparent persistence mechanism, where classes are unaware of their own persistence capability, it is possible to write application logic that is unaware of whether the data it operates on represents a persistent state or a temporary state that exists only in memory. The application shouldn't necessarily need to care that an instance is persistent when invoking its methods. We can, for example, invoke the `Item#calculateTotalPrice()` business method without having to consider persistence at all (such as in a unit test). The method may be unaware of any persistence concept while its executing.

Any application with a persistent state must interact with the persistence service whenever it needs to propagate the state held in memory to the database (or vice versa). In other words, we have to call the Jakarta Persistence interfaces to store and load data.

When interacting with the persistence mechanism that way, the application must concern itself with the state and lifecycle of an entity instance with respect to persistence. We refer to this as the *persistence lifecycle*: the states an entity instance goes through during its life, and we'll analyze them in a moment. We also use the term *unit of work*: a set of (possibly) state-changing operations considered one (usually atomic) group. Another piece of the puzzle is the *persistence context* provided by the persistence service. Think of the persistence context as a service that remembers all the modifications and state changes we made to the data in a particular unit of work (this is somewhat simplified, but it's a good starting point).

We'll now dissect the following terms: *entity states, persistence contexts,* and *managed scope.* You're probably more accustomed to thinking about which SQL statements you have to manage to get stuff in and out of the database, but one of the key factors of the success of Java Persistence is the analysis of *state management,* so stick with us through this section.

10.1.1 *Entity instance states*

Different ORM solutions use different terminology and define different states and state transitions for the persistence lifecycle. Moreover, the states used internally may be different from those exposed to the client application. JPA defines four states, hiding the complexity of Hibernate's internal implementation from the client code. Figure 10.1 shows these states and their transitions.

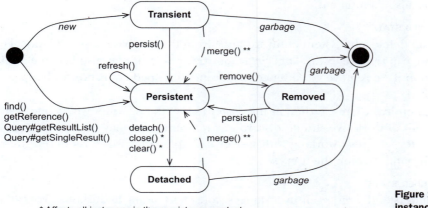

Figure 10.1   Entity instance states and their transitions

* Affects all instances in the persistence context
** Merging returns a persistent instance, original doesn't change state

Figure 10.1 also includes the method calls to the `EntityManager` (and `Query`) API that triggers transitions. We'll discuss this chart in this chapter; refer to it whenever you need an overview.

Now, let's explore the states and transitions in more detail.

TRANSIENT STATE

Instances created with the `new` Java operator are *transient*, which means their state is lost and garbage-collected as soon as they're no longer referenced. For example, `new Item()` creates a transient instance of the `Item` class, just like `new Long()` and `new BigDecimal()` create transient instances of those classes. Hibernate doesn't provide any rollback functionality for transient instances; if we modify the price of a transient `Item`, we can't automatically undo the change.

For an entity instance to transition from transient to *persistent* state requires either a call to the `EntityManager#persist()` method or the creation of a reference from an already-persistent instance and enabled cascading of state for that mapped association.

PERSISTENT STATE

A *persistent* entity instance has a representation in the database. It's stored in the database—or it will be stored when the unit of work completes. It's an instance with a database identity, as defined in section 5.2; its database identifier is set to the primary key value of the database representation.

The application may have created instances and then made them persistent by calling `EntityManager#persist()`. Instances may have also become persistent when the application created a reference to the object from another persistent instance that the JPA provider already manages. A persistent entity instance may be an instance retrieved from the database by executing a query, an identifier lookup, or navigating the object graph starting from another persistent instance.

Persistent instances are always associated with a persistence context. We'll see more about this in a moment.

REMOVED STATE

We can delete a persistent entity instance from the database in several ways. For example, we can remove it with `EntityManager#remove()`. It may also become available for deletion if we remove a reference to it from a mapped collection with *orphan removal* enabled.

An entity instance is then in the *removed* state: the provider will delete it at the end of a unit of work. We should discard any references we may hold to it in the application after we finish working with it—for example, after we've rendered the removal-confirmation screen the users see.

DETACHED STATE

To understand *detached* entity instances, consider loading an instance. We call `EntityManager#find()` to retrieve an entity instance by its (known) identifier. Then we end our unit of work and close the persistence context. The application still has a *handle*—a reference to the instance we loaded. It's now in a detached state, and the data is becoming stale. We could discard the reference and let the garbage collector reclaim the memory. Or, we could continue working with the data in the detached state and later call the `merge()` method to save our modifications in a new unit of work. We'll discuss detachment and merging in section 10.3.

You should now have a basic understanding of entity instance states and their transitions. Our next topic is the persistence context: an essential service of any Jakarta Persistence provider.

10.1.2 *The persistence context*

In a Java Persistence application, an `EntityManager` has a persistence context. We create a persistence context when we call `EntityManagerFactory#createEntityManager()`. The context is closed when we call `EntityManager#close()`. In JPA terminology, this is an *application-managed* persistence context; our application defines the scope of the persistence context, demarcating the unit of work.

The persistence context monitors and manages all entities in the persistent state. The persistence context is the centerpiece of much of the functionality of a JPA provider.

The persistence context also allows the persistence engine to perform *automatic dirty checking*, detecting which entity instances the application modified. The provider then synchronizes with the database the state of instances monitored by a persistence context, either automatically or on demand. Typically, when a unit of work completes, the provider propagates state that's held in memory to the database through the execution of SQL `INSERT`, `UPDATE`, and `DELETE` statements (all part of the Data Manipulation Language, DML). This *flushing* procedure may also occur at other times. For example, Hibernate may synchronize with the database before the execution of a query. This ensures that queries are aware of changes made earlier during the unit of work.

The persistence context also acts as a *first-level cache*; it remembers all entity instances handled in a particular unit of work. For example, if we ask Hibernate to load an entity instance using a primary key value (a lookup by identifier), Hibernate can first check the current unit of work in the persistence context. If Hibernate finds the entity instance in the persistence context, no database hit occurs—this is a repeatable read for an application. Consecutive `em.find(Item.class, ITEM_ID)` calls with the same persistence context will yield the same result.

This cache also affects the results of arbitrary queries, such as those executed with the `javax.persistence.Query` API. Hibernate reads the SQL result set of a query and transforms it into entity instances. This process first tries to resolve every entity instance in the persistence context by identifier lookup. Only if an instance with the same identifier value can't be found in the current persistence context does Hibernate read the rest of the data from the result-set row. Hibernate ignores any potentially newer data in the result set, due to read-committed transaction isolation at the database level, if the entity instance is already present in the persistence context.

The persistence context cache is always on—it can't be turned off. It ensures the following:

- The persistence layer isn't vulnerable to stack overflows in the case of circular references in an object graph.
- There can never be conflicting representations of the same database row at the end of a unit of work. The provider can safely write all changes made to an entity instance to the database.
- Likewise, changes made in a particular persistence context are always immediately visible to all other code executed inside that unit of work and its persistence context. JPA guarantees repeatable entity-instance reads.

The persistence context provides a *guaranteed scope of object identity*; in the scope of a single persistence context, only one instance represents a particular database row. Consider the comparison of references `entityA == entityB`. This is `true` only if both are references to the same Java instance on the heap. Now consider the comparison `entityA.getId().equals(entityB.getId())`. This is `true` if both have the same database identifier value. Within one persistence context, Hibernate guarantees that both comparisons will yield the same result. This solves one of the fundamental object/relational mismatch problems we discussed in section 1.2.3.

The lifecycle of entity instances and the services provided by the persistence context can be difficult to understand at first. Let's look at some code examples of dirty checking, caching, and how the guaranteed identity scope works in practice. To do this, we'll work with the persistence manager API.

Would process-scoped identity be better?

For a typical web or enterprise application, persistence context-scoped identity is preferred. Process-scoped identity, where only one in-memory instance represents the row in the entire process (JVM), offers some potential advantages in terms of cache utilization. In a pervasively multithreaded application, though, the cost of always synchronizing shared access to persistent instances in a global identity map is too high a price to pay. It's simpler and more scalable to have each thread work with a distinct copy of the data in each persistence context.

10.2   *The EntityManager interface*

Any transparent persistence tool includes a persistence manager API. This persistence manager usually provides services for basic CRUD (create, read, update, delete) operations, query execution, and controlling the persistence context. In Jakarta Persistence applications, the main interface we interact with is the `EntityManager` to create units of work.

> **NOTE**   To execute the examples from the source code, you'll first need to run the Ch10.sql script. The source code that follows can be found in the managing-data and managing-data2 folders.

We will not use Spring Data JPA in this chapter, not even the Spring framework. The examples that follow will use JPA and, sometimes, the Hibernate API, without any Spring integration—they are finer-grained for our demonstrations and analysis.

10.2.1   *The canonical unit of work*

In Java SE and some EE architectures (if we only have plain servlets, for example), we get an `EntityManager` by calling `EntityManagerFactory#createEntityManager()`. The application code shares the `EntityManagerFactory`, representing one persistence unit, or one logical database. Most applications have only one shared `EntityManagerFactory`.

We use the `EntityManager` for a single unit of work in a single thread, and it's inexpensive to create. The following listing shows the canonical, typical form of a unit of work.

Listing 10.1   A typical unit of work

```
Path: managing-data/src/test/java/com/manning/javapersistence/ch10
➥  /SimpleTransitionsTest.java

EntityManagerFactory emf =
      Persistence.createEntityManagerFactory("ch10");
```

```
// . . .
EntityManager em = emf.createEntityManager();

try {
    em.getTransaction().begin();

    // . . .
    em.getTransaction().commit();
} catch (Exception ex) {
    // Transaction rollback, exception handling
    // . . .
} finally {
    if (em != null && em.isOpen())
        em.close();
}
```

Everything between `em.getTransaction().begin()` and `em.getTransaction()` `.commit()` occurs in one transaction. For now, keep in mind that all database operations in a transaction scope, such as the SQL statements executed by Hibernate, either completely succeed or completely fail. Don't worry too much about the transaction code for now; you'll read more about concurrency control in the next chapter. We'll look at the same example there with a focus on the transaction and exception-handling code. Don't write empty `catch` clauses in the code, though—you'll have to roll back the transaction and handle exceptions.

Creating an `EntityManager` starts its persistence context. Hibernate won't access the database until necessary; the `EntityManager` doesn't obtain a JDBC `Connection` from the pool until SQL statements have to be executed. We can even create and close an `EntityManager` without hitting the database. Hibernate executes SQL statements when we look up or query data and when it flushes changes detected by the persistence context to the database. Hibernate joins the in-progress system transaction when an `EntityManager` is created and waits for the transaction to commit. When Hibernate is notified of the commit, it performs dirty checking of the persistence context and synchronizes with the database. We can also force dirty checking synchronization manually by calling `EntityManager#flush()` at any time during a transaction.

We determine the scope of the persistence context by choosing when to `close()` the `EntityManager`. We have to close the persistence context at some point, so always place the `close()` call in a `finally` block.

How long should the persistence context be open? Let's assume for the following examples that we're writing a server, and each client request will be processed with one persistence context and system transaction in a multithreaded environment. If you're familiar with servlets, imagine the code in listing 10.1 embedded in a servlet's `service()` method. Within this unit of work, you access the `EntityManager` to load and store data.

10.2.2 *Making data persistent*

Let's create a new instance of an entity and bring it from transient into persistent state. You will do this whenever you want to save the information from a newly created object to the database. We can see the same unit of work and how the Item instances change state in figure 10.2.

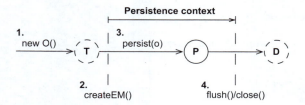

Figure 10.2 Making an instance persistent in a unit of work

To make an instance persistent, you can use a piece of code like the following:

```
Path: managing-data/src/test/java/com/manning/javapersistence/ch10
    /SimpleTransitionsTest.java - makePersistent()

Item item = new Item();
item.setName("Some Item");
em.persist(item);
Long ITEM_ID = item.getId();
```

A new transient Item is instantiated as usual. Of course, we could also instantiate it before creating the EntityManager. A call to persist() makes the transient instance of Item persistent. It's then managed by and associated with the current persistence context.

To store the Item instance in the database, Hibernate has to execute an SQL INSERT statement. When the transaction of this unit of work commits, Hibernate flushes the persistence context, and the INSERT occurs at that time. Hibernate may even batch the INSERT at the JDBC level with other statements. When we call persist(), only the identifier value of the Item is assigned. Alternatively, if the identifier generator isn't *pre-insert*, the INSERT statement will be executed immediately when persist() is called. You may want to review section 5.2.5 for a refresher on the identifier generator strategies.

Detecting entity state using the identifier

Sometimes we need to know whether an entity instance is persistent, transient, or detached.

- *Persistent*—An entity instance is in persistent state if EntityManager# contains(e) returns true.
- *Transient*—It's in transient state if PersistenceUnitUtil#getIdentifier(e) returns null.
- *Detached*—It's in the detached state if it's not persistent, and PersistenceUnit-Util#getIdentifier(e) returns the value of the entity's identifier property.

We can get to `PersistenceUnitUtil` from the `EntityManagerFactory`.

There are two concerns to look out for. First, be aware that the identifier value may not be assigned and available until the persistence context is flushed. Second, Hibernate (unlike some other JPA providers) never returns `null` from `Persistence-UnitUtil#getIdentifier()` if the identifier property is a primitive (a `long` and not a `Long`).

It's better (but not required) to fully initialize the `Item` instance before managing it with a persistence context. The SQL INSERT statement contains the values that were held by the instance at the point when `persist()` was called. If we don't set the `name` of the `Item` before making it persistent, a NOT NULL constraint may be violated. We can modify the `Item` after calling `persist()`, and the changes will be propagated to the database with an additional SQL UPDATE statement.

If one of the INSERT or UPDATE statements fails during flushing, Hibernate causes a rollback of changes made to persistent instances in this transaction at the database level. But Hibernate doesn't roll back in-memory changes to persistent instances. If we change the `Item#name` after `persist()`, a commit failure won't roll back to the old name. This is reasonable, because a failure of a transaction is normally non-recoverable, and we have to discard the failed persistence context and `EntityManager` immediately. We'll discuss exception handling in the next chapter.

Next, we'll load and modify the stored data.

10.2.3 *Retrieving and modifying persistent data*

We can retrieve persistent instances from the database with the `EntityManager`. In a real-life use case, we would have kept the identifier value of the `Item` stored in the previous section somewhere, and we are now looking up the same instance in a new unit of work by identifier. Figure 10.3 shows this transition graphically.

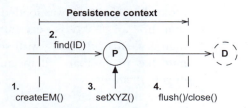

Figure 10.3   Making an instance persistent in a unit of work

To make an instance persistent in a unit of work, you can use a piece of code like the following:

```
Path: managing-data/src/test/java/com/manning/javapersistence/ch10
  /SimpleTransitionsTest.java – retrievePersistent()

Item item = em.find(Item.class, ITEM_ID);        ⬅ A
if (item != null)
    item.setName("New Name");        ⬅ B
```

Ⓐ The instruction will hit the database if `item` is not already in the persistence context.

Ⓑ Then we modify the name.

We don't need to cast the returned value of the find() operation; it's a generified method, and its return type is set as a side effect of the first parameter. The retrieved entity instance is in a persistent state, and we can now modify it inside the unit of work.

If no persistent instance with the given identifier value can be found, find() returns null. The find() operation always hits the database if there is no hit for the given entity type and identifier in the persistence context cache. The entity instance is always initialized during loading. We can expect to have all of its values available later in a detached state, such as when rendering a screen after we close the persistence context. (Hibernate may not hit the database if its optional second-level cache is enabled.)

We can modify the Item instance, and the persistence context will detect these changes and record them in the database automatically. When Hibernate flushes the persistence context during commit, it executes the necessary SQL DML statements to synchronize the changes with the database. Hibernate propagates state changes to the database as late as possible, toward the end of the transaction. DML statements usually create locks in the database that are held until the transaction completes, so Hibernate keeps the lock duration in the database as short as possible.

Hibernate writes the new Item#name to the database with an SQL UPDATE. By default, Hibernate includes all columns of the mapped ITEM table in the SQL UPDATE statement, updating unchanged columns to their old values. Hence, Hibernate can generate these basic SQL statements at startup, not at runtime. If we want to include only modified (or non-nullable for INSERT) columns in SQL statements, we can enable dynamic SQL generation as demonstrated in section 5.3.2.

Hibernate detects the changed name by comparing the Item with a snapshot copy it took when the Item was loaded from the database. If the Item is different from the snapshot, an UPDATE is necessary. This snapshot in the persistence context consumes memory. Dirty checking with snapshots can also be time-consuming because Hibernate has to compare all instances in the persistence context with their snapshots during flushing.

We mentioned earlier that the persistence context enables repeatable reads of entity instances and provides an object-identity guarantee:

```
Path: managing-data/src/test/java/com/manning/javapersistence/ch10
    /SimpleTransitionsTest.java - retrievePersistent()
```

A

B

```
Item itemA = em.find(Item.class, ITEM_ID);
Item itemB = em.find(Item.class, ITEM_ID);
assertTrue(itemA == itemB);
assertTrue(itemA.equals(itemB));
assertTrue(itemA.getId().equals(itemB.getId()));
```

A The first find() operation hits the database and retrieves the Item instance with a SELECT statement.

B The second find() is a repeatable read and is resolved in the persistence context, and the same cached Item instance is returned.

Sometimes we need an entity instance but we don't want to hit the database.

10.2.4 *Getting a reference*

If we don't want to hit the database when loading an entity instance, because we aren't sure we need a fully initialized instance, we can tell the EntityManager to attempt the retrieval of a hollow placeholder—a proxy.

If the persistence context already contains an Item with the given identifier, that Item instance is returned by getReference() without hitting the database. Furthermore, if *no* persistent instance with that identifier is currently managed, Hibernate produces the hollow placeholder: the proxy. This means getReference() won't access the database, and it doesn't return null, unlike find(). JPA offers the PersistenceUnitUtil helper methods. The isLoaded() helper method is used to detect whether we're working with an uninitialized proxy.

As soon as we call any method, such as Item#getName(), on the proxy, a SELECT is executed to fully initialize the placeholder. The exception to this rule is a mapped database identifier getter method, such as getId(). A proxy may look like the real thing, but it's only a placeholder carrying the identifier value of the entity instance it represents. If the database record no longer exists when the proxy is initialized, an EntityNotFoundException is thrown. Note that the exception can be thrown when Item#getName() is called. The Hibernate class has a convenient static initialize() method that loads the proxy's data.

After the persistence context is closed, item is in a detached state. If we don't initialize the proxy while the persistence context is still open, we get a LazyInitialization-Exception if we access the proxy, as demonstrated in the following code. We can't load data on demand once the persistence context is closed. The solution is simple: load the data before closing the persistence context.

```
Path: managing-data/src/test/java/com/manning/javapersistence/ch10
➡ /SimpleTransitionsTest.java - retrievePersistentReference()

Item item = em.getReference(Item.class, ITEM_ID);          B
PersistenceUnitUtil persistenceUtil =
    emf.getPersistenceUnitUtil();
assertFalse(persistenceUtil.isLoaded(item));               C
// assertEquals("Some Item", item.getName());
// Hibernate.initialize(item);                             E
em.getTransaction().commit();
em.close();                                                                  G
assertThrows(LazyInitializationException.class, () -> item.getName());
```

A The persistence context.

B The helper methods.

C Detecting an uninitialized proxy.

D Mapping the exception to the rule.

E Load the proxy data.

F `item` is in a detached state.

G Load data after closing the persistence context.

We'll have much more to say about proxies, lazy loading, and on-demand fetching in chapter 12.

Next, if we want to remove the state of an entity instance from the database, we have to make it transient.

10.2.5 *Making data transient*

To make an entity instance transient and delete its database representation, we can call the `remove()` method on the `EntityManager`. Figure 10.4 shows this process.

If we call `find()`, Hibernate executes a `SELECT` to load the `Item`. If we call `get-Reference()`, Hibernate attempts to

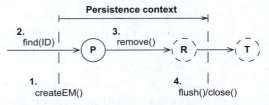

Figure 10.4 **Removing an instance in a unit of work**

avoid the `SELECT` and returns a proxy. Calling `remove()` queues the entity instance for deletion when the unit of work completes; it's now in *removed* state. If `remove()` is called on a proxy, Hibernate executes a `SELECT` to load the data. An entity instance must be fully initialized during lifecycle transitions. We may have lifecycle callback methods or an entity listener enabled (see section 13.2), and the instance must pass through these interceptors to complete its full lifecycle.

An entity in a removed state is no longer in a persistent state. We can check this with the `contains()` operation. We can make the removed instance persistent again, canceling deletion.

When the transaction commits, Hibernate synchronizes the state transitions with the database and executes the SQL `DELETE`. The JVM garbage collector detects that the `item` is no longer referenced by anything and finally deletes the last trace of the data. We can finally close `EntityManager`:

```
Path: managing-data/src/test/java/com/manning/javapersistence/ch10
  ➥ /SimpleTransitionsTest.java - makeTransient()
```

```
Item item = em.find(Item.class, ITEM_ID);
em.remove(item);
assertFalse(em.contains(item));
// em.persist(item);
assertNull(item.getId());
em.getTransaction().commit();
em.close();
```

A Call `find()`; Hibernate executes a `SELECT` to load the `Item`.

B Call `remove()`; Hibernate queues the entity instance for deletion when the unit of work completes.

Ⓒ An entity in a removed state is no longer contained in the persistence context.

Ⓓ Canceling deletion makes the removed instance persistent again.

Ⓔ `item` will now look like a transient instance.

Ⓕ The transaction commits; Hibernate synchronizes the state transitions with the database and executes the SQL `DELETE`.

Ⓖ Close `EntityManager`.

By default, Hibernate won't alter the identifier value of a removed entity instance. This means the `item.getId()` method still returns the now outdated identifier value. Sometimes it's useful to work with the "deleted" data further: for example, we might want to save the removed `Item` again if our user decides to undo. As shown in the example, we can call `persist()` on a removed instance to cancel the deletion before the persistence context is flushed. Alternatively, if we set the property `hibernate .use_identifier_rollback` to `true` in persistence.xml, Hibernate will reset the identifier value after the removal of an entity instance. In the previous code example, the identifier value is reset to the default value of `null` (it's a `Long`). The `Item` is now the same as in a transient state, and we can save it again in a new persistence context.

Let's say we load an entity instance from the database and work with the data. For some reason, we know that another application or maybe another thread of the application has updated the underlying row in the database. Next we'll see how to refresh the data held in memory.

10.2.6 *Refreshing data*

It is possible that, after you have loaded an entity instance, some other process changes the information corresponding to the instance in the database. The following example demonstrates refreshing a persistent entity instance:

```
Path: managing-data/src/test/java/com/manning/javapersistence/ch10
➥ /SimpleTransitionsTest.java - refresh()

Item item = em.find(Item.class, ITEM_ID);
item.setName("Some Name");
// Someone updates this row in the database with "Concurrent UpdateName"
em.refresh(item);
em.close();
assertEquals("Concurrent UpdateName", item.getName());
```

After we load the entity instance, we realize (it isn't important how) that someone else changed the data in the database. Calling `refresh()` causes Hibernate to execute a `SELECT` to read and marshal a whole result set, overwriting changes we already made to the persistent instance in application memory. As a result, the `item`'s `name` is updated with the value set from the other side. If the database row no longer exists (if someone deleted it), Hibernate throws an `EntityNotFoundException` on `refresh()`.

Most applications don't have to manually refresh the in-memory state; concurrent modifications are typically resolved at transaction commit time. The best use case for refreshing is with an extended persistence context, which might span several request/response cycles or system transactions. While we wait for user input with an open persistence context, data gets stale, and selective refreshing may be required depending on the duration of the conversation and the dialogue between the user and the system. Refreshing can be useful to undo changes made in memory during a conversation if the user cancels the dialogue.

Another infrequently used operation is the replication of an entity instance.

10.2.7 *Replicating data*

Replication is useful, for example, when we need to retrieve data from one database and store it in another. Replication takes detached instances loaded in one persistence context and makes them persistent in another persistence context. We usually open these contexts from two different `EntityManagerFactory` configurations, enabling two logical databases. We have to map the entity in both configurations.

The `replicate()` operation is only available on the Hibernate `Session` API. Here is an example that loads an `Item` instance from one database and copies it into another:

```
Path: managing-data/src/test/java/com/manning/javapersistence/ch10
➦ /SimpleTransitionsTest.java – replicate()

EntityManager emA = getDatabaseA().createEntityManager();
emA.getTransaction().begin();
Item item = emA.find(Item.class, ITEM_ID);
emA.getTransaction().commit();

EntityManager emB = getDatabaseB().createEntityManager();
emB.getTransaction().begin();
emB.unwrap(Session.class)
        .replicate(item, org.hibernate.ReplicationMode.LATEST_VERSION);
Item item1 = emB.find(Item.class, ITEM_ID);
assertEquals("Some Item", item1.getName());
emB.getTransaction().commit();
emA.close();
emB.close();
```

`ReplicationMode` controls the details of the replication procedure:

- `IGNORE`—Ignores the instance when there is an existing database row with the same identifier in the database.
- `OVERWRITE`—Overwrites any existing database row with the same identifier in the database.
- `EXCEPTION`—Throws an exception if there is an existing database row with the same identifier in the target database.
- `LATEST_VERSION`—Overwrites the row in the database if its version is older than the version of the given entity instance, or ignores the instance otherwise. Requires enabled optimistic concurrency control with entity versioning (discussed in section 11.2.2).

We may need replication when we reconcile data entered into different databases. One use case is a product upgrade: if the new version of the application requires a new database (schema), we may want to migrate and replicate the existing data once.

The persistence context does many things for you: automatic dirty checking, guaranteed scope of object identity, and so on. It's equally important that you know some of the details of its management, and that you sometimes influence what goes on behind the scenes.

10.2.8   *Caching in the persistence context*

The persistence context is a cache of persistent instances. Every entity instance in a persistent state is associated with the persistence context.

Many Hibernate users who ignore this simple fact run into an `OutOfMemoryError`. This is typically the case when we load thousands of entity instances in a unit of work but never intend to modify them. Hibernate still has to create a snapshot of each instance in the persistence context cache, which can lead to memory exhaustion. (Obviously, we should execute a bulk data operation if we modify thousands of rows.)

The persistence context cache never shrinks automatically, so you should keep the size of the persistence context to the minimum necessary. Often, many persistent instances in the context are there by accident—for example, because we needed only a few items but queried for many. Extremely large graphs can have a serious performance consequence and require significant memory for state snapshots. Check that queries return only the data you need, and consider the following ways to control Hibernate's caching behavior.

You can call `EntityManager#detach(i)` to evict a persistent instance manually from the persistence context. You can call `EntityManager#clear()` to detach all persistent entity instances, leaving you with an empty persistence context.

The native `Session` API has some extra operations you might find useful. You can set the entire persistence context to read-only mode. This disables state snapshots and dirty checking, and Hibernate won't write modifications to the database:

```
Path: managing-data2/src/test/java/com/manning/javapersistence/ch10
➥ /ReadOnly.java - selectiveReadOnly()
                                                                        Ⓐ
em.unwrap(Session.class).setDefaultReadOnly(true);  ⟵
Item item = em.find(Item.class, ITEM_ID);
Ⓑ   item.setName("New Name");
➥ em.flush();
```

Ⓐ Set the persistence context to read-only.

Ⓑ Consequently, `flush()` will not update the database.

You can disable dirty checking for a single entity instance:

```
Path: managing-data2/src/test/java/com/manning/javapersistence/ch10
➥ /ReadOnly.java - selectiveReadOnly()
```

```
Item item = em.find(Item.class, ITEM_ID);                          A
em.unwrap(Session.class).setReadOnly(item, true);    ←┘
item.setName("New Name");
em.flush();
```

A Set `item` in the persistence context to read-only.

B Consequently, `flush()` will not update the database.

A query with the `org.hibernate.Query` interface can return read-only results, which Hibernate doesn't check for modifications:

Path: managing-data2/src/test/java/com/manning/javapersistence/ch10
➥ /ReadOnly.java - selectiveReadOnly()

```
org.hibernate.query.Query query = em.unwrap(Session.class)
    .createQuery("select i from Item i");
query.setReadOnly(true).list();
List<Item> result = query.list();
for (Item item : result)
    item.setName("New Name");                B
em.flush();                       ←┘
```

A Set the query to read-only.

B Consequently, `flush()` will not update the database.

With query hints you can also disable dirty checking for instances obtained with the JPA standard `javax.persistence.Query` interface:

```
Query query = em.createQuery(queryString)
    .setHint(
        org.hibernate.annotations.QueryHints.READ_ONLY,
        true
    );
```

Be careful with read-only entity instances: you can still delete them, and modifications to collections are tricky! The Hibernate manual has a long list of special cases you need to read if you use these settings with mapped collections.

So far, flushing and synchronization of the persistence context have occurred automatically, when the transaction commits. In some cases, though, we need more control over the synchronization process.

10.2.9 *Flushing the persistence context*

By default, Hibernate flushes the persistence context of an `EntityManager` and synchronizes changes with the database whenever the joined transaction is committed. All the previous code examples, except some in the last section, have used that strategy. JPA allows implementations to synchronize the persistence context at other times if they wish.

Hibernate, as a JPA implementation, synchronizes at the following times:

- When a joined Java Transaction API (JTA) system transaction is committed.
- Before a query is executed—we don't mean a lookup with `find()` but a query with `javax.persistence.Query` or the similar Hibernate API.
- When the application calls `flush()` explicitly.

We can control this behavior with the `FlushModeType` setting of an `EntityManager`:

```
Path: managing-data/src/test/java/com/manning/javapersistence/ch10
➥ /SimpleTransitionsTest.java – flushModeType()

em.getTransaction().begin();
Item item = em.find(Item.class, ITEM_ID);
item.setName("New Name");

em.setFlushMode(FlushModeType.COMMIT);

assertEquals(
        "Original Name",
        em.createQuery("select i.name from Item i where i.id = :id",
    String.class)
                .setParameter("id", ITEM_ID).getSingleResult()
);

em.getTransaction().commit(); // Flush!
em.close();
```

Here, we load an `Item` instance and change its name. Then we query the database, retrieving the item's name. Usually, Hibernate recognizes that data has changed in memory and synchronizes these modifications with the database before the query. This is the behavior of `FlushModeType.AUTO`, the default if we join the `EntityManager` with a transaction. With `FlushModeType.COMMIT` we disable flushing before queries, so we may see different data returned by the query than what we have in memory. The synchronization then occurs only when the transaction commits.

We can, at any time while a transaction is in progress, force dirty checking and synchronization with the database by calling `EntityManager#flush()`.

This concludes our discussion of the *transient, persistent*, and *removed* entity states, and the basic usage of the `EntityManager` API. Mastering these state transitions and API methods is essential; every JPA application is built with these operations.

Next we'll look at the *detached* entity state. We already mentioned some problems we'll see when entity instances aren't associated with a persistence context anymore, such as disabled lazy initialization. Let's explore the detached state with some examples, so we know what to expect when we work with data outside of a persistence context.

10.3 Working with detached state

If a reference leaves the scope of guaranteed identity, we call it a *reference* to a *detached entity instance*. When the persistence context is closed, it no longer provides an identity-mapping service. You'll run into aliasing problems when you work with detached entity instances, so make sure you understand how to handle the identity of detached instances.

10.3.1 *The identity of detached instances*

If we look up data using the same database identifier value in the same persistence context, the result is two references to the same in-memory instance on the JVM heap. When different references are obtained from the same persistence context, they have the same Java identity. The references may be equal because by default equals() relies on Java identity comparison. They obviously have the same database identity. They reference the same instance, in persistent state, managed by the persistence context for that unit of work.

References are in a detached state when the first persistence context is closed. We may be dealing with instances that live outside of a guaranteed scope of object identity.

Listing 10.2   Guaranteed scope of object identity in Java Persistence

```
Path: managing-data/src/test/java/com/manning/javapersistence/ch10
   /SimpleTransitionsTest.java - scopeOfIdentity()

em = emf.createEntityManager();
em.getTransaction().begin();
Item a = em.find(Item.class, ITEM_ID);
Item b = em.find(Item.class, ITEM_ID);
assertTrue(a == b);
assertTrue(a.equals(b));
assertEquals(a.getId(), b.getId());
em.getTransaction().commit();
em.close();
em = emf.createEntityManager();
em.getTransaction().begin();
Item c = em.find(Item.class, ITEM_ID);
assertTrue(a != c);
assertFalse(a.equals(c));
assertEquals(a.getId(), c.getId());
em.getTransaction().commit();
em.close();
```

A Create a persistence context.

B Begin the transaction.

C Load some entity instances.

D References a and b are obtained from the same persistence context; they have the same Java identity.

E equals() relies on Java identity comparison.

F a and b reference the same Item instance, in persistent state, managed by the persistence context for that unit of work.

G Commit the transaction.

H Close the persistence context. References a and b are in a detached state when the first persistence context is closed.

I a and c, loaded in different persistence contexts, aren't identical.

J a.equals(c) is also `false`, because the equals() method has not been overridden, which means it uses instance equality (==).

K A test for database identity still returns `true`.

If we treat entity instances as equal in detached state, this can lead to problems. For example, consider the following extension of the code, after the second unit of work has ended:

```
em.close();
Set<Item> allItems = new HashSet<>();
allItems.add(a);
allItems.add(b);
allItems.add(c);
assertEquals(2, allItems.size());
```

This example adds all three references to a `Set`, and all are references to detached instances. Now if we check the size of the collection—the number of elements—what result should we expect?

A `Set` doesn't allow duplicate elements. Duplicates are detected by the `Set`; whenever we add a reference to a `HashSet`, the `Item#equals()` method is called automatically against all other elements already in the collection. If equals() returns true for any element already in the collection, the addition doesn't occur.

By default, all Java classes inherit the equals() method of java.lang.Object. This implementation uses a double-equals (==) comparison to check whether two references refer to the same in-memory instance on the Java heap.

You might guess that the number of elements in the collection will be 2. After all, a and b are references to the same in-memory instance; they were loaded in the same persistence context. We obtained reference c from another persistence context; it refers to a different instance on the heap. We have three references to two instances, but we know this only because we've seen the code that loaded the data. In a real application, we may not know that a and b are loaded in a different context than c. Furthermore, we might expect that the collection has exactly one element because a, b, and c represent the same database row, the same `Item`.

Whenever we work with instances in a detached state and test them for equality (usually in hash-based collections), we need to supply our own implementation of the equals() and hashCode() methods for our mapped entity class. This is an important issue: if we don't work with entity instances in a detached state, no action is needed, and the default equals() implementation of java.lang.Object is fine. We'll rely on Hibernate's guaranteed scope of object identity within a persistence context. Even if we work with detached instances, if we never check whether they're equal, or we never put them in a `Set` or use them as keys in a `Map`, we don't have to worry. If all we do is render a detached `Item` on the screen, we aren't comparing it to anything.

Let's assume that we want to use detached instances and that we have to test them for equality with our own method.

10.3.2 *Implementing equality methods*

We can implement `equals()` and `hashCode()` methods several ways. Keep in mind that when we override `equals()`, we also need to override `hashCode()` so the two methods are consistent. If two instances are equal, they must have the same hash value.

A seemingly clever approach is to implement `equals()` to compare just the database identifier property, which is often a surrogate primary key value. Basically, if two `Item` instances have the same identifier returned by `getId()`, they must be the same. If `getId()` returns `null`, it must be a transient `Item` that hasn't been saved.

Unfortunately, this solution has one huge problem: identifier values aren't assigned by Hibernate until an instance becomes persistent. If a transient instance were added to a `Set` before being saved, then when we save it, its hash value would change while it's contained by the `Set`. This is contrary to the contract of `java.util.Set`, breaking the collection. In particular, this problem makes cascading persistent states useless for mapped associations based on sets. We strongly discourage database identifier equality.

To get to the solution that we recommend, you need to understand the notion of a *business key*. A business key is a property or some combination of properties, that is unique for each instance with the same database identity. Essentially, it's the natural key that we would use if we weren't using a surrogate primary key instead. Unlike a natural primary key, it isn't an absolute requirement that the business key never changes—as long as it changes rarely, that's enough.

We argue that essentially every entity class should have a business key, even if it includes all properties of the class (which would be appropriate for some immutable classes). If our users are looking at a list of items on the screen, how do they differentiate between items A, B, and C? The same property, or combination of properties, is our business key. The business key is what the user thinks of as uniquely identifying a particular record, whereas the surrogate key is what the application and database systems rely on. The business key property or properties are most likely constrained `UNIQUE` in our database schema.

Let's write custom equality methods for the `User` entity class; this is easier than comparing `Item` instances. For the `User` class, `username` is a great candidate business key. It's always required, it's unique with a database constraint, and it changes rarely, if ever.

Listing 10.3 Custom implementation of `User` equality

```
@Entity
@Table(name = "USERS",
       uniqueConstraints =
```

```
        @UniqueConstraint(columnNames = "USERNAME"))
public class User {
    @Override
    public boolean equals(Object other) {
        if (this == other) return true;
        if (other == null) return false;
        if (!(other instanceof User)) return false;
        User that = (User) other;
        return this.getUsername().equals(that.getUsername());
    }
    @Override
    public int hashCode() {
        return getUsername().hashCode();
    }
    //   . . .
}
```

You may have noticed that the equals() method code always accesses the properties of the "other" reference via getter methods. This is extremely important because the reference passed as other may be a Hibernate proxy, not the actual instance that holds the persistent state. We can't access the username field of a User proxy directly. To initialize the proxy to get the property value, we need to access it with a getter method. This is one point where Hibernate isn't *completely* transparent, but it's good practice anyway to use getter methods instead of direct instance variable access.

Check the type of the other reference with instanceof, rather than by comparing the values of getClass(). Again, the other reference may be a proxy, which is a runtime-generated subclass of User, so this and other may not be exactly the same type but a valid supertype or subtype. You'll learn more about proxies in section 12.1.1.

We can now safely compare User references in persistent state:

```
em = emf.createEntityManager();
em.getTransaction().begin();
User a = em.find(User.class, USER_ID);
User b = em.find(User.class, USER_ID);
assertTrue(a == b);
assertTrue(a.equals(b));
assertEquals(a.getId(), b.getId());
em.getTransaction().commit();
em.close();
```

We also, of course, get correct behavior if we compare references to instances in the persistent and detached state:

```
em = emf.createEntityManager();
em.getTransaction().begin();
User c = em.find(User.class, USER_ID);
assertFalse(a == c);
assertTrue(a.equals(c));                          ←── B
assertEquals(a.getId(), c.getId());
em.getTransaction().commit();
```

```
em.close();
Set<User> allUsers = new HashSet();
allUsers.add(a);
allUsers.add(b);
allUsers.add(c);                                    C
assertEquals(1, allUsers.size());
```

A Comparing the two references will, of course, still be false.

B Now they are equal.

C The size of the set is finally correct.

For some other entities, the business key may be more complex, consisting of a combination of properties. Here are some hints that should help you identify a business key in the domain model classes:

- Consider what attributes users of the application will refer to when they have to identify an object (in the real world). How do users tell the difference between one element and another if they're displayed on the screen? This is probably the business key to look for.

- Every immutable attribute is probably a good candidate for the business key. Mutable attributes may be good candidates, too, if they're updated rarely or if you can control the case when they're updated, such as by ensuring the instances aren't in a Set at the time.

- Every attribute that has a UNIQUE database constraint is a good candidate for the business key. Remember that the precision of the business key has to be good enough to avoid overlaps.

- Any date or time-based attribute, such as the creation timestamp of the record, is usually a good component of a business key, but the accuracy of System .currentTimeMillis() depends on the virtual machine and operating system. Our recommended safety buffer is 50 milliseconds, which may not be accurate enough if the time-based property is the single attribute of a business key.

- You can use database identifiers as part of the business key. This seems to contradict our previous statements, but we aren't talking about the database identifier value of the given entity. You may be able to use the database identifier of an associated entity instance. For example, a candidate business key for the Bid class is the identifier of the Item it matches, together with the bid amount. You may even have a unique constraint that represents this composite business key in the database schema. You can use the identifier value of the associated Item because it never changes during the lifecycle of a Bid—the Bid constructor can require an already-persistent Item.

If you follow this advice, you shouldn't have much difficulty finding a good business key for all your business classes. If you encounter a difficult case, try to solve it without considering Hibernate. After all, it's purely an object-oriented problem. Notice that it's extremely rarely correct to override equals() on a subclass and include another property in the comparison. It's a little tricky to satisfy the `Object` identity and equality requirements that equality is both symmetric and transitive in this case, and more important, the business key may not correspond to any well-defined candidate natural key in the database (subclass properties may be mapped to a different table). For more information on customizing equality comparisons, see *Effective Java*, third edition, by Joshua Bloch (Bloch, 2017), a mandatory book for all Java programmers.

The `User` class is now prepared for the detached state; we can safely put instances loaded in different persistence contexts into a `Set`. Next we'll look at some examples that involve the detached state, and you'll see some of the benefits of this concept.

10.3.3   *Detaching entity instances*

Sometimes we might want to detach an entity instance manually from the persistence context. We don't have to wait for the persistence context to close. We can evict entity instances manually:

```
Path: managing-data/src/test/java/com/manning/javapersistence/ch10
➥ /SimpleTransitionsTest.java - detach()

User user = em.find(User.class, USER_ID);
em.detach(user);
assertFalse(em.contains(user));
```

This example also demonstrates the `EntityManager#contains()` operation, which returns `true` if the given instance is in the managed persistent state in this persistence context.

We can now work with the `user` reference in a detached state. Many applications only read and render the data after the persistence context is closed.

Modifying the loaded `user` after the persistence context is closed has no effect on its persistent representation in the database. JPA allows us to merge any changes back into the database in a new persistence context, though.

10.3.4   *Merging entity instances*

Let's assume we've retrieved a `User` instance in a previous persistence context, and now we want to modify it and save these modifications:

```
Path: managing-data/src/test/java/com/manning/javapersistence/ch10
➥ /SimpleTransitionsTest.java - mergeDetached()

detachedUser.setUsername("johndoe");
em = emf.createEntityManager();
em.getTransaction().begin();
User mergedUser = em.merge(detachedUser);
mergedUser.setUsername("doejohn");
em.getTransaction().commit();
em.close();
```

Consider the graphical representation of this procedure in figure 10.5. The goal is to record the new `username` of the detached `User`. It's not as difficult as it seems.

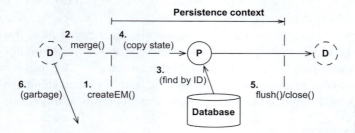

Figure 10.5   **Making an instance persistent in a unit of work**

First, when we call `merge()`, Hibernate checks whether a persistent instance in the persistence context has the same database identifier as the detached instance we merging. In this example, the persistence context is empty; nothing has been loaded from the database. Hibernate, therefore, loads an instance with this identifier from the database. Then `merge()` copies the detached entity instance *onto* this loaded persistent instance. In other words, the new `username` we have set on the detached `User` is also set on the persistent merged `User`, which `merge()` returns to us.

Now we discard the old reference to the stale and outdated detached state; the `detachedUser` no longer represents the current state. We can continue modifying the returned `mergedUser`; Hibernate will execute a single `UPDATE` when it flushes the persistence context during commit.

If there is no persistent instance with the same identifier in the persistence context, and a lookup by identifier in the database is negative, Hibernate instantiates a fresh `User`. Hibernate then copies our detached instance onto this fresh instance, which it inserts into the database when we synchronize the persistence context with the database.

If the instance we're giving to `merge()` is not detached but rather is transient (it doesn't have an identifier value), Hibernate instantiates a fresh `User`, copies the values of the transient `User` onto it, and then makes it persistent and returns it to us. In simpler terms, the `merge()` operation can handle detached *and* transient entity instances. Hibernate always returns the result to us as a persistent instance.

An application architecture based on detachment and merging may not call the `persist()` operation. We can merge new and detached entity instances to store data. The important difference is the returned current state and how we handle this switch of references in our application code. We have to discard the `detachedUser` and from now on reference the current `mergedUser`. Every other component in our application still holding on to `detachedUser` has to switch to `mergedUser`.

Can I reattach a detached instance?

The Hibernate `Session` API has a method for reattachment called `saveOrUpdate()`. It accepts either a transient or a detached instance and doesn't return anything. The given instance will be in a persistent state after the operation, so we don't have to switch references. Hibernate will execute an `INSERT` if the given instance was transient or an `UPDATE` if it was detached. We recommend that you rely on merging instead, because it's standardized and therefore easier to integrate with other frameworks. In addition, instead of an `UPDATE`, merging may only trigger a `SELECT` if the detached data wasn't modified. If you're wondering what the `saveOrUpdateCopy()` method of the `Session` API does, it's the same as `merge()` on the `EntityManager`.

If we want to delete a detached instance, we have to merge it first. Then we can call `remove()` on the persistent instance returned by `merge()`.

Summary

- The lifecycle of entity instances includes the transient, persistent, detached, and removed states.
- The most important interface in JPA is `EntityManager`.
- We can use the `EntityManager` to make data persistent, retrieve and modify persistent data, get a reference, make data transient, refresh and replicate data, cache in the persistence context, and flush the persistence context.
- We can work with the detached state, using the identity of detached instances and implementing equality methods.

Transactions
and concurrency

This chapter covers

- Defining database and system transaction essentials
- Controlling concurrent access with Hibernate and JPA
- Using non-transactional data access
- Managing transactions with Spring and Spring Data

In this chapter, we'll finally talk about transactions: how we create and control concurrent units of work in an application. A *unit of work* is an atomic group of operations, and transactions allow us to set unit of work boundaries and help us isolate one unit of work from another. In a multiuser application, we may also be processing these units of work concurrently.

To handle concurrency, we'll first focus on units of work at the lowest level: database and system transactions. You'll learn the APIs for transaction demarcation and how to define units of work in Java code. We'll demonstrate how to preserve isolation and control concurrent access with pessimistic and optimistic strategies. The overall architecture of the system affects the scope of a transaction; a bad architecture may lead to fragile transactions.

Then we'll analyze some special cases and JPA features, based on accessing the database without explicit transactions. Finally we'll demonstrate how to work with transactions with Spring and Spring Data.

Let's start with some background information.

Major new features in JPA 2

There are new lock modes and exceptions for pessimistic locking:

- You can set a lock mode, pessimistic or optimistic, on a `Query`.
- You can set a lock mode when calling `EntityManager#find()`, `refresh()`, or `lock()`. A lock timeout hint for pessimistic lock modes is also standardized.

When the new `QueryTimeoutException` or `LockTimeoutException` is thrown, the transaction doesn't have to be rolled back.

The persistence context can now be in an *unsynchronized* mode with disabled automatic flushing. This allows us to queue modifications until we join a transaction and to decouple the `EntityManager` usage from transactions.

11.1 Transaction essentials

Application functionality requires that several things be done in one go. For example, when an auction finishes, the CaveatEmptor application must perform three different tasks:

1 Find the winning bid (highest amount) for the auction item.
2 Charge the seller of the item the cost of the auction.
3 Notify the seller and successful bidder.

What happens if we can't bill the auction costs because of a failure in the external credit card system? The business requirements may state that either all listed actions must succeed or none must succeed. If so, we call these steps collectively a *transaction* or *unit of work*. If only a single step fails, the entire unit of work must fail.

11.1.1 ACID attributes

ACID stands for *atomicity, consistency, isolation, durability*. *Atomicity* is the notion that all operations in a transaction execute as an atomic unit. Furthermore, transactions allow multiple users to work concurrently with the same data without compromising the *consistency* of the data (consistent with database integrity rules). A particular transaction should not be visible to other concurrently running transactions; they should run in *isolation*. Changes made in a transaction should be *durable*, even if the system fails after the transaction has been completed successfully.

In addition, we want the *correctness* of a transaction. For example, the business rules dictate that the application charges the seller once, not twice. This is a reasonable assumption, but we may not be able to express it with database constraints. Hence, the correctness of a transaction is the responsibility of the application, whereas consistency is the responsibility of the database. Together, these transaction attributes define the *ACID* criteria.

11.1.2 *Database and system transactions*

We've also mentioned *system* and *database* transactions. Consider the last example again: during the unit of work ending an auction, we might mark the winning bid in a database system. Then, in the same unit of work, we talk to an external system to bill the seller's credit card. This is a transaction spanning several systems, with coordinated subordinate transactions on possibly several resources, such as a database connection and an external billing processor. This chapter focuses on transactions spanning one system and one database.

Database transactions have to be short because open transactions consume database resources and potentially prevent concurrent access due to exclusive locks on data. A single database transaction usually involves only a single batch of database operations.

To execute all of the database operations inside a system transaction, we have to set the boundaries of that unit of work. We must start the transaction and, at some point, commit the changes. If an error occurs (either while executing database operations or when committing the transaction), we have to roll back the changes to leave the data in a consistent state. This process defines a *transaction demarcation* and, depending on the technique we use, involves manually defining transaction boundaries in the code. In general, transaction boundaries that begin and end a transaction can be set either programmatically in the application code or declaratively. We'll demonstrate both ways, focusing on declarative transactions while working with Spring and Spring Data.

> **NOTE**   All examples in this chapter work in any Java SE environment, without a special runtime container. Hence, from now on you'll see programmatic transaction demarcation code until we move on to specific Spring application examples.

Next we'll focus on the most complex aspect of ACID properties: how you can *isolate* concurrently running units of work from each other.

11.2 *Controlling concurrent access*

Databases (and other transactional systems) attempt to ensure transaction *isolation*, meaning that, from the point of view of each concurrent transaction, it appears that no other transactions are in progress. Traditionally, database systems have implemented isolation with locking. A transaction can place a lock on a particular item of data in the database, temporarily preventing read and/or write access to that item by other transactions. Some modern database engines implement transaction isolation with multi-version concurrency control (MVCC), which vendors generally consider more scalable. We'll analyze isolation assuming a locking model, but most of our observations are also applicable to MVCC.

How databases implement concurrency control is of the utmost importance in the Java Persistence application. Applications may inherit the isolation guarantees provided by the database management system, but frameworks may come on top of them and allow you to start, commit, and roll back transactions in a resource-agnostic way. If you consider the many years of experience that database vendors have with implementing concurrency control, you'll see the advantage of this approach. Additionally, some features in Java Persistence can improve the isolation guarantee beyond what the database provides, either because you explicitly use the features or by design.

We'll discuss concurrency control in several steps. First we'll explore the lowest layer: the transaction isolation guarantees provided by the database. After that, you'll see the Java Persistence features for pessimistic and optimistic concurrency control at the application level, and other isolation guarantees that Hibernate can provide.

11.2.1 Understanding database-level concurrency

When we talk about isolation, you can assume that two transactions are either isolated or not. When we talk about database transactions, complete isolation comes at a high price. You can't stop the world in order to access data exclusively in a multiuser online transaction processing (OLTP) system. Therefore, several isolation levels are available, which, naturally, weaken full isolation but increase the performance and scalability of the system.

TRANSACTION ISOLATION PROBLEMS

First, let's examine several problems that may occur when you weaken full transaction isolation. The ANSI SQL standard defines the standard transaction isolation levels in terms of which of these phenomena are permissible.

A *lost update* occurs when two concurrent transactions simultaneously update the same information in a database. The first transaction reads a value. The second transaction starts shortly after and reads the same value. The first transaction changes and writes the updated value, and the second transaction overwrites that value with its own update. Thus, the update of the first transaction is lost, being overwritten by the second transaction. *The last commit wins.* This occurs in systems that don't implement concurrency control, where concurrent transactions aren't isolated. This is shown in figure 11.1. The buyNowPrice field is updated from two transactions, but only one update occurred, the other update was lost.

A *dirty read* occurs if transaction 2 reads changes made by transaction 1, and it hasn't yet been committed. This is dangerous because the changes made by transaction 1 may later be rolled back, and invalid data will have been read by transaction 2. This is illustrated in figure 11.2.

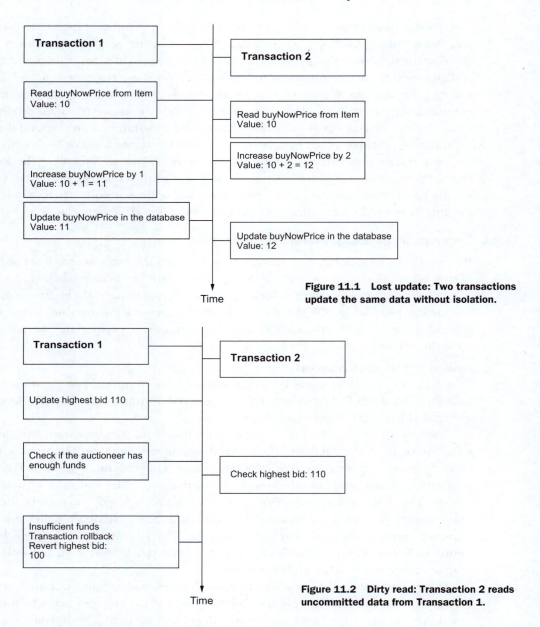

Figure 11.1   Lost update: Two transactions update the same data without isolation.

Figure 11.2   Dirty read: Transaction 2 reads uncommitted data from Transaction 1.

An *unrepeatable read* occurs if a transaction reads a data item twice and reads different states each time. For example, another transaction may have written to the data item and committed between the two reads, as shown in figure 11.3.

A *phantom read* is said to occur when a transaction executes a query twice, and the second result includes data that wasn't visible in the first result because something was added, or it includes less data because something was deleted. This need not necessarily

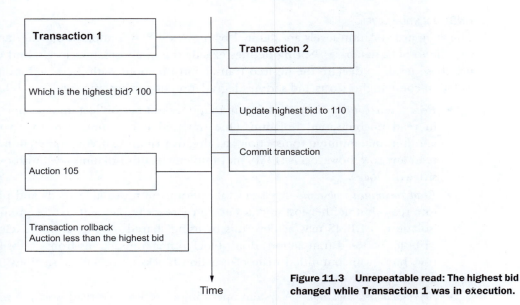

Figure 11.3   Unrepeatable read: The highest bid changed while Transaction 1 was in execution.

refer to the exact same query. Another transaction inserting or deleting data between the executions of the two queries causes this situation, as shown in figure 11.4.

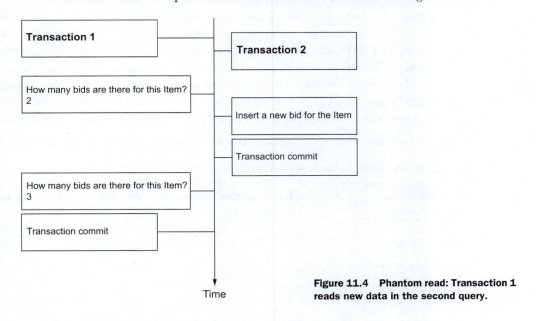

Figure 11.4   Phantom read: Transaction 1 reads new data in the second query.

Now that you understand all the bad things that can occur, we can define the transaction isolation levels and see what problems they prevent.

ANSI ISOLATION LEVELS

The standard isolation levels are defined by the ANSI SQL standard, but they aren't specific to SQL databases. Spring defines exactly the same isolation levels, and we'll use these levels to declare the desired transaction isolation. With increased levels of isolation come higher costs and serious degradation of performance and scalability:

- *Read uncommitted isolation*—A system that does not permit lost updates operates in read uncommitted isolation. One transaction may not write to a row if another uncommitted transaction has already written to it. Any transaction may read any row, however. A DBMS may implement this isolation level with exclusive write locks.

- *Read committed isolation*—A system that permits unrepeatable reads and phantom reads but neither lost updates nor dirty reads implements read committed isolation. A DBMS may achieve this by using shared read locks and exclusive write locks. Read transactions don't block other transactions from accessing a row, but an uncommitted write transaction blocks all other transactions from accessing the row.

- *Repeatable read isolation*—A system operating in repeatable read isolation mode does not permit lost updates, dirty reads, or unrepeatable reads. Phantom reads may occur. Read transactions block write transactions but do not block other read transactions, and write transactions block all other transactions.

- *Serializable isolation*—The strictest isolation, serializable, emulates serial execution as if transactions were executed one after another, rather than concurrently. A DBMS may not implement serializable isolation using only row-level locks. A DBMS must instead provide some other mechanism that prevents a newly inserted row from becoming visible to a transaction that has already executed a query that would return the row. A crude mechanism is exclusively locking the entire database table after a write so that no phantom reads can occur.

Table 11.1 summarizes the ANSI isolation levels and the problems that they address.

Table 11.1   ANSI isolation levels and the problems that they address

Isolation level	Phantom read	Unrepeatable read	Dirty read	Lost update
READ_UNCOMMITTED	–	–	–	+
READ_COMMITTED	–	–	+	+
REPEATABLE_READ	–	+	+	+
SERIALIZABLE	+	+	+	+

How exactly a DBMS implements its locking system varies significantly; each vendor has a different strategy. You should study the documentation of your DBMS to find out more about its locking system, how locks are escalated (from row-level to pages to entire tables, for example), and what effect each isolation level has on the performance and scalability of the system.

It's nice to know how all these technical terms are defined, but how does that help us choose an isolation level for the application?

CHOOSING AN ISOLATION LEVEL

Developers (ourselves included) are often unsure what transaction isolation level to use in a production application. Too high an isolation level harms the scalability of a highly concurrent application. Insufficient isolation may cause subtle, difficult-to-reproduce bugs that we won't discover until the system is working under heavy load.

Note that we'll refer to *optimistic locking* (with versioning) in the following explanation, which is a concept analyzed later in this chapter. You may want to revisit this section when it's time to pick an isolation level for your application. Choosing the correct isolation level is, after all, highly dependent on the particular scenario. The following discussion should be read as recommendations, not dictums carved in stone.

Hibernate tries hard to be as transparent as possible regarding the transactional semantics of the database. Nevertheless, persistence context caching and versioning affect these semantics. What is a sensible database isolation level to choose in a JPA application?

First, for almost all scenarios, eliminate the *read uncommitted* isolation level. It's extremely dangerous to allow one transaction's uncommitted changes to be used in a different transaction. The rollback or failure of one transaction will affect other concurrent transactions. The rollback of the first transaction could bring other transactions down with it, or perhaps even cause them to leave the database in an incorrect state (the seller of an auction item might be charged twice—consistent with database integrity rules but incorrect). It's possible that changes made by a transaction that ends up being rolled back could be committed anyway because they could be read and then propagated by another successful transaction! You can use the *read uncommitted* isolation level for debugging purposes, to follow the execution of long insert queries, make some rough estimates of aggregate functions (such as SUM(*) or COUNT(*)).

Second, most applications don't need *serializable* isolation. Phantom reads aren't usually problematic, and this isolation level tends to scale poorly. Few existing applications use serializable isolation in production, but rather rely on selectively applied pessimistic locks that effectively force a serialized execution of operations in certain situations.

Next, let's consider *repeatable read*. This level provides reproducibility for query result sets for the duration of a database transaction. This means we won't read committed updates from the database if we query it several times, but phantom reads are still possible: new rows might appear, and rows we thought existed might disappear if another transaction committed changes concurrently. Although we may sometimes want repeatable reads, we typically don't need them in every transaction.

The JPA specification assumes that *read committed* is the default isolation level. This means we have to deal with unrepeatable reads and phantom reads.

Let's assume we're enabling versioning of our domain model entities, which is something Hibernate can do for us automatically. The combination of the (mandatory) persistence context cache and versioning already gives us most of the nice features of repeatable read isolation. The persistence context cache ensures that the state of the entity instances loaded by one transaction is isolated from changes made by other transactions. If we retrieve the same entity instance twice in a unit of work, the second lookup will be resolved within the persistence context cache and not hit the database. Hence, our read *is* repeatable, and we won't see conflicting committed data. (We can still get phantom reads, though, which are typically much easier to deal with.) Additionally, versioning switches to *first commit wins*. Hence, for almost all multiuser JPA applications, *read committed* isolation for all database transactions is acceptable with enabled entity versioning.

Hibernate retains the isolation level of the database connection; it doesn't change the level. Most products default to read committed isolation, though MySQL defaults to repeatable read. There are several ways we can change either the default transaction isolation level or the settings of the current transaction.

First, we can check whether the DBMS has a global transaction isolation level setting in its proprietary configuration. If the DBMS supports the standard SQL statement SET SESSION CHARACTERISTICS, we can execute it to set the transaction settings of all transactions started in this particular database *session* (which means a particular connection to the database, not a Hibernate Session). SQL also standardizes the SET TRANSACTION syntax, which sets the isolation level of the current transaction. Finally, the JDBC Connection API offers the setTransactionIsolation() method, which (according to its documentation) "attempts to change the transaction isolation level for this connection." In a Hibernate/JPA application, we can obtain a JDBC Connection from the native Session API.

Frequently, the database connections are, by default, in read committed isolation levels. From time to time, a particular unit of work in the application may require a different, usually stricter, isolation level. Instead of changing the isolation level of the entire transaction, we should use the Jakarta Persistence API to obtain additional locks on the relevant data. This fine-grained locking is more scalable in a highly concurrent application. JPA offers optimistic version checking and database-level pessimistic locking.

11.2.2 *Optimistic concurrency control*

Handling concurrency in an optimistic way is appropriate when concurrent modifications are rare and it's feasible to detect conflicts late in a unit of work. JPA offers automatic version checking as an optimistic conflict-detection procedure.

The previous sections have been somewhat dry; it's time for some code. First we'll enable versioning, because it's turned off by default. Most multiuser applications, especially web applications, should rely on versioning for any concurrently modified @Entity instances, enabling the more user-friendly *first commit wins*.

After enabling automatic version checking, we'll see how manual version checking works and when we have to use it.

NOTE To be able to execute the examples from the source code, you'll first need to run the Ch11.sql script.

ENABLING VERSIONING

We can enable versioning with an @Version annotation on a special additional property of the entity class, as demonstrated next.

Listing 11.1 Enabling versioning on a mapped entity

Path: Ch11/transactions/src/main/java/com/manning/javapersistence/ch11
➡ /concurrency/Item.java

```
@Entity
public class Item {
    @Version
    private long version;
    //  . . .
}
```

In this example, each entity instance carries a numeric version. It's mapped to an additional column of the ITEM database table; as usual, the column name defaults to the property name, here VERSION. The actual names of the property and column don't matter—we could rename it if VERSION is a reserved keyword in the DBMS.

We could add a getVersion() method to the class, but we shouldn't have a setter method, and the application shouldn't modify the value. Hibernate automatically changes the version value: it increments the version number whenever an Item instance has been found to be dirty during the flushing of the persistence context. The version is a simple counter without any useful semantic value beyond concurrency control. We can use an int, an Integer, a short, a Short, or a Long instead of a long; Hibernate wraps and starts from zero again if the version number reaches the limit of the data type.

After incrementing the version number of a detected dirty Item during flushing, Hibernate compares versions when executing the UPDATE and DELETE SQL statements. For example, assume that in a unit of work we load an Item and change its name, as follows.

Listing 11.2 Hibernate incrementing and checking the version automatically

Path: /Ch11/transactions/src/test/java/com/manning/javapersistence/ch11
➡ /concurrency/Versioning.java – firstCommitWins()

```
EntityManager em1 = emf.createEntityManager();           A
em1.getTransaction().begin();
Item item = em1.find(Item.class, ITEM_ID);           ←
```

```
// select * from ITEM where ID = ?
assertEquals(0, item.getVersion());          ◄──B
item.setName("New Name");
// . . .   Another transaction changes the record          C
assertThrows(OptimisticLockException.class, () -> em1.flush());   ◄──┘
// update ITEM set NAME = ?, VERSION = 1 where ID = ? and VERSION = 0
```

A Retrieving an entity instance by identifier loads the current version from the database with a SELECT.

B The current version of the Item instance is 0.

C When the persistence context is flushed, Hibernate detects the dirty Item instance and increments its version to 1. SQL UPDATE now performs the version check, storing the new version in the database, but only if the database version is still 0.

Pay attention to the SQL statements, in particular, the UPDATE and its WHERE clause. This update will be successful only if there *is* a row with VERSION = 0 in the database. JDBC returns the number of updated rows to Hibernate; if that result is zero, it means the ITEM row is either gone or doesn't have version 0 anymore. Hibernate detects this conflict during flushing, and a javax.persistence.OptimisticLockException is thrown.

Now imagine two users executing this unit of work at the same time, as shown previously in figure 11.1. The first user to commit will update the name of the Item and flush the incremented version 1 to the database. The second user's flush (and commit) will fail because their UPDATE statement can't find the row in the database with version 0. The database version is 1. Hence, the *first commit wins*, and we can catch the OptimisticLockException and handle it specifically. For example, we could show the following message to the second user: "The data you have been working with has been modified by someone else. Please start your unit of work again with fresh data. Click the Restart button to proceed."

What modifications trigger the increment of an entity's version? Hibernate increments the version whenever an entity instance is dirty. This includes all dirty value-typed properties of the entity, no matter whether they're single-valued (like a String or int property), embedded (like an Address), or collections. The exceptions are @OneToMany and @ManyToMany association collections that have been made read-only with mappedBy. Adding or removing elements in these collections doesn't increment the version number of the owning entity instance. You should know that none of this is standardized in JPA—don't rely on two JPA providers to implement the same rules when accessing a shared database.

If we don't want to increment the version of the entity instance when a particular property's value has changed, we can annotate the property with @org.hibernate .annotations.OptimisticLock(excluded = true).

You may not like the additional VERSION column in the database schema. Alternatively, you may already have a "last updated" timestamp property on the entity class and a matching database column. Hibernate can check versions with timestamps instead of using the extra counter field.

Versioning with a shared database

If several applications access the database, and they don't all use Hibernate's versioning algorithm, we'll have concurrency problems. An easy solution is to use database-level triggers and stored procedures: an INSTEAD OF trigger can execute a stored procedure when any UPDATE is made; it runs instead of the update. In the procedure, we can check whether the application incremented the version of the row; if the version isn't updated or the version column isn't included in the update, we know the statement wasn't sent by a Hibernate application. We can then increment the version in the procedure before applying the UPDATE.

VERSIONING WITH TIMESTAMPS

If the database schema already contains a timestamp column such as LASTUPDATED or MODIFIED_ON, we can map it for automatic version checking instead of using a numeric counter.

Listing 11.3   Enabling versioning with timestamps

```
Path: Ch11/transactions2/src/main/java/com/manning/javapersistence/ch11
➡ /timestamp/Item.java

@Entity
public class Item {
    @Version
        // Optional: @org.hibernate.annotations.Type(type = "dbtimestamp")
    private LocalDateTime lastUpdated;
    //  . . .
}
```

This example maps the LASTUPDATED column to a java.time.LocalDateTime property; a Date or Calendar type would also work with Hibernate. The JPA standard doesn't define these types for version properties; JPA only considers java.sql.Timestamp portable. This is less attractive, because we'd have to import that JDBC class in the domain model. We should try to keep implementation details such as JDBC out of the domain model classes so they can be tested, instantiated, serialized, and deserialized in as many environments as possible.

In theory, versioning with a timestamp is slightly less safe, because two concurrent transactions may both load and update the same Item in the same millisecond; this is exacerbated by the fact that a JVM usually doesn't have millisecond accuracy (you should check your JVM and operating system documentation for the guaranteed precision). Furthermore, retrieving the current time from the JVM isn't necessarily safe in a clustered environment, where the system time of nodes may not be synchronized, or time synchronization isn't as accurate as you'd need for your transactional load.

You can switch to retrieving the current time from the database machine by placing an @org.hibernate.annotations.Type(type="dbtimestamp") annotation on the version property. Hibernate now asks the database for the current time before updating, which gives a single source of time for synchronization. Not all Hibernate SQL dialects support this, so check the source of the configured dialect. In addition, there is always the overhead of hitting the database for every increment.

We recommend that new projects rely on versioning with a numeric counter, not timestamps. If you're working with a legacy database schema or existing Java classes, it may be impossible to introduce a version or timestamp property and column. If that's the case, Hibernate provides an alternative strategy.

VERSIONING WITHOUT VERSION NUMBERS OR TIMESTAMPS

If you don't have version or timestamp columns, Hibernate can still perform automatic versioning. This alternative implementation of versioning checks the current database state against the unmodified values of persistent properties at the time Hibernate retrieved the entity instance (or the last time the persistence context was flushed).

You can enable this functionality with the proprietary Hibernate annotation @org.hibernate.annotations.OptimisticLocking:

```
Path: Ch11/transactions3/src/main/java/com/manning/javapersistence/ch11
➡ /versionall/Item.java

@Entity
@org.hibernate.annotations.OptimisticLocking(
    type = org.hibernate.annotations.OptimisticLockType.ALL)
@org.hibernate.annotations.DynamicUpdate
public class Item {
    // . . .
}
```

For this strategy, you also have to enable dynamic SQL generation of UPDATE statements, using @org.hibernate.annotations.DynamicUpdate, as explained in section 5.3.2.

Hibernate now executes the following SQL to flush a modification of an Item instance:

```
update ITEM set NAME = 'New Name'
    where ID = 123
        and NAME = 'Old Name'
        and PRICE = '9.99'
        and DESCRIPTION = 'Some item for auction'
        and ...
        and SELLER_ID = 45
```

Hibernate lists all columns and their last known values in the WHERE clause. If any concurrent transaction has modified any of these values or even deleted the row, this statement returns with zero updated rows. Hibernate then throws an exception at flush time.

Alternatively, Hibernate includes only the modified properties in the restriction (only NAME, in this example) if you switch to OptimisticLockType.DIRTY. This means two units of work can modify the same Item concurrently, and Hibernate detects a conflict only if they both modify the same value-typed property (or a foreign key value). The WHERE clause of the last SQL excerpt would be reduced to where ID = 123 and NAME = 'Old Name'. Someone else could concurrently modify the price, and Hibernate wouldn't detect any conflict. Only if the application modified the name concurrently would we get a javax.persistence.OptimisticLockException.

In most cases, checking only dirty properties isn't a good strategy for business entities. It's probably not OK to change the price of an item if the description changes! This strategy also doesn't work with detached entities and merging: if we merge a detached entity into a new persistence context, the "old" values aren't known. The detached entity instance will have to carry a version number or timestamp for optimistic concurrency control.

Automatic versioning in Java Persistence prevents lost updates when two concurrent transactions try to commit modifications on the same piece of data. Versioning can also help us obtain additional isolation guarantees manually when we need them.

MANUAL VERSION CHECKING

Here's a scenario that requires repeatable database reads: imagine there are some categories in the auction system and that each Item is in a Category. This is a regular @ManyToOne mapping of an Item#category entity association.

Let's say you want to sum up all item prices in several categories. This requires a query for all items in each category, to add up the prices. The problem is, what happens if someone moves an Item from one Category to another Category while you're still querying and iterating through all the categories and items? With read-committed isolation, the same Item might show up twice while your procedure runs!

To make the "get items in each category" reads repeatable, JPA's Query interface has a setLockMode() method. Look at the procedure in the following listing.

> **Listing 11.4 Requesting a version check at flush time to ensure repeatable reads**

Path: /Ch11/transactions/src/test/java/com/manning/javapersistence/ch11
➡ /concurrency/Versioning.java - manualVersionChecking()

```
EntityManager em = emf.createEntityManager();
em.getTransaction().begin();

BigDecimal totalPrice = BigDecimal.ZERO;                          Ⓐ
for (Long categoryId : CATEGORIES) {                           ⟵┐
    List<Item> items =
        em.createQuery("select i from Item i where i.category.id = :catId",
        ➡ Item.class)
            .setLockMode(LockModeType.OPTIMISTIC)
            .setParameter("catId", categoryId)
            .getResultList();
    for (Item item : items)
```

```
        totalPrice = totalPrice.add(item.getBuyNowPrice());
   }
    em.getTransaction().commit();                          ◄──── Ⓑ
  em.close();
  assertEquals("108.00", totalPrice.toString());
```

Ⓐ For each `Category`, query all `Item` instances with an `OPTIMISTIC` lock mode. Hibernate now knows it has to check each `Item` at flush time.

Ⓑ For each `Item` loaded earlier with the locking query, Hibernate executes a `SELECT` during flushing. It checks whether the database version of each `ITEM` row is still the same as when it was loaded. If any `ITEM` row has a different version or the row no longer exists, an `OptimisticLockException` is thrown.

Don't be confused by the *locking* terminology: The JPA specification leaves open how exactly each `LockModeType` is implemented. For `OPTIMISTIC`, Hibernate performs version checking; there are no actual locks involved. We'll have to enable versioning on the `Item` entity class as explained earlier; otherwise, we can't use the optimistic `LockModeTypes` with Hibernate.

Hibernate doesn't batch or otherwise optimize the `SELECT` statements for manual version checking; if we sum up 100 items, we get 100 additional queries at flush time. A pessimistic approach, as we'll demonstrate later in this chapter, may be a better solution for this particular case.

Why can't the persistence context cache prevent the concurrent modification problem?

The "get all items in a particular category" query returns item data in a `ResultSet`. Hibernate then looks at the primary key values in this data and first tries to resolve the rest of the details of each `Item` in the persistence context cache—it checks whether an `Item` instance has already been loaded with that identifier.

This cache, however, doesn't help in the example procedure: if a concurrent transaction moved an item to another category, that item might be returned several times in different `ResultSets`. Hibernate will perform its persistence context lookup and say, "Oh, I've already loaded that `Item` instance; let's use what we already have in memory." Hibernate isn't even aware that the category assigned to the item changed or that the item appeared again in a different result.

Hence, this is a case where the repeatable-read feature of the persistence context hides concurrently committed data. We need to manually check the versions to find out if the data changed while we were expecting it not to change.

As shown in the preceding example, the `Query` interface accepts a `LockModeType`. Explicit lock modes are also supported by the `TypedQuery` and `NamedQuery` interfaces, with the same `setLockMode()` method.

An additional optimistic lock mode is available in JPA, forcing an increment of an entity's version.

FORCING A VERSION INCREMENT

What happens if two users place a bid for the same auction item at the same time? When a user makes a new bid, the application must do two things:

1 Retrieve the currently highest `Bid` for the `Item` from the database.
2 Compare the new `Bid` with the highest `Bid`; if the new `Bid` is higher, it must be stored in the database.

There is the potential for a race condition between these two steps. If, between reading the highest `Bid` and placing the new `Bid`, another `Bid` is made, you won't see it. This conflict isn't visible, and even enabling versioning of the `Item` doesn't help. The `Item` is never modified during the procedure. However, forcing a version increment of the `Item` makes the conflict detectable.

Listing 11.5   Forcing a version increment of an entity instance

```
Path: /Ch11/transactions/src/test/java/com/manning/javapersistence/ch11
    /concurrency/Versioning.java - forceIncrement()
```

```
    EntityManager em = emf.createEntityManager();
    em.getTransaction().begin();
Item item = em.find(
    Item.class,
    ITEM_ID,
    LockModeType.OPTIMISTIC_FORCE_INCREMENT
);
Bid highestBid = queryHighestBid(em, item);
// . . . Another transaction changes the record
Bid newBid = new Bid(
        new BigDecimal("45.45"),
        item,
        highestBid);
em.persist(newBid);
assertThrows(RollbackException.class,
                () -> em.getTransaction().commit());
em.close();
```

Ⓐ `find()` accepts a `LockModeType`. The `OPTIMISTIC_FORCE_INCREMENT` mode tells Hibernate that the version of the retrieved `Item` should be incremented after loading, even if it's never modified in the unit of work.

Ⓑ The code persists a new `Bid` instance; this doesn't affect any values of the `Item` instance. A new row is inserted into the `BID` table. Hibernate wouldn't detect concurrently made bids without a forced version increment of the `Item`.

Ⓒ When flushing the persistence context, Hibernate executes an `INSERT` for the new `Bid` and forces an `UPDATE` of the `Item` with a version check. If someone modified the `Item` concurrently or placed a `Bid` concurrently with this procedure, Hibernate throws an exception.

For the auction system, placing bids concurrently is certainly a frequent operation. Incrementing a version manually is useful in many situations where we insert or modify data and want the version of some root instance of an aggregate to be incremented.

Note that if instead of a `Bid#item` entity association with `@ManyToOne`, we have an `@ElementCollection` of `Item#bids`, adding a `Bid` to the collection *will* increment the `Item` version. The forced increment then isn't necessary. You may want to review the discussion of parent/child ambiguity and how aggregates and composition work with ORM in section 8.3.

So far, we've focused on optimistic concurrency control: we expect that concurrent modifications are rare, so we don't prevent concurrent access and detect conflicts late. Sometimes, however, we know that conflicts will happen frequently, and we want to place an exclusive lock on some data. This calls for a pessimistic approach.

11.2.3 *Explicit pessimistic locking*

Let's repeat the procedure demonstrated in the previous "Manual version checking" section, but this time with a pessimistic lock instead of optimistic version checking. We'll again summarize the total price of all items in several categories. This is the same code as shown earlier in listing 11.5, with a different `LockModeType`.

> **Listing 11.6 Locking data pessimistically**

```
Path: /Ch11/transactions/src/test/java/com/manning/javapersistence/ch11
    /concurrency/Locking.java - pessimisticReadWrite()

    EntityManager em = emf.createEntityManager();
    em.getTransaction().begin();

BigDecimal totalPrice = BigDecimal.ZERO;
for (Long categoryId : CATEGORIES) {                           (A)
    List<Item> items =
        em.createQuery("select i from Item i where i.category.id = :catId",
            Item.class)
            .setLockMode(LockModeType.PESSIMISTIC_READ)
            .setHint("javax.persistence.lock.timeout", 5000)
            .setParameter("catId", categoryId)
            .getResultList();                                  (B)
    for (Item item : items)
        totalPrice = totalPrice.add(item.getBuyNowPrice());
    // . . . Another transaction tries to obtain a lock and fails
}                                                              (C)
    em.getTransaction().commit();
    em.close();
    assertEquals(0, totalPrice.compareTo(new BigDecimal("108")));
```

(A) For each `Category`, query all `Item` instances in `PESSIMISTIC_READ` lock mode. Hibernate locks the rows in the database with the SQL query. If another transaction holds a conflicting lock, wait 5 seconds if possible. If the lock can't be obtained, the query throws an exception.

B If the query returns successfully, we know that we hold an exclusive lock on the data, and no other transaction can access it with an exclusive lock or modify it until this transaction commits.

C The locks are released after committing, when the transaction completes.

The JPA specification defines that the PESSIMISTIC_READ lock mode guarantees repeatable reads. JPA also standardizes the PESSIMISTIC_WRITE mode, with additional guarantees: in addition to repeatable reads, the JPA provider must serialize data access, and no phantom reads can occur.

It's up to the JPA provider to implement these requirements. For both modes, Hibernate appends a FOR UPDATE clause to the SQL query when loading data. This places a lock on the rows at the database level. What kind of lock Hibernate uses depends on the LockModeType and the Hibernate database dialect:

- On H2 the query is SELECT * FROM ITEM ... FOR UPDATE. Because H2 supports only one type of exclusive lock, Hibernate generates the same SQL for all pessimistic modes.
- PostgreSQL, on the other hand, supports shared read locks: the PESSIMISTIC_READ mode appends FOR SHARE to the SQL query. PESSIMISTIC_WRITE uses an exclusive write lock with FOR UPDATE.
- On MySQL, PESSIMISTIC_READ translates to LOCK IN SHARE MODE, and PESSIMISTIC_WRITE to FOR UPDATE.

Check your database dialect. The lock is configured with the getReadLockString() and getWriteLockString() methods.

The duration of a pessimistic lock in JPA is a single database transaction. This means we can't use an exclusive lock to block concurrent access for longer than a single database transaction. When the database lock can't be obtained, an exception is thrown.

Compare this with an optimistic approach, where Hibernate throws an exception at commit time, not when you query. With a pessimistic strategy, we know that we can read and write the data safely as soon as the locking query succeeds. With an optimistic approach, we hope for the best and may be surprised later, when we commit.

> **Offline locks**
>
> Pessimistic database locks are held only for a single transaction. Other lock implementations are possible: for example, a lock held in memory, or a so-called *lock table* in the database. A common name for these kinds of locks is *offline locks*.
>
> Locking pessimistically for longer than a single database transaction is usually a performance bottleneck: every data access involves additional lock checks to a globally synchronized lock manager. Optimistic locking, however, is the perfect concurrency control strategy for long-running conversations (as you'll see in the next chapter), and it performs well. Depending on the conflict-resolution strategy—which determines what happens after a conflict is detected—the application's users may be just as happy with optimistic locking as with blocked concurrent access. They may also appreciate the application not locking them out of particular screens while others look at the same data.

We can configure how long the database will wait to obtain the lock and block the query in milliseconds with the `javax.persistence.lock.timeout` hint. As usual with hints, Hibernate might ignore it, depending on the database product. H2, for example, doesn't support lock timeouts for specific queries, only a global lock timeout for the connection (defaulting to 1 second). With some dialects, such as PostgreSQL and Oracle, a lock timeout of `0` appends the `NOWAIT` clause to the SQL string.

We've demonstrated the lock timeout hint applied to a `Query`. We can also set the timeout hint for `find()` operations:

```
Path: /Ch11/transactions/src/test/java/com/manning/javapersistence/ch11
    /concurrency/Locking.java - findLock()

EntityManager em = emf.createEntityManager();
em.getTransaction().begin();

Map<String, Object> hints = new HashMap<>();
hints.put("javax.persistence.lock.timeout", 5000);

Category category =                        ◁──Ⓐ
        em.find(
                Category.class,
                CATEGORY_ID,
                LockModeType.PESSIMISTIC_WRITE,
                Hints
        );

category.setName("New Name");

em.getTransaction().commit();
em.close();
```

Ⓐ Executes `SELECT ... FOR UPDATE WAIT 5000`, if supported by the dialect.

When a lock can't be obtained, Hibernate throws either a `javax.persistence.LockTimeoutException` or a `javax.persistence.PessimisticLockException`. If Hibernate throws a `PessimisticLockException`, the transaction must be rolled back, and the unit of work ends. A timeout exception, on the other hand, isn't fatal for the transaction. Which exception Hibernate throws again depends on the SQL dialect. For example, because H2 doesn't support per-statement lock timeouts, we always get a `PessimisticLockException`.

We can use both the `PESSIMISTIC_READ` and `PESSIMISTIC_WRITE` lock modes even if we haven't enabled entity versioning. They translate to SQL statements with database-level locks.

The special `PESSIMISTIC_FORCE_INCREMENT` mode requires versioned entities. In Hibernate, this mode executes a `FOR UPDATE NOWAIT` lock (or whatever the dialect supports; check its `getForUpdateNowaitString()` implementation). Then, immediately after the query returns, Hibernate increments the version and makes an `UPDATE` for each returned entity instance. This indicates to any concurrent transaction that we have updated these rows, even if we haven't so far modified any data. This mode is rarely useful, except for aggregate locking as discussed in the "Forcing a version increment" section earlier in this chapter.

What about lock modes READ and WRITE?

These are older lock modes from JPA 1.0, and you should no longer use them. `Lock-ModeType.READ` is equivalent to `OPTIMISTIC`, and `LockModeType.WRITE` is equivalent to `OPTIMISTIC_FORCE_INCREMENT`.

If we enable pessimistic locking, Hibernate locks only rows that correspond to entity instance state. In other words, if we lock an `Item` instance, Hibernate will lock its row in the `ITEM` table. If we have a joined inheritance mapping strategy, Hibernate will recognize this and lock the appropriate rows in supertable and subtables. This also applies to any secondary table mappings of an entity. Because Hibernate locks entire rows, any relationship where the foreign key is in that row will also effectively be locked: the `Item#seller` association is locked if the `SELLER_ID` foreign key column is in the `ITEM` table, but the actual `Seller` instance isn't locked! Neither are collections or other associations of the `Item` where the foreign keys are in other tables.

Extending lock scope

JPA 2.0 defines the `PessimisticLockScope.EXTENDED` option. It can be set as a query hint with `javax.persistence.lock.scope`. If enabled, the persistence engine expands the scope of locked data to include any data in collections and association join tables of locked entities.

With exclusive locking in the DBMS, you may experience transaction failures because you run into deadlock situations. Let's look at how you can avoid that.

11.2.4 Avoiding deadlocks

Deadlocks can occur if the DBMS relies on exclusive locks to implement transaction isolation. Consider the following unit of work, updating two `Item` entity instances in a particular order:

```
EntityManager em = emf.createEntityManager();
em.getTransaction().begin();
Item itemOne = em.find(Item.class, ITEM_ONE_ID);
itemOne.setName("First new name");
Item itemTwo = em.find(Item.class, ITEM_TWO_ID);
itemTwo.setName("Second new name");
em.getTransaction().commit();
em.close();
```

Hibernate executes two SQL UPDATE statements when the persistence context is flushed. The first UPDATE locks the row representing Item one, and the second UPDATE locks Item two:

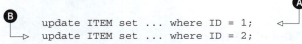

```
update ITEM set ... where ID = 1;
update ITEM set ... where ID = 2;
```

Ⓐ Locks row 1

Ⓑ Attempts to lock row 2

A deadlock may (or may not!) occur if a similar procedure, with the opposite order of Item updates, executes in a concurrent transaction:

```
update ITEM set ... where ID = 2;
update ITEM set ... where ID = 1;
```

Ⓐ Locks row 2

Ⓑ Attempts to lock row 1

With a deadlock, both transactions are blocked and can't move forward, each waiting for a lock to be released. The chance of a deadlock is usually small, but in highly concurrent applications, two Hibernate applications may execute this kind of interleaved update. Note that we may not see deadlocks during testing (unless we write the right kinds of tests). Deadlocks can suddenly appear when the application has to handle a high transaction load in production. Usually the DBMS terminates one of the deadlocked transactions after a timeout period and this transaction fails; the other transaction can then proceed. Alternatively, the DBMS may detect a deadlock situation automatically and immediately abort one of the transactions.

You should try to avoid transaction failures because they're difficult to recover from in application code. One solution is to run the database connection in *serializable* mode when updating a single row will lock the entire table. The concurrent transaction has to wait until the first transaction completes its work. Alternatively, the first transaction can obtain an exclusive lock on all data when you SELECT the data, as demonstrated in the previous section. Then any concurrent transaction also has to wait until these locks are released.

An alternative pragmatic optimization that significantly reduces the probability of deadlocks is to order the UPDATE statements by primary key value: Hibernate should always update the row with primary key 1 before updating row 2, no matter in what order the data was loaded and modified by the application. You can enable this optimization for the entire persistence unit with the hibernate.order_updates configuration property. Hibernate then orders all UPDATE statements it executes in ascending order by the primary key value of the modified entity instances and collection elements detected during flushing. (As mentioned earlier, make sure you fully understand the transactional and locking behavior of your DBMS product. Hibernate inherits most of its transaction guarantees from the DBMS; for example, your MVCC database product may avoid read locks but probably depends on exclusive locks for writer isolation, and you may see deadlocks.)

We didn't have an opportunity to mention the `EntityManager#lock()` method. It accepts an already-loaded persistent entity instance and a lock mode. It performs the same locking you've seen with `find()` and a `Query`, except that it doesn't load the instance. Additionally, if a versioned entity is being locked pessimistically, the `lock()` method performs an immediate version check on the database and potentially throws an `OptimisticLockException`. If the database representation is no longer present, Hibernate throws an `EntityNotFoundException`. Finally, the `EntityManager#refresh()` method also accepts a lock mode, with the same semantics.

We've now covered concurrency control at the lowest level—the database—and the optimistic and pessimistic locking features of JPA. We still have one more aspect of concurrency to examine: accessing data outside of a transaction.

11.3 *Non-transactional data access*

A JDBC `Connection` is by default in *auto-commit* mode. This mode is useful for executing ad hoc SQL.

Imagine that you connect to a database with an SQL console, and you run a few queries, and maybe even update and delete rows. This interactive data access is ad hoc; most of the time you don't have a plan or a sequence of statements that you consider a unit of work. The default auto-commit mode on the database connection is perfect for this kind of data access—after all, you don't want to type `begin transaction` and `end transaction` for every SQL statement you write and execute.

In auto-commit mode, a (short) database transaction begins and ends for each SQL statement you send to the database. You're effectively working in the non-transactional mode because there are no atomicity or isolation guarantees for your session with the SQL console. (The only guarantee is that a single SQL statement is atomic.)

An application, by definition, always executes a planned sequence of statements. It seems reasonable that you can therefore always create transaction boundaries to group the statements into units that are atomic and isolated from each other. In JPA, however, special behavior is associated with auto-commit mode, and you may need it to implement long-running conversations. You can access the database in auto-commit mode and read data.

11.3.1 *Reading data in auto-commit mode*

Consider the following example, which loads an `Item` instance, changes its `name`, and then rolls back that change by refreshing.

No transaction is active when we create the `EntityManager`. The persistence context will be in a special unsynchronized mode; Hibernate won't flush automatically. You can access the database to read data, and such an operation executes a `SELECT`, which is sent to the database in auto-commit mode.

Usually Hibernate flushes the persistence context when you execute a `Query`. If the context is unsynchronized, flushing doesn't occur and the query returns the old, original database value. Queries with scalar results aren't repeatable: you see whatever values are in the database and given to Hibernate in the `ResultSet`. This also isn't a repeatable read if you're in synchronized mode.

Retrieving a managed entity instance involves a lookup during JDBC result-set marshaling in the current persistence context. The already-loaded instance with the changed name is returned from the persistence context; values from the database are ignored. This is a repeatable read of an entity instance, even without a system transaction.

If you try to flush the persistence context manually to store a new `Item#name`, Hibernate throws a `javax.persistence.TransactionRequiredException`. You can't execute an `UPDATE` in unsynchronized mode, because you wouldn't be able to roll back the change.

You can roll back the change you made with the `refresh()` method. It loads the current `Item` state from the database and overwrites the change you made in memory.

Listing 11.7   Reading data in auto-commit mode

```
Path: Ch11/transactions4/src/test/java/com/manning/javapersistence/ch11
➥ /concurrency/NonTransactional.java
                                                                    A
EntityManager em = emf.createEntityManager();      ⟵
Item item = em.find(Item.class, ITEM_ID);
item.setName("New Name");
assertEquals(                          ⟵ C
    "Original Name",
    em.createQuery("select i.name from Item i where i.id = :id",
    String.class)
      .setParameter("id", ITEM_ID).getSingleResult()
);
assertEquals(              ⟵ D
    "New Name",
    em.createQuery("select i from Item i where i.id = :id". Item.class)
              .setParameter("id", ITEM_ID).getSingleResult().getName()
);                                      F
// em.flush();
em.refresh(item);                          ⟵
assertEquals("Original Name", item.getName());
em.close();
```

A No transaction is active when creating the `EntityManager`.

B Access the database to read data.

C Because the context is unsynchronized, flushing doesn't occur, and the query returns the old, original database value.

D The already-loaded `Item` instance with the changed name is returned from the persistence context; values from the database are ignored.

E You cannot execute an UPDATE in unsynchronized mode, because you wouldn't be able to roll back the change.

F Roll back the change you made with the refresh() method.

With an unsynchronized persistence context, you read data in auto-commit mode with find(), getReference(), refresh(), or queries. You can load data on demand as well: proxies are initialized if you access them, and collections are loaded if you start iterating through their elements. But if you try to flush the persistence context or lock data with anything but LockModeType.NONE, a TransactionRequiredException will occur.

So far, the auto-commit mode doesn't seem very useful. Indeed, many developers often rely on auto-commit for the wrong reasons:

- Many small per-statement database transactions (that's what auto-commit means) won't improve the performance of the application.
- You won't improve the scalability of the application. You might think that a longer-running database transaction, instead of many small transactions for every SQL statement, may hold database locks for a longer time, but this is a minor concern, because Hibernate writes to the database as late as possible within a transaction (flush at commit), so the database already holds write locks for a short time.
- Auto-commit provides weaker isolation guarantees if the application modifies data concurrently. Repeatable reads based on read locks are impossible with auto-commit mode. (The persistence context cache helps here, naturally.)
- If your DBMS has MVCC (for example, Oracle or PostgreSQL), you'll likely want to use its capability for *snapshot isolation* to avoid unrepeatable and phantom reads. Each transaction gets its own snapshot of the data; you only see a (database-internal) version of the data as it was before your transaction started. With auto-commit mode, snapshot isolation makes no sense, because there is no transaction scope.
- Your code will be more difficult to understand if you use auto-commit. Any reader of your code will have to pay special attention to whether a persistence context is joined with a transaction, or if it's in unsynchronized mode. If you always group operations within a system transaction, even if you only read data, everyone can follow this simple rule, and the likelihood of difficult-to-find concurrency problems is reduced.

So what are the benefits of an unsynchronized persistence context? If flushing doesn't happen automatically, you can prepare and *queue* modifications outside of a transaction.

11.3.2   Queuing modifications

The following example stores a new Item instance with an unsynchronized EntityManager.

You can call persist() to save a transient entity instance with an unsynchronized persistence context. Hibernate only fetches a new identifier value, typically by calling a database sequence, and assigns it to the instance. The instance will be in a persistent state in the context, but the SQL INSERT hasn't happened. Note that this is only possible with *pre-insert* identifier generators; see section 5.2.5.

When you're ready to store the changes, you must join the persistence context with a transaction. Synchronization and flushing occur as usual when the transaction commits. Hibernate writes all queued operations to the database.

Path: Ch11/transactions4/src/test/java/com/manning/javapersistence/ch11
➡ /concurrency/NonTransactional.java

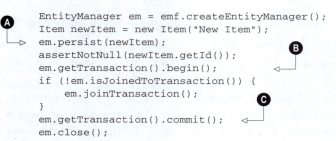

```
EntityManager em = emf.createEntityManager();
Item newItem = new Item("New Item");
em.persist(newItem);
assertNotNull(newItem.getId());
em.getTransaction().begin();
if (!em.isJoinedToTransaction()) {
    em.joinTransaction();
}
em.getTransaction().commit();
em.close();
```

A Call persist() to save a transient entity instance with an unsynchronized persistence context.

B Join the persistence context with a transaction.

C Synchronization and flushing occur when the transaction commits.

Merged changes of a detached entity instance can also be queued:

Path: Ch11/transactions4/src/test/java/com/manning/javapersistence/ch11
➡ /concurrency/NonTransactional.java

```
detachedItem.setName("New Name");
EntityManager em = emf.createEntityManager();
Item mergedItem = em.merge(detachedItem);
em.getTransaction().begin();
em.joinTransaction();
em.getTransaction().commit();
em.close();
```

A Hibernate executes a SELECT in auto-commit mode when you merge().

B Hibernate defers the UPDATE until a joined transaction commits.

Queuing also works for the removal of entity instances and DELETE operations:

Path: Ch11/transactions4/src/test/java/com/manning/javapersistence/ch11
➡ /concurrency/NonTransactional.java

```
EntityManager em = emf.createEntityManager();
Item item = em.find(Item.class, ITEM_ID);
em.remove(item);
em.getTransaction().begin();
```

```
em.joinTransaction();
em.getTransaction().commit();
em.close();
```

An unsynchronized persistence context, therefore, allows you to decouple persistence operations from transactions. The ability to queue data modifications, independent of transactions (and client/server requests), is a major feature of the persistence context.

Hibernate's MANUAL flush mode

Hibernate offers a `Session#setFlushMode()` method, with the additional `FlushMode.MANUAL`. It's a much more convenient switch that disables any automatic flushing of the persistence context, even when a joined transaction commits. With this mode, you have to call `flush()` explicitly to synchronize with the database. In JPA, the idea was that a "transaction commit should always write any outstanding changes," so reading was separated from writing with the *unsynchronized* mode. If you don't agree with this or don't want auto-committed statements, enable manual flushing with the `Session` API. You can then have regular transaction boundaries for all units of work, with repeatable reads and even snapshot isolation from your MVCC database, but still queue changes in the persistence context for later execution and manually `flush()` before your transaction commits.

11.4 *Managing transactions with Spring and Spring Data*

We'll now move on and demonstrate how to implement transactions with Spring and Spring Data. The transactional model used by Spring is applicable to different APIs, such as Hibernate, JPA, and Spring Data JPA. The management of the transactions can be either programmatic (as we have already demonstrated) or declarative, with the help of annotations (which is what we'll mostly use for this section of the chapter).

The key Spring transaction abstraction is defined by the `org.springframework.transaction.PlatformTransactionManager` interface.

```
public interface PlatformTransactionManager extends TransactionManager {
    TransactionStatus getTransaction(
    ➥ @Nullable TransactionDefinition definition)
                                    throws TransactionException;
    void commit(TransactionStatus status) throws TransactionException;
    void rollback(TransactionStatus status) throws TransactionException;
}
```

Typically, this interface is not used directly. You will either mark transactions declaratively, through annotations, or you may eventually use `TransactionTemplate` for the programmatic transaction definition.

Spring uses the previously discussed ANSI isolation levels. For a refresher, take a look back at section 11.2.1 and particularly table 11.1, which summarizes the isolation levels and the problems that they address.

11.4.1 *Transaction propagation*

Spring deals with the transaction propagation problem. In brief, if method-A is transactional and it calls method-B, how will the latter behave, from the transactional point of view? Take a look at figure 11.5:

1 bean-1 contains method-A, which is transactional, executed in transaction TX1.

2 method-A calls bean-2.method-B(), which is also transactional.

In which transaction will be method-B executed?

Spring defines the list of possible propagations through the org.springframework.transaction .annotation.Propagation enum:

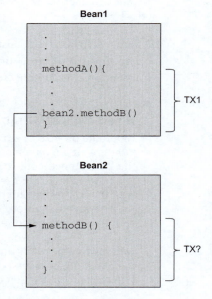

Figure 11.5   The transaction propagation concept

- REQUIRED—If a transaction is in progress, the execution will continue within that transaction. Otherwise, a new transaction will be created. REQUIRED is the default propagation for transactions in Spring.

- SUPPORTS—If a transaction is in progress, the execution will continue within that transaction. Otherwise, no transaction will be created.

- MANDATORY—If a transaction is in progress, the execution will continue within that transaction. Otherwise, a TransactionRequiredException exception will be thrown.

- REQUIRES_NEW—If a transaction is in progress, it will be suspended and a new transaction will be started. Otherwise, a new transaction will be created anyway.

- NOT_SUPPORTED—If a transaction is in progress, it will be suspended and a non-transactional execution will continue. Otherwise, the execution will simply continue.

- NEVER—If a transaction is in progress, an IllegalTransactionStateException will be thrown. Otherwise, the execution will simply continue.

- NESTED—If a transaction is in progress, a subtransaction of this one will be created, and at the same time a savepoint will be created. If the subtransaction fails, the execution will roll back to this savepoint. If no transaction was originally in progress, a new transaction will be created.

Table 11.2 summarizes the possible transaction propagations in Spring (T1 and T2 are transactions 1 and 2).

Table 11.2   Transaction propagation in Spring

Transaction propagation	Transaction in the caller method	Transaction in the called method
REQUIRED	No	T1
T1	T1	SUPPORTS
No	No	T1
T1	MANDATORY	No
Exception	T1	T1
REQUIRES_NEW	No	T1
T1	T2	NOT_SUPPORTED
No	No	T1
No	NEVER	No
No	T1	Exception
NESTED	No	T1
T1	T2 with savepoint	

11.4.2 Transaction rollback

Spring transactions define the default rollback rules: a transaction will be rolled back for RuntimeException. This behavior can be overwritten and we can specify which exceptions automatically roll back the transaction and which will not. This is done with the help of the @Transactional annotation properties rollbackFor, rollback-ForClassName, noRollbackFor, noRollbackForClassName. The behavior determined by these properties is summarized in table 11.3.

Table 11.3   Transaction rollback rules

Property	Type	Behavior
rollbackFor	Array of Class objects extending Throwable	Defines exception classes that must cause rollback
rollbackForClassName	Array of class names extending Throwable	Defines exception class names that must cause rollback
noRollbackFor	Array of Class objects extending Throwable	Defines exception classes that must not cause rollback
noRollbackForClassName	Array of class names extending Throwable	Defines exception class names that must not cause rollback

11.4.3 *Transaction properties*

The @Transactional annotation defines the properties in table 11.4. We'll deal here with the already examined isolation and propagation and with other properties. All the meta-information will be transposed at the level of how the transactional operation is executed.

Table 11.4 @Transactional annotation properties

Property	Type	Behavior
isolation	Isolation enum	Declares the isolation levels, following the ANSI standard.
propagation	Propagation enum	Propagation settings following the values from table 11.2.
timeout	int (seconds)	Timeout after which the transaction will automatically roll back.
readOnly	boolean	Declares if the transaction is read-only or read-write. Read-only transactions allow optimizations that can make them faster.

The @Transactional annotation can be applied to interfaces, to methods in interfaces, to classes, or to methods in classes. Once applied to an interface or to a class, the annotation is taken over by all methods from that class or from that interface. You can change the behavior by annotating particular methods in a different way. Also, once it's applied to an interface or to a method in an interface, the annotation is taken over by the classes implementing that interface or by the corresponding methods from the classes implementing that interface. The behavior can be overwritten. Consequently, for fine-grained behavior, it is advisable to apply the @Transactional annotation to methods from classes.

11.4.4 *Programmatic transaction definition*

Declarative transaction management is generally the way to go when using Spring in an application. It requires less code to write, and the behavior is determined through the meta-information provided by the annotations. However, programmatic transaction management is still possible, using the TransactionTemplate class.

Once a TransactionTemplate object is created, the behavior of the transaction can be defined programmatically, as follows:

```
TransactionTemplate transactionTemplate;
// . . .
transactionTemplate.setIsolationLevel(
        TransactionDefinition.ISOLATION_REPEATABLE_READ);
transactionTemplate.setPropagationBehavior(
        TransactionDefinition.PROPAGATION_REQUIRES_NEW);
transactionTemplate.setTimeout(5);
transactionTemplate.setReadOnly(false);
```

Once defined, a TransactionTemplate object supports the callback approach through the execute method, which receives a TransactionCallback as an argument, as in the

following code. The operations to be executed in the transaction are defined in the
doInTransaction method.

```
transactionTemplate.execute(new TransactionCallback() {
    public Object doInTransaction(TransactionStatus status) {
      //operations to be executed in transaction
    }
});
```

As TransactionCallback is a functional interface (it even bears the @Functional-
Interface annotation), the preceding snippet could be shortened as follows:

```
transactionTemplate.execute(status -> {
  // operations to be executed in transaction
});
```

11.4.5 *Transactional development with Spring and Spring Data*

We have been working on the CaveatEmptor application, and now we're going to
implement a feature that logs the results of our actions when we work with items.
We'll start the implementation using Spring Data JPA, and we'll first create the Item-
RepositoryCustom interface and its methods, as shown in listing 11.8. Such an interface is known as a *fragment interface,* and its purpose is to extend a repository with
custom functionality, which will be provided by a later implementation.

> **Listing 11.8   The ItemRepositoryCustom interface**

```
Path: Ch11/transactions5-springdata/src/main/java/com/manning
 /javapersistence/ch11/repositories/ItemRepositoryCustom.java

public interface ItemRepositoryCustom {
    void addItem(String name, LocalDate creationDate);
    void checkNameDuplicate(String name);
    void addLogs();
    void showLogs();
    void addItemNoRollback(String name, LocalDate creationDate);
}
```

Next, we'll create an ItemRepository interface, extending both JpaRepository and
the previously declared ItemRepositoryCustom interface. Additionally, we'll declare
the findByName method, following the Spring Data JPA naming conventions.

> **Listing 11.9   The ItemRepository interface**

```
Path: Ch11/transactions5-springdata/src/main/java/com/manning
 /javapersistence/ch11/repositories/ItemRepository.java

public interface ItemRepository extends JpaRepository<Item, Long>,
                ItemRepositoryCustom {
    Optional<Item> findByName(String name);
}
```

We'll then create the `LogRepositoryCustom` interface and its methods, as shown in listing 11.10. Again, this is a fragment interface, and its purpose is to extend a repository with custom functionality that will be provided by a later implementation.

Listing 11.10   The `LogRepositoryCustom` interface

Path: Ch11/transactions5-springdata/src/main/java/com/manning
➥ /javapersistence/ch11/repositories/LogRepositoryCustom.java

```
public interface LogRepositoryCustom {
    void log(String message);
    void showLogs();
    void addSeparateLogsNotSupported();
    void addSeparateLogsSupports();
}
```

We'll now create the `LogRepository` interface, extending both `JpaRepository` and the previously declared `LogRepositoryCustom` interface.

Listing 11.11   The `LogRepository` interface

Path: Ch11/transactions5-springdata/src/main/java/com/manning
➥ /javapersistence/ch11/repositories/LogRepository.java

```
public interface LogRepository extends JpaRepository<Log, Integer>,
                LogRepositoryCustom {
}
```

We'll provide an implementation class for `ItemRepository` next. The key part of this class name is the `Impl` ending. It is not connected to Spring Data and it only implements `ItemRepositoryCustom`. When injecting an `ItemRepository` bean, Spring Data will have to create a proxy class; it will detect that `ItemRepository` implements `ItemRepositoryCustom` and will look up a class called `ItemRepositoryImpl` to act as a custom repository implementation. Consequently, the methods of the injected `ItemRepository` bean will have the same behavior as the methods of the `ItemRepositoryImpl` class.

Listing 11.12   The `ItemRepositoryImpl` class

Path: Ch11/transactions5-springdata/src/main/java/com/manning
➥ /javapersistence/ch11/repositories/ItemRepositoryImpl.java

```
public class ItemRepositoryImpl implements ItemRepositoryCustom {

    @Autowired
    private ItemRepository itemRepository;

    @Autowired
    private LogRepository logRepository;
```

A

```
@Override
@Transactional(propagation = Propagation.MANDATORY)      ⬅ Ⓑ
public void checkNameDuplicate(String name) {
    if (itemRepository.findAll().stream().map(item ->
        item.getName()).filter(n -> n.equals(name)).count() > 0) {     Ⓒ
        throw new DuplicateItemNameException("Item with name " + name +
            " already exists");
    }
}


                                        Ⓓ
@Override
@Transactional                  ⬅
public void addItem(String name, LocalDate creationDate) {
    logRepository.log("adding item with name " + name);
    checkNameDuplicate(name);
    itemRepository.save(new Item(name, creationDate));
}


                                                             Ⓔ
@Override
@Transactional(noRollbackFor = DuplicateItemNameException.class)    ⬅
public void addItemNoRollback(String name, LocalDate creationDate) {
    logRepository.save(new Log(
        "adding log in method with no rollback for item " + name));
    checkNameDuplicate(name);
    itemRepository.save(new Item(name, creationDate));
}


                              Ⓓ
@Override
@Transactional          ⬅
public void addLogs() {
    logRepository.addSeparateLogsNotSupported();
}


                              Ⓓ
@Override
@Transactional          ⬅
public void showLogs() {
    logRepository.showLogs();
}

}
```

Ⓐ Autowiring an `ItemRepository` and a `LogRepository` bean.

Ⓑ `MANDATORY` propagation: Spring Data will check if a transaction is already in progress and will continue with it. Otherwise, an exception will be thrown.

Ⓒ Throw a `DuplicateItemNameException` if an `Item` with the given name already exists.

Ⓓ Default propagation is `REQUIRED`.

Ⓔ No rollback of the transaction in the case of a `DuplicateItemNameException`.

Next we'll provide an implementation class for `LogRepository`. As was the case for `Item-RepositoryImpl`, the key part of this class name is the `Impl` ending. It only implements

LogRepositoryCustom. When we inject a LogRepository bean, Spring Data will detect that LogRepository implements LogRepositoryCustom and will look up a class called LogRepositoryImpl to act as a custom repository implementation. Consequently, the methods of the injected LogRepository bean will have the same behavior as the methods of the LogRepositoryImpl class.

Listing 11.13   The `LogRepositoryImpl` class

Path: Ch11/transactions5-springdata/src/main/java/com/manning
⟹ /javapersistence/ch11/repositories/LogRepositoryImpl.java

```
public class LogRepositoryImpl implements LogRepositoryCustom {
    @Autowired                                                              A
    private LogRepository logRepository;

B
    @Override
    @Transactional(propagation = Propagation.REQUIRES_NEW)
    public void log(String message) {
        logRepository.save(new Log(message));                 C
    }
                                                                            D
    @Override
    @Transactional(propagation = Propagation.NOT_SUPPORTED)
    public void addSeparateLogsNotSupported() {
        logRepository.save(new Log("check from not supported 1"));
        if (true) throw new RuntimeException();
        logRepository.save(new Log("check from not supported 2"));
    }
                                                                  E
    @Override
    @Transactional(propagation = Propagation.SUPPORTS)
    public void addSeparateLogsSupports() {
        logRepository.save(new Log("check from supports 1"));
        if (true) throw new RuntimeException();
        logRepository.save(new Log("check from supports 2"));
    }
                                                                  F
    @Override
    @Transactional(propagation = Propagation.NEVER)
    public void showLogs() {
        System.out.println("Current log:");
        logRepository.findAll().forEach(System.out::println);
    }

}
```

Ⓐ Autowiring a LogRepository bean.

Ⓑ REQUIRES_NEW propagation. Spring Data will execute the logging in a separate transaction, independent of the eventual transaction of the method that called log.

Ⓒ The log method will save a message to the repository.

D NOT_SUPPORTED propagation. If a transaction is in progress, it will be suspended and a non-transactional execution will continue. Otherwise, the execution will simply continue.

E SUPPORTS propagation. If a transaction is in progress, the execution will continue within that transaction. Otherwise, no transaction will be created.

F NEVER propagation. If a transaction is in progress, an IllegalTransactionState-Exception will be thrown. Otherwise, the execution will simply continue.

We'll now write a series of tests to verify the behavior of the transactional methods we have just written.

Listing 11.14   The `TransactionPropagationTest` class

Path: Ch11/transactions5-springdata/src/test/java/com/manning
➥ /javapersistence/ch11/concurrency/TransactionPropagationTest.java

```
@ExtendWith(SpringExtension.class)
@ContextConfiguration(classes = {SpringDataConfiguration.class})
public class TransactionPropagationTest {

    @Autowired
    private ItemRepository itemRepository;                          A

    @Autowired
    private LogRepository logRepository;

    @BeforeEach
    public void clean() {                                           B
        itemRepository.deleteAll();
        logRepository.deleteAll();
    }

    @Test
    public void notSupported() {
        assertAll(
                () -> assertThrows(RuntimeException.class, () ->    C
                                itemRepository.addLogs()),
                () -> assertEquals(1, logRepository.findAll().size()),   D
                () -> assertEquals("check from not supported 1",
                        logRepository.findAll().get(0).getMessage())
        );
        logRepository.showLogs();    ←───┐
    }                                    E

    @Test
    public void supports() {
        assertAll(
                () -> assertThrows(RuntimeException.class, () ->    F
                        logRepository.addSeparateLogsSupports()),
                () -> assertEquals(1, logRepository.findAll().size()),   G
                () -> assertEquals("check from supports 1",
                        logRepository.findAll().get(0).getMessage())
```

```
    );
    logRepository.showLogs();    ◁━━━━┓
}                                      Ⓗ

@Test
public void mandatory() {
    IllegalTransactionStateException ex =
        assertThrows(IllegalTransactionStateException.class,
            () -> itemRepository.checkNameDuplicate("Item1"));       Ⓘ
    assertEquals("No existing transaction found for transaction marked
      with propagation 'mandatory'", ex.getMessage());
}

@Test
public void never() {
    itemRepository.addItem("Item1", LocalDate.of(2022, 5, 1));       Ⓙ
    logRepository.showLogs();

    IllegalTransactionStateException ex =
        assertThrows(IllegalTransactionStateException.class,
                    () -> itemRepository.showLogs());                Ⓚ
    assertEquals(
    "Existing transaction found for transaction marked with propagation
     'never'", ex.getMessage());
}

@Test
public void requiresNew() {
    itemRepository.addItem("Item1", LocalDate.of(2022, 5, 1));
    itemRepository.addItem("Item2", LocalDate.of(2022, 3, 1));
    itemRepository.addItem("Item3", LocalDate.of(2022, 1, 1));

    DuplicateItemNameException ex =
        assertThrows(DuplicateItemNameException.class, () ->           Ⓛ
          itemRepository.addItem("Item2", LocalDate.of(2016, 3, 1)));
    assertAll(
            () -> assertEquals("Item with name Item2 already exists",  Ⓜ
                            ex.getMessage()),
            () -> assertEquals(4, logRepository.findAll().size()),     Ⓝ
            () -> assertEquals(3, itemRepository.findAll().size())
    );

    System.out.println("Logs: ");
    logRepository.findAll().forEach(System.out::println);

    System.out.println("List of added items: ");
    itemRepository.findAll().forEach(System.out::println);
}

@Test
public void noRollback() {
    itemRepository.addItemNoRollback("Item1",
    ➥ LocalDate.of(2022, 5, 1));
    itemRepository.addItemNoRollback("Item2",
    ➥ LocalDate.of(2022, 3, 1));
```

```
itemRepository.addItemNoRollback("Item3",
 ⇒  LocalDate.of(2022, 1, 1));

DuplicateItemNameException ex =
    assertThrows(DuplicateItemNameException.class,
       () -> itemRepository.addItem("Item2",
            LocalDate.of(2016, 3, 1)));
assertAll(
    () -> assertEquals("Item with name Item2 already exists",
                       ex.getMessage()),
    () -> assertEquals(4, logRepository.findAll().size()),
    () -> assertEquals(3, itemRepository.findAll().size())
);

System.out.println("Logs: ");
logRepository.findAll().forEach(System.out::println);

System.out.println("List of added items: ");
itemRepository.findAll().forEach(System.out::println);
   }
}
```

A Autowiring an `ItemRepository` and a `LogRepository` bean.

B Before the execution of each test, all `Item` entities and all `Log` entities are removed from the repositories.

C The `addLogs` method starts a transaction, but it calls the `addSeparateLogsNot-Supported` method, which will suspend the started transaction before explicitly throwing an exception.

D Before an exception was thrown, the `logRepository` was able to save one message.

E The `showLog` method will display one message in a non-transactional way.

F The `addSeparateLogsSupports` method will explicitly throw an exception.

G Before an exception was thrown, the `logRepository` was able to save one message.

H The `showLog` method will display one message in a non-transactional way.

I The `checkNameDuplicate` method can be executed only in a transaction, so an `IllegalTransactionStateException` will be thrown when calling it without a transaction. We also check the message from the exception.

J After adding an `Item` to the repository, it is safe to call the `showLogs` method from `LogRepository` without a transaction.

K However, we cannot call the `showLogs` method from `LogRepository` within a transaction, as the calling method `showLogs` from `ItemRepository` is transactional.

L Trying to insert a duplicate `Item` in the repository will throw a `DuplicateItemNameException`.

M However, a log message is persisted in the logs even after exception, because it was added in a separate transaction.

N The repository will contain 4 `Log` messages (one for each attempt to insert an `Item`, successful or unsuccessful), but only 3 `Items` (the duplicate `Item` was rejected).

O Trying to insert a duplicate `Item` in the repository will throw a `DuplicateItem-NameException`.

P However, a log message is persisted in the logs even after the exception, because the transaction was not rolled back. The `addItemNoRollback` method from `Item-Repository` does not roll back for `DuplicateItemNameException`.

Q The repository will contain 4 `Log` messages (one for each attempt to insert an `Item`, successful or unsuccessful), but only 3 `Items` (the duplicate `Item` was rejected).

Summary

- Hibernate relies on a database's concurrency-control mechanism but provides better isolation guarantees in a transaction, thanks to automatic versioning and the persistence context cache.
- Transaction boundaries can be set programmatically, and you can handle exceptions.
- You can use optimistic concurrency control and explicit pessimistic locking.
- You can work with auto-commit mode and an unsynchronized persistence context outside of a transaction.
- You can work with transactions with Spring and Spring Data, defining and configuring transactions using various properties.

Fetch plans, strategies, and profiles

This chapter covers

- Working with lazy and eager loading
- Applying fetch plans, strategies, and profiles
- Optimizing SQL execution

In this chapter, we'll explore Hibernate's solution for the fundamental ORM problem of navigation, as introduced in section 1.2.5: the difference in how you access data in Java code and within a relational database. We'll demonstrate how to retrieve data from the database and how to optimize this loading.

Hibernate provides the following ways to get data out of the database and into memory:

- We can retrieve an entity instance by identifier. This is the most convenient method when the unique identifier value of an entity instance is known, such as `entityManager.find(Item.class, 123)`.
- We can navigate the entity graph, starting from an already-loaded entity instance, by accessing the associated instances through property accessor methods such as `someItem.getSeller().getAddress().getCity()`, and so

on. Elements of mapped collections are also loaded on demand when we start iterating through a collection. Hibernate automatically loads nodes of the graph if the persistence context is still open. What data is loaded when we call accessors and iterate through collections, and how it's loaded, is the focus of this chapter.

- We can use the Jakarta Persistence Query Language (JPQL), a full object-oriented query language based on strings such as `select i from Item i where i.id = ?`.

- The `CriteriaQuery` interface provides a type-safe and object-oriented way to perform queries without string manipulation.

- We can write native SQL queries, call stored procedures, and let Hibernate take care of mapping the JDBC result sets to instances of the domain model classes.

In our JPA applications, we'll use a combination of these techniques. By now you should be familiar with the basic Jakarta Persistence API for retrieving by identifier. We'll keep our JPQL and `CriteriaQuery` examples as simple as possible, and you won't need the SQL query-mapping features.

Major new features in JPA 2

We can manually check the initialization state of an entity or an entity property with the new `PersistenceUtil` static helper class. We can also create standardized declarative fetch plans with the new `EntityGraph` API.

This chapter analyzes what happens behind the scenes when we navigate the graph of the domain model and Hibernate retrieves data on demand. In all the examples, we'll interpret the SQL executed by Hibernate in a comment right immediately after the operation that triggered the SQL execution.

What Hibernate loads depends on the *fetch plan*: we define the sub-graph of the network of objects that should be loaded. Then we pick the right *fetch strategy*, defining *how* the data should be loaded. We can store the selection of plan and strategy as a *fetch profile* and reuse it.

Defining fetch plans and what data should be loaded by Hibernate relies on two fundamental techniques: *lazy* and *eager* loading of nodes in the network of objects.

12.1 Lazy and eager loading

At some point we must decide what data should be loaded into memory from the database. When we execute `entityManager.find(Item.class, 123)`, what is available in memory and loaded into the persistence context? What happens if we use `EntityManager#getReference()` instead?

In the domain-model mapping, we define the global *default fetch plan*, with the `FetchType.LAZY` and `FetchType.EAGER` options on associations and collections. This plan is the default setting for all operations involving the persistent domain model classes. It's always active when we load an entity instance by identifier and when we navigate the entity graph by following associations and iterating through persistent collections.

Our recommended strategy is a *lazy* default fetch plan for all entities and collections. If we map all of the associations and collections with `FetchType.LAZY`, Hibernate will only load the data we're accessing. As we navigate the graph of the domain model instances, Hibernate will load data on demand, bit by bit. We can then override this behavior on a per-case basis when necessary.

To implement lazy loading, Hibernate relies on runtime-generated entity placeholders called *proxies* and on *smart wrappers* for collections.

12.1.1 Understanding entity proxies

Consider the `getReference()` method of the `EntityManager` API. In section 10.2.4, we took a first look at this operation and at how it may return a proxy. Let's further explore this important feature and find out how proxies work.

> **NOTE** To execute the examples from the source code, you'll first need to run the Ch12.sql script.

The following code doesn't execute any SQL against the database. All Hibernate does is create an `Item` proxy: it looks (and smells) like the real thing, but it's only a placeholder:

Path: Ch12/proxy/src/test/java/com/manning/javapersistence/ch12/proxy
➥ /LazyProxyCollections.java

```
Item item = em.getReference(Item.class, ITEM_ID);   ⟵Ⓐ
assertEquals(ITEM_ID, item.getId());
```

Ⓐ There is no database hitting, meaning there is no `SELECT`.

Ⓑ Calling the identifier getter (no field access!) doesn't trigger initialization.

In the persistence context, in memory, we now have this proxy available in persistent state, as shown in figure 12.1.

The proxy is an instance of a runtime-generated subclass of `Item`, carrying the identifier value of the entity instance it represents. This is why Hibernate (in line with JPA) requires that entity classes have at least a public or protected no-argument constructor (the class may have other constructors too). The entity class and its methods must not be final; otherwise, Hibernate can't produce a proxy. Note that the JPA specification doesn't mention proxies; it's up to the JPA provider how lazy loading is implemented.

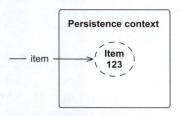

Figure 12.1 The persistence context, under the control of Hibernate, contains an `Item` proxy.

If we call any method on the proxy that isn't the "identifier getter," we'll trigger initialization of the proxy and hit the database. If we call `item.getName()`, the SQL

SELECT to load the Item will be executed. The previous example called item.getId() without triggering initialization because getId() *is* the identifier getter method in the given mapping; the getId() method was annotated with @Id. If @Id was on a field, then calling getId(), just like calling any other method, would initialize the proxy. (Remember that we usually prefer mappings and access on fields, because this allows more freedom when designing accessor methods; see section 3.2.3. It's up to you whether calling getId() without initializing a proxy is more important.)

With proxies, be careful how you compare classes. Because Hibernate generates the proxy class, it has a funny-looking name, and it is *not* equal to Item.class:

Path: Ch12/proxy/src/test/java/com/manning/javapersistence/ch12/proxy
➥ /LazyProxyCollections.java

```
                                                           A
assertNotEquals(Item.class, item.getClass());  ⬅
assertEquals(
    Item.class,
    HibernateProxyHelper.getClassWithoutInitializingProxy(item)
);
```

A The class is runtime generated and named something like Item$Hibernate-Proxy$BLsrPly8.

If we really must get the actual type represented by a proxy, we can use the HibernateProxyHelper.

JPA provides PersistenceUtil, which we can use to check the initialization state of an entity or any of its attributes:

Path: Ch12/proxy/src/test/java/com/manning/javapersistence/ch12/proxy
➥ /LazyProxyCollections.java

```
PersistenceUtil persistenceUtil = Persistence.getPersistenceUtil();
assertFalse(persistenceUtil.isLoaded(item));
assertFalse(persistenceUtil.isLoaded(item, "seller"));
assertFalse(Hibernate.isInitialized(item));           A
// assertFalse(Hibernate.isInitialized(item.getSeller()));  ⬅
```

A Executing this line of code would effectively trigger the initialization of the item.

The isLoaded() method also accepts the name of a property of the given entity (proxy) instance, checking its initialization state. Hibernate offers an alternative API with Hibernate.isInitialized(). If we call item.getSeller(), though, the item proxy is initialized first.

Hibernate also offers a utility method for quick-and-dirty initialization of proxies:

Path: Ch12/proxy/src/test/java/com/manning/javapersistence/ch12/proxy
➥ /LazyProxyCollections.java

```
                                        A
Hibernate.initialize(item);     ⬅
// select * from ITEM where ID = ?
```

```
assertFalse(Hibernate.isInitialized(item.getSeller()));        ← Ⓑ
Hibernate.initialize(item.getSeller());  ←
// select * from USERS where ID = ?       Ⓒ
```

Ⓐ The first call hits the database and loads the `Item` data, populating the proxy with the item's name, price, and so on.

Ⓑ Make sure the `@ManyToOne` default of `EAGER` has been overridden with `LAZY`. That is why the `seller` of the `item` is not yet initialized.

Ⓒ By initializing the `seller` of the `item`, we hit the database and load the `User` data.

The `seller` of the `Item` is a `@ManyToOne` association mapped with `FetchType.LAZY`, so Hibernate creates a `User` proxy when the `Item` is loaded. We can check the `seller` proxy state and load it manually, just like with the `Item`. Remember that the JPA default for `@ManyToOne` is `FetchType.EAGER`! We usually want to override this to get a lazy default fetch plan, as we demonstrated in section 8.3.1 and again here:

Path: Ch12/proxy/src/main/java/com/manning/javapersistence/ch12/proxy
➡ /Item.java

```
@Entity
public class Item {
    @ManyToOne(fetch = FetchType.LAZY)
    public User getSeller() {
        return seller;
    }
    //  . . .
}
```

With such a lazy fetch plan, we might run into a `LazyInitializationException`. Consider the following code:

Path: Ch12/proxy/src/test/java/com/manning/javapersistence/ch12/proxy
➡ /LazyProxyCollections.java

```
                                                             Ⓐ
Item item = em.find(Item.class, ITEM_ID);       ←
// select * from ITEM where ID = ?
em.detach(item);                ← Ⓑ
em.detach(item.getSeller());
// em.close();                                                        Ⓒ
PersistenceUtil persistenceUtil = Persistence.getPersistenceUtil();  ←
assertTrue(persistenceUtil.isLoaded(item));
Ⓓ  assertFalse(persistenceUtil.isLoaded(item, "seller"));
    assertEquals(USER_ID, item.getSeller().getId());
    //assertNotNull(item.getSeller().getUsername());     ← Ⓔ
```

Ⓐ An `Item` entity instance is loaded in the persistence context. Its `seller` isn't initialized; it's a User proxy.

Ⓑ We can manually detach the data from the persistence context or close the persistence context and detach everything.

C The `PersistenceUtil` helper works without a persistence context. We can check at any time whether the data we want to access has been loaded.

D In detached state, we can call the identifier getter method of the `User` proxy.

E Calling any other method on the proxy, such as `getUsername()`, will throw a `Lazy-InitializationException`. Data can only be loaded on demand while the persistence context manages the proxy, not in detached state.

How does lazy loading of one-to-one associations work?

Lazy loading for one-to-one entity associations is sometimes confusing for new Hibernate users. If we consider one-to-one associations based on shared primary keys (see section 9.1.1), an association can be proxied only if it's `optional=false`. For example, an `Address` always has a reference to a `User`. If this association is nullable and optional, Hibernate must first hit the database to find out whether it should apply a proxy or a null, and the purpose of lazy loading is to not hit the database at all.

Hibernate proxies are useful beyond simple lazy loading. For example, we can store a new `Bid` without loading any data into memory.

Path: Ch12/proxy/src/test/java/com/manning/javapersistence/ch12/proxy
➥ /LazyProxyCollections.java

```
Item item = em.getReference(Item.class,  ITEM_ID);
User user = em.getReference(User.class,  USER_ID);
Bid newBid = new Bid(new BigDecimal("99.00"));
newBid.setItem(item);
newBid.setBidder(user);
em.persist(newBid);
// insert into BID values (?, ? ,? ,  . . . )
```

A There is no SQL `SELECT` in this procedure, only one `INSERT`.

The first two calls produce proxies of `Item` and `User`, respectively. Then the `item` and `bidder` association properties of the transient `Bid` are set with the proxies. The `persist()` call queues one SQL `INSERT` when the persistence context is flushed, and no `SELECT` is necessary to create the new row in the `BID` table. All key values are available as identifier values of the `Item` and `User` proxy.

Runtime proxy generation, as provided by Hibernate, is an excellent choice for transparent lazy loading. The domain model classes don't have to implement any special type or supertype, as some older ORM solutions require. No code generation or post-processing of bytecode is needed either, simplifying the build procedure. But you should be aware of some potentially negative aspects:

- Some runtime proxies aren't completely transparent, such as polymorphic associations that are tested with `instanceof`. This problem was demonstrated in section 7.8.1.

- With entity proxies, you have to be careful not to access fields directly when writing custom `equals()` and `hashCode()` methods, as discussed in section 10.3.2.
- Proxies can only be used to lazy-load entity associations. They can't be used to lazy-load individual basic properties or embedded components, such as `Item# description` or `User#homeAddress`. If you set the `@Basic(fetch = FetchType .LAZY)` hint on such a property, Hibernate ignores it; the value is eagerly loaded when the owning entity instance is loaded. Optimizing at the level of individual columns selected in SQL is unnecessary if you aren't working with either a significant number of optional or nullable columns, or columns containing large values that have to be retrieved on demand because of the physical limitations of the system. Large values are best represented with large objects (LOBs) instead; they provide lazy loading by definition (see "Binary and large value types" in section 6.3.1).

Proxies enable lazy loading of entity instances. For persistent collections, Hibernate has a slightly different approach.

12.1.2 *Lazy persistent collections*

We map persistent collections with either `@ElementCollection` for a collection of elements of basic or embeddable types or with `@OneToMany` and `@ManyToMany` for many-valued entity associations. These collections are, unlike `@ManyToOne`, lazy-loaded by default. We don't have to specify the `FetchType.LAZY` option on the mapping.

The lazy `bids` one-to-many collection is only loaded when accessed:

```
Path: Ch12/proxy/src/test/java/com/manning/javapersistence/ch12/proxy
  ➥ /LazyProxyCollections.java                          Ⓐ

Item item = em.find(Item.class, ITEM_ID);   ◄───┘
// select * from ITEM where ID = ?
Set<Bid> bids = item.getBids();
PersistenceUtil persistenceUtil = Persistence.getPersistenceUtil();
assertFalse(persistenceUtil.isLoaded(item, "bids"));
assertTrue(Set.class.isAssignableFrom(bids.getClass()));   ◄───Ⓒ
assertNotEquals(HashSet.class, bids.getClass());
assertEquals(org.hibernate.collection.internal.PersistentSet.class,
  ➥ bids.getClass());
```

Ⓐ The `find()` operation loads the `Item` entity instance into the persistence context, as you can see in figure 12.2.

Ⓑ The `Item` instance has a reference to an uninitialized `Set` of bids. It also has a reference to an uninitialized `User` proxy: the `seller`.

Ⓒ The `bids` field is a `Set`.

Ⓓ However, the `bids` field is not a `HashSet`.

Ⓔ The `bids` field is a Hibernate proxy class.

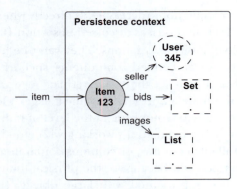

Figure 12.2   **Proxies and collection wrappers are the boundary of the loaded graph under Hibernate control.**

Hibernate implements lazy loading (and dirty checking) of collections with its own special implementations called *collection wrappers*. Although the bids certainly look like a Set, Hibernate replaced the implementation with an org.hibernate.collection .internal.PersistentSet while we weren't looking. It's not a HashSet, but it has the same behavior. That's why it's so important to program with interfaces in the domain model and only rely on Set and not HashSet. Lists and maps work the same way.

These special collections can detect when we access them, and they load their data at that time. As soon as we start iterating through the bids, the collection and all bids made for the item are loaded:

Path: Ch12/proxy/src/test/java/com/manning/javapersistence/ch12/proxy
➥ /LazyProxyCollections.java

```
Bid firstBid = bids.iterator().next();
// select * from BID where ITEM_ID = ?
// Alternative: Hibernate.initialize(bids);
```

Alternatively, just as for entity proxies, we can call the static Hibernate.initialize() utility method to load a collection. It will be completely loaded; we can't say "only load the first two bids," for example. To do that, we'd have to write a query.

For convenience, so we don't have to write many trivial queries, Hibernate offers a proprietary LazyCollectionOption.EXTRA setting on collection mappings:

Path: Ch12/proxy/src/main/java/com/manning/javapersistence/ch12/proxy
➥ /Item.java

```
@Entity
public class Item {
    @OneToMany(mappedBy = "item")
    @org.hibernate.annotations.LazyCollection(
        org.hibernate.annotations.LazyCollectionOption.EXTRA
    )
    public Set<Bid> getBids() {
        return bids;
    }
    //  . . .
}
```

With `LazyCollectionOption.EXTRA`, the collection supports operations that don't trigger initialization. For example, we could ask for the collection's size:

Path: Ch12/proxy/src/test/java/com/manning/javapersistence/ch12/proxy
➡ /LazyProxyCollections.java

```
Item item = em.find(Item.class, ITEM_ID);
// select * from ITEM where ID = ?
assertEquals(3, item.getBids().size());
// select count(b) from BID b where b.ITEM_ID = ?
```

The `size()` operation triggers a `SELECT COUNT()` SQL query but doesn't load the `bids` into memory. On all extra-lazy collections, similar queries are executed for the `isEmpty()` and `contains()` operations. An extra-lazy `Set` checks for duplicates with a simple query when we call `add()`. An extra-lazy `List` only loads one element if we call `get(index)`. For `Map`, extra-lazy operations are `containsKey()` and `containsValue()`.

12.1.3   Eager loading of associations and collections

We've recommended a lazy default fetch plan, with `FetchType.LAZY` on all the association and collection mappings. Sometimes, although not often, we want the opposite: to specify that a particular entity association or collection should always be loaded. We want the guarantee that this data is available in memory without an additional database hit.

More important, we want a guarantee that, for example, we can access the `seller` of an `Item` once the `Item` instance is in detached state. When the persistence context is closed, lazy loading is no longer available. If `seller` were an uninitialized proxy, we'd get a `LazyInitializationException` when we accessed it in detached state. For data to be available in detached state, we need to either load it manually while the persistence context is still open or, if we *always* want it loaded, change the fetch plan to be eager instead of lazy.

Let's assume that we always require the `seller` and the `bids` of an `Item` to be loaded:

Path: Ch12/eagerjoin/src/main/java/com/manning/javapersistence/ch12
➡ /eagerjoin/Item.java

```
@Entity
public class Item {                                    Ⓐ
    @ManyToOne(fetch = FetchType.EAGER)    ←┘
    private User seller;
    @OneToMany(mappedBy = "item", fetch = FetchType.EAGER)    ←┘  Ⓑ
    private Set<Bid> bids = new HashSet<>();
    //  . . .
}
```

Ⓐ `FetchType.EAGER` is the default for entity instances.

B Generally, `FetchType.EAGER` on a collection is not recommended. Unlike `Fetch-Type.LAZY`, which is a hint the JPA provider can ignore, `FetchType.EAGER` is a hard requirement. The provider has to guarantee that the data is loaded and available in detached state; it can't ignore the setting.

Consider the collection mapping: is it really a good idea to say "whenever an item is loaded into memory, load the bids of the item right away too"? Even if we only want to display the item's name or find out when the auction ends, all bids will be loaded into memory. Always eager-loading collections, with `FetchType.EAGER` as the default fetch plan in the mapping, usually isn't a great strategy. (Later in this chapter, we'll analyze the *Cartesian product problem*, which appears if we eagerly load several collections.) It's best if we leave collections set with the default `FetchType.LAZY`.

If we now `find()` an `Item` (or force the initialization of an `Item` proxy), both the `seller` and all the `bids` are loaded as persistent instances into the persistence context:

Path: Ch12/eagerjoin/src/test/java/com/manning/javapersistence/ch12
➥ /eagerjoin/EagerJoin.java

```
Item item = em.find(Item.class, ITEM_ID);
// select i.*, u.*, b.*
//   from ITEM i
//     left outer join USERS u on u.ID = i.SELLER_ID
//     left outer join BID b on b.ITEM_ID = i.ID
//   where i.ID = ?
em.detach(item);
assertEquals(3, item.getBids().size());
assertNotNull(item.getBids().iterator().next().getAmount());
assertEquals("johndoe", item.getSeller().getUsername());
```

A When calling `detach()`, the fetching is done. There will be no more lazy loading.

B In detached state, the `bids` collection is available, so we can check its size.

C In detached state, the `seller` is available, so we can check its name.

For the `find()`, Hibernate executes a single SQL `SELECT` and `JOIN`s three tables to retrieve the data. You can see the contents of the persistence context in figure 12.3. Note how the boundaries of the loaded graph are represented: each `Bid` has a reference to an uninitialized `User` proxy, the `bidder`. If we now detach the `Item`, we access the loaded `seller` and bids without causing a `LazyInitializationException`. If we try to access one of the `bidder` proxies, we'll get an exception.

Next, we'll investigate *how* data should be loaded when we find an entity instance by identity and when we navigate the network, using the pointers of the mapped associations and collections. We're interested in what SQL is executed and in finding the ideal *fetch strategy*.

In the following examples, we'll assume that the domain model has a lazy default fetch plan. Hibernate will only load the data we explicitly request and the associations and collections we access.

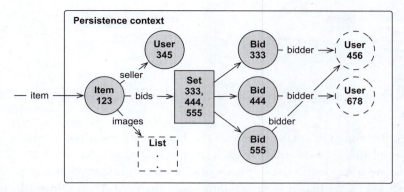

Figure 12.3 The seller and the bids of an `Item` are loaded in the Hibernate persistence context.

12.2 Selecting a fetch strategy

Hibernate executes SQL `SELECT` statements to load data into memory. If we load an entity instance, one or more `SELECT`s are executed, depending on the number of tables involved and the *fetching strategy* we've applied. Our goal is to minimize the number of SQL statements and to simplify the SQL statements so that querying can be as efficient as possible.

Consider our recommended fetch plan from earlier in this chapter: every association and collection should be loaded on demand, lazily. This default fetch plan will most likely result in too many SQL statements, each loading only one small piece of data. This will lead to the *n+1 selects problem*, so we'll look at this first. The alternative fetch plan, using eager loading, will result in fewer SQL statements, because larger chunks of data will be loaded into memory with each SQL query. We might then see the Cartesian product problem, as SQL result sets become too large.

We need to find a middle ground between these two extremes: the ideal fetching strategy for each procedure and use case in our application. Like with fetch plans, we can set a global fetching strategy in the mappings: a default setting that is always active. Then, for a particular procedure, we might override the default fetching strategy with a custom JPQL `CriteriaQuery`, or even a SQL query.

First, let's investigate the fundamental issues, starting with the n+1 selects problem.

12.2.1 The n+1 selects problem

This problem is easy to understand with some example code. Let's assume that we mapped a lazy fetch plan, so everything is loaded on demand. The following code checks whether the `seller` of each `Item` has a username:

Path: Ch12/nplusoneselects/src/test/java/com/manning/javapersistence/ch12
➥ /nplusoneselects/NPlusOneSelects.java

```
List<Item> items =
        em.createQuery("select i from Item i").getResultList();
```

```
// select * from ITEM
for (Item item : items) {                                    A
    assertNotNull(item.getSeller().getUsername());    ◄──┘
    // select * from USERS where ID = ?
}
```

A Whenever we access a seller, each of them must be loaded with an additional SELECT.

You can see the one SQL SELECT that load the Item entity instances. Then, as we iterate through all the items, retrieving each User requires an additional SELECT. This amounts to one query for the Item plus *n* queries depending on how many items we have and whether a particular User is selling more than one Item. Obviously, this is a very inefficient strategy if we know we'll be accessing the seller of each Item.

We can see the same problem with lazily loaded collections. The following example checks whether each Item has any bids:

Path: Ch12/nplusoneselects/src/test/java/com/manning/javapersistence/ch12
➥ /nplusoneselects/NPlusOneSelects.java

```
List<Item> items = em.createQuery("select i from Item i").getResultList();
// select * from ITEM
for (Item item : items) {                            A
    assertTrue(item.getBids().size() > 0);    ◄──┘
    // select * from BID where ITEM_ID = ?
}
```

A Each bids collection has to be loaded with an additional SELECT.

Again, if we know we'll be accessing each bids collection, loading only one at a time is inefficient. If we have 100 bids, we'll execute 101 SQL queries!

With what we know so far, we might be tempted to change the default fetch plan in the mappings and put a FetchType.EAGER on the seller or bids associations. But doing so can lead to our next topic: the Cartesian product problem.

12.2.2 *The Cartesian product problem*

If we look at the domain and data model and say, "Every time I need an Item, I also need the seller of that Item," we can map the association with FetchType.EAGER instead of a lazy fetch plan. We want a guarantee that whenever an Item is loaded, the seller will be loaded right away—we want that data to be available when the Item is detached and the persistence context is closed:

Path: Ch12/cartesianproduct/src/main/java/com/manning/javapersistence/ch12
➥ /cartesianproduct/Item.java

```
@Entity
public class Item {
    @ManyToOne(fetch = FetchType.EAGER)
```

```
    private User seller;
    //  . . .
}
```

To implement the eager fetch plan, Hibernate uses an SQL JOIN operation to load an Item and a User instance in one SELECT:

```
 item = em.find(Item.class, ITEM_ID);
// select i.*, u.*
//   from ITEM i
//     left outer join USERS u on u.ID = i.SELLER_ID
//   where i.ID = ?
```

The result set contains one row with data from the ITEM table combined with data from the USERS table, as shown in figure 12.4.

i.ID	i.NAME	i.SELLER_ID	...	u.ID	u.USERNAME	...
1	One	2	...	2	johndoe	...

Figure 12.4   Hibernate joins two tables to eagerly fetch associated rows.

Eager fetching with the default JOIN strategy isn't problematic for @ManyToOne and @OneToOne associations. We can eagerly load, with one SQL query and JOINs, an Item, its seller, the User's Address, the City they live in, and so on. Even if we map all these associations with FetchType.EAGER, the result set will have only one row.

Hibernate has to stop following the FetchType.EAGER plan at *some* point. The number of tables joined depends on the global hibernate.max_fetch_depth configuration property, and by default, no limit is set. Reasonable values are small, usually from 1 to 5. We can even disable JOIN fetching of @ManyToOne and @OneToOne associations by setting the property to 0. If Hibernate reaches the limit, it will still eagerly load the data according to the fetch plan, but with additional SELECT statements. (Note that some database dialects may preset this property; for example, MySQLDialect sets it to 2.)

Eagerly loading collections with JOINs, on the other hand, can lead to serious performance concerns. If we also switched to FetchType.EAGER for the bids and images collections, we'd run into the Cartesian product problem.

This problem appears when we eagerly load two collections with one SQL query and a JOIN operation. First, let's create such a fetch plan and then look at the problem:

Path: Ch12/cartesianproduct/src/main/java/com/manning/javapersistence/ch12
➥ /cartesianproduct/Item.java

```
@Entity
public class Item {
    @OneToMany(mappedBy = "item", fetch = FetchType.EAGER)
    private Set<Bid> bids = new HashSet<>();
    @ElementCollection(fetch = FetchType.EAGER)
    @CollectionTable(name = "IMAGE")
    @Column(name = "FILENAME")
```

```
        private Set<String> images = new HashSet<>();
        //  . . .
}
```

It doesn't matter whether both collections are @OneToMany, @ManyToMany, or @Element-Collection. Eager fetching more than one collection at once with the SQL JOIN operator is the fundamental problem, no matter what the collection's content is. If we load an Item, Hibernate executes the problematic SQL statement:

Path: Ch12/cartesianproduct/src/test/java/com/manning/javapersistence/ch12
➥ /cartesianproduct/CartesianProduct.java

```
Item item = em.find(Item.class, ITEM_ID);
// select i.*, b.*, img.*
//  from ITEM i
//   left outer join BID b on b.ITEM_ID = i.ID
//   left outer join IMAGE img on img.ITEM_ID = i.ID
// where i.ID = ?
em.detach(item);
assertEquals(3, item.getImages().size());
assertEquals(3, item.getBids().size());
```

As you can see, Hibernate obeyed the eager fetch plan, and we can access the bids and images collections in detached state. The problem is *how* they were loaded, with an SQL JOIN that results in a product. Look at the result set in figure 12.5.

i.ID	i.NAME	...	b.ID	b.AMOUNT	img.FILENAME
1	One	...	1	99.00	foo.jpg
1	One	...	1	99.00	bar.jpg
1	One	...	1	99.00	baz.jpg
1	One	...	2	100.00	foo.jpg
1	One	...	2	100.00	bar.jpg
1	One	...	2	100.00	baz.jp
1	One	...	3	101.00	foo.jpg
1	One	...	3	101.00	bar.jpg
1	One	...	3	101.00	baz.jpg

Figure 12.5 A product is the result of two joins with many rows.

This result set contains many redundant data items, and only the shaded cells are relevant for Hibernate. The Item has three bids and three images. The size of the product depends on the size of the collections we're retrieving: 3 × 3 is 9 rows total. Now imagine that we have an Item with 50 bids and 5 images—we'd see a result set with possibly 250 rows! We can create even larger SQL products when we write our own queries with JPQL or CriteriaQuery; imagine what would happen if we load 500 items and eager fetch dozens of bids and images with JOINs.

Considerable processing time and memory are required on the database server to create such results, which then must be transferred across the network. If you're hoping that the JDBC driver will compress the data on the wire somehow, you're probably expecting too much from database vendors. Hibernate immediately removes all duplicates when it marshals the result set into persistent instances and collections; the information in cells that aren't shaded in figure 12.5 will be ignored. Obviously, we can't remove these duplicates at the SQL level; the SQL `DISTINCT` operator doesn't help here.

Instead of using one SQL query with an extremely large result, three separate queries would be faster for retrieving an entity instance and two collections at the same time. We'll focus on this kind of optimization next and see how we can find and implement the best fetch strategy. We'll start again with a default lazy fetch plan and try to solve the *n+1* selects problem first.

12.2.3 Prefetching data in batches

If Hibernate fetches every entity association and collection only on demand, many additional SQL `SELECT` statements may be needed to complete a particular procedure. As before, consider a routine that checks whether the `seller` of each `Item` has a username. With lazy loading, this would require one `SELECT` to get all `Item` instances and *n* more `SELECT`s to initialize the `seller` proxy of each `Item`.

Hibernate offers algorithms that can prefetch data. The first algorithm we'll look at is *batch fetching*, and it works as follows: if Hibernate must initialize one `User` proxy, it can go ahead and initialize several with the same `SELECT`. In other words, if we already know that there are several `Item` instances in the persistence context and that they all have a proxy applied to their `seller` association, we may as well initialize several proxies instead of just one when we make the round trip to the database.

Let's see how this works. First, enable batch fetching of `User` instances with a proprietary Hibernate annotation:

```
Path: Ch12/batch/src/main/java/com/manning/javapersistence/ch12/batch
➡ /User.java
```

```
@Entity
@org.hibernate.annotations.BatchSize(size = 10)
@Table(name = "USERS")
public class User {
    //  . . .
}
```

This setting tells Hibernate that it may load up to 10 `User` proxies if one has to be loaded, all with the same `SELECT`. Batch fetching is often called a *blind-guess optimization* because we don't know how many uninitialized `User` proxies may be in a particular persistence context. We can't say for sure that 10 is an ideal value—it's a guess. We know that instead of *n+1* SQL queries, we'll now see queries, a significant reduction.

Reasonable values are usually small because we don't want to load too much data into memory either, especially if we aren't sure we'll need it.

This is the optimized procedure, which checks the `username` of each `seller`:

Path: Ch12/batch/src/test/java/com/manning/javapersistence/ch12/batch
➡ /Batch.java

```java
List<Item> items = em.createQuery("select i from Item i",
➡ Item.class).getResultList();
// select * from ITEM
for (Item item : items) {
    assertNotNull(item.getSeller().getUsername());
    // select * from USERS where ID in (?, ?, ?, ?, ?, ?, ?, ?, ?, ?)
}
```

Note the SQL query that Hibernate executes while we iterate through the `items`. When we call `item.getSeller().getUserName()` for the first time, Hibernate must initialize the first `User` proxy. Instead of only loading a single row from the `USERS` table, Hibernate retrieves several rows, and up to 10 `User` instances are loaded. Once we access the eleventh `seller`, another 10 are loaded in one batch, and so on, until the persistence context contains no uninitialized `User` proxies.

> ### What is the real batch-fetching algorithm?
>
> Our explanation of batch loading in section 12.2.3 is somewhat simplified, and you may see a slightly different algorithm in practice.
>
> As an example, imagine a batch size of 32. At startup time, Hibernate creates several batch loaders internally. Each loader knows how many proxies it can initialize. The goal is to minimize the memory consumption for loader creation and to create enough loaders that every possible batch fetch can be produced. Another goal is obviously to minimize the number of SQL queries. To initialize 31 proxies, Hibernate executes 3 batches (you probably expected 1, because 32 > 31). The batch loaders that are applied are 16, 10, and 5, as automatically selected by Hibernate.
>
> You can customize this batch-fetching algorithm with the `hibernate.batch_fetch_style` property in the persistence unit configuration. The default is `LEGACY`, which builds and selects several batch loaders on startup. Other options are `PADDED` and `DYNAMIC`. With `PADDED`, Hibernate builds only one batch loader SQL query on startup with placeholders for 32 arguments in the `IN` clause and then repeats bound identifiers if fewer than 32 proxies have to be loaded. With `DYNAMIC`, Hibernate dynamically builds the batch SQL statement at runtime, when it knows the number of proxies to initialize.

Batch fetching is also available for collections:

Path: Ch12/batch/src/main/java/com/manning/javapersistence/ch12/batch
➡ /Item.java

```java
@Entity
```

```
public class Item {
    @OneToMany(mappedBy = "item")
    @org.hibernate.annotations.BatchSize(size = 5)
    private Set<Bid> bids = new HashSet<>();
    //  . . .
}
```

If we now force the initialization of one `bids` collection, up to five more `Item#bids` collections, if they're uninitialized in the current persistence context, are loaded right away:

Path: Ch12/batch/src/test/java/com/manning/javapersistence/ch12/batch
➥ /Batch.java

```
List<Item> items = em.createQuery("select i from Item i",
➥ Item.class).getResultList();
// select * from ITEM
for (Item item : items) {
    assertTrue(item.getBids().size() > 0);
    // select * from BID where ITEM_ID in (?, ?, ?, ?, ?)
}
```

When we call `item.getBids().size()` for the first time while iterating, a whole batch of `Bid` collections are preloaded for the other `Item` instances.

Batch fetching is a simple and often smart optimization that can significantly reduce the number of SQL statements that would otherwise be necessary to initialize all the proxies and collections. Although we may prefetch data we won't need, and consume more memory, the reduction in database round trips can make a huge difference. Memory is cheap, but scaling database servers isn't.

Another prefetching algorithm that isn't a blind guess uses subselects to initialize many collections with a single statement.

12.2.4   Prefetching collections with subselects

A potentially better strategy for loading all the `bids` of several `Item` instances is prefetching with a subselect. To enable this optimization, add a `Fetch` Hibernate annotation to the collection mapping, having the `SUBSELECT` parameter:

Path: Ch12/subselect/src/main/java/com/manning/javapersistence/ch12
➥ /subselect/Item.java

```
@Entity
public class Item {
    @OneToMany(mappedBy = "item")
    @org.hibernate.annotations.Fetch(
        org.hibernate.annotations.FetchMode.SUBSELECT
    )
    private Set<Bid> bids = new HashSet<>();
    //  . . .
}
```

Hibernate now initializes all `bids` collections for all loaded `Item` instances as soon as we force the initialization of one `bids` collection:

Path: Ch12/subselect/src/test/java/com/manning/javapersistence/ch12
➡ /subselect/Subselect.java

```
List<Item> items = em.createQuery("select i from Item i",
➡ Item.class).getResultList();
// select * from ITEM
for (Item item : items) {
    assertTrue(item.getBids().size() > 0);
    // select * from BID where ITEM_ID in (
    //   select ID from ITEM
    // )
}
```

Hibernate remembers the original query used to load the `items`. It then embeds this initial query (slightly modified) in a subselect, retrieving the collection of `bids` for each `Item`.

Note that the original query that is rerun as a subselect is only remembered by Hibernate for a particular persistence context. If we detach an `Item` instance without initializing the collection of `bids`, and then merge it with a new persistence context and start iterating through the collection, no prefetching of other collections occurs.

Batch and subselect prefetching reduce the number of queries necessary for a particular procedure if you stick with a global lazy fetch plan in the mappings, helping mitigate the *n*+1 selects problem. If, instead, your global fetch plan has eager loaded associations and collections, you'll have to avoid the Cartesian product problem—for example, by breaking down a `JOIN` query into several `SELECT`s.

12.2.5 *Eager fetching with multiple SELECTs*

When trying to fetch several collections with one SQL query and `JOIN`s, we'll run into the Cartesian product problem, as discussed earlier. Instead of a `JOIN` operation, we can tell Hibernate to eagerly load data with additional `SELECT` queries and hence avoid large results and SQL products with duplicates:

Path: Ch12/eagerselect/src/main/java/com/manning/javapersistence/ch12
➡ /eagerselect/Item.java

```
@Entity
public class Item {
    @ManyToOne(fetch = FetchType.EAGER)
    @org.hibernate.annotations.Fetch(                           Ⓐ
        org.hibernate.annotations.FetchMode.SELECT       ⟵┐
    )
    private User seller;
    @OneToMany(mappedBy = "item", fetch = FetchType.EAGER)
    @org.hibernate.annotations.Fetch(                           Ⓐ
        org.hibernate.annotations.FetchMode.SELECT       ⟵┐
    )
```

```
    private Set<Bid> bids = new HashSet<>();
    //  . . .
}
```

Ⓐ `FetchMode.SELECT` means that the property should be loaded lazily. The default value is `FetchMode.JOIN`, meaning the property would be retrieved eagerly, via a `JOIN`.

Now when an `Item` is loaded, the `seller` and `bids` have to be loaded as well:

Path: Ch12/eagerselect/src/test/java/com/manning/javapersistence/ch12
➥ /eagerselect/EagerSelect.java

```
Item item = em.find(Item.class, ITEM_ID);      ⟵   Ⓐ
// select * from ITEM where ID = ?
// select * from USERS where ID = ?
// select * from BID where ITEM_ID = ?
em.detach(item);
assertEquals(3, item.getBids().size());
assertNotNull(item.getBids().iterator().next().getAmount());      Ⓑ
assertEquals("johndoe", item.getSeller().getUsername());
```

Ⓐ Hibernate uses one `SELECT` to load a row from the `ITEM` table. It then immediately executes two more `SELECT`s: one loading a row from the `USERS` table (the `seller`) and the other loading several rows from the `BID` table (the `bids`). The additional `SELECT` queries aren't executed lazily; the `find()` method produces several SQL queries.

Ⓑ Hibernate followed the eager fetch plan; all data is available in detached state.

Still, all of these settings are global; they're always active. The danger is that adjusting one setting for one problematic case in the application might have negative side effects on some other procedure. Maintaining this balance can be difficult, so our recommendation is to map every entity association and collection as `FetchType.LAZY`, as mentioned before.

A better approach is to *dynamically* use eager fetching and `JOIN` operations only when needed, for a particular procedure.

12.2.6 *Dynamic eager fetching*

As in the previous sections, let's say we have to check the `username` of each `Item#seller`. With a lazy global fetch plan, we can load the needed data for this procedure and apply a dynamic eager fetch strategy in a query:

Path: Ch12/eagerselect/src/test/java/com/manning/javapersistence/ch12
➥ /eagerselect/EagerQueryUsers.java

Ⓐ
```
List<Item> items =
    em.createQuery("select i from Item i join fetch i.seller", Item.class)
        .getResultList();
// select i.*, u.*
```

```
//  from ITEM i
//   inner join USERS u on u.ID = i.SELLER_ID
//  where i.ID = ?
em.close();
for (Item item : items) {
    assertNotNull(item.getSeller().getUsername());
}
```

A Apply a dynamic eager strategy in a query.

B Detach all.

C Hibernate followed the eager fetch plan; all data is available in detached state.

The important keywords in this JPQL query are `join fetch`, telling Hibernate to use a SQL `JOIN` (an `INNER JOIN`, actually) to retrieve the `seller` of each `Item` in the same query. The same query can be expressed with the `CriteriaQuery` API instead of a JPQL string:

Path: Ch12/eagerselect/src/test/java/com/manning/javapersistence/ch12
➥ /eagerselect/EagerQueryUsers.java

```
CriteriaBuilder cb = em.getCriteriaBuilder();
CriteriaQuery<Item> criteria = cb.createQuery(Item.class);
Root<Item> i = criteria.from(Item.class);
i.fetch("seller");
criteria.select(i);
List<Item> items = em.createQuery(criteria).getResultList();
em.close();
for (Item item : items) {
    assertNotNull(item.getSeller().getUsername());
}
```

A Apply an eager strategy in a query dynamically constructed with the `Criteria-Query` API.

B Detach all.

C Hibernate followed the eager fetch plan; all data is available in detached state.

Dynamic eager join fetching also works for collections. Here we load all `bids` of each `Item`:

Path: Ch12/eagerselect/src/test/java/com/manning/javapersistence/ch12
➥ /eagerselect/EagerQueryBids.java

```
List<Item> items =
    em.createQuery("select i from Item i left join fetch i.bids",
    ➥ Item.class)
        .getResultList();
// select i.*, b.*
//  from ITEM i
//   left outer join BID b on b.ITEM_ID = i.ID
//  where i.ID = ?
em.close();
```

```
for (Item item : items) {
    assertTrue(item.getBids().size() > 0);          ←─ C
}
```

A Apply a dynamic eager strategy in a query.

B Detach all.

C Hibernate followed the eager fetch plan; all data is available in detached state.

Now let's do the same with the `CriteriaQuery` API:

Path: Ch12/eagerselect/src/test/java/com/manning/javapersistence/ch12
➥ /eagerselect/EagerQueryBids.java

```
CriteriaBuilder cb = em.getCriteriaBuilder();
CriteriaQuery<Item> criteria = cb.createQuery(Item.class);
Root<Item> i = criteria.from(Item.class);
i.fetch("bids", JoinType.LEFT);
criteria.select(i);                                          A
List<Item> items = em.createQuery(criteria).getResultList(); ←─
em.close();                                         C
for (Item item : items) {
    assertTrue(item.getBids().size() > 0);          ←─
}
```

A Apply an eager strategy in a query dynamically constructed with the `Criteria-Query` API.

B Detach all.

C Hibernate followed the eager fetch plan; all data is available in detached state.

Note that for collection fetching, a `LEFT OUTER JOIN` is necessary, because we also want rows from the `ITEM` table if there are no `bids`.

Writing queries by hand isn't the only available option if we want to override the global fetch plan of the domain model dynamically. We can write *fetch profiles* declaratively.

12.3 Using fetch profiles

Fetch profiles complement the fetching options in the query languages and APIs. They allow us to maintain the profile definitions in either XML or annotation metadata. Early Hibernate versions didn't have support for special fetch profiles, but today Hibernate supports the following:

- *Fetch profiles*—A proprietary API based on the declaration of the profile with `@org.hibernate.annotations.FetchProfile` and execution with `Session #enableFetchProfile()`. This simple mechanism currently supports overriding lazy-mapped entity associations and collections selectively, enabling a `JOIN` eager fetching strategy for a particular unit of work.

- *Entity graphs*—Specified in JPA 2.1, we can declare a graph of entity attributes and associations with the @EntityGraph annotation. This fetch plan, or a combination of plans, can be enabled as a hint when executing EntityManager #find() or queries (JPQL, criteria). The provided graph controls *what* should be loaded; unfortunately, it doesn't control *how* it should be loaded.

It's fair to say that there is room for improvement here, and we expect future versions of Hibernate and JPA to offer a unified and more powerful API.

We can externalize JPQL and SQL statements and move them to metadata. A JPQL query *is* a declarative (named) fetch profile; what we're missing is the ability to overlay different plans easily on the same base query. We've seen some creative solutions with string manipulation that are best avoided. With criteria queries, on the other hand, we already have the full power of Java available to organize the query-building code. The value of entity graphs is being able to reuse fetch plans across any kind of query.

Let's talk about Hibernate fetch profiles first and how we can override a global lazy fetch plan for a particular unit of work.

12.3.1 *Declaring Hibernate fetch profiles*

Hibernate fetch profiles are global metadata; they're declared for the entire persistence unit. Although we could place the @FetchProfile annotation on a class, we prefer it as package-level metadata in a package-info.java file:

```
Path: Ch12/profile/src/main/java/com/manning/javapersistence/ch12/profile
      /package-info.java

@org.hibernate.annotations.FetchProfiles({                        A
    @FetchProfile(name = Item.PROFILE_JOIN_SELLER,          <┘
        fetchOverrides = @FetchProfile.FetchOverride(
   ┌>        entity = Item.class,            C
   B          association = "seller",
            mode = FetchMode.JOIN           <┘
    )),
    @FetchProfile(name = Item.PROFILE_JOIN_BIDS,
        fetchOverrides = @FetchProfile.FetchOverride(
            entity = Item.class,
            association = "bids",
            mode = FetchMode.JOIN
    ))
})
```

Ⓐ Each profile has a name. This is a simple string isolated in a constant.

Ⓑ Each override in a profile names one entity association or collection.

Ⓒ FetchMode.JOIN means the property will be retrieved eagerly, via a JOIN.

The profiles can now be enabled for a unit of work. We need the Hibernate API to enable a profile. It's then active for any operation in that unit of work. The Item#seller may be fetched with a join in the same SQL statement whenever an Item is loaded with this EntityManager.

We can overlay another profile on the same unit of work. In the following example, the `Item#seller` and the `Item#bids` collections will be fetched with a join in the same SQL statement whenever an `Item` is loaded.

Path: Ch12/profile/src/test/java/com/manning/javapersistence/ch12/profile
➥ /Profile.java

Ⓐ

```
Item item = em.find(Item.class, ITEM_ID);          ⟵
em.clear();                                                      Ⓑ
em.unwrap(Session.class).enableFetchProfile(Item.PROFILE_JOIN_SELLER);   ⟵
item = em.find(Item.class, ITEM_ID);                            Ⓒ
em.clear();
em.unwrap(Session.class).enableFetchProfile(Item.PROFILE_JOIN_BIDS);   ⟵
item = em.find(Item.class, ITEM_ID);
```

Ⓐ The `Item#seller` is mapped lazily, so the default fetch plan only retrieves the `Item` instance.

Ⓑ Fetch the `Item#seller` with a join in the same SQL statement whenever an `Item` is loaded with this `EntityManager`.

Ⓒ Fetch `Item#seller` and `Item#bids` with a join in the same SQL statement whenever an `Item` is loaded.

Basic Hibernate fetch profiles can be an easy solution for fetching optimization in smaller or simpler applications. Starting with JPA 2.1, the introduction of *entity graphs* enables similar functionality in a standard fashion.

12.3.2 *Working with entity graphs*

An entity graph is a declaration of entity nodes and attributes, overriding or augmenting the default fetch plan when we execute an `EntityManager#find()` or put a hint on query operations. This is an example of a retrieval operation using an entity graph:

Path: Ch12/fetchloadgraph/src/test/java/com/manning/javapersistence/ch12
➥ /fetchloadgraph/FetchLoadGraph.java

```
Map<String, Object> properties = new HashMap<>();
properties.put(                                         Ⓐ
    "javax.persistence.loadgraph",
    em.getEntityGraph(Item.class.getSimpleName()))   ⟵
);
Item item = em.find(Item.class, ITEM_ID, properties);
// select * from ITEM where ID = ?
```

Ⓐ The name of the entity graph we're using is `Item`, and the hint for the `find()` operation indicates it should be the *load graph*. This means attributes that are specified by attribute nodes of the entity graph are treated as `FetchType.EAGER`, and attributes that aren't specified are treated according to their specified or default `FetchType` in the mapping.

The following code shows the declaration of this graph and the default fetch plan of the entity class:

Path: Ch12/fetchloadgraph/src/main/java/com/manning/javapersistence/ch12
➡ /fetchloadgraph/Item.java

```
@NamedEntityGraphs({                     Ⓐ
    @NamedEntityGraph          ←──┐
})
@Entity
public class Item {
    @NotNull
    @ManyToOne(fetch = FetchType.LAZY)
    private User seller;
    @OneToMany(mappedBy = "item")
    private Set<Bid> bids = new HashSet<>();
    @ElementCollection
    private Set<String> images = new HashSet<>();
    //  . . .
}
```

Ⓐ Entity graphs in metadata have names and are associated with an entity class; they're usually declared in annotations at the top of an entity class. We can alternatively put them in XML if we like. If we don't give an entity graph a name, it gets the simple name of its owning entity class, which here is Item.

If we don't specify any attribute nodes in the graph, like the empty entity graph in the preceding example, the defaults of the entity class are used. In Item, all associations and collections are mapped lazily; this is the default fetch plan. Hence, what we've done so far makes little difference, and the find() operation without any hints will produce the same result: the Item instance is loaded, and the seller, bids, and images aren't.

Alternatively, we can build an entity graph with an API:

Path: Ch12/fetchloadgraph/src/test/java/com/manning/javapersistence/ch12
➡ /fetchloadgraph/FetchLoadGraph.java

```
EntityGraph<Item> itemGraph = em.createEntityGraph(Item.class);
Map<String, Object> properties = new HashMap<>();
properties.put("javax.persistence.loadgraph", itemGraph);
Item item = em.find(Item.class, ITEM_ID, properties);
```

This is again an empty entity graph with no attribute nodes, given directly to a retrieval operation.

Let's say we want to write an entity graph that changes the lazy default of Item#seller to eager fetching when it's enabled:

Path: Ch12/fetchloadgraph/src/main/java/com/manning/javapersistence/ch12
➡ /fetchloadgraph/Item.java

```
@NamedEntityGraphs({
    @NamedEntityGraph(
        name = "ItemSeller",
        attributeNodes = {
            @NamedAttributeNode("seller")
        }
    )
})
@Entity
public class Item {
    //  . . .
}
```

We can now enable this graph by name when we want the `Item` and the `seller` eagerly loaded:

Path: Ch12/fetchloadgraph/src/test/java/com/manning/javapersistence/ch12
➥ /fetchloadgraph/FetchLoadGraph.java

```
Map<String, Object> properties = new HashMap<>();
properties.put(
    "javax.persistence.loadgraph",
    em.getEntityGraph("ItemSeller")
);
Item item = em.find(Item.class, ITEM_ID, properties);
// select i.*, u.*
//   from ITEM i
//   inner join USERS u on u.ID = i.SELLER_ID
// where i.ID = ?
```

If we don't want to hardcode the graph in annotations, we can build it with the API instead:

Path: Ch12/fetchloadgraph/src/test/java/com/manning/javapersistence/ch12
➥ /fetchloadgraph/FetchLoadGraph.java

```
EntityGraph<Item> itemGraph = em.createEntityGraph(Item.class);
itemGraph.addAttributeNodes(Item_.seller);
Map<String, Object> properties = new HashMap<>();
properties.put("javax.persistence.loadgraph", itemGraph);
Item item = em.find(Item.class, ITEM_ID, properties);
// select i.*, u.*
//   from ITEM i
//   inner join USERS u on u.ID = i.SELLER_ID
// where i.ID = ?
```

A The `Item_` class belongs to the static metamodel. It is automatically generated by including the Hibernate JPA2 Metamodel Generator dependency in the project. Take a look back at section 3.3.4 for more details.

So far we've seen only properties for the `find()` operation. Entity graphs can also be enabled for queries, as hints:

```
Path: Ch12/fetchloadgraph/src/test/java/com/manning/javapersistence/ch12
➥ /fetchloadgraph/FetchLoadGraph.java

List<Item> items =
    em.createQuery("select i from Item i", Item.class)
        .setHint("javax.persistence.loadgraph", itemGraph)
        .getResultList();
// select i.*, u.*
//   from ITEM i
//    left outer join USERS u on u.ID = i.SELLER_ID
```

Entity graphs can be complex. The following declaration shows how to work with reusable subgraph declarations:

```
Path: Ch12/fetchloadgraph/src/main/java/com/manning/javapersistence/ch12
➥ /fetchloadgraph/Bid.java

@NamedEntityGraphs({
    @NamedEntityGraph(
        name = "BidBidderItemSellerBids",
        attributeNodes = {
            @NamedAttributeNode(value = "bidder"),
            @NamedAttributeNode(
                value = "item",
                subgraph = "ItemSellerBids"
            )
        },
        subgraphs = {
            @NamedSubgraph(
                name = "ItemSellerBids",
                attributeNodes = {
                    @NamedAttributeNode("seller"),
                    @NamedAttributeNode("bids")
                })
        }
    )
})
@Entity
public class Bid {
    //  . . .
}
```

This entity graph, when enabled as a load graph when retrieving `Bid` instances, also triggers eager fetching of `Bid#bidder`, the `Bid#item`, and furthermore the `Item#seller` and all `Item#bids`. Although you're free to name your entity graphs any way you like, we recommend that you develop a convention that everyone in your team can follow, and move the strings to shared constants.

With the entity graph API, the previous plan looks like this:

```
Path: Ch12/fetchloadgraph/src/test/java/com/manning/javapersistence/ch12
➥ /fetchloadgraph/FetchLoadGraph.java
```

```
EntityGraph<Bid> bidGraph = em.createEntityGraph(Bid.class);
bidGraph.addAttributeNodes(Bid_.bidder, Bid_.item);
Subgraph<Item> itemGraph = bidGraph.addSubgraph(Bid_.item);
itemGraph.addAttributeNodes(Item_.seller, Item_.bids);
Map<String, Object> properties = new HashMap<>();
properties.put("javax.persistence.loadgraph", bidGraph);
Bid bid = em.find(Bid.class, BID_ID, properties);
```

We've only seen entity graphs as *load graphs* so far. There is another option: we can enable an entity graph as a *fetch graph* with the `javax.persistence.fetchgraph` hint. If we execute a `find()` or query operation with a fetch graph, any attributes and collections not in the plan will be made `FetchType.LAZY`, and any nodes in the plan will be `FetchType.EAGER`. This effectively ignores all `FetchType` settings in the entity attribute and collection mappings.

Two weak points of the JPA entity graph operations are worth mentioning, because you'll run into them quickly. First, you can only modify fetch plans, not the Hibernate fetch strategy (batch/subselect/join/select). Second, declaring an entity graph in annotations or XML isn't fully type-safe: the attribute names are strings. The `EntityGraph` API at least is type-safe.

Summary

- A fetch profile combines a fetch plan (identifying what data should be loaded) with a fetch strategy (how the data should be loaded), encapsulated in reusable metadata or code.

- You can create a global fetch plan and define which associations and collections should be loaded into memory at all times.

- You can define the fetch plan based on use cases, how to access associated entities and iterate through collections in the application, and which data should be available in detached state.

- You can select the right fetching strategy for the fetch plan. The goal is to minimize the number of SQL statements and the complexity of each SQL statement that must be executed.

- You can use fetching strategies especially to avoid the $n+1$ selects and Cartesian product problems.

Filtering data

This chapter covers

- Cascading state transitions
- Listening to and intercepting events
- Auditing and versioning with Hibernate Envers
- Filtering data dynamically

In this chapter, we'll analyze many different strategies for *filtering* data as it passes through the Hibernate engine. When Hibernate loads data from the database, we can transparently restrict the data seen by the application with a filter. When Hibernate stores data in the database, we can listen to the event and execute secondary routines: for example, we could write an audit log or assign a tenant identifier to a record.

In the four main sections of this chapter, we'll explore the following data-filtering features and APIs:

- First you'll learn to react to state changes of an entity instance and *cascade the state change* to associated entities. For example, when a `User` is saved, Hibernate can transitively and automatically save all related `BillingDetails`. When an `Item` is deleted, Hibernate can delete all `Bid` instances associated with that `Item`. We can enable this standard JPA feature with special attributes in the entity association and collection mappings.

358

- The Jakarta Persistence standard includes lifecycle *callbacks* and *event listeners*. An event listener is a class we write with special methods, called by Hibernate when an entity instance changes state, such as after Hibernate loads it or is about to delete it from the database. These callback methods can also be on the entity classes and marked with special annotations. This gives us an opportunity to execute custom side effects when a transition occurs. Hibernate also has several proprietary extension points that allow interception of lifecycle events at a lower level within its engine.

- A common side effect is writing an *audit log*; such a log typically contains information about the data that was changed, when the change was made, and who made the modification. A more sophisticated auditing system might require storing several versions of data and *temporal views*; for example, we might want to ask Hibernate to load data "as it was last week." This being a complex problem, we'll introduce Hibernate Envers, a subproject dedicated to versioning and auditing in JPA applications.

- Finally, we'll examine *data filters*, which are also available as a proprietary Hibernate API. These filters add custom restrictions to SQL SELECT statements executed by Hibernate. Hence, we can effectively define a custom limited view of the data in the application tier. For example, we could apply a filter that restricts loaded data by sales region or any other authorization criteria.

We'll start with cascading options for transitive state changes.

> **NOTE**   To be able to execute the examples from the source code, you'll first need to run the Ch13.sql script.

13.1   *Cascading state transitions*

When an entity instance changes state—such as when goes from being *transient* to *persistent*—associated entity instances may also be included in this state transition. This *cascading* of state transitions isn't enabled by default; each entity instance has an independent lifecycle. But for some associations between entities, we may want to implement fine-grained lifecycle dependencies.

For example, in section 8.3 we created an association between the Item and Bid entity classes. In this case, not only did we make the bids of an Item automatically persistent when they were added to an Item, but they were also automatically deleted when the owning Item was deleted. We effectively made Bid an entity class that was dependent on another entity, Item.

The cascading settings we enabled in that association mapping were CascadeType .PERSIST and CascadeType.REMOVE. We also investigated the special orphanRemoval switch and how cascading deletion at the database level (with the foreign key ON DELETE option) affects the application.

So we briefly pointed out how we could work with *cascading* state in chapter 8. In this section, we'll analyze some other, rarely used, cascading options.

13.1.1 *Available cascading options*

Table 13.1 summarizes the most important cascading options available in Hibernate. Note how each is linked with an `EntityManager` or `Session` operation.

Table 13.1   Cascading options for entity association mappings

Option	Description
CascadeType.PERSIST	When an entity instance is stored with `EntityManager #persist()`, at flush time any associated entity instances are also made persistent.
CascadeType.REMOVE	When an entity instance is deleted with `EntityManager #remove()`, at flush time any associated entity instances are also removed.
CascadeType.DETACH	When an entity instance is evicted from the persistence context with `EntityManager#detach()`, any associated entity instances are also detached.
CascadeType.MERGE	When a transient or detached entity instance is merged into a persistence context with `EntityManager#merge()`, any associated transient or detached entity instances are also merged.
CascadeType.REFRESH	When a persistent entity instance is refreshed with `EntityManager#refresh()`, any associated persistent entity instances are also refreshed.
CascadeType.REPLICATE	When a detached entity instance is copied into a database with `Session#replicate()`, any associated detached entity instances are also copied.
CascadeType.ALL	This is shorthand to enable all cascading options for the mapped association.

There are more cascading options defined in the `org.hibernate.annotations.CascadeType` enumeration. Today, though, the only interesting option is `REPLICATE` and the `Session#replicate()` operation. All other `Session` operations have a standardized equivalent or an alternative on the `EntityManager` API, so we can ignore these settings.

We've already examined the `PERSIST` and `REMOVE` options. Let's analyze transitive detachment, merging, refreshing, and replication.

13.1.2 *Transitive detachment and merging*

We want to retrieve an `Item` and its `bids` from the database and work with this data in detached state. The `Bid` class maps this association with a `@ManyToOne`. It's bidirectional with this `@OneToMany` collection mapping in `Item`:

```
Path: Ch13/cascade/src/main/java/com/manning/javapersistence/ch13/filtering
➥ /cascade/Item.java

@Entity
public class Item {
```

```
@OneToMany(
    mappedBy = "item",
    cascade = {CascadeType.DETACH, CascadeType.MERGE}
)
private Set<Bid> bids = new HashSet<>();
//  . . .
}
```

Transitive detachment and merging is enabled with the `DETACH` and `MERGE` cascade types. Now we can load the `Item` and initialize its `bids` collection:

Path: Ch13/cascade/src/test/java/com/manning/javapersistence/ch13/filtering
➡ /Cascade.java

```
Item item = em.find(Item.class, ITEM_ID);                    Ⓐ
assertEquals(2, item.getBids().size());                   ⟵
em.detach(item);
```

Ⓐ Accessing `item.getBids()` initializes the bids collection (it is lazily initialized).

Ⓑ The `EntityManager#detach()` operation is cascaded: it evicts the `Item` instance from the persistence context as well as all `bids` in the collection. If the `bids` aren't loaded, they aren't detached. (Of course, we could have closed the persistence context, effectively detaching *all* loaded entity instances.)

In detached state, we can change the `Item#name`, create a new `Bid`, and link it with the `Item`:

Path: Ch13/cascade/src/test/java/com/manning/javapersistence/ch13/filtering
➡ /Cascade.java

```
item.setName("New Name");
Bid bid = new Bid(new BigDecimal("101.00"), item);
item.addBid(bid);
```

Because we're working with detached entity state and collections, we have to pay extra attention to identity and equality. As discussed in section 10.3, we should override the `equals()` and `hashCode()` methods on the `Bid` entity class:

Path: Ch13/cascade/src/main/java/com/manning/javapersistence/ch13/filtering
➡ /cascade/Bid.java

```
@Entity
public class Bid {
    @Override
    public boolean equals(Object o) {
 if (this == o) return true;
 if (o instanceof Bid bid) {
            return Objects.equals(id, bid.id) &&
                    Objects.equals(amount, bid.amount) &&
                    Objects.equals(item, bid.item);
    }
```

```
            return false;
        }

        @Override
        public int hashCode() {
            return Objects.hash(id, amount, item);
        }
    }
```

Two Bid instances are *equal* when they have the same id, the same amount, and are linked with the same Item.

Once we're done with the modifications in detached state, the next step is to store the changes. Using a new persistence context, we can merge the detached Item and let Hibernate detect the changes.

Using the merge method, Hibernate will merge a detached instance. First it checks whether the persistence context already contains an entity with the given identifier value. If there isn't any, the entity is loaded from the database. Hibernate is smart enough to know that it will also need the referenced entities during merging, so it fetches them right away in the same SQL query.

When flushing the persistence context, Hibernate detects whether some property of the entity changed during merging. Referenced entities may also be stored:

Path: Ch13/cascade/src/test/java/com/manning/javapersistence/ch13/filtering
➡ /Cascade.java

```
Item mergedItem = em.merge(item);     ⬅──🅐
// select i.*, b.*
//   from ITEM i
//     left outer join BID b on i.ID = b.ITEM_ID
//   where i.ID = ?
for (Bid b : mergedItem.getBids()) {     ⬅──┐
    assertNotNull(b.getId());                🅑
}
em.flush();     🅒
// update ITEM set NAME = ? where ID = ?
// insert into BID values (?, ?, ?,  . . . )
```

🅐 Hibernate merges the detached item. There isn't any Item with the given identifier value, so the Item is loaded from the database. Hibernate fetches the bids during merging in the same SQL query. Hibernate then copies the detached item values into the loaded instance, which it returns to us in persistent state. The same procedure is applied to every Bid, and Hibernate will detect that one of the bids is new.

🅑 Hibernate made the new Bid persistent during merging. It now has an identifier value assigned.

🅒 When we flush the persistence context, Hibernate detects that the name of the Item changed during merging. The new Bid will also be stored.

Cascaded merging with collections is a powerful feature; consider how much code we would have to write without Hibernate to implement this functionality.

Eagerly fetching associations when merging

In the final code example in section 13.1.2, we said that Hibernate is smart enough to load the `Item#bids` collection when we merge a detached `Item`. Hibernate always loads entity associations eagerly with a `JOIN` when merging if `CascadeType.MERGE` is enabled for the association. This is smart in the aforementioned case, where the `Item#bids` were initialized, detached, and modified. It's necessary and optimal for Hibernate to load the collection when merging with a `JOIN`, but if we merge an `Item` instance with an uninitialized `bids` collection or an uninitialized `seller` proxy, Hibernate will fetch the collection and proxy with a `JOIN` when merging. The merge initializes these associations on the managed `Item` it returns. `CascadeType.MERGE` causes Hibernate to ignore and effectively override any `FetchType.LAZY` mapping (as allowed by the JPA specification).

Our next example is less sophisticated, enabling cascaded refreshing of related entities.

13.1.3 Cascading refresh

The `User` entity class has a one-to-many relationship with `BillingDetails`: each user of the application may have several credit cards, bank accounts, and so on. If you would like to review the `BillingDetails` class, take a look at the mappings in chapter 7.

We can map the relationship between `User` and `BillingDetails` as a unidirectional one-to-many entity association:

Path: Ch13/cascade/src/main/java/com/manning/javapersistence/ch13/filtering
➡ /cascade/User.java

```
@Entity
@Table(name = "USERS")
public class User {
    @OneToMany(cascade = {CascadeType.PERSIST, CascadeType.REFRESH})
    @JoinColumn(name = "USER_ID", nullable = false)
    private Set<BillingDetails> billingDetails = new HashSet<>();
    //  . . .
}
```

The cascading options enabled for this association are `PERSIST` and `REFRESH`. The `PERSIST` option simplifies storing billing details; they become persistent when we add an instance of `BillingDetails` to the collection of an already persistent `User`.

The `REFRESH` cascading option ensures that when we reload the state of a `User` instance, Hibernate will also refresh the state of each `BillingDetails` instance linked to the `User`. For example, when we `refresh()` the managed `User` instance, Hibernate cascades the operation to the managed `BillingDetails` and refreshes each with an SQL `SELECT`. If none of these instances remain in the database, Hibernate throws an

EntityNotFoundException. Then, Hibernate refreshes the User instance and eagerly loads the entire billingDetails collection to discover any new BillingDetails:

Path: Ch13/cascade/src/test/java/com/manning/javapersistence/ch13/filtering
➥ /Cascade.java

```
                                                         Ⓐ
User user = em.find(User.class, USER_ID);            ←──┘
assertEquals(2, user.getBillingDetails().size());    ←──┐
for (BillingDetails bd : user.getBillingDetails()) {    Ⓑ
    assertEquals("John Doe", bd.getOwner());
}
// Someone modifies the billing information in the database!
em.refresh(user);
// select * from CREDITCARD join BILLINGDETAILS where ID = ?
// select * from BANKACCOUNT join BILLINGDETAILS where ID = ?
// select * from USERS
//   left outer join BILLINGDETAILS
//   left outer join CREDITCARD
//   left outer JOIN BANKACCOUNT
// where ID = ?
for (BillingDetails bd : user.getBillingDetails()) {
    assertEquals("Doe John", bd.getOwner());
}
```

Ⓒ (marker pointing to `em.refresh(user);`)

Ⓐ An instance of User is loaded from the database.

Ⓑ Its lazy billingDetails collection is initialized when we iterate through the elements or when we call size().

Ⓒ When we refresh() the managed User instance, Hibernate cascades the operation to the managed BillingDetails and refreshes each with an SQL SELECT.

This is a case where Hibernate isn't as smart as it could be. First, it executes an SQL SELECT for each BillingDetails instance that's in the persistence context and referenced by the collection. Then it loads the entire collection again to find any added BillingDetails. Hibernate could obviously do this with one SELECT.

We would like to refresh the record after it's modified by another transaction, so we have to keep in mind that the default transaction isolation level for MySQL is REPEATABLE_READ, while for most other databases it is READ_COMMITTED. We started one transaction and then a second, which committed its changes before the first one performed the refresh operation. For the first transaction to be able to see the changes from the second, we need to change the isolation level on the JDBC driver. That is why we provided the following configuration URL:

Path: Ch13/cascade/src/main/resources/META-INF/persistence.xml

```
<property name="javax.persistence.jdbc.url"
value="jdbc:mysql://localhost:3306/CH13_CASCADE?
➥ sessionVariables=transaction_isolation=
➥ 'READ-COMMITTED'&amp;serverTimezone=UTC"/>
```

As the change is made only at the configuration level, the code will continue to work correctly using different databases, as long as the persistence.xml file contains the correct configuration.

The last cascading option is for the Hibernate-only `replicate()` operation.

13.1.4 Cascading replication

We first examined replication in section 10.2.7. This nonstandard operation is available on the Hibernate `Session` API. Its main use case is copying data from one database into another.

Consider this many-to-one entity association mapping between `Item` and `User`:

Path: Ch13/cascade/src/main/java/com/manning/javapersistence/ch13/filtering
➥ /cascade/Item.java

```
@Entity
public class Item {
    @ManyToOne(fetch = FetchType.LAZY)
    @JoinColumn(name = "SELLER_ID", nullable = false)
    @org.hibernate.annotations.Cascade(
        org.hibernate.annotations.CascadeType.REPLICATE
    )
    private User seller;
    //  . . .
}
```

Here we enable the `REPLICATE` cascading option with a Hibernate annotation. Next, we'll load an `Item` and its `seller` from the source database:

Path: Ch13/cascade/src/test/java/com/manning/javapersistence/ch13/filtering
➥ /Cascade.java

```
em = emf.createEntityManager();
em.getTransaction().begin();
Item item = em.find(Item.class, ITEM_ID);          Ⓐ
assertNotNull(item.getSeller().getUsername());  ◄┘
em.getTransaction().commit();
em.close();
```

Ⓐ Initialize `Item#seller` lazily.

After we close the persistence context, the `Item` and the `User` entity instances are in detached state. Next, we connect to the database and write the detached data:

Path: Ch13/cascade/src/test/java/com/manning/javapersistence/ch13/filtering
➥ /Cascade.java

```
EntityManager otherDatabase = //  . . .   get EntityManager
otherDatabase.getTransaction().begin();
otherDatabase.unwrap(Session.class)
    .replicate(item, ReplicationMode.OVERWRITE);
```

```
// select ID from ITEM where ID = ?
// select ID from USERS where ID = ?
otherDatabase.getTransaction().commit();
// update ITEM set NAME = ?, SELLER_ID = ?,  . . .  where ID = ?
// update USERS set USERNAME = ?,  . . .  where ID = ?
otherDatabase.close();
```

When we call `replicate()` on the detached `Item`, Hibernate executes SQL `SELECT` statements to find out whether the `Item` and its `seller` are already present in the database. Then, on commit, when the persistence context is flushed, Hibernate writes the values of the `Item` and the `seller` into the target database. In the previous example, these rows were already present, so we'd see an `UPDATE` of each, overwriting the values in the database. If the target database doesn't contain the `Item` or `User`, two `INSERT`s are made.

13.2 *Listening to and intercepting events*

In this section, we'll analyze three different APIs for custom event listeners and persistence lifecycle interceptors available in JPA and Hibernate. They allow us to do several things:

- Use the standard JPA lifecycle callback methods and event listeners.
- Write a proprietary `org.hibernate.Interceptor` and activate it on a `Session`.
- Use extension points of the Hibernate core engine with the `org.hibernate.event` service provider interface (SPI).

Let's start with the standard JPA callbacks. They offer easy access to persist, load, and remove lifecycle events.

13.2.1 *JPA event listeners and callbacks*

Let's say we want to log a message whenever a new entity instance is stored. An entity listener class must have an implicit or explicit public no-argument constructor. It doesn't have to implement any special interfaces. An entity listener is stateless; the JPA engine automatically creates and destroys it. This means it can be difficult to get more contextual information when we need it, but we'll demonstrate some possibilities.

First we'll write a lifecycle event listener with a callback method, annotated with `@PostPersist`, as shown in the following listing. We can annotate any method of an entity listener class as a callback method for persistence lifecycle events.

> **Listing 13.1   Notifying an admin when an entity instance was stored**

Path: Ch13/callback/src/main/java/com/manning/javapersistence/ch13
➥ /filtering/callback/PersistEntityListener.java

```
public class PersistEntityListener {                          Ⓐ
    @PostPersist
    public void logMessage(Object entityInstance) {
        User currentUser = CurrentUser.INSTANCE.get();       Ⓑ
```

```
        Log log = Log.INSTANCE;
        log.save(
            "Entity instance persisted by "
                + currentUser.getUsername()
                + ": "
                + entityInstance
        );
    }
}
```

Ⓐ The `logMessage()` method, annotated with `@PostPersist`, is invoked after a new entity instance is stored in the database.

Ⓑ We want the contextual information of the currently logged-in user and access to log information. A primitive solution is to use thread-local variables and singletons; the source for `CurrentUser` and `Log` is in the example code.

A callback method of an entity listener class has a single `Object` parameter: the entity instance involved in the state change. If we only enable the callback for a particular entity type, we may declare the argument as that specific type. The callback method can have any kind of access; it doesn't have to be public. It must not be static or final and return nothing. If a callback method throws an unchecked `RuntimeException`, Hibernate will abort the operation and mark the current transaction for rollback. If a callback method declares and throws a checked `Exception`, Hibernate will wrap and treat it as a `RuntimeException`.

We can only use each callback annotation once in an entity listener class; that is, only one method may be annotated `@PostPersist`. Table 13.2 summarizes all the available callback annotations.

Table 13.2 Lifecycle callback annotations

Annotation	Description
`@PostLoad`	Triggered after an entity instance is loaded into the persistence context, either by identifier lookup, through navigation and proxy/collection initialization, or with a query. Also called after refreshing an already-persistent instance.
`@PrePersist`	Called immediately when `persist()` is called on an entity instance. Also called for `merge()` when an entity is discovered as transient, after the transient state is copied into a persistent instance. Also called for associated entities if we enable `CascadeType.PERSIST`.
`@PostPersist`	Called after the database operation for making an entity instance persistent is executed and an identifier value is assigned. This may be when `persist()` or `merge()` is invoked, or later when the persistence context is flushed if the identifier generator is *pre-insert* (see section 5.2.5). Also called for associated entities if we enable `CascadeType.PERSIST`.
`@PreUpdate`, `@PostUpdate`	Executed before and after the persistence context is synchronized with the database; that is, before and after flushing. Triggered only when the state of the entity requires synchronization (for example, because it's considered dirty).

Table 13.2   Lifecycle callback annotations *(continued)*

Annotation	Description
`@PreRemove,` `@PostRemove`	Triggered when `remove()` is called or the entity instance is removed by cascading, and after deletion of the record in the database when the persistence context is flushed.

An entity listener class must be enabled for any entity we'd like to intercept, such as this `Item`:

Path: Ch13/callback/src/main/java/com/manning/javapersistence/ch13
➡ /filtering/callback/Item.java

```
@Entity
@EntityListeners(
    PersistEntityListener.class
)
public class Item {
    //  . . .
}
```

The `@EntityListeners` annotation accepts an array of listener classes if we have several interceptors. If several listeners define callback methods for the same event, Hibernate invokes the listeners in the declared order.

We don't have to write a separate entity listener class to intercept lifecycle events. We can, for example, implement the `logMessage()` method on the `User` entity class:

Path: Ch13/callback/src/main/java/com/manning/javapersistence/ch13
➡ /filtering/callback/User.java

```
@Entity
@Table(name = "USERS")
public class User {
    @PostPersist
    public void logMessage(){
        User currentUser = CurrentUser.INSTANCE.get();
        Log log = Log.INSTANCE;
        log.save(
                        "Entity instance persisted by "
            + currentUser.getUsername()
            + ": "
            + this
        );
    }
    //  . . .
}
```

Note that callback methods on an entity class don't have any arguments: the "current" entity involved in the state changes is `this`. Duplicate callbacks for the same event aren't allowed in a single class, but we can intercept the same event with callback methods in several listener classes or in a listener and an entity class.

We can also add callback methods on an entity superclass for the entire hierarchy. If, for a particular entity subclass, we want to disable the superclass's callbacks, we can annotate the subclass with `@ExcludeSuperclassListeners`. If we want to disable a default entity listener for a particular entity, we can mark it with the `@ExcludeDefault-Listeners` annotation:

```
Path: Ch13/callback/src/main/java/com/manning/javapersistence/ch13
 /filtering/callback/User.java

@Entity
@Table(name = "USERS")
@ExcludeDefaultListeners
public class User {
    //  . . .
}
```

JPA event listeners and callbacks provide a rudimentary framework for reacting to lifecycle events with our own procedures. Hibernate also has a more fine-grained and powerful alternative API: `org.hibernate.Interceptor`.

13.2.2   Implementing Hibernate interceptors

Let's assume that we want to write an audit log of data modifications in a separate database table. For example, we may want to record information about creation and update events for each `Item`. The audit log includes the user, the date and time of the event, what type of event occurred, and the identifier of the `Item` that was changed.

Audit logs are often handled using database triggers. On the other hand, it's sometimes better for the application to take responsibility, especially if portability between different databases is required.

We need several elements to implement audit logging. First, we have to mark the entity classes for which we want to enable audit logging. Next, we define what information to log, such as the user, date, time, and type of modification. Finally, we'll tie it all together with an `org.hibernate.Interceptor` that automatically creates the audit trail.

First we'll create a marker interface, `Auditable`:

```
Path: Ch13/interceptor/src/main/java/com/manning/javapersistence/ch13
 /filtering/interceptor/Auditable.java

public interface Auditable {
    Long getId();
}
```

This interface requires that a persistent entity class exposes its identifier with a getter method; we need this property to log the audit trail. Enabling audit logging for a particular persistent class is then trivial. We add it to the class declaration, such as for `Item`:

```
Path: /model/src/main/java/org/jpwh/model/filtering/interceptor/Item.java

@Entity
public class Item implements Auditable {
    //  . . .
}
```

Now we can create a new persistent entity class, `AuditLogRecord`, with the information we want to log in the audit database table:

```
Path: Ch13/interceptor/src/main/java/com/manning/javapersistence/ch13
➥ /filtering/interceptor/AuditLogRecord.java

@Entity
public class AuditLogRecord {
    @Id
    @GeneratedValue(generator = Constants.ID_GENERATOR)
    private Long id;
    @NotNull
    private String message;
    @NotNull
    private Long entityId;
    @NotNull
    private Class<? extends Auditable> entityClass;
    @NotNull
    private Long userId;
    @NotNull
    private LocalDateTime createdOn = LocalDateTime.now();
    //  . . .
}
```

We want to store an instance of `AuditLogRecord` whenever Hibernate inserts or updates an `Item` in the database. A Hibernate interceptor can handle this automatically. Instead of implementing all methods in `org.hibernate.Interceptor`, we extend the `EmptyInterceptor` and override only the methods we need, as demonstrated in listing 13.2. We need to access the database to write the audit log, so the interceptor needs a Hibernate `Session`.

We'll also want to store the identifier of the currently logged-in user in each audit log record. The `inserts` and `updates` instance variables that we'll declare will be collections where this interceptor will hold its internal state.

> **Listing 13.2   Hibernate interceptor logging modification events**

```
Path: Ch13/interceptor/src/test/java/com/manning/javapersistence/ch13
➥ /filtering/AuditLogInterceptor.java

public class AuditLogInterceptor extends EmptyInterceptor {
    private Session currentSession;
    private Long currentUserId;
    private Set<Auditable> inserts = new HashSet<>();
    private Set<Auditable> updates = new HashSet<>();
```

```
    public void setCurrentSession(Session session) {
        this.currentSession = session;
    }
    public void setCurrentUserId(Long currentUserId) {
        this.currentUserId = currentUserId;
    }                                                                    Ⓐ
    public boolean onSave(Object entity, Serializable id,    ◁
                          Object[] state, String[] propertyNames,
                          Type[] types)
        throws CallbackException {
        if (entity instanceof Auditable aud) {
            inserts.add(aud);
        }
        return false;   ◁──Ⓑ
    }                                                                              Ⓒ
    public boolean onFlushDirty(Object entity, Serializable id,    ◁
                                Object[] currentState,
                                Object[] previousState,
                                String[] propertyNames, Type[] types)
        throws CallbackException {
        if (entity instanceof Auditable aud) {
            updates.add(aud);
        }
        return false;   ◁──
    }                        Ⓓ
    //   . . .
}
```

Ⓐ This method is called when an entity instance is made persistent.

Ⓑ The state was not modified.

Ⓒ This method is called when an entity instance is detected as dirty during flushing of the persistence context.

Ⓓ The currentState was not modified.

The interceptor collects the modified Auditable instances in inserts and updates. Note that in onSave(), there may not be an identifier value assigned to the given entity instance. Hibernate guarantees to set entity identifiers during flushing, so the actual audit log trail is written in the postFlush() callback, which isn't shown in listing 13.2. This method is called after the flushing of the persistence context is complete.

Now we'll write the audit log records for all insertions and updates we collected earlier:

Path: Ch13/interceptor/src/test/java/com/manning/javapersistence/ch13
➡ /filtering/AuditLogInterceptor.java

```
public class AuditLogInterceptor extends EmptyInterceptor {
    //   . . .
    public void postFlush(@SuppressWarnings("rawtypes") Iterator iterator)
    ➡ throws CallbackException {
        Session tempSession =                                ◁──Ⓐ
            currentSession.sessionWithOptions()
```

```
            .connection()
            .openSession();
    try {
        for (Auditable entity : inserts) {        ←──┐ B
            tempSession.persist(
                new AuditLogRecord("insert", entity, currentUserId)
            );
        }
        for (Auditable entity : updates) {
            tempSession.persist(
                new AuditLogRecord("update", entity, currentUserId)
            );                            C
        }
        tempSession.flush();              ←──┐
    } finally {
        tempSession.close();
        inserts.clear();
        updates.clear();
    }
    }
}
```

A We can't access the original persistence context—the `Session` that is currently executing this interceptor. The `Session` is in a fragile state during interceptor calls. Hibernate lets us create a new `Session` that inherits some information from the original `Session` with the `sessionWithOptions()` method. The new temporary `Session` works with the same transaction and database connection as the original `Session`.

B We store a new `AuditLogRecord` for each insertion and update using the temporary `Session`.

C We flush and close the temporary `Session` independently of the original `Session`.

We're now ready to enable this interceptor:

Path: Ch13/interceptor/src/test/java/com/manning/javapersistence/ch13
➥ /filtering/AuditLogging.java

```
EntityManager em = emf.createEntityManager();
SessionFactory sessionFactory = emf.unwrap(SessionFactory.class);
Session session = sessionFactory.withOptions().
        interceptor(new AuditLogInterceptor()).openSession();
```

> **Enabling default interceptors**
>
> If we want to enable an interceptor by default for any `EntityManager`, we can set the `hibernate.ejb.interceptor` property in persistence.xml to a class that implements `org.hibernate.Interceptor`. Note that, unlike a session-scoped interceptor, Hibernate shares this default interceptor, so it must be thread-safe! The example `AuditLogInterceptor` is *not* thread-safe.

This `Session` now has an enabled `AuditLogInterceptor`, but the interceptor must also be configured with the current `Session` and logged-in user identifier. This involves some typecasts to access the Hibernate API:

```
Path: Ch13/interceptor/src/test/java/com/manning/javapersistence/ch13
    /filtering/AuditLogging.java
```

```
AuditLogInterceptor interceptor =
    (AuditLogInterceptor) ((SessionImplementor) session).getInterceptor();
interceptor.setCurrentSession(session);
interceptor.setCurrentUserId(CURRENT_USER_ID);
```

The `Session` is now ready for use, and an audit trail will be written whenever we store or modify an `Item` instance with it.

Hibernate interceptors are flexible, and, unlike JPA event listeners and callback methods, we have access to much more contextual information when an event occurs. Having said that, Hibernate allows us to hook even deeper into its core with the extensible event system it's based on.

13.2.3 *The core event system*

The Hibernate core engine is based on a model of events and listeners. For example, if Hibernate needs to save an entity instance, it triggers an event. Whoever listens to this kind of event can catch it and handle saving the data. Hibernate, therefore, implements all of its core functionality as a set of default listeners, which can handle all Hibernate events.

Hibernate is open by design: we can write and enable our own listeners for Hibernate events. We can either replace the existing default listeners or extend them and execute a side effect or additional procedure. Replacing the event listeners is rare; doing so implies that our own listener implementation can take care of a piece of Hibernate's core functionality.

Essentially, all the methods of the `Session` interface (and its narrower cousin, the `EntityManager`) correlate to an event. The `find()` and `load()` methods trigger a `Load-Event`, and by default this event is processed with the `DefaultLoadEventListener`.

A custom listener should implement the appropriate interface for the event it wants to process and/or extend one of the convenience base classes provided by Hibernate, or any of the default event listeners. Here's an example of a custom load event listener.

Listing 13.3 Custom load event listener

```
Path: Ch13/interceptor/src/test/java/com/manning/javapersistence/ch13
    /filtering/SecurityLoadListener.java
```

```java
public class SecurityLoadListener extends DefaultLoadEventListener {
    public void onLoad(LoadEvent event, LoadType loadType)
        throws HibernateException {
```

```
        boolean authorized =
            MySecurity.isAuthorized(
                event.getEntityClassName(), event.getEntityId()
            );
        if (!authorized) {
            throw new MySecurityException("Unauthorized access");
        }
        super.onLoad(event, loadType);
    }
}
```

This listener performs custom authorization code. A listener should be considered effectively a singleton, meaning it's shared between persistence contexts and thus shouldn't save any transaction-related state as instance variables. For a list of all events and listener interfaces in native Hibernate, see the API Javadoc of the `org.hibernate` `.event` package.

We enable listeners for each core event in persistence.xml:

Path: Ch13/interceptor/src/main/resources/META-INF/persistence.xml

```
<properties>
    // . . .
    <property name="hibernate.ejb.event.load" value=
        "com.manning.javapersistence.ch13.filtering.SecurityLoadListener"/>
</properties>
```

The property name of the configuration settings always starts with `hibernate.ejb` `.event`, followed by the type of event we want to listen to. You can find a list of all event types in `org.hibernate.event.spi.EventType`. The value of the property can be a comma-separated list of listener class names; Hibernate will call each listener in the specified order.

We rarely have to extend the Hibernate core event system with our own functionality. Most of the time, an `org.hibernate.Interceptor` is flexible enough. However, it helps to have more options and to be able to replace any piece of the Hibernate core engine in a modular fashion.

The audit-logging implementation we demonstrated in the previous section was very simple. If we needed to log more information for auditing, such as the actually changed property values of an entity, we would consider Hibernate Envers.

13.3   *Auditing and versioning with Hibernate Envers*

Envers is a project of the Hibernate suite dedicated to audit logging and keeping multiple versions of data in the database. This is similar to version control systems you may already be familiar with, such as Subversion and Git.

With Envers enabled, a copy of the data is automatically stored in separate database tables when we add, modify, or delete data in the main tables of the application. Envers internally uses the Hibernate event SPI you saw in the previous section. Envers listens to Hibernate events, and when Hibernate stores changes in the database, Envers creates a copy of the data and logs a revision in its own tables.

Envers groups all data modifications in a unit of work—that is, in a transaction—as a change set with a revision number. We can write queries with the Envers API to retrieve historical data, given a revision number or timestamp; for example, "find all `Item` instances as they were last Friday."

Once you enable Envers in your application, you will be able to easily work with it, as it is based on annotations. It will provide you with the option to keep multiple versions of data in the database with little effort on your part. The tradeoff is that it will create a lot of additional tables (but you will be able to control which tables you want to audit).

13.3.1 Enabling audit logging

Envers is available without further configuration as soon as we put its JAR file on the classpath (we'll include it as a Maven dependency). We can enable audit logging selectively for an entity class with the `@org.hibernate.envers.Audited` annotation.

Listing 13.4   Enabling audit logging for the `Item` entity

```
Path: Ch13/envers/src/main/java/com/manning/javapersistence/ch13
⮑ /filtering/envers/Item.java

@Entity
@org.hibernate.envers.Audited
public class Item {
    @NotNull
    private String name;
    @OneToMany(mappedBy = "item")
    @org.hibernate.envers.NotAudited
    private Set<Bid> bids = new HashSet<>();
    @ManyToOne(fetch = FetchType.LAZY)
    @JoinColumn(name = "SELLER_ID", nullable = false)
    private User seller;
    //  . . .
}
```

We've now enabled audit logging for `Item` instances and all properties of the entity. To disable audit logging for a particular property, we can annotate it with `@NotAudited`. In this case, Envers ignores the `bids` but audits the `seller`. We also have to enable auditing with `@Audited` on the `User` class.

Hibernate will now generate (or expect) additional database tables to hold historical data for each `Item` and `User`. Figure 13.1 shows the schema for these tables.

The `ITEM_AUD` and `USERS_AUD` tables are where the modification history of `Item` and `User` instances is stored. When we modify data and commit a transaction, Hibernate inserts a new revision number with a timestamp into the `REVINFO` table. Then, for each modified and audited entity instance involved in the change set, a copy of its data is stored in the audit tables. Foreign keys on revision number columns link the

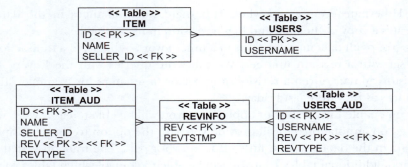

Figure 13.1   Audit logging tables for the `Item` and `User` entities

change set together. The `REVTYPE` column holds the type of change: whether the entity instance was inserted, updated, or deleted in the transaction. Envers never automatically removes any revision information or historical data; even after we `remove()` an `Item` instance, we still have its previous versions stored in `ITEM_AUD`.

Let's run through some transactions to see how this works.

13.3.2   *Creating an audit trail*

In the following code examples, we'll look at several transactions involving an `Item` and its `seller`, a `User`. We'll create and store an `Item` and `User`, then modify both, and then finally delete the `Item`.

You should already be familiar with this code. Envers automatically creates an audit trail when we work with the `EntityManager`:

Path: Ch13/envers/src/test/java/com/manning/javapersistence/ch13/filtering
➥ /Envers.java

```
EntityManager em = emf.createEntityManager();
em.getTransaction().begin();
User user = new User("johndoe");
em.persist(user);
Item item = new Item("Foo", user);
em.persist(item);
em.getTransaction().commit();
em.close();
```

Path: Ch13/envers/src/test/java/com/manning/javapersistence/ch13/filtering
➥ /Envers.java

```
EntityManager em = emf.createEntityManager();
em.getTransaction().begin();
Item item = em.find(Item.class, ITEM_ID);
item.setName("Bar");
item.getSeller().setUsername("doejohn");
em.getTransaction().commit();
em.close();
```

Path: Ch13/envers/src/test/java/com/manning/javapersistence/ch13/filtering
➡ /Envers.java

```
EntityManager em = emf.createEntityManager();
em.getTransaction().begin();
EntityManager em = JPA.createEntityManager();
Item item = em.find(Item.class, ITEM_ID);
em.remove(item);
em.getTransaction().commit();
em.close();
```

Envers transparently writes the audit trail for this sequence of transactions by logging three change sets. To access this historical data, we first have to obtain the number of the revision, representing the change set we'd like to access.

13.3.3 Finding revisions

With the Envers `AuditReader` API, we can find the revision number of each change set. The main Envers API is `AuditReader`. It can be accessed with an `EntityManager`. Given a timestamp, we can find the revision number of a change set made before or on that timestamp. If we don't have a timestamp, we can get all the revision numbers in which a particular audited entity instance was involved.

Listing 13.5   Obtaining the revision numbers of change sets

Path: Ch13/envers/src/test/java/com/manning/javapersistence/ch13/filtering
➡ /Envers.java

```
                                                                   Ⓐ
AuditReader auditReader = AuditReaderFactory.get(em);          ◀──┘
Number revisionCreate =
            auditReader.getRevisionNumberForDate(TIMESTAMP_CREATE);
Number revisionUpdate =
         auditReader.getRevisionNumberForDate(TIMESTAMP_UPDATE);
Number revisionDelete =
      auditReader.getRevisionNumberForDate(TIMESTAMP_DELETE);
List<Number> itemRevisions =
        auditReader.getRevisions(Item.class, ITEM_ID);      ◀──┐
assertEquals(3, itemRevisions.size());
for (Number itemRevision : itemRevisions) {           Ⓒ              Ⓓ
  Date itemRevisionTimestamp = auditReader.getRevisionDate(itemRevision); ◀──┘
  //  . . .
}
                                                      Ⓔ
List<Number> userRevisions =
        auditReader.getRevisions(User.class, USER_ID);    ◀──┘
assertEquals(2, userRevisions.size());
```

Ⓑ (left margin, pointing to `Number revisionCreate`)

Ⓐ Access the `AuditReader` Envers API.

Ⓑ Find the revision number of a change set made before or on that timestamp.

Ⓒ Without a timestamp, this operation finds all change sets where the given `Item` was created, modified, or deleted. In our example, we created, modified, and then deleted the `Item`. Hence, we have three revisions.

D If we have a revision number, we can get the timestamp when Envers logged the change set.

E We created and modified the User, so there are two revisions.

In listing 13.5, we assumed that either we know the (approximate) timestamp for a transaction or we have the identifier value of an entity so we can obtain its revisions. If we have neither, we may want to explore the audit log with queries. This is also useful if we have to show a list of all change sets in the user interface of the application.

The following code discovers all revisions of the Item entity class and loads each Item version and the audit log information for that change set:

Path: Ch13/envers/src/test/java/com/manning/javapersistence/ch13/filtering
➥ /Envers.java   **A**

```
AuditQuery query = auditReader.createQuery()
    .forRevisionsOfEntity(Item.class, false, false);
@SuppressWarnings("unchecked")
List<Object[]> result = query.getResultList();
for (Object[] tuple : result) {
    Item item = (Item) tuple[0];
    DefaultRevisionEntity revision = (DefaultRevisionEntity)tuple[1];
    RevisionType revisionType = (RevisionType)tuple[2];
    if (revision.getId() == 1) {
        assertEquals(RevisionType.ADD, revisionType);
        assertEquals("Foo", item.getName());
    } else if (revision.getId() == 2) {
        assertEquals(RevisionType.MOD, revisionType);
        assertEquals("Bar", item.getName());
    } else if (revision.getId() == 3) {
        assertEquals(RevisionType.DEL, revisionType);
        assertNull(item);
    }
}
```

A If we don't know the modification timestamps or revision numbers, we can write a query with forRevisionsOfEntity() to obtain all audit trail details of a particular entity.

B This query returns the audit trail details as a List of Object[].

C Each result tuple contains the entity instance for a particular revision, the revision details (including revision number and timestamp), as well as the revision type.

D The revision type indicates why Envers created the revision—whether the entity instance was inserted, modified, or deleted in the database.

Revision numbers are sequentially incremented; a higher revision number is always a more recent version of an entity instance. We now have revision numbers for the three change sets in the audit trail, giving us access to historical data.

13.3.4 Accessing historical data

With a revision number, we can access different versions of the Item and its seller.

Listing 13.6 Loading historical versions of entity instances

Path: Ch13/envers/src/test/java/com/manning/javapersistence/ch13/filtering
➥ /Envers.java

```
Item item = auditReader.find(Item.class, ITEM_ID, revisionCreate);   ◄───┘  Ⓐ
assertEquals("Foo", item.getName());                         Ⓑ
assertEquals("johndoe", item.getSeller().getUsername());
Item modifiedItem = auditReader.find(Item.class,             ◄───┘
        ITEM_ID, revisionUpdate);
assertEquals("Bar", modifiedItem.getName());
assertEquals("doejohn", modifiedItem.getSeller().getUsername());
Item deletedItem = auditReader.find(Item.class, ◄───
        ITEM_ID, revisionDelete);                            ⒞
assertNull(deletedItem);
User user = auditReader.find(User.class,
        USER_ID, revisionDelete);
assertEquals("doejohn", user.getUsername());
```

Ⓐ The find() method returns an audited entity instance version, given a revision. This operation loads the Item as it was after creation.

Ⓑ The seller of this change set is also retrieved automatically.

Ⓒ In this revision, the Item was deleted, so find() returns null.

Ⓓ The example didn't modify the User in this revision, so Envers returns its closest historical revision.

The AuditReader#find() operation retrieves only a single entity instance, like EntityManager#find(). But the returned entity instances are *not* in persistent state: the persistence context doesn't manage them. If we modify an older version of Item, Hibernate won't update the database. Consider the entity instances returned by the AuditReader API to be detached, or read-only.

AuditReader also has an API for the execution of arbitrary queries, similar to the native Hibernate Criteria API.

Listing 13.7 Querying historical entity instances

Path: Ch13/envers/src/test/java/com/manning/javapersistence/ch13/filtering
➥ /Envers.java

```
AuditQuery query = auditReader.createQuery()                         ◄───┘  Ⓐ
    .forEntitiesAtRevision(Item.class, revisionUpdate);             Ⓑ
query.add(AuditEntity.property("name").like("Ba", MatchMode.START)); ◄───┘  Ⓒ
query.add(AuditEntity.relatedId("seller").eq(USER_ID));
query.addOrder(AuditEntity.property("name").desc());                ◄─── Ⓓ
query.setFirstResult(0);   ◄───┐
query.setMaxResults(10);       Ⓔ
```

```
assertEquals(1, query.getResultList().size());
Item result = (Item)query.getResultList().get(0);
assertEquals("doejohn", result.getSeller().getUsername());
```

A This query returns `Item` instances restricted to a particular revision and change set.

B We can add further restrictions to the query; here the `Item#name` must start with "Ba".

C Restrictions can include entity associations; for example, we're looking for the revision of an `Item` sold by a particular `User`.

D We can order query results.

E We can paginate through large results.

Envers supports projection. The following query retrieves only the `Item#name` of a particular version:

Path: Ch13/envers/src/test/java/com/manning/javapersistence/ch13/filtering
➡ /Envers.java

```
AuditQuery query = auditReader.createQuery()
    .forEntitiesAtRevision(Item.class, revisionUpdate);
query.addProjection(AuditEntity.property("name"));
assertEquals(1, query.getResultList().size());
String result = (String)query.getSingleResult();
assertEquals("Bar", result);
```

Finally, we may want to roll back an entity instance to an older version. This can be accomplished with the `Session#replicate()` operation and overwriting an existing row. The following example loads the `User` instance from the first change set and then overwrites the current `User` in the database with the older version:

Path: Ch13/envers/src/test/java/com/manning/javapersistence/ch13/filtering
➡ /Envers.java

```
User user = auditReader.find(User.class, USER_ID, revisionCreate);
em.unwrap(Session.class)
    .replicate(user, ReplicationMode.OVERWRITE);
em.flush();
em.clear();
user = em.find(User.class, USER_ID);
assertEquals("johndoe", user.getUsername());
```

Envers will also track this change as an update in the audit log; it's just another new revision of the `User` instance.

Temporal data is a complex subject, and we encourage you to read the Envers reference documentation for more information. Adding details to the audit log, such as the user who made a change, isn't difficult. The documentation also shows how to configure different tracking strategies and customize the database schema used by Envers.

Next, imagine that you don't want to see all the data in the database. For example, the currently logged-in application user may not have the rights to see everything. Usually, we add a condition to the queries and restrict the results dynamically. But this becomes difficult if we have to handle a concern such as security, because we'd have to customize most of the queries in the application. We can centralize and isolate these restrictions with Hibernate's dynamic data filters.

13.4 Dynamic data filters

The first use case for dynamic data filtering relates to data security. A User in Caveat-Emptor may have a `ranking` property, which is a simple integer:

Path: /model/src/main/java/org/jpwh/model/filtering/dynamic/User.java

```
@Entity
@Table(name = "USERS")
public class User {
    @NotNull
    private int ranking = 0;
    //  . . .
}
```

Now assume that users can only bid on items that other users offer with an equal or lower ranking. In business terms, we may have several groups of users that are defined by an arbitrary ranking (a number), and users can trade only with people who have the same or a lower ranking.

To implement this requirement, we'd have to customize all queries that load Item instances from the database. We'd check whether the Item#seller we want to load has an equal or lower ranking than the currently logged-in user. Hibernate can do this work for us with a dynamic filter.

13.4.1 Defining dynamic filters

First we'll define our filter with a name and the dynamic runtime parameters it accepts. We can place the Hibernate annotation for this definition on any entity class of our domain model or in a package-info.java metadata file:

Path: Ch13/dynamic/src/main/java/com/manning/javapersistence/ch13/filtering
➥ /dynamic/package-info.java

```
@org.hibernate.annotations.FilterDef(
    name = "limitByUserRanking",
    parameters = {
        @org.hibernate.annotations.ParamDef(
            name = "currentUserRanking", type = "int"
        )
    }
)
```

This example names this filter `limitByUserRanking`; note that filter names must be unique in a persistence unit. It accepts one runtime argument of type `int`. If we have several filter definitions, we declare them within `@org.hibernate.annotations` `.FilterDefs`.

The filter is inactive now; nothing indicates that it's supposed to apply to `Item` instances. We must apply and implement the filter on the classes or collections we want to filter.

13.4.2 Applying a dynamic filter

We want to apply the defined filter on the `Item` class so that no items are visible if the logged-in user doesn't have the necessary rank:

Path: Ch13/dynamic/src/main/java/com/manning/javapersistence/ch13/filtering
➡ /dynamic/Item.java

```
@Entity
@org.hibernate.annotations.Filter(
    name = "limitByUserRanking",
    condition = """
        :currentUserRanking >= (
                select u.RANKING from USERS u
                where u.ID = SELLER_ID
            )"""
)
public class Item {
    //  . . .
}
```

The `condition` in the preceding code is an SQL expression that's passed through directly to the database system, so we can use any SQL operator or function. It must evaluate to `true` if a record should pass the filter. In this example, we are using a subquery to obtain the `ranking` of the seller of the item. Unqualified columns, such as `SELLER_ID`, refer to the table mapped to the entity class. If the currently logged-in user's ranking isn't greater than or equal to the ranking returned by the subquery, the `Item` instance is filtered out. We can apply several filters by grouping them in an `@org.hibernate.annotations.Filters`.

A defined and applied filter, if enabled for a particular unit of work, filters out any `Item` instance that doesn't pass the condition. Let's enable it.

13.4.3 Enabling a dynamic filter

We've defined a data filter and applied it to a persistent entity class. It's still not filtering anything—it must be enabled and parameterized in the application for a particular unit of work, with the `Session` API:

Path: Ch13/dynamic/src/test/java/com/manning/javapersistence/ch13/filtering
➡ /DynamicFilter.java

```
org.hibernate.Filter filter = em.unwrap(Session.class)
    .enableFilter("limitByUserRanking");
filter.setParameter("currentUserRanking", 0);
```

We enable the filter by name, and the method returns a `Filter` on which we set the runtime arguments dynamically. We must set the parameters we've defined; here it's set to ranking 0. This example then filters out `Items` sold by a `User` with a higher ranking in this `Session`.

Other useful methods of the `Filter` are `getFilterDefinition()`, which allows us to iterate through the parameter names and types, and `validate()`, which throws a `HibernateException` if we forget to set a parameter. We can also set a list of arguments with `setParameterList()`; this is mostly useful if our SQL restriction contains an expression with a quantifier operator (the `IN` operator, for example).

Now every JPQL or criteria query that we execute on the filtered persistence context restricts the returned `Item` instances:

Path: Ch13/dynamic/src/test/java/com/manning/javapersistence/ch13/filtering
➥ /DynamicFilter.java

```
List<Item> items = em.createQuery("select i from Item i",
    Item.class).getResultList();
// select * from ITEM where 0 >=
//  (select u.RANKING from USERS u where u.ID = SELLER_ID)
```

Path: Ch13/dynamic/src/test/java/com/manning/javapersistence/ch13/filtering
➥ /DynamicFilter.java

```
CriteriaBuilder cb = em.getCriteriaBuilder();
CriteriaQuery<Item> criteria = cb.createQuery(Item.class);
criteria.select(criteria.from(Item.class));
List<Item> items = em.createQuery(criteria).getResultList();
// select * from ITEM where 0 >=
//  (select u.RANKING from USERS u  where u.ID = SELLER_ID)
```

Note how Hibernate dynamically appends the SQL restriction conditions to the statement generated.

When you first experiment with dynamic filters, you'll most likely run into a problem with retrieval by identifier. You might expect that `em.find(Item.class, ITEM_ID)` will be filtered as well. This is not the case, though: Hibernate doesn't apply filters to retrieval by identifier operations. One of the reasons is that data-filter conditions are SQL fragments, and lookup by identifier may be resolved completely in memory in the first-level persistence context cache. Similar reasoning applies to filtering of many-to-one or one-to-one associations. If a many-to-one association was filtered (for example, by returning `null` if you called `anItem.getSeller()`), the multiplicity of the association would change! You won't know if the item has a seller or if you aren't allowed to see it.

But you can dynamically filter collection access.

13.4.4 *Filtering collection access*

Until now, calling `someCategory.getItems()` has returned all `Item` instances that are referenced by that `Category`. This can be restricted with a filter applied to a collection:

Path: Ch13/dynamic/src/main/java/com/manning/javapersistence/ch13/filtering
➥ /dynamic/Category.java

```
@Entity
public class Category {
    @OneToMany(mappedBy = "category")
    @org.hibernate.annotations.Filter(
        name = "limitByUserRanking",
        condition = """
            :currentUserRanking >= (
                    select u.RANKING from USERS u
                    where u.ID = SELLER_ID
                    )"""
    )
    private Set<Item> items = new HashSet<>();
    //  . . .
}
```

If we now enable the filter in a `Session`, all iteration through a collection of `Category#` `items` is filtered:

Path: Ch13/dynamic/src/test/java/com/manning/javapersistence/ch13/filtering
➥ /DynamicFilter.java

```
filter.setParameter("currentUserRanking", 0);
Category category = em.find(Category.class, CATEGORY_ID);
assertEquals(1, category.getItems().size());
```

If the current user's ranking is 0, only one `Item` is loaded when we access the collection. With a ranking of 100, we can see more data:

Path: Ch13/dynamic/src/test/java/com/manning/javapersistence/ch13/filtering
➥ /DynamicFilter.java

```
filter.setParameter("currentUserRanking", 100);
category = em.find(Category.class, CATEGORY_ID);
assertEquals(2, category.getItems().size());
```

You probably noticed that the SQL condition for both filter applications is the same. If the SQL restriction is the same for all filter applications, we can set it as the default condition when we define the filter, so we don't have to repeat it:

Path: Ch13/dynamic/src/main/java/com/manning/javapersistence/ch13/filtering
➥ /dynamic/package-info.java

```
@org.hibernate.annotations.FilterDef(
    name = "limitByUserRankingDefault",
```

```
        defaultCondition= """
               :currentUserRanking >= (
                       select u.RANKING from USERS u
                       where u.ID = SELLER_ID
                  )""",
        parameters = {
           @org.hibernate.annotations.ParamDef(
               name = "currentUserRanking", type = "int"
           )
        }
    )
```

There are many other excellent use cases for dynamic data filters. We've seen a restriction of data access given an arbitrary security-related condition. This can be the user ranking, a particular group the user must belong to, or a role the user has been assigned. Data might be stored with a regional code (for example, all business contacts of a sales team). Or perhaps each salesperson works only on data that covers their region.

Summary

- Cascading state transitions are predefined reactions to lifecycle events in the persistence engine.
- Cascading provides options: the transitive detachment and merging, the cascading refresh and replication.
- You can implement event listeners and interceptors to add custom logic when Hibernate loads and stores data.
- You can use Hibernate Envers for audit logging and keeping multiple versions of data in the database (like a version control system).
- You can query Envers to retrieve historical data.
- You can use dynamic data filters so that Hibernate can automatically append arbitrary SQL restrictions to queries it generates.
- You can define dynamic filters, apply and enable the filters, and filter collection access.

Part 4

Building Java persistence applications with Spring

In part 4, you'll connect Java Persistence with the most widely used Java framework nowadays: Spring.

In chapter 14, you'll learn the most important strategies for creating a JPA or Hibernate application and integrating it with Spring. You'll see various alternatives for making this integration, you'll work in more depth with the DAO (data access object) pattern, and you'll build generic persistence applications.

Next, chapter 15 introduces and analyzes the possibilities of developing persistence applications using another part of the large Spring Data framework: Spring Data JDBC. In chapter 16, we'll work with Spring Data REST to build applications in the representational state transfer (REST) architectural style. After reading this part of the book, you'll know how to efficiently work with JPA, Hibernate, and Spring, and how to decide between the alternatives to integrate your persistence application with Spring.

14

Integrating JPA and Hibernate with Spring

This chapter covers

- Introducing Spring Framework and dependency injection
- Examining the data access object (DAO) design pattern
- Creating and generifying a Spring JPA application using the DAO design pattern
- Creating and generifying a Spring Hibernate application using the DAO design pattern

In this chapter, we'll analyze a few different possibilities for integrating Spring and Hibernate. Spring is a lightweight but also flexible and universal Java framework. It is open source, and it can be used at the level of any layer in a Java application. We'll investigate the principles behind the Spring Framework (*dependency injection*, also known as *inversion of control*), and we'll use Spring together with JPA or Hibernate to build Java persistence applications.

> **NOTE** To execute the examples from the source code, you'll first need to run the Ch14.sql script.

14.1   *Spring Framework and dependency injection*

Spring Framework provides a comprehensive infrastructure for developing Java applications. It handles the infrastructure so that you can focus on your application, and it enables you to build applications from plain old Java objects (POJOs).

Rod Johnson created Spring in 2002, beginning with his book *Expert One-on-One J2EE Design and Development* (Johnson, 2002). The basic idea behind Spring is that it simplifies the traditional approach to designing enterprise applications. For a quick introduction to the capabilities of the Spring Framework, the book *Spring Start Here* by Laurenţiu Spilcă (Spilcă, 2021) is a good source.

A Java application typically consists of objects that collaborate to solve a problem. The objects in a program depend on each other. You can use design patterns (factory, builder, proxy, decorator, and so on) to compose classes and objects, but this burden is on the side of the developer.

Spring implements various design patterns. Spring Framework's *dependency injection* pattern (also known as *inversion of control*, or IoC) supports the creation of an application consisting of different components and objects.

The key characteristic of a framework is exactly this dependency injection or IoC. When you call a method from JDK or a library, you are in control. In contrast, with a framework, control is inverted: the framework calls *you* (see figure 14.1). You must follow the paradigm provided by the framework and fill out your own code. The framework defines a skeleton, and you insert the features to fill out that skeleton. Your code is under the control of the framework, and the framework calls it. This way, you can focus on implementing the business logic rather than on the design.

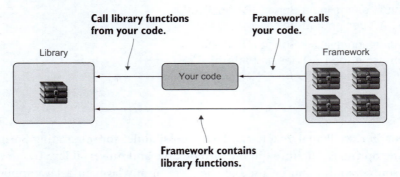

Figure 14.1   Your code calls a library. A framework calls your code.

The creation, dependency injection, and general lifecycle of objects under the control of the Spring Framework are managed by a container. The container will combine the application classes and the configuration information (metadata) to get a ready-to-run application (figure 14.2). The container is thus at the core of the IoC principle.

The objects under the management of the IoC container are called *beans*. The beans form the backbone of the Spring application.

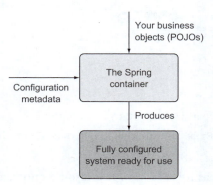

Figure 14.2   **The functionality of the Spring IoC container**

14.2   *JPA application using Spring and the DAO pattern*

In this section, we'll look at how we can build a JPA application using Spring and the data access object (DAO) design pattern. The DAO design pattern creates an abstract interface to a database, supporting access operations without exposing any internals of the database.

You may argue that the Spring Data JPA repositories we have created and worked with already do this, and that is true. We'll demonstrate in this chapter how to build a DAO class, and we'll discuss when we should prefer this approach instead of using Spring Data JPA.

The CaveatEmptor application contains the Item and Bid classes (listings 14.1 and 14.2). The entities will now be managed with the help of the Spring Framework. The relationship between the BID and ITEM tables will be kept through a foreign key field on the BID table side. A field marked with the @javax.persistence.Transient annotation is excluded from persistence.

Listing 14.1   The Item class

```
Path: Ch14/spring-jpa-dao/src/main/java/com/manning/javapersistence/ch14
➡ /Item.java

@Entity
public class Item {

    @Id
    @GeneratedValue(generator = "ID_GENERATOR")          Ⓐ
    private Long id;

    @NotNull
    @Size(
            min = 2,
            max = 255,                                    Ⓑ
            message = "Name is required, maximum 255 characters."
    )
    private String name;
```

```
    @Transient                                          C
    private Set<Bid> bids = new HashSet<>();

    // . . .
}
```

A The `id` field is a generated identifier.

B The `name` field is not null and must have a size from 2 to 255 characters.

C Each `Item` has a reference to its set of `Bids`. The field is marked as `@Transient`, so it is excluded from persistence.

We'll move our attention to the `Bid` class, as it looks now. It is also an entity, and the relationship between `Item` and `Bid` is one-to-many.

Listing 14.2 | **The `Bid` class**

Path: Ch14/spring-jpa-dao/src/main/java/com/manning/javapersistence/ch14
➡ /Bid.java

```
@Entity
public class Bid {

    @Id
    @GeneratedValue(generator = "ID_GENERATOR")         A
    private Long id;

    @NotNull                             B
    private BigDecimal amount;

    @ManyToOne(optional = false, fetch = FetchType.LAZY)      C
    @JoinColumn(name = "ITEM_ID")
    private Item item;
    // . . .
}
```

A The `Bid` entity class contains the `id` field as the generated identifier.

B The `amount` field should not be null.

C Each `Bid` has a non-optional reference to its `Item`. The fetching will be lazy, and the name of the joining column is `ITEM_ID`.

To implement the DAO design pattern, we'll start by creating two interfaces, `ItemDao` and `BidDao`, and we'll declare the access operations that will be implemented:

Path: Ch14/spring-jpa-dao/src/main/java/com/manning/javapersistence/ch14
➡ /dao/ItemDao.java

```
public interface ItemDao {
    Item getById(long id);

    List<Item> getAll();
```

```
    void insert(Item item);

    void update(long id, String name);

    void delete(Item item);

    Item findByName(String name);
}
```

The `BidDao` interface is declared as follows:

Path: Ch14/spring-jpa-dao/src/main/java/com/manning/javapersistence/ch14
➡ /dao/BidDao.java

```
public interface BidDao {
    Bid getById(long id);

    List<Bid> getAll();

    void insert(Bid bid);

    void update(long id, String amount);

    void delete(Bid bid);

    List<Bid> findByAmount(String amount);
}
```

`@Repository` is a marker annotation indicating that the component represents a DAO. Besides marking the annotated class as a Spring component, `@Repository` will catch the persistence-specific exceptions and will translate them to Spring unchecked exceptions. `@Transactional` will make all the methods from inside the class transactional, as discussed in section 11.4.3.

An `EntityManager` is not thread-safe by itself. We'll use `@PersistenceContext` so that the container injects a proxy object that is thread-safe. Besides injecting the dependency on a container-managed entity manager, the `@PersistenceContext` annotation has parameters. Setting the persistence type to `EXTENDED` keeps the persistence context for the whole lifecycle of a bean.

The implementation of the `ItemDao` interface, `ItemDaoImpl`, is shown in the following listing.

Listing 14.3   The `ItemDaoImpl` class

Path: Ch14/spring-jpa-dao/src/main/java/com/manning/javapersistence/ch14
➡ /dao/ItemDaoImpl.java

```
@Repository                      Ⓐ
@Transactional
public class ItemDaoImpl implements ItemDao {
```

```
    @PersistenceContext(type = PersistenceContextType.EXTENDED)       B
    private EntityManager em;

    @Override
    public Item getById(long id) {                    C
        return em.find(Item.class, id);
    }

    @Override
    public List<Item> getAll() {                                          D
        return (List<Item>) em.createQuery("from Item", Item.class)
                             .getResultList();
    }

    @Override
    public void insert(Item item) {
        em.persist(item);                             E
        for (Bid bid : item.getBids()) {
            em.persist(bid);
        }
    }

    @Override
    public void update(long id, String name) {               F
        Item item = em.find(Item.class, id);
        item.setName(name);
        em.persist(item);
    }

    @Override
    public void delete(Item item) {
        for (Bid bid : item.getBids()) {              G
            em.remove(bid);
        }
        em.remove(item);
    }

    @Override
    public Item findByName(String name) {                                 H
        return em.createQuery("from Item where name=:name", Item.class)
                .setParameter("name", name).getSingleResult();
    }
}
```

Ⓐ The `ItemDaoImpl` class is annotated with `@Repository` and `@Transactional`.

Ⓑ The `EntityManager` em field is injected in the application, as annotated with `@PersistenceContext`. Persistence type `EXTENDED` means the persistence context is kept for the whole lifecycle of a bean.

Ⓒ Retrieve an `Item` by its id.

Ⓓ Retrieve all `Item` entities.

Ⓔ Persist an `Item` and all its `Bids`.

F Update the name field of an Item.

G Remove all the bids belonging to an Item and the Item itself.

H Search for an Item by its name.

The implementation of the BidDao interface, BidDaoImpl, is shown in the next listing.

Listing 14.4 The BidDaoImpl class

Path: Ch14/spring-jpa-dao/src/main/java/com/manning/javapersistence/ch14
➥ /dao/BidDaoImpl.java

```
@Repository                                   A
@Transactional
public class BidDaoImpl implements BidDao {
    @PersistenceContext(type = PersistenceContextType.EXTENDED)      B
    private EntityManager em;

    @Override
    public Bid getById(long id) {             C
        return em.find(Bid.class, id);
    }

    @Override
    public List<Bid> getAll() {                                         D
        return em.createQuery("from Bid", Bid.class).getResultList();
    }

    @Override
    public void insert(Bid bid) {             E
        em.persist(bid);
    }

    @Override
    public void update(long id, String amount) {          F
        Bid bid = em.find(Bid.class, id);
        bid.setAmount(new BigDecimal(amount));
        em.persist(bid);
    }

    @Override
    public void delete(Bid bid) {             G
        em.remove(bid);
    }

    @Override
    public List<Bid> findByAmount(String amount) {                     H
        return em.createQuery("from Bid where amount=:amount", Bid.class)
          .setParameter("amount", new BigDecimal(amount)).getResultList();
    }
}
```

Ⓐ The `BidDaoImpl` class is annotated with `@Repository` and `@Transactional`.

Ⓑ The `EntityManager` em field is injected in the application, as it is annotated with `@PersistenceContext`. Setting the persistence type to `EXTENDED` keeps the persistence context for the whole lifecycle of a bean.

Ⓒ Retrieve a `Bid` by its id.

Ⓓ Retrieve all `Bid` entities.

Ⓔ Persist a `Bid`.

Ⓕ Update the amount field of a `Bid`.

Ⓖ Remove a `Bid`.

Ⓗ Search for a `Bid` by its amount.

To work with the database, we'll provide a special class, `DatabaseService`, that will be responsible for populating the database and for removing the information from it.

Listing 14.5   **The `DatabaseService` class**

Path: Ch14/spring-jpa-dao/src/test/java/com/manning/javapersistence/ch14
➥ /DatabaseService.java

```java
public class DatabaseService {

    @PersistenceContext(type = PersistenceContextType.EXTENDED)   Ⓐ
    private EntityManager em;

    @Autowired                Ⓑ
    private ItemDao itemDao;

    @Transactional
    public void init() {
        for (int i = 0; i < 10; i++) {
            String itemName = "Item " + (i + 1);
            Item item = new Item();
            item.setName(itemName);                                    Ⓒ
            Bid bid1 = new Bid(new BigDecimal(1000.0), item);
            Bid bid2 = new Bid(new BigDecimal(1100.0), item);

            itemDao.insert(item);
        }
    }

    @Transactional
    public void clear() {                                          Ⓓ
        em.createQuery("delete from Bid b").executeUpdate();
        em.createQuery("delete from Item i").executeUpdate();
    }

}
```

Ⓐ The `EntityManager` em field is injected in the application, as it is annotated with
`@PersistenceContext`. Setting the persistence type to `EXTENDED` keeps the persistence context for the whole lifecycle of a bean.

Ⓑ The `ItemDao` itemDao field is injected in the application, as it is annotated with
`@Autowired`. Because the `ItemDaoImpl` class is annotated with `@Repository`, Spring
will create the needed bean belonging to this class, to be injected here.

Ⓒ Generate 10 `Item` objects, each of them having 2 `Bids`, and insert them in the
database.

Ⓓ Delete all previously inserted `Bid` and `Item` objects.

The standard configuration file for Spring is a Java class that creates and sets up the
needed beans. The `@EnableTransactionManagement` annotation will enable Spring's
annotation-driven transaction management capability. When using XML configuration, this annotation is mirrored by the `tx:annotation-driven` element. Every interaction with the database should occur within transaction boundaries and Spring
needs a transaction manager bean.

We'll create the following configuration file for the application.

Listing 14.6 The `SpringConfiguration` class

Path: Ch14/spring-jpa-dao/src/test/java/com/manning/javapersistence/ch14
➡ /configuration/SpringConfiguration.java

```
@EnableTransactionManagement            ←─ Ⓐ
public class SpringConfiguration {
    @Bean
    public DataSource dataSource() {                                              Ⓑ
        DriverManagerDataSource dataSource = new DriverManagerDataSource();
   ┌─▷ dataSource.setDriverClassName("com.mysql.cj.jdbc.Driver");
 Ⓒ     dataSource.setUrl(
          "jdbc:mysql://localhost:3306/CH14_SPRING_HIBERNATE               Ⓓ
            ➡ ?serverTimezone=UTC");
 Ⓔ─▷   dataSource.setUsername("root");
        dataSource.setPassword("");          ←─ Ⓕ
        return dataSource;          ←─┐
    }                                 Ⓑ

    @Bean
    public DatabaseService databaseService() {             Ⓖ
        return new DatabaseService();
    }

    @Bean
    public JpaTransactionManager
            transactionManager(EntityManagerFactory emf){       Ⓗ
        return new JpaTransactionManager(emf);
    }
```

```
    @Bean
    public LocalContainerEntityManagerFactoryBean entityManagerFactory() {
        LocalContainerEntityManagerFactoryBean
        localContainerEntityManagerFactoryBean =
                new LocalContainerEntityManagerFactoryBean();
        localContainerEntityManagerFactoryBean
                .setPersistenceUnitName("ch14");
        localContainerEntityManagerFactoryBean.setDataSource(dataSource());
        localContainerEntityManagerFactoryBean.setPackagesToScan(
            "com.manning.javapersistence.ch14");
        return localContainerEntityManagerFactoryBean;
    }

    @Bean
    public ItemDao itemDao() {
        return new ItemDaoImpl();
    }

    @Bean
    public BidDao bidDao() {
        return new BidDaoImpl();
    }
}
```

A The `@EnableTransactionManagement` annotation enables Spring's annotation-driven transaction management capability.

B Create a data source bean.

C Indicate the JDBC properties—the driver.

D The URL of the database.

E The username.

F There is no password in this configuration. Modify the credentials to correspond to the ones on your machine and use a password in practice.

G The `DatabaseService` bean that Spring will use to populate and clear the database.

H Create a transaction manager bean based on an entity manager factory.

I `LocalContainerEntityManagerFactoryBean` is a factory bean that produces an `EntityManagerFactory` following the JPA standard container bootstrap contract.

J Set the persistence unit name, defined in persistence.xml.

K Set the data source.

L Set the packages to scan for entity classes. Beans are located in `com.manning` `.javapersistence.ch14`, so we set this package to be scanned.

M Create an `ItemDao` bean.

N Create a `BidDao` bean.

This configuration information is used by Spring to create and inject the beans that form the backbone of the application. We can use the alternative XML configuration, and the application-context.xml file mirrors the work done in SpringConfiguration

.java. We would just like to emphasize one thing we mentioned previously: in XML, we enable Spring's annotation-driven transaction management capability with the help of the `tx:annotation-driven` element, referencing a transaction manager bean:

Path: `Ch14/spring-jpa-dao/src/test/resources/application-context.xml`

```
<tx:annotation-driven transaction-manager="txManager"/>
```

The `SpringExtension` extension is used to integrate the Spring test context with the JUnit 5 Jupiter test by implementing several JUnit Jupiter extension model callback methods.

It is important to use the type `PersistenceContextType.EXTENDED` for all injected `EntityManager` beans. If we used the default `PersistenceContextType.TRANSACTION` type, the returned object would become detached at the end of a transaction's execution. Passing it to the `delete` method would result in an "IllegalArgumentException: Removing a detached instance" exception.

It is time to test the functionality we've developed for persisting the `Item` and `Bid` entities.

Listing 14.7 The `SpringJpaTest` class

Path: `Ch14/spring-jpa-dao/src/test/java/com/manning/javapersistence/ch14`
➡ `/SpringJpaTest.java`   **A**

                                                                                                            B
```java
@ExtendWith(SpringExtension.class)          ←
@ContextConfiguration(classes = {SpringConfiguration.class})      ←
//@ContextConfiguration("classpath:application-context.xml")
public class SpringJpaTest {

    @Autowired
    private DatabaseService databaseService;
                                                            D
    @Autowired
    private ItemDao itemDao;

    @Autowired
    private BidDao bidDao;

    @BeforeEach                                        E
    public void setUp() {
        databaseService.init();
    }

    @Test
    public void testInsertItems() {
        List<Item> itemsList = itemDao.getAll();
        List<Bid> bidsList = bidDao.getAll();       F
        assertAll(
                () -> assertNotNull(itemsList),
                () -> assertEquals(10, itemsList.size()),
```

C

```
                    () -> assertNotNull(itemDao.findByName("Item 1")),
                    () -> assertNotNull(bidsList),
                    () -> assertEquals(20, bidsList.size()),
                    () -> assertEquals(10,
                                    bidDao.findByAmount("1000.00").size())
        );
    }


    @Test
    public void testDeleteItem() {
        itemDao.delete(itemDao.findByName("Item 2"));
        assertThrows(NoResultException.class,
                    () -> itemDao.findByName("Item 2"));
    }



    // . . .

    @AfterEach
    public void dropDown() {
        databaseService.clear();
    }


}
```

F

G

H

I

A Extend the test using `SpringExtension`. As previously mentioned, this will integrate the Spring TestContext Framework into JUnit 5 by implementing several JUnit Jupiter extension model callback methods.

B The Spring test context is configured using the beans defined in the previously presented `SpringConfiguration` class.

C Alternatively, we can configure the test context using XML. Only one of the **B** or **C** lines should be active in the code.

D Autowire one `DatabaseService` bean, one `ItemDao` bean, and one `BidDao` bean.

E Before the execution of each test, the content of the database is initialized by the `init` method from the injected `DatabaseService`.

F Retrieve all `Items` and all `Bids` and do verifications.

G Find an `Item` by its `name` field and delete it from the database. We will use `PersistenceContextType.EXTENDED` for all injected `EntityManager` beans. Otherwise, passing it to the `delete` method would result in an "IllegalArgument-Exception: Removing a detached instance" exception.

H After the successful deletion of the `Item` from the database, trying to find it again will throw a `NoResultException`. The rest of the tests can be easily investigated in the source code.

I After the execution of each test, the content of the database is erased by the `clear` method from the injected `DatabaseService`.

When should we apply such a solution using the Spring Framework and the DAO design pattern? There are a few situations when we would recommend it:

- You would like to hand off the task of controlling the entity manager and the transactions to the Spring Framework (remember that this is done through the *inversion of control*). The tradeoff is that you lose the possibility of debugging the transactions. Just be aware of that.
- You would like to create your own API for managing persistence and either you cannot or you do not want to use Spring Data. This might happen when you have very particular operations that you need to control, or you want to remove the Spring Data overhead (including the ramp-up time for the team to adopt it, introducing new dependencies in an already existing project, and the execution delay of Spring Data, as was discussed in section 2.7).
- In particular situations, you may want to handle the entity manager and the transactions to the Spring Framework and still not implement your own DAO classes.

We would like to improve on the design of our Spring persistence application. The next sections are dedicated to making it more generic and using the Hibernate API instead of JPA. We'll focus on the differences between this first solution and our new versions, and we'll discuss how to introduce the changes.

14.3   Generifying a JPA application that uses Spring and DAO

If we take a closer look at the `ItemDao` and `BidDao` interfaces and `ItemDaoImpl` and `BidDaoImpl` classes we've created, we'll find a few shortcomings:

- There are similar operations, such as `getById`, `getAll`, `insert`, and `delete`, that differ mainly in the type of argument they receive or in the returned result.
- The `update` method receives as a second argument the value of a particular property. We may need to write multiple methods if we need to update different properties of an entity.
- Methods such as `findByName` or `findByAmount` are tied to particular properties. We may need to write different methods for finding an entity using different properties.

Consequently, we'll introduce a `GenericDao` interface.

Listing 14.8   The `GenericDao` interface

Path: Ch14/spring-jpa-dao-gen/src/main/java/com/manning/javapersistence
➥ /ch14/dao/GenericDao.java

```
public interface GenericDao<T> {
    T getById(long id);                          Ⓐ

    List<T> getAll();
```

```
        void insert(T entity);              B

        void delete(T entity);

        void update(long id, String propertyName, Object propertyValue);              C

        List<T> findByProperty(String propertyName, Object propertyValue);

}
```

A The getById and getAll methods have a generic return type.

B The insert and update methods have generic input, T entity.

C The update and findByProperty methods will receive as arguments the property-Name and the new propertyValue.

We'll create an abstract implementation of the GenericDao interface, called AbstractGenericDao, as shown in listing 14.9. Here we'll write the common functionality of all DAO classes, and we'll let concrete classes implement their specifics.

We'll inject an EntityManager em field in the application, annotating it with @PersistenceContext. Setting the persistence type to EXTENDED keeps the persistence context for the whole lifecycle of a bean.

Listing 14.9 The **AbstractGenericDao** class

Path: Ch14/spring-jpa-dao-gen/src/main/java/com/manning/javapersistence
➥ /ch14/dao/AbstractGenericDao.java

```
@Repository
@Transactional                                                                    A
public abstract class AbstractGenericDao<T> implements GenericDao<T> {

    @PersistenceContext(type = PersistenceContextType.EXTENDED)                    B
    protected EntityManager em;
    private Class<T> clazz;

    public void setClazz(Class<T> clazz) {                                        C
        this.clazz = clazz;
    }

    @Override
    public T getById(long id) {                                                    D
        return em.createQuery(
                "SELECT e FROM " + clazz.getName() + " e WHERE e.id = :id",
                clazz).setParameter("id", id).getSingleResult();
    }

    @Override
    public List<T> getAll() {                                                      E
        return em.createQuery("from " +
                            clazz.getName(), clazz).getResultList();
    }
```

```
@Override
public void insert(T entity) {              F
    em.persist(entity);
}

@Override
public void delete(T entity) {              G
    em.remove(entity);
}

@Override
public void update(long id, String propertyName, Object propertyValue) {
    em.createQuery("UPDATE " + clazz.getName() + " e SET e." +
            propertyName + " = :propertyValue WHERE e.id = :id")    H
            .setParameter("propertyValue", propertyValue)
            .setParameter("id", id).executeUpdate();
}

@Override
public List<T> findByProperty(String propertyName,
                              Object propertyValue) {
    return em.createQuery(
            "SELECT e FROM " + clazz.getName() + " e WHERE e." +     I
            propertyName + " = :propertyValue", clazz)
            .setParameter("propertyValue", propertyValue)
            .getResultList();
}
}
```

A The `AbstractGenericDao` class is annotated with `@Repository` and `@Transactional`.

B The `EXTENDED` persistence type of the `EntityManager` will keep the persistence context for the whole lifecycle of a bean. The field is `protected`, to be eventually inherited and used by subclasses.

C `clazz` is the effective `Class` field on which the DAO will work.

D Execute a `SELECT` query using the `clazz` entity and setting the `id` as a parameter.

E Execute a `SELECT` query using the `clazz` entity and get the list of the results.

F Persist the `entity`.

G Remove the `entity`.

H Execute an `UPDATE` using the `propertyName`, the `propertyValue`, and the `id`.

I Execute a `SELECT` using the `propertyName` and the `propertyValue`.

The `AbstractGenericDao` class provides most of the general DAO functionality. It only needs to be customized a little for particular DAO classes. The `ItemDaoImpl` class will extend the `AbstractGenericDao` class and will override some of the methods.

Listing 14.10 The `ItemDaoImpl` class extending `AbstractGenericDao`

Path: Ch14/spring-jpa-dao-gen/src/main/java/com/manning/javapersistence
➡ /ch14/dao/ItemDaoImpl.java

Ⓐ

```java
public class ItemDaoImpl extends AbstractGenericDao<Item> {        ⟵──Ⓐ

    public ItemDaoImpl() {              Ⓑ
        setClazz(Item.class);
    }

    @Override
    public void insert(Item item) {
        em.persist(item);
        for (Bid bid : item.getBids()) {          Ⓒ
            em.persist(bid);
        }
    }

    @Override
    public void delete(Item item) {
        for (Bid bid: item.getBids()) {          Ⓓ
            em.remove(bid);
        }
        em.remove(item);
    }

}
```

Ⓐ `ItemDaoImpl` extends `AbstractGenericDao` and is generified by `Item`.

Ⓑ The constructor sets `Item.class` as the entity class to be managed.

Ⓒ Persist the `Item` entity and all its `Bid` entities. The `EntityManager` em field is inherited from the `AbstractGenericDao` class.

Ⓓ Remove all the bids belonging to an `Item` and the `Item` itself.

The `BidDaoImpl` class will simply extend the `AbstractGenericDao` class and set the entity class to manage.

Listing 14.11 The `BidDaoImpl` class extending `AbstractGenericDao`

Path: Ch14/spring-jpa-dao-gen/src/main/java/com/manning/javapersistence
➡ /ch14/dao/BidDaoImpl.java

Ⓐ

```java
public class BidDaoImpl extends AbstractGenericDao<Bid> {        ⟵──Ⓐ

    public BidDaoImpl() {              Ⓑ
        setClazz(Bid.class);
    }

}
```

Ⓐ `BidDaoImpl` extends `AbstractGenericDao` and is generified by `Bid`.

Ⓑ The constructor sets `Bid.class` as the entity class to be managed. All other methods are inherited from `AbstractGenericDao` and are fully reusable this way.

Some small changes are needed for the configuration and testing classes. The `SpringConfiguration` class will now declare the two DAO beans as `GenericDao`:

Path: Ch14/spring-jpa-dao-gen/src/test/java/com/manning/javapersistence
➡ /ch14/configuration/SpringConfiguration.java

```
@Bean
public GenericDao<Item> itemDao() {
    return new ItemDaoImpl();
}

@Bean
public GenericDao<Bid> bidDao() {
    return new BidDaoImpl();
}
```

The `DatabaseService` class will inject the `itemDao` field as `GenericDao`:

Path: Ch14/spring-jpa-dao-gen/src/test/java/com/manning/javapersistence
➡ /ch14/DatabaseService.java

```
@Autowired
private GenericDao<Item> itemDao;
```

The `SpringJpaTest` class will inject the `itemDao` and `bidDao` fields as `GenericDao`:

Path: Ch14/spring-jpa-dao-gen/src/test/java/com/manning/javapersistence
➡ /ch14/SpringJpaTest.java

```
@Autowired
private GenericDao<Item> itemDao;

@Autowired
private GenericDao<Bid> bidDao;
```

We have now developed an easily extensible DAO class hierarchy using the JPA API. We can reuse the already written generic functionality or we can quickly overwrite some methods for particular entities (as was the case for `ItemDaoImpl`).

Let's now move on to the alternative of implementing a Hibernate application using Spring and the DAO pattern.

14.4 Hibernate application using Spring and the DAO pattern

We'll now demonstrate how to use Spring and the DAO pattern with the Hibernate API. As we previously mentioned, we'll emphasize only the changes between this approach and the previous applications.

Calling `sessionFactory.getCurrentSession()` will create a new `Session`, if one does not exist. Otherwise, it will use the existing session from the Hibernate context. The session will be automatically flushed and closed when a transaction ends. Using `sessionFactory.getCurrentSession()` is ideal in single-threaded applications, as using a single session will boost performance. In a multithreaded application, the session is not thread-safe, so you should use `sessionFactory.openSession()` and explicitly close the opened session. Or, as `Session` implements `AutoCloseable`, it can be used in try-with-resources blocks.

As the `Item` and `Bid` classes and the `ItemDao` and `BidDao` interfaces remain unchanged, we'll move on to `ItemDaoImpl` and `BidDaoImpl` and see what they look like now.

Listing 14.12   The `ItemDaoImpl` class using the Hibernate API

Path: Ch14/spring-hibernate-dao/src/main/java/com/manning/javapersistence
➡ /ch14/dao/ItemDaoImpl.java

```java
@Repository                                               A
@Transactional
public class ItemDaoImpl implements ItemDao {
    @Autowired                                            B
    private SessionFactory sessionFactory;

    @Override
    public Item getById(long id) {                        C
        return sessionFactory.getCurrentSession().get(Item.class, id);
    }

    @Override
    public List<Item> getAll() {                          D
        return sessionFactory.getCurrentSession()
                .createQuery("from Item", Item.class).list();
    }

    @Override
    public void insert(Item item) {
        sessionFactory.getCurrentSession().persist(item);     E
        for (Bid bid : item.getBids()) {
            sessionFactory.getCurrentSession().persist(bid);
        }
    }

    @Override
    public void update(long id, String name) {
        Item item = sessionFactory.getCurrentSession().get(Item.class, id);   F
        item.setName(name);
        sessionFactory.getCurrentSession().update(item);
    }

    @Override
    public void delete(Item item) {                       G
        sessionFactory.getCurrentSession()
```

```
            .createQuery("delete from Bid b where b.item.id = :id")
            .setParameter("id", item.getId()).executeUpdate();
        sessionFactory.getCurrentSession()
            .createQuery("delete from Item i where i.id = :id")
            .setParameter("id", item.getId()).executeUpdate();
    }

    @Override
    public Item findByName(String name) {
        return sessionFactory.getCurrentSession()
                .createQuery("from Item where name=:name", Item.class)
                .setParameter("name", name).uniqueResult();
    }
}
```

Ⓖ

Ⓗ

Ⓐ The `ItemDaoImpl` class is annotated with `@Repository` and `@Transactional`.

Ⓑ The `SessionFactory` `sessionFactory` field is injected in the application, as it is annotated with `@Autowired`.

Ⓒ Retrieve an `Item` by its `id`. Calling `sessionFactory.getCurrentSession()` will create a new `Session` if one does not exist.

Ⓓ Retrieve all `Item` entities.

Ⓔ Persist an `Item` and all its `Bids`.

Ⓕ Update the `name` field of an `Item`.

Ⓖ Remove all the bids belonging to an `Item` and the `Item` itself.

Ⓗ Search for an `Item` by its `name`.

The `BidDaoImpl` class will also mirror the previously implemented functionality that used JPA and `EntityManager`, but it will use the Hibernate API and `SessionFactory`.

There are also important changes in the `SpringConfiguration` class. Moving from JPA to Hibernate, the `EntityManagerFactory` bean to be injected will be replaced with a `SessionFactory`. Similarly, the `JpaTransactionManager` bean to be injected will be replaced with a `HibernateTransactionManager`.

Listing 14.13   The `SpringConfiguration` class using the Hibernate API

Path: Ch14/spring-hibernate-dao/src/test/java/com/manning/javapersistence
➥ /ch14/configuration/SpringConfiguration.java

```
@EnableTransactionManagement                    ⟵—— Ⓐ
public class SpringConfiguration {

    @Bean
    public LocalSessionFactoryBean sessionFactory() {        Ⓑ
        LocalSessionFactoryBean sessionFactory =
            new LocalSessionFactoryBean();
        sessionFactory.setDataSource(dataSource());
        sessionFactory.setPackagesToScan(                           Ⓒ
            new String[]{"com.manning.javapersistence.ch14"});
```

```
        sessionFactory.setHibernateProperties(hibernateProperties());

        return sessionFactory;

    }

    private Properties hibernateProperties() {
        Properties hibernateProperties = new Properties();
        hibernateProperties.setProperty(AvailableSettings.HBM2DDL_AUTO,
                                                       "create");
        hibernateProperties.setProperty(AvailableSettings.SHOW_SQL,
                                                       "true");
        hibernateProperties.setProperty(AvailableSettings.DIALECT,
                            "org.hibernate.dialect.MySQL8Dialect");

        return hibernateProperties;

    }

    @Bean
    public DataSource dataSource() {
        DriverManagerDataSource dataSource = new DriverManagerDataSource();
        dataSource.setDriverClassName("com.mysql.cj.jdbc.Driver");
        dataSource.setUrl(
      "jdbc:mysql://localhost:3306/CH14_SPRING_HIBERNATE?serverTimezone=
        ➥ UTC ");
        dataSource.setUsername("root");
        dataSource.setPassword("");
        return dataSource;

    }

    @Bean
    public DatabaseService databaseService() {
        return new DatabaseService();

    }

    @Bean
    public HibernateTransactionManager transactionManager(
                                    SessionFactory sessionFactory) {
        HibernateTransactionManager transactionManager
            = new HibernateTransactionManager();
        transactionManager.setSessionFactory(sessionFactory);
        return transactionManager;

    }

    @Bean
    public ItemDao itemDao() {
        return new ItemDaoImpl();

    }

    @Bean
    public BidDao bidDao() {
        return new BidDaoImpl();

    }

}
```

Ⓐ The `@EnableTransactionManagement` annotation will enable Spring's annotation-driven transaction management capability.

Ⓑ A `LocalSessionFactoryBean` is the `sessionFactory` object to be injected.

Ⓒ Set the data source and the packages to scan.

Ⓓ Set the Hibernate properties that will be provided from a separate method.

Ⓔ Create the Hibernate properties in a separate method.

Ⓕ Create a data source bean.

Ⓖ Indicate the JDBC properties—the driver.

Ⓗ The URL of the database.

Ⓘ The username.

Ⓙ There is no password in this configuration. Modify the credentials to correspond to the ones on your machine, and use a password in practice.

Ⓚ A `DatabaseService` bean will be used by Spring to populate and clear the database.

Ⓛ Create a transaction manager bean based on a session factory. Every interaction with the database should occur within transaction boundaries, so Spring needs a transaction manager bean.

Ⓜ Create an `ItemDao` bean.

Ⓝ Create a `BidDao` bean.

We can use the alternative of XML configuration, and the application-context.xml file should mirror the work done in SpringConfiguration.java. Enabling Spring's annotation-driven transaction management capability is done with the help of the `tx:annotation-driven` element, referencing a transaction manager bean, instead of the `@EnableTransactionManagement` annotation.

We'll now demonstrate how to generify this application that uses the Hibernate API instead of JPA. As usual, we'll focus on the differences from the initial solution and how to introduce the changes.

14.5 Generifying a Hibernate application that uses Spring and DAO

Keep in mind the shortcomings that we previously identified for the JPA solution using Data Access Object:

- There are similar operations, such as `getById`, `getAll`, `insert`, and `delete`, that differ mainly in the type of argument they receive or in the returned result.
- The `update` method receives as a second argument the value of a particular property. We may need to write multiple methods if we need to update different properties of an entity.
- Methods such as `findByName` or `findByAmount` are tied to particular properties. We may need to write different methods for finding an entity using different properties.

To address these shortcomings, we introduced the GenericDao interface, shown earlier in listing 14.8. This interface was implemented by the AbstractGenericDao class (listing 14.9), which now needs to be rewritten using the Hibernate API.

Listing 14.14   The AbstractGenericDao class using the Hibernate API

Path: Ch14/spring-hibernate-dao-gen/src/main/java/com/manning
➥ /javapersistence/ch14/dao/AbstractGenericDao.java

```java
@Repository
@Transactional                                              A
public abstract class AbstractGenericDao<T> implements GenericDao<T> {

    @Autowired                                              B
    protected SessionFactory sessionFactory;
    private Class<T> clazz;
                                                            C
    public void setClazz(Class<T> clazz) {
        this.clazz = clazz;
    }

    @Override
    public T getById(long id) {
        return sessionFactory.getCurrentSession()           D
            .createQuery("SELECT e FROM " + clazz.getName() +
                        " e WHERE e.id = :id", clazz)
            .setParameter("id", id).getSingleResult();
    }

    @Override
    public List<T> getAll() {                               E
        return sessionFactory.getCurrentSession()
            .createQuery("from " + clazz.getName(), clazz).getResultList();
    }

    @Override
    public void insert(T entity) {                         F
        sessionFactory.getCurrentSession().persist(entity);
    }

    @Override
    public void delete(T entity) {                         G
        sessionFactory.getCurrentSession().delete(entity);
    }

    @Override
    public void update(long id, String propertyName, Object propertyValue) {
        sessionFactory.getCurrentSession()                 H
            .createQuery("UPDATE " + clazz.getName() + " e SET e." +
                    propertyName + " = :propertyValue WHERE e.id = :id")
            .setParameter("propertyValue", propertyValue)
            .setParameter("id", id).executeUpdate();
    }
```

```
    @Override
    public List<T> findByProperty(String propertyName,
  Object propertyValue) {
        return sessionFactory.getCurrentSession()
      .createQuery("SELECT e FROM " + clazz.getName() + " e WHERE e." +
          propertyName + " = :propertyValue", clazz)
      .setParameter("propertyValue", propertyValue).getResultList();
    }
}
```

Ⓐ The `AbstractGenericDao` class is annotated with `@Repository` and `@Transactional`.

Ⓑ The `SessionFactory sessionFactory` field is injected in the application, as it is annotated with `@Autowired`. It is `protected`, to be inherited and used by subclasses.

Ⓒ `clazz` is the effective `Class` field on which the DAO will work.

Ⓓ Execute a `SELECT` query using the `clazz` entity and setting the `id` as a parameter.

Ⓔ Execute a `SELECT` query using the `clazz` entity and get the list of the results.

Ⓕ Persist the `entity`.

Ⓖ Remove the `entity`.

Ⓗ Execute an `UPDATE` using the `propertyName`, the `propertyValue`, and the `id`.

Ⓘ Execute a `SELECT` using the `propertyName` and the `propertyValue`.

We'll customize the `AbstractGenericDao` class when it is extended by `ItemDaoImpl` and `BidDaoImpl`, this time using the Hibernate API.

The `ItemDaoImpl` class will extend the `AbstractGenericDao` class and will override some of the methods.

Listing 14.15 The `ItemDaoImpl` class using the Hibernate API

Path: Ch14/spring-jpa-hibernate-gen/src/main/java/com/manning
➡ /javapersistence/ch14/dao/ItemDaoImpl.java

```
public class ItemDaoImpl extends AbstractGenericDao<Item> {   ⟵

    public ItemDaoImpl() {          Ⓑ
        setClazz(Item.class);
    }

    @Override
    public void insert(Item item) {
        sessionFactory.getCurrentSession().persist(item);          Ⓒ
        for (Bid bid : item.getBids()) {
            sessionFactory.getCurrentSession().persist(bid);
        }
    }

    @Override
    public void delete(Item item) {          Ⓓ
        sessionFactory.getCurrentSession()
```

```
            .createQuery("delete from Bid b where b.item.id = :id")
            .setParameter("id", item.getId()).executeUpdate();
        sessionFactory.getCurrentSession()
            .createQuery("delete from Item i where i.id = :id")
            .setParameter("id", item.getId()).executeUpdate();
    }

}
```

(A) `ItemDaoImpl` extends `AbstractGenericDao` and is generified by `Item`.

(B) The constructor sets `Item.class` as the entity class to be managed.

(C) Persist the `Item` entity and all its `Bid` entities. The `sessionFactory` field is inherited from the `AbstractGenericDao` class.

(D) Remove all the bids belonging to an `Item` and the `Item` itself.

The `BidDaoImpl` class will simply extend the `AbstractGenericDao` class and set the entity class to manage.

Listing 14.16   The `BidDaoImpl` class using the Hibernate API

Path: Ch14/spring-hibernate-dao-gen/src/main/java/com/manning
➥ /javapersistence/ch14/dao/BidDaoImpl.java

```
public class BidDaoImpl extends AbstractGenericDao<Bid> {    ⟵ (A)

    public BidDaoImpl() {          (B)
        setClazz(Bid.class);
    }

}
```

(A) `BidDaoImpl` extends `AbstractGenericDao` and is generified by `Bid`.

(B) The constructor sets `Bid.class` as the entity class to be managed. All other methods are inherited from `AbstractGenericDao` and are fully reusable this way.

We have developed an easily extensible DAO class hierarchy using the Hibernate API. We can reuse the already written generic functionality or we can quickly overwrite some methods for particular entities (as we did for `ItemDaoImpl`).

Summary

- The dependency injection design pattern is the base of the Spring Framework, supporting the creation of applications consisting of different components and objects.
- You can develop a JPA application using the Spring Framework and the DAO pattern. Spring controls the `EntityManager`, the transaction manager, and other beans used by the application.

- You can generify a JPA application to provide a generic and easily extensible DAO base class. The DAO base class contains the common behavior to be inherited by all derived DAOs and will allow them to implement only their particular behavior.
- You can develop a Hibernate application using the Spring Framework and the DAO pattern. Spring controls the `SessionFactory`, the transaction manager, and other beans used by the application.
- You can generify a Hibernate application to provide a generic and easily extensible DAO base class. The DAO base class contains the common behavior to be inherited by all derived DAOs and will allow them to implement only their particular behavior.

15
Working with Spring Data JDBC

This chapter covers

- Starting a Spring Data JDBC project
- Working with queries and query methods in Spring Data JDBC
- Building relationships using Spring Data JDBC
- Modeling embedded entities with Spring Data JDBC

We introduced Spring Data in chapter 2: it's an umbrella project containing many projects whose purpose is to simplify access to both relational and NoSQL databases by adhering to the Spring framework principles. In chapter 4, we looked in detail at the principles and capabilities of the Spring Data JPA project. The purpose of Spring Data JDBC is to efficiently deal with JDBC-based repositories. It is a younger project in the family, and it does not offer all the JPA capabilities, such as caching or lazy loading, resulting in a simpler and more limited ORM. However, it is growing and introducing new features with each version.

Why would we need Spring Data JDBC, when we already have alternatives such as JPA, Hibernate, and Spring Data JPA? The truth is that object/relational mapping (ORM) makes projects complex, and you clearly saw this in the previous chapters. There are situations when we'll want to eliminate this complexity and take the benefits of working with Spring, the most popular Java framework today. What alternatives do we have?

If we look back to the old-style JDBC, we have to remember its shortcomings, such as opening and closing connections by yourself or manually handling exceptions—overall, we would have to deal with a lot of service code.

Spring Data JDBC allows us to create our own queries to be executed against the database, but it also has its own ORM and uses concepts already used by JPA, Hibernate, and Spring Data JPA: entities, repositories, and `@Query` annotations. Spring Data JDBC does not use JPQL and there is no portability. Queries must be written in plain SQL and be specific to the database vendor. Entity loading must be done through SQL queries, and it is either complete or absent. Caching and lazy loading are not available. Sessions and dirty tracking do not exist; we have to explicitly save entities.

Also, at the time of writing this chapter, Spring Data JDBC does not support schema generation. We can declare our entities as we do in Hibernate or Spring Data JPA, but the DDL commands need to be written and run.

Let's create a project that uses Spring Data JDBC and analyze its capabilities to support us as we introduce new features.

15.1 Creating a Spring Data JDBC project

In this chapter, we'll create an application that will manage and persist CaveatEmptor users with Spring Data JDBC as a persistence framework, much like we did using Spring Data JPA in chapter 4. We'll create a Spring Boot application to use Spring Data JDBC.

To get started, we'll use the Spring Initializr website (https://start.spring.io/) to create a new Spring Boot project (figure 15.1) with the following characteristics:

- Group: com.manning.javapersistence
- Artifact: spring-data-jdbc
- Description: Spring Data JDBC project

We'll also add the following dependencies:

- Spring Data JDBC (this will add `spring-boot-starter-data-jdbc` in the Maven pom.xml file)
- MySQL Driver (this will add `mysql-connector-java` in the Maven pom.xml file)

NOTE   To execute the examples from the source code, you'll first need to run the Ch15.sql script.

Figure 15.1   Creating a new Spring Boot project using Spring Data JDBC and MySQL

The skeleton of the project contains four files:

- SpringDataJdbcApplication, including a skeleton `main` method
- SpringDataJdbcApplicationTests, including a skeleton test method
- application.properties, which is empty at the beginning
- pom.xml, including the management information needed by Maven

The pom.xml file, shown in the following listing, includes the dependencies that we added to start the Spring Data JDBC project: we'll use the Spring Data JDBC framework to access a MySQL database, for which we need the driver.

Listing 15.1   The pom.xml Maven file

Path: Ch15/spring-data-jdbc/pom.xml

```
<dependencies>
    <dependency>
        <groupId>org.springframework.boot</groupId>            A
        <artifactId>spring-boot-starter-data-jdbc</artifactId>
    </dependency>

    <dependency>
        <groupId>mysql</groupId>
        <artifactId>mysql-connector-java</artifactId>          B
        <scope>runtime</scope>
    </dependency>
    <dependency>
        <groupId>org.springframework.boot</groupId>           C
        <artifactId>spring-boot-starter-test</artifactId>
```

```
        <scope>test</scope>
    </dependency>
</dependencies>
```

A `spring-boot-starter-data-jdbc` is the starter dependency used by Spring Boot to connect to a relational database through Spring Data JDBC.

B `mysql-connector-java` is the JDBC driver for MySQL. It is a runtime dependency, meaning it is needed in the classpath only at runtime.

C `spring-boot-starter-test` is the Spring Boot starter dependency for testing. It is needed only for the test compilation and execution phases.

The application.properties file can include various properties that will be used by the application. Spring Boot will automatically find and load the application.properties file from the classpath, and the src/main/resources folder is added by Maven to the classpath. As the initialization script is run by default only for embedded databases, and we are using MySQL, we'll have to force the execution of the script by setting the initialization mode, `spring.sql.init.mode`, to be `always`. The configuration file is shown in the following listing.

Listing 15.2   The application.properties file

Path: `Ch15/spring-data-jdbc/src/main/resources/application.properties`

```
spring.datasource.url=jdbc:mysql://localhost:3306/CH15_SPRINGDATAJDBC
    ?serverTimezone=UTC
spring.datasource.username=root
spring.datasource.password=
spring.jpa.properties.hibernate.dialect=org.hibernate.dialect.MySQL8Dialect
spring.sql.init.mode=always
```
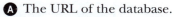 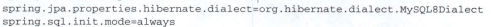

A The URL of the database.

B The credentials to access the database. Replace them with the credentials on your machine, and use a password in real life.

C The dialect of the database, MySQL.

D The SQL initialization mode is `always`, so the SQL file will be always executed, recreating the database schema.

The SQL script that is automatically executed will look like the one in the following listing, dropping and recreating the USERS table. At startup, Spring Boot will always execute the schema.sql and data.sql files on the classpath.

Listing 15.3   The schema.sql file

Path: `Ch15/spring-data-jdbc/src/main/resources/schema.sql`

```
DROP TABLE IF EXISTS USERS;
```

```
CREATE TABLE USERS (
    ID INTEGER AUTO_INCREMENT PRIMARY KEY,
    USERNAME VARCHAR(30),
    REGISTRATION_DATE DATE
);
```

We'll now define the entity class corresponding to the USERS table as demonstrated in listing 15.4. We'll use some Spring-specific annotations to configure how the class is mapped to the table in the database:

- org.springframework.data.relational.core.mapping.Table—This is different from the previously used javax.persistence.Table, which is JPA-specific.
- org.springframework.data.annotation.Id—This is different from the previously used javax.persistence.Id, which is JPA-specific. We defined the corresponding column in the database as ID INTEGER AUTO_INCREMENT PRIMARY KEY, so the database will take care of generating the auto-incremented values.
- org.springframework.data.relational.core.mapping.Column—This is different from the previously used javax.persistence.Column, which is JPA-specific. For the column names, Spring Data JDBC will convert the camel case used for the definition of class fields into the snake case used for the definition of table columns.

Listing 15.4   The User class

Path: Ch15/spring-data-jdbc/src/main/java/com/manning/javapersistence/ch15
➥ /model/User.java

```
@Table("USERS")                      A
public class User {
                                   C
    @Id
    @Column("ID")          ←
    private Long id;
                                D
    @Column("USERNAME")    ←
    private String username;
                                  E
    @Column("REGISTRATION_DATE")   ←
    private LocalDate registrationDate;

    //constructors, getters and setters
}
```

A Annotate the User class with the @Table annotation, explicitly indicating that the corresponding table is USERS.

B Annotate the id field with the @Id annotation.

C Annotate the id field with the @Column("ID") annotation, specifying the corresponding column in the database. This is the default value.

D Annotate the username field with the `@Column("USERNAME")` annotation, specifying the corresponding column in the database. This is the default value.

E Annotate the `registrationDate` field with the `@Column("REGISTRATION_DATE")` annotation, specifying the corresponding column in the database. This is the default value.

We'll also create the `UserRepository` interface that extends `CrudRepository` and thus provides access to the database.

Listing 15.5   The `UserRepository` interface

Path: Ch15/spring-data-jdbc/src/main/java/com/manning/javapersistence/ch15
➥ /repositories/UserRepository.java

```
@Repository
public interface UserRepository extends CrudRepository<User, Long> {
    List<User> findAll();
}
```

The `UserRepository` interface extends `CrudRepository<User, Long>`. This means that it is a repository of `User` entities, having a `Long` identifier. Remember, the `User` class has an `id` field annotated as `@Id` of type `Long`. We can directly call methods such as `save`, `findAll`, or `findById`, inherited from `CrudRepository`, and we can use them without any other additional information to execute the usual operations against a database. Spring Data JDBC will create a proxy class implementing the `UserRepository` interface and implement its methods.

> **NOTE**   It is worth recalling what we mentioned in section 4.3: `CrudRepository` is a generic technology-agnostic persistence interface that we can use not only for JPA/relational databases, as you've seen so far.

We are only overriding the `findAll` method so that it returns `List<User>` instead of `Iterable<User>`. This will simplify our future tests. As a base class for all future tests, we'll write the `SpringDataJdbcApplicationTests` abstract class.

The `@SpringBootTest` annotation, added by Spring Boot to the initially created class, will tell Spring Boot to search the main configuration class (the `@SpringBoot-Application` annotated class, for instance) and create the `ApplicationContext` to be used in the tests. As you'll recall, the `@SpringBootApplication` annotation added by Spring Boot to the class containing the `main` method will enable the Spring Boot auto-configuration mechanism, enable the scan on the package where the application is located, and allow us to register extra beans in the context.

Using the `@TestInstance(TestInstance.Lifecycle.PER_CLASS)` annotation, we'll ask JUnit 5 to create a single instance of the test class and reuse it for all test methods. This will allow us to make the `@BeforeAll` and `@AfterAll` annotated methods non-static and to directly use inside them the autowired `UserRepository` instance field. The `@BeforeAll` annotated non-static method is executed once before all tests from any class extending SpringDataJdbcApplicationTests, and it saves the list of users created inside the generateUsers method to the database. The @AfterAll annotated non-static method is executed once after all tests from any class extending SpringDataJdbcApplicationTests, and it deletes all users from the database.

Listing 15.6   The `SpringDataJdbcApplicationTests` abstract class

Path: Ch15/spring-data-jdbc/src/test/java/com/manning/javapersistence/ch15
➥ /SpringDataJdbcApplicationTests.java

```
@SpringBootTest
@TestInstance(TestInstance.Lifecycle.PER_CLASS)
abstract class SpringDataJdbcApplicationTests {
    @Autowired
    UserRepository userRepository;              A

    @BeforeAll
    void beforeAll() {
        userRepository.saveAll(generateUsers());
    }

    private static List<User> generateUsers() {
        List<User> users = new ArrayList<>();

        User john = new User("john", LocalDate.of(2020, Month.APRIL, 13));

        //create and set a total of 10 users

        users.add(john);
        //add a total of 10 users to the list

        return users;
    }

    @AfterAll
    void afterAll() {
        userRepository.deleteAll();
    }

}
```

🅐 Autowire a UserRepository instance. This is possible due to the @SpringBoot-Application annotation, which enables the scan on the package where the application is located and registers the beans in the context.

The next tests will extend this class and use the already populated database. To test the methods that now belong to UserRepository, we'll create the FindUsersUsing-QueriesTest class and follow the same recipe for writing tests: we'll call the repository method and verify its results.

Path: Ch15/spring-data-jdbc/src/test/java/com/manning/javapersistence/ch15
➡ /FindUsersUsingQueriesTest.java

```
public class FindUsersUsingQueriesTest extends
➡ SpringDataJdbcApplicationTests{

    @Test
    void testFindAll() {
        List<User> users = userRepository.findAll();
        assertEquals(10, users.size());
    }
}
```

15.2 Working with queries in Spring Data JDBC

We'll now look at working with queries in Spring Data JDBC. We'll start by defining queries with the query builder mechanism, and move on to limiting query results, sorting and paging, streaming results, using modifying queries, and creating customized queries.

15.2.1 Defining query methods with Spring Data JDBC

We'll extend the `User` class by adding the fields `email`, `level`, and `active`. A user may have different levels, which will allow them to execute particular actions, such as bidding above some amount. A user may be active or retired (meaning they are no longer active in the CaveatEmptor auction system).

Our goal is to write a program that can address use cases that involve finding users with some particular level, users who are active or not, users with a given username or email, or users with a registration date in a given interval.

Path: Ch15/spring-data-jdbc2/src/main/java/com/manning/javapersistence/ch15
➡ /model/User.java

```
@Table(name = "USERS")
public class User {

    @Id
    private Long id;

    private String username;

    private LocalDate registrationDate;

    private String email;

    private int level;
```

```
    private boolean active;

    //constructors, getters and setters
}
```

As we are now responsible for the DDL commands to be executed, we can modify the content of the schema.sql file on the classpath.

Path: Ch15/spring-data-jdbc2/src/main/resources/schema.sql

```
DROP TABLE IF EXISTS USERS;

CREATE TABLE USERS (
    ID INTEGER AUTO_INCREMENT PRIMARY KEY,
    ACTIVE BOOLEAN,
    USERNAME VARCHAR(30),
    EMAIL VARCHAR(30),
    LEVEL INTEGER,
    REGISTRATION_DATE DATE
);
```

We'll now add new methods to the UserRepository interface that query the database, and we'll use them in newly created tests.

Path: Ch15/spring-data-jdbc2/src/main/java/com/manning/javapersistence/ch15
➡ /repositories/UserRepository.java

```
public interface UserRepository extends CrudRepository<User, Long> {
    List<User> findAll();
    Optional<User> findByUsername(String username);
    List<User> findAllByOrderByUsernameAsc();
    List<User> findByRegistrationDateBetween(LocalDate start,
    ➡ LocalDate end);
    List<User> findByUsernameAndEmail(String username, String email);
    List<User> findByUsernameOrEmail(String username, String email);
    List<User> findByUsernameIgnoreCase(String username);
    List<User> findByLevelOrderByUsernameDesc(int level);
    List<User> findByLevelGreaterThanEqual(int level);
    List<User> findByUsernameContaining(String text);
    List<User> findByUsernameLike(String text);
    List<User> findByUsernameStartingWith(String start);
    List<User> findByUsernameEndingWith(String end);
    List<User> findByActive(boolean active);
    List<User> findByRegistrationDateIn(Collection<LocalDate> dates);
    List<User> findByRegistrationDateNotIn(Collection<LocalDate> dates);
    // . . .
}
```

The purpose of the query methods is to retrieve information from the database. Starting with version 2.0, Spring Data JDBC provides a query builder mechanism similar to the one in Spring Data JPA—it creates the behavior of the repository methods based on their names. Remember that the query mechanism removes prefixes and suffixes such as `find...By`, `get...By`, `query...By`, `read...By`, and `count...By` from the name of the method and then parses the remainder of it.

Just like Spring Data JPA, Spring Data JDBC will look at the return type of the method. If we want to find a `User` and return it in an `Optional` container, the method return type will be `Optional<User>`.

The names of the methods need to follow the rules to determine the resulting query. Defined query methods may currently only use properties that can be included in a `WHERE` clause, but without joins. If the method naming is wrong (for example, the entity property does not match in the query method), we'll get an error when the application context is loaded. Table 15.1 summarizes the use of the essential keywords in building Spring Data JDBC query methods and the resulting conditions. For a more comprehensive list, see appendix C.

Table 15.1   Keyword usage in Spring Data JDBC and resulting conditions

Keyword	Example	Condition

Is, Equals	`findByUsername(String name)`
	`findByUsernameIs(String name)`
	`findByUsernameEquals(String name)`
		username = name

And	`findByUsernameAndRegistrationDate` `(String name, LocalDate date)`	username = name and registration_date = date
Or	`findByUsernameOrRegistrationDate` `(String name, LocalDate date)`	username = name or registrationdatev= name
LessThan	`findByRegistrationDateLessThan` `(LocalDate date)`	registrationdate < date
LessThanEqual	`findByRegistrationDateLessThanEqual` `(LocalDate date)`	registrationdate <= date
GreaterThan	`findByRegistrationDateGreaterThan` `(LocalDate date)`	registrationdate > date
GreaterThanEqual	`findByRegistrationDateGreaterThanEqual` `(LocalDatevdate)`	registrationdate >= date
Between	`findByRegistrationDateBetween` `(LocalDate from, LocalDate to)`	registrationdate between from and to
OrderBy	`findByRegistrationDateOrderByUsernameDesc` `(LocalDate date)`	registrationdate = date order by username desc
Like	`findByUsernameLike(String name)`	username like name
NotLike	`findByUsernameNotLike(String name)`	username not like name

Table 15.1   Keyword usage in Spring Data JDBC and resulting conditions *(continued)*

Keyword	Example	Condition
Before	findByRegistrationDateBefore (LocalDate date)	registrationdate < date
After	findByRegistrationDateAfter (LocalDate date)	registrationdate > date
Null, IsNull	findByRegistrationDate(Is)Null()	registrationdate is null
NotNull, IsNotNull	findByRegistrationDate(Is)NotNull()	registrationdate is not null
Not	findByUsernameNot(String name)	username <> name

We'll extend the `SpringDataJdbcApplicationTests` abstract class, the base class for our tests, by configuring the newly introduced fields `email`, `level`, and `active` for each user.

Listing 15.11   The updated `SpringDataJdbcApplicationTests` abstract class

```
Path: Ch15/spring-data-jdbc2/src/test/java/com/manning/javapersistence/ch15
➥ /SpringDataJdbcApplicationTests.java

@SpringBootTest
@TestInstance(TestInstance.Lifecycle.PER_CLASS)
abstract class SpringDataJdbcApplicationTests {
    // . . .
    private static List<User> generateUsers() {
        List<User> users = new ArrayList<>();

        User john = new User("john", LocalDate.of(2020, Month.APRIL, 13));
        john.setEmail("john@somedomain.com");
        john.setLevel(1);
        john.setActive(true);

        //create and set a total of 10 users

        users.add(john);
        //add a total of 10 users to the list

        return users;
    }

    // . . .
}
```

The next tests extend this class and use the already populated database. The use case we want to solve is getting a user or a list of users fulfilling a particular condition (such as a registration date within a given interval) or ordered by username. To test the methods that now belong to `UserRepository`, we'll create the `FindUsersUsingQueriesTest` class and follow the same recipe for writing tests: call the repository method and verify its results.

Listing 15.12   The `FindUsersUsingQueriesTest` class

```
Path: Ch15/spring-data-jdbc2/src/test/java/com/manning/javapersistence/ch15
➡ /FindUsersUsingQueriesTest.java

public class FindUsersUsingQueriesTest extends
➡ SpringDataJdbcApplicationTests{

    @Test
    void testFindAll() {
        List<User> users = userRepository.findAll();
        assertEquals(10, users.size());
    }

    @Test
    void testFindUser() {
        User beth = userRepository.findByUsername("beth").get();
        assertEquals("beth", beth.getUsername());
    }

    @Test
    void testFindAllByOrderByUsernameAsc() {
        List<User> users = userRepository.findAllByOrderByUsernameAsc();
        assertAll(() -> assertEquals(10, users.size()),
                  () -> assertEquals("beth", users.get(0).getUsername()),
                  () -> assertEquals("stephanie",
                          users.get(users.size() - 1).getUsername()));
    }

    @Test
    void testFindByRegistrationDateBetween() {
        List<User> users = userRepository.findByRegistrationDateBetween(
                LocalDate.of(2020, Month.JULY, 1),
                LocalDate.of(2020, Month.DECEMBER, 31));
        assertEquals(4, users.size());
    }

    //more tests
}
```

15.2.2 *Limiting query results, sorting, and paging*

As in Spring Data JPA, the `first` and `top` keywords (used equivalently) can limit the results of query methods. The `top` and `first` keywords may be followed by an optional numeric value to indicate the maximum result size to be returned. If this numeric value is missing, the result size will be 1.

`Pageable` is an interface for pagination information. In practice, we use the `Page-Request` class that implements it. This class can specify the page number, the page size, and the sorting criterion.

The use cases we want to solve here are getting a limited number of users (such as the first user by username or by registration date) or the first users with a given level, sorted by registration date, or a large bunch of users in pages, so we can easily manipulate them.

We'll add the following methods to the `UserRepository` interface.

Listing 15.13   Limiting query results, sorting, and paging in `UserRepository`

Path: Ch15/spring-data-jdbc2/src/main/java/com/manning/javapersistence/ch15
➡ /repositories/UserRepository.java

```
Optional<User> findFirstByOrderByUsernameAsc();
Optional<User> findTopByOrderByRegistrationDateDesc();
Page<User> findAll(Pageable pageable);
List<User> findFirst2ByLevel(int level, Sort sort);
List<User> findByLevel(int level, Sort sort);
List<User> findByActive(boolean active, Pageable pageable);
```

These methods follow the pattern required by the query builder mechanism (summarized in table 15.1), but this time their purpose is to limit the results of the query, so we can do sorting and paging. For example, the `Optional<User> findFirstByOrder-ByUsernameAsc()` method will get the first user by its username (the result is an `Optional`, so eventually it may not exist). The `Page<User> findAll(Pageable page-able)` method will get all users but in pages. We'll write the following tests to verify how these newly added methods work.

Listing 15.14   Testing limiting query results, sorting, and paging

Path: Ch15/spring-data-jdbc2/src/test/java/com/manning/javapersistence/ch15
➡ /FindUsersSortingAndPagingTest.java

```
public class FindUsersSortingAndPagingTest extends
            SpringDataJdbcApplicationTests {

    @Test
    void testOrder() {

        User user1 = userRepository.findFirstByOrderByUsernameAsc().get();        Ⓐ
        User user2 =                                                           Ⓑ
            userRepository.findTopByOrderByRegistrationDateDesc().get();
        Page<User> userPage = userRepository.findAll(PageRequest.of(1, 3));
        List<User> users = userRepository.findFirst2ByLevel(2,               Ⓒ
                                      Sort.by("registrationDate"));

        assertAll(
                () -> assertEquals("beth", user1.getUsername()),
                () -> assertEquals("julius", user2.getUsername()),
                () -> assertEquals(2, users.size()),
                () -> assertEquals(3, userPage.getSize()),
                () -> assertEquals("beth", users.get(0).getUsername()),
```

```
                    () -> assertEquals("marion", users.get(1).getUsername())
        );

    }

    @Test
    void testFindByLevel() {
        Sort.TypedSort<User> user = Sort.sort(User.class);

        List<User> users = userRepository.findByLevel(3,
                user.by(User::getRegistrationDate).descending());
        assertAll(
                () -> assertEquals(2, users.size()),
                () -> assertEquals("james", users.get(0).getUsername())
        );

    }

    @Test
    void testFindByActive() {
        List<User> users = userRepository.findByActive(true,
                PageRequest.of(1, 4, Sort.by("registrationDate")));
        assertAll(
                () -> assertEquals(4, users.size()),
                () -> assertEquals("burk", users.get(0).getUsername())
        );

    }
}
```

Ⓐ The first test finds the first user by ascending order of username and the first user by descending order of registration date.

Ⓑ Find all users, split them into pages, and return page number 1 of size 3 (the page numbering starts with 0).

Ⓒ Find the first 2 users with level 2, ordered by registration date.

Ⓓ The second test defines a sorting criterion on the `User` class. `Sort.TypedSort` extends `Sort` and can use method handles to define properties to sort by.

Ⓔ Find users of level 3 and sort by registration date, descending.

Ⓕ The third test finds the active users sorted by registration date, splits them into pages, and returns page number 1 of size 4 (page numbering starts with 0).

15.2.3 *Streaming results*

Query methods returning more than one result can use standard Java interfaces, such as `Iterable`, `List`, and `Set`. Like Spring Data JPA, Spring Data JDBC supports `Streamable`, which can be used as an alternative to `Iterable` or any collection type. It allows us to concatenate `Streamables` and to directly filter and map over the elements.

The use case we'll solve here is getting the results as a stream, without waiting for the whole collection of users or a page of users to be obtained. This way, we can quickly start processing the first results as they flow in. Unlike collections, a stream can be consumed only once and is immutable.

We'll add the following methods to the `UserRepository` interface.

Listing 15.15   Adding methods that return `Streamable` in `UserRepository`

Path: Ch15/spring-data-jdbc2/src/main/java/com/manning/javapersistence/ch15
➥ /repositories/UserRepository.java

```
Streamable<User> findByEmailContaining(String text);
Streamable<User> findByLevel(int level);
```

We'll write the following test to verify how these newly added methods interact with the database and provide results as streams. A stream is given as a resource of the `try` block, so it is automatically closed. An alternative is to explicitly call the `close()` method. Otherwise the stream would keep the underlying connection to the database.

Listing 15.16   Testing methods that return `Streamable`

Path: Ch15/spring-data-jdbc2/src/test/java/com/manning/javapersistence/ch15
➥ /QueryResultsTest.java

```
@Test
void testStreamable() {
    try(Stream<User> result =                                        A
            userRepository.findByEmailContaining("someother")
 B ─→      .and(userRepository.findByLevel(2))
           .stream().distinct()) {            ◄──  C
        assertEquals(6, result.count());    ◄─┐
    }                                         │
}                                             D
```

A The test will call the `findByEmailContaining` method to search for emails containing the `someother` word.

B The test will concatenate the resulting `Streamable` with the `Streamable` providing users of level 2.

C It will transform this into a stream and will keep the distinct users.

D Check that the resulting stream contains 6 users.

15.2.4 *The @Query annotation*

We can use the `@Query` annotation to create methods for which a custom query can be specified. With the `@Query` annotation, the method name does not need to follow any naming convention. The custom query can be parameterized, but unlike for Spring Data JPA, the parameters can be identified only by name, and they must be bound in the query with the `@Param` annotation. Unlike with Spring Data JPA, we do not use JPQL but SQL. Consequently, there is no portability—if you change the database vendor, you will have to rewrite the queries.

We'll add two new methods to the `UserRepository` interface. These methods will be annotated with the `@Query` annotation, and their generated behavior will depend on the definition of these queries.

Listing 15.17 Methods annotated with `@Query` in the `UserRepository` interface

Path: Ch15/spring-data-jdbc2/src/main/java/com/manning/javapersistence/ch15
➥ /repositories/UserRepository.java

```
@Query("SELECT COUNT(*) FROM USERS WHERE ACTIVE = :ACTIVE")
int findNumberOfUsersByActivity(@Param("ACTIVE") boolean active);
```

```
@Query("SELECT * FROM USERS WHERE LEVEL = :LEVEL AND ACTIVE = :ACTIVE")
List<User> findByLevelAndActive(@Param("LEVEL") int level, @Param("ACTIVE")
                                boolean active);
```

Ⓐ The `findNumberOfUsersByActivity` method will return the number of active users.

Ⓑ The `findByLevelAndActive` method will return users with the `level` and `active` status given as named parameters. The `@Param` annotation will match the `:LEVEL` parameter of the query with the `level` argument of the method and the `:ACTIVE` parameter of the query with the `active` argument of the method.

Writing tests for these query methods is pretty straightforward and similar to the previous examples. They can be found in the source code for the book.

15.2.5 Modifying queries

We can define modifying methods with the `@Modifying` annotation. For example, `INSERT`, `UPDATE`, and `DELETE` queries and DDL statements modify the content of the database. The `@Query` annotation can take as an argument the modifying query, and it may need binding parameters. At the time of writing, Spring Data JDBC does not support query derivation for delete methods (unlike Spring Data JPA).

We'll add the new methods, annotated with the `@Query` annotation, to the `User-Repository` interface, but this time the queries will update or delete records from the `USERS` table.

Listing 15.18 Adding modifying methods to the `UserRepository` interface

Path: Ch15/spring-data-jdbc2/src/main/java/com/manning/javapersistence/ch15
➥ /repositories/UserRepository.java

```
@Modifying
@Query("UPDATE USERS SET LEVEL = :NEW_LEVEL WHERE LEVEL = :OLD_LEVEL")
int updateLevel(@Param("OLD_LEVEL") int oldLevel,
➥ @Param("NEW_LEVEL")int newLevel);

@Modifying
@Query("DELETE FROM USERS WHERE LEVEL = :LEVEL")
int deleteByLevel(@Param("LEVEL") int level);
```

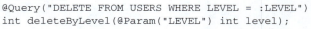

Ⓐ The updateLevel method will change the level of the users having the oldLevel and set it to the newLevel. The method is also annotated with @Modifying.

Ⓑ The deleteByLevel method will remove all users with the level given as a parameter, as the argument of the @Query annotation indicates. The method is also annotated with @Modifying.

Writing the tests for these query methods is pretty straightforward and similar to the previous examples. They can be found in the source code for the book.

15.3 *Modeling relationships with Spring Data JDBC*

Managing the associations between classes and the relationships between tables is at the heart of ORM problems. We examined the possible solutions to these problems using JPA and Spring Data JPA in chapter 8, and we'll now look at the approaches provided by Spring Data JDBC.

15.3.1 *Modeling a one-to-one relationship with Spring Data JDBC*

Spring Data JPA can model relationships between entities with the JPA annotations @OneToOne, @OneToMany, @ManyToMany. Spring Data JDBC uses a different mechanism than JPA. We'll start with modeling one-to-one relationships between entities in Spring Data JDBC using the User and Address entities. Each User will have only one Address, and each Address will belong to one User.

As previously stated, Spring Boot will always execute the schema.sql file on the classpath at startup. As shown in the following listing, it drops and recreates the ADDRESSES and USERS tables.

> Listing 15.19   The schema.sql file for one-to-one relationships

```
Path: Ch15/spring-data-jdbc3/src/main/resources/schema.sql

DROP TABLE IF EXISTS ADDRESSES;
DROP TABLE IF EXISTS USERS;

CREATE TABLE USERS (
    ID INTEGER AUTO_INCREMENT PRIMARY KEY,
    ACTIVE BOOLEAN,
    USERNAME VARCHAR(30),
    EMAIL VARCHAR(30),
    LEVEL INTEGER,
    REGISTRATION_DATE DATE
);

CREATE TABLE ADDRESSES (
  USER_ID INTEGER AUTO_INCREMENT PRIMARY KEY,
  STREET VARCHAR(30) NOT NULL,
  CITY VARCHAR(20) NOT NULL
);
```

The @MappedCollection annotation (introduced in Spring Data JDBC 1.1) can be used on a reference type for a one-to-one relationship. The ID field of the USERS table will be a foreign key in the ADDRESSES table, the corresponding field from the ADDRESSES table being USER_ID. Having one single Address reference inside User will make the relationship one-to-one. In the User class, the reference to the Address field will look like this:

Path: Ch15/spring-data-jdbc3/src/main/java/com/manning/javapersistence/ch15
➥ /model/User.java

```
@Table("USERS")
public class User {

    @Id
    private Long id;

    // . . .

    @MappedCollection(idColumn = "USER_ID")
    private Address address;
```

The Address class will also be annotated with @Table, because it will correspond to a different table from the database:

Path: Ch15/spring-data-jdbc3/src/main/java/com/manning/javapersistence/ch15
➥ /model/Address.java

```
@Table("ADDRESSES")
public class Address {
// . . .
```

We'll create two repositories. The first is for the User entity:

Path: Ch15/spring-data-jdbc3/src/main/java/com/manning/javapersistence/ch15
➥ /repositories/UserOneToOneRepository.java

```
public interface UserOneToOneRepository extends
➥ CrudRepository<User, Long> {

}
```

The second is for the Address entity:

Path: Ch15/spring-data-jdbc3/src/main/java/com/manning/javapersistence/ch15
➥ /repositories/AddressOneToOneRepository.java

```
public interface AddressOneToOneRepository extends
                CrudRepository<Address, Long> {
}
```

We'll use these repositories to populate the database and execute the tests:

```
Path: Ch15/spring-data-jdbc3/src/test/java/com/manning/javapersistence/ch15
  /UserAddressOneToOneTest.java

@SpringBootTest
@TestInstance(TestInstance.Lifecycle.PER_CLASS)
public class UserAddressOneToOneTest {

    @Autowired
    private UserOneToOneRepository userOneToOneRepository;

    @Autowired
    private AddressOneToOneRepository addressOneToOneRepository;

    // . . .

    @Test
    void oneToOneTest() {

        assertAll(
                () -> assertEquals(10, userOneToOneRepository.count()),
                () -> assertEquals(10, addressOneToOneRepository.count())
        );

    }
    // . . .
}
```

15.3.2 *Modeling embedded entities with Spring Data JDBC*

We now move on to the modeling of embedded entities in Spring Data JDBC. We want to embed the User entity and the Address class in User.

The SQL script that's automatically executed is shown in the following listing. There will be only one table, USERS, which will embed the information about addresses.

Listing 15.20   The schema.sql file for embedded entities

```
Path: Ch15/spring-data-jdbc4/src/main/resources/schema.sql

DROP TABLE IF EXISTS USERS;

CREATE TABLE USERS (
    ID INTEGER AUTO_INCREMENT PRIMARY KEY,
    ACTIVE BOOLEAN,
    USERNAME VARCHAR(30),
    EMAIL VARCHAR(30),
    LEVEL INTEGER,
    REGISTRATION_DATE DATE,
    STREET VARCHAR(30) NOT NULL,
     CITY VARCHAR(20) NOT NULL
);
```

The address will be embedded in the USERS table. If the embedded STREET and CITY columns are empty, the address field is null. In the User class, the reference to the Address field will look like this:

Path: Ch15/spring-data-jdbc4/src/main/java/com/manning/javapersistence/ch15
➡ /model/User.java

```java
@Table("USERS")
public class User {

    @Id
    private Long id;

    // . . .

    @Embedded(onEmpty = Embedded.OnEmpty.USE_NULL)
    private Address address;
```

The Address class will not be annotated with @Table, as it will no longer correspond to a different table from the database—all its information will be embedded in the USERS table.

Path: Ch15/spring-data-jdbc4/src/main/java/com/manning/javapersistence/ch15
➡ /model/Address.java

```java
public class Address {
// . . .
```

We'll create a single repository for the User entity.

Path: Ch15/spring-data-jdbc4/src/main/java/com/manning/javapersistence/ch15
➡ /repositories/UserAddressEmbeddedRepository.java

```java
public interface UserAddressEmbeddedRepository extends
            CrudRepository<User, Long> {

}
```

We'll then use this repository to populate the database and execute the tests.

Path: Ch15/spring-data-jdbc4/src/test/java/com/manning/javapersistence/ch15
➡ /UserAddressEmbeddedTest.java

```java
@SpringBootTest
@TestInstance(TestInstance.Lifecycle.PER_CLASS)
public class UserAddressEmbeddedTest {

    @Autowired
    private UserAddressEmbeddedRepository userAddressEmbeddedRepository;

    // . . .
```

```
@Test
void embeddedTest() {

    assertEquals(10, userAddressEmbeddedRepository.count());

}
// . . .
}
```

15.3.3 Modeling a one-to-many relationship with Spring Data JDBC

We'll now move on to the modeling of a one-to-many relationship in Spring Data JDBC. We have the User entity and the Address entity. Each user can have many addresses.

The SQL script that's automatically executed is shown in the following listing. There will be two tables, USERS and ADDRESSES.

Listing 15.21   The schema.sql file for one-to-many relationships

```
Path: Ch15/spring-data-jdbc5/src/main/resources/schema.sql

DROP TABLE IF EXISTS ADDRESSES;
DROP TABLE IF EXISTS USERS;

CREATE TABLE USERS (
    ID INTEGER AUTO_INCREMENT PRIMARY KEY,
    ACTIVE BOOLEAN,
    USERNAME VARCHAR(30),
    EMAIL VARCHAR(30),
    LEVEL INTEGER,
    REGISTRATION_DATE DATE
);

CREATE TABLE ADDRESSES (
    ID INTEGER AUTO_INCREMENT PRIMARY KEY,
    USER_ID INTEGER,
    STREET VARCHAR(30) NOT NULL,
    CITY VARCHAR(20) NOT NULL,
    FOREIGN KEY (USER_ID)
        REFERENCES USERS(ID)
            ON DELETE CASCADE
    );
```

The ID field of the USERS table will be a foreign key in the ADDRESSES table, the corresponding field from the ADDRESSES table being USER_ID. Having a set of Address references inside User will indicate that a User has many Addresses. In the User class, the reference to the Addresses will look like this:

```
Path: Ch15/spring-data-jdbc5/src/main/java/com/manning/javapersistence/ch15
➥ /model/User.java

@Table("USERS")
```

```
public class User {

    @Id
    private Long id;

    // . . .

    @MappedCollection(idColumn = "USER_ID")
    private Set<Address> addresses = new HashSet<>();
```

The `Address` class will also be annotated with `@Table`, as it will correspond to a different table from the database:

Path: Ch15/spring-data-jdbc5/src/main/java/com/manning/javapersistence/ch15
➡ /model/Address.java

```
@Table("ADDRESSES")
public class Address {
    // . . .
```

We'll create two repositories: one for the `User` entity and one for the `Address` entity. The second repository will contain an additional method. Even if the name of the `countByUserId` method follows the pattern discussed both for Spring Data JDBC and Spring Data JPA, the method needs to be annotated with `@Query`, as `userId` does not exist in the `Address` class:

Path: Ch15/spring-data-jdbc5/src/main/java/com/manning/javapersistence/ch15
➡ /repositories/AddressOneToManyRepository.java

```
public interface AddressOneToManyRepository
                extends CrudRepository<Address, Long> {

    @Query("SELECT COUNT(*) FROM ADDRESSES WHERE USER_ID = :USER_ID")
    int countByUserId(@Param("USER_ID") Long userId);
}
```

We'll use the repositories to populate the database and execute the tests:

Path: Ch15/spring-data-jdbc5/src/test/java/com/manning/javapersistence/ch15
➡ /UserAddressOneToManyTest.java

```
@SpringBootTest
@TestInstance(TestInstance.Lifecycle.PER_CLASS)
public class UserAddressOneToManyTest {

    @Autowired
    private UserOneToManyRepository userOneToManyRepository;

    @Autowired
    private AddressOneToManyRepository addressOneToManyRepository;

    // . . .
```

```
    @Test
    void oneToManyTest() {

        assertAll(
                () -> assertEquals(10, userOneToManyRepository.count()),
                () -> assertEquals(20, addressOneToManyRepository.count()),
                () -> assertEquals(2,

➡  addressOneToManyRepository.countByUserId(users.get(0).getId()))
        );

    }
    // . . .
}
```

15.3.4   Modeling a many-to-many relationship with Spring Data JDBC

We'll now move on to modeling a many-to-many relationship in Spring Data JDBC. We have the User and Address entities. Each User can have many Addresses, and each Address may have many Users. We'll also need to manually introduce a class corresponding to the USERS_ADDRESSES intermediary table, which will model the many-to-many relationship.

The SQL script that's automatically executed will look like the following listing. There will be three tables: USERS, ADDRESSES, and USERS_ADDRESSES.

Listing 15.22   The schema.sql file for many-to-many relationships

```
Path: Ch15/spring-data-jdbc6/src/main/resources/schema.sql

DROP TABLE IF EXISTS USERS_ADDRESSES;
DROP TABLE IF EXISTS USERS;
DROP TABLE IF EXISTS ADDRESSES;

CREATE TABLE USERS (
    ID INTEGER AUTO_INCREMENT PRIMARY KEY,
    ACTIVE BOOLEAN,
    USERNAME VARCHAR(30),
    EMAIL VARCHAR(30),
    LEVEL INTEGER,
    REGISTRATION_DATE DATE
);

CREATE TABLE ADDRESSES (
  ID INTEGER AUTO_INCREMENT PRIMARY KEY,
  STREET VARCHAR(30) NOT NULL,
  CITY VARCHAR(20) NOT NULL
);

CREATE TABLE USERS_ADDRESSES (
  USER_ID INTEGER,
  ADDRESS_ID INTEGER,
```

```
FOREIGN KEY (USER_ID)
   REFERENCES USERS(ID)
      ON DELETE CASCADE,
FOREIGN KEY (ADDRESS_ID)
   REFERENCES ADDRESSES(ID)
      ON DELETE CASCADE
);
```

To model many-to-many relationships, the `User` class will be connected to the intermediary class `UserAddress`. Having a set of `UserAddress` references inside `User` will indicate that a `User` has many `UserAddresses`. The `ID` field of the `USERS` table will be a foreign key in the `USERS_ADDRESSES` table, the corresponding field from the `USERS_ADDRESSES` table being `USER_ID`. In the `User` class, the reference to the `Addresses` will look like this:

Path: Ch15/spring-data-jdbc6/src/main/java/com/manning/javapersistence/ch15
➡ /model/User.java

```java
@Table("USERS")
public class User {

    @Id
    private Long id;

    // . . .

    @MappedCollection(idColumn = "USER_ID")
    private Set<UserAddress> addresses = new HashSet<>();
```

The `Address` class will also be annotated with `@Table`, as it will correspond to a different table from the database:

Path: Ch15/spring-data-jdbc6/src/main/java/com/manning/javapersistence/ch15
➡ /model/Address.java

```java
@Table("ADDRESSES")
public class Address {
// . . .
```

Also, we'll create the `UserAddress` class and annotate it with `@Table`, as it will correspond to a different table from the database. It will hold only the ID of the `Address`, as the `User` class keeps a set of references of `UserAddress` type.

Path: Ch15/spring-data-jdbc6/src/main/java/com/manning/javapersistence/ch15
➡ /model/UserAddress.java

```java
@Table("USERS_ADDRESSES")
public class UserAddress {
    private Long addressId;

    public UserAddress(Long addressId) {
```

```
        this.addressId = addressId;
    }

    public Long getAddressId() {
        return addressId;
    }
}
```

We'll create three repositories: one for the User entity, one for the Address entity, and one for the UserAddress entity. The third repository will contain an additional method: even though the name of the countByUserId method follows the pattern discussed both for Spring Data JDBC and Spring Data JPA, the method needs to be annotated with @Query, because the userId does not exist in the UserAddress class.

Path: Ch15/spring-data-jdbc6/src/main/java/com/manning/javapersistence/ch15
➥ /repositories/UserAddressManyToManyRepository.java

```
public interface UserAddressManyToManyRepository extends
                CrudRepository<UserAddress, Long> {

    @Query("SELECT COUNT(*) FROM USERS_ADDRESSES WHERE USER_ID = :USER_ID")
    int countByUserId(@Param("USER_ID") Long userId);

}
```

We'll use the repositories to populate the database and execute the tests:

Path: Ch15/spring-data-jdbc6/src/test/java/com/manning/javapersistence/ch15
➥ /UserAddressManyToManyTest.java

```
@SpringBootTest
@TestInstance(TestInstance.Lifecycle.PER_CLASS)
public class UserAddressManyToManyTest {

    @Autowired
    private UserAddressManyToManyRepository
    ➥ userAddressManyToManyRepository;

    @Autowired
    private AddressManyToManyRepository addressManyToManyRepository;

    @Autowired
    private UserManyToManyRepository userManyToManyRepository;

    // . . .

    @Test
    void manyToManyTest() {

        assertAll(
                () -> assertEquals(10, userManyToManyRepository.count()),
                () -> assertEquals(3, addressManyToManyRepository.count()),
```

```
          () -> assertEquals(20,
                   userAddressManyToManyRepository.count()),
          () -> assertEquals(2,
                  userAddressManyToManyRepository.countByUserId(
                                                users.get(0).getId())))
      );

  }

  // . . .
}
```

To conclude and finally compare and contrast the current capabilities of Spring Data JPA and Spring Data JDBC, take a look at table 15.2. We've summarized here the most important capabilities, such as portability, the complexity of learning and adopting it in projects, query derivation, native SQL usage, annotation usage, relationship modeling, caching and lazy loading, sessions, and dirty tracking.

Table 15.2 Spring Data JPA capabilities vs. Spring Data JDBC capabilities

Spring Data JPA	Spring Data JDBC
Database-independent and portable	Generally, database-specific
Introduces complexity through object/relational mapping (ORM)	Less complex, but still adheres to the Spring Framework principles
Automatic schema generation based on the entities	Schema generation through DDL commands on the side of the programmer
Query derivation since the first version	Query derivation since version 2.0
Queries annotated with JPQL code and native SQL	Only queries using native SQL
Can reuse classes with JPA annotations	Uses annotations from the `org.springframework.data` package
Models relationships between entities through annotations such as `@OneToMany`, `@Embedded`, etc.	Models relationships mostly on the side of the programmer, through the design of the classes
Caching and lazy loading	No caching, no lazy loading
Sessions and dirty tracking	No sessions, no dirty tracking

NOTE Spring Data JDBC is a young project, and it is in full development. It is expected to add considerable new features in the near future.

Summary

- You can create and configure a Spring Data JDBC project using Spring Boot, adding step-by-step methods that query the database and model different types of relationships.

- You can define and use a series of query methods to access repositories by following the Spring Data JDBC query builder mechanisms, as introduced in version 2.0 of the framework.
- Spring Data JDBC capabilities include limiting query results, sorting, paging, streaming results, and the `@Query` annotation.
- You can create and use modifying queries to update and delete entities.
- You can model one-to-one, one-to-many, and many-to-many relationships between entities as well as embedded entities with Spring Data JDBC.

Working with
Spring Data REST

Representational state transfer (REST) is a software architectural style for creating web services; it also provides a set of constraints. The American computer scientist Roy Fielding, who is also one of the authors of the HTTP specification, first defined REST, presenting the REST principles in his PhD dissertation (Fielding, 2000). Web services following this REST architectural style are called *RESTful web services*, and they allow interoperability between the internet and computer systems. Requesting systems can access and manipulate web resources represented as text using a well-known set of stateless operations (GET, POST, PUT, PATCH, DELETE). A stateless operation does not depend on any other prior operation; it must contain all the information needed to be understood by the server.

16.1 *Introducing REST applications*

We will first define the terms *client* and *resource* to describe what makes an API RESTful. A *client* is a person or software using the RESTful API. For example, a programmer using a RESTful API to execute actions against the LinkedIn website is a client, but the client can also be a web browser. When we go to the LinkedIn website, our browser is the client that calls the website API and that displays the obtained information on the screen. A *resource* can be any object about which the API can obtain information. In the LinkedIn API, a resource can be a message, a photo, or a user. Each resource has a unique identifier.

The REST architecture style defines six constraints (https://restfulapi.net/rest-architectural-constraints/):

- *Client-server*—Clients are separated from servers, and each has its own concerns. Most frequently, a client is concerned with the representation of the user, and a server is concerned with data storage and domain model logic—the conceptual model of a domain including data and behavior.
- *Stateless*—The server does not keep any information about the client between requests. Each request from a client contains all of the information necessary to respond to that request. The client keeps the state on its side.
- *Uniform interface*—The client and the server may evolve independently of each other. The uniform interface between them makes them loosely coupled.
- *Layered systems*—The client does not have any way to determine if it is interacting directly with the server or with an intermediary. Layers can be dynamically added and removed. They can provide security, load balancing, or shared caching.
- *Cacheable*—Clients are able to cache responses. Responses define themselves as cacheable or not.
- *Code on demand (optional)*—Servers are able to temporarily customize or extend the functionality of a client. The server can transfer some logic to the client that the client can execute, such as JavaScript client-side scripts.

A RESTful web application provides information about its resources, which are identified with the help of URLs. The client can execute actions against such a resource; it can create, read, update, or delete a resource.

The REST architectural style is not protocol-specific, but the most widely used protocol is REST over HTTP. HTTP is a synchronous application network protocol based on requests and responses.

To make our API RESTful, we have to follow a set of rules while developing it. A RESTful API will transfer information to the client, which uses that information as a representation of the state of the accessed resource. For example, when we call the

LinkedIn API to access a specific user, the API will return the state of that user (name, biography, professional experience, posts). The REST rules make the API easier to understand and simpler for new programmers to use when they join a team.

The representation of the state can be in JSON, XML, or HTML format. The client uses the API to send the following information to the server:

- The identifier (URL) of the resource we want to access.
- The operation we want the server to perform on that resource. This is an HTTP method, the most common of which are GET, POST, PUT, PATCH, and DELETE.

For example, using the LinkedIn RESTful API to fetch a specific LinkedIn user requires that we have a URL that identifies the user and that we use the HTTP method GET.

16.2   Creating a Spring Data REST application

Our first goal is to create a Spring Data REST application that will provide a browser interface to interact with the database and to manage and persist CaveatEmptor users. To do this, we'll access the Spring Initializr website (https://start.spring.io/) and create a new Spring Boot project (figure 16.1), having the following characteristics:

- Group: com.manning.javapersistence
- Artifact: spring-data-rest
- Description: Spring Data REST

Figure 16.1   Creating a new Spring Boot project using Spring Data REST and MySQL

We'll also add the following dependencies:

- Spring Web (this will add `spring-boot-starter-web` in the Maven pom.xml file)

- Spring Data JPA (this will add `spring-boot-starter-data-jpa` in the Maven pom.xml file)
- REST Repositories (this will add `spring-boot-starter-data-rest` in the Maven pom.xml file)
- MySQL Driver (this will add `mysql-connector-java` in the Maven pom.xml file)

NOTE To execute the examples from the source code, you'll first need to run the Ch16.sql script.

The pom.xml file in the following listing includes the dependencies we added to start the Spring Data REST project. This Spring Data REST application will access a MySQL database, so we need the driver.

Listing 16.1 The pom.xml Maven file

Path: Ch16/spring-data-rest/pom.xml

```
<dependency>
    <groupId>org.springframework.boot</groupId>         A
    <artifactId>spring-boot-starter-web</artifactId>
</dependency>
<dependency>
    <groupId>org.springframework.boot</groupId>         B
    <artifactId>spring-boot-starter-data-jpa</artifactId>
</dependency>
<dependency>
    <groupId>org.springframework.boot</groupId>         C
    <artifactId>spring-boot-starter-data-rest</artifactId>
</dependency>
<dependency>
    <groupId>mysql</groupId>                             D
    <artifactId>mysql-connector-java</artifactId>
    <scope>runtime</scope>
</dependency>
```

A `spring-boot-starter-web` is the starter dependency used by Spring Boot to build web applications.

B `spring-boot-starter-data-jpa` is the starter dependency used by Spring Boot to connect to a relational database through Spring Data JPA.

C `spring-boot-starter-data-rest` is the starter dependency used by Spring Boot for Spring Data REST applications.

D `mysql-connector-java` is the JDBC driver for MySQL. It is a runtime dependency, so it is needed in the classpath only at runtime.

The next step is to fill in the Spring Boot application.properties file, which can include various properties to be used by the application. Spring Boot will automatically find and load the application.properties file from the classpath—the src/main/resources folder is added by Maven to the classpath.

There are several ways to provide parameters in a Spring Boot application, and the .properties file is just one of them. Parameters can also come from the source code or as command-line arguments—see the Spring Boot documentation for details.

For our application, the application.properties configuration file will look like the following listing.

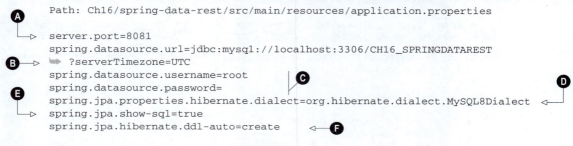

Listing 16.2   The application.properties file

Path: Ch16/spring-data-rest/src/main/resources/application.properties

```
server.port=8081
spring.datasource.url=jdbc:mysql://localhost:3306/CH16_SPRINGDATAREST
    ?serverTimezone=UTC
spring.datasource.username=root
spring.datasource.password=
spring.jpa.properties.hibernate.dialect=org.hibernate.dialect.MySQL8Dialect
spring.jpa.show-sql=true
spring.jpa.hibernate.ddl-auto=create
```

Ⓐ The application will start on port 8081.

Ⓑ The URL of the database.

Ⓒ The credentials to access the database. Replace them with the credentials on your machine, and use a password in real life.

Ⓓ The dialect of the database, MySQL.

Ⓔ Show the SQL queries when they are executed.

Ⓕ Recreate the tables for each execution of the application.

The User class will now contain a @Version annotated field. As discussed in section 11.2.2, the field value is incremented whenever a modified User instance has been persisted. Section 16.3 will demonstrate how this field can be used for conditional REST requests using ETags.

Listing 16.3   The modified User class

Path: Ch16/spring-data-rest/src/main/java/com/manning/javapersistence/ch16
    /model/User.java

```
@Entity
public class User {

    @Id
    @GeneratedValue
    private Long id;

    @Version
    private Long version;

    private String name;
```

```
    private boolean isRegistered;

    private boolean isCitizen;

    //constructors, getters and setters
}
```

Users will participate in an auction that is represented by the `Auction` class. An auction is described by the `auctionNumber`, the number of `seats`, and the set of `users`.

Listing 16.4   The `Auction` class

Path: Ch16/ spring-data-rest/src/main/java/com/manning/javapersistence/ch16
➡ /model/Auction.java

```
public class Auction {

    private String auctionNumber;
    private int seats;
    private Set<User> users = new HashSet<>();

    //constructors, getters and methods
}
```

The users participating in the auction will be read from a CSV file, in the `CsvData-Loader` class. We'll use the `@Bean` annotation to create a bean that will be managed and injected into the application by Spring.

Listing 16.5   The `CsvDataLoader` class

Path: Ch16/spring-data-rest/src/main/java/com/manning/javapersistence/ch16
➡ /beans/CsvDataLoader.java

```
public class CsvDataLoader {                         Ⓐ

    @Bean
    public Auction buildAuctionFromCsv() throws IOException {        Ⓑ
        Auction auction = new Auction("1234", 20);
        try (BufferedReader reader = new BufferedReader(                    Ⓒ
            new FileReader("src/main/resources/users_information.csv"))) {
            String line = null;
            do {                                              Ⓓ
                line = reader.readLine();
                if (line != null) {
                    User user = new User(line);
                    user.setIsRegistered(false);               Ⓔ
                    auction.addUser(user);
                }
            } while (line != null);

        }
    }
```

```
        return auction;
    }
}
```
F

A The result of the method will be a bean managed by Spring.

B Create the `Auction` object.

C Use the information from the CSV file.

D Read line by line.

E Create the user from the read information, configure it, and add it to the auction.

F Return the `Auction` bean.

The `UserRepository` interface extends `JpaRepository<User, Long>`, inheriting the JPA-related methods and managing the `User` entity, having IDs of type `Long`.

Listing 16.6   The `UserRepository` interface

Path: Ch16/spring-data-rest/src/main/java/com/manning/javapersistence/ch16
➡ /repositories/UserRepository.java

```java
public interface UserRepository extends JpaRepository<User, Long> {

}
```

The Spring Boot application will import the bean created in the `CsvDataLoader` class and autowire it. It will also create a bean of type `ApplicationRunner`. This is a Spring Boot functional interface (an interface with a single abstract method) that gives access to application arguments. This `ApplicationRunner` interface is created, and its single method is executed, just before the `run()` method from `SpringApplication` completes.

Listing 16.7   The `Application` class

Path: Ch16/spring-data-rest/src/main/java/com/manning/javapersistence/ch16
➡ /Application.java

```java
@SpringBootApplication

@Import(CsvDataLoader.class)          ⟵  A
public class Application {

    @Autowired                         B
    private Auction auction;

    public static void main(String[] args) {
        SpringApplication.run(Application.class, args);
    }

    @Bean                                                            C
    ApplicationRunner configureRepository(UserRepository userRepository) {
        return args -> {
```

```
                    for (User user : auction.getUsers()) {
                        userRepository.save(user);
                    }

              };
          }
      }
```

A Import the `CsvDataLoader` class and the `Auction` bean it creates.

B Autowire the imported `Auction` bean.

C Browse all users from the auction, and save them in the repository.

We can access the Spring Data REST application in the browser (http://localhost:8081/users) as shown in figure 16.2. We get the information about users and the option to easily navigate between the records. Spring Data REST will expose information about the API to be accessed, providing links to each record.

Figure 16.2   Accessing the Spring Data REST application from the browser

We can test this REST API endpoint using a REST client. IntelliJ IDEA Ultimate edition provides such a REST client, but you can use a different client (such as cURL or Postman). We can execute commands like the following (see figure 16.3):

```
GET http://localhost:8081/users/1
```

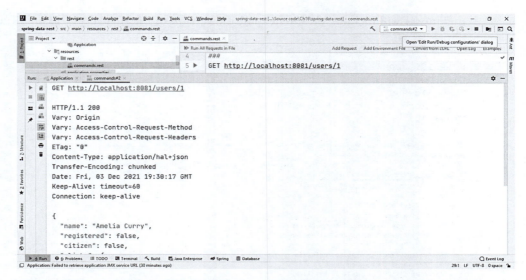

Figure 16.3   The result of executing the `GET http://localhost:8081/users/1` command in the IntelliJ IDEA Ultimate edition REST client

16.3 Using ETags for conditional requests

Any exchange of information across the network requires time. The smaller the information is, the quicker our program will work. But when and how can we reduce the amount of information retrieved from the server and transferred across the network?

Suppose we need to execute a command such as the following one multiple times:

```
GET http://localhost:8081/users/1
```

We'll access the server each time, and the same information will be sent across the network. This is inefficient, and we'd like to limit the amount of data exchanged between the client and server.

We can use ETags to make conditional requests and avoid sending information that has not changed. An ETag is an HTTP response header returned by a web server. It will help us determine if the content at a given URL has been modified, and consequently allow us to make a conditional request.

In the `User` class, there is a field annotated with the `@Version` annotation:

```
@Version
    private Long version;
```

This field will also be used as an ETag. When we execute this request to the server,

```
GET http://localhost:8081/users/1
```

the answer will include, on the header, the version of the record (0), as an ETag (see figure 16.4):

```
HTTP/1.1 200
Vary: Origin
Vary: Access-Control-Request-Method
Vary: Access-Control-Request-Headers
ETag: "0"
```

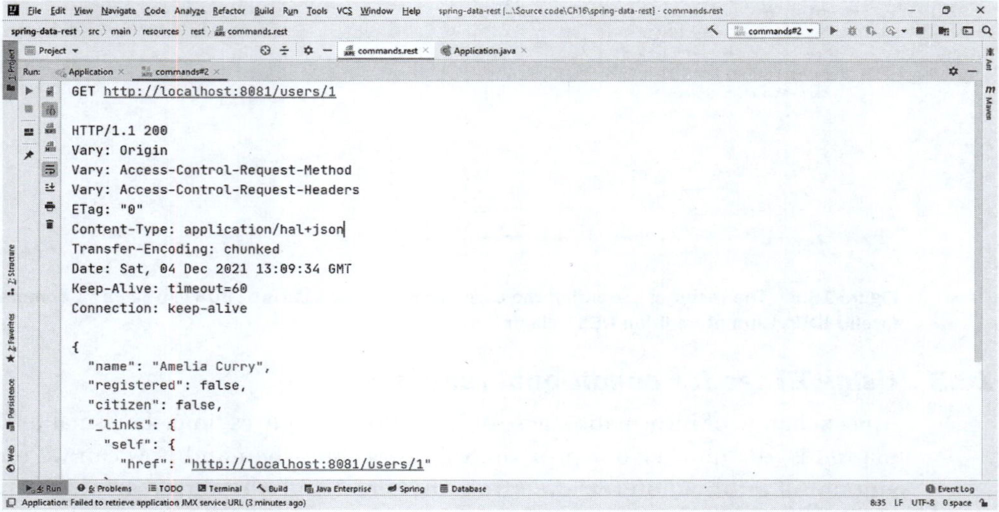

Figure 16.4   The server's answer, including the ETag on the header, representing the entity version

Using this information, we can now execute a conditional request and get the information about the user with ID 1 only if the ETag is different than 0.

```
GET http://localhost:8081/users/1
If-None-Match: "0"
```

The answer from the server will be the 304 (Not Modified) response code, together with an empty body (see figure 16.5):

```
HTTP/1.1 304
Vary: Origin
Vary: Access-Control-Request-Method
Vary: Access-Control-Request-Headers
ETag: "0"
Date: Sat, 04 Dec 2021 13:19:11 GMT
Keep-Alive: timeout=60
Connection: keep-alive

<Response body is empty>
```

Figure 16.5   The server's answer for a record matching the existing ETag does not have a body.

We can now modify the content from the user with ID 1, executing a PATCH command. We use a PATCH instead of a PUT, as PATCH will update only the fields that are included in the request, whereas PUT will replace an entire entity with a new one.

```
PATCH http://localhost:8081/users/1
Content-Type: application/json
{
  "name": "Amelia Jones",
  "isRegistered": "true"
}
```

The answer from the server will be 204 (No Content) success response code, and the ETag will be the increased version of the record (1) (see figure 16.6):

```
HTTP/1.1 204
Vary: Origin
Vary: Access-Control-Request-Method
Vary: Access-Control-Request-Headers
ETag: "1"
Date: Sat, 04 Dec 2021 13:25:57 GMT
Keep-Alive: timeout=60
Connection: keep-alive

<Response body is empty>
```

We can now re-execute the conditional request, to get the information about user with ID 1 only if the ETag is different from 0:

```
GET http://localhost:8081/users/1
If-None-Match: "0"
```

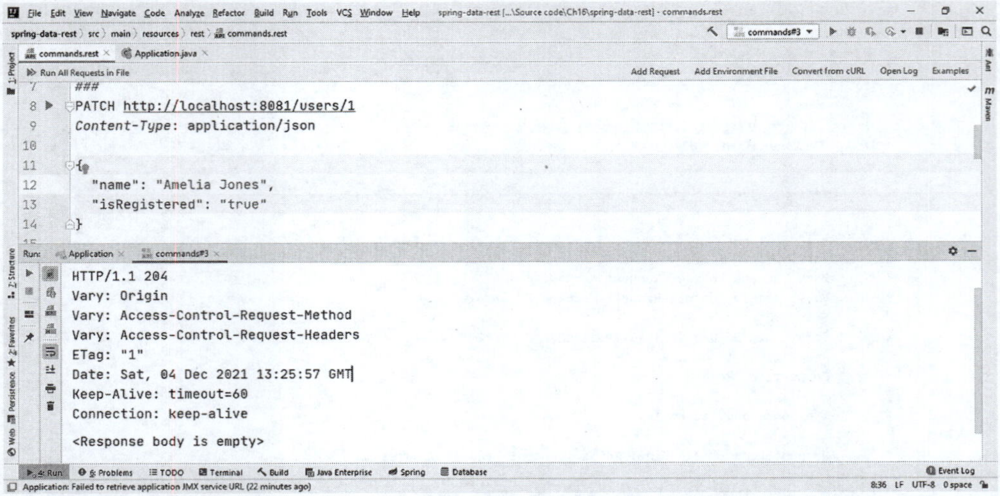

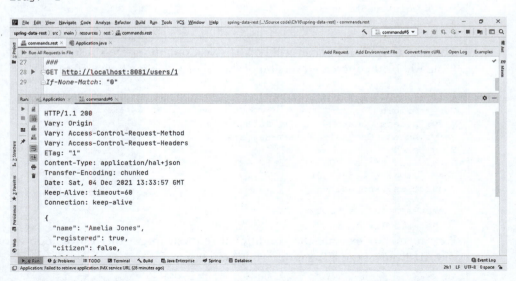

Figure 16.6   The server's answer after patching a user increases the ETag to 1.

As the version of the record was changed from 0 to 1, the conditional request will get an answer with the 200 (Success) response code and the full information about the user (see figure 16.7):

```
HTTP/1.1 200
Vary: Origin
Vary: Access-Control-Request-Method
Vary: Access-Control-Request-Headers
ETag: "1"
```

Figure 16.7   The server's answer includes the full information about the user, with the ETag changed from 0 to 1.

16.4 *Limiting access to repositories, methods, and fields*

Spring Data REST will export all public top-level repository interfaces by default. But real-world use cases will frequently require limiting access to particular methods, fields, or even whole repositories. We can use the @RepositoryRestResource annotation to block an *interface* from being exported or to customize access to an endpoint.

For example, if the managed entity is User, Spring Data REST will export it to the /users path. We can block the export of the entire repository by using the exported = false option of the @RepositoryRestResource annotation. The repository will look like this:

```
@RepositoryRestResource(path = "users", exported = false)

public interface UserRepository extends JpaRepository<User, Long> {

}
```

Any command executed against this repository will result in an error. For example, executing

```
GET http://localhost:8081/users/1
```

will generate the 404 (Not Found) response code from the server (see figure 16.8):

```
HTTP/1.1 404
Vary: Origin
Vary: Access-Control-Request-Method
Vary: Access-Control-Request-Headers
Content-Type: application/json
```

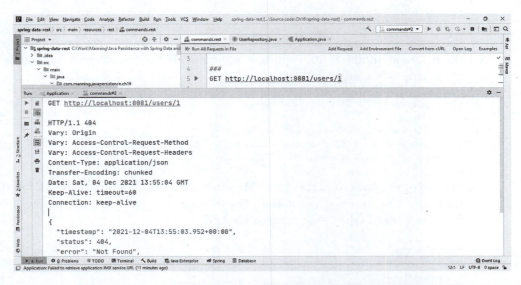

Figure 16.8 Blocking the export of the repository will prevent any interaction from the REST interface.

For convenience, we'll use the @RepositoryRestResource annotation with its default options for the UserRepository interface.

By default, Spring Data REST will also export all methods from a repository interface, but we can block access to these *methods* with the @RestResource(exported = false) annotation. For the UserRepository interface, we won't export the deletion methods.

Listing 16.8   The UserRepository interface

```
Path: Ch16/spring-data-rest/src/main/java/com/manning/javapersistence/ch16
➡ /repositories/UserRepository.java                    Ⓐ

@RepositoryRestResource(path = "users")           ◄─┐
public interface UserRepository extends JpaRepository<User, Long> {
                                                   Ⓑ
    @Override
    @RestResource(exported = false)               ◄─┐
    void deleteById(Long id);
                                                   Ⓑ
    @Override
    @RestResource(exported = false)               ◄─┐
    void delete(User· entity);
}
```

Ⓐ Use the @RepositoryRestResource annotation to export the repository to the /users path. This is the default option.

Ⓑ Use the @RestResource(exported = false) annotation to not export the delete methods of the repositories.

If we now execute the DELETE command,

```
DELETE http://localhost:8081/users/1
```

the server will respond with the 405 (Method Not Allowed) response code, because the delete method was not exported (see figure 16.9). The allowed methods are GET, HEAD, PUT, PATCH, and OPTIONS:

```
HTTP/1.1 405
Vary: Origin
Vary: Access-Control-Request-Method
Vary: Access-Control-Request-Headers
Allow: GET,HEAD,PUT,PATCH,OPTIONS
```

We can limit access to particular fields and not expose them in the REST interface by using the @JsonIgnore annotation. For example, we can use this annotation inside the User class, on the isRegistered method:

```
@JsonIgnore
public boolean isRegistered() {
    return isRegistered;
}
```

Figure 16.9   The delete method is no longer exported by Spring Data REST and is not allowed by the server.

Accessing the repository through the browser will no longer provide the `isRegistered` field information. You can see this in figure 16.10 and compare it to figure 16.2.

Figure 16.10   The REST client no longer gets the `isRegistered` information.

16.5   Working with REST events

In some situations, we may need to add side effects to the behavior of the application when a particular event occurs. The REST application can emit 10 different types of events when working with an entity. All of them extend the `org.springframework.data` `.rest.core.event.RepositoryEvent` class and belong to the same `org.springframework.data.rest.core.event` package:

- `BeforeCreateEvent`
- `AfterCreateEvent`
- `BeforeSaveEvent`
- `AfterSaveEvent`
- `BeforeLinkSaveEvent`
- `AfterLinkSaveEvent`
- `BeforeDeleteEvent`
- `AfterDeleteEvent`
- `BeforeLinkDelete`
- `AfterLinkDelete`

These events can be treated in two ways:

- Write an annotated handler
- Write an `ApplicationListener`

Let's look at these two options.

16.5.1 *Writing an AnnotatedHandler*

To add side effects by writing an `AnnotatedHandler`, we can create a POJO class with the `@RepositoryEventHandler` annotation on it. This annotation tells the `BeanPostProcessor` managed by Spring that this class must be inspected for handler methods. The `BeanPostProcessor` will browse the methods of the class carrying this annotation and detect annotations that correspond to different events.

The event handler bean must be under the control of the container. We can annotate the class as a `@Service` (which is a `@Component` stereotype), so it will be considered by `@ComponentScan` or `@SpringBootApplication`.

The entity whose events we are following is provided by the type of the first parameter of the annotated methods. In the following examples, the methods of the handler will have a `User` entity as a parameter.

The association between the annotated methods and the events is summarized in table 16.1.

Table 16.1   `AnnotatedHandler` annotations and corresponding events

Annotations	Events
`@HandleBeforeCreate` `@HandleAfterCreate`	POST event
`@HandleBeforeSave` `@HandleAfterSave`	PUT and PATCH events

Table 16.1 `AnnotatedHandler` annotations and corresponding events *(continued)*

Annotations	Events
@HandleBeforeDelete @HandleAfterDelete	DELETE events
@HandleBeforeLinkSave @HandleAfterLinkSave	A linked object is saved to the repository
@HandleBeforeLinkDelete @HandleAfterLinkDelete	A linked object is deleted from the repository

The `UserRepositoryEventHandler` class, a POJO class with the `@RepositoryEvent-Handler` annotation on it, is shown in the following listing.

Listing 16.9 The `UserRepositoryEventHandler` class

Path: Ch16/spring-data-rest-events/src/main/java/com/manning
➡ /javapersistence/ch16/events/UserRepositoryEventHandler.java

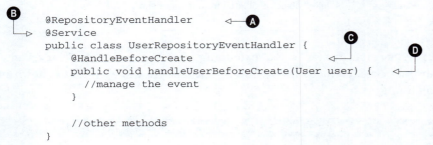

```
@RepositoryEventHandler        ◄── A
@Service
public class UserRepositoryEventHandler {
    @HandleBeforeCreate                           C          D
    public void handleUserBeforeCreate(User user) {  ◄──
      //manage the event
    }

    //other methods
}
```

Ⓐ Annotate the class with the `@RepositoryEventHandler` annotation to tell the Spring `BeanPostProcessor` to inspect it for handler methods.

Ⓑ Annotate the class with the `@Service` annotation to bring it under the control of the container.

Ⓒ Annotate the method with `@HandleBeforeCreate` to associate it with the POST event.

Ⓓ The method has an entity `User` as a first parameter, indicating the type whose events we are following.

16.5.2 *Writing an ApplicationListener*

To add side effects by writing an `ApplicationListener`, we'll extend the `Abstract-RepositoryEventListener` abstract class. This class is generified by the type of entity on which the events happen. It will listen for the events and call the corresponding methods. We'll annotate the custom listener as a `@Service` (which is a `@Component` stereotype), so it will be considered by `@ComponentScan` or `@SpringBootApplication`.

The `AbstractRepositoryEventListener` abstract class already contains a series of empty protected methods to address events. We'll need to override and make public only the ones we are interested in.

The association between the methods and events is summarized in table 16.2.

Table 16.2 `ApplicationListener` methods and corresponding events

Methods	Events
onBeforeCreate onAfterCreate	POST event
onBeforeSave onAfterSave	PUT and PATCH events
onBeforeDelete onAfterDelete	DELETE events
onBeforeLinkSave onAfterLinkSave	A linked object is saved to the repository
onBeforeLinkDelete onAfterLinkDelete	A linked object is deleted from the repository

The `RepositoryEventListener` class, extending the `AbstractRepositoryEvent-Listener` abstract class, contains the methods that react to the events. It's shown in the following listing.

Listing 16.10   The `RepositoryEventListener` class

Path: Ch16/spring-data-rest-events/src/main/java/com/manning
➡ /javapersistence/ch16/events/RepositoryEventListener.java

```
Ⓐ
@Service
public class RepositoryEventListener extends            Ⓑ
        AbstractRepositoryEventListener<User> {

    @Override                                          Ⓒ
    public void onBeforeCreate(User user) {
        //manage the event
    }
    //other methods
}
```

Ⓐ Annotate the class with the `@Service` annotation to bring it under the control of the container.

Ⓑ Extend the `AbstractRepositoryEventListener`, generified by the `User` entity— the entity on which the events happen.

Ⓒ The method has a `User` entity as the first parameter, indicating the type whose events we are following.

Now we can run the application and execute a REST command as follows:

```
POST http://localhost:8081/users
Content-Type: application/json
{
   "name": "John Smith"
}
```

The handler and the listener will react to the events and generate additional behavior as a side effect, as shown in figure 16.11.

Figure 16.11   Additional behavior (side effects) from the handler and listener reacting to a REST event

The two approaches of addressing events (with handlers and with listeners) provide similar behavior and they treat the same types of events. All other things being equal, handlers provide the advantage of working only at a declarative level (annotations on classes and methods), while listeners require us to extend an existing abstract class, so they hang in an existing hierarchy, which means less freedom of hierarchy design.

16.6   Using projections and excerpts

Spring Data REST provides a default view of the domain model you are working with, but real-world use cases may require it to be changed or adapted to particular needs. You can do this using projections and excerpts, providing specific views of the information that is exported.

We'll add the new Address class to the project. It will contain a few fields, and we'd like to display the information inside it with the toString method.

Listing 16.11   The `Address` class

```
Path: Ch16/spring-data-rest-projections/src/main/java/com/manning
➡ /javapersistence/ch16/model/Address.java

@Entity
public class Address {

    @GeneratedValue
    @Id
    private Long id;
    private String street, zipCode, city, state;

    //constructors and methods

    public String toString() {
        return String.format("%s, %s %s, %s", street, zipCode, city, state);
    }
}
```

There is a one-to-one relationship between `User` and `Address`, as we introduced a new field in the `User` entity:

```
@OneToOne(cascade = CascadeType.ALL, orphanRemoval = true)
private Address address;
```

The `CascadeType.ALL` option will cause the persistence operations to be cascaded to the related entities. The `orphanRemoval=true` argument specifies that we want to permanently remove an `Address` when it is no longer referenced by the `User`. You can revisit chapter 8 for more details about these options.

If we access the http://localhost:8081/users/1 URL, we'll get the default view of the user with ID 1, displaying all its fields and the fields from the address, as shown in figure 16.12.

Figure 16.12   The default view of a user with an address

We'll now add the new `UserProjection` interface to the project (listing 16.12). With the help of the `@Projection` annotation, we can create the `summary` projection on the `User` entity, which will export only the name of the user and the address according to how it is displayed by the `toString` method. We'll do this using Spring Expression Language (SpEL).

```
Path: Ch16/spring-data-rest-projections/src/main/java/com/manning
    /javapersistence/ch16/model/UserProjection.java            A

@Projection(name = "summary", types = User.class)    ⟵──┐
public interface UserProjection {

    String getName();    ⟵──B

    @Value("#{target.address.toString()}")
    String getAddress();                      C
}
```

Ⓐ The projection is named `summary`, and it applies to the `User` entities.

Ⓑ As the field is called `name`, we need to write a `getName` method to export it, following the getter names convention.

Ⓒ Export the `address` according to how it is displayed by the `toString` method. We use the `@Value` annotation, containing a SpEL expression. We also need to follow the getter names convention, so the method is called `getAddress`.

If we access the http://localhost:8081/users/1?projection=summary URL (with the projection name included as a parameter), we'll get a view of the user with ID 1, displaying the `name` field and the address provided by the `toString` method. This is shown in figure 16.13.

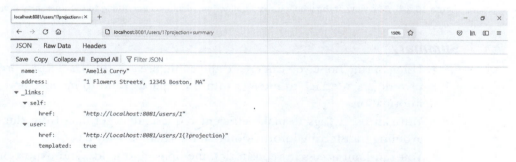

Figure 16.13   The view of a user with an address provided by the `summary` projection

We may want to apply the default view of a projection at the level of a whole collection. In this case, we'll have to go to the already defined repository and use the `excerptProjection = UserProjection.class` option of the `@RepositoryRest-Resource` annotation, as shown in listing 16.13.

Listing 16.13   The modified `UserRepository` interface

```
Path: Ch16/spring-data-rest-projections/src/main/java/com/manning
  /javapersistence/ch16/repositories/UserRepository.java

@RepositoryRestResource(path = "users",
                        excerptProjection = UserProjection.class)
public interface UserRepository extends JpaRepository<User, Long> {
}
```

If we access the http://localhost:8081/users/ URL, we'll get a view of all users, displayed according to the projection definition, as shown in figure 16.14.

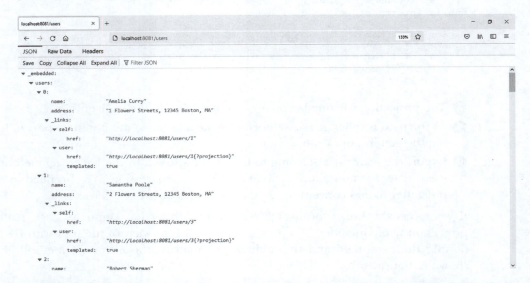

Figure 16.14   The view of the whole `users` collection, displayed according to the `summary` projection

Summary

- Using Spring Boot, you can create and configure a Spring Data REST project to provide an interface to interact with the database and to manage and persist information.

- You can use ETags to make efficient requests that get data from the server, avoiding transferring information that the client already has.

- You can limit access to repositories, methods, and fields, and export only the information and actions that you would like to allow.

- You can work with REST events and manage them through handlers and listeners. They can work through meta-information or by extending an existing class.

- You can use projections and excerpts to provide customized views of the information exported by the repository, according to the needs of different users.

Part 5

Building Java persistence applications with Spring

In part 5, you'll connect Java applications to frequently used NoSQL databases: MongoDB and Neo4j.

In chapter 17, you'll learn the most important features of the Spring Data MongoDB framework, and we'll compare them with the already used Spring Data JPA and Spring Data JDBC. You'll connect to a MongoDB database using two alternatives: `MongoRepository` and `MongoTemplate`. We'll emphasize the advantages, drawbacks, and best use cases for both of these alternatives.

Next, chapter 18 introduces the Hibernate OGM framework and demonstrates how to use JPA code to connect to different NoSQL databases (MongoDB and Neo4j) that have different storage paradigms (document-oriented and graph-oriented). We'll migrate between the two databases changing only the configuration and without touching the Java code.

After reading this part of the book, you'll know how to work with NoSQL databases from Java programs and you'll be able to choose between the alternative frameworks you can use.

17
Working with
Spring Data MongoDB

This chapter covers

- Introducing MongoDB
- Examining Spring Data MongoDB
- Accessing a database with MongoRepository
- Accessing a database with MongoTemplate

Document-oriented databases are one type of NoSQL database, where the information is kept as a key/value store. MongoDB is such a database program. Spring Data MongoDB, as part of the larger Spring Data umbrella project, facilitates the interaction of Java programs with MongoDB document databases.

17.1 Introducing MongoDB

MongoDB is an open source, document-oriented NoSQL database. MongoDB uses JSON-like documents to store the information, and it uses the concepts of databases, collections, and documents.

- *Database*—A database represents a container for collections. After installing MongoDB, you will generally get a set of databases.

465

- *Collection*—A collection is similar to a table in the world of relational database management systems (RDBMSs). A collection may contain a set of documents.
- *Document*—A document represents a set of key/value pairs, equivalent to rows in RDBMSs. Documents belonging to the same collection may have different sets of fields. Fields that are common to multiple documents in a collection may contain data of different types—such situations are known as dynamic schemas.

Table 17.1 summarizes the terminology equivalences between relational databases and the NoSQL database MongoDB.

Table 17.1   Compared terminology: RDBMS vs. MongoDB

Relational databases	MongoDB
Database	Database
Table	Collection
Row	Document
Column	Field

You can download the MongoDB Community Edition installation kit here: https://www.mongodb.com/try/download/community. Installation instructions, depending on your operating system, can be found here: https://docs.mongodb.com/manual/administration/install-community/.

After installing MongoDB, you can open the MongoDB Compass program, as in figure 17.1. MongoDB Compass is a GUI for interacting with and querying MongoDB databases.

Figure 17.1   Opening the MongoDB Compass program

Click the Connect button, and you will connect to the local server, as demonstrated in figure 17.2.

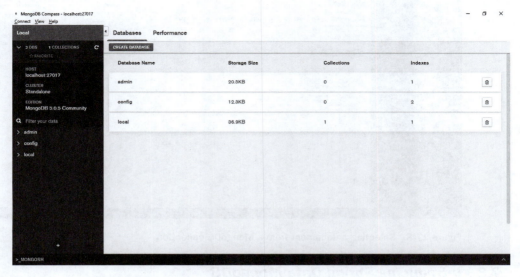

Figure 17.2   The connection to the local MongoDB server

Data in a MongoDB collection is represented in JSON format. A typical MongoDB document describing a user of our CaveatEmptor application might look like this:

```
{
"_id":{
    "$oid":"61c9e17e382deb3ba55d65ac"
},
"username":"john",
"firstName":"John",
"lastName":"Smith",
"registrationDate":{
    "$date":"2020-04-12T21:00:00.000Z"
},
"email":"john@somedomain.com",
"level":1,
"active":true,
"_class":"com.manning.javapersistence.springdatamongodb.model.User"
}
```

To select documents fulfilling particular conditions, you can use the Filter edit box in the MongoDB Compass program to insert a query filter parameter. For example, to select documents with the username "john", you would insert the query filter {"user-name":"john"} and click the Find button, as demonstrated in figure 17.3.

For details about MongoDB CRUD operations you may want to execute, refer to the official documentation: https://docs.mongodb.com/manual/crud/.

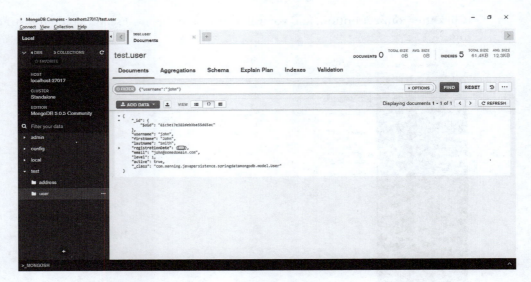

Figure 17.3   Selecting a document from a MongoDB collection

17.2   *Introducing Spring Data MongoDB*

Spring Data MongoDB is part of the umbrella Spring Data project, and it allows for MongoDB to be used from Java programs, following the Spring Data approach: repositories and custom object-mapping abstractions, annotations, dynamic query creation based on repository method names, integration with other Spring projects, and Spring Boot.

To demonstrate Spring Data MongoDB, we'll create an application that will manage and persist CaveatEmptor users. We'll create a Spring Boot application that uses Spring Data MongoDB. To do this, go to the Spring Initializr website (https:// start.spring.io/) and create a new Spring Boot project (see figure 17.4), having the following characteristics:

- Group: com.manning.javapersistence
- Artifact: springdatamongodb
- Description: Spring Data MongoDB

We'll also add the following dependencies:

- Spring Data MongoDB (this will add `spring-boot-starter-data-mongodb` in the Maven pom.xml file)
- Lombok (this will add `org.projectlombok,lombok` in the Maven pom.xml file)

The pom.xml file (listing 17.1) includes the dependencies that we previously added to start the project: the dependency on the Spring Data MongoDB framework and on Lombok. Lombok is a Java library that can be used to automatically create constructors, getters, and setters through annotations, thus reducing the boilerplate code.

Figure 17.4   Creating a new Spring Boot project using Spring Data MongoDB

Lombok has its shortcomings, including these: you will need a plugin for the IDE to understand the annotations and not complain about missing constructors, getters, and setters; and you cannot set breakpoints and debug inside the generated methods (but debugging inside these methods is pretty rare).

> **Listing 17.1   The pom.xml Maven file**

```
Path: Ch17/springdatamongodb/pom.xml

<dependency>
    <groupId>org.springframework.boot</groupId>
    <artifactId>spring-boot-starter-data-mongodb</artifactId>
</dependency>
<dependency>
    <groupId>org.projectlombok</groupId>
    <artifactId>lombok</artifactId>
</dependency>
```

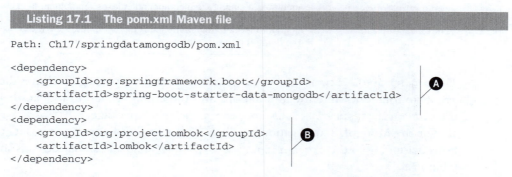

Ⓐ `spring-boot-starter-data-mongodb` is the starter dependency used by Spring Boot to connect to a MongoDB database through Spring Data.

Ⓑ Lombok allows us to reduce boilerplate code and instead rely on automatically generated constructors, getters, and setters.

Our next step is to fill in the Spring Boot application.properties file, which can include various properties that will be used by the application. Spring Boot will automatically find and load application.properties from the classpath, and the src/main/resources folder is added by Maven to the classpath. The application.properties configuration file is shown in listing 17.2.

Listing 17.2   The application.properties file

Path: Ch17/springdatamongodb/src/main/resources/application.properties

```
logging.level.org.springframework.data.mongodb.core.MongoTemplate=DEBUG
spring.data.mongodb.auto-index-creation=true
```

A Queries are logged by the Spring Data MongoDB application at DEBUG level. So, to enable query logging, we have to set the log level to DEBUG.

B The creation of indexes is disabled by default in Spring Data MongoDB. Enable it by setting the `spring.data.mongodb.auto-index-creation` property to `true`.

The `User` class will now contain annotations that are specific to Spring Data MongoDB. Table 17.2 examines a few annotations and classes, and then we'll look at them in action while working with the `User` class.

Table 17.2   Spring Data MongoDB annotations and classes

Spring Data MongoDB annotation/class	Meaning
@Document	A domain object to be persisted to MongoDB
@Indexed	A field indexed by MongoDB
@CompoundIndexes	A container annotation for compound indexes; it defines a collection of multiple @CompoundIndex annotations
@CompoundIndex	Annotates a class to use compound indexes on multiple fields
IndexDirection	An enum that determines the index direction: ASCENDING (the default) or DESCENDING

The `org.springframework.data.mongodb.core.mapping` package includes the `@Document` annotation, while the annotations and the enum related to indexes belong to the `org.springframework.data.mongodb.core.index` package.

For the MongoDB application, we'll also use a series of core Spring Data annotations belonging to the `org.springframework.data.annotation` package, as shown in table 17.3.

Table 17.3   Spring Data core annotations

Spring Data annotation	Meaning
@Id	Marks the field as an identifier
@Transient	A transient field that will not be persisted and will not be examined by the persistence framework
@PersistenceConstructor	Marks the constructor to be the primary one used by the persistence framework when retrieving information from the database

This chapter uses the Lombok library to automatically create constructors, getters, and setters through annotations, thus reducing the boilerplate code. The most important Lombok annotations belonging to the `lombok` package are listed in table 17.4.

Table 17.4 Lombok annotations

Lombok annotation	Meaning
`@NoArgsConstructor`	Automatically creates a public no arguments constructor for the class it annotates
`@Getter`	Automatically creates a public getter for the field it annotates
`@Setter`	Automatically creates a public setter for the field it annotates

The `User` class used by the Spring Data MongoDB application is presented in listing 17.3. The `password` field annotated with `@Transient` will not be saved to the MongoDB database—there are many cases where you would like secret information, such as a password, not to be persisted. The constructor annotated with `@Persistence-Constructor` will be used by Spring Data MongoDB when retrieving the information from the database. The `ip` parameter of the constructor is annotated with `@Value` (`"#root.ip ?: '192.168.1.100'"`), which means that if the `ip` value is absent when retrieving the document from the database, it will automatically take this default value.

Listing 17.3 The `User` class

Path: Ch17/springdatamongodb/src/main/java/com/manning/javapersistence
➥ /springdatamongodb/model/User.java

```
@NoArgsConstructor
@Document
@CompoundIndexes({
        @CompoundIndex(name = "username_email",
                        def = "{'username' : 1, 'email': 1}"),
        @CompoundIndex(name = "lastName_firstName",
                        def = "{'lastName' : 1, 'firstName': 1}")
})
public class User {

    @Id
    @Getter
    private String id;

    @Getter
    @Setter
    @Indexed(direction = IndexDirection.ASCENDING)
    private String username;

    //fields annotated with @Getter and @Setter
```

```
@Getter
@Setter
@Transient
private String password;

//another constructor

@PersistenceConstructor
public User(String username, String firstName, String lastName,
            @Value("#root.ip ?: '192.168.1.100'") String ip) {
    this.username = username;
    this.firstName = firstName;
    this.lastName = lastName;
    this.ip = ip;
    }
}
```

17.3   *Using MongoRepository to access a database*

The `UserRepository` interface extends `MongoRepository<User, String>`, inheriting the MongoDB-related methods and managing the `User` document, which has IDs of type `String`.

Listing 17.4   **The `UserRepository` interface**

Path: Ch17/springdatamongodb/src/main/java/com/manning/javapersistence
➡ /springdatamongodb/repositories/UserRepository.java

```
public interface UserRepository extends MongoRepository<User, String> {
}
```

17.3.1   *Defining query methods with Spring Data MongoDB*

We'll add new methods to the `UserRepository` interface so we can query the database for some particular documents and use them in tests.

The purpose of the query methods is to retrieve information from the database. Spring Data MongoDB provides a query builder mechanism similar to the one provided by Spring Data JPA—it will create the behavior of repository methods based on their names. Remember that the query mechanism removes prefixes and suffixes such as `find...By`, `get...By`, `query...By`, `read...By`, and `count...By` from the name of the method, and it then parses the remainder.

Just like Spring Data JPA, Spring Data MongoDB will look at the return type of the method. If we want to find a `User` and return it in an `Optional` container, the method's return type will be `Optional<User>`.

Listing 17.5   **The `UserRepository` interface with new methods**

Path: Ch17/springdatamongodb/src/main/java/com/manning/javapersistence
➡ /springdatamongodb/repositories/UserRepository.java

```
public interface UserRepository extends MongoRepository<User, String> {
    Optional<User> findByUsername(String username);
    List<User> findByLastName(String lastName);
    List<User> findAllByOrderByUsernameAsc();
    List<User> findByRegistrationDateBetween(LocalDate start,
    ➡ LocalDate end);
List<User> findByUsernameAndEmail(String username, String email);
List<User> findByUsernameOrEmail(String username, String email);
List<User> findByUsernameIgnoreCase(String username);
List<User> findByLevelOrderByUsernameDesc(int level);
List<User> findByLevelGreaterThanEqual(int level);
List<User> findByUsernameContaining(String text);
List<User> findByUsernameLike(String text);
List<User> findByUsernameStartingWith(String start);
List<User> findByUsernameEndingWith(String end);
List<User> findByActive(boolean active);
List<User> findByRegistrationDateIn(Collection<LocalDate> dates);
List<User> findByRegistrationDateNotIn(Collection<LocalDate> dates);
}
```

The names of the methods need to follow the rules to determine the resulting query. If the method naming is wrong (for example, the entity property does not match in the query method), we'll get an error when the application context is loaded. Table 17.5 summarizes the usage of the essential keywords in building Spring Data MongoDB query methods and the resulting conditions. For a more comprehensive list, see appendix D.

Table 17.5 Keyword usage in Spring Data MongoDB and the resulting conditions

Keyword	Example	Condition
Is, Equals	findByUsername(String name) findByUsernameIs(String name) findByUsernameEquals(String name)	{"username":"name"}
And	findByUsernameAndEmail(String username, String email)	{"username":"username", "email":"email"}
Or	findByUsernameOrEmail (String username, String email)	{ "$or" : [{ "username" : "username"}, { "email" : "email"}]}
LessThan	findByRegistrationDateLessThan (LocalDate date)	{ "registrationDate" : { "$lt" : { "$date" : "date"}}}
LessThanEqual	findByRegistrationDateLessThanEqual (LocalDate date)	{ "registrationDate" : { "$lte" : { "$date" : "date"}}}
GreaterThan	findByRegistrationDateGreaterThan (LocalDate date)	{ "registrationDate" : { "$gt" : { "$date" : "date"}}}

Table 17.5   Keyword usage in Spring Data MongoDB and the resulting conditions *(continued)*

Keyword	Example	Condition
GreaterThanEqual	findByRegistrationDateGreaterThanEqual (LocalDate date)	{ "registrationDate" : { "$gte" : { "$date" : "date"}}}
Between	findByRegistrationDateBetween (LocalDate from, LocalDate to)	"registrationDate" : { "$gte" : { "$date" : "from"}, "$lte" : { "$date" : "to"}}}
OrderBy	findByRegistrationDateOrderByUsernameDesc (LocalDate date)	"registrationDate" : { "$date" : "date"}}
Like	findByUsernameLike(String name)	{ "username" : { "$regularExpression" : { "pattern" : "name", "options" : ""}}}
NotLike	findByUsernameNotLike(String name)	{ "username" : { "$not" : { "$regularExpression" : { "pattern" : "name", "options" : ""}}}}
Before	findByRegistrationDateBefore (LocalDate date)	{ "registrationDate" : { "$lt" : { "$date" : "date"}}}
After	findByRegistrationDateAfter (LocalDate date)	{ "registrationDate" : { "$gt" : { "$date" : "date"}}}
Null, IsNull	findByRegistrationDate(Is)Null()	{ "registrationDate" : null}
NotNull, IsNotNull	findByRegistrationDate(Is)NotNull()	{ "registrationDate" : { "$ne" :vnull}}
Not	findByUsernameNot(String name)	{ "username" : { "$ne" : "name"}}

As a base class for all future tests, we'll write the SpringDataJdbcApplicationTests abstract class (listing 17.6).

The @SpringBootTest annotation is added by Spring Boot to the initially created class, and it will tell Spring Boot to search the main configuration class (the @Spring-BootApplication annotated class, for instance) and create the ApplicationContext to be used in the tests. As you'll recall, the @SpringBootApplication annotation added by Spring Boot to the class containing the main method will enable the Spring Boot autoconfiguration mechanism, enable the scan on the package where the application is located, and allow registering extra beans in the context.

Using the `@TestInstance(TestInstance.Lifecycle.PER_CLASS)` annotation, we'll ask JUnit 5 to create a single instance of the test class and reuse it for all test methods. This will allow us to make the `@BeforeAll` and `@AfterAll` annotated methods non-static and to directly use the autowired `UserRepository` instance field inside them. The `@BeforeAll` annotated non-static method is executed once before all tests from any class extending `SpringDataJdbcApplicationTests`, and it saves the list of users created inside the `generateUsers` method to the database. The `@AfterAll` annotated non-static method is executed once after all tests from any class extending `SpringDataJdbcApplicationTests`, and it deletes all users from the database.

Listing 17.6 The `SpringDataJdbcApplicationTests` abstract class

Path: Ch17/springdatamongodb/src/test/java/com/manning/javapersistence
➡ /springdatamongodb/SpringDataMongoDBApplicationTests.java

```java
@SpringBootTest
@TestInstance(TestInstance.Lifecycle.PER_CLASS)
abstract class SpringDataJdbcApplicationTests {
    @Autowired
    UserRepository userRepository;                          Ⓐ

    @BeforeAll
    void beforeAll() {
        userRepository.saveAll(generateUsers());
    }

    private static List<User> generateUsers() {
        List<User> users = new ArrayList<>();

        User john = new User("john", "John", "Smith");
        john.setRegistrationDate(LocalDate.of(2020, Month.APRIL, 13));
        john.setEmail("john@somedomain.com");
        john.setLevel(1);
        john.setActive(true);
        john.setPassword("password1");


        //create and set a total of 10 users

        users.add(john);
        //add a total of 10 users to the list

        return users;
    }
    @AfterAll
    void afterAll() {
        userRepository.deleteAll();
    }

}
```

Ⓐ Autowire a `UserRepository` instance. This is possible due to the `@SpringBoot-Application` annotation, which enables the scan on the package where the application is located and registers the beans in the context.

The next tests will extend this class and use the already populated database. To test the methods that belong now to `UserRepository`, we'll create the `FindUsersTest` class and follow the same recipe for writing tests: call the repository method and verify its results. Recall that, in JUnit 5, it is enough that test classes and methods are package private; they are not required to be public.

Listing 17.7   The `FindUsersTest` class

Path: Ch17/springdatamongodb/src/test/java/com/manning/javapersistence
➥ /springdatamongodb/FindUsersTest.java

```java
class FindUsersTest extends SpringDataJdbcApplicationTests{

    @Test
    void testFindAll() {
        List<User> users = userRepository.findAll();
        assertEquals(10, users.size());
    }

    @Test
    void testFindUser() {
        User beth = userRepository.findByUsername("beth").get();
        assertAll(
            () -> assertNotNull(beth.getId()),
            () -> assertEquals("beth", beth.getUsername())
        );
    }

    @Test
    void testFindAllByOrderByUsernameAsc() {
        List<User> users = userRepository.findAllByOrderByUsernameAsc();
        assertAll(() -> assertEquals(10, users.size()),
                  () -> assertEquals("beth", users.get(0).getUsername()),
                  () -> assertEquals("stephanie", users.get(users.size() -
                                                   1).getUsername()));
    }

    @Test
    void testFindByRegistrationDateBetween() {
        List<User> users = userRepository.findByRegistrationDateBetween(
                LocalDate.of(2020, Month.JULY, 1),
                LocalDate.of(2020, Month.DECEMBER, 31));
        assertEquals(4, users.size());
    }

    //more tests
}
```

17.3.2 *Limiting query results, sorting, and paging*

As in Spring Data JPA and Spring Data JDBC, the first and top keywords (used equivalently) can limit the results of query methods. The top and first keywords can be followed by an optional numeric value to indicate the maximum result size to be returned. If this numeric value is missing, the result size will be 1.

Pageable is an interface for pagination information, and in practice we use the PageRequest class that implements it. This class can specify the page number, the page size, and the sorting criterion.

The use cases we'll solve here will be getting a limited number of users (such as the first user by username or by registration date, or the first users with a given level, sorted by registration date), or a large bunch of users in pages, so we can easily manipulate them.

To limit the query results and do sorting and paging, we'll add the following methods to the UserRepository interface.

Listing 17.8 Limiting query results, sorting, and paging in UserRepository

Path: Ch17/springdatamongodb/src/main/java/com/manning/javapersistence
➥ /springdatamongodb/repositories/UserRepository.java

```
Optional<User> findFirstByOrderByUsernameAsc();
Optional<User> findTopByOrderByRegistrationDateDesc();
Page<User> findAll(Pageable pageable);
List<User> findFirst2ByLevel(int level, Sort sort);
List<User> findByLevel(int level, Sort sort);
List<User> findByActive(boolean active, Pageable pageable);
```

These methods use the query builder mechanism presented in table 17.5, but this time with the purpose of limiting the results of the query, to do sorting and paging. For example, the Optional<User> findFirstByOrderByUsernameAsc() method will get the first user by its username (the result is an Optional, so eventually it may not exist). The Page<User> findAll(Pageable pageable) method will get all users but in pages. We'll write the following tests to verify that these newly added methods work.

Listing 17.9 Testing limiting query results, sorting, and paging

Path: Ch17/springdatamongodb/src/test/java/com/manning/javapersistence
➥ /springdatamongodb/FindUsersSortingAndPagingTest.java

```
class FindUsersSortingAndPagingTest extends SpringDataJdbcApplicationTests {
    @Test
    void testOrder() {

        User user1 = userRepository.findFirstByOrderByUsernameAsc().get();
        User user2 =
            userRepository.findTopByOrderByRegistrationDateDesc().get();
        Page<User> userPage = userRepository.findAll(PageRequest.of(1, 3));
```

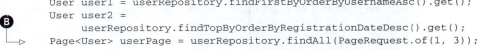

```
        List users = userRepository.findFirst2ByLevel(2,
                                    Sort.by("registrationDate"));

        assertAll(
                () -> assertEquals("beth", user1.getUsername()),
                () -> assertEquals("julius", user2.getUsername()),
                () -> assertEquals(2, users.size()),
                () -> assertEquals(3, userPage.getSize()),
                () -> assertEquals("beth", users.get(0).getUsername()),
                () -> assertEquals("marion", users.get(1).getUsername())
        );

    }

    @Test
    void testFindByLevel() {
        Sort.TypedSort<User> user = Sort.sort(User.class);

        List<User> users = userRepository.findByLevel(3,
                user.by(User::getRegistrationDate).descending());
        assertAll(
                () -> assertEquals(2, users.size()),
                () -> assertEquals("james", users.get(0).getUsername())
        );

    }

    @Test
    void testFindByActive() {
        List<User> users = userRepository.findByActive(true,
                PageRequest.of(1, 4, Sort.by("registrationDate")));
        assertAll(
                () -> assertEquals(4, users.size()),
                () -> assertEquals("burk", users.get(0).getUsername())
        );
    }
}
```

Ⓐ The first test will find the first user by ascending order of username and the first user by descending order of registration date.

Ⓑ Find all users, split them into pages, and return page number 1 of size 3 (the page numbering starts with 0).

Ⓒ Find the first 2 users with level 2, ordered by registration date.

Ⓓ The second test will define a sorting criterion on the User class. Sort.TypedSort extends Sort and can use method handles to define properties to sort by.

Ⓔ Find the users of level 3 and sort by registration date, descending.

Ⓕ The third test will find active users, sorted by registration date, and will split them into pages, and return page number 1 of size 4 (page numbering starts with 0).

17.3.3   Streaming results

Query methods returning more than one result can use standard Java interfaces such as `Iterable`, `List`, `Set`. Like Spring Data JPA and Spring Data JDBC, Spring Data MongoDB supports `Streamable`, which can be used as an alternative to `Iterable` or any collection type. It allows us to concatenate `Streamables` and to directly filter and map over the elements.

The use case we'll solve here is getting the results as a stream, without waiting for the whole collection of users or a page of users to be obtained. This way we'll be able to quickly start processing the first results as they flow to us. Unlike collections, a stream can be consumed only once and is immutable.

We'll add the following methods to the `UserRepository` interface.

Listing 17.10   Adding methods that return `Streamable` in `UserRepository` interface

Path: Ch17/springdatamongodb/src/main/java/com/manning/javapersistence
➥ /springdatamongodb/repositories/UserRepository.java

```
Streamable<User> findByEmailContaining(String text);
Streamable<User> findByLevel(int level);
```

We'll write the following test to verify how these newly added methods work to interact with the database and to provide results as streams. A stream is given as a resource of the `try` block to be automatically closed. An alternative is to explicitly call the `close()` method. Otherwise the stream would keep the underlying connection to the database.

Listing 17.11   Testing methods that return `Streamable`

Path: Ch17/springdatamongodb/src/test/java/com/manning/javapersistence
➥ /springdatamongodb/QueryResultsTest.java

```
@Test
void testStreamable() {
    try(Stream<User> result =                                      A
            userRepository.findByEmailContaining("someother")
            .and(userRepository.findByLevel(2))            ←        B
 C  →       .stream().distinct())  {
        assertEquals(7, result.count());                   ←
    }                                                              D
}
```

Ⓐ The test will call the `findByEmailContaining` method, searching for emails containing the `"someother"` word.

Ⓑ The test will concatenate the resulting `Streamable` with the `Streamable`, providing the users of level 2.

Ⓒ It will transform this into a stream and keep the distinct users.

Ⓓ Check that the resulting stream contains 7 users.

17.3.4 *The @Query annotation*

We can create methods for which a custom query can be specified by using the `@org.springframework.data.mongodb.repository.Query` annotation. With this `@Query` annotation, the method name does not need to follow any naming convention. The custom query will have a MongoDB query filter as an argument, and this query filter can be parameterized.

We'll add new methods to the `UserRepository` interface: they will be annotated with the `@Query` annotation, and their generated behavior will depend on the definitions of these queries. The `value` parameter will indicate the query filter to be executed. The `fields` parameter will indicate the fields to be included or excluded from the result. Table 17.6 summarizes the query operations and the corresponding `@Query` parameters for the most frequent situations. For a comprehensive list, consult the Spring Data MongoDB documentation.

Table 17.6   Query operations and corresponding `@Query` parameters

Operation	`@Query` parameters
Fetch data for a given field	`value = { 'field' : ?0}`
Fetch data for a given regular expression	`value = { 'lastName' : { $regex: ?0 } }`
Fetch data having a field greater than a parameter	`value = { 'field' : { $gt: ?0 } }`
Fetch data having a field greater than or equal to a parameter	`value = { 'field' : { $gte: ?0 } }`
Fetch data having a field less than a parameter	`value = { 'field' : { $lt: ?0 } }`
Fetch data having a field less than or equal to a parameter	`value = { 'field' : { $lte: ?0 } }`
Include only one field in the query	`fields = "{field : 1}"`
Exclude a field from the query	`fields = "{field : 0}"`

The query filter is the argument of the `@Query` annotation: the `?0` placeholder will reference the first parameter of the method, the `?1` placeholder will reference the second parameter of the method, and so on, as shown in the following listing.

Listing 17.12   Limiting query results, sorting, and paging in `UserRepository`

Path: Ch17/springdatamongodb/src/main/java/com/manning/javapersistence
➥ /springdatamongodb/repositories/UserRepository.java

```
@Query("{ 'active' : ?0 }")                                    A
List<User> findUsersByActive(boolean active);

@Query("{ 'lastName' : ?0 }")                                  B
List<User> findUsersByLastName(String lastName);
```

```
@Query("{ 'lastName' : { $regex: ?0 } }")
List<User> findUsersByRegexpLastName(String regexp);
```
Ⓒ

```
@Query("{ 'level' : { $gte: ?0, $lte: ?1 } }")
List<User> findUsersByLevelBetween(int minLevel, int maxLevel);
```
Ⓓ

```
@Query(value = "{}", fields = "{username : 1}")
List<User> findUsernameAndId();
```
Ⓔ

```
@Query(value = "{}", fields = "{_id : 0}")
List<User> findUsersExcludeId();
```
Ⓕ

```
@Query(value = "{'lastName' : { $regex: ?0 }}", fields = "{_id : 0}")
List<User> findUsersByRegexpLastNameExcludeId(String regexp);
```
Ⓖ

Ⓐ The findUsersByActive method will return the users with a given active status.

Ⓑ The findUsersByLastName method will return the users with a given lastName.

Ⓒ The findUsersByRegexpLastName method will return the users with a lastName matching the ?0 placeholder, referencing the regular expression that is the first parameter of the method.

Ⓓ The findUsersByLevelBetween method will return the users with a level greater than or equal to the ?0 placeholder, referencing the first parameter of the method, and less than or equal to the ?1 placeholder, referencing the second parameter of the method.

Ⓔ The findUsernameAndId method will select all users (because the value parameter is {}) and will return only the id and the username fields (because the fields parameter is {username : 1}).

Ⓕ The findUsersExcludeId method will select all users (because the value parameter is {}) and will exclude the id from the returned fields (because the fields parameter is {_id : 0}).

Ⓖ The findUsersByRegexpLastNameExcludeId method will select users with a lastName matching a given regular expression and will exclude the id from the returned fields.

Writing tests for these query methods is pretty straightforward and similar to the previous examples. They can be found in the source code for the book.

17.4   Query by Example

Query by Example (QBE) was discussed in chapter 4 when we examined Spring Data JPA. It is a querying technique that does not require writing classical queries to include entities and properties. It allows dynamic query creation and consists of three pieces: a probe, an ExampleMatcher, and an Example.

A probe is a domain object with already set properties. The ExampleMatcher provides the rules about matching particular properties. The Example puts the probe and the ExampleMatcher together and generates the query. Multiple Examples can reuse a single ExampleMatcher.

As discussed before, these are the most appropriate use cases for QBE:

- When you want to decouple work on the code from the underlying data store API
- When you want to make frequent changes to the internal structure of the domain objects without propagating them to the existing queries
- When you are building a set of static or dynamic constraints to query a repository

QBE has some limitations:

- It supports only starting/ending/containing/regex matching for `String` properties and only exact matching for other types.
- It does not support nested or grouped property constraints, such as `{"$or":[ {"username":"username"},{{"lastName":"lastName", "email":"email"}}]}`.

We won't add any more methods to the `UserRepository` interface. Instead we'll write tests to build the probe, the `ExampleMatchers`, and the `Examples`. The following listing will create a simple probe and a user having with the `lastName` set.

Listing 17.13   Query By Example tests

```
Path: Ch17/springdatamongodb/src/test/java/com/manning/javapersistence
➥ /springdatamongodb/QueryByExampleTest.java                          Ⓐ
                                                                         Ⓑ
User probe = new User(null, null, "Smith");           ◄───┘
List<User> result = userRepository.findAll(Example.of(probe));    ◄───┘
assertThat(result).hasSize(2)                              Ⓒ
        .extracting("username").contains("john", "burk");    │
```

Ⓐ Initialize a `User` instance and set up a `lastName` for it. This will represent the probe.

Ⓑ Execute the query to find all users matching the probe.

Ⓒ Verify that the query to find all users matching the probe returned 2 documents, and it contains the `usernames` john and burk.

We can now create an `ExampleMatcher` with the help of the builder pattern. Any `null` reference property will be ignored by the matcher. However, we'll need to explicitly ignore properties that are primitives. If they are not ignored, they will be included in the matcher with their default values, and that would change the generated query.

Listing 17.14   Query By Example with matcher tests

```
Path: Ch17/springdatamongodb/src/test/java/com/manning/javapersistence
➥ /springdatamongodb/QueryByMatcherTest.java

ExampleMatcher matcher = ExampleMatcher.matching()
                                .withIgnorePaths("level")          Ⓐ
                                .withIgnorePaths("active");
```

```
User probe = new User();
probe.setLastName("Smith");
List<User> result = userRepository.findAll(Example.of(probe, matcher));

assertThat(result).hasSize(2)
        .extracting("username").contains("john", "burk");
```

Ⓑ

Ⓒ

Ⓓ

Ⓐ Create the `ExampleMatcher` with the help of the builder pattern. We explicitly ignore the `level` and `active` properties, which are primitives. If they were not ignored, they would be included in the matcher with their default values (0 for `level` and `false` for `active`) and would change the generated query.

Ⓑ Create and set a `User` probe.

Ⓒ Execute the query to find all users matching the probe.

Ⓓ Verify that the query to find all users matching the probe returned 2 documents, and it contains the usernames `john` and `burk`.

17.5 *Referencing other MongoDB documents*

Spring Data MongoDB does not support relationships in the sense of the one-to-one, one-to-many, and many-to-many relationships we examined for relational databases. The framework does not support embedding a document inside another document. However, a document may be referenced from another document using DBRefs. A DBRef will include the collection name and the value of the other document's ID field, and optionally another database name.

To use DBRefs, we'll create another class annotated with `@Document` and another MongoDB repository, and we'll use the `@DBRef` annotation inside the class referencing the newly added document.

The new `Address` class we'll add is shown in the following listing. It is annotated with `@Document`, like any class corresponding to a MongoDB document, and the fields are annotated with the Lombok `@Getter` annotation, indicating the automatic generation of the getters.

Listing 17.15   The modified `Address` class

Path: Ch17/springdatamongodb2/src/main/java/com/manning/javapersistence
➥ /springdatamongodb/model/Address.java

```
@Document
public class Address {

    @Id
    @Getter
    private String id;

    @Getter
    private String street, zipCode, city, state;

    // . . .

}
```

The new `AddressRepository` interface is shown in the next listing. It extends `MongoRepository<Address, String>`, inheriting the MongoDB-related methods and managing the `Address` document, having IDs of type `String`.

Listing 17.16   The `AddressRepository` interface

```
Path: Ch17/springdatamongodb2/src/main/java/com/manning/javapersistence
➡ /springdatamongodb/repositories/AddressRepository.java

public interface AddressRepository extends
➡ MongoRepository<Address, String> {
}
```

We'll modify the `User` class to include an `address` field that references the `Address` document. We'll use the `@DBRef` annotation, indicating that this field will be stored using a DBRef. We'll also annotate the field with the `@Field` annotation, which can provide a custom name inside the document.

Listing 17.17   The modified `User` class

```
Path: Ch17/springdatamongodb2/src/main/java/com/manning/javapersistence
➡ /springdatamongodb/model/User.java

@NoArgsConstructor
@Document
@CompoundIndexes({
        @CompoundIndex(name = "username_email",
                        def = "{'username' : 1, 'email': 1}"),
        @CompoundIndex(name = "lastName_firstName",
                        def = "{'lastName' : 1, 'firstName': 1}")
})
public class User {

    // . . .

    @DBRef
    @Field("address")
    @Getter
    @Setter
    private Address address;

        // . . .

}
```

A MongoDB document describing a user with an address could look like this:

```
{
    "_id": {
        "$oid": "61cb2fcfff98d570824fef66"
    },
```

```
    "username": "john",
    "firstName": "John",
    "lastName": "Smith",
    "registrationDate": {
        "$date": "2020-04-12T21:00:00.000Z"
    },
    "email": "john@somedomain.com",
    "level": 1,
    "active": true,
    "address": {
        "$ref": "address",
        "$id": {
            "$oid": "61cb2fcbff98d570824fef30"
        }
    },
    "_class": "com.manning.javapersistence.springdatamongodb.model.User"
}
```

A MongoDB document describing an address could look like this:

```
{
    "_id": {
        "$oid": "61cb2fcbff98d570824fef30"
    },
    "street": "Flowers Street",
    "zipCode": "1234567",
    "city": "Boston",
    "state": "MA",
    "_class": "com.manning.javapersistence.springdatamongodb.model.Address"
}
```

Note that operations such as save and delete are not cascaded between documents. If we save or delete a document, we have to explicitly save or delete the referenced documents.

Writing tests for working with MongoDB documents that reference other documents is pretty straightforward and similar to the previous examples. They can be found in the source code for the book.

17.6   Using MongoTemplate to access a database

`MongoTemplate` is a class that provides access to CRUD operations against MongoDB databases. `MongoTemplate` implements the `MongoOperations` interface. The methods from `MongoOperations` are named similarly to the MongoDB driver `Collection` object methods, to facilitate understanding and use of the API.

17.6.1   Configuring access to the database through MongoTemplate

To connect our Spring Boot application to MongoDB, we'll extend the `Abstract-MongoClientConfiguration` class. This class provides support for the Java configuration of Spring Data MongoDB. We can connect to MongoDB through an implementation of the `MongoDatabaseFactory` interface and a `MongoTemplate`.

The `AbstractMongoClientConfiguration` class provides two beans that can be used in the Spring Boot application:

```
@Bean
public MongoTemplate mongoTemplate(MongoDatabaseFactory databaseFactory,
                                   MappingMongoConverter converter) {
    return new MongoTemplate(databaseFactory, converter);
}

@Bean
public MongoDatabaseFactory mongoDbFactory() {
    return new SimpleMongoClientDatabaseFactory(this.mongoClient(),
                                                this.getDatabaseName());
}
```

We'll create a `MongoDBConfig` class that extends `AbstractMongoClientConfiguration`, and we'll only override the `getDatabaseName()` method to indicate that our Spring Boot application connects to the `test` database, as shown in the following listing.

> **Listing 17.18   The `MongoDBConfig` class**

```
Path: Ch17/springdatamongodb3/src/main/java/com/manning/javapersistence
➡ /springdatamongodb/configuration/MongoDBConfig.java

@Configuration
public class MongoDBConfig extends AbstractMongoClientConfiguration {
    @Override
    public String getDatabaseName() {
        return "test";
    }
}
```

17.6.2   *Executing CRUD operations using MongoTemplate*

To insert documents in a database, we can use the `MongoTemplate` insert method. The method is overloaded, and the following snippet uses the methods that have an object as an argument, or a collection of objects and their class.

```
Path: Ch17/springdatamongodb3/src/test/java/com/manning/javapersistence
➡ /springdatamongodb/template/SpringDataMongoDBApplicationTests.java

mongoTemplate.insert(GenerateUsers.address);
mongoTemplate.insert(generateUsers(), User.class);
```

The `save` method has different behavior: if the `id` is already present in the database, it executes an update; otherwise, it executes an insert. The method is also overloaded; the following snippet uses the methods that have an object and the collection name as arguments:

Path: Ch17/springdatamongodb3/src/test/java/com/manning/javapersistence
➥ /springdatamongodb/template/SaveUpdateTest.java

```
mongoTemplate.save(user, "user");
```

We'll use `org.springframework.data.mongodb.core.query.Query` objects to define criteria, projection, and sorting for retrieving MongoDB documents. Such a `Query` initiated using the default constructor will correspond to all documents in a collection. For example, we can remove all documents from a collection with a snippet like this:

Path: Ch17/springdatamongodb3/src/test/java/com/manning/javapersistence
➥ /springdatamongodb/template/SpringDataMongoDBApplicationTests.java

```
mongoTemplate.remove(new Query(), User.class);
mongoTemplate.remove(new Query(), Address.class);
```

We can modify `Query` objects using different criteria. Here we'll build a query to look for users having `level` 1:

Path: Ch17/springdatamongodb3/src/test/java/com/manning/javapersistence
➥ /springdatamongodb/template/FindAndModifyTest.java

```
Query query = new Query();
query.addCriteria(Criteria.where("level").is(1));
```

We can build a query to look for users with a given `username` *and* email:

Path: Ch17/springdatamongodb3/src/test/java/com/manning/javapersistence
➥ /springdatamongodb/template/FindUsersTest.java

```
Query query1 = new Query();
query1.addCriteria(Criteria.where("username").is("mike")
      .andOperator(Criteria.where("email").is("mike@somedomain.com")));
```

We can similarly build a query to look for users with a given `username` *or* email:

Path: Ch17/springdatamongodb3/src/test/java/com/manning/javapersistence
➥ /springdatamongodb/template/FindUsersTest.java

```
Query query2 = new Query(new Criteria().
            orOperator(Criteria.where("username").is("mike"),
                 Criteria.where("email").is("beth@somedomain.com")));
```

To update a document, we can use an object belonging to the `org.springframework` `.data.mongodb.core.query.Update` class. Such an object must be set with the new values to replace the old ones. `updateFirst` updates the first document found that matches the given criteria. The following code will find the first document from the `User` class having `level` 1 and will update it to `level` 2. We can then get all the remaining users having `level` 1 using the `find` method:

```
Path: Ch17/springdatamongodb3/src/test/java/com/manning/javapersistence
➥ /springdatamongodb/template/UpdateFirstTest.java

Query query = new Query();
query.addCriteria(Criteria.where("level").is(1));

Update update = new Update();
update.set("level", 2);
mongoTemplate.updateFirst(query, update, User.class);

List<User> users = mongoTemplate.find(query, User.class);
```

updateMulti updates all the documents found that match the given criteria. The following code will find all the documents from the User class having level 1 and will update them to level 2:

```
Path: Ch17/springdatamongodb3/src/test/java/com/manning/javapersistence
➥ /springdatamongodb/template/UpdateMultiTest.java

Query query = new Query();
query.addCriteria(Criteria.where("level").is(1));

Update update = new Update();
update.set("level", 2);
mongoTemplate.updateMulti(query, update, User.class);
```

The findAndModify method is similar to updateMulti, but it returns the object before it's modified. In the following snippet, we check that the object returned by the findAndModify method still has the old level value:

```
Path: Ch17/springdatamongodb3/src/test/java/com/manning/javapersistence
➥ /springdatamongodb/template/FindAndModifyTest.java

Query query = new Query();
query.addCriteria(Criteria.where("level").is(1));

Update update = new Update();
update.set("level", 2);
User user = mongoTemplate.findAndModify(query, update, User.class);

assertEquals(1, user.getLevel());
```

The upsert method will look for a document matching some given criteria. If it finds one, it will update it; otherwise, it will create a new document combining the query and update object. The name of the method is a combination of update and insert, and MongoDB will decide what to do depending on whether the document already exists. The following snippet uses the getMatchedCount() method to check that one document matched the query and the getModifiedCount() method to check that one document was modified by the update:

```
Path: Ch17/springdatamongodb3/src/test/java/com/manning/javapersistence
➥ /springdatamongodb/template/UpsertTest.java

Query query = new Query();
query.addCriteria(Criteria.where("level").is(1));

Update update = new Update();
update.set("level", 2);
UpdateResult result = mongoTemplate.upsert(query, update, User.class);

assertAll(
        () -> assertEquals(1, result.getMatchedCount()),
        () -> assertEquals(1, result.getModifiedCount())
);
```

You can find comprehensive tests accessing MongoDB through `MongoTemplate` in the source code for the book.

For a comparison of the two approaches, `MongoRepository` and `MongoTemplate`, see table 17.7.

Table 17.7 Comparing `MongoRepository` and `MongoTemplate`

	Strong points	Weak points
`MongoRepository`	▪ Follows the approach of Spring Data JPA and Spring Data JDBC repositories. ▪ Allows us to quickly create methods with the query builder mechanism pattern, defining their behavior through their names.	▪ Provides methods that perform basic CRUD operations working with all the fields of a document. ▪ Updating a document must be executed either in steps (find, modify the relevant fields, save) or using methods annotated with `@Query`.
`MongoTemplate`	▪ Provides atomic operations such as `updateFirst`, `updateMulti`, `findAndModify`, `upsert`. ▪ Atomic operations favor the work in concurrent applications. ▪ The `Update` object allows us to choose only the fields to be updated.	▪ More verbose and more code to write, especially for simple operations.

Summary

- You can create and configure a Spring Data MongoDB project using Spring Boot.
- You can create document classes and use the Spring Data MongoDB annotations to define simple and compound indexes, to mark fields as transient, and to define the persistence constructor.
- You can build custom interfaces extending `MongoRepository` and create custom methods following the query builder mechanism to interact with the MongoDB database.

- You can use the Spring Data MongoDB capabilities for limiting query results, sorting, paging, and streaming the results.
- You can use the `@Query` annotation to define custom queries, and you can work with the Query by Example (QBE) querying technique.
- You can configure an application to use `MongoTemplate` to execute CRUD operations against a MongoDB database.

Working with
Hibernate OGM

This chapter covers

- Introducing Hibernate OGM
- Building a simple MongoDB Hibernate OGM application
- Switching to the Neo4j NoSQL database

The world of databases is extremely diverse and complex. Besides the challenges of working with different relational database systems, the NoSQL world may add to these challenges. One goal of the persistence frameworks is to ensure portability of the code, so we'll now look at the Hibernate OGM alternative and how it tries to support the JPA solution working with NoSQL databases.

18.1 Introducing Hibernate OGM

A NoSQL database is a database that keeps data in a format different than relational tables. In general, NoSQL databases provide the advantage of flexible schemas, meaning that the designer of the database does not have to determine the schema before persisting data. In applications that quickly change their requirements, this may be an important advantage for development speed.

491

NoSQL databases can be classified according to the format they use to keep data:

- Document-oriented databases, like MongoDB, which we introduced in chapter 17, use JSON-like documents to keep the information.
- Graph-oriented databases store information using graphs. A graph consists of nodes and edges: the role of the nodes is to keep the data, and the edges represent the relationships between nodes. Neo4j is an example of such a database.
- Key/value databases store data using a map structure. The key identifies the record, while the value represents the data. Redis is an example of such a database.
- Wide-column stores keep data using tables, rows, and columns. The difference between these and traditional relational databases is that the name and format of a column can vary between rows belonging to the same table. This capability is known as dynamic columns. Apache Cassandra is an example of such a database.

A significant part of our previous demonstrations used JPA and Hibernate to interact with relational databases. This allowed us to write portable applications, independent of the relational database vendor, and to manage the differences between providers through the framework.

Hibernate OGM extends the portability concept from relational databases to NoSQL databases. Portability may come with the tradeoff of influencing execution speed, but overall it provides more advantages than shortcomings. OGM stands for Object-Grid Mapper. It reuses the Hibernate Core engine, the API, and JPQL to interact not only with relational databases but also with NoSQL ones.

Hibernate OGM supports a series of NoSQL databases, and in this chapter we'll use MongoDB and Neo4j.

18.2   *Building a simple MongoDB Hibernate OGM application*

We'll start building a simple Hibernate OGM application managed by Maven. We'll examine the steps involved, the dependencies that need to be added to the project, and the persistence code that needs to be written.

We'll work first with MongoDB as a document-oriented NoSQL database. Then we'll modify our application to use Neo4j, a graph-oriented NoSQL database. We'll change only some needed dependencies and configurations—we won't touch the code that uses JPA and JPQL.

18.2.1   *Configuring the Hibernate OGM application*

In the Maven pom.xml file, we'll add `org.hibernate.ogm:hibernate-ogm-bom` to the `dependencyManagement` section. BOM is an acronym for *bill of materials*. Adding a BOM to the `dependencyManagement` block will not actually add the dependency to the project, but it is a declaration of intention. The transitive dependencies that will later be found in the dependencies section will have their versions controlled by this initial declaration.

Next we'll add two other things to the dependencies section: `hibernate-ogm-mongodb`, which is needed to work with MongoDB, and `org.jboss.jbossts:jbossjta`, a JTA (Java Transaction API) implementation that Hibernate OGM will need to support transactions.

We'll also use JUnit 5 for testing and Lombok, a Java library that can be used to automatically create constructors, getters, and setters through annotations, thus reducing the boilerplate code. As previously mentioned (in section 17.2), Lombok comes with its own shortcomings: you will need a plugin for the IDE to understand the annotations and not complain about missing constructors, getters, and setters; and you cannot set breakpoints and debug inside the generated methods (but the need to debug generated methods is pretty rare).

The resulting Maven pom.xml file is shown in the following listing.

Listing 18.1   The pom.xml Maven file

```
Path: Ch18/hibernate-ogm/pom.xml

<dependencyManagement>
    <dependencies>
        <dependency>
            <groupId>org.hibernate.ogm</groupId>
            <artifactId>hibernate-ogm-bom</artifactId>
            <type>pom</type>
            <version>4.2.0.Final</version>
            <scope>import</scope>
        </dependency>
    </dependencies>
</dependencyManagement>

<dependencies>
    <dependency>
        <groupId>org.hibernate.ogm</groupId>
        <artifactId>hibernate-ogm-mongodb</artifactId>
    </dependency>
    <dependency>
        <groupId>org.jboss.jbossts</groupId>
        <artifactId>jbossjta</artifactId>
    </dependency>
    <dependency>
        <groupId>org.projectlombok</groupId>
        <artifactId>lombok</artifactId>
        <version>1.18.24</version>
    </dependency>
    <dependency>
        <groupId>org.junit.jupiter</groupId>
        <artifactId>junit-jupiter-engine</artifactId>
        <version>5.8.2</version>
        <scope>test</scope>
    </dependency>
</dependencies>
```

We'll now move on to the standard configuration file for persistence units, src/main/resources/META-INF/persistence.xml.

Listing 18.2   The persistence.xml configuration file

Path: Ch18/hibernate-ogm/src/main/resources/META-INF/persistence.xml

Ⓐ

Ⓑ

```
<persistence-unit name="ch18.hibernate_ogm">
    <provider>org.hibernate.ogm.jpa.HibernateOgmPersistence</provider>     <─
    <properties>
        <property name="hibernate.ogm.datastore.provider" value="mongodb"/>
        <property name="hibernate.ogm.datastore.database"
                    value="hibernate_ogm"/>
        <property name="hibernate.ogm.datastore.create_database"
                        value="true"/>
    </properties>
</persistence-unit>
```

Ⓒ Ⓓ Ⓔ

Ⓐ The persistence.xml file configures the ch18.hibernate_ogm persistence unit.

Ⓑ The vendor-specific provider implementation of the API is Hibernate OGM.

Ⓒ The data store provider is MongoDB.

Ⓓ The name of the database is hibernate_ogm.

Ⓔ The database will be created if it does not exist.

18.2.2 *Creating the entities*

We'll now create the classes that represent the entities of the application: User, Bid, Item, and Address. The relationships between them will be of type one-to-many, many-to-one, or embedded.

Listing 18.3   The User class

Path: Ch18/hibernate-ogm/src/main/java/com/manning/javapersistence
➡ /hibernateogm/model/User.java

```
@Entity
@NoArgsConstructor
public class User {

    @Id
    @GeneratedValue(generator = "ID_GENERATOR")                          Ⓐ
    @GenericGenerator(name = "ID_GENERATOR", strategy = "uuid2")
    @Getter
    private String id;

                    Ⓑ
    @Embedded        <─
    @Getter
    @Setter          Ⓑ
    private Address address;     <─
```

```
@OneToMany(mappedBy = "user", cascade = CascadeType.PERSIST)
private Set<Bid> bids = new HashSet<>();

// . . .
```

}

Ⓐ The ID field is an identifier generated by the ID_GENERATOR generator. This one uses the uuid2 strategy, which produces a unique 128-bit UUID. For a review of the generator strategies, refer to section 5.2.5.

Ⓑ The address does not have its own identity; it is embeddable.

Ⓒ There is a one-to-many relationship between User and Bid, with this being mapped by the user field on the Bid side. CascadeType.PERSIST indicates that the persist operation will be propagated from the parent User to the child Bid.

The Address class does not have its own persistence identity, and it will be embeddable.

Listing 18.4   The Address class

Path: Ch18/hibernate-ogm/src/main/java/com/manning/javapersistence
➡ /hibernateogm/model/Address.java

```
@Embeddable
@NoArgsConstructor
public class Address {

    //fields with Lombok annotations, constructor
}
```

The Item class will contain an id field with a similar generation strategy as in User. The relationship between Item and Bid will be one-to-many, and the cascade type will propagate persist operations from parent to child.

Listing 18.5   The Item class

Path: Ch18/hibernate-ogm/src/main/java/com/manning/javapersistence
➡ /hibernateogm/model/Item.java

```
@Entity
@NoArgsConstructor
public class Item {

    @Id
    @GeneratedValue(generator = "ID_GENERATOR")
    @GenericGenerator(name = "ID_GENERATOR", strategy = "uuid2")
    @Getter
    private String id;
```

```
@OneToMany(mappedBy = "item", cascade = CascadeType.PERSIST)
private Set<Bid> bids = new HashSet<>();
 // . . .


}
```

18.2.3 *Using the application with MongoDB*

To persist entities from the application to MongoDB, we'll write code that uses the regular JPA classes and JPQL. This means that our application can work with relational databases and with various NoSQL databases. We'd just need to change some configuration.

To work with JPA the way we did with relational databases, we'll first initialize an `EntityManagerFactory`. The `ch18.hibernate_ogm` persistence unit was previously declared in persistence.xml.

Listing 18.6 Initializing the `EntityManagerFactory`

Path: Ch18/hibernate-ogm/src/test/java/com/manning/javapersistence
➡ /hibernateogm/HibernateOGMTest.java

```
public class HibernateOGMTest {

    private static EntityManagerFactory entityManagerFactory;

    @BeforeAll
    static void setUp() {
        entityManagerFactory =
                Persistence.createEntityManagerFactory("ch18.hibernate_ogm");
    }
     // . . .


}
```

After the execution of each test from the `HibernateOGMTest` class, we'll close the `EntityManagerFactory`.

Listing 18.7 Closing the `EntityManagerFactory`

Path: Ch18/hibernate-ogm/src/test/java/com/manning/javapersistence
➡ /hibernateogm/HibernateOGMTest.java

```
@AfterAll
static void tearDown() {
    entityManagerFactory.close();
}
```

Before the execution of each test from the `HibernateOGMTest` class, we'll persist a few entities to the NoSQL MongoDB database. Our code will use JPA for these operations,

which is unaware of whether it is interacting with a relational or a non-relational
database.

Listing 18.8   Persisting the data to test on

Path: Ch18/hibernate-ogm/src/test/java/com/manning/javapersistence
➥ /hibernateogm/HibernateOGMTest.java

```java
@BeforeEach
void beforeEach() {
    EntityManager entityManager =
                entityManagerFactory.createEntityManager();          Ⓐ

    try {                                                    Ⓑ
        entityManager.getTransaction().begin();      ←

        john = new User("John", "Smith");
        john.setAddress(new Address("Flowers Street", "12345", "Boston"));

        bid1 = new Bid(BigDecimal.valueOf(1000));
        bid2 = new Bid(BigDecimal.valueOf(2000));

        item = new Item("Item1");

        bid1.setItem(item);                                          Ⓒ
        item.addBid(bid1);

        bid2.setItem(item);
        item.addBid(bid2);

        bid1.setUser(john);
        john.addBid(bid1);

        bid2.setUser(john);
        john.addBid(bid2);

        entityManager.persist(item);          Ⓓ
        entityManager.persist(john);
                                                  Ⓔ
        entityManager.getTransaction().commit();     ←
    } finally {
        entityManager.close();      ←
    }
}                                       Ⓕ
```

Ⓐ Create an `EntityManager` with the help of the existing `EntityManagerFactory`.

Ⓑ Start a transaction. As you'll recall, operations with JPA need to be transactional.

Ⓒ Create and set up the entities to be persisted.

D Persist the Item entity and the User entity. As the Bid entities from an Item and a User are referenced using CascadeType.PERSIST, the persist operation will be propagated from parent to child.

E Commit the previously started transaction.

F Close the previously created EntityManager.

We'll query the database using JPA. We'll use the entityManager.find method, as we do when interacting with a relational database. As previously discussed, every interaction with a database should occur within transaction boundaries, even if we're only reading data, so we'll start and commit transactions.

> Listing 18.9 Querying the MongoDB database using JPA

Path: Ch18/hibernate-ogm/src/test/java/com/manning/javapersistence
➥ /hibernateogm/HibernateOGMTest.java

```java
@Test
void testCRUDOperations() {
    EntityManager entityManager =
                            entityManagerFactory.createEntityManager();      A

    try {
        entityManager.getTransaction().begin();    ←—B

        User fetchedUser = entityManager.find(User.class, john.getId());
        Item fetchedItem = entityManager.find(Item.class, item.getId());     C
        Bid fetchedBid1 = entityManager.find(Bid.class, bid1.getId());
        Bid fetchedBid2 = entityManager.find(Bid.class, bid2.getId());
            assertAll(
              () -> assertNotNull(fetchedUser),
              () -> assertEquals("John", fetchedUser.getFirstName()),
              () -> assertEquals("Smith", fetchedUser.getLastName()),
              () -> assertNotNull(fetchedItem),
              () -> assertEquals("Item1", fetchedItem.getName()),          D
              () -> assertNotNull(fetchedBid1),
              () -> assertEquals(new BigDecimal(1000),
                                    fetchedBid1.getAmount()),
              () -> assertNotNull(fetchedBid2),
              () -> assertEquals(new BigDecimal(2000),
                                    fetchedBid2.getAmount())
        );
            entityManager.getTransaction().commit();    ←—E
    } finally {
        entityManager.close();    ←—F
    }
}
```

A Create an EntityManager with the help of the existing EntityManagerFactory.

B Start a transaction; the operations need to be transactional.

C Fetch the previously persisted User, Item, and Bids based on the ids of the entities.

D Check that the fetched information contains what we previously persisted.

E Commit the previously started transaction.

F Close the previously created `EntityManager`.

We can examine the content of the MongoDB database after executing this test. Open the MongoDB Compass program, as shown in figure 18.1. MongoDB Compass is a GUI for interacting with and querying MongoDB databases. It will show us that three collections were created after executing the test. This demonstrates that the code written using JPA was able to interact with the NoSQL MongoDB database, with the help of Hibernate OGM.

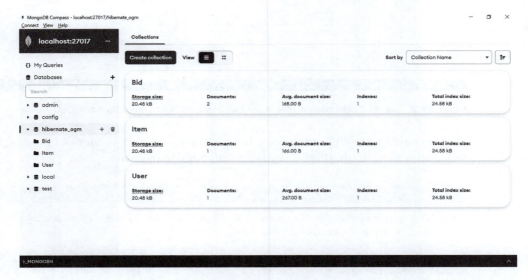

Figure 18.1   The test written using JPA and Hibernate OGM created three collections inside MongoDB.

We can also inspect the collections that were created and see that they contain the documents persisted from the test (this should be viewed before the `afterEach()` method, which removes the newly added documents, runs). For example, the `Bid` collection contains two documents, as shown in figure 18.2.

We'll also query the database using JPQL. JPQL (Jakarta Persistence Query Language, previously Java Persistence Query Language) is an object-oriented query language independent of the platform.

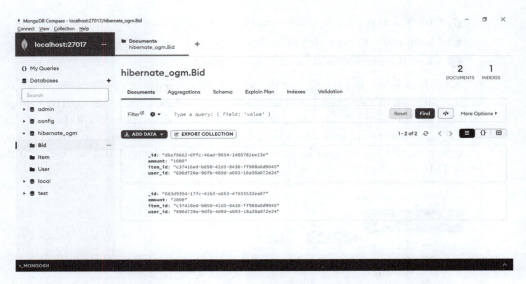

Figure 18.2   The `Bid` collection contains the two documents persisted from the test.

We previously used JPQL to query relational databases independent of their SQL dialect, and now we'll use JPQL to interact with NoSQL databases.

Listing 18.10   Querying the MongoDB database using JPQL

Path: Ch18/hibernate-ogm/src/test/java/com/manning/javapersistence
➡ /hibernateogm/HibernateOGMTest.java

```java
@Test
void testJPQLQuery() {
    EntityManager entityManager =
            entityManagerFactory.createEntityManager();          A
    try {
        entityManager.getTransaction().begin();    ←—B
        List<Bid> bids = entityManager.createQuery(                C
            "SELECT b FROM Bid b ORDER BY b.amount DESC", Bid.class)
            .getResultList();
        Item item = entityManager.createQuery(
            "SELECT i FROM Item i", Item.class)        D
                .getSingleResult();
        User user = entityManager.createQuery(                    E
            "SELECT u FROM User u", User.class).getSingleResult();
        assertAll(() -> assertEquals(2, bids.size()),
                () -> assertEquals(new BigDecimal(2000),
                                    bids.get(0).getAmount()),
                () -> assertEquals(new BigDecimal(1000),          F
                                    bids.get(1).getAmount()),
                () -> assertEquals("Item1", item.getName()),
                () -> assertEquals("John", user.getFirstName()),
                () -> assertEquals("Smith", user.getLastName())
```

```
    );
    entityManager.getTransaction().commit();    ◄──Ⓖ
} finally {
    entityManager.close();    ◄───┐
}                                  Ⓗ
}
```

Ⓐ Create an `EntityManager` with the help of the existing `EntityManagerFactory`.

Ⓑ Start a transaction; the operations need to be transactional.

Ⓒ Create a JPQL query to get all `Bids` from the database, in descending order of amount.

Ⓓ Create a JPQL query to get the `Item` from the database.

Ⓔ Create a JPQL query to get the `User` from the database.

Ⓕ Check that the information obtained through JPQL contains what we previously persisted.

Ⓖ Commit the previously started transaction.

Ⓗ Close the previously created `EntityManager`.

As previously stated, we want to keep the database clean and the tests independent, so we'll clean up the data inserted after the execution of each test in the `HibernateOGM-Test` class. Our code will use JPA for these operations, which is unaware of whether it is interacting with a relational or non-relational database.

Listing 18.11   Cleaning the database after the execution of each test

Path: Ch18/hibernate-ogm/src/test/java/com/manning/javapersistence
➥ /hibernateogm/HibernateOGMTest.java

```
@AfterEach
void afterEach() {
    EntityManager entityManager =
            entityManagerFactory.createEntityManager();    Ⓐ
    try {
        entityManager.getTransaction().begin();
        User fetchedUser = entityManager.find(User.class, john.getId());
        Item fetchedItem = entityManager.find(Item.class, item.getId());    Ⓒ
        Bid fetchedBid1 = entityManager.find(Bid.class, bid1.getId());
        Bid fetchedBid2 = entityManager.find(Bid.class, bid2.getId());

        entityManager.remove(fetchedBid1);
        entityManager.remove(fetchedBid2);
        entityManager.remove(fetchedItem);    Ⓓ
        entityManager.remove(fetchedUser);

        entityManager.getTransaction().commit();    ◄──Ⓔ
    } finally {
        entityManager.close();    ◄──Ⓕ
    }
}
```

Ⓐ Create an `EntityManager` with the help of the existing `EntityManagerFactory`.

Ⓑ Start a transaction; the operations need to be transactional.

Ⓒ Fetch the previously persisted `User`, `Item`, and `Bids` based on the `ids` of the entities.

Ⓓ Remove the previously persisted entities.

Ⓔ Commit the previously started transaction.

Ⓕ Close the previously created `EntityManager`.

18.3 *Switching to the Neo4j NoSQL database*

Neo4j is also a NoSQL database, and specifically a graph-oriented database. Unlike MongoDB, which uses JSON-like documents to store the data, Neo4j uses graphs to store it. A graph consists of nodes that keep the data and edges that represent the relationships. Neo4j can run in a desktop version or an embedded version (which we'll use for our demonstrations). For a comprehensive guide of Neo4j's capabilities, see the Neo4j website: https://neo4j.com/.

Hibernate OGM facilitates the quick and efficient switching between different NoSQL databases, even if they internally use different paradigms to store data. Currently, Hibernate OGM supports both MongoDB, the document-oriented database that we already demonstrated how to work with, and Neo4j, a graph-oriented database that we would like to quickly switch to.

The efficiency of Hibernate OGM consists of the fact that we can still use the JPA code that we previously presented to define the entities and describe the interaction with the database. That code remains unchanged. We only need to make changes at the level of the configuration: we need to replace the Hibernate OGM MongoDB dependency with Hibernate OGM Neo4j, and we need to change the persistence unit configuration from MongoDB to Neo4j.

We'll update the Maven pom.xml file to include the Hibernate OGM Neo4j dependency.

Listing 18.12   The pom.xml file with the Hibernate OGM Neo4j dependency

Path: Ch18/hibernate-ogm/pom.xml

```
<dependency>
    <groupId>org.hibernate.ogm</groupId>
    <artifactId>hibernate-ogm-neo4j</artifactId>
</dependency>
```

We'll also replace the persistence unit configuration in src/main/resources/META-INF/persistence.xml.

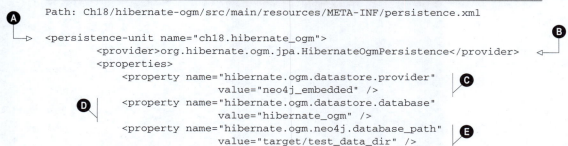

Listing 18.13   The persistence.xml configuration file for Neo4j

Path: `Ch18/hibernate-ogm/src/main/resources/META-INF/persistence.xml`

```
<persistence-unit name="ch18.hibernate_ogm">
        <provider>org.hibernate.ogm.jpa.HibernateOgmPersistence</provider>
        <properties>
            <property name="hibernate.ogm.datastore.provider"
                        value="neo4j_embedded" />
            <property name="hibernate.ogm.datastore.database"
                        value="hibernate_ogm" />
            <property name="hibernate.ogm.neo4j.database_path"
                        value="target/test_data_dir" />
        </properties>
    </persistence-unit>
```

A The persistence.xml file configures the `ch18.hibernate_ogm` persistence unit.

B The vendor-specific provider implementation of the API is Hibernate OGM.

C The data store provider is Neo4j; the database is embedded.

D The name of the database is `hibernate_ogm`.

E The database path is in test_data_dir, in the target folder created by Maven.

The functionality of the application will be the same with Neo4j as with MongoDB. Using Hibernate OGM, the code is untouched, and JPA can access different kinds of NoSQL databases. The changes are only at the level of configuration.

Summary

- You can create a simple Hibernate OGM application using MongoDB and set the Maven dependencies it needs to interact with the database.
- You can configure the persistence unit with the MongoDB provider and a MongoDB database.
- You can create entities that use only JPA annotations and functionality and persist them against the MongoDB database, verifying the insertion of the entities in MongoDB.
- You can switch from the document-oriented MongoDB database to the graph-oriented Neo4j database, changing only the Maven dependencies and the persistence unit configuration.
- You can persist the previously created entities that use only JPA annotations against the Neo4j database without touching the existing code.

Part 6

Writing queries and testing Java persistence applications

In part 6, you'll learn how to write queries and how to test Java persistence applications.

In chapter 19, you'll learn to work with Querydsl, one of the alternatives for querying a database using Java programs. We'll examine its most important capabilities and we'll apply them in a Java persistence project.

Next, chapter 20 examines how to test Java persistence applications. We'll introduce the testing pyramid and examine persistence testing in its context. We'll use the Spring TestContext Framework and its annotations, we'll work with Spring profiles, and we'll use test execution listeners to test Java persistence applications.

After reading this part of the book, you'll know how to write queries using Querydsl and how to test persistence applications using the Spring TestContext Framework.

Querying JPA with Querydsl

This chapter covers

- Introducing Querydsl
- Creating a Querydsl application
- Querying a database with Querydsl

Querying a database is essential to retrieve information that meets certain criteria. This chapter focuses on Querydsl, one of the alternatives for querying a database from Java programs. The "dsl" part of the Querydsl name refers to domain specific languages (DSLs), which are languages dedicated to particular application domains. For example, querying a database is such a domain.

In this chapter we'll examine the most important capabilities of Querydsl, and we'll apply them in a Java persistence project. For comprehensive documentation of Querydsl, see its website: http://querydsl.com/.

19.1 Introducing Querydsl

There are various alternatives for querying a database from within Java programs. You can use SQL, as has been possible since the early days of JDBC. The drawbacks

507

of this approach are the lack of portability (the queries are dependent on the database and the particular SQL dialect) and the lack of type safety and static query verification.

JPQL (Jakarta Persistence Query Language) was a step forward, being an object-oriented query language that is independent of the database. This means there's no lack of portability, but there's still a lack of type safety and static query verification.

Spring Data allows us to create methods with the query builder mechanism and to annotate methods with JPQL and SQL queries (though these still have their previously mentioned drawbacks). The query builder mechanism also has the disadvantage of requiring the methods to be defined in advance, and their names are not statically checked at compile time.

The Criteria API allows you to build type safe and portable queries using a Java API. While it solved the drawbacks of the previously presented alternatives, it ended up being extremely verbose and created code that was difficult to read.

Querydsl keeps the important ideas of type safety and portability. Furthermore, it reduces the verboseness of Criteria API, and the code it creates is much easier to read and understand than that built with Criteria API.

19.2 *Creating a Querydsl application*

We'll start by creating a Querydsl application whose dependencies are managed by Maven. We'll examine the steps involved, the dependencies that need to be added to the project, the entities that will be managed, and how to write queries with the help of Querydsl.

> **NOTE**   To execute the examples from the source code, you'll first need to run the Ch19.sql script.

19.2.1 *Configuring the Querydsl application*

We'll add two dependencies in the Maven pom.xml file: `querydsl-jpa` and `querydsl-apt`. The `querydsl-jpa` dependency is needed to use the Querydsl API inside a JPA application. The `querydsl-apt` dependency is needed to process annotations from Java files before code compilation.

The APT in `querydsl-apt` stands for Annotation Processing Tool, and using it, the entities that are managed by the application will be replicated in the so-called Q-types (Q standing for "query"). This means that each `Entity` entity will have a corresponding `QEntity` that will be generated at build time, which Querydsl will use to query the database. Also, each field of the entity will be mirrored in the `QEntity` using the specific Querydsl classes. For example, `String` fields will be mirrored to `StringPath` fields, `Long` fields to `NumberPath<Long>` fields, `Integer` fields to `NumberPath<Integer>` fields, and so on.

The resulting Maven pom.xml file will have the dependencies shown in the following listing.

Listing 19.1   The pom.xml Maven file

Path: Ch19/querydsl/pom.xml

```
<dependency>
    <groupId>com.querydsl</groupId>
    <artifactId>querydsl-jpa</artifactId>
    <version>5.0.0</version>
</dependency>
<dependency>
    <groupId>com.querydsl</groupId>
    <artifactId>querydsl-apt</artifactId>
    <version>5.0.0</version>
    <scope>provided</scope>
</dependency>
```

The scope of the `querydsl-apt` dependency is specified as `provided`. This means that the dependency is needed only at build time when Maven generates the previously introduced Q-types. Then it is no longer needed, so it won't be included in the application artifacts.

To work with Querydsl we also need to include the Maven APT plugin in the Maven pom.xml file. This plugin will take care of generating the Q-types during the build process. As we are using JPA annotations in our project, the class that effectively does this is `com.querydsl.apt.jpa.JPAAnnotationProcessor`. If we were using the Hibernate API and annotations, we would have to use `com.querydsl.apt.hibernate.HibernateAnnotationProcessor` instead.

We'll also have to indicate the output directory where the generated Q-types will reside: inside the `target` Maven folder. The pom.xml file with all this added is shown in the following listing.

Listing 19.2   The pom.xml Maven file with the APT plugin

Path: Ch19/querydsl/pom.xml

```
<plugin>
  <groupId>com.mysema.maven</groupId>
  <artifactId>apt-maven-plugin</artifactId>
  <version>1.1.3</version>
  <executions>
    <execution>
      <goals>
        <goal>process</goal>
      </goals>
      <configuration>
        <outputDirectory>target/generated-sources/java</outputDirectory>    ◄─┐ Ⓐ
    Ⓑ─►   <processor>com.querydsl.apt.jpa.JPAAnnotationProcessor</processor>
      </configuration>
    </execution>
  </executions>
</plugin>
```

A The generated Q-types will be located in the target/generated-sources/java folder.

B Use the `com.querydsl.apt.jpa.JPAAnnotationProcessor` class to generate Q-types.

We'll now move on to the standard configuration file for persistence units, in src/main/resources/META-INF/persistence.xml. This file is shown in the following listing.

Listing 19.3   **The persistence.xml configuration file**

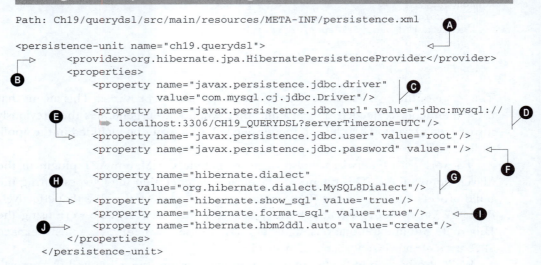

```
Path: Ch19/querydsl/src/main/resources/META-INF/persistence.xml          A

<persistence-unit name="ch19.querydsl">                                  ⊲
        <provider>org.hibernate.jpa.HibernatePersistenceProvider</provider>
        <properties>
            <property name="javax.persistence.jdbc.driver"               C
                      value="com.mysql.cj.jdbc.Driver"/>
            <property name="javax.persistence.jdbc.url" value="jdbc:mysql://   D
                localhost:3306/CH19_QUERYDSL?serverTimezone=UTC"/>
            <property name="javax.persistence.jdbc.user" value="root"/>
            <property name="javax.persistence.jdbc.password" value=""/>  ⊲
                                                                             F
            <property name="hibernate.dialect"
                    value="org.hibernate.dialect.MySQL8Dialect"/>         G
            <property name="hibernate.show_sql" value="true"/>
            <property name="hibernate.format_sql" value="true"/>         ⊲   I
            <property name="hibernate.hbm2ddl.auto" value="create"/>
        </properties>
    </persistence-unit>
```

A The persistence.xml file configures the ch19.querydsl persistence unit.

B As JPA is only a specification, we need to indicate the vendor-specific `Persistence-Provider` implementation of the API. The persistence we define will be backed by a Hibernate provider.

C The JDBC properties—the driver.

D The URL of the database.

E The username.

F No password for access. The machine we are running the programs on has MySQL 8 installed, and the access credentials are the ones from persistence.xml. You should modify the credentials to correspond to the ones on your machine.

G The Hibernate dialect is MySQL8, as the database we'll interact with is MySQL Release 8.0.

H While executing, show the SQL code.

I Hibernate will format the SQL nicely and generate comments in the SQL string so we know why Hibernate executed the SQL statement.

J Every time the program is executed, the database will be created from scratch. This is ideal for automated testing when we want to work with a clean database for every test run.

19.2.2 Creating the entities

We'll now create the classes that represent the entities of the application: User, Bid, and Address. The relationships between them will be of type one-to-many, many-to-one, or embedded.

Listing 19.4 The User class

Path: Ch19/querydsl/src/main/java/com/manning/javapersistence/querydsl
➥ /model/User.java

```
@Entity
@NoArgsConstructor
public class User {

    @Id
    @GeneratedValue(generator = Constants.ID_GENERATOR)        A
    @Getter
    private Long id;


    @Embedded        ◄──B
    @Getter
    @Setter
    private Address address;        ◄──B

    @OneToMany(mappedBy = "user", cascade = CascadeType.ALL)        C
    private Set<Bid> bids = new HashSet<>();

    // . . .
}
```

Ⓐ The ID field is an identifier generated by the Constants.ID_GENERATOR generator. For a review of generators, revisit chapter 5.

Ⓑ The address does not have its own identity; it is embeddable.

Ⓒ There is a one-to-many relationship between User and Bid, which is mapped by the user field on the Bid side. CascadeType.ALL indicates that all operations will be propagated from the parent User to the child Bid.

The Address class does not have its own persistence identity, and it will be embeddable.

Listing 19.5 The Address class

Path: Ch19/querydsl/src/main/java/com/manning/javapersistence/querydsl
➥ /model/User.java

```
@Embeddable
@NoArgsConstructor
public class Address {

    //fields with Lombok annotations, constructor
}
```

The `Bid` class will contain an `id` field having a similar generation strategy as for `User`. The relationship between `Bid` and `User` will be many-to-one, not optional, and the fetch type will be lazy.

Listing 19.6   The `Bid` class

Path: Ch19/querydsl/src/main/java/com/manning/javapersistence/querydsl
➥ /model/Bid.java

```java
@Entity
@NoArgsConstructor
public class Bid {

    @Id
    @GeneratedValue(generator = Constants.ID_GENERATOR)
    private Long id;


    @ManyToOne(optional = false, fetch = FetchType.LAZY)
    @Getter
    @Setter
    private User user;

    // . . .

}
```

The `UserRepository` interface extends `JpaRepository<User, Long>`. It manages the `User` entity and has IDs of type `Long`. We'll use this Spring Data JPA interface only to conveniently populate the database to test Querydsl on.

Listing 19.7   The `UserRepository` interface

Path: Ch19/querydsl/src/main/java/com/manning/javapersistence/querydsl
➥ /repositories/UserRepository.java

```java
public interface UserRepository extends JpaRepository<User, Long> {

}
```

19.2.3 *Creating the test data to query*

To populate and work with the database, we'll need a `SpringDataConfiguration` class and a `GenerateUsers` class. We have used this approach repeatedly, so we'll only quickly review the capabilities of these classes here.

Listing 19.8   The `SpringDataConfiguration` class

Path: Ch19/querydsl/src/test/java/com/manning/javapersistence/querydsl
➥ /configuration/SpringDataConfiguration.java

```
@EnableJpaRepositories("com.manning.javapersistence.querydsl.repositories")
public class SpringDataConfiguration {
    @Bean
    public DataSource dataSource() {
        // . . .
        return dataSource;
    }

    @Bean
    public JpaTransactionManager
            transactionManager(EntityManagerFactory emf) {
        return new JpaTransactionManager(emf);
    }

    @Bean
    public JpaVendorAdapter jpaVendorAdapter() {
        HibernateJpaVendorAdapter jpaVendorAdapter = new
                HibernateJpaVendorAdapter();
        //...
        return jpaVendorAdapter;
    }

    @Bean
    public LocalContainerEntityManagerFactoryBean entityManagerFactory() {
        LocalContainerEntityManagerFactoryBean
          localContainerEntityManagerFactoryBean =
                new LocalContainerEntityManagerFactoryBean();
        // . . .
        return localContainerEntityManagerFactoryBean;
    }
}
```

Ⓐ The `@EnableJpaRepositories` annotation will scan the package of the annotated configuration class for Spring Data repositories.

Ⓑ Create a data source bean to keep the JDBC properties: the driver, the URL of the database, the username, and the password.

Ⓒ Create a transaction manager bean based on an entity manager factory. Every interaction with the database should occur within transaction boundaries, and Spring Data needs a transaction manager bean.

Ⓓ Create and configure a JPA vendor adapter bean, which is needed by JPA to interact with Hibernate.

Ⓔ Create and configure a `LocalContainerEntityManagerFactoryBean`—this is a factory bean that produces an `EntityManagerFactory`.

The `GenerateUsers` class contains the `generateUsers` method, which creates a list of users and their related bids.

Listing 19.9   The `GenerateUsers` class

Path: Ch19/querydsl/src/test/java/com/manning/javapersistence/querydsl
➡ /GenerateUsers.java

```
public class GenerateUsers {

    public static Address address = new Address("Flowers Street",
                                        "1234567", "Boston", "MA");

    public static List<User> generateUsers() {
        List<User> users = new ArrayList<>();

        User john = new User("john", "John", "Smith");
        john.setRegistrationDate(LocalDate.of(2020, Month.APRIL, 13));
        john.setEmail("john@somedomain.com");
        john.setLevel(1);
        john.setActive(true);
        john.setAddress(address);

        Bid bid1 = new Bid(new BigDecimal(100));
        bid1.setUser(john);
        john.addBid(bid1);

        Bid bid2 = new Bid(new BigDecimal(110));
        bid2.setUser(john);
        john.addBid(bid2);

        // . . . .
    }
}
```

19.3   *Querying a database with Querydsl*

As we mentioned previously, the Maven APT plugin will generate the Q-types during the build process. According to the provided configuration (see listing 19.2), these sources will be generated in the target/generated-sources/java folder (see figure 19.1). We'll use these generated classes to query the database.

First, though, we have to populate the database, and to do this, we'll use the User-Repository interface. We'll also use an EntityManagerFactory and the created EntityManager to start working with a JPAQueryFactory and a JPAQuery. We'll need a JPAQueryFactory instance to work with queries, and it will be created by the constructor that takes an EntityManager argument. Then, JPAQueryFactory will create JPAQuery instances, to effectively query the database.

We'll extend the test using SpringExtension. This extension is used to integrate the Spring test context with the JUnit 5 Jupiter test.

Before executing the tests, we'll populate the database with previously generated users and their corresponding bids. Before each test, we'll create an EntityManager and start a transaction. Thus, every interaction with the database will occur within transaction boundaries. For the moment, we won't execute queries from inside this

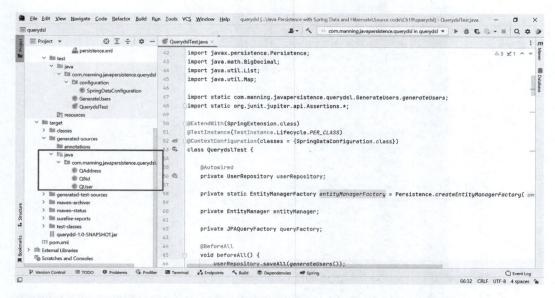

Figure 19.1   The generated Q-types in the `target` folder

class, but as tests and queries will be immediately added (starting with listing 19.11), we'll name our class `QuerydslTest`.

Listing 19.10   The `QuerydslTest` class

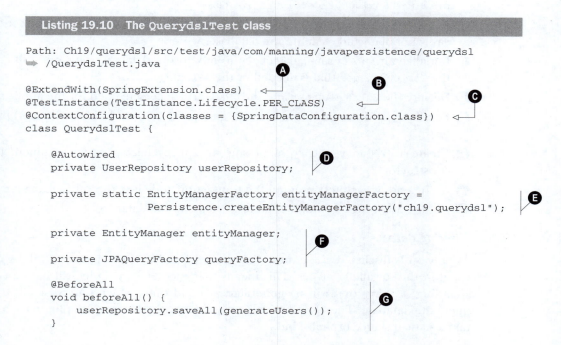

```
Path: Ch19/querydsl/src/test/java/com/manning/javapersistence/querydsl
⇒ /QuerydslTest.java

@ExtendWith(SpringExtension.class)            ⬅  Ⓐ
@TestInstance(TestInstance.Lifecycle.PER_CLASS)    ⬅  Ⓑ
@ContextConfiguration(classes = {SpringDataConfiguration.class})   ⬅  Ⓒ
class QuerydslTest {

    @Autowired
    private UserRepository userRepository;        |  Ⓓ

    private static EntityManagerFactory entityManagerFactory =
                    Persistence.createEntityManagerFactory("ch19.querydsl");   |  Ⓔ

    private EntityManager entityManager;    |  Ⓕ

    private JPAQueryFactory queryFactory;

    @BeforeAll
    void beforeAll() {                         |  Ⓖ
        userRepository.saveAll(generateUsers());
    }
```

```
@BeforeEach
void beforeEach() {
    entityManager = entityManagerFactory.createEntityManager();
    entityManager.getTransaction().begin();
    queryFactory = new JPAQueryFactory(entityManager);
}

@AfterEach
void afterEach() {
    entityManager.getTransaction().commit();
    entityManager.close();
}

@AfterAll
void afterAll() {
    userRepository.deleteAll();
}
```

Ⓐ Extend the test using `SpringExtension`.

Ⓑ JUnit will create only one instance of the test class for executing all tests, instead of one instance per test. This way we'll be able to autowire the `UserRepository` field as an instance variable.

Ⓒ The Spring test context is configured using the beans defined in the previously presented `SpringDataConfiguration` class.

Ⓓ A `UserRepository` bean is injected by Spring through autowiring. It will be used to easily populate and clean up the database.

Ⓔ Initialize an `EntityManagerFactory` to talk to the database. This one will create the `EntityManager` that is needed by the `JPAQueryFactory`.

Ⓕ Declare the `EntityManager` and the `JPAQueryFactory` needed for the application.

Ⓖ Populate the database with previously generated users and bids, to be used by the tests.

Ⓗ Create a `JPAQueryFactory` by passing an `EntityManager` as an argument to its constructor.

Ⓘ At the end of each test, commit the transaction and close the `EntityManager`.

Ⓙ At the end of the execution of all tests, clean up the database.

19.3.1 *Filtering data*

As previously discussed, the entities that are managed by the application will be replicated in the so-called Q-types. This means that each `Entity` entity will have a corresponding `QEntity` that will be generated at build time, which Querydsl will use to query the database. The Q-type classes generated by the Maven APT plugin each contain a static instance of their kind:

```
public static final QUser user = new QUser("user");
public static final QBid bid = new QBid("bid");
public static final QAddress address = new QAddress("address");
```

These instances will be used to query the database. We'll first get a JPAQuery instance by calling queryFactory.selectFrom(user). Then we'll use this JPAQuery instance to build the clauses of the query. We'll use the where method to filter by a given Predicate and the fetchOne method to fetch a single element from the database. fetchOne returns null if no element to fulfill a condition is found, and it throws NonUniqueResult-Exception if multiple elements that fulfill a condition are found.

For example, to get the User with a given username, we'll write the code in the following listing.

Listing 19.11 Finding a User by username

Path: Ch19/querydsl/src/test/java/com/manning/javapersistence/querydsl
➥ /QuerydslTest.java

```
@Test
void testFindByUsername() {

    User fetchedUser = queryFactory.selectFrom(QUser.user)        ◀─┐ Ⓐ
              .where(QUser.user.username.eq("john"))    ┌─▷
              .fetchOne();        ◀─┐
    Ⓑ
                        Ⓒ
    assertAll(
            () -> assertNotNull(fetchedUser),
            () -> assertEquals("john", fetchedUser.getUsername()),
            () -> assertEquals("John", fetchedUser.getFirstName()),        Ⓓ
            () -> assertEquals("Smith", fetchedUser.getLastName()),
            () -> assertEquals(2, fetchedUser.getBids().size())
    );

}
```

Ⓐ Start building the query using the selectFrom method belonging to the JPAQuery-Factory class. This method will get the created Q-type instance QUser.user as an argument and will return a JPAQuery.

Ⓑ The where method will filter by the given Predicate related to the username.

Ⓒ The fetchOne method will try to fetch a single element from the database.

Ⓓ Verify that the fetched data is the expected data.

The following SQL queries are generated by Hibernate:

```
select
    *
from
    User user0_
where
    user0_.username=?
```

```
select
    *
from
    Bid bids0_
where
    bids0_.user_id=?
```

We can filter by multiple `Predicates` using methods such as `and` or `or`, which each receive a `Predicate`. For example, to filter by the `level` and `active` fields, we could write the following piece of code:

```
List<User> users = (List<User>)queryFactory.from(QUser.user)
                       .where(QUser.user.level.eq(3)
                       .and(QUser.user.active.eq(true))).fetch();
```

The following SQL query is generated by Hibernate:

```
select
    *
from
    User user0_
where
    user0_.level=?
    and user0_.active=?
```

19.3.2 *Ordering data*

To order data, we'll use the `orderBy` method, which can receive multiple arguments representing the criteria to order by. For example, to get the `User` instances ordered by `username`, we'll write the following code.

Listing 19.12   Ordering `User` instances by `username`

Path: Ch19/querydsl/src/test/java/com/manning/javapersistence/querydsl
➡ /QuerydslTest.java

```
@Test
void testOrderByUsername() {                                         Ⓐ

    List<User> users = queryFactory.selectFrom(QUser.user)      ⟵
            .orderBy(QUser.user.username.asc())
    ⟶      .fetch();                       ⟵
  Ⓑ                                       Ⓒ

    assertAll(
            () -> assertEquals(users.size(), 10),
            () -> assertEquals("beth", users.get(0).getUsername()),
            () -> assertEquals("burk", users.get(1).getUsername()),      Ⓓ
            () -> assertEquals("mike", users.get(8).getUsername()),
            () -> assertEquals("stephanie", users.get(9).getUsername())
    );
}
```

Ⓐ Start building the query using the `selectFrom` method belonging to the `JPAQuery-Factory` class. This method will get the created Q-type instance `QUser.user` as an argument and will return a `JPAQuery`.

Ⓑ Order the results by `username`, ascending. The `orderBy` method is overloaded and can receive multiple criteria to order by.

Ⓒ The `fetch` method will fetch the list of `User` instances.

Ⓓ Verify that the fetched data is the expected data.

The following SQL query is generated by Hibernate:

```
select
    *
from
    User user0_
order by
    user0_.username asc
```

19.3.3 Grouping data and working with aggregates

To group data, we'll use the `groupBy` method, which receives the expression to group by. Such a query will return a `List<Tuple>`. A `com.querydsl.core.Tuple` object is a key/value pair that contains the key to group by and its corresponding value. For example, the following code counts `Bid` instances grouped by `amount`.

Listing 19.13 Grouping bids by amount

Path: Ch19/querydsl/src/test/java/com/manning/javapersistence/querydsl
➥ /QuerydslTest.java

```
@Test
void testGroupByBidAmount() {

    NumberPath<Long> count = Expressions.numberPath(Long.class, "bids");    ← Ⓐ

    List<Tuple> userBidsGroupByAmount =
        queryFactory.select(QBid.bid.amount,
                            QBid.bid.id.count().as(count))
                .from(QBid.bid)
                .groupBy(QBid.bid.amount)
                .orderBy(count.desc())    ← Ⓔ
                .fetch();    ←
                                Ⓕ
    assertAll(
            () -> assertEquals(new BigDecimal("120.00"),
                    userBidsGroupByAmount.get(0).get(QBid.bid.amount)),
            () -> assertEquals(2, userBidsGroupByAmount.get(0).get(count))
    );

}
```
Ⓑ Ⓒ Ⓓ Ⓖ

Ⓐ Keep the `count()` expression, as we'll need it multiple times later when building the query.

Ⓑ Return a `List<Tuple>`, the key/value pairs with the key to group by and its corresponding value.

Ⓒ Select the `amount` and the count of the same `amounts` from `Bid`.

Ⓓ Group by the `amount` value.

Ⓔ Order by the count of records having the same amount.

Ⓕ Fetch the `List<Tuple>` objects.

Ⓖ Verify that the fetched data is the expected data.

The following SQL query is generated by Hibernate:

```
select
    bid0_.amount as col_0_0_,
    count(bid0_.id) as col_1_0_
from
    Bid bid0_
group by
    bid0_.amount
order by
    col_1_0_ desc
```

To work with aggregation and get the maximum, minimum, and average values of the `Bids`, we can use the `max`, `min`, and `avg` methods, as in the following code:

```
queryFactory.from(QBid.bid).select(QBid.bid.amount.max()).fetchOne();
queryFactory.from(QBid.bid).select(QBid.bid.amount.min()).fetchOne();
queryFactory.from(QBid.bid).select(QBid.bid.amount.avg()).fetchOne();
```

The following SQL queries are generated by Hibernate:

```
select
    max(bid0_.amount) as col_0_0_
    from
    Bid bid0_

    select
        min(bid0_.amount) as col_0_0_
    from
        Bid bid0_

    select
        avg(bid0_.amount) as col_0_0_ ·
    from
        Bid bid0_
```

19.3.4 *Working with subqueries and joins*

To work with subqueries, we'll create a subquery with the `JPAExpressions` static factory methods (such as `select`), and we'll define the query parameters using methods such as from and where. We'll pass the subquery to the where method of the main query. For example, the following listing selects the Users having Bids with a given amount.

Listing 19.14 Working with subqueries

Path: Ch19/querydsl/src/test/java/com/manning/javapersistence/querydsl
➡ /QuerydslTest.java

```
@Test
void testSubquery() {                                              Ⓐ

    List<User> users = queryFactory.selectFrom(QUser.user)   ←──┘
            .where(QUser.user.id.in(
                JPAExpressions.select(QBid.bid.user.id)
                    .from(QBid.bid)                                Ⓒ
                    .where(QBid.bid.amount.eq(
                            new BigDecimal("120.00")))))
        .fetch();          ←──Ⓓ
Ⓑ

    List<User> otherUsers = queryFactory.selectFrom(QUser.user)
            .where(QUser.user.id.in(
                JPAExpressions.select(QBid.bid.user.id)
                    .from(QBid.bid)                                Ⓔ
                    .where(QBid.bid.amount.eq(
                            new BigDecimal("105.00")))))
        .fetch();

    assertAll(
            () -> assertEquals(2, users.size()),
            () -> assertEquals(1, otherUsers.size()),             Ⓕ
            () -> assertEquals("burk", otherUsers.get(0).getUsername())
    );
}
```

Ⓐ Start building the query using the selectFrom method belonging to the JPAQuery-Factory class.

Ⓑ Pass the subquery as a parameter of the where method.

Ⓒ Create the subquery to get the Bids having amount 120.00.

Ⓓ Fetch the result.

Ⓔ Create a similar query and subquery for the Bids having amount 105.00.

Ⓕ Verify that the fetched data is as expected.

The following SQL query is generated by Hibernate:

```
select
    *
from
    User user0_
where
```

```
    user0_.id in (
        select
            bid1_.user_id
        from
            Bid bid1_
        where
            bid1_.amount=?
    )
```

To work with joins, we'll use the methods innerJoin, leftJoin, and outerJoin to define the join, and we'll use the on method to declare the condition (a Predicate) to join on.

Listing 19.15   Working with joins

Path: Ch19/querydsl/src/test/java/com/manning/javapersistence/querydsl
➥ /QuerydslTest.java

```
@Test
void testJoin() {                                                    Ⓐ

Ⓑ  List<User> users = queryFactory.selectFrom(QUser.user)           ⟵
           .innerJoin(QUser.user.bids, QBid.bid)
           .on(QBid.bid.amount.eq(new BigDecimal("120.00")))        ⟵ Ⓒ
Ⓓ ▷       .fetch();

    List<User> otherUsers = queryFactory.selectFrom(QUser.user)
           .innerJoin(QUser.user.bids, QBid.bid)                    Ⓔ
           .on(QBid.bid.amount.eq(new BigDecimal("105.00")))
           .fetch();

    assertAll(
           () -> assertEquals(2, users.size()),
           () -> assertEquals(1, otherUsers.size()),               Ⓕ
           () -> assertEquals("burk", otherUsers.get(0).getUsername())
    );
}
```

Ⓐ Start building the query using the selectFrom method belonging to the JPAQueryFactory class.

Ⓑ Make the inner join to Bids.

Ⓒ Define the join on condition as a Predicate to have the Bid amount 120.00.

Ⓓ Fetch the result.

Ⓔ Create a similar join for the Bids having amount 105.00.

Ⓕ Verify that the fetched data is as expected.

The following SQL query is generated by Hibernate:

```
select
    *
from
```

```
        User user0_
inner join
    Bid bids1_
        on user0_.id=bids1_.user_id
        and (
            bids1_.amount=?
        )
```

19.3.5 *Updating entities*

To update the entities, we'll use the `update` method of the `JPAQueryFactory` class, the `where` method to define the `Predicate` that will filter the entities to be updated (optional), the `set` method to define the changes to be made, and the `execute` method to effectively execute the update.

> **Listing 19.16   Updating the information**

```
Path: Ch19/querydsl/src/test/java/com/manning/javapersistence/querydsl
➡ /QuerydslTest.java

@Test
void testUpdate() {                              Ⓐ

    queryFactory.update(QUser.user)     ←⏋          Ⓑ
          .where(QUser.user.username.eq("john"))  ←⏋           Ⓒ
 Ⓓ       .set(QUser.user.email, "john@someotherdomain.com")   ←⏋
 └⏵      .execute();                           Ⓔ

    entityManager.getTransaction().commit();   ←⏋

    entityManager.getTransaction().begin();   ←Ⓕ

    assertEquals("john@someotherdomain.com",
            queryFactory.select(QUser.user.email)
                    .from(QUser.user)                    Ⓖ
                    .where(QUser.user.username.eq("john"))
                    .fetchOne());

}
```

Ⓐ Start building the query using the `update` method belonging to the `JPAQuery-Factory` class.

Ⓑ Define the `where` condition to update on (optional).

Ⓒ Define the changes to be made to the entities with the `set` method.

Ⓓ Effectively execute the update.

Ⓔ Commit the transaction that was started in the `@BeforeEach` annotated method.

Ⓕ Start a new transaction that will be committed in the `@AfterEach` annotated method.

Ⓖ Check the result of the update by fetching the modified entity.

The following SQL query is generated by Hibernate:

```
update
    User
set
    email=?
where
    username=?
```

19.3.6 *Deleting entities*

To delete entities, we'll use the `update` method of the `JPAQueryFactory` class, the `where` method to define the `Predicate` that will filter the entities to be deleted (optional), and the `execute` method to effectively execute the delete.

There's a big problem with Querydsl here. In the Querydsl reference documentation (http://querydsl.com/static/querydsl/latest/reference/html/), section 2.1.11 on `DELETE` queries using JPA notes, "DML clauses in JPA don't take JPA level cascade rules into account and don't provide fine-grained second level cache interaction." Therefore, the cascade attribute of the bids `@OneToMany` annotation in the `User` class is ignored; it is necessary to select a user and manually delete their bids before deleting it through a Querydsl delete query.

As an extra proof that the issue comes from Querydsl, if a user was to be deleted through a `userRepository.delete(burk);` instruction, the `@OneToMany` cascade attribute would be properly taken into account, and no manual handling of the user's bids would be needed.

> **Listing 19.17   Deleting the information**

Path: Ch19/querydsl/src/test/java/com/manning/javapersistence/querydsl
➥ /QuerydslTest.java

```
@Test
void testDelete() {

    User burk = (User) queryFactory.from(QUser.user)
                    .where(QUser.user.username.eq("burk"))      Ⓐ
                    .fetchOne();
    if (burk != null) {
        queryFactory.delete(QBid.bid)
                    .where(QBid.bid.user.eq(burk))              Ⓑ
                    .execute();
Ⓒ  }
                                                                Ⓓ
    queryFactory.delete(QUser.user)
                .where(QUser.user.username.eq("burk"))  ◄─┘
Ⓔ              .execute();
                                                        Ⓕ
    entityManager.getTransaction().commit();   ◄─┘
Ⓖ  entityManager.getTransaction().begin();
```

```
assertNull(queryFactory.selectFrom(QUser.user)
        .where(QUser.user.username.eq("burk"))
        .fetchOne());
```
ⓗ

```
}
```

Ⓐ Find user `burk`.

Ⓑ Delete the bids belonging to the previously found user.

Ⓒ Start building the query using the `delete` method belonging to the `JPAQueryFactory` class.

Ⓓ Define the `where` condition to delete on (optional).

Ⓔ Effectively execute the delete.

Ⓕ Commit the transaction that was started in the `@BeforeEach` annotated method.

Ⓖ Start a new transaction that will be committed in the `@AfterEach` annotated method. This is why in this listing a `commit` transaction appears before a `begin` transaction.

Ⓗ Check the result of the delete by trying to fetch the entity. If the entity no longer exists, the `fetchOne` method will return `null`.

The following SQL query is generated by Hibernate:

```
delete
from
    User
where
    username=?
```

This query is not enough if the `User` has child `Bids` that need to be deleted first. This reveals another problem specific to MySQL: when Hibernate creates the schema, no `ON DELETE CASCADE` clause is added when defining the foreign key constraint on the `user_id` column in the `bid` table. Otherwise, this single `DELETE` query would be sufficient regardless of Querydsl ignoring `@OneToMany` cascade attributes.

No insert capability is provided by the Querydsl API. For inserting entities, you may use an `EntityManager` (JPA), `Session` (Hibernate), or repository (Spring Data JPA).

Summary

- Query alternatives such as SQL, JPQL, Criteria API, Spring Data have drawbacks: lack of portability, lack of type safety and static query verification, and verboseness. Querydsl addresses the important ideas of type safety and portability, and it reduces the verboseness.

- You can create a persistence application to use Querydsl, define its configuration and entities, and persist and query data.

- To work with Querydsl, its dependencies need to be added to the application. The Maven APT (Annotation Processing Tool) is required for the creation, at build time, of the Q-types that replicate the entities.
- You can work with the core Querydsl classes, `JPAQueryFactory` and `JPAQuery`, to build the queries to retrieve, update, and delete data.
- You can create queries to filter, order, and group data and queries to execute joins, updates, and deletes.

Testing Java
persistence applications

This chapter covers

- Introducing the testing pyramid and examining persistence testing in its context
- Creating a persistence application to test using Spring Boot
- Using the Spring TestContext Framework
- Working with Spring profiles to test Java persistence applications
- Using execution listeners to test Java persistence applications

All code needs to be tested. During development, we code, compile, and run. When we run, we may sometimes test how our code works. Testing persistence applications involves more than this. In those cases, our code interacts with the external database, and how our program works may be dependent on it.

20.1 *Introducing the test pyramid*

In previous chapters, we focused on developing code that interacts with a database. We examined different alternatives for doing this, and different frameworks, and we interacted with various databases. Now we need to make sure that our programs are safe and bug-free. We need to be able to introduce changes without creating bugs, add new features without affecting the old features, and refactor code without breaking existing functionality. That is the purpose of this final chapter.

Applications can be tested manually, but nowadays most tests are executed automatically and they address different levels. The different levels of software tests for monolithic applications can be regarded as a pyramid, as shown in figure 20.1. We can define the following levels of software testing (from lowest to highest):

- *Unit testing*—Unit testing is at the foundation of the pyramid. It focuses on methods or classes (individual units) by testing each one in isolation to determine whether it works according to expectations.
- *Integration testing*—Individual, verified software components are combined in larger aggregates and tested together.
- *System testing*—Testing is performed on a complete system, to evaluate its compliance with the specification. System testing requires no knowledge of the design or code but focuses on the functionality of the entire system.
- *Acceptance testing*—Acceptance testing uses scenarios and test cases to check whether the application satisfies the expectations of the end user.

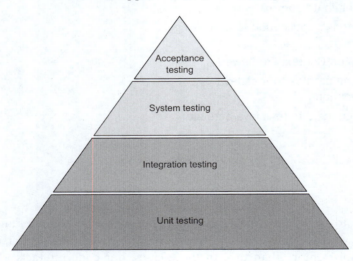

Figure 20.1   The testing pyramid has a larger bottom level (unit tests), while the higher testing levels are smaller. They start with checking individual units and go up to verifying how software addresses the user's needs.

Testing persistence applications belongs to the integration level. We combine our code with the database interaction, and we are dependent on how the database works. We would like to keep the behavior of our tests consistent between repeated test executions and to keep the content of the database the same as it was before running the tests. We'll examine the best ways to achieve these goals in the following sections.

20.2   *Creating the persistence application to test*

We'll create a Spring Boot persistence application so we can test its functionality. To do this, go to the Spring Initializr website (https://start.spring.io/) and create a new Spring Boot project (figure 20.2), having the following characteristics:

- Group: com.manning.javapersistence
- Artifact: testing
- Description: Persistence Testing

We'll also add the following dependencies:

- Spring Data JPA (this will add `spring-boot-starter-data-jpa` in the Maven pom.xml file).
- MySQL Driver (this will add `mysql-connector-java` in the Maven pom.xml file).
- Lombok (this will add `org.projectlombok,lombok` in the Maven pom.xml file).
- Bean Validation with Hibernate validator (this will add `spring-boot-starter-validation` in the Maven pom.xml file).
- The `spring-boot-starter-test` dependency will be automatically added.

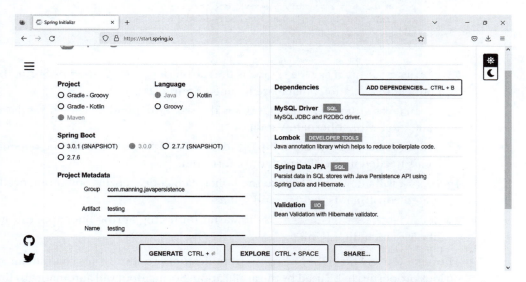

Figure 20.2   Creating a new Spring Boot project that will use a MySQL database through Spring Data JPA

NOTE   To execute the examples from the source code, you'll first need to run the Ch20.sql script.

The pom.xml file in the following listing includes the dependencies that we added when we created the Spring Boot project. We'll create a Spring persistence application that accesses a MySQL database, for which we'll need the driver and we'll also need to validate some fields.

Listing 20.1   The pom.xml Maven file

Path: Ch20/1 spring testing/pom.xml

```
<dependency>
    <groupId>org.springframework.boot</groupId>        Ⓐ
    <artifactId>spring-boot-starter-data-jpa</artifactId>
</dependency>
<dependency>
    <groupId>org.springframework.boot</groupId>        Ⓑ
    <artifactId>spring-boot-starter-validation</artifactId>
</dependency>
<dependency>
    <groupId>mysql</groupId>
    <artifactId>mysql-connector-java</artifactId>       Ⓒ
    <scope>runtime</scope>
</dependency>
<dependency>
    <groupId>org.projectlombok</groupId>
    <artifactId>lombok</artifactId>                     Ⓓ
    <optional>true</optional>
</dependency>
<dependency>
    <groupId>org.springframework.boot</groupId>
    <artifactId>spring-boot-starter-test</artifactId>   Ⓔ
    <scope>test</scope>
</dependency>
```

Ⓐ spring-boot-starter-data-jpa is the starter dependency used by Spring Boot to connect to a relational database through Spring Data JPA.

Ⓑ spring-boot-starter-validation is the starter dependency for using Java Bean Validation with Hibernate Validator.

Ⓒ mysql-connector-java is the JDBC driver for MySQL. It's a runtime dependency, so it's needed in the classpath only at runtime.

Ⓓ Lombok will allow us to reduce the boilerplate code, relying on automatically generated constructors, getters, and setters.

Ⓔ spring-boot-starter-test is the starter for testing Spring Boot applications with libraries including JUnit 5.

The next step is to fill in the Spring Boot application.properties file. This file can include various properties to be used by the application. Spring Boot will automatically find and load application.properties from the classpath; the src/main/resources folder is added by Maven to the classpath. For this chapter's demonstration, the application.properties configuration file will look like listing 20.2.

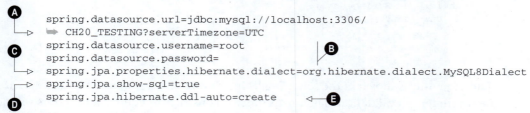

Listing 20.2 The application.properties file

Path: `Ch20/1 spring testing/src/main/resources/application.properties`

```
spring.datasource.url=jdbc:mysql://localhost:3306/
    CH20_TESTING?serverTimezone=UTC
spring.datasource.username=root
spring.datasource.password=
spring.jpa.properties.hibernate.dialect=org.hibernate.dialect.MySQL8Dialect
spring.jpa.show-sql=true
spring.jpa.hibernate.ddl-auto=create
```

Ⓐ The URL of the database.

Ⓑ The credentials to access the database. Replace them with the credentials on your machine, and use a password in real life.

Ⓒ The dialect of the database, MySQL.

Ⓓ Show the SQL queries while they are executed.

Ⓔ Recreate the tables for each execution of the application.

> **NOTE** There are several ways to provide parameters in a Spring Boot application, and the .properties file is just one of them. Among the alternatives, the parameters may come from the source code or as command-line arguments. Refer to the Spring Boot documentation for details.

The application that we'll test will include two entities, `User` and `Log`. The `User` entity is shown in the following listing. It will have a generated `id` and a `name` field with length validation. The no-arguments constructor, getters, and setters will be generated by Lombok.

Listing 20.3 The User class

Path: `Ch20/1 spring testing/src/main/java/com/manning/javapersistence`
`/testing/model/User.java`

```java
@Entity
@NoArgsConstructor
public class User {

    @Id
    @GeneratedValue
    @Getter
    private Long id;

    @NotNull
    @Size(
            min = 2,
            max = 255,
            message = "Name is required, maximum 255 characters."
    )
    @Getter
```

```
@Setter
private String name;

public User(String name) {
    this.name = name;
}

}
```

The `Log` entity is shown in the following listing. It will have a generated `id` and an `info` field with length validation. The no-arguments constructor, getters, and setters will be generated by Lombok.

Listing 20.4   The `Log` class

Path: Ch20/1 spring testing/src/main/java/com/manning/javapersistence
➥ /testing/model/Log.java

```
@Entity
@NoArgsConstructor
public class Log {

    @Id
    @GeneratedValue
    @Getter
    private Long id;

    @NotNull
    @Size(
            min = 2,
            max = 255,
            message = "Info is required, maximum 255 characters."
    )
    @Getter
    @Setter
    private String info;

    public Log(String info) {
        this.info = info;
    }
}
```

To manage the two entities, we'll create two repository interfaces to extend `JpaRepos-itory`: `UserRepository` and `LogRepository`:

```
public interface UserRepository extends JpaRepository<User, Long> {
}

public interface LogRepository extends JpaRepository<Log, Long> {

}
```

20.3 Using the Spring TestContext Framework

The Spring TestContext Framework is designed to provide integration testing support, so it is ideal for testing the persistence layer. It is agnostic of the testing framework we use with it, and we'll work with JUnit 5. We'll examine its essential classes and annotations, which belong to the `org.springframework.test.context` package.

The entry point into the Spring TestContext Framework is the `TestContext-Manager` class. Its goal is to manage a single `TestContext` and to send events to the registered listeners. We'll examine listeners in detail in section 20.8.

We'll write a first test that will save a `User` entity to the database and retrieve it again, using an injected `UserRepository`.

Listing 20.5 The `SaveRetrieveUserTest` class

Path: Ch20/1 spring testing/src/test/java/com/manning/javapersistence
➡ /testing/SaveRetrieveUserTest.java

```java
@SpringBootTest
class SaveRetrieveUserTest {

    @Autowired
    private UserRepository userRepository;

    @Test
    void saveRetrieve() {
        userRepository.save(new User("User1"));
        List<User> users = userRepository.findAll();

        assertAll(
                () -> assertEquals(1, users.size()),
                () -> assertEquals("User1", users.get(0).getName())
        );
    }

}
```

If we repeatedly run this test several times, it will always succeed, so we might try to modify it and annotate the `saveRetrieve` test method with the `@RepeatedTest(2)` JUnit 5 annotation. This will run it twice in one execution of the class. The modified test will look like the following listing.

Listing 20.6 The `SaveRetrieveUserTest` class using `@RepeatedTest`

Path: Ch20/1 spring testing/src/test/java/com/manning/javapersistence
➡ /testing/SaveRetrieveUserTest.java

```java
@SpringBootTest
class SaveRetrieveUserTest {

    @Autowired
```

```
    private UserRepository userRepository;

    @RepeatedTest(2)
    void saveRetrieve() {
        userRepository.save(new User("User1"));
        List<User> users = userRepository.findAll();

        assertAll(
                () -> assertEquals(1, users.size()),
                () -> assertEquals("User1", users.get(0).getName())
        );
    }

}
```

Let's run the modified test now. Surprising or not, it will succeed for the first execution and will fail for the second, getting two Users from the database instead of one (see figure 20.3).

Figure 20.3   The @RepeatedTest will succeed the first time and will fail the second time, as the database was left dirty after the execution of the first test.

This happens because the row that was inserted by the execution of the first test was not removed, and the second test found it in the table, adding one more. We can follow the SQL commands that are executed when the class is run.

Before running the two tests, the SQL commands that are executed deal with the (re)creation of tables:

```
drop table if exists hibernate_sequence
drop table if exists log
drop table if exists user
```

```
create table hibernate_sequence (next_val bigint)
insert into hibernate_sequence values ( 1 )
create table log (id bigint not null, info varchar(255) not null,
➡ primary key (id))
create table user (id bigint not null, name varchar(255) not null,
➡ primary key (id))
```

Before running each test, the following SQL commands are executed, inserting a new row into the table:

```
select next_val as id_val from hibernate_sequence for update
update hibernate_sequence set next_val= ? where next_val=?
insert into user (name, id) values (?, ?)
select user0_.id as id1_1_, user0_.name as name2_1_ from user user0_
```

The execution of the second test will find an existing row in the table, will add a new one, and so will fail because it expects to find a single row. We'll have to look for alternatives to leave the content of the database at the end of each test the same as it was before running it.

20.4   The @DirtiesContext annotation

One alternative, provided by the Spring TestContext Framework, is to use the @DirtiesContext annotation. @DirtiesContext acknowledges that the test method or the test class changes the Spring context, and the Spring TestContext Framework will recreate it from scratch and provide it to the next test. The annotation can be applied to a method or a class. Its effects can be applied before or after the execution of each test method, or before or after the execution of the test class.

We'll modify the test class as shown in the following listing.

Listing 20.7   The `SaveRetrieveUserTest` class using `@DirtiesContext`

Path: Ch20/1 spring testing/src/test/java/com/manning/javapersistence
➡ /testing/SaveRetrieveUserTest.java

```
@SpringBootTest
@DirtiesContext(classMode =                                    Ⓐ
➡ DirtiesContext.ClassMode.AFTER_EACH_TEST_METHOD)   ←─┐
class SaveRetrieveUserTest {

    @Autowired
    private UserRepository userRepository;

    @RepeatedTest(2)
    void saveRetrieve() {
        // . . .
    }

}
```

Ⓐ Recreate the Spring context after the execution of each test method.

If we run the modified test now, it will succeed for the first and second executions (see figure 20.4). This means that after running the first test, the execution of the second test will no longer encounter a dirtied database.

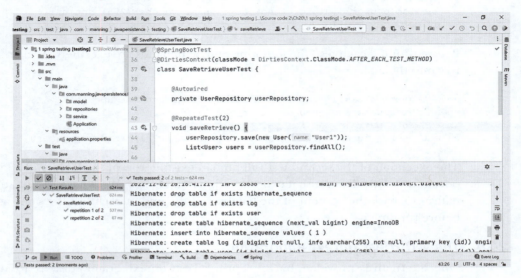

Figure 20.4   The @DirtiesContext annotated test will succeed both the first and second time.

Before running each test, the SQL commands that are executed deal with both the (re)creation of tables and inserting a row in the table:

```
drop table if exists hibernate_sequence
drop table if exists log
drop table if exists user
create table hibernate_sequence (next_val bigint)
insert into hibernate_sequence values ( 1 )
create table log (id bigint not null, info varchar(255) not null,
➡ primary key (id))
create table user (id bigint not null, name varchar(255) not null,
➡ primary key (id))
select next_val as id_val from hibernate_sequence for update
update hibernate_sequence set next_val= ? where next_val=?
insert into user (name, id) values (?, ?)
select user0_.id as id1_1_, user0_.name as name2_1_ from user user0_
```

These commands are executed twice, once before each test. More than this, the Spring Boot banner (also displayed at the bottom of figure 20.4) will be shown twice as well—once each time the application is started.

The functionality of the @DirtiesContext annotation at the method level is demonstrated in figure 20.5.

This solution works, but it comes with a performance cost related to the recreation of tables and reinitialization of the application for each test execution. Let's explore more alternatives.

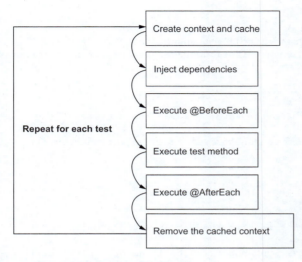

Figure 20.5   The `@DirtiesContext` annotation at the method level will create the context and cache before the execution of each test method and will remove them after the execution.

20.5   *@Transactional execution*

We examined transactions in detail in chapter 11. Transactions control atomic groups of operations that either fully succeed or fully fail. Managing transactions with Spring and Spring Data and the `@Transactional` annotation were detailed in section 11.4. The idea that we'll apply now is to run each test transactionally and to roll back the transaction at the end of the execution.

By default, when executing a test, our transactions will automatically be rolled back due to the `TransactionalTestExecutionListener`. We'll deal in detail with listeners in section 20.8; for now, just note that they can provide some additional action at the execution of a test. The default behavior can be modified with the help of the `@Commit` and `@Rollback` annotations. So if we want a test to commit at the end of the execution, we can annotate it either with `@Commit` or with `@Rollback(false)`.

To keep track of when a transaction is active during the execution of a test, we'll use the `TransactionSynchronizationManager` class. This class manages resources and transaction synchronizations for a thread. Its `isActualTransactionActive()` method will check whether a `Transaction` object is currently active.

In the following listing, we'll create a test class, annotate it with `@Transactional`, and follow the status of the transaction inside the methods of the class.

Listing 20.8   The `TransactionalTest` class

Path: Ch20/1 spring testing/src/test/java/com/manning/javapersistence
➡ /testing/TransactionalTest.java

```
@SpringBootTest
@Transactional
class TransactionalTest {

    // . . .
```

```
@BeforeAll
static void beforeAll() {
    System.out.println("beforeAll, transaction active = " +
            TransactionSynchronizationManager.isActualTransactionActive());
}

@BeforeEach
void beforeEach() {
    System.out.println("beforeEach, transaction active = " +

 TransactionSynchronizationManager.isActualTransactionActive());
}


@RepeatedTest(2)
void storeRetrieve() {
    // . . .
    System.out.println("end of method, transaction active = " +

 TransactionSynchronizationManager.isActualTransactionActive());
}

@AfterEach
void afterEach() {
    System.out.println("afterEach, transaction active = " +

 TransactionSynchronizationManager.isActualTransactionActive());
}

@AfterAll
static void afterAll() {
    System.out.println("afterAll, transaction active = " +

 TransactionSynchronizationManager.isActualTransactionActive());
}

}
```

The log of the execution will tell us that the transaction is not active in the `@BeforeAll` and `@AfterAll` methods, but it is active in the `@BeforeEach` and `@AfterEach` methods and inside the test method itself. As previously stated, the transaction will be rolled back by default at the end of the test, so `@RepeatedTest` will succeed for all executions:

```
beforeAll, transaction active = false
beforeEach, transaction active = true
end of method, transaction active = true
afterEach, transaction active = true
beforeEach, transaction active = true
end of method, transaction active = true
afterEach, transaction active = true
afterAll, transaction active = false
```

There is still a pitfall of this approach that we will demonstrate. We introduced a separate `UserService` class with a transactional method, as shown in the following listing.

> **Listing 20.9   The `UserService` class**

Path: Ch20/1 spring testing/src/main/java/com/manning/javapersistence
➡ /testing/service/UserService.java

```
@Service
public class UserService {

    @Autowired
    private UserRepository userRepository;

    @Transactional
    public void saveTransactionally(User user) {
        userRepository.save(user);
    }
}
```

We'll call this method from inside the @RepeatedTest from the TransactionalTest
class, to persist a user in a transactional way.

> **Listing 20.10   Calling the `saveTransactionally` method**

Path: Ch20/1 spring testing/src/test/java/com/manning/javapersistence
➡ /testing/TransactionalTest.java

```
@SpringBootTest
@Transactional
class TransactionalTest {

    // . . .

    @RepeatedTest(2)
    void storeRetrieve() {
        List<User> users = buildUsersList();
        userRepository.saveAll(users);
        assertEquals(getIterations(), userRepository.findAll().size());

        userService.saveTransactionally(users.get(0));

        System.out.println("end of method, transaction active = " +

    TransactionSynchronizationManager.isActualTransactionActive());
    }

    // . . .

}
```

The saveTransactionally method from UserService has the annotation @Transac-
tional with no other argument. The default propagation is REQUIRED (see section
11.4). As there is already a transaction running for the test, the saveTransactionally
method will execute within the same transaction, and everything will be rolled back at
the end of the test.

We can change the `saveTransactionally` method annotation to be `@Transac-tional(propagation = Propagation.REQUIRES_NEW)`. This will suspend the transaction executed in the test, start a new transaction, and commit it, as figure 20.6 shows.

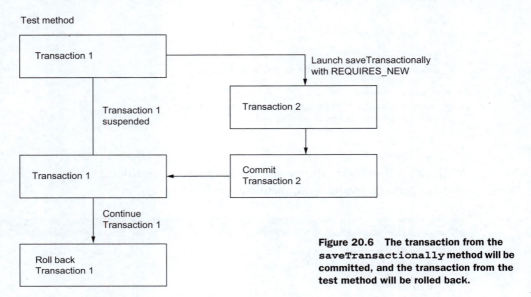

Figure 20.6   The transaction from the `saveTransactionally` method will be committed, and the transaction from the test method will be rolled back.

The transaction from `saveTransactionally` was committed. As a consequence, running the test for a second time will encounter an existing record in the database, and the test will fail (see figure 20.7).

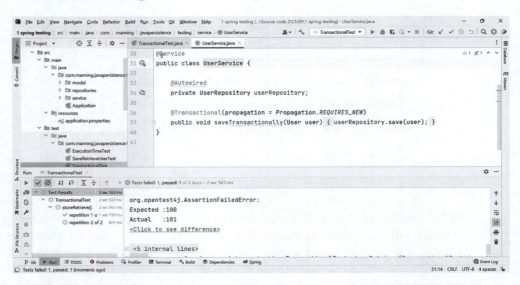

Figure 20.7   Running two tests in a row while the `saveTransactionally` method commits its transaction separately will make the second test fail.

The conclusion is that even if you run your tests transactionally, beware of the pitfall of launching methods in separate transactions. It can lead to strange bugs. Also, debugging might be difficult with this approach.

To make a performance comparison between using `@DirtiesContext` and using `@Transactional`, we executed a series of 10 tests, progressively increasing the number of records from 100 to 2,000. The results on MySQL are provided in figure 20.8.

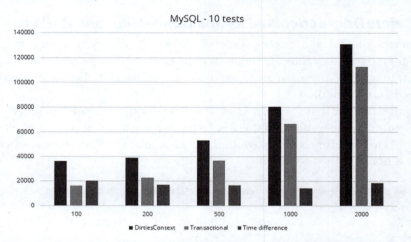

Figure 20.8 The execution times (in ms) on MySQL using `@DirtiesContext` and `@Transactional` and varying the number of records from 100 to 2,000

The results on H2 are provided in figure 20.9. We executed the same series of 10 tests using this in-memory database, progressively increasing the number of records from 100 to 2,000.

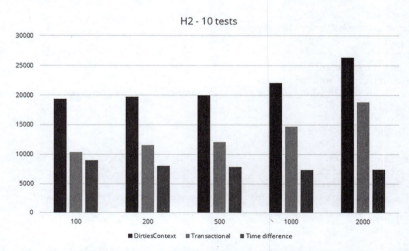

Figure 20.9 The execution times (in ms) on H2 using `@DirtiesContext` and `@Transactional` and varying the number of records from 100 to 2,000

Analyzing the results for both MySQL and H2, we can see that the difference between the execution with @DirtiesContext and with @Transactional is approximately constant. It does not depend on the number of records, but on the number of times the context is reinitialized. The conclusion is that you should use @DirtiesContext sparingly. Pushing tests with this annotation to the CI/CD (continuous integration/continuous development) environment will seriously increase the time of their execution.

20.6   *The @BeforeTransaction and @AfterTransaction annotations*

We'll now examine the @BeforeTransaction and @AfterTransaction annotations. As their names suggest, they indicate methods to be executed before and after the execution of a transaction. For our analysis, we'll check that, indeed, there is no transaction active inside such a method.

Using the Assumptions.assumeFalse JUnit 5 method, we'll indicate that a precondition for running the tests is that there is no transaction active at that moment; otherwise the tests will not run. So if an assumption is not met, the test will be aborted. If an assertion is not met, the test will fail.

Listing 20.11   Using @BeforeTransaction and @AfterTransaction

Path: Ch20/1 spring testing/src/test/java/com/manning/javapersistence
➥ /testing/TransactionsManagementTest.java

```
@SpringBootTest
@Transactional
class TransactionsManagementTest {

    @Autowired
    private UserRepository userRepository;

    @Autowired
    private LogRepository logRepository;

    @BeforeTransaction
    void beforeTransaction() {
        Assumptions.assumeFalse(
            TransactionSynchronizationManager.isActualTransactionActive());
    }

    // . . .

    @AfterTransaction
    void afterTransaction() {
        Assumptions.assumeFalse(
            TransactionSynchronizationManager.isActualTransactionActive());

    }

}
```

There is still one pitfall to avoid here: the possibility of persisting data in the `@Before-Transaction` or `@AfterTransaction` methods. Because these are executed outside transactions, data will not be rolled back and will affect the content of the database. Even more, if we persist data that we do not check in the tests (for example, `Log` entities, while our tests verify `User` entities), our tests will always execute correctly but will leave committed data behind them, as happens in the following listing.

Listing 20.12 Persisting entities in `@BeforeTransaction`/`@AfterTransaction`

Path: Ch20/1 spring testing/src/test/java/com/manning/javapersistence
➡ /testing/TransactionsManagementTest.java

```
@SpringBootTest
@Transactional
class TransactionsManagementTest {

    @Autowired
    private UserRepository userRepository;

    @Autowired
    private LogRepository logRepository;

    @BeforeTransaction
    void beforeTransaction() {
        Assumptions.assumeFalse(
            TransactionSynchronizationManager.isActualTransactionActive());
        logRepository.save(new Log("@BeforeTransaction"));
    }

    // . . .

    @AfterTransaction
    void afterTransaction() {
        Assumptions.assumeFalse(
            TransactionSynchronizationManager.isActualTransactionActive());
        logRepository.save(new Log("@AfterTransaction"));
    }

}
```

20.7 Working with Spring profiles

By default, Spring Boot creates a main/resources/application.properties file to keep the configuration of the application. But there are frequent situations where we'll need to differentiate between properties depending on a user's profile. Spring Boot will allow us to separate the properties in this case, in files named, by default, main/resources/application-profilename.properties, and it will allow us to switch between profiles.

A real-life use case would be when you have a profile for programmers, using an embedded database during development, and another profile for production, using a real database. Programmers would like to be able to quickly execute their tests, while in production the tests will run in the real environment.

The configuration for development is shown in the following listing. It addresses an H2 database and will display SQL queries during execution, because the programmer is interested in following them.

Listing 20.13   The application-dev.properties file

```
Path: Ch20/2 spring profiles/src/main/resources
➡ /application-dev.properties

spring.datasource.url=jdbc:h2:mem:ch20_testing
spring.datasource.username=sa
spring.datasource.password=
spring.jpa.properties.hibernate.dialect=org.hibernate.dialect.H2Dialect
spring.jpa.show-sql=true
spring.jpa.hibernate.ddl-auto=create
```

The configuration for production is shown in the following listing. It addresses a MySQL database and will not display the SQL queries during execution, as this would consume resources in production.

Listing 20.14   The application-prod.properties file

```
Path: Ch20/2 spring profiles/src/main/resources
➡ /application-prod.properties

spring.datasource.url=
➡ jdbc:mysql://localhost:3306/CH20_TESTING?serverTimezone=UTC
spring.datasource.username=root
spring.datasource.password=
spring.jpa.properties.hibernate.dialect=org.hibernate.dialect.MySQL8Dialect
spring.jpa.show-sql=false
spring.jpa.hibernate.ddl-auto=create
```

To run the tests on the H2 database during development, we'll have to choose the dev profile. This can be done, for example, from within the application.properties file.

Listing 20.15   The application.properties file with the dev profile

```
Path: Ch20/2 spring profiles/src/main/resources/application.properties

spring.profiles.active=dev
```

To demonstrate how to easy it is to switch between profiles, we'll run one test that will save and retrieve an entity from the database.

Listing 20.16   The `SpringProfilesTest` class

```
Path: Ch20/2 spring profiles/src/test/java/com/manning/javapersistence
➥ /testing/SpringProfilesTest.java

@SpringBootTest
@Transactional
class SpringProfilesTest {

    @Autowired
    private UserRepository userRepository;

    @Test
    void storeUpdateRetrieve() {
        List<User> users = buildUsersList();
        userRepository.saveAll(users);

        assertEquals(getIterations(), userRepository.findAll().size());
    }

}
```

To successfully run this test, we'll need to have the H2 driver dependency in the pom.xml file.

Listing 20.17   The pom.xml file with the H2 driver dependency

```
Path: Ch20/2 spring profiles/pom.xml

<dependency>
    <groupId>com.h2database</groupId>
    <artifactId>h2</artifactId>
    <version>1.4.200</version>
    <scope>runtime</scope>
</dependency>
```

The result of running the test on the dev profile is shown in figure 20.10: the dev profile uses the in-memory H2 database.

To run the tests on the MySQL database in production, we'll have to choose the prod profile. This can be done, for example, from within the application.properties file.

Listing 20.18   The application.properties file with the prod profile

```
Path: Ch20/2 spring profiles/src/main/resources/application.properties

spring.profiles.active=prod
```

As an alternative to modifying the active profile, we can use the `@ActiveProfiles` annotation at the level of the test, as shown in listing 20.19. This annotation will

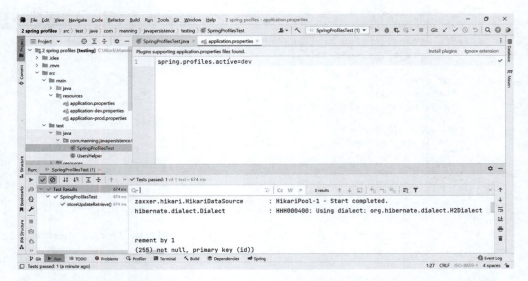

Figure 20.10   The result of running the test on the `dev` profile, using an H2 database and displaying the execution of the SQL queries

override the profile that is set in application.properties, but it will require us to modify and recompile the code.

Listing 20.19   The `SpringProfilesTest` class

Path: Ch20/2 spring profiles/src/test/java/com/manning/javapersistence
➥ /testing/SpringProfilesTest.java

```
@SpringBootTest
@Transactional
@ActiveProfiles("prod")
class SpringProfilesTest {
    // . . .
}
```

To successfully run this test, we'll need to have the MySQL driver dependency in the pom.xml file.

Listing 20.20   The pom.xml file with the MySQL driver dependency

Path: Ch20/2 spring profiles/pom.xml

```
<dependency>
    <groupId>mysql</groupId>
    <artifactId>mysql-connector-java</artifactId>
    <scope>runtime</scope>
</dependency>
```

The result of running the test on the prod profile is shown in figure 20.11. Unlike the dev profile, this profile uses the MySQL database.

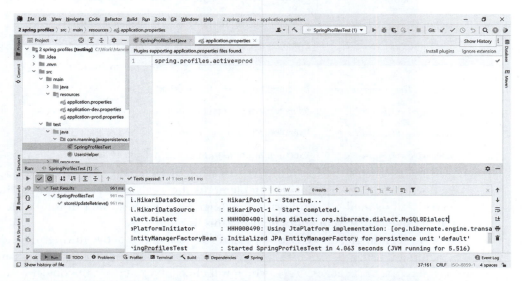

Figure 20.11   The result of running the test on the prod profile, using a MySQL database and not displaying the execution of the SQL queries

20.8   *Working with test execution listeners*

One way to control the lifecycle of a test's execution is to work with the JUnit 5 annotations: @BeforeAll, @AfterAll, @BeforeEach, and @AfterEach. This may be inconvenient in some situations. For example, if we need the same @BeforeEach and @AfterEach behavior for several tests, we would need to create a base class containing these methods and to create multiple subclasses that will inherit and execute them when running the tests. This has the inconvenience of hanging our tests in a hierarchy of classes. Alternatively, we can consider working with test execution listeners, with the TestExecutionListener interface, and with the @TestExecutionListeners annotation, thus separating the behavior that controls the lifecycle of the test.

By default, Spring provides some already implemented TestExecutionListeners for each test. The ones of most interest to us here are DependencyInjectionTestExecutionListener, which supports dependency injection for the test instance, and TransactionalTestExecutionListener, which supports the transactional execution of a test with rollback. We mentioned in section 20.3.2 that, by default, when executing a test, the transaction will automatically be rolled back due to the TransactionalTestExecutionListener—this is essential when testing persistence and striving to leave a clean database after executing the tests.

The TestExecutionListener interface defines a series of empty default methods that are more fine-grained than the JUnit 5 lifecycle methods, and that are executed in the order shown in table 20.1.

Table 20.1   The default methods from the `TestExecutionListener` interface

Method	Description
beforeTestClass	Executed before the @BeforeAll method of JUnit 5
prepareTestInstance	Prepares the test instance of the supplied test context
beforeTestMethod	Executed before the @BeforeEach method of JUnit 5
beforeTestExecution	Executed before the test method
afterTestExecution	Executed after the test method
afterTestMethod	Executed after the @AfterEach method of JUnit 5
afterTestClass	Executed after the @AfterAll method of JUnit 5

We'll write our own listener that implements the `TestExecutionListener` interface, override all its methods, and print a message from each, so we can follow the execution of the test that we'll annotate using this listener.

As in section 20.3.2, we'll follow when a transaction is active during the execution of a test by using the `TransactionSynchronizationManager` class and its method `isActualTransactionActive()`, which will check if a `Transaction` object is currently active. Our listener is shown in the following listing.

Listing 20.21   The `DatabaseOperationsListener` class

Path: Ch20/3 spring listeners/src/test/java/com/manning/javapersistence
➥ /testing/listeners/DatabaseOperationsListener.java

```
public class DatabaseOperationsListener implements TestExecutionListener {

    @Override
    public void beforeTestClass(TestContext testContext) {
        System.out.println("beforeTestClass, transaction active = " +
            TransactionSynchronizationManager.isActualTransactionActive());
    }

    @Override
    public void afterTestClass(TestContext testContext) {
        System.out.println("afterTestClass, transaction active = " +
            TransactionSynchronizationManager.isActualTransactionActive());
    }

    @Override
    public void beforeTestMethod(TestContext testContext) {
        System.out.println("beforeTestMethod, transaction active = " +
            TransactionSynchronizationManager.isActualTransactionActive());
    }

    @Override
    public void afterTestMethod(TestContext testContext) {
```

```
        System.out.println("afterTestMethod, transaction active = " +
            TransactionSynchronizationManager.isActualTransactionActive());
    }

    @Override
    public void beforeTestExecution(TestContext testContext) {
        System.out.println("beforeTestExecution, transaction active = " +
            TransactionSynchronizationManager.isActualTransactionActive());
    }

    @Override
    public void afterTestExecution(TestContext testContext) {
        System.out.println("afterTestExecution, transaction active = " +
            TransactionSynchronizationManager.isActualTransactionActive());
    }

    @Override
    public void prepareTestInstance(TestContext testContext) {
        System.out.println("prepareTestInstance, transaction active = " +
            TransactionSynchronizationManager.isActualTransactionActive());
    }

}
```

We'll create our own test, annotate it to use the new DatabaseOperationsListener, and print messages from the lifecycle methods and the test itself, to follow its execution.

Listing 20.22 The ListenersTest class

Path: Ch20/3 spring listeners/src/test/java/com/manning/javapersistence
➥ /testing/ListenersTest.java

```
@SpringBootTest
@Transactional
@TestExecutionListeners(value = {DatabaseOperationsListener.class})
class ListenersTest {

    @Autowired
    private UserRepository userRepository;

    @BeforeAll
    static void beforeAll() {
        System.out.println("@BeforeAll");
    }

    @BeforeEach
    void beforeEach() {
        System.out.println("@BeforeEach");
    }

    @Test
    void storeUpdateRetrieve() {
        TestContextManager testContextManager = new
                        TestContextManager(getClass());
```

```
        System.out.println(
            "testContextManager.getTestExecutionListeners().size() = "
          + testContextManager.getTestExecutionListeners().size());
        List<User> users = buildUsersList();
        userRepository.saveAll(users);
        assertEquals(getIterations(), userRepository.findAll().size());

    }

    @AfterEach
    void afterEach() {
        System.out.println("@AfterEach");
    }

    @AfterAll
    static void afterAll() {
        System.out.println("@AfterAll");
    }

}
```

If we run this test now, it will fail with `NullPointerException`, as in figure 20.12.

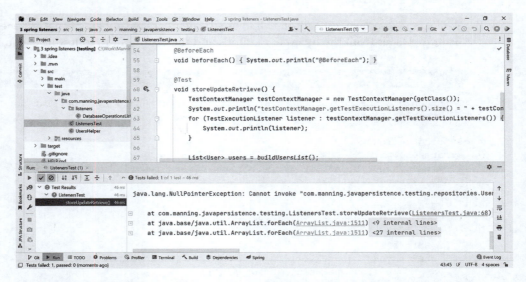

Figure 20.12   The test initially annotated with our custom listener fails with `NullPointerException`.

If we examine what is happening, we'll notice that the `userRepository` reference to the object that interacts with the database is `null`. As the messages from the console demonstrate, there is only one listener registered in the `TestContextManager`, our `DatabaseOperationsListener`. The previously needed `DependencyInjectionTest-ExecutionListener`, which supports dependency injection for the test instance, and consequently for the userRepository, is no longer registered. This is because, once we introduce our own listeners, the default listeners are no longer automatically registered.

To fix this, we'll use the MERGE_WITH_DEFAULTS option as merge mode, as follows.

Listing 20.23   Merging the default listeners with our custom listener

```
Path: Ch20/3 spring listeners/src/test/java/com/manning/javapersistence
➥ /testing/ListenersTest.java

@SpringBootTest
@Transactional
@TestExecutionListeners(value = {
        DatabaseOperationsListener.class}, mergeMode =
            TestExecutionListeners.MergeMode.MERGE_WITH_DEFAULTS)
class ListenersTest {
        // . . .
}
```

If we run the test again now, we'll be able to follow the sequence of the methods' execution, both from the listener and from the lifecycle methods of JUnit 5. We'll also notice that the number of registered listeners is now 15, meaning 14 default listeners and our custom listener:

```
beforeTestClass, transaction active = false
@BeforeAll
prepareTestInstance, transaction active = false
beforeTestMethod, transaction active = true
@BeforeEach
beforeTestExecution, transaction active = true
testContextManager.getTestExecutionListeners().size() = 15
afterTestExecution, transaction active = true
@AfterEach
afterTestMethod, transaction active = true
@AfterAll
afterTestClass, transaction active = false
```

Table 20.2 summarizes the most important annotations from the Spring TestContext Framework, to be used in testing persistence applications. You will be able to use these annotations from the Spring TestContext Framework for your persistence applications. This framework provides strong support for integration testing, to which persistence application testing belongs. On this base, you can continue to build system tests and acceptance tests, as we demonstrated at the beginning of this chapter when we introduced the testing pyramid. For more information about testing Java applications in general and about acceptance tests in particular, you can refer to my book *JUnit in Action*, third edition (Tudose, 2020).

With predictable and safe tests that fail only when there are problems in your code and not due to external factors (such as inappropriate content in a dirtied database), your life as a programmer will be much better!

Table 20.2   The most important Spring TestContext Framework annotations to be used in testing persistence applications

Annotation	Description
@DirtiesContext	The underlying Spring context was changed during the execution of a test and should be reinitialized.
@BeforeTransaction	The void method should be executed before any method having the Spring @Transactional annotation.
@AfterTransaction	The void method should be executed after any method having the Spring @Transactional annotation.
@Rollback	The transaction for a transactional test will be rolled back after the test completes. This is the default behavior and may be changed using @Rollback(false) or @Commit.
@Commit	The transaction for a transactional test will be committed after the test completes.
@ActiveProfiles	Specifies which configuration profiles will be active in the Spring context.
@TestExecutionListeners	Configures the test execution listeners to be registered with the TestContextManager.

Summary

- The testing pyramid consists of the unit, integration, system, and acceptance levels. Persistence testing can be classified at the integration level.
- You can create and configure a persistence application using Spring Boot and manage entities and repositories inside it.
- You can use the Spring TestContext Framework to create persistence tests and manage them using either @DirtiesContext or @Transactional.
- You can use Spring profiles to test Java persistence applications that access various databases and have different configurations.
- You can create a custom test execution listener to follow the lifecycle of a test and work with it and with the default listeners.

appendix A
Maven

Maven (https://maven.apache.org) can be regarded as a source-building *environment*. To better understand how Maven works, you need to understand the key points (principles) that stand behind Maven. From the very beginning of the Maven project, certain ground rules were created for software architecture. These rules aimed to simplify development with Maven and make it easier for developers to implement the build system.

One of the fundamental ideas of Maven is that the build system should be as simple as possible: software engineers should not spend a lot of time implementing the build system. It should be easy to start a new project from scratch and then to rapidly begin developing the software. This appendix describes the core Maven principles in detail and explains what they mean from a developer's point of view.

A.1 Convention over configuration

Convention over configuration is a software design principle that aims to decrease the number of configurations a software engineer needs to make, instead of introducing conventional rules that we must follow strictly. This way, we can skip tedious project configuration and focus on the more important parts of our work.

Convention over configuration is one of the strongest principles of the Maven project. One example of its application is the folder structure for the build process. With Maven, all the directories we need are already defined for us. src/main/java/, for example, is the Maven convention for where Java code for the project resides, src/test/java is where the unit tests for the project reside, target is the build folder, and so on.

That sounds great, but aren't we losing the flexibility in the project? What if we want our source code to reside in another folder? Maven is easy to configure: it provides the convention, but we can override the convention at any point and use the configuration of our choice.

A.2   Strong dependency management

Strong dependency management is the second key point that Maven introduced. When the Maven project began, the de facto build system for Java projects was another build tool, Ant. With Ant, we have to distribute the dependencies of our project, which means each project must take care of the dependencies it requires, and the dependencies of a single project may be distributed across different locations. Also, the same dependency may be used by different projects but located in different places for each project, causing duplication of resources.

Maven introduced the notion of a *central repository*: a location on the internet where all kinds of artifacts (dependencies) are stored. The Maven build tool resolves these artifacts by reading a project's build descriptor, downloading the necessary versions of the artifacts, and including them in the classpath of the application. This way, we need to list our dependencies only once, in the dependencies section of our build descriptor. Here's an example:

```
<dependencies>
    <dependency>
        <groupId>mysql</groupId>
        <artifactId>mysql-connector-java</artifactId>
        <version>8.0.29</version>
    </dependency>
    <dependency>
        <groupId>org.springframework.data</groupId>
        <artifactId>spring-data-jpa</artifactId>
        <version>2.7.0</version>
    </dependency>
</dependencies>
```

Thereafter, we are free to build the software on any other machine. We don't need to bundle the dependencies with our project.

Maven also introduced the concept of the local repository: a folder on a hard disk (~/.m2/repository/ in UNIX and C:\Users\<UserName>\.m2\repository\ in Windows) where Maven keeps the artifacts that it downloads from the central repository. After we build our project, our artifacts are installed in the local repository for later use by other projects, which is simple and neat.

A developer might join a project managed by Maven and need access only to the sources of the project. Maven downloads the needed dependencies from the central repository and brings them to the local repository, where they will be available for other projects that the same developer may work on.

A.3   Maven build lifecycles

Another very strong principle in Maven is the *build lifecycle*. A Maven project is built around the idea of defining the process of building, testing, and distributing a particular artifact. A Maven project can produce only one artifact. This way, we can use

Maven to build the project artifact, clean the project's folder structure, or generate the project documentation. These are the three built-in Maven lifecycles:

- *Default*—For generating the project artifact
- *Clean*—For cleaning the project
- *Site*—For generating the project documentation

Each of these lifecycles is composed of several phases. To navigate a certain lifecycle, the build follows its phases (see figure A.1).

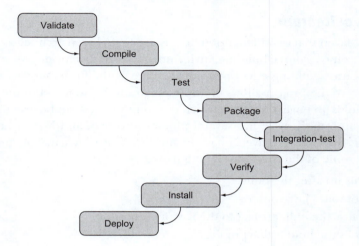

Figure A.1 The phases of Maven's default lifecycle, from validate to deploy

These are the phases of the default lifecycle:

1. *Validate*—Validate that the project is correct and all necessary information is available.
2. *Compile*—Compile the source code of the project.
3. *Test*—Test the compiled source code using a suitable unit testing framework (perhaps JUnit 5, in this case). The test should not require the code to be packaged or deployed.
4. *Package*—Package the compiled code in its distributable format, such as a .jar file.
5. *Integration-test*—Process and deploy the package (if necessary) into an environment where integration tests can be run.
6. *Verify*—Run any checks to verify that the package is valid and meets quality criteria.
7. *Install*—Install the package in the local repository for use as a dependency in other projects locally.
8. *Deploy*—In an integration or release environment, copy the final package to the remote repository for sharing with other developers and projects.

Here, again, is the convention-over-configuration principle promoted by Maven. These phases are already defined in the order in which they are listed here. Maven invokes these phases in a very strict order; the phases are executed sequentially, in the order in which they are listed here, to complete the lifecycle. If we invoke any of these phases—if we type `mvn compile` on the command line in our project home directory, for example—Maven first validates the project and then tries to compile the sources of the project.

One last thing: it is useful to think of all these phases as extension points. We can attach additional Maven plugins to the phases and orchestrate the order and how these plugins are executed.

A.4   *Plugin-based architecture*

The last feature of Maven that we will mention here is its plugin-based architecture. We mentioned that Maven is a source-building environment. More specifically, Maven is a plugin-execution source-building environment. The core of the project is very small, but the architecture of the project allows multiple plugins to be attached to the core. This way, Maven builds an environment in which different plugins can be executed.

Each phase in a given lifecycle has several plugins attached, and Maven invokes them when passing through the given phase in the order in which the plugins are declared. Here are some of the core Maven plugins:

- *Clean*—Cleans up after the build
- *Compiler*—Compiles Java sources
- *Deploy*—Deploys the built artifact to the remote repository
- *Install*—Installs the built artifact in the local repository
- *Resources*—Copies the resources to the output directory for inclusion in the .jar file
- *Site*—Generates a site that includes information about the current project
- *Surefire*—Runs the JUnit tests in an isolated classloader
- *Verifier*—Verifies the existence of certain conditions (useful for integration tests)

In addition to these core Maven plugins, other Maven plugins are available for many situations, such as WAR (for packaging a web application) and Javadoc (for generating project documentation).

Plugins are declared in the `plugins` section of the build configuration file, as in this example:

```
<build>
    <plugins>
        <plugin>
            <artifactId>maven-surefire-plugin</artifactId>
            <version>2.22.2</version>
        </plugin>
    </plugins>
</build>
```

A plugin declaration can have a `groupId`, `artifactId`, and `version`. This way, the plugins look like dependencies. In fact, plugins are handled the same way as dependencies; they are downloaded to the local repository like dependencies. When we specify a plugin, the `groupId` and `version` parameters are optional; if we do not declare them, Maven looks for a plugin with the specified `artifactId` and one of the following `groupId`s: `org.apache.maven.plugins` or `org.codehaus.mojo`. As the version is optional, Maven tries to download the latest available plugin version. Specifying the plugin versions is highly recommended to prevent auto-updates and nonreproducible builds. We may have built our project with the most recently updated Maven plugin; but later, if another developer tries to make the same build with the same configuration, and if the Maven plugin has since been updated, using the most current update may result in a nonreproducible build.

A.5   *The Maven project object model (POM)*

Maven has a build descriptor called pom.xml (short for *project object model*) by default. We do not imperatively specify the things we want to do; we declaratively specify general information for the project itself, as in the following listing.

> Listing A.1   Very simple pom.xml

```
<project>
    <modelVersion>4.0.0</modelVersion>
    <groupId>com.manning.javapersistence</groupId>
    <artifactId>example-pom</artifactId>
    <packaging>jar</packaging>
    <version>1.0-SNAPSHOT</version>
</project>
```

This code looks really simple, doesn't it? But one big question may arise: how is Maven capable of building source code with that little information?

The answer lies in the inheritance feature of the pom.xml files. Every simple pom.xml inherits most of its functionality from a Super POM. As in Java, in which every class inherits certain methods from the `java.lang.Object` class, the Super POM empowers each pom.xml file with Maven features.

To take the analogy between Java and Maven even further, Maven pom.xml files can inherit from one another; just as in Java, some classes can act as parents for others. If we want to use the pom from listing A.1 as our parent, all we have to do is change its `packaging` value to `pom`. Parent and aggregation (multimodule) projects can have `pom` only as a packaging value. We also need to define in our parent which modules are the children.

Listing A.2 **Parent pom.xml with a child module**

```
<project>
    <modelVersion>4.0.0</modelVersion>
    <groupId>com.manning.javapersistence</groupId>
    <artifactId>example-pom</artifactId>
    <packaging>pom</packaging>
    <version>1.0-SNAPSHOT</version>
    <modules>
        <module>example-module</module>
    </modules>
</project>
```

Listing A.2 is an extension of listing A.1. We declare that this pom is an aggregation module by declaring the package to be of pom type and adding a modules section. The modules section lists all the child modules that our module has by providing the relative path to the project folder (example-module in this case).

The following listing shows the child pom.xml.

Listing A.3 **A pom.xml that inherits the parent pom.xml**

```
<project>
  <modelVersion>4.0.0</modelVersion>
  <parent>
    <groupId>com.manning.javapersistence</groupId>
    <artifactId>example-pom</artifactId>
    <version>1.0-SNAPSHOT</version>
  </parent>
  <artifactId>example-child</artifactId>
</project>
```

Remember that this pom.xml resides in the folder that the parent XML has declared (example-module in this case).

Two things are worth noticing here. First, because we inherit from some other pom, we don't need to specify groupId and version for the child pom; second, Maven expects the values to be the same as in the parent.

Going further with the analogy of Java, it seems reasonable to ask what kinds of objects poms can inherit from their parents. Here are all the elements that a pom can inherit from its parent:

- Dependencies
- Developers and contributors
- Plugins and their configurations
- Reports lists

Each of these elements specified in the parent pom is automatically specified in the child pom.

A.6   *Installing Maven*

Installing Maven is a three-step process:

1 Download the latest distribution from https://maven.apache.org, and unzip/untar it in the directory of your choice.

2 Define an M2_HOME environment variable pointing to where you have installed Maven.

3 Add M2_HOME\bin (M2_HOME/bin on UNIX) to your PATH environment variable so that you can type mvn from any directory.

appendix B Spring Data JPA keyword usage

Table B.1 describes the keywords that Spring Data JPA supports and how each method name is transposed in JPQL.

Table B.1   Keyword usage in Spring Data JPA and generated JPQL

Keyword	Example	Generated JPQL

Is, Equals	`findByUsername`
	`findByUsernameIs`
	`findByUsernameEquals`
		`. . . where e.username = ?1`

And	`findByUsernameAndRegistrationDate`	`. . . where e.username = ?1` `and e.registrationDate = ?2`
Or	`findByUsernameOrRegistrationDate`	`. . . where e.username = ?1` `or e.registrationDate = ?2`
LessThan	`findByRegistrationDateLessThan`	`. . . where` `e.registrationDate < ?1`
LessThanEqual	`findByRegistrationDateLessThanEqual`	`. . . where` `e.registrationDate <= ?1`
GreaterThan	`findByRegistrationDateGreaterThan`	`. . . where` `e.registrationDate > ?1`
GreaterThanEqual	`findByRegistrationDateGreaterThanEqual`	`. . . where` `e.registrationDate >= ?1`

Between	`findByRegistrationDateBetween`	`. . . where`
		`e.registrationDate between`
		`?1 and ?2`

Table B.1 Keyword usage in Spring Data JPA and generated JPQL *(continued)*

Keyword	Example	Generated JPQL
OrderBy	findByRegistrationDateOrderByUsernameDesc	. . . where e.registrationDate = ?1 order by e.username desc
Like	findByUsernameLike	. . . where e.username like ?1
NotLike	findByUsernameNotLike	. . . where e.username not like ?1
Before	findByRegistrationDateBefore	. . . where e.registrationDate < ?1
After	findByRegistrationDateAfter	. . . where e.registrationDate > ?1
Null, IsNull	findByRegistrationDate(Is)Null	. . . where e.registrationDate is null
NotNull, IsNotNull	findByRegistrationDate(Is)NotNull	. . . where e.registrationDate is not null
Not	findByUsernameNot	. . . where e.username <> ?1
In	findByRegistrationDateIn (Collection<LocalDate> dates)	. . . where e.registrationDate in ?1
NotIn	findByRegistrationDateNotIn (Collection<LocalDate> dates)	. . . where e.registrationDate not in ?1
True	findByActiveTrue	. . . where e.active = true
False	findByActiveFalse	. . . where e.active = false
StartingWith	findByUsernameStartingWith	. . . where e.username like ?1%
EndingWith	findByUsernameEndingWith	. . . where e.username like %?1
Containing	findByUsernameContaining	. . . where e.username like %?1%
IgnoreCase	findByUsernameIgnoreCase	. . . where UPPER(e.username) = UPPER(?1)

appendix C
Spring Data
JDBC keyword usage

Table C.1 describes the keywords that Spring Data JDBC supports and how each method name generates query conditions.

Table C.1   Keyword usage in Spring Data JDBC and resulting conditions

Keyword	Example	Condition
Is, Equals	findByUsername(String name) findByUsernameIs(String name) findByUsernameEquals(String name)	username = name
And	findByUsernameAndRegistrationDate (String name, LocalDate date)	username = name and registrationDate = date
Or	findByUsernameOrRegistrationDate (String name, LocalDate date)	username = name or registrationDate = name
LessThan	findByRegistrationDateLessThan (LocalDate date)	registrationDate < date
LessThanEqual	findByRegistrationDateLessThanEqual (LocalDate date)	registrationDate <= date
GreaterThan	findByRegistrationDateGreaterThan (LocalDate date)	registrationDate > date
GreaterThanEqual	findByRegistrationDateGreaterThanEqual (LocalDate date)	registrationDate >= date
Between	findByRegistrationDateBetween (LocalDate from, LocalDate to)	registrationDate between from and to

Table C.1 Keyword usage in Spring Data JDBC and resulting conditions *(continued)*

Keyword	Example	Condition
OrderBy	findByRegistrationDateOrderByUsernameDesc (LocalDate date)	registrationDate = date order by username desc
Like	findByUsernameLike(String name)	username like name
NotLike	findByUsernameNotLike(String name)	username not like name
Before	findByRegistrationDateBefore (LocalDate date)	registrationDate < date
After	findByRegistrationDateAfter (LocalDate date)	registrationDate > date
Null, IsNull	findByRegistrationDate(Is)Null()	registrationDate is null
NotNull, IsNotNull	findByRegistrationDate(Is)NotNull()	registrationDate is not null
Not	findByUsernameNot(String name)	username <> name
In	findByRegistrationDateIn (Collection<LocalDate> dates)	registrationDate in (date1, . . . dateN)
NotIn	findByRegistrationDateNotIn (Collection<LocalDate> dates)	registrationDate not in (date1, . . . dateN)
True, IsTrue	findByActiveTrue()	active is true
False, IsFalse	findByActiveFalse()	active is false
StartingWith	findByUsernameStartingWith(String name)	username like name%
EndingWith	findByUsernameEndingWith(String name)	username like %name
Containing	findByUsernameContaining(String name)	username like %name%
IgnoreCase	findByUsernameIgnoreCase(String name)	UPPER(username) = UPPER(name)

appendix D
Spring Data
MongoDB keyword usage

Table D.1 describes the keywords that Spring Data MongoDB supports and how each method name generates query conditions.

Table D.1   Keyword usage in Spring Data MongoDB and resulting conditions

Keyword	Example	Condition

Is, Equals	`findByUsername(String name)`
	`findByUsernameIs(String name)`
	`findByUsernameEquals(String name)`
		`{"username":"name"}`

And	`findByUsernameAndEmail(String username, String email)`	`{"username":"username", "email":"email"}`
Or	`findByUsernameOrEmail (String username, String email)`	`{ "$or" : [{ "username" : "username"}, { "email" : "email"}]}`
LessThan	`findByRegistrationDateLessThan (LocalDate date)`	`{ "registrationDate" : { "$lt" : { "$date" : "date"}}}`
LessThanEqual	`findByRegistrationDateLessThanEqual (LocalDate date)`	`{ "registrationDate" : { "$lte" : { "$date" : "date"}}}`
GreaterThan	`findByRegistrationDateGreaterThan (LocalDate date)`	`{ "registrationDate" : { "$gt" : { "$date" : "date"}}}`
GreaterThanEqual	`findByRegistrationDateGreaterThanEqual (LocalDate date)`	`{ "registrationDate" : { "$gte" : { "$date" : "date"}}}`

Table D.1 Keyword usage in Spring Data MongoDB and resulting conditions *(continued)*

Keyword	Example	Condition
Between	findByRegistrationDateBetween (LocalDate from, LocalDate to)	"registrationDate" : { "$gte" : { "$date" : "date"}, "$lte" : { "$date" : "date"}}}
OrderBy	findByRegistrationDateOrderByUsernameDesc (LocalDate date)	"registrationDate" : { "$date" : "date"}}
Like	findByUsernameLike(String name)	{ "username" : { "$regularExpression" : { "pattern" : "name", "options" : ""}}}
NotLike	findByUsernameNotLike(String name)	{ "username" : { "$not" : { "$regularExpression" : { "pattern" : "name", "options" : ""}}}}
Before	findByRegistrationDateBefore (LocalDate date)	{ "registrationDate" : { "$lt" : { "$date" : "date"}}}
After	findByRegistrationDateAfter (LocalDate date)	{ "registrationDate" : { "$gt" : { "$date" : "date"}}}
Null, IsNull	findByRegistrationDate(Is)Null()	{ "registrationDate" : null}
NotNull, IsNotNull	findByRegistrationDate(Is)NotNull()	{ "registrationDate" : { "$ne" : null}}
Not	findByUsernameNot(String name)	{ "username" : { "$ne" : "name"}}
In	findByRegistrationDateIn (Collection<LocalDate> dates)	"registrationDate" : { "$in" : [{ "$date" : "date1"}, . { "$date" : "daten"}]}}
NotIn	findByRegistrationDateNotIn (Collection<LocalDate> dates)	"registrationDate" : { "$nin" : [{ "$date" : "date1"}, . . . { "$date" : "daten"}]}}
True, IsTrue	findByActiveTrue()	{ "active" : true}
False, IsFalse	findByActiveFalse()	{ "active" : false}
StartingWith	findByUsernameStartingWith(String name)	{ "username" : { "$regularExpression" : { "pattern" : "^name", "options" : ""}}}
EndingWith	findByUsernameEndingWith(String name)	{ "username" : { "$regularExpression" : { "pattern" : "name$", "options" : ""}}}
Containing	findByUsernameContaining(String name)	{ "pattern" : ".*name.*", "options" : ""}}}

Table D.1   Keyword usage in Spring Data MongoDB and resulting conditions *(continued)*

Keyword	Example	Condition
IgnoreCase	findByUsernameIgnoreCase(String name)	{ "username" : { "$regularExpression" : { "pattern" : "^name$", "options" : "i"}}}

references

Bernard, E., and J. Griffin. 2008. *Hibernate Search in Action*. Manning Publications.

Bloch, J. 2017. *Effective Java*, third edition. Addison-Wesley Professional.

Codd, E.F. 1970. "A Relational Model of Data for Large Shared Data Banks." *Communications of the ACM* 13 (6): 377-387. https://dl.acm.org/doi/10.1145/362384.362685.

Date, C.J. 2015. *SQL and Relational Theory: How to Write Accurate SQL Code,* third edition. O'Reilly Media.

Elmasri, R., and S. Navathe. 2016. *Fundamentals of Database Systems*. Pearson.

Fielding, R. 2000. "Architectural Styles and the Design of Network-based Software Architecture." PhD dissertation, University Of California, Irvine. https://www.ics.uci.edu/~fielding/pubs/dissertation/top.htm.

Gamma, E., R. Helm, R. Johnson, and J. Vlissides. 1994. *Design Patterns: Elements of Reusable Object-Oriented Software*. Addison-Wesley Professional.

Johnson, R. 2002. *Expert One-on-One J2EE Design and Development*. Wrox.

Karwin, B. 2010. *SQL Antipatterns: Avoiding the Pitfalls of Database Programming*. The Pragmatic Bookshelf.

Spilcă, L. 2021. *Spring Start Here*. Manning Publications.

Tow, D. 2003. *SQL Tuning*. O'Reilly Media.

Tudose, C. 2020. *JUnit in Action*, third edition. Manning Publications.

Tudose, C., and C. Odubășteanu. 2021. "Object-Relational Mapping Using JPA, Hibernate and Spring Data JPA." *Proceedings 2021 23rd International Conference on Control Systems and Computer Science* (CSCS 2021): 424–431.

index

Q